Practice 111

THE PRACTICE OF SOCIAL WORK

A Comprehensive Worktext

TENTH EDITION

THE PRACTICE OF SOCIAL WORK

A Comprehensive Worktext

Brooks/Cole Empowerment Series

Charles H. Zastrow
George Williams College of Aurora University

BROOKS/COLE
CENGAGE Learning

Australia • Brazil • Japan • Korea • Mexico • Singapore • Spain • United Kingdom • United States

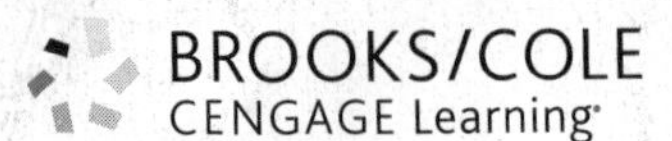

Brooks/Cole Empowerment Series: *The Practice of Social Work: A Comprehensive Worktext*, Tenth Edition
Charles H. Zastrow

Publisher: Linda Schreiber-Ganster

Acquisitions Editor: Seth Dobrin

Editorial Assistant: Suzanna Kincaid

Media Editor: Elizabeth Momb

Marketing Program Manager: Tami Strang

Content Project Manager: Michelle Clark

Art Director: Caryl Gorska

Manufacturing Planner: Judy Inouye

Rights Acquisitions Specialist: Tom McDonough

Production and Composition: S4Carlisle Publishing Services

Text Researcher: Isabel Saraiva

Copy Editor: Kirsten Balayti

Text Designer: Diane Beasley

Cover Designer: Gia Giasullo

Cover Image: (clockwise from top) JLP/Jose L. Pelaez/Corbis; Paula Connelly; Imageegaml; 67photo/Alamy

Library of Congress Control Number: 2011944308

Student Edition:
ISBN-13: 978-0-8400-2918-8

ISBN-10: 0-8400-2918-7

Brooks/Cole
20 Davis Drive
Belmont, CA 94002-3098
USA

Cengage Learning is a leading provider of customized learning solutions with office locations around the globe, including Singapore, the United Kingdom, Australia, Mexico, Brazil, and Japan. Locate your local office at: **www.cengage.com/global.**

Cengage Learning products are represented in Canada by Nelson Education, Ltd.

To learn more about Brooks/Cole, visit **www.cengage.com/brookscole**

Purchase any of our products at your local college store or at our preferred online store **www.CengageBrain.com**

Printed in the United States of America
1 2 3 4 5 6 7 16 15 14 13 12

Contents

Preface

The Council on Social Work Education (CSWE) is the national organization in the United States that accreditates baccalaureate and master's degree programs in social work education. In 2008, CSWE published *Educational Policy and Accreditation Standards (EPAS)* for baccalaureate and master's degree programs. A major thrust of *The Practice of Social Work: A Comprehensive Workbook* is to present material that is consistent with the following mandated content on social work practice in *EPAS*:

> Professional practice involves the dynamic and interactive processes of engagement, assessment, intervention, and evaluation at multiple levels. Social workers have the knowledge and skills to practice with individuals, families, groups, organizations, and communities. Practice knowledge includes identifying, analyzing, and implementing evidence-based interventions designed to achieve client goals; using research and technological advances; evaluating program outcomes and practice effectiveness; developing, analyzing, advocating, and providing leadership for policies and services; and promoting social and economic justice.

Also, consistent with *EPAS* requirements, content is presented on social work values and ethics, the promotion of social and economic justice, critical thinking to inform and communicate professional judgments, diversity and difference in practice, human rights, research-informed practice and practice-informed research, policy practice to advance social and economic well-being and to deliver effective social work services, and contexts that shape practice.

This text provides the theoretical and practical knowledge needed for entry levels of practice in social work. Material is presented covering generalist practice, social work values, confidentiality, principles of interviewing, contemporary theories of counseling, social work with individuals, social work with groups, social work with families, social work with organizations, social work community practice, assessment, evaluation, evidence-based practice, general systems theory, cross-cultural social work, working within a bureaucratic system, burnout, and the frustrations and satisfactions of being a social worker. Numerous case examples are included to illustrate the theory that is presented.

The Practice of Social Work is designed for use in practice courses in social work at both undergraduate and graduate levels. Social work practitioners also will find the text valuable because it describes a variety of approaches to social work practice, including relaxation approaches, mediation, milieu therapy, task-centered practice, family counseling concepts, feminist intervention, reality therapy, rational therapy, and behavior therapy. An eclectic approach is used in presenting these diverse types of therapies. After each therapy approach is described, a critical review of the theory is presented to help the reader assess its merits and shortcomings.

The skill-building exercises in this text may be used in a variety of ways. The instructor may request that students complete certain exercises as a homework assignment before the next class period; the exercises are then reviewed when the class next meets. The instructor may have students complete one or more exercises during class. The instructor may assign certain exercises as written homework to be submitted for evaluation. The pages of this workbook are perforated for easy removal. The instructor may have each student complete several exercises and then place them in a portfolio, which the instructor may periodically review for evaluation purposes.

This book is unique in that it combines the key components of existing practice texts, both traditional and contemporary, into one volume. As much as possible, jargon-free language is used so the reader can more readily grasp the theory. Exercises for students are presented in each chapter to illustrate key concepts and to help students learn how to apply the theoretical material to social work practice. These exercises are largely skill-building exercises that are designed to facilitate students' developing social work practice skills. Exercises also are presented at the end of each chapter to facilitate students' learning how to apply the theoretical material to social work practice.

PLAN OF THE BOOK

Part 1 is an introductory section with two chapters. Chapter 1 conceptualizes social work practice. It describes what social workers do, explains how social work is distinct from other professions, and summarizes the knowledge, values, and skills needed for beginning-level social work practice. This chapter also describes the goals of social work practice, gives a brief history of social work, indicates that social work is a multiskilled profession, and summarizes professional activities performed by social workers, including casework, case management, group work, group counseling, family counseling, and community organization. Various role models of social work practice are defined, including that of an enabler, broker, advocate, and activist. Generalist practice in social work is also defined and described.

Chapter 2 summarizes social work values. Values described include self-determination, individualization, confidentiality, belief in the institutional approach for the delivery of services, focus on family, advocacy for those being discriminated against, and accountability.

Part 2 has several chapters that describe generalist social work practice. Social work with individuals, social work with groups, social work with families, social work with organizations, and social work community practice are covered in depth. Techniques for interviewing and counseling clients are given considerable attention. Eight stages of a problem-solving approach to counseling clients are presented. Guidelines are also provided on how to begin and end interviews, how to phrase interview questions, and how to take notes while interviewing. Chapters are also included on assessment and on evaluating social work practice. Material is summarized on computer applications in social work practice and on systems analysis. This part covers material on changing the delivery system to serve clients better, cross-cultural social work (for example, white workers and Native American clients), spirituality, and social work practice.

Part 3 focuses on taking care of oneself. To be of help to others, social workers must first take care of themselves. Suggestions are presented for resolving common concerns of students receiving professional training in social work. Techniques to manage stress and prevent burnout are described. Safety guidelines for social workers are described. This part concludes with a discussion of the importance for social workers (as well as other people) of developing a positive identity and provides guidelines on how to develop a positive sense of self.

The final section of the book is a Counseling Theories Resource Manual (CTRM). To highlight the uniqueness of the CTRM, material is presented in modules, rather than chapters. This CTRM presents and critiques the prominent theories of counseling that are widely used by social workers, including reality therapy, rational therapy, and behavior therapy. Specific intervention techniques are also described, including assertiveness training, token economies, aversive techniques, milieu therapy, psychodrama, crisis intervention, parent effectiveness training, mediation, task-centered practice, solution-focused therapy, and narrative therapy.

The instructor does not have to cover all the theories of intervention presented in this text. Rather, he or she (with the consultation of other faculty in the program) should decide which of the intervention theories described in the CTRM are most important for students to learn to best serve clients in the school's geographic area.

NEW TO THIS EDITION

Content has been added on:

- Motivational interviewing
- Assessing bio-psycho-social and cultural components
- The law of attraction
- Improving one's self-concept
- Material and exercises on assessing the extent to which students are attaining the competencies and practice behaviors of the 2008 *EPAS*
- Crisis intervention
- Elaine Congress's ETHIC process model of decision making
- Letting go and forgiving as strategies for resolving conflicts
- The impact of the changing technological landscape on community practice
- Bisexual and transgendered clients
- Clients with a disability
- Traumas and stress disorders

COUNSELING AS A COMPONENT OF GENERALIST PRACTICE

A small minority of social work educators assert that counseling is not a component of generalist social work practice. I, however, strongly assert that counseling is a key component of generalist practice. A generalist practitioner uses the problem-solving approach to bring about positive changes when working with individuals, families, groups, organizations, and communities. Much of social work practice with individuals, treatment groups, and families requires the social worker to use counseling principles and theories extensively. Competence in counseling is as essential for generalist-practice social workers to have as are competencies in other areas (such as brokering, policy making, lobbying, and planning). Most baccalaureate and master's degree social workers are engaged primarily in providing direct services to individuals, treatment groups, and families—and the provision of counseling services is a major component of the direct services provided. Conversely, when a social worker identifies himself or herself as a clinical social worker or a psychotherapist, it does not mean that the person is uninvolved in other areas of generalist practice. Every clinical social worker (at times) works with changing organizations and communities to benefit clients. And because I believe that counseling is a key component of generalist social work practice, I provide the Counseling Theories Resource Manual (CTRM), which presents contemporary theories of counseling that are useful in working with individuals, treatment groups, and families.

From one point of view, the 14 chapters of Parts 1, 2, and 3 focus on generalist practice, whereas the CTRM focuses exclusively on counseling. However, the reader will note that in describing social work practice with individuals, families, and groups, it is essential to discuss aspects of counseling. Not surprisingly, most of the 14 "generalist" chapters describe some aspects of counseling, as the following list indicates:

Chapter 1, "Overview of Social Work Practice," links the social work goal "Enhance people's problem-solving, coping, and developmental capacities" with counseling. It also describes how counseling is an integral component of "social casework," "group therapy," and "family therapy."

Chapter 2, "Social Work Values," describes a number of values that relate to counseling—such as confidentiality, privileged communication, whether to inform partners of clients in counseling that a client is HIV-positive, and establishing professional boundaries with clients.

Chapter 3, "Assessment," discusses strategies and approaches to assessing the issues of clients in counseling and features counseling case examples.

Chapter 4, "Social Work with Individuals: Interviewing," focuses on interviewing, which is directly related to counseling.

Chapter 5, "Social Work with Individuals: Counseling," focuses exclusively on counseling.

Chapter 6, "Social Work with Groups: Types of Groups and Guidelines for Leading Them," presents considerable content on counseling groups.

Chapter 7, "Social Work with Groups: Concepts and Skills," presents a section on starting, leading, and ending counseling groups.

Chapter 8, "Social Work with Families," describes family counseling and features a lengthy family counseling case example.

Chapter 11, "Evaluating Social Work Practice," primarily focuses on describing evaluation approaches to assess the effectiveness of counseling and other direct practice services. It also features content on counseling services provided on the Internet.

Chapter 12, "Social Work Practice with Diverse Groups," provides considerable content on cultural competence for social workers who provide culturally sensitive services to clients who receive counseling and other services.

Chapter 13, "Spirituality and Religion in Social Work Practice," describes the importance of assessing the religious and spiritual aspects of clients, including clients receiving counseling. Also described are religious and spiritual interventions with clients receiving counseling.

Chapter 14, "Surviving and Enjoying Social Work," features content on common concerns of social work students who are preparing to provide services to clients, including clients receiving counseling. (In covering this material, some instructors may choose to assign this chapter after chapter 2 or 3 because it covers material that is essential to thriving as a social work practitioner.)

ACKNOWLEDGMENTS

I wish to express my deep appreciation to the following people who made this book possible: to the contributing authors listed below, and to Vicki Vogel, who assisted in conceptualizing various chapters and helped in a number of ways with the writing of this text. My thanks also go to the reviewers of this edition:

A final thank-you to the staff at Brooks/Cole for their support and highly professional assistance with the texts I have authored.

Charles H. Zastrow

ABOUT THE AUTHOR

Charles H. Zastrow, MSW and PhD, is Assistant Director and Professor in the Social Work Program at George Williams College of Aurora University at Williams Bay, Wisconsin. He has worked as a practitioner in a variety of public and private social welfare agencies and chaired 22 social work accreditation site visit teams for the Council on Social Work Education (CSWE). He served two terms as a Commissioner on the Commission on Accreditation of CSWE. Dr. Zastrow is a Licensed Clinical Social Worker in the state of Wisconsin. In addition to *The Practice of Social Work*, he has written four other textbooks: *Introduction to Social Work and Social Welfare* (10th ed.), *Social Work with Groups* (8th ed.), *Social Problems: Issues and Solutions* (5th ed.), and *Understanding Human Behavior and the Social Environment* (8th ed.) (with Dr. Karen Krist-Ashman).

CONTRIBUTING AUTHORS

Wallace J. Gingerich, MSW, Ph.D.
Professor, Mandel School of Applied Social Sciences
Case Western Reserve University
Cleveland, OH

Grafton H. Hull, Jr., MSW, Ed.D.
Professor
University of Utah
Salt Lake City, UT

Karen K. Kirst-Ashman, MSW, Ph.D.
Professor Emeritus Social Work Department
University of Wisconsin—Whitewater
Whitewater, WI

Carolyn Wells, MSW, Ph.D.
Professor Emeritus, Social Work Department
University of Wisconsin—Oshkosh
Oshkosh, WI

James P. Winship, MSW, DPA
Chair and Professor, Social Work Department
University of Wisconsin—Whitewater
Whitewater, WI

CHAPTER 1

Overview of Social Work Practice

The Practice of Social Work, Tenth Edition, is intended for use in social work practice courses. The focus of this book is on the theoretical and practical knowledge students need to perform the tasks of workers in entry-level positions that require either a bachelor's (BSW) or master's (MSW) degree in social work. This book is designed to be read by students preparing for, or already in, field placement. This chapter will:

A. Present a history of social work
B. Define social work
C. Describe the relationship between social work and social welfare
D. Define generalist social work practice
E. Describe the change process in working with clients
F. Identify the roles in social work practice
G. Emphasize that social workers use a systems perspective
H. Illustrate that counseling is a component of generalist practice
I. Discuss the relationship between counseling and therapy
J. Compare the medical model of human behavior to the ecological model
K. Present the goals of social work practice
L. Identify the knowledge, skills, and values needed for social work practice

THE HISTORY OF SOCIAL WORK

Social work as a profession is of relatively recent origin. The first social welfare agencies appeared in urban areas in the early 1800s. These agencies, or services, were private and were developed primarily at the initiation of the clergy and religious groups. Until the early 1900s, these services were provided exclusively by the clergy and affluent "do-gooders" who had no formal training and little understanding of human behavior or of how to help people. The focus of these private services was on meeting such basic physical needs as food and shelter and on attempting to cure emotional and personal difficulties with religious admonitions.

An example of an early social welfare organization is the Society for the Prevention of Pauperism, founded by John Griscom in 1820 (Bemner, 1962, p. 13). This society investigated the habits and circumstances of the poor, suggested plans by which the poor could help themselves, and encouraged the poor to save and economize. One of the remedies used was house-to-house visitation (a very elementary type of social work).

By the latter half of the 1800s, a fairly large number of private relief agencies had been established in large cities to help the unemployed, the poor, the ill, persons with physical or mental disabilities, and orphans. Their programs were uncoordinated and sometimes overlapping, and so an English invention—the Charity Organization

Society (COS)—soon caught the interest of a number of American cities (Cohen, 1958). Starting in Buffalo, New York, in 1877, COS was rapidly adopted in many cities. In charity organization societies, private agencies joined together (1) to provide direct services to individuals and families—in this respect, they were the forerunners of social casework and of family counseling approaches—and (2) to plan and coordinate the efforts of private agencies to meet pressing urban social problems—in this respect, they were the precursors of community organization and social-planning approaches. Charity organizations conducted a detailed investigation of each applicant for services and financial help, maintained a central client registration system to avoid duplication, and used volunteer *friendly visitors* extensively to work with those in difficulty. The friendly visitors were primarily "doers of good works," as they generally gave sympathy rather than money and encouraged the poor to save and to seek employment. Poverty was viewed as a personal shortcoming. Most of the friendly visitors were women.

Concurrent with the COS movement was the establishment of settlement houses in the late 1800s. Toynbee Hall was the first settlement house, established in 1884 in London; many others were soon formed in larger U.S. cities. Many of the early settlement house workers were the daughters of ministers. The workers, who were from the middle and upper classes, lived in poor neighborhoods to experience the harsh realities of poverty. Simultaneously, in cooperation with neighborhood residents, they sought to develop ways to improve living conditions. In contrast to friendly visitors, they lived in impoverished neighborhoods and used the missionary approach of teaching residents how to live moral lives and improve their circumstances. They sought to improve housing, health, and living conditions; find jobs; teach English, hygiene, and occupational skills; and change environmental surroundings through cooperative efforts. The change techniques that settlement houses used are now called social group work, social action, and community organization.

Settlement houses emphasized "environmental reform" while "they continued to struggle to teach the poor the prevailing middle-class values of work, thrift, and abstinence as the keys to success" (Becker, 1968, p. 85). In addition to dealing with local problems by local action, settlement houses played important roles in drafting legislation and in organizing to influence social policy and legislation. The most noted leader in the settlement house movement was Jane Addams of Hull House in Chicago, who summarized settlement houses as follows: "The Settlement, then, is an experimental effort to aid in the solution of the social and industrial problems which are engendered by the modern conditions of life in a great city" (Addams, 1959, pp. 125–126). Settlement house leaders believed that by changing neighborhoods they would improve communities, and through altering communities they would develop a better society.

The first paid social workers were executive secretaries of charity organization societies (Dolgoff & Feldstein, 1980, pp. 233–234). In the late 1800s charity organization societies received some contracts from the cities in which they were located to administer relief funds. To administer these programs, COS hired people as executive secretaries to organize and train the friendly visitors and to establish accounting procedures to show accountability for the funds received. To improve the services of friendly visitors, the executive secretaries established standards and training courses. In 1898, a training course was first offered by the New York Charity Organization Society. By 1904, the New York School of Philanthropy offered a one-year program. Soon after, colleges and universities began offering training programs in social work. Initially, social work education focused on environmental reform approaches to meet social problems. (Such approaches focus on changing the system to better meet people's needs. The enactment in 1935 of the Social Security Act to meet the needs of the poor and the unemployed is an example of an environmental reform approach.)

Richard Cabot introduced medical social work into Massachusetts General Hospital in 1905 (Dolgoff & Feldstein, 1980, pp. 233–234). Gradually, social workers were employed in schools, courts, child guidance clinics, and other settings.

In 1917 Mary Richmond published *Social Diagnosis,* a text that presented for the first time a theory and methodology for social work. The book focused on how the worker should intervene with individuals. The process is still used today and involves study (collecting information), diagnosis (stating what is wrong), prognosis, and treatment planning (stating what should be done to help clients improve). This book was important because it formulated a common body of knowledge for casework.

In the 1920s, Freud's theories of personality development and therapy became popular. The concepts and explanations of psychiatrists appeared particularly appropriate for social workers, who also worked in one-to-one relationships with clients. The psychiatric approach emphasized intrapsychic processes and focused on enabling clients to adapt and adjust to their social situations. For the next three decades, social workers switched their emphasis from reform to therapy. In the 1960s, however, social workers expressed renewed interest in sociological approaches, or reform. Several reasons account for this change. Questions arose about the relevance and appropriateness of talking approaches with low-income clients who have urgent social and economic pressures. Furthermore, the effectiveness of many psychotherapeutic approaches was questioned (Eysenck, 1961). Other reasons for the renewed interest included the increase in status of sociology and the mood of the 1960s, which raised questions about the relevance of social institutions in meeting the needs of the population. Social work at the present time embraces both reform and therapy approaches.[1]

Not until the end of World War I did social work begin to be recognized as a distinct profession. The Depression of the 1930s and enactment of the Social Security Act in 1935 brought about an extensive expansion of public social services and job opportunities for social workers. Since 1900, there has been a growing awareness by social agency boards and the public that professionally trained social workers are needed to provide social services competently. In 1955, the National Association of Social Workers was formed to represent the social work profession in this country. Its purpose is to improve social conditions and to promote high-quality and effective social work practice.

In recent years, considerable energy has been expended to develop a system of registration or licensing of social workers. Such a system helps assure the public that qualified personnel are providing social work services and also advances the recognition of social work as a profession. All states have passed legislation to license or certify the practice of social work. Currently there is an effort to merge the different social work organizations into one organization. Included in the proposed merger would be the Council on Social Work Education and the National Association of Social Workers.

Social work is one of the most important professions in our society in terms of the number of people affected, the human misery treated, and the amount of money spent.

A DEFINITION OF SOCIAL WORK

The National Association of Social Workers (NASW) defines *social work* as follows:

> Social work is the professional activity of helping individuals, groups, or communities to enhance or restore their capacity for social functioning and to create societal conditions favorable to their goals.
>
> Social work practice consists of the professional application of social work values, principles, and techniques to one or more of the following ends: helping people obtain tangible services; providing counseling and psychotherapy for individuals, families, and groups; helping communities or groups provide or improve social and health services; and participating in relevant legislative processes.

---

[1]I believe there is little difference between therapy and counseling (for emotional and behavioral problems); therefore, these terms are used interchangeably in this text. In addition, because counseling (or therapy) is an intervention with a client, sometimes the term *intervention* is used to refer to *counseling*.

> The practice of social work requires knowledge of human development and behavior; of social, economic, and cultural institutions; and of the interaction of all these factors. (Barker, 2003, p. 408)

The term *social worker* is generally applied to graduates of educational programs (either with bachelor's or master's degrees) in social work who are employed in the field of social welfare. A social worker is a *change agent,* a helper who is specifically employed for the purpose of creating planned change (Pincus & Minahan, 1973, p. 54). As a change agent, a social worker is expected to be skilled at working with individuals, groups, families, and organizations and at bringing about community changes.

THE RELATIONSHIP BETWEEN SOCIAL WORK AND SOCIAL WELFARE

The goal of social welfare is to fulfill the social, financial, health, and recreational requirements of all individuals in a society. Social welfare seeks to enhance the social functioning of all age groups, both rich and poor. When other institutions in our society (such as the market economy and the family) fail at times to meet the basic needs of individuals or groups of people, social services are needed and demanded. Barker (2003) defined *social welfare* as follows:

> A nation's system of programs, benefits, and services that help people meet those social, economic, educational, and health needs that are fundamental to the maintenance of society. (p. 408)

Examples of social welfare programs and services are foster care, adoption, day care, Head Start, probation and parole, public assistance programs, public health nursing, sex therapy, suicide counseling, recreational services (Boy Scouts and YWCA programs), services to minority groups and veterans, school social services, medical and legal services to the poor, family planning services, Meals on Wheels, nursing home services, shelters for battered spouses, services to persons with acquired immune deficiency syndrome (AIDS), protective services for victims of child abuse and neglect, assertiveness training, public housing projects, family counseling, Alcoholics Anonymous, runaway services, services to people with developmental disabilities, and rehabilitation services.

Almost all social workers are employed in the social welfare field. There are, however, many other professional and occupational groups working in the field, as illustrated in Figure 1.1.

WHAT IS THE PROFESSION OF SOCIAL WORK?

The National Association of Social Workers (NASW) describes the social work profession as follows:

> The social work profession exists to provide humane and effective social services to individuals, families, groups, communities, and society so that social functioning may be enhanced and the quality of life improved. . . .
>
> The profession of social work, by both traditional and practical definition, is the profession that provides the formal knowledge base, theoretical concepts, specific functional skills, and essential social values which are used to implement society's mandate to provide safe, effective, and constructive social services.[2]

Social work is thus distinct from other professions (such as psychology and psychiatry) because it has the responsibility and mandate to provide social services.

A social worker needs training and expertise in a wide range of areas to effectively handle problems faced by individuals, groups, families, organizations, and the larger

[2]Published 1982, National Association of Social Workers, Inc. Reprinted with permission, from *Standards for the Classification of Social Work Practice,* Policy Statement 4, p. 5. Copyright material reprinted with permission from the National Association of Social Workers, Inc.

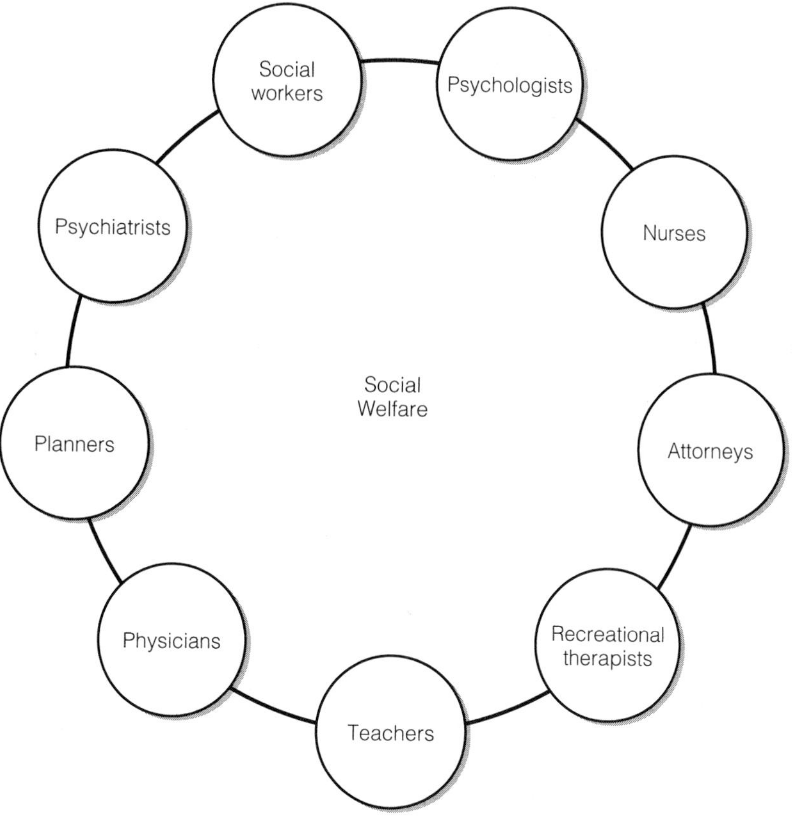

Figure 1.1
Examples of professional groups within the field of social welfare include attorneys providing legal services to the poor; urban planners in social planning agencies; physicians in public health agencies; teachers in residential treatment facilities for those with emotional and behavioral disorders; psychologists, nurses, and recreational therapists in mental hospitals; and psychiatrists in mental health clinics.

Source: © Cengage Learning, 2013.

EP 2.1.1.b

community. Although most professions are increasingly becoming more specialized (for example, most medical doctors now specialize in one or two areas), social work continues to emphasize a generic (broad-based) approach. The practice of social work is analogous to the old general practice of medicine. A general (or family) practitioner has professional education to handle a wide range of common medical problems; a social worker has professional education to handle a wide range of common social and personal problems. The Case Example "Rape" highlights some of the skills that social workers need.

Exercise 1.1: Your Areas of Interest in Social Work

Goal: This exercise is designed to help you identify the social work areas that you desire to work in.

Step 1: Rank the following five client systems that you prefer to work with (with one being your first choice).

____ Individuals

____ Families

____ Groups

____ Organizations

____ The larger community

(continued)

CASE EXAMPLE Rape

Dr. Richard Carr referred Kay Barber to Lakeside Counseling Center (a mental health center). Kay is 17 years old and a senior at West High School. The previous evening she had been raped by four males in a parking lot near West High. The rape had occurred after Kay left a school dance, about 1:00 a.m. The intake worker assigned the case to Karen Bowman, a social worker who had in the recent past counseled most of the agency's sexual assault cases. Ms. Bowman immediately met with Kay.

In tears, badly bruised, and still shaking from terror, Kay was angry, confused, and deeply hurt emotionally. In the next 50 minutes, she briefly described the details of the assault and some of her feelings. She was getting into her dad's car, alone, when she was grabbed by two youths and pulled into some bushes. Behind the bushes were two other youths, one of whom she recognized as the son of a college professor in the community. Following the assault, the youths warned her there would be serious trouble if she informed anyone. Hurt (emotionally and physically) and terrified, she returned home. Her mother was awake when she returned and immediately recognized that something had happened. Kay informed her parents. Kay's mother was horrified and angry but attempted to comfort Kay. Kay indicated that her father was even more upset, and even today was talking about shooting the rapists if he could find out who they were. (Kay had not as yet informed him that she knew one of the attackers for fear of what her father might do.)

Kay indicated that on hearing of the assault her parents took her to the police station. There she was questioned by two male police officers. Kay indicated that she revealed only sketchy details of the rape to the police officers as she was in tears, still terrified, and on the defensive because she felt many of the officers' questions suggested she contributed to the rape. She also felt that the officers did not believe she was assaulted.

Earlier this morning her parents took her to the family doctor, Richard Carr, who provided medical attention and then referred the case to the counseling center. Medical attention included a PERK (Physical Evidence Recovery Kit) procedure, in which hair, fluid, and tissue samples were taken. PERK is used to collect physical evidence of a sexual assault, in case the victim decides to initiate criminal charges against the assailants.

Kay was especially confused about a number of issues. Should she inform the police that she knows one of the youths who assaulted her? If she reveals his identity, would she have to appear in court? If she appears in court, what effect might this have on her reputation? If she doesn't inform the police of the identity of one of her assailants, might not these youths rape others, or perhaps even her again, in the future? In either case, how would she face the other students in school who she felt would hear, one way or the other, about the attack? Why did the police officers doubt her story about being raped, and why did the officers imply she may have contributed to the assault? What were her chances of getting pregnant? If she were pregnant, what would she do then? (Ms. Bowman indicated that the medical services she received might well have prevented her from now being pregnant—and this could be checked with Dr. Carr.) Should she inform her father that she knew one of the assailants? If she did, what might be the consequences? How could she ever learn to deal with the terror she experienced? She also indicated that she felt she would never go out in the evening, alone or with anyone else, in the future, unless she went with a member of her family. And, she wondered why this had to happen to her.

Ms. Bowman listened attentively and conveyed warmth, empathy, support, and a sincere sense of caring. After Kay had ventilated her concerns, Ms. Bowman expressed her understanding that Kay had been deeply hurt and was now feeling overwhelmed by this situation. Ms. Bowman gradually informed Kay that something could be done about all of her present concerns. The way to proceed would be to take her concerns, one by one, and work on resolving them. Ms. Bowman asked Kay to indicate her most urgent concerns. Kay thought awhile and said they were whether to inform her parents that she knew one of the attackers, and how to react to schoolmates who might make cruel remarks related to the rape.

Kay was then asked to elaborate her concerns in each of these two areas. Her concerns about telling her parents centered around what her father might do. With regard to cruel remarks from others, Ms. Bowman suggested to Kay that they role-play how she might respond to such remarks. Ms. Bowman first played Kay's role to model a few assertive strategies to respond to cruel remarks. The roles were then reversed, with Ms. Bowman role-playing someone giving a crude remark, and Kay practicing responding to it.

After this initial hour and 40-minute meeting, Kay became a little more relaxed. Kay mentioned that she was really worried about what her father might do. Ms. Bowman suggested that her parents (who were in the waiting room) might be brought in to discuss their concerns. Kay agreed. A rather lengthy meeting was then held with the Barbers. They began by ventilating a great deal of anger, wanting to find out who did this. Mr. Barber indicated he was going to shoot whoever did this. Ms. Bowman mentioned that Kay was partially upset, now, by what her father might do if he found out, and she asked Mr. Barber if he was aware of this. Following a lengthy discussion of the negative consequences of taking the law into one's own hands, Mr. Barber cried and acknowledged that he would not carry out his threats and that he was only making the threats because he felt so helpless. After Mr. Barber gave full assurance that he would not do anything illegal, he

CASE EXAMPLE *(continued)*

was informed that Kay thought she knew one of the attackers. Another meeting was arranged with the Barbers for the next day to talk further about their concerns. Time was also set aside for Kay and Ms. Bowman to meet the next day to continue to discuss her concerns.

As indicated earlier, this case was only one of several sexual assault cases that Ms. Bowman was handling. These cases led her to conclude that the area she was living in (320,000 population) needed a well-publicized rape crisis center. She began by gathering data on the incidence of sexual assault in the community—from the police department (many cases go unreported) and from other social service agencies in the community. She then convinced the director of the counseling center to form a committee of representatives from other interested social service agencies in the community and from certain women's organizations in the community. After formation of the committee (of which Ms. Bowman was a member), a questionnaire to obtain further information on the incidence of sexual assault was constructed. Committee members distributed the questionnaire to women shoppers at a large shopping center (respondents in this way remained entirely anonymous). The results suggested less than 1 rape in 10 was being reported to the police, which further documented the need for a rape crisis center that would be well publicized so that victims would know where help was available. Another proposed service of the center would be to provide speakers to schools and other organizations on how to seek to avoid becoming a victim and on what to do if an assault occurred. The center would also work with the police department and the court system to "humanize" the reporting and processing of sexual assault cases. The committee then wrote a grant proposal. After 11 months of searching for funding, the proposal was funded for a 3-year test period by the city and the United Way. Because of her interest and capacities in this area, Karen Bowman was appointed assistant director of this rape crisis center.

Counseling Skills at Work in Generalist Practice

This case illustration documents the wide range of generalist practice skills displayed by Ms. Bowman: interviewing skills, ability to effectively counsel individuals with families during a crisis, ability to work effectively with other agencies, research and grant-writing skills, public speaking capacities, program development and fund-raising skills, and knowledge of how to handle ethical and legal issues that arise.

Perhaps the most basic skill a social worker needs is to be able to counsel clients effectively. An individual who is not able to do this should probably not be in social work, certainly not in direct service. Another key skill is to be able to interact effectively with other groups and professionals in the area. Social workers need to learn a wide range of skills and intervention techniques that will enable them to intervene effectively with (1) the client's common personal and emotional problems and (2) the common social problems faced by groups, organizations, and the larger community.

Step 2: Describe the reasons for your ranking.

Step 3: Describe the areas of social work (such as services to battered spouses) that you prefer to work in. Also specify your reasons for your selected areas.

GENERALIST SOCIAL WORK PRACTICE

There used to be an erroneous belief that a social worker was a caseworker, a group worker, or a community organizer. Practicing social workers know that such a belief is faulty because every social worker is a change agent working with individuals, groups, families, organizations, and the larger community. The amount of time spent at these levels varies from worker to worker, but every worker will, at times, work at each of these levels and therefore needs training in all of them.

The Council on Social Work Education (CSWE, the national accrediting entity for baccalaureate and master's programs in social work) requires that all bachelor's and master's programs train students in generalist social work practice. (MSW programs, in addition, usually require students to select and study in an area of concentration. They generally offer several choices, such as family therapy, administration, corrections, or clinical social work.)

A generalist social worker is trained to use problem solving to assess and intervene in the problems confronting individuals, families, groups, organizations, and communities. Brieland, Costin, and Atherton (1985) defined and described *generalist practice* as follows:

> The generalist social worker, the equivalent of the general practitioner in medicine, is characterized by a wide repertoire of skills to deal with basic conditions, backed up by specialists to whom referrals are made. This role is a fitting one for the entry-level social worker.
>
> The generalist model involves identifying and analyzing the interventive behaviors appropriate to social work. The worker must perform a wide range of tasks related to the provision and management of direct service, the development of social policy, and the facilitation of social change. The generalist should be well grounded in systems theory that emphasizes interaction and independence. The major system that will be used is the local network of services. . . .
>
> The public welfare worker in a small county may be a classic example of the generalist. He or she knows the resources of the county, is acquainted with the key people, and may have considerable influence to accomplish service goals, including obtaining jobs, different housing, or emergency food and clothing. The activities of the urban generalist are more complex, and more effort must be expended to use the array of resources. (pp. 120–121)

Hull (1990) defined *generalist practice* as follows:

> The basic principle of generalist practice is that baccalaureate social workers are able to utilize the problem solving process to intervene with various size systems including individuals, families, groups, organizations, and communities. The generalist operates within a systems and person-in-the-environment framework (sometimes referred to as an ecological model). The generalist expects that many problems will require intervention with more than one system (e.g., individual work with [a] delinquent adolescent plus work with the family or school) and that single explanations of problem situations are frequently unhelpful. The generalist may play several roles simultaneously or sequentially depending upon the needs of the client (e.g., facilitator, advocate, educator, broker, enabler, case manager, and/or mediator). They may serve as leaders/facilitators of task groups, socialization groups, information groups, and self-help groups. They are capable of conducting needs assessments and evaluating their own practice and the programs with which they are associated. They make referrals when client problems so dictate and know when to utilize supervision from more experienced staff. Generalists operate within the ethical guidelines prescribed by the NASW Code of Ethics and must be able to work with clients, coworkers and colleagues from different ethnic, cultural, and professional orientations. The knowledge and skills of the generalist are transferable from one setting to another and from one problem to another. (p. 7)

The crux of generalist practice involves a view of the situation through the person-in-environment conceptualization (described in an upcoming section of this chapter) and the capacity and willingness to intervene at several different levels, if necessary, while assuming any number of roles. The Case Example "Rape" illustrates how social workers respond at several different levels in a variety of roles.

The Baccalaureate Program Directors Organization (BPD, 2006, p. 2) defined *generalist practice* as follows:

> Generalist social work practitioners work with individuals, families, groups, communities and organizations in a variety of social work and host settings. Generalist practitioners view clients and client systems from a strengths perspective in order to recognize, support, and build upon the innate capabilities of all human beings. They use a professional problem solving process to engage, assess, broker services, advocate, counsel, educate, and organize with and on behalf of client and client systems. In addition, generalist practitioners engage in community and organizational development. Finally, generalist practitioners evaluate service outcomes in order to continually improve the provision and quality of services most appropriate to client needs.
>
> Generalist social work practice is guided by the NASW Code of Ethics and is committed to improving the well-being of individuals, families, groups, communities and organizations and furthering the goals of social justice.

The Council on Social Work Education, in *Educational Policy and Accreditation Standards* (2008), also defined *generalist practice*:

> Generalist practice is grounded in the liberal arts and the person and environment construct. To promote human and social well-being, generalist practitioners use a range of prevention and intervention methods in their practice with individuals, families, groups, organizations, and communities. The generalist practitioner identifies with the social work profession and applies ethical principles and critical thinking in practice. Generalist practitioners incorporate diversity in their practice and advocate for human rights and social and economic justice. They recognize, support, and build on the strengths and resiliency of all human beings. They engage in research-informed practice and are proactive in responding to the impact of context on professional practice.

This text teaches the generalist-practice approach in social work by describing a variety of assessment and intervention strategies. Once you have learned these strategies, you can select the approaches that hold the most promise in facilitating positive changes in your clients.

In working with individuals, families, groups, organizations, and communities, social workers use a problem-solving approach. The process can be described in a variety of ways but includes these steps:

1. Identify as precisely as possible the problem or problems.
2. Generate possible alternative solutions.
3. Evaluate the alternative solutions.
4. Select a solution or solutions to be used and set goals.
5. Implement the solution.
6. Follow up to evaluate how the solution worked.

EP 2.1.7.a

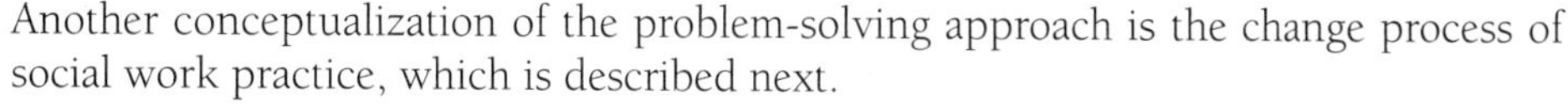

Another conceptualization of the problem-solving approach is the change process of social work practice, which is described next.

Exercise 1.2: Applying the Problem-Solving Approach

Goal: This exercise is designed to help you understand the problem-solving approach.

Step 1: Identify a situation in your past where you faced a challenge or an issue in which you used the problem-solving approach. What was the situation?

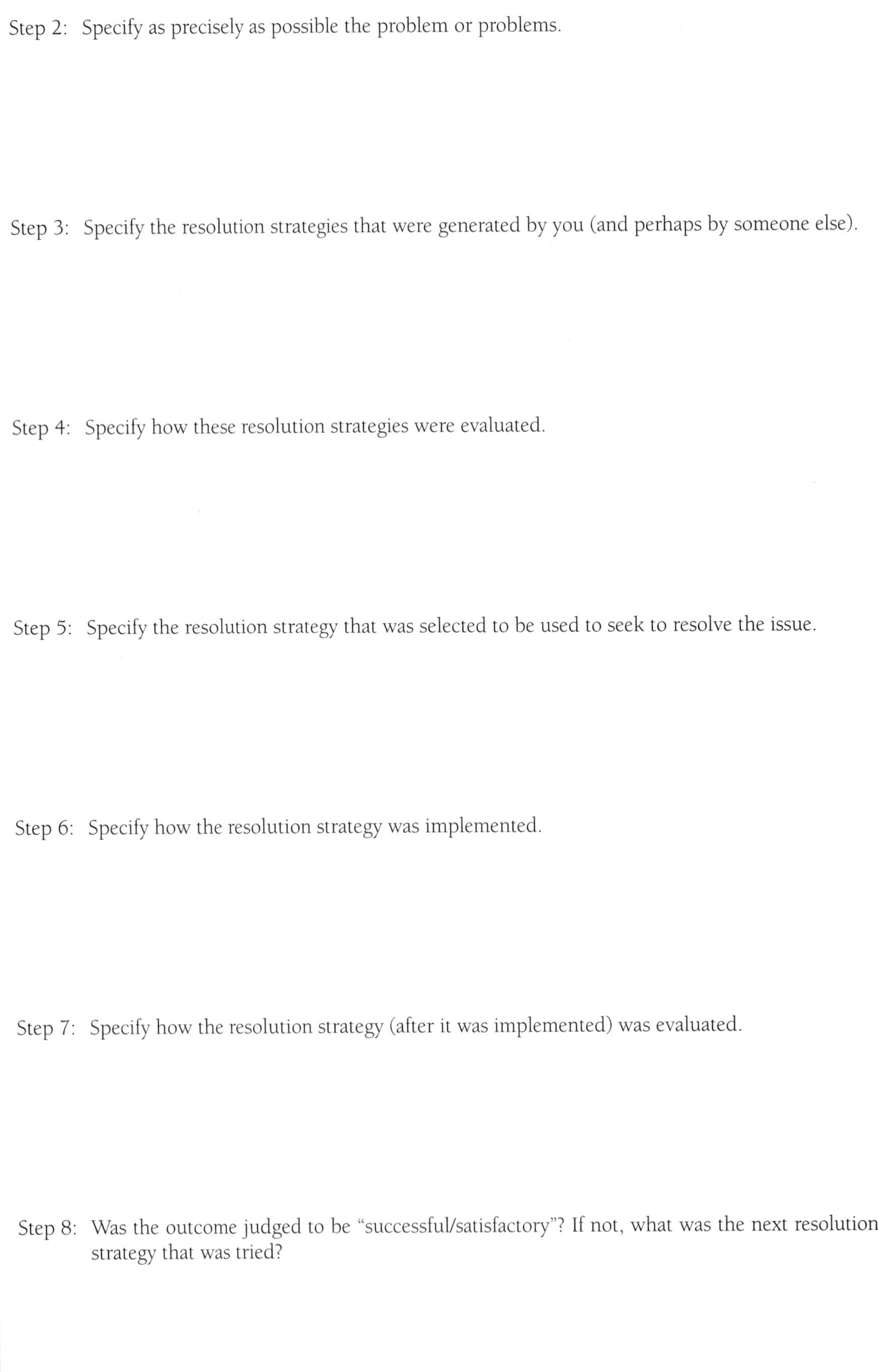
Step 2: Specify as precisely as possible the problem or problems.

Step 3: Specify the resolution strategies that were generated by you (and perhaps by someone else).

Step 4: Specify how these resolution strategies were evaluated.

Step 5: Specify the resolution strategy that was selected to be used to seek to resolve the issue.

Step 6: Specify how the resolution strategy was implemented.

Step 7: Specify how the resolution strategy (after it was implemented) was evaluated.

Step 8: Was the outcome judged to be "successful/satisfactory"? If not, what was the next resolution strategy that was tried?

Step 9: What do you see as the strengths and shortcomings of the problem-solving approach?

The Change Process

EP 2.1.10.a.b. c.e.f.g.h.i.j. k.l.m

A social worker uses a *change process* in working with clients. (Clients include individuals, groups, families, organizations, and communities.) The Council on Social Work Education (2008), in *Educational Policy and Accreditation Standards,* defined professional *social work practice*:

> Professional practice involves the dynamic and interactive processes of engagement, assessment, intervention, and evaluation at multiple levels. Social workers have the knowledge and skills to practice with individuals, families, groups, organizations, and communities. Practice knowledge includes identifying, analyzing, and implementing evidence-based interventions designed to achieve client goals; using research and technological advances; evaluating program outcomes and practice effectiveness; developing, analyzing, advocating, and providing leadership for policies and services; and promoting social and economic justice.
>
> **Educational Policy 2.1.10(a)—Engagement**
> Social workers
>
> - substantively and affectively prepare for action with individuals, families, groups, organizations, and communities;
> - use empathy and other interpersonal skills; and
> - develop a mutually agreed-on focus of work and desired outcomes.
>
> **Educational Policy 2.1.10(b)—Assessment**
> Social workers
>
> - collect, organize, and interpret client data;
> - assess client strengths and limitations;
> - develop mutually agreed-on intervention goals and objectives; and
> - select appropriate intervention strategies.
>
> **Educational Policy 2.1.10(c)—Intervention**
> Social workers
>
> - initiate actions to achieve organizational goals;
> - implement prevention interventions that enhance client capacities;
> - help clients resolve problems;
> - negotiate, mediate, and advocate for clients; and
> - facilitate transitions and endings.
>
> **Educational Policy 2.1.10(d)—Evaluation**
> Social workers critically analyze, monitor, and evaluate interventions.[3]

In reviewing this conceptualization of professional social work practice, we can identify eight skills needed by social work practitioners:

1. Engaging clients in an appropriate working relationship
2. Identifying issues, problems, needs, resources, and assets
3. Collecting and assessing information
4. Planning for service delivery

---

[3]Reprinted from *Educational Policy and Accreditation Standards* (Alexandria, VA: Council on Social Work Education, 2008).

5. Using communication skills, supervision, and consultation
6. Identifying, analyzing, and implementing empirically based interventions designed to achieve client goals
7. Applying empirical knowledge and technology
8. Evaluating program outcomes and practice effectiveness

The following case example illustrates the use of these skills in the change process in social work.

Phase 1: Engaging Clients in an Appropriate Working Relationship Debra Singer has been a protective services worker for the past 4½ years. She holds a BSW degree. Her agency, Walworth County Human Services Department, uses a traditional protective services approach when a complaint comes into the office that a child is suspected of being abused or neglected by his or her parents. This traditional approach will briefly be described.

The complaint is first investigated by a protective services worker. Those interviewed when a complaint is investigated include the child and the parents. When there is no evidence of neglect or abuse, the case may be closed after the initial interview. For families with serious problems, continued services may be provided for years.

If the child is clearly in danger (for example, is a victim of repeated severe abuse) or if the parents are unable or unwilling to make changes essential for the long-term well-being of the child, the youngster may have to be removed from the home. If the social worker decides it is necessary to remove the child from the home, the parents' voluntary consent is first sought. If it is not received, a petition is made to the court requesting that the child receive protection. Protective services agencies view court action as a means of protecting the child rather than prosecuting the parents.

After a petition is filed, a preliminary hearing is held within a few weeks. Parents are permitted to be represented by an attorney, and the normal adversarial court procedures are followed. The social worker must support the petition with documented facts. The judge has the responsibility of protecting the rights not only of the child but also of the parents. At the preliminary hearing, the parents are asked if they will consent to, or contest, the petition. If they decide to contest and if evidence of abuse and neglect is substantiated, a trial is held.

Numerous avenues are open to the judge when making a disposition. She or he may decide that there is not sufficient evidence of neglect or abuse to warrant any action. Or the judge can place the child under supervision of the court while permitting the child to remain at home. Such supervision puts pressure on the family to make needed changes, with the threat of the child being removed if the changes are not made. The judge also has the option of placing the child into protective legal custody. Under this arrangement, legal custody is assigned to a social agency, which then has the authority to remove the child from the parents' control if essential changes are not made. The judge also can terminate the parents' legal rights and place the child under guardianship of the agency. Under this disposition, the child is automatically removed from the home.

For children who are in imminent danger, many jurisdictions have provisions that allow either the protective services agency or the family court to remove the child immediately. Such children are then usually placed in a temporary foster home. When a child is removed for emergency reasons, a court hearing must be held within 24 hours to determine the appropriateness of the action. Unless the court is satisfied that protection of the child requires removal from the home, the child must be returned to his or her parents.

Protective services cannot withdraw from the situation if it finds that the parents are uncooperative or resistant. For most social services, clients are voluntary recipients. Protective services is one of the few services in which participation is involuntary (probation and parole are other examples).

Because protective services is involuntary, and because provision of services is based on an "outside" complaint, the recipients are likely to view the services as an invasion of privacy. The initial contact by the social worker may arouse hostility, be viewed as a threat to family autonomy, and perhaps raise some guilt about incidents in which the parents mistreated their children in the past. Having one's functioning as a parent questioned and explored arouses substantial emotional feelings. Although in theory the focus of protective services is rehabilitative and nonpunitive, protective services clients generally view the services as punitive and investigatory.

Some recipients of protective services remain hostile and resistant throughout the time services are provided. Others eventually form a productive working relationship with the agency, in which case positive changes are much more likely to occur. A few individuals are cooperative from the beginning, perhaps because they recognize that their family needs help.

In working with parents who neglect or abuse their children, the social worker must show respect for the parents as people while in no way conveying acceptance of their mistreatment. The worker needs to convey empathy with their situation, and be warm, yet be firm about the need for positive changes.

Numerous treatment resources are used in attempting to make the needed changes. Crisis nurseries, extended day-care centers, and emergency foster homes provide short-term shelter to relieve a potentially damaging crisis situation. Parent effectiveness training programs (see CTRM Module 4), group counseling, and family-life education programs sometimes are useful in curbing abuse or neglect. Homemakers relieve the frustrated, overburdened mother of some of the daily load of child care. Emergency relief funds are sometimes provided to meet immediate rent, heat, food, and electricity expenses. Behavior modification programs, such as modeling and role-playing (see Module 2), have been used to change the behaviors of parents toward their children. *Emergency parents* have been used in some communities to go into a home and stay with a child who has been left unsupervised and unprotected. Psychotherapy and counseling have been provided by protective services workers and other professionals. (Very few communities have the resources to provide all of these services. In many cities, the primary intervention resources available to protective services workers are their own counseling capacities and their ability to remove children who are in danger from the home.)

Debra Singer sees two major problems with this traditional approach. First, the adult clients (the parents) tend to view the services of the protective services worker and agency as adversarial. They are often reluctant to become engaged with the worker and agency in a respectful manner, and they often view the whole protective services process as an invasion of their parental rights. Second, Ms. Singer is concerned that a large number of the neglected or abused children who are placed in foster homes tend to languish in foster care (sometimes until age 18), and some of them are moved from one foster home to another. Thus, Ms. Singer urges the protective services agency to appoint a study committee to seek to problem-solve these issues.

To be effective, a worker must seek to form appropriate, professional relationships with all potential clients. A working relationship is facilitated when the worker reflects empathy, warmth, and sincerity. (Chapter 5 contains additional information on forming and maintaining professional relationships with clients.)

Phase 2: Identifying Issues, Problems, Needs, Resources, and Assets The first step in phase 2 is to identify issues, problems, and needs. The two issues identified by Ms. Singer have already been mentioned. Based on the initial identification of issues, problems, and needs, the social worker must determine what resources and assets are available to confront the situation.

Ms. Singer is aware that Walworth County has five protective services workers who investigate cases and then provide services to cases in which abuse or neglect has been substantiated. In addition, the county spends considerable funds on foster care. Ms. Singer concludes that if an alternative intervention approach to providing protective services can be identified, some of the current funds being spent on protective services by the county could be allocated to the alternative approach.

Phase 3: Collecting and Assessing Information In this phase, an in-depth collection and analysis of data are undertaken to provide the social worker with answers to the issues and problems raised in phase 1.

Ms. Singer receives approval from the supervisor of the protective services unit to study these issues. The study committee is composed of three of the five protective services workers in the county. Assessment is the process of analyzing the data to make sense of it. The processes of collecting data and arriving at valid assessments are described in Chapter 3.

The study committee begins by reviewing the research conducted on the traditional protective services approach. The research supports Ms. Singer's concerns about the difficulties in engaging parents in protective services cases and the high costs and adverse effects of long-term foster care.

Phase 4: Planning for Service Delivery This phase involves making a decision about whether services should be provided. In this case example, the decision is easily made, for the county is mandated by the state to provide protective services. The bigger question for this case is what intervention approaches should be used. Can an alternative approach be found to better engage the parents in protective services cases, and can the number of children being sent to foster care be sharply reduced?

Phase 5: Using Communication Skills, Supervision, and Consultation Effectiveness as a social worker is highly dependent on the worker's communication skills—both oral and writing skills. (Many agency directors assert that writing skills are as important as interviewing and counseling skills—because workers need to document assessment and treatment plans, as well as write court reports and the other reports required by the agency.) Also important are the worker's capacities to give presentations; to be a witness in court; and to communicate effectively with clients, staff, and professionals at other agencies.

Every agency administrator wants social workers who are team players and who respond to supervision in a positive manner—that is, who do not become defensive when critical comments and suggestions are given. (Ms. Singer has frequent meetings with her supervisor about what courses of action she should take.)

Workers also need to know when consultation may be beneficial and then be willing to use such consultation. Thus, after contacting the state's Department of Health and Human Services, Ms. Singer is informed that a state department consultant, Dr. Raul Gomez, has considerable expertise in innovative approaches to providing protective services. Dr. Gomez is available to protective services units in the state at no direct charge. The two arrange to meet.

Phase 6: Identifying, Analyzing, and Implementing Empirically Based Interventions Designed to Achieve Client Goals Ms. Singer and Dr. Gomez meet. Ms. Singer shares her concerns. Dr. Gomez says he is aware of a program that may be of interest to Ms. Singer. He describes *family group conferencing*. The family group conferencing approach with abused or neglected children originated in New Zealand but has been adopted in many other countries, including the United States.

When evidence of child abuse has been documented by child protective services or the police, some child protective services agencies offer parents of the affected children the option of using family group conferencing to attempt to improve their parenting and end abuse. The process is first explained to the parents. If the parents agree to involve their extended kinship network in planning, the process is then implemented.

The family decision-making conference is facilitated by a professional person (often associated with child protective services). The professional person is usually called the *family group coordinator*. Three characteristics are central to family group conferencing:

1. The word *family* is broadly defined to include extended family members, as well as other people who are significant to the family.
2. The family is given the opportunity to prepare the plan.
3. The professionals working with the family must agree to the plan.

The coordinator prepares and plans for the first meeting of the extended family. Such planning may take weeks. Downs, Moore, McFadden, and Costin (2000) describe the initial planning process:

> This involves working with the family; identifying concerned parties and members of the extended kinship network; clarifying their roles and inviting them to a family group meeting; establishing the location, time, and other logistics; and managing other unresolved issues. At the meeting the coordinator welcomes and introduces participants in a culturally appropriate manner, establishes the purpose of the meeting, and helps participants reach agreement about roles, goals, and ground rules. Next, information is shared with the family, which may involve the child protection workers and other relevant professionals such as a doctor or teacher involved with the child. (p. 295)

In the New Zealand model, the coordinator and other professionals withdraw from the meeting in the next stage, to allow the family privacy for their deliberations. (Some programs in the United States and other countries allow the coordinator to remain in the meeting.) The kinship network makes plans to respond to the issues that are raised, including developing a plan for the safety and the care of the child. The coordinator or protective services retain the right to veto a family plan if they believe the child will not be protected. (In reality, a veto is rarely used.) Several meetings (over several days) may be necessary to develop the family plan.

Downs et al. (2000) summarize the challenges faced by social workers with this approach:

> Working with family group decision making requires a new approach to family-centered practice. The social worker must expand his or her ideas about the family to recognize the strength and centrality of the extended kinship network, particularly in communities of color. Use of the strengths perspective is critical. The worker must understand the greater investment of kin in the well-being of the child and should also understand that, even when parts of the kinship system may seem to be compromised or dysfunctional, the healthier kinfolk can assess and deal with the problem. One of the greatest challenges for the social worker is incorporating the sharing of power or returning of power to the kinship network. Many social workers trained as family therapists or child welfare workers have assumed a power role and may find it difficult to relinquish a sense of control. (p. 295)

Family group conferencing has several advantages: It facilitates getting the extended family involved in meeting the needs of the abused or neglected child or children and in meeting the needs of their parents. It reduces government interventions in people's lives. It recognizes the strengths of kinship networks to provide assistance to at-risk families. It reduces the number of children placed in foster homes. (Frequently, with this approach one or more extended family members temporarily take in the abused or neglected child, which then gives the parents an opportunity to receive whatever they need to become more stable and to learn better parenting skills.)

Ms. Singer is very interested in family group conferencing. It appears to meet her two main objectives: to find an approach that better engages parents in the protective services process when abuse or neglect is substantiated and to find an approach that reduces the number of children going into foster care. She indicates she will inform her study committee and her supervisor about this approach. (Identifying and implementing alternative interventions is described in further detail in Chapters 5, 7, 8, and 10.)

Phase 7: Applying Empirical Knowledge and Technology Ms. Singer, her study committee, and her supervisor review research conducted on family group conferencing.

The Internet provides ready access to a number of research studies. The articles support Dr. Gomez's assertion that family group conferencing (compared with the traditional protective services approach) will better engage parents in protective services cases and will reduce the number of children going into foster care. The protective services unit at Walworth County Human Services decides to try family group conferencing on a trial basis. Ms. Singer is designated the family group coordinator at this agency. (Additional information on research in social work practice is described in Chapters 5, 7, and 11.)

Phase 8: Evaluating Program Outcomes and Practice Effectiveness To evaluate the cost-benefit effectiveness of family group conferencing, Ms. Singer compares the costs and outcomes of the traditional protective services approach with the costs and outcomes of the family group conferencing alternative. She calculates an "average" cost for the traditional approach. The calculation includes costs for foster care, incurred when a child is removed for his or her protection. She also tabulates the amount of money spent on parents who choose family group conferencing. Ms. Singer realizes it is harder to quantify the benefits to a child on family group conferencing of staying with his or her parents (or with a relative or family friend) than it is to calculate the benefits of placing the child in foster care. But after a year of implementing the family group conferencing approach, she is able to document that it is cost-effective for the county to offer family group conferencing as an alternative to the traditional protective services approach, and the protective services unit decides to offer family group conferencing to all parents in protective services cases where abuse or neglect has been substantiated.

The final phase of any intervention is termination. (Chapters 5–8 and 11 describe termination and evaluation in greater detail.)

EP 2.1.1.c

A Variety of Roles

In working with individuals, groups, families, organizations, and communities, a social worker is expected to be knowledgeable and skillful in filling a variety of roles. Particular roles should (ideally) be determined by what will be most effective, given the circumstances. The following list identifies some, but certainly not all, of the roles assumed by social workers.

Enabler In this role, a worker *helps* individuals or groups articulate their needs, clarify and identify their problems, explore resolution strategies, select and apply a strategy, and develop their capacities to deal with their own problems more effectively. The enabler is perhaps the most frequently used role in counseling individuals, groups, and families. The model is also used in community practice, primarily when the objective is to help people organize to help themselves.

(This definition of *enabler* is very different from the definition used in the context of chemical dependency. There the term refers to a family member or friend who facilitates the substance abuser in continuing to use and abuse the drug of his or her choice.)

Broker A broker links individuals and groups who need help (and do not know where to obtain it) with community services. For example, a wife who is frequently physically abused by her husband might be referred to a shelter for battered women. Nowadays even moderate-size communities have 200 or 300 social service agencies/organizations providing community services. Even human services professionals are often only partially aware of the total service network in their community.

Advocate This role is borrowed from the law profession. It is an active directive role—that is, the social worker advocates for a client or for a citizen's group. When a client or a citizen's group is in need of help and existing institutions are uninterested (and sometimes openly negative and hostile) in providing services, the advocate's role may be appropriate. The advocate provides leadership for collecting information, arguing the correctness of the client's need and request, and challenging the institution's decision not to provide services. The object is not to ridicule or censure a particular institution but to modify or change one or more of its service policies. In this role, the social worker is a partisan who serves the interests of a client or of a citizen's group exclusively.

Empowerer A key goal of social work practice is *empowerment,* the process of helping individuals, families, groups, organizations, and communities increase their personal, interpersonal, socioeconomic, and political strength and influence by improving their circumstances. Social workers who engage in empowerment-focused practice seek to develop the capacity of clients to understand their environment, make choices, take responsibility for their choices, and influence their life situations through organization and advocacy. Empowerment-focused social workers also seek to gain a more equitable distribution of resources and power among different groups in society. This focus on equity and social justice is a hallmark of the social work profession, as evidenced through the early settlement workers such as Jane Addams.

Activist An activist seeks basic institutional change; often the objective involves a shift in power and resources to a disadvantaged group. An activist is concerned about social injustice, inequity, and deprivation. Tactics involve conflict, confrontation, and negotiation. Social action is concerned with changing the social environment to better meet the recognized needs of individuals. The methods used are assertive and action oriented (for example, organizing welfare recipients to work toward improvements in services and increases in money payments). Activities of social action include fact finding, analysis of community needs, research, dissemination and interpretation of information, organization of activities with people, and other efforts to mobilize public understanding and support on behalf of some existing or proposed social program. Social action can be geared toward a problem that is local, statewide, or national in scope.

Mediator Mediators intervene in disputes between parties to help them find compromises, reconcile differences, or reach mutually satisfactory agreements. Social workers use their value orientations and unique skills in many forms of mediation between opposing parties (for example, divorcing spouses, neighbors in conflict, landlord-tenant disputes, labor–management disputes, and child custody disputes). A mediator remains neutral, not siding with either party in the dispute. Mediators make sure they understand the positions of both parties. They clarify positions, recognize miscommunication, and help the parties present their cases clearly.

Negotiator A negotiator brings together those who are in conflict over one or more issues, then helps them bargain and compromise to arrive at mutually acceptable agreements. Somewhat like mediation, negotiation involves finding a middle ground that all sides can live with. However, unlike a mediator (which is a neutral role), a negotiator usually is allied with one of the sides involved.

Educator Educators give information to clients and teach them adaptive skills. To be an effective educator, the worker must first be knowledgeable. In addition, the worker must be a good communicator so that information is conveyed clearly and is readily understood by the receiver. Examples include teaching parenting skills to young parents, instructing teenagers in job-hunting strategies, and teaching anger-control techniques to individuals with difficulties in this area.

Initiator An initiator calls attention to a problem or to a potential problem. A problem does not have to exist before attention can be called to it. For example, a proposal to renovate a low-income neighborhood by building middle-income housing units may raise the problem of dispossessing current residents who cannot afford the cost of the new units. Because calling attention to problems usually does not resolve them, the initiator role must often be followed by other kinds of work.

Coordinator In this role, the worker brings components together in an organized manner. For example, in the case of a multiproblem family, several agencies often work together to meet the complicated financial, emotional, legal, health, social, educational, recreational, and interactional needs of the family members. Frequently, one social worker assumes the role of case manager and coordinates services from the different agencies to avoid duplication of services and conflicting objectives.

Researcher At times, every worker is a researcher. Research in social work practice includes researching the literature on topics of interest, evaluating the outcomes of one's practice, assessing the merits and shortcomings of programs, and studying community needs.

Group Facilitator A group facilitator is a leader for some group experience. The group may be a counseling group, an educational group, a self-help group, a sensitivity group, a family counseling group, or a group with some other focus.

EP 2.1.1.b.c

Public Speaker Social workers occasionally talk to a variety of groups (for example, high school classes, public service organizations such as Kiwanis, police officers, staff at other agencies) to inform them of available services or to advocate developing new services for clients whose needs are not being met. In recent years, various new services have been identified as being needed (for example, family preservation programs and services for persons with AIDS). Social workers who have public speaking skills are better able to explain services to groups of potential clients and also are likely to be rewarded (including financially) by their employers for their public speaking services.

Exercise 1.3: Your Interest in Various Social Work Roles

Goal: This exercise is designed to help you identify the social work roles that you want to become involved in.

Step 1: With a check, indicate your interest in each of the indicated roles.

	I want to become involved in	Uncertain	I do not want to become involved in
Enabler			
Broker			
Advocate			
Empowerer			
Activist			
Mediator			
Negotiator			
Educator			
Initiator			
Coordinator			
Researcher			
Group Facilitator			
Public Speaker			

Step 2: Describe your reasons for wanting to become involved in some roles.

Step 3: Describe your reasons for not wanting to become involved in other roles.

A Systems Perspective

Social workers are trained to have a systems perspective in their dealings with individuals, groups, families, organizations, and communities. A systems perspective emphasizes looking beyond presenting the problems of the client to assess the complexities and interrelationships of problems. Wholeness, relationship, and homeostasis are key concepts in systems theory.

The concept of *wholeness* means that the objects or elements within a system produce an entity that is greater than the sum of the parts. Systems theory is antireductionistic; it asserts that no system can be adequately understood or totally explained once it has been broken down into its component parts. (For example, the central nervous system carries out thought processes that would not occur if only parts were used.)

The concept of *relationship* asserts that the patterning and structuring among the elements in a system are as important as the elements themselves. For example, Masters and Johnson (1970) found that sexual dysfunctions occur primarily because of the nature of the husband–wife relationship rather than the psychological makeup of each partner.

Systems theory opposes simple cause-and-effect explanations. For instance, whether a child will be abused in a family is determined by a variety of variables and the patterning of these variables: the parents' capacity to control their anger, relationships between the child and the parents, relationships between the parents, degree of psychological stress, characteristics of the child, and opportunities for socially acceptable ways for parents to ventilate anger.

The concept of *homeostasis* suggests that most living systems endeavor to maintain and preserve the current system. Jackson (1965), for example, noted that families tend to establish a behavior balance or stability and to resist any change from that predetermined level of stability. Thus, a state of imbalance typically is driven back toward the previous state of balance *or* is driven forward to a new balance. If one child is abused in a family, that abuse often serves a function in the family as indicated by the fact that if that child is removed a second child is often selected to be abused. Or, if one family member improves through counseling, the improvement often upsets the balance within the family; other family members will have to change (which may be adaptive or maladaptive) to adjust to the new behavior of the improved family member.

Ecological theory is a subcategory of systems theory. Ecological theory has emerged as a prominent force in social work practice, as discussed in the next section.

COUNSELING AS A COMPONENT OF GENERALIST PRACTICE

A small minority of social work educators assert that counseling and clinical social work are not components of generalist social work practice. For instance, in *Understanding Generalist Practice,* Kirst-Ashman and Hull (2008) do not use the terms *counseling* and *clinical social work,* nor do they describe contemporary theories of counseling (such as rational therapy, reality therapy, and behavior therapy). In *Social Work Practice: A Generalist Approach,* Johnson (1986) does not use the terms *counseling* and *clinical social work* either, although she does give a half-page introduction to each of the contemporary theories of counseling.

I believe that counseling and clinical social work are key components in generalist practice. A generalist practitioner uses the problem-solving approach to bring about positive changes when working with individuals, families, groups, organizations, and communities. Much of social work practice with individuals, intervention groups, and families involves counseling and what has been called clinical social work. Clinical social workers diagnose and treat a wide variety of clients, using different treatment techniques and strategies to address different emotional and behavioral problems. Licensure for independent clinical social workers has been achieved in all 50 states, with the specific requirements varying from state to state (Groshong, 2009).

Every social worker who provides services to individuals, intervention groups, and families uses counseling principles and theories extensively. Competence in counseling is as essential for generalist-practice social workers to have as are competencies in other areas (such as brokering, policy making, lobbying, and planning). The vast majority of baccalaureate degree and master's degree social workers is engaged primarily in providing direct services to individuals, intervention groups, and families—with counseling services a major component of the direct services provided (Hopps & Collins, 1995). More social workers are psychotherapists in the United States than psychologists or psychiatrists are psychotherapists (Hepworth, Rooney, Rooney, Stromm-Gottfried, & Larsen, 2010). For many social workers, the term *clinical social worker* is synonymous with *social work psychotherapist.*

When a social worker identifies himself or herself as a clinical social worker or a psychotherapist, it does not mean that the person is uninvolved in other areas of generalist practice. In fact, in providing quality services to individuals, intervention groups, and families, every clinical social worker at times seeks to make positive changes in organizations and communities to benefit clients. One example would be advocating that social service agencies in the community change their eligibility guidelines for services so that clients (and individuals with similar needs in the community) can receive services to meet their health, welfare, and recreational needs.

Because counseling is a key component of generalist social work practice, in this text I emphasize principles and guidelines for counseling and present contemporary theories of counseling that are useful in working with individuals, intervention groups, and families.

Modules 1–4 in the Counseling Theories Resource Manual present and critique the prominent theories of counseling that are widely used by social workers, including reality therapy, rational therapy, and behavior therapy. Numerous specific intervention techniques are also described, including assertiveness training, token economies, aversive techniques, milieu therapy, psychodrama, crisis intervention, parent effectiveness training, meditation, task-centered practice, and solution-focused therapy.

COUNSELING VERSUS THERAPY/PSYCHOTHERAPY

One of the reviewers of a draft of this text commented that I needed to make it clear that graduates of accredited baccalaureate social work programs can counsel clients but cannot provide therapy/psychotherapy to clients. As far as the profession of social work is concerned, it is accurate to say that only licensed clinical social workers can be reimbursed by third-party payers (usually health insurance companies) for providing psychotherapy. (Other helping professionals, such as clinical psychologists and psychiatrists, also are reimbursed for providing psychotherapy.)

The question that arises is, What differentiates "counseling" from "therapy" or from "psychotherapy"? I believe this question is very important because graduates of accredited baccalaureate programs are supposed to limit the services they provide to "counseling." So I researched a variety of sources, seeking a definition that would differentiate "counseling" from "therapy" and "psychotherapy," including three state licensing/certification boards in social work and the Association of Social Work Boards. I also asked baccalaureate social work educators who are on the Baccalaureate Program Directors (BPD) listserv to respond to this question.

I received a variety of definitions of these three terms. A definition of each of these terms follows:

> **Counseling—**Professional guidance of individuals, families or groups to assist them in coping with life challenges through such techniques as problem solving, identifying alternatives, articulating goals, and providing needed information.
>
> **Therapy—**Therapeutic treatment, especially of bodily, emotional or behavioral disorders. Social workers frequently use this term as a synonym for psychotherapy.
>
> **Psychotherapy—**Treatment of emotional or behavioral disorders, or of related bodily ills by professional therapists—such as clinical social workers, psychologists, and psychiatrists. Psychotherapists are licensed in all 50 states in the United States.

From the BPD listserv, I received a variety of responses regarding what differentiates "counseling" from "therapy" or "psychotherapy." The following are illustrative:

- The licensed professions should limit the use of the term *psychotherapy* to only the licensed mental health professions for the protection of the public.
- In this state, there is no control of therapy/psychotherapy. We may think that these terms convey work that is done by only the most skilled professionals; however, in reality anybody off the street can perform the duties of a therapist/psychotherapist.
- No difference among them.
- Although psychotherapy and counseling overlap considerably, there are also some differences. The work with clients may be of considerable depth in both modalities; however, the focus of counseling is more likely to be on specific problems or changes in life adjustment. Psychotherapy is more concerned with the restructuring of the personality or self.
- Although both psychotherapists and counselors work with a wide variety of clients, psychotherapists are more likely to work very intensively with more deeply disturbed individuals who are seen more frequently over a longer period of time.
- Counseling is an educative modality, and therapy is an emotional, understanding restorative modality.
- Counseling is problem solving, and therapy/psychotherapy deals with deeper psychological or mental health issues.
- Psychotherapy is concerned with some type of personality change whereas counseling is concerned with helping individuals utilize full coping potential.
- Counseling is best for routine maintenance, and psychotherapy is best for a major overhaul of the client's personality.
- The distinction between counseling and psychotherapy is murky at best, even at the master's and doctoral level.
- Licensed clinical social workers can diagnose clients, using the classifications in *Diagnostic and Statistical Manual of Mental Disorders-IV, Revised* (American Psychiatric Association, 2000), but BSW persons cannot. (It should be noted that some states require that licensed clinical social workers need to be supervised by a psychiatrist or by a clinical psychologist.)

Given this list, what can be concluded is that there is considerable overlap between "counseling" and "therapy/psychotherapy." At the present time, there appear to be no major clear-cut distinctions between these terms. It is true that licensed clinical social workers can diagnose clients using *DSM-IV, Revised,* but BSW persons cannot.

Some key unanswered questions are the following: First, are some intervention techniques (such as hypnosis) beyond the limit of authority for a BSW graduate to use? If so, what are they? Also, how do we determine if a BSW graduate has exceeded the limit of his or her authority?

I put this last question to a social worker in my state who is a member of the state social work certification/licensing board. This person responded, "To date, the board has only concluded that a BSW person is acting outside the scope of his or her certification when that person states in a résumé or in an ad that s/he provides psychotherapy."

THE MEDICAL MODEL VERSUS THE ECOLOGICAL MODEL OF HUMAN BEHAVIOR

The Medical Model

EP 2.1.7.a

From the 1920s to the 1960s, most social workers used a medical model for assessing and changing human behavior. This model, initiated primarily by Sigmund Freud, views clients as *patients.* The service provider first diagnoses the causes of a patient's problems and then provides treatment. The patient's problems are viewed as being inside the patient.

The medical model has a lengthy classification of mental disorders defined by the American Psychiatric Association. The major categories of mental disorders are listed in Exhibit 1.1.

Exercise 1.4: Understanding the Major Mental Disorders

Goal: This exercise is designed to assist you in understanding the major mental disorders.

Briefly describe people you know who have the mental disorders identified in Exhibit 1.1. For confidentiality reasons, do not use their real names. Here is an example of a desired brief description: Jenny, age 22 and a college student, has been bulimic for at least the past three years. She has been binging and purging four or more times a week. Recently, she stated some of her vomit sometimes contains blood (which may suggest a serious medical issue).

EP 2.1.7.a

The medical model conceptualizes emotional and behavioral problems as *mental illnesses.* People with emotional or behavioral problems are then given medical labels such as schizophrenia, paranoia, psychosis, and insanity. Adherents of the medical approach believe the disturbed person's mind is affected by some generally unknown internal condition that is thought to result from a variety of possible causative factors: genetic endowment, metabolic disorders, infectious diseases, internal conflicts, unconscious uses of defense mechanisms, and traumatic early experiences that cause emotional fixations and prevent future psychological growth.

Several specific mental disorders are described briefly here.

Schizophrenia This malady encompasses a large group of disorders, usually of psychotic proportion, manifested by characteristic disturbances of language and communication, thought, perception, affect, and behavior and lasting longer than 6 months.

Exhibit 1.1 Major Mental Disorders According to the American Psychiatric Association

Disorders usually first diagnosed in infancy, childhood, or adolescence include, but are not limited to, mental retardation, learning disorders, communication disorders (such as stuttering), autism, attention-deficit/hyperactivity disorders, and separation anxiety disorder.
Delirium, dementia, and amnestic and other cognitive disorders include delirium due to alcohol and other drug intoxication, dementia due to Alzheimer's disease or Parkinson's disease, dementia due to head trauma, and amnestic disorder.
Substance-related disorders include mental disorders related to abuse of alcohol, caffeine, amphetamines, cocaine, hallucinogens, nicotine, and other mind-altering substances.
Schizophrenia and other psychotic disorders include delusional disorders and all forms of schizophrenia (such as paranoid, disorganized, and catatonic).
Mood disorders—emotional disorders such as depression and bipolar disorders.
Anxiety disorders include phobias, post-traumatic stress disorder, and anxiety disorders.
Somatoform disorders—psychological problems that manifest themselves as symptoms of physical disease (for example, hypochondria).
Dissociative disorders—problems in which part of the personality is dissociated from the rest (for example, dissociative identity disorder, formerly called multiple personality disorder).
Sexual and gender identity disorders include sexual dysfunctions (such as hypoactive sexual desire, premature ejaculation, male erectile disorder, male and female orgasmic disorders, and vaginismus), exhibitionism, fetishism, pedophilia (child molestation), sexual masochism, sexual sadism, voyeurism, and gender identity disorders (such as cross-gender identification).
Eating disorders include anorexia nervosa and bulimia nervosa.
Sleep disorders—insomnia and other problems with sleep (such as nightmares and sleepwalking).
Impuse-control disorders—the inability to control certain undesirable impulses (for example, kleptomania, pyromania, and pathological gambling).
Adjustment disorders—difficulty in adjusting to the stress created by such common events as unemployment or divorce.
Personality disorders—an enduring pattern of inner experience and behavior that deviates markedly from the expectations of the individual's culture, is pervasive and inflexible, has an onset in adolescence or early adulthood, is stable over time, and leads to distress or impairment, examples include paranoid personality disorder, antisocial personality disorder, and obsessive-compulsive personality disorder.
Other conditions—cover a variety of disorders including parent-child relational problems; partner relational problems; sibling relational problems; child victims of physical abuse, sexual abuse, and neglect; adult victims of physical abuse and sexual abuse; malingering; bereavement; academic problems; occupational problems; identity problems; and religious or spiritual problems.

Source: Reprinted with permission from the *Diagnostic and Statistical Manual of Mental Diorders, Fourth Edition, Text Revision*, (Copyright © 2000). American Psychiatric Association.

Delusional Disorder The essential feature is the presence of one or more delusions that persist for at least 1 month. A delusion is something that is falsely believed or propagated. An example is the persecutory type, in which an individual erroneously believes that he or she is being conspired against, cheated, spied on, followed, poisoned or drugged, maliciously maligned, harassed, or obstructed in the pursuit of long-term goals.

Hypochondriasis This is a chronic maladaptive style of relating to the environment through preoccupation with shifting somatic concerns and symptoms, a fear or conviction that one has a serious physical illness, the search for medical treatment, inability to accept reassurance, and either hostile or dependent relationships with caregivers and family.

Bipolar Disorder This is a major affective disorder characterized by episodes of both mania and depression; it was formerly called manic-depressive psychosis. Bipolar disorder may be subdivided into manic, depressed, or mixed types on the basis of currently presenting symptoms.

Phobia A phobia is characterized by an obsessive, persistent, unrealistic, intense fear of an object or situation. Common phobias include *acrophobia* (fear of heights), *algophobia* (fear of pain), *claustrophobia* (fear of closed spaces), and *erythrophobia* (fear of blushing).

Personality Disorders Some of the most common personality disorders and their characteristics are as follows:

- *Paranoid.* A pattern of distrust and suspicion such that others' motives are interpreted as malevolent
- *Schizoid.* A pattern of detachment from social relationships and a restricted range of emotional expression
- *Schizotypal.* A pattern of acute discomfort in close relationships, cognitive or perceptual distortions, and eccentricities of behavior
- *Antisocial.* A pattern of disregard for, and violation of, the rights of others
- *Borderline.* A pattern of instability in interpersonal relationships, self-image, and affect; also characterized by marked impulsivity
- *Histrionic.* A pattern of excessive emotionality and attention seeking
- *Narcissistic.* A pattern of grandiosity, need for admiration, and lack of empathy
- *Avoidant.* A pattern of social inhibition, feelings of inadequacy, and hypersensitivity to negative evaluation
- *Dependent.* A pattern of submissive and clinging behavior related to an excessive need to be taken care of
- *Obsessive-compulsive.* A pattern of preoccupation with orderliness, perfectionism, and control

The medical model arose in reaction to the historical notion that the emotionally disturbed were possessed by demons, were mad, and were to be blamed for their disturbances. These people were "treated" by being beaten, locked up, or killed. The medical model viewed the disturbed as in need of help, stimulated research into the nature of emotional problems, and promoted the development of therapeutic approaches.

The major evidence for the validity of the medical model comes from studies that suggest that some mental disorders, such as schizophrenia, may be influenced by genetics (heredity). The bulk of the evidence on the case for heredity comes from studies of twins. For example, in some studies identical twins have been found to have a concordance rate (that is, if one twin has it, both have it) for schizophrenia of about 50% (Comer, 2005, pp. 251–260). Keep in mind that the rate of schizophrenia in the general population is about 1% (p. 251). When one identical twin is schizophrenic, the other is 50 times more likely than the average to be schizophrenic. This suggests a causal influence of genes, but not genetic determination, for concordance for identical twins is only 50%, not 100%.

The Ecological Model

In the 1960s, some social work scholars began to question the usefulness of the medical model. Environmental factors were shown to be at least as important as internal factors in causing a client's problems. Research also was demonstrating that psychoanalysis was probably ineffective in treating clients' problems (Stuart, 1970).

In the 1960s, social work shifted at least some of its emphasis to a *reform approach,* which seeks to change systems to benefit clients. Enactment of antipoverty programs (such as Head Start) is an example of an effort to change systems to benefit clients.

In the past several years, social work has increasingly focused on an *ecological model.* This model integrates both treatment and reform by conceptualizing and emphasizing the dysfunctional transactions between people and their physical and social environments. Human beings are viewed as developing and adapting through transactions with all elements of their environments. An ecological model gives attention to both internal and external factors. It does not view people as passive reactors to their environments but, rather, as being involved in dynamic and reciprocal interactions with them.

This model tries to improve the coping patterns of people and their environments so that a better match can be attained between an individual's needs and the

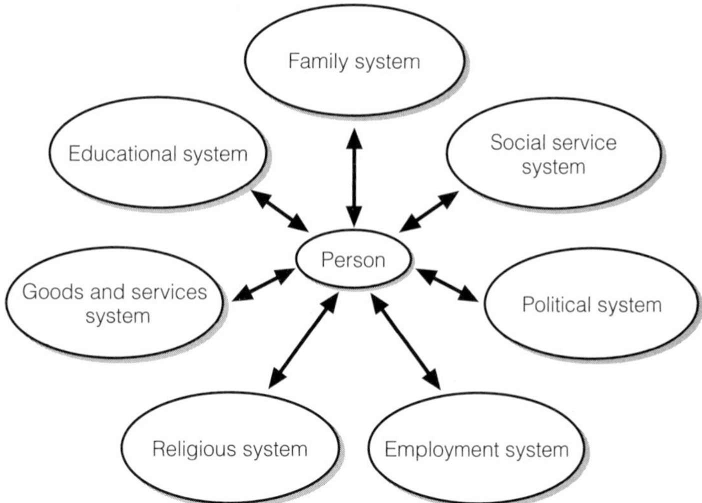

Figure 1.2
Person-in-environment conceptualization.

Source: © Cengage Learning, 2013.

characteristics of his or her environment. One emphasis of the model is on the person-in-environment. The person-in-environment conceptualization is depicted in Figure 1.2.

As is evident in the figure, people interact with many systems. With this conceptualization, social work can focus on three separate areas. First, it can focus on the person and seek to develop his or her problem-solving, coping, and developmental capacities. Second, it can focus on the relationship between a person and the systems he or she interacts with and link the person with needed resources, services, and opportunities. Third, it can focus on the systems and seek to reform them to meet the needs of the individual more effectively.

The ecological model views individuals, families, and small groups as having transitional problems and needs as they move from one life stage to another. Individuals face many transitional changes as they grow older, such as learning to walk, entering first grade, adjusting to puberty, graduating from school, finding a job, getting married, having children, having children leave home, and retiring.

Families also have a life cycle. Here are only a few of the events that require adjustment: engagement, marriage, birth of children, parenting, children going to school, children leaving home, and loss of a parent (perhaps through death or divorce).

Small groups have transitional phases of development as well. Members of small groups spend time getting acquainted, gradually learn to trust one another, begin to self-disclose more, learn to work together on tasks, develop approaches to handle interpersonal conflict, and face adjustments to the group eventually terminating or some members leaving.

The model's central concern is to articulate the transitional problems and needs of individuals, families, and small groups. Once these problems and needs are identified, intervention approaches are then selected and applied to help individuals, families, and small groups resolve the transitional problems and meet their needs.

An ecological model can also focus on maladaptive interpersonal problems and needs in families and groups, including communication processes and dysfunctional relationship patterns. These difficulties cover an array of areas, including interpersonal conflicts, power struggles, double binds, distortions in communicating, scapegoating, and discrimination. The consequences of such difficulties are usually maladaptive for some members. An ecological model seeks to identify such interpersonal obstacles and then apply appropriate intervention strategies. For example, parents may set the price for honesty too high for their children. In such families, children gradually learn to hide certain behaviors and thoughts, and even learn to lie. If the parents discover such dishonesty, an uproar usually occurs. An appropriate intervention is to open up communication patterns and help the parents understand that, if they really want honesty from their children, they need to learn to be more accepting of their children's thoughts and actions.

EP 2.1.7.a

Two centuries ago, people interacted primarily within the family system. Families were nearly self-sufficient. In those days, the person-in-family was a way of conceptualizing the main system that individuals interacted with. Our society has become much more complex. Today, a person's life and quality of life are interwoven with and inter-dependent on many systems, as shown in Figure 1.2.

Exercise 1.5: Understanding the Medical Model and the Ecological Model

Goal: This exercise is designed to help you understand the medical model and the ecological model. In understanding why people become involved in dysfunctional behavior (such as being anorexic, committing a crime, or becoming a batterer), which model (the medical model or the ecological model) do you believe is more useful? State the reasons for your choice.

GOALS OF SOCIAL WORK PRACTICE

EP 2.1.7.a

The National Association of Social Workers (1982) has conceptualized social work practice as having five major goals.

Goal 1: Enhance People's Problem-Solving, Coping, and Developmental Capacities

Using the person-in-environment concept, social work practice at this level focuses on the "person." With this focus, a social worker serves primarily as an *enabler*. In this role, the worker may take on the activities of a counselor, teacher, caregiver (providing supportive services to those who cannot fully solve their problems and meet their own needs), and behavior changer (that is, changing specific parts of a client's behavior).

Goal 2: Link People with Systems That Provide Them with Resources, Services, and Opportunities

Using the person-in-environment concept, social work practice at this level focuses on the relationships between individuals and the systems they interact with. In this situation, a social worker serves primarily as a *broker*.

Goal 3: Promote the Effective and Humane Operation of Systems That Provide People with Resources and Services

Using the person-in-environment concept, the focus of social work practice at this level is on the systems people interact with. One role a worker may fill at this level is an *advocate*. Additional roles include

Program developer: The worker seeks to promote or design programs or technologies to meet social needs.

Supervisor: The worker seeks to increase the effectiveness and efficiency of the delivery of services through supervising other staff.

Coordinator: The worker seeks to improve a delivery system by increasing communications and coordination between human service resources.

Consultant: The worker seeks to provide guidance to agencies and organizations by suggesting ways to increase the effectiveness and efficiency of services.

Goal 4: Develop and Improve Social Policy

Similar to goal 3, social work practice at this level focuses on the systems people interact with. The distinction between goal 3 and goal 4 is that the focus of goal 3 is on the available resources for serving people. Goal 4 works on the statutes and broader social policies that underlie such resources. The major roles at this level are *planner* and *policy developer*. In these roles, workers develop and seek adoption of new statutes or policies and propose elimination of ineffective or inappropriate ones. In these planning and policy development processes, social workers may take on an advocate role and, in some instances, an activist role.

The Council on Social Work Education (CSWE) is the national accreditating body for social work education in the United States. It describes the purpose of social work as follows (CSWE, 2008):

> The purpose of the social work profession is to promote human and community well-being. Guided by a person and environment construct, a global perspective, respect for human diversity, and knowledge based on scientific inquiry, social work's purpose is actualized through its quest for social and economic justice, the prevention of conditions that limit human rights, the elimination of poverty, and the enhancement of the quality of life for all persons.

This description of the purpose of social work is consistent with the four goals of social work mentioned earlier. However, it adds one additional goal, as follows.

Goal 5: Promote Human and Community Well-Being

The social work profession is committed to enhancing the well-being of all human beings and to promoting community well-being. It is particularly committed to alleviating poverty, oppression, and other forms of social injustice. About 15% of the U.S. population has an income below the poverty line. Social work has always advocated for developing programs to alleviate poverty, and many practitioners focus on providing services to the poor.

Poverty is global; every society has members who are poor. In some societies, as much as 95% of the population lives in poverty. Social workers are committed to alleviating poverty not only in the United States but also worldwide. Alleviating poverty is obviously complex and difficult. Social work professionals work with a variety of systems to make progress in alleviating poverty, including educational systems, health-care systems, political systems, business and employment systems, religious systems, and human services systems.

Oppression is the unjust or cruel exercise of authority or power. In our society, numerous groups have been oppressed—including African Americans, Latinos, Chinese Americans, Native Americans, women, persons with disabilities, gays and lesbians, various religious groups, and people living in poverty. (The listing of these groups is only illustrative and certainly not exhaustive.) Social injustice occurs when some members of a society have less protection, fewer basic rights and opportunities, or fewer social benefits than other members of that society. Social work is a profession that is committed not only to alleviating poverty but also to combating oppression and other forms of social injustice.

Social justice is an ideal condition in which all members of a society have the same basic rights, protection, opportunities, obligations, and social benefits. Economic justice is also an ideal condition in which all members of a society have the same opportunities to attain material goods, income, and wealth. Social workers have an obligation to help groups at risk increase their personal, interpersonal, socioeconomic, and political strength and influence through improving their circumstances. Empowerment-focused social workers seek a more equitable distribution of resources and power among the various groups in society. Diverse groups that may be at risk include those distinguished by "age, class, color, culture, disability, ethnicity, gender, gender identity and expression, immigration status, political ideology, race, religion, sex, and sexual orientation" (CSWE, 2008).

EP 2.1.1.b

Exercise 1.6: Your Interest in Achieving the Goals of Social Work

Goal: This exercise is designed to assist you in identifying your interest in becoming involved in activities that are consistent with the five goals of social work.

Step 1: Check which of the following identifies your interest level in each of the five goals of social work.

	Highly Interested	Somewhat Interested	Uncertain	Somewhat Disinterested	Not Interested
Goal 1					
Goal 2					
Goal 3					
Goal 4					
Goal 5					

Step 2: For the goals that you checked "Highly Interested," state the reasons for these selections.

Step 3: For the goals that you checked "Somewhat Disinterested" or "Not Interested," state your reasons for these markings.

MICRO, MEZZO, AND MACRO LEVELS OF PRACTICE

EP 2.1.7.a

Social workers practice at three levels: (1) *micro*—working on a one-to-one basis with an individual; (2) *mezzo*—working with families and other small groups; and (3) *macro*—working with organizations and communities or seeking changes in statutes and social policies.

The specific activities performed by workers include, but are not limited to, the following categories.

Social Casework

Aimed at helping individuals on a one-to-one basis to meet personal and social problems, casework may be geared to helping the client adjust to his or her environment or to changing certain social and economic pressures that adversely affect an individual. Social casework services are provided by nearly every social welfare agency that provides direct services to people. *Social casework* encompasses a wide variety of activities, such as counseling runaway youths; helping unemployed people secure training or employment; counseling someone who is suicidal; placing a homeless child in an adoptive or foster home; providing protective services to abused children and their families; finding nursing homes for stroke victims who no longer need to be hospitalized; counseling individuals with sexual dysfunctions; helping alcoholics acknowledge they have a drinking problem; counseling those with a terminal illness; being a probation and parole officer; providing services to single parents; and working in medical and mental hospitals as a member of a rehabilitation team.

Case Management

Many social service agencies have labeled their social workers *case managers*. The tasks performed by case managers are similar to those of caseworkers. The job descriptions of case managers vary from service area to service area. For example, case managers in a juvenile probation setting supervise clients, provide some counseling, monitor clients to make certain they are following the rules of probation, link clients and their families with needed services, prepare court reports, and testify in court. Case managers at a sheltered workshop are likely to provide job training and counseling, arrange transportation, discipline clients for unacceptable behavior, act as an advocate, and act as liaison with the people who supervise clients during their nonwork hours (which may be at a group home, foster home, residential treatment facility, or their parents' home). Hepworth and Larsen (1986) described the role of a case manager this way:

> Case managers link clients to needed resources that exist in complex service delivery networks and orchestrate the delivery of services in a timely fashion. Case managers function as brokers, facilitators, linkers, mediators, and advocates. A case manager must have extensive knowledge of community resources, rights of clients, and policies and procedures of various agencies and must be skillful in mediation and advocacy. (p. 563)

Group Work

The intellectual, emotional, and social development of individuals may be furthered through group activities. In contrast to casework or group counseling, *group work* is not primarily therapeutic, except in a broad sense. Different groups have different objectives, such as socialization, information exchange, curbing delinquency, recreation, changing socially unacceptable values, and helping achieve better relations between cultural and racial groups. For example, through group activities a group worker at a neighborhood center may seek to curb delinquency patterns and change socially unacceptable values, or a worker at an adoption agency may meet with a group of applicants to explain adoption procedures and help applicants prepare for becoming adoptive parents. Activities and focuses of groups vary: arts and crafts, dancing, games, dramatics, music, photography, sports, nature study, woodwork, first aid, home management, information exchange, and discussion of such topics as politics, sex, marriage, religion, and selecting a career.

Group Counseling

Group counseling is aimed at facilitating the social, behavioral, and emotional adjustment of individuals through the group process. Participants in group counseling usually have emotional, interactional, or behavioral difficulties. Group counseling has several advantages over one-to-one counseling, such as the operation of the helper therapy principle, which maintains it is therapeutic for the helper (who can be any member of a group) to feel he or she has been helpful to others. In contrast to one-to-one counseling, group pressure is often more effective in changing individuals' maladaptive behavior, and group counseling is a time saver because it enables the group facilitator to treat several people simultaneously. For example, group counseling might be used for individuals who are severely depressed, have drinking problems, are rape victims, are psychologically addicted to drugs, have a relative who is terminally ill, are single and pregnant, are recently divorced, or have an eating disorder.

Family Counseling

A type of group counseling aimed at helping families with interactional, behavioral, and emotional problems, *family counseling* can be used with parent–child interaction problems, marital conflicts, and conflicts with grandparents. A wide variety of problems are dealt with in family treatment or family counseling, such as communication problems and disagreements between parents and youths on choice of friends, drinking and other drug use, domestic tasks, curfew hours, sexual values and behavior, study habits and grades received, and choice of dates.

Community Organization

The aim of *community organization* is stimulating and assisting the local community to evaluate, plan, and coordinate efforts to provide for the community's health, welfare, and recreation needs. Although it is not possible to define precisely the activities of a community organizer, they often include encouraging and fostering citizen participation, coordinating efforts between agencies or groups, public relations and public education, research, planning, and being a resource person. A community organizer acts as a catalyst in stimulating and encouraging community action. Such specialists are apt to be employed in community welfare councils, social planning agencies, health planning councils, and community action agencies. The term *community organization* is now being replaced in some settings by *planning, social planning, program development, policy development,* and *macro practice*.

Barker (2003) defined *community organization* as:

> An intervention process used by social workers and other professionals to help individuals, groups, and collectives of people with common interests or from the same geographic areas to deal with social problems and to enhance social well-being through planned collective action. Methods include identifying problem areas, analyzing causes, formulating plans, developing strategies, mobilizing necessary resources, identifying and recruiting community leaders, and encouraging interrelationships between them to facilitate their efforts. (p. 84)

Policy Analysis

Policy analysis involves systematic evaluation of a policy and the process by which it was formulated. Those who conduct such an analysis consider whether the process and result were clear, equitable, legal, rational, compatible with social values, superior to other alternatives, cost-effective, and explicit. Such an analysis frequently identifies shortcomings in the policy. Those conducting the policy analysis then usually recommend modifications in the policy that are designed to alleviate these shortcomings.

Administration

Administration involves directing the overall program of a social service agency. Administrative functions include setting agency program objectives; analyzing social conditions in the community; making decisions about what services will be provided; employing and supervising staff members; setting up an organizational structure; administering financial affairs; and securing funds for the agency's operations. Administration also involves setting organizational goals; coordinating activities to achieve the selected goals; and monitoring and making necessary changes in processes and structure to improve the effectiveness and efficiency of processes that contribute to transforming social policy into social services. In social work, the term *administration* is often used synonymously with *management*. In a small agency, administrative functions may be carried out by one person, whereas several people may be involved in administrative affairs in a larger agency.

EP 2.1.1.b

Exercise 1.7: Identifying Your Interest in Various Social Work Activities

Goal: This exercise is designed to help you reflect on the kinds of activities you want to engage in as a social worker.

Step 1: Check which of the following indicates your interest in engaging in a variety of social work activities.

	Highly Interested	Somewhat Interested	Uncertain	Somewhat Disinterested	Not Interested
1. Social Casework					
2. Case Management					
3. Group Work					
4. Group Counseling					
5. Family Counseling					
6. Community Organization					
7. Policy Analysis					
8. Administration					

Step 2: For the activities that you checked "Highly Interested," state the reasons for these selections.

Step 3: For the activities that you checked "Somewhat Disinterested" or "Not Interested," state your reasons for these markings.

Other areas of professional activity in social work include research, consulting, supervising, planning, program development, policy development, and teaching (primarily at the college level). Social casework, case management, group work, group counseling, family counseling, and community organization constitute the primary professional activities that beginning-level social workers are likely to provide. All of these activities require social workers to have counseling skills. (Counseling involves helping individuals or groups resolve social and personal problems through the process of developing a relationship, exploring the problems in depth, and exploring alternative solutions. This process is described in Chapter 5.) Caseworkers, case managers, group workers, group counselors, and family counselors need high levels of counseling skills to work with individuals and groups. Community organizers need to be perceptive, and they need skills in relating to other people in assessing problems and developing resolution strategies—skills that parallel or are analogous to counseling skills. Therefore, a major emphasis of this text is on counseling.

Counseling skills, however, are not the only skills social workers need. For example, caseworkers also need to be able to construct social histories and to link clients with other human services. Some agencies require skills in public speaking, preparing and presenting reports to courts and to other agencies, and teaching parents better parenting techniques. Research capacities to evaluate one's own practice and other programs are also important. The essential skills needed for social work practice are further described in the next section. As you will see, generalist social workers are expected to have an extensive knowledge base and numerous skills and to adhere to a well-defined set of professional social work values.

KNOWLEDGE, SKILLS, AND VALUES NEEDED FOR SOCIAL WORK PRACTICE

EP 2.1.1.a through 2.1.10.m

In *Educational Policy and Accreditation Standards (EPAS)*, the Council on Social Work Education (2008) identified knowledge, skills, and values that accredited baccalaureate and master's degree programs are mandated to convey to social work students. *EPAS* is based on a competency approach. The following material is reprinted with permission from *EPAS* (CSWE, 2008).

> The BSW curriculum prepares its graduates for generalist practice through mastery of the core competencies. The MSW curriculum prepares its graduates for advanced practice through mastery of the core competencies augmented by knowledge and practice behaviors specific to a concentration.

EDUCATIONAL POLICY 2.1—CORE COMPETENCIES

Competency-based education is an outcome performance approach to curriculum design. Competencies are measurable practice behaviors that are comprised of knowledge, values, and skills. The goal of the outcome approach is to demonstrate the integration and application of the competencies in practice with individuals, families, groups, organizations, and communities. The ten core competencies are listed below [EP 2.1.1–EP 2.1.10(d)], followed by a description of characteristic knowledge, values, skills, and the resulting practice behaviors that may be used to operationalize the curriculum and assessment methods. Programs may add competencies consistent with their missions and goals.

Educational Policy 2.1.1—Identify as a professional social worker and conduct oneself accordingly.

Social workers serve as representatives of the profession, its mission, and its core values. They know the profession's history. Social workers commit themselves to the profession's enhancement and to their own professional conduct and growth. Social workers

- advocate for client access to the services of social work;
- practice personal reflection and self-correction to assure continual professional development;
- attend to professional roles and boundaries;
- demonstrate professional demeanor in behavior, appearance, and communication;
- engage in career-long. learning; and
- use supervision and consultation.

Educational Policy 2.1.2—Apply social work ethical principles to guide professional practice.

Social workers have an obligation to conduct themselves ethically and to engage in ethical decision making. Social workers are knowledgeable about the value base of the profession, its ethical standards, and relevant law. Social workers

- recognize and manage personal values in a way that allows professional values to guide practice;
- make ethical decisions by applying standards of the National Association of Social Workers Code of Ethics[4] and, as applicable, of the International Federation of Social Workers/International Association of Schools of Social Work Ethics in Social Work, Statement of Principles;[5]
- tolerate ambiguity in resolving ethical conflicts; and
- apply strategies of ethical reasoning to arrive at principled decisions.

Educational Policy 2.1.3—Apply critical thinking to inform and communicate professional judgments.

Social workers are knowledgeable about the principles of logic, scientific inquiry, and reasoned discernment. They use critical thinking augmented by creativity and curiosity. Critical thinking also requires the synthesis and communication of relevant information. Social workers

- distinguish, appraise, and integrate multiple sources of knowledge, including research-based knowledge, and practice wisdom;
- analyze models of assessment, prevention, intervention, and evaluation; and
- demonstrate effective oral and written communication in working with individuals, families, groups, organizations, communities, and colleagues.

Educational Policy 2.1.4—Engage diversity and difference in practice.

Social workers understand how diversity characterizes and shapes the human experience and is critical to the formation of identity. The dimensions of diversity are understood as the intersectionality of multiple factors including age, class, color, culture, disability,

---

[4]National Association of Social Workers (approved 1996, revised 1999), *Code of Ethics for Social Workers*. Washington, DC: NASW.

[5]International Federation of Social Workers and International Association of Schools of Social W (2004), *Ethics in Social Work, Statement of Principles*. Retrieved January 2, 2008, from http://www.ifsw.

ethnicity, gender identity and expression, immigration status, political ideology, race, religion, sex, and sexual orientation. Social workers appreciate that, as a consequence of difference, a person's life experiences may include oppression, poverty, marginalization, and alienation as well as privilege, power, and acclaim. Social workers

- recognize the extent to which a culture's structures and values may oppress, marginalize, alienate, or create or enhance privilege and power;
- gain sufficient self-awareness to eliminate the influence of personal biases and values in working with diverse groups;
- recognize and communicate their understanding of the importance of difference in shaping life experiences; and
- view themselves a learner and engage those with whom they work as informants.

Educational Policy 2.1.5—Advance human rights and social and economic justice.
Each person, regardless of position in society, has basic human rights, such as freedom, safety, privacy, an adequate standard of living, health care, and education. Social workers recognize the global interconnections of oppression and are knowledgeable about theories of justice and strategies to promote human and civil rights. Social work incorporates social justice practices in organizations, institutions, and society to ensure that these basic human rights are distributed equitably and without prejudice. Social workers

- understand the forms and mechanisms of oppression and discrimination;
- advocate for human rights and social and economic justice; and
- engage in practices that advance social and economic justice.

Educational Policy 2.1.6—Engage in research-informed practice and practice-informed research.
Social workers use practice experience to inform research, employ evidence-based interventions, evaluate their own practice, and use research findings to improve practice, policy, and social service delivery. Social workers comprehend quantitative and qualitative research and understand scientific and ethical approaches to building knowledge. Social workers

- use practice experience to inform scientific inquiry; and
- use research evidence to inform practice.

Educational Policy 2.1.7—Apply knowledge of human behavior and the social environment.
Social workers are knowledgeable about human behavior across the life course; the range of social systems in which people live; and the ways social systems promote or deter people in maintaining or achieving health and well-being. Social workers apply theories and knowledge from the liberal arts to understand biological, social, cultural, psychological, and spiritual development. Social workers

- utilize conceptual frameworks to guide the processes of assessment, intervention, and evaluation; and
- critique and apply knowledge to understand person and environment.

Educational Policy 2.1.8—Engage in policy practice to advance social and economic well-being and to deliver effective social work services.
Social work practitioners understand that policy affects service delivery, and they actively engage in policy practice. Social workers know the history and current structures of social policies and services; the role of policy in service delivery; and the role of practice in policy development. Social workers

- analyze, formulate, and advocate for policies that advance social well-being; and
- collaborate with colleagues and clients for effective policy action.

Educational Policy 2.1.9—Respond to contexts that shape practice.
Social workers are informed, resourceful, and proactive in responding to evolving organizational, community, and societal contexts at all levels of practice. Social workers recognize that the context of practice is dynamic, and use knowledge and skill to respond proactively. Social workers

- continuously discover, appraise, and attend to changing locales, populations, scientific and technological developments, and emerging societal trends to provide relevant services; and
- provide leadership in promoting sustainable changes in service delivery and practice to improve the quality of social services.

Educational Policy 2.1.10(a)–(d)—Engage, assess, intervene, and evaluate with individuals, families, groups, organizations, and communities.
Professional practice involves the dynamic and interactive processes of engagement, assessment, intervention, and evaluation at multiple levels. Social workers have the knowledge and skills to practice with individuals, families, groups, organizations, and communities. Practice knowledge includes identifying, analyzing, and implementing evidence-based interventions designed to achieve client goals; using research and technological advances; evaluating program outcomes and practice effectiveness; developing, analyzing, advocating, and providing leadership for policies and services; and promoting social and economic justice.

Educational Policy 2.1.10(a)—Engagement
Social workers

- substantively and affectively prepare for action with individuals, families, groups, organizations, and communities;
- use empathy and other interpersonal skills; and
- develop a mutually agreed-on focus of work and desired outcomes.

Educational Policy 2.1.10(b)—Assessment
Social workers

- collect, organize, and interpret client data;
- assess client strengths and limitations;
- develop mutually agreed-on intervention goals and objectives; and
- select appropriate intervention strategies.

Educational Policy 2.1.10(c)—Intervention
Social workers

- initiate actions to achieve organizational goals;
- implement prevention interventions that enhance client capacities;
- help clients resolve problems;
- negotiate, mediate, and advocate for clients; and
- facilitate transitions and endings.

Educational Policy 2.1.10(d)—Evaluation
Social workers critically analyze, monitor, and evaluate interventions.

EDUCATIONAL POLICY B2.2—GENERALIST PRACTICE

Generalist practice is grounded in the liberal arts and the person and environment construct. To promote human and social well-being, generalist practitioners use a range of prevention and intervention methods in their practice with individuals, families, groups, organizations, and communities. The generalist practitioner identifies with the social work profession and applies ethical principles and critical thinking in practice. Generalist practitioners incorporate diversity in their practice and advocate for human rights and social and economic justice. They recognize, support, and build on the strengths and resiliency of all human beings. They engage in research-informed practice and are proactive in responding to the impact of context on professional practice. BSW practice incorporates all of the core competencies.

EDUCATIONAL POLICY M2.2—ADVANCED PRACTICE

Advanced practitioners refine and advance the quality of social work practice and that of the larger social work profession. They synthesize and apply a broad range of interdisciplinary and multidisciplinary knowledge and skills. In areas of specialization, advanced practitioners assess, intervene, and evaluate to promote human and social well-being. To do so they suit each action to the circumstances at hand, using the discrimination learned through experience and self-improvement. Advanced practice incorporates all of the core competencies augmented by knowledge and practice behaviors specific to a concentration.

EDUCATIONAL POLICY 2.3—SIGNATURE PEDAGOGY: FIELD EDUCATION

Signature pedagogy represents the central form of instruction and learning in which a profession socializes its students to perform the role of practitioner. Professionals have pedagogical norms with which they connect and integrate theory and practice.[6] In social

---

[6]Shulman, L. S. (2005, Summer). Signature pedagogies in the professions. *Daedelus,* 52–159.

work, the signature pedagogy is field education. The intent of field education is to connect the theoretical and conceptual contribution of the classroom with the practical world of the practice setting. It is a basic precept of social work education that the two interrelated components of curriculum—classroom and field—are of equal importance within the curriculum, and each contributes to the development of the requisite competencies of professional practice. Field education is systematically designed, supervised, coordinated, and evaluated based on criteria by which students demonstrate the achievement of program competencies.

TEXT OBJECTIVES

This text uses an integrative approach to present prominent methods in social work practice. Thus, the key objectives of this text are as follows:

- Provide content on social work practice, social work values and ethics, diversity, human rights, and promotion of social and economic justice that is consistent with *EPAS*.
- Prepare students for generalist social work practice by informing them of contemporary assessment and intervention strategies.
- Develop students' interviewing and counseling skills and capacities so they can intervene effectively with individuals, families, and groups.
- Develop students' macro practice skills and capacities in intervening with organizations and communities.
- Help students develop a philosophical value orientation that is consistent with social work practice.
- Develop students' capacities to function effectively in a variety of social work roles, including enabler, empowerer, broker, advocate, activist, mediator, negotiator, educator, initiator, coordinator, researcher, and group facilitator.
- Foster in students an awareness, understanding, and appreciation of how to intervene effectively with people of diverse racial, ethnic, cultural, social, and class backgrounds.
- Expand students' capacities to evaluate and modify human service programs and systems to make human services more equitable, humane, and responsive to consumers.
- Foster philosophical conceptual skills so that graduates can critically evaluate and further develop their own practice capacities throughout life.
- Help students develop a positive sense of self and an awareness and appreciation of the importance of continuing to evaluate their professional skills and professional growth.

WHICH INTERVENTION STRATEGIES SHOULD SOCIAL WORKERS LEARN?

EP 2.1.7.a

Literally hundreds of intervention approaches have been developed at the micro, mezzo, and macro levels of practice. A partial list of available techniques that can be used at the micro and mezzo levels of practice appears in Exhibit 1.2.

It is impossible for social workers to have an effective working knowledge of all of these intervention approaches. What social workers can do, however, is continue to learn additional approaches throughout their careers and also learn to apply the approaches they already use more effectively. Social work agencies encourage this continual learning by offering in-service training and workshops, sending workers to conferences, and encouraging workers to take additional college courses in the helping professions.

Exhibit 1.2 Partial List of Intervention Therapies at the Micro and Mezzo Levels

Task-centered therapy	Solution-focused therapy
Psychoanalysis	Gestalt therapy
Client-centered therapy	Assertiveness training
Transactional analysis	Token economies
Feminist intervention	Contingency contracting
Rational-emotive therapy	Systematic desensitization
Reality therapy	In vivo desensitization
Crisis intervention	Implosive therapy
Behavior modification	Covert sensitization
Provocative therapy	Aversive techniques
Radical therapy	Thought-stopping
Adlerian therapy	Sex therapy
Analytical therapy	Milieu therapy
Existential therapy	Play therapy
Encounter therapies	Parent effectiveness training
Ego psychology approaches	Muscle relaxation
Cognitive approaches	Deep breathing relaxation
General systems approaches	Imagery relaxation
Role theory approaches	Meditation
Time management	Hypnosis
Biofeedback	Self-hypnosis
Marathon groups	Encounter groups
Alcoholics Anonymous	Sensitivity groups
Weight Watchers	Parents Anonymous
Psychodrama	Neuro-linguistic programming

Workers should continue to learn a wide variety of intervention approaches so they can select from their "bag of tricks" the approach that is likely to be most effective (given each client's unique set of problems and circumstances). Workers soon become aware that their own personalities also partially determine which intervention approaches they are most comfortable with and effective in applying.

Because there are so many intervention techniques (as suggested in Exhibit 1.2), students may be bewildered about which intervention approaches to learn. It is therefore crucial that faculty guide students by (1) making carefully thought-out decisions, as a group, regarding the intervention theories that are most useful for students in their geographic area to learn; (2) giving an overview so that students are familiar with a wide number of theories; and (3) conveying material on each theory's merits and shortcomings. Later chapters in this text summarize many of the intervention approaches listed in Exhibit 1.2. The instructor of this course, along with the other social work faculty members, should decide which intervention approaches to cover in this class.

Once you graduate and obtain employment, your work setting will be a deciding factor in which intervention approaches you should use. If you are working with shy or aggressive people, assertiveness training may be appropriate. Alcoholics Anonymous may be appropriate for people with drinking problems, rational therapy for people who are depressed, in vivo desensitization for people who have phobias, and so on.

A competent social worker generally has a working knowledge of a variety of intervention approaches. In working with clients, the worker should focus on selecting effective intervention approaches that help clients solve their problems rather than trying to redefine the problems in terms of the worker's favorite intervention approach (see the material on evidence-based practice in Chapter 11).

SUMMARY

Social work is the professional activity of helping individuals, families, groups, organizations, and communities enhance or restore their capacity for social functioning and create societal conditions favorable to their goals. The term *social worker* is generally applied to graduates of bachelor's- or master's-level social work programs who are employed in the field of social welfare. A social worker is a change agent who is skilled at working with individuals, groups, families, organizations, and communities. Almost all social workers are employed in the field of social welfare.

The profession of social work is distinct from other helping professions because it has the responsibility and mandate to provide social services and it uses the person-in-environment concept. Social work has a number of goals, including to (1) enhance the problem-solving, coping, and developmental capacities of people; (2) link people with systems that provide them with resources, services, and opportunities; (3) promote the effectiveness and humane operation of systems that provide people with resources and services; (4) develop and improve social policy; and (5) promote human and community well-being.

A social worker needs training and expertise in a wide range of areas to effectively handle problems faced by individuals, groups, families, organizations, and the larger community. Most professions are becoming increasingly specialized, but social work continues to emphasize a generalist (broad-based) approach.

Social work uses a problem-solving approach. Social workers practice at three levels: micro, mezzo, and macro. Specific activities include social casework, case management, group work, group counseling, family counseling, community organization, policy analysis, planning, program development, policy development, research, consulting, supervision, and administration. The knowledge, skills, and values needed for social work practice were summarized.

EP 2.1.10.b

Literally hundreds of intervention approaches have been developed for social work practice. It is impossible for any social worker to have an effective working knowledge of all of these theories. Educational programs have an obligation to provide social work students with an overview of the commonly used theories and to convey information on the merits and shortcomings of these approaches. Social workers have an obligation to continue throughout their careers to learn a variety of intervention approaches. In working with clients, a worker should focus on selecting the most effective intervention approaches for solving clients' problems rather than redefining clients' problems to fit the worker's favorite intervention approach.

EXERCISES

1. Breaking the Ice

Goal: To get acquainted and to reduce anxiety.

Step 1: Starting a new class can be exciting and anxiety producing for both students and instructors Brainstorm about what you would like to know about other members of the class. Examples might include marital status, hometown, work or volunteer experience in social work, and most unforgettable experience. List these questions on the blackboard.

Step 2: Answer the questions developed in step 1.

Step 3: Ask your instructor questions you may have about her or his educational background and professional experiences.

Step 4: (Optional) In groups of two, share an experience that has had a profound effect on your life. Listeners should be encouraged to ask questions to seek clarification. After each person has had a chance to speak, class re-forms to report on what students have learned about their partners.

Note: An alternative icebreaker is to ask everyone to share "what is something surprising that we do not know about you?" (Additional option) Each student is asked to "tell us something that would surprise us about you."

EP 2.1.10.b

2. Searching for Descriptors

Goal: To facilitate student interaction and to establish a positive class atmosphere.

Step 1: A list of descriptors is distributed to the class. (A descriptor is a word or phrase that identifies an item.) Some possibilities are listed below.

Step 2: Each student finds one student (or two or three students in large classes) who says "yes" to having specific descriptors. (Each student can be listed only once on the sheet by each "searcher.")

Step 3: After several minutes the instructor indicates time is up. The instructor then reads each descriptor and asks for the names of those who were listed by at least one "searcher."

Step 4: The instructor ends the exercise by finding out who has the largest list and then giving a small prize (such as a nutritious candy bar) to the winner.

SAMPLE DESCRIPTORS

Plays golf

Likes classical music

Is a fan of the Dallas Cowboys

Has had a paid or volunteer job in social work

Was born west of the Mississippi River

Has traveled in Mexico

Has traveled in Europe

Is married

Likes to jog

Has never flown in an airplane

Has meditated

Has water-skied

Likes the psychoanalytic approach to therapy

Has been hypnotized

Has been to a gay pride festival

Has traveled in Canada

Enjoys fishing

Attends church regularly

Has received a speeding ticket

Has visited, or lived on, a reservation

EP 2.1.1 through 2.1.10.m

3. Assessing Core Competencies and Practice Behaviors

Goal: This exercise is designed to help students self-assess the extent to which they have acquired the core competencies and core practice behaviors in social work.

Step 1: The instructor states the purpose of this exercise. The instructor instructs the students to review the material, presented earlier in this chapter, on the core competencies and core practice behaviors identified by the CSWE in 2008 (*EPAS*) for effective social work practice.

Step 2: The instructor makes photocopies of the following list of core competencies and core practice behaviors. Each student is given one of these lists.

Step 3: Each student anonymously rates him/herself on the extent to which he or she has attained each of these competencies and practice behaviors according to the following five-point scale.

1.	I have attained this competency/practice behavior (in the range of 80 to 100%)
2.	I have largely attained this competency/practice behavior (in the range of 60 to 80%)
3.	I have partially attained this competency/practice behavior (in the range of 40 to 60%)
4.	I have made a little progress in attaining this competency/practice behavior (in the range of 20 to 40%)
5.	I have made almost no progress in attaining this competency/practice behavior (in the range of 0 to 20%)

EPAS 2008 Core Competencies & Core Practice Behaviors	Student Self-Assessment					Evaluator Feedback
Student and Evaluator Assessment Scale and Comments	**1**	**2**	**3**	**4**	**5**	**Agree/Disagree/ Comments**
2.1.1 IDENTITY AS A PROFESSIONAL SOCIAL WORKER AND CONDUCT ONESELF ACCORDINGLY:						
Advocate for client access to the services of social work						
Practice personal reflection and self-correction to assure continual professional development						
Attend to professional roles and boundaries						
Demonstrate professional demeanor in behavior, appearance, and communication						
Engage in career-long learning						
Use supervision and consultation						
2.1.2 APPLY SOCIAL WORK ETHICAL PRINCIPLES TO GUIDE PROFESSIONAL PRACTICE:						
Recognize and manage personal values in a way that allows professional values to guide practice						
Make ethical decisions by applying NASW Code of Ethics and, as applicable, IFSW/IASSW Ethics in Social Work, Statement of Principles						
Tolerate ambiguity in resolving ethical conflicts						
Apply strategies of ethical reasoning to arrive at principled decisions						
2.1.3 APPLY CRITICAL THINKING TO INFORM AND COMMUNICATE PROFESSIONAL JUDGMENTS:						
Distinguish, appraise, and integrate multiple sources of knowledge, including research-based knowledge and practice wisdom						
Analyze models of assessment, prevention, intervention, and evaluation						
Demonstrate effective oral and written communication in working with individuals, families, groups, organizations, communities, and colleagues						
2.1.4 ENGAGE DIVERSITY AND DIFFERENCE IN PRACTICE:						
Recognize the extent to which a culture's structures and values may oppress, marginalize, alienate, or create or enhance privilege and power						

EPAS 2008 Core Competencies & Core Practice Behaviors	Student Self-Assessment					Evaluator Feedback
Student and Evaluator Assessment Scale and Comments	**1**	**2**	**3**	**4**	**5**	**Agree/Disagree/ Comments**
Gain sufficient self-awareness to eliminate the influence of personal biases and values in working with diverse groups						
Recognize and communicate their understanding of the importance of difference in shaping life experiences						
View themselves as learners and engage those with whom they work as informants						
2.1.5 ADVANCE HUMAN RIGHTS AND SOCIAL AND ECONOMIC JUSTICE:						
Understand forms and mechanisms of oppression and discrimination						
Advocate for human rights and social and economic justice						
Engage in practices that advance social and economic justice						
2.1.6 ENGAGE IN RESEARCH-INFORMED PRACTICE AND PRACTICE-INFORMED RESEARCH:						
Use practice experience to inform scientific inquiry						
Use research evidence to inform practice						
2.1.7 APPLY KNOWLEDGE OF HUMAN BEHAVIOR AND THE SOCIAL ENVIRONMENT:						
Utilize conceptual frameworks to guide the processes of assessment, intervention, and evaluation						
Critique and apply knowledge to understand person and environment						
2.1.8 ENGAGE IN POLICY PRACTICE TO ADVANCE SOCIAL AND ECONOMIC WELL-BEING AND TO DELIVER EFFECTIVE SOCIAL WORK SERVICES:						
Analyze, formulate, and advocate for policies that advance social well-being						
Collaborate with colleagues and clients for effective policy action						
2.1.9 RESPOND TO CONTEXTS THAT SHAPE PRACTICE:						
Continuously discover, appraise, and attend to changing locales, populations, scientific and technological developments, and emerging societal trends to provide relevant services						

EPAS 2008 Core Competencies & Core Practice Behaviors	Student Self-Assessment					Evaluator Feedback
Student and Evaluator Assessment Scale and Comments	**1**	**2**	**3**	**4**	**5**	**Agree/Disagree/ Comments**
Provide leadership in promoting sustainable changes in service delivery and practice to improve the quality of social services						
2.1.10 ENGAGE, ASSESS, INTERVENE, AND EVALUATE WITH INDIVIDUALS, FAMILIES, GROUPS, ORGANIZATIONS, AND COMMUNITIES:						
Substantively and affectively prepare for action with individuals, families, groups, organizations, and communities						
Use empathy and other interpersonal skills						
Develop a mutually agreed-on focus of work and desired outcomes						
Collect, organize, and interpret client data						
Assess client strengths and limitations						
Develop mutually agreed-on intervention goals and objectives						
Select appropriate intervention strategies						
Initiate actions to achieve organizational goals						
Implement prevention interventions that enhance client capacities						
2.1.10 ENGAGE, ASSESS, INTERVENE, AND EVALUATE WITH INDIVIDUALS, FAMILIES, GROUPS, ORGANIZATIONS, AND COMMUNITIES:						
Help clients resolve problems						
Negotiate, mediate, and advocate for clients						
Facilitate transitions and endings						
Critically analyze, monitor, and evaluate interventions						

EP 2.1.1.a through 2.1.10.m

Step 4: The instructor collects each of the lists and then calculates the mean scores on each item. At a future class period, the instructor shares this information with the students and holds a discussion with the students that is focused on the students providing information on changes in the program/curriculum that the students believe will improve the ratings on low-rated items.

NOTE TO FACULTY

This exercise may be very valuable in obtaining assessment information for reaffirmation of accreditation by the Commission on Accreditation of the CSWE.

4. Assessing Core Competencies and Practice Behaviors in Class and in Field Placement

Goal: This exercise is designed to facilitate students and the social work program in assessing the extent to which students have acquired the core competencies and core practice behaviors in social work.

Step 1: In class, distribute the following instrument to the students. Indicate this is an instrument that may be used in field placement to assess the extent to which students are attaining the competencies and practice behaviors identified in 2008 *EPAS* (which is described earlier in this chapter).

Rating Scale for Evaluation of Field Placement Performance

Midterm **Final**

Name of Intern ____________________ **Date**________________

Instructions for Rating Interns on the 10 Competencies in the First Part of the Evaluation:

The standard by which an intern is to be compared is that of a new beginning-level social worker. The 10 competencies that are specified in this evaluation form are those established by our national accrediting organization (the Council on Social Work Education). Under each competency statement are several items that we ask that you rate according to the following criteria.

1	The intern has excelled in this area
2	The intern is functioning above expectations for interns in this area
3	The intern has met the expectations for interns in this area
4	The intern has not as yet met the expectations in this area, but there is hope that the intern will meet the expectations in the near future
5	The intern has not met the expectations in this area, and there is not much hope that the intern will meet the expectations in this area in the near future
n/a	Not applicable, as the intern has not had the opportunity to demonstrate competence in this area

Comments may be made under any competency statement, if desired. Please be sure to indicate those areas in which you think the intern is particularly strong and those areas that need improvement.

This evaluation is intended to give the intern feedback about her or his performance. The agency supervisor's rating of these items will not directly be used to calculate the grade that is given to the intern. The faculty supervisor has the responsibility of assigning the grade for the course. The grade that is assigned will be based on: **the faculty supervisor's overall evaluation of the student's performance in placement in conjunction with the agency supervisor's evaluation (65%); intern logs (10%); seminar participation (5%); two papers (10% each—20% total).**

If you prefer to use another evaluation system **in addition** to this form to evaluate a student's performance, please discuss this with the faculty supervisor.

COMPETENCE #1: INTERN IDENTIFIES AS A PROFESSIONAL SOCIAL WORKER AND CONDUCTS HIMSELF/ HERSELF ACCORDINGLY.

1.1	Knows the profession's history	1	2	3	4	5	na
1.2	Has a commitment to enhancing the profession	1	2	3	4	5	na

1.3	Has a commitment to conducting himself/herself as a professional social worker	1	2	3	4	5	na
1.4	Has a commitment to career-long learning and growth	1	2	3	4	5	na
1.5	Advocates well for client access to the services of social work	1	2	3	4	5	na
1.6	Practices personal reflection and self-correction to assure continual professional development	1	2	3	4	5	na
1.7	Attends well to professional roles and boundaries	1	2	3	4	5	na
1.8	Demonstrates professional demeanor in appearance	1	2	3	4	5	na
1.9	Demonstrates professional demeanor in communication	1	2	3	4	5	na
1.10	Uses supervision and consultation effectively	1	2	3	4	5	na

Comments:

COMPETENCE #2: INTERN APPLIES SOCIAL WORK ETHICAL PRINCIPLES TO GUIDE HIS OR HER PROFESSIONAL PRACTICE.

2.1	Is knowledgeable about the value base of the profession	1	2	3	4	5	na
2.2	Is knowledgeable of, and abides by, the ethical standards of the profession	1	2	3	4	5	na
2.3	Is knowledgeable, and abides by, laws relevant to social work	1	2	3	4	5	na
2.4	Recognizes and manages personal values in a way that allows professional values to guide practice (e.g., on such issues as abortion and gay rights)	1	2	3	4	5	na
2.5	Tolerates well ambiguity in resolving ethical conflicts	1	2	3	4	5	na
2.6	Is able to apply strategies of ethical reasoning to arrive at principled decisions	1	2	3	4	5	na

Comments:

COMPETENCE #3: INTERN APPLIES CRITICAL THINKING TO INFORM AND COMMUNICATE PROFESSIONAL JUDGMENTS.

3.1	Is knowledgeable about the principles of logic and scientific inquiry	1	2	3	4	5	na
3.2	Is able to grasp and comprehend what is obscure	1	2	3	4	5	na

3.3	Is skilled in using critical thinking augmented by creativity and curiosity	1	2	3	4	5	na
3.4	Has good assessment skills	1	2	3	4	5	na
3.5	Has good problem-solving skills	1	2	3	4	5	na
3.6	Has good data-gathering skills	1	2	3	4	5	na
3.7	Analyzes complex material well	1	2	3	4	5	na
3.8	Is skilled at appraising and integrating multiple sources of knowledge; including research-based knowledge and practice wisdom	1	2	3	4	5	na
3.9	Is skilled at analyzing models of assessment, prevention, intervention, and evaluation	1	2	3	4	5	na
3.10	Demonstrates effective oral communication in working with individuals, families, groups, organizations, communities, and colleagues	1	2	3	4	5	na
3.11	Demonstrates effective written communication in working with individuals, families, groups, organizations, communities, and colleagues	1	2	3	4	5	na

Comments:

COMPETENCE #4: INTERN ENGAGES DIVERSITY AND DIFFERENCE IN PRACTICE.

4.1	Treats diverse clients with dignity and respect	1	2	3	4	5	na
4.2	Is knowledgeable and respectful of clients who differ by such factors as age, class, color, culture, disability, ethnicity, gender identity and expression, immigration status, political ideology, race, religion, sex, and sexual orientation	1	2	3	4	5	na
4.3	Recognizes the extent to which a culture's structures and values may oppress, marginalize, alienate, or create or enhance privilege and power	1	2	3	4	5	na
4.4	Has sufficient self-awareness to eliminate the influence of personal biases and values in working with diverse groups	1	2	3	4	5	na
4.5	Recognizes and communicates her or his understanding of the importance of difference in shaping life experiences	1	2	3	4	5	na
4.6	Views herself or himself as a learner and engages those he or she works with as informants	1	2	3	4	5	na

Comments:

COMPETENCE #5: INTERN ADVANCES HUMAN RIGHTS AND SOCIAL AND ECONOMIC JUSTICE.

5.1	Recognizes that each person, regardless of position in society, has basic human rights, such as freedom, safety, privacy, an adequate standard of living, health care, and education	1	2	3	4	5	na
5.2	Recognizes the global interconnections of oppression and is knowledgeable about theories of justice and strategies to promote human and civil rights	1	2	3	4	5	na
5.3	Understands the forms and mechanisms of oppression and discrimination	1	2	3	4	5	na
5.4	Is skilled at advocating for human rights and social and economic justice	1	2	3	4	5	na
5.5	Is skilled at engaging in practices that advance social and economic justice	1	2	3	4	5	na

Comments:

COMPETENCE #6: INTERN ENGAGES IN RESEARCH-INFORMED PRACTICE AND PRACTICE-INFORMED RESEARCH.

6.1	Is skilled at using practice experience to inform research	1	2	3	4	5	na
6.2	Is skilled at employing evidence-based interventions	1	2	3	4	5	na
6.3	Is skilled at evaluating her or his practice	1	2	3	4	5	na
6.4	Is skilled at using research findings to improve practice, policy, and social service delivery	1	2	3	4	5	na
6.5	Comprehends quantitative research	1	2	3	4	5	na
6.6	Comprehends qualitative research	1	2	3	4	5	na
6.7	Understands scientific and ethical approaches to building knowledge	1	2	3	4	5	na

Comments:

COMPETENCE #7: INTERN APPLIES KNOWLEDGE OF HUMAN BEHAVIOR AND THE SOCIAL ENVIRONMENT.

7.1	Is knowledgeable about human behavior across the life course	1	2	3	4	5	na
7.2	Is knowledgeable about the range of social systems in which people live	1	2	3	4	5	na

7.3	Is knowledgeable about the ways social systems promote or deter people in maintaining or achieving health and well-being	1	2	3	4	5	na
7.4	Is skilled at applying theories and knowledge about biological variables, social variables, cultural variables, psychological variables, and spiritual development	1	2	3	4	5	na
7.5	Is skilled at utilizing conceptual frameworks to guide the processes of assessment, intervention, and evaluation	1	2	3	4	5	na

Comments:

COMPETENCE #8: INTERN ENGAGES IN POLICY PRACTICE TO ADVANCE SOCIAL AND ECONOMIC WELL-BEING AND TO DELIVER EFFECTIVE SOCIAL WORK SERVICES.

8.1	Understands that policy affects service delivery	1	2	3	4	5	na
8.2	Actively engages in policy practice	1	2	3	4	5	na
8.3	Is knowledgeable about the history of social policies and services	1	2	3	4	5	na
8.4	Is knowledgeable about current social policies and services	1	2	3	4	5	na
8.5	Is knowledgeable about the role of practice in policy development	1	2	3	4	5	na
8.6	Is skilled at analyzing, formulating, and advocating for policies that advance social well-being	1	2	3	4	5	na
8.7	Is skilled at collaborating with colleagues and client for effective policy action	1	2	3	4	5	Na

Comments:

COMPETENCE #9: INTERN RESPONDS TO CONTEXTS THAT SHAPE PRACTICE.

9.1	Is informed, resourceful, and proactive in responding to evolving organizational, community, and societal contexts at all levels of practice	1	2	3	4	5	na
9.2	Recognizes that the context of practice is dynamic, and has the knowledge and skills to respond proactively	1	2	3	4	5	na
9.3	Is skilled at continuously discovering, appraising, and attending to changing locales, populations, scientific and technological developments, and emerging societal trends in order to provide relevant services	1	2	3	4	5	na

9.4	Is skilled at providing leadership in promoting sustainable changes in service delivery and practice to improve the quality of social services	1	2	3	4	5	na

Comments:

COMPETENCE #10: INTERN ENGAGES, ASSESSES, INTERVENES, AND EVALUATES WITH INDIVIDUALS, FAMILIES, GROUPS, ORGANIZATIONS, AND COMMUNITIES.

10.1	Is skilled at identifying, analyzing, and implementing evidence-based interventions designed to achieve client goals	1	2	3	4	5	na
10.2	Is skilled at using research and technological advances	1	2	3	4	5	na
10.3	Is skilled at evaluating program outcomes	1	2	3	4	5	na
10.4	Is skilled at evaluating the effectiveness of her or his practice	1	2	3	4	5	na
10.5	Is skilled at developing, analyzing, advocating, and providing leadership for policies and services	1	2	3	4	5	na
10.6	Is skilled at promoting social and economic justice	1	2	3	4	5	na
10.7	Is skilled at engaging (developing a positive relationship) with individuals	1	2	3	4	5	na
10.8	Is skilled at engaging families	1	2	3	4	5	na
10.9	Is skilled at engaging groups	1	2	3	4	5	na
10.10	Is skilled at engaging organizations	1	2	3	4	5	na
10.11	Is skilled at engaging communities	1	2	3	4	5	na
10.12	Is skilled at assessing individuals	1	2	3	4	5	na
10.13	Is skilled at assessing families	1	2	3	4	5	na
10.14	Is skilled at assessing groups	1	2	3	4	5	na
10.15	Is skilled at assessing organizations	1	2	3	4	5	na
10.16	Is skilled at assessing communities	1	2	3	4	5	na
10.17	Is skilled at providing effective services to individuals	1	2	3	4	5	na
10.18	Is skilled at providing effective services to families	1	2	3	4	5	na
10.19	Is skilled at providing effective services to groups	1	2	3	4	5	na

10.20	Is skilled at providing effective services to organizations	1	2	3	4	5	na
10.21	Is skilled at providing effective services to communities	1	2	3	4	5	na

Comments:

OVERALL EVALUATION AT MIDTERM:

Please check one of the following at the midterm evaluation. At the final evaluation do NOT complete this section.	
❑	This intern is excelling in field placement by performing above expectations for interns.
❑	This intern is meeting the expectations of a field placement intern.
❑	This intern is functioning somewhat below the expectations of a field placement intern. There is a question whether this intern will be ready for beginning-level social work practice by the end of placement.
❑	This intern is functioning below the expectations of a field placement intern. There is considerable concern that this intern will not be ready for beginning-level social work practice by the end of placement. This intern should perhaps be encouraged to pursue another major.

Comments/Elaboration:

FINAL OVERALL EVALUATION:

Please check one of the following at the final evaluation. At the midterm evaluation do NOT complete this section.	
❑	This intern has excelled in field placement by performing above expectations for interns. If an appropriate position were open at this agency, for a beginning-level social worker, this intern would be considered among the top candidates for this position.
❑	This intern has met the expectations of the field placement. This intern is ready for beginning-level social work practice.
❑	This intern is not yet ready for beginning-level social work practice.
❑	This intern is not yet ready for beginning-level social work practice, and has demonstrated serious problems in performance, and perhaps should be encouraged to pursue another major.

Comments/Elaboration:

Signature of Agency Field Instructor ______________________________

Agency ______________________________ **Date** ______________

The following section should be completed by the intern:

My agency supervisor and faculty supervisor have discussed this evaluation with me, and I have received a copy. My agreement or disagreement follows:

I agree with the evaluation	❑
I do not agree with evaluation	❑

Intern's Signature ____________________________ **Date** __________________

❑	If the intern disagrees with the evaluation, she or he should state that disagreement in writing and submit a copy to both the agency supervisor and the faculty supervisor. A meeting between the student, agency supervisor, and faculty supervisor should then be held to discuss the disagreement.

Step 2: Ask the students, using the indicated rating scale, to self-assess the extent to which they have attained the indicated competencies and practice behaviors.

Step 3: After the students complete Step 2, ask them to form groups of four or five and identify the five items on which they rated themselves lowest.

Step 4: Have a representative from each subgroup indicate to the class the five items. (These items from each subgroup may be written on the board.) The class then holds a discussion on what changes in the program/curriculum would be desirable to make so that the students would rate themselves higher on these items. (This exercise helps students to assess their strengths and shortcomings in acquiring social work competencies and practice behaviors.)

ALTERNATIVE USE OF THIS INSTRUMENT

This field instrument may be used in field placement to assess the extent to which agency supervisors rate the competencies and practice behaviors of interns. Program faculty may choose to administer this instrument at the end of field placement, completed by the field instructor and reviewed with the student intern and faculty liaison for the dual purposes of providing a grade for the field placement as well as assessing the individual student's attainment of practice behaviors and core competencies. Another approach is for field instructors to complete the evaluation mid-way through the length of the field placement (i.e., mid-semester for a one-semester field placement or mid-year for a two-term field placement), then again at termination of the field placement. With either approach, benchmarks (as specified in 2008 *EPAS*) need to be established. Some programs may prefer an "acceptable" or passing mean score, whereas others may prefer to establish a percentage of students who will be evaluated as competent relative to specific core or concentration practice behaviors. To use the "mean score" example, if a program chooses to establish an acceptable "mean score" approach, means for all interns in the same level of placement (for example, all baccalaureate foundation field students, or all MSW foundation field students etc.) are tabulated in the aggregate. The "acceptable" benchmarks range provides an indication of the achievement of the practice behaviors and competencies appropriate to that level of field. "Unacceptable" benchmarks indicate the program is not successfully preparing field students in the requisite practice behaviors and competencies for that level of field instruction.

NOTE TO FACULTY

This exercise may be very valuable in obtaining assessment information for reaffirmation of accreditation by the Commission on Accreditation of the CSWE.

COMPETENCY NOTES

The following identifies where Educational Policy (EP) competencies and practice behaviors are discussed in the chapter.

EP 2.1.1b *Practice personal reflection and self-correction to assure continual professional development.* (pp. 5, 7).

Exercise 1.1 allows students to reflect on their areas of interest in social work.

EP 2.1.7a *Utilize conceptual frameworks to guide the process of assessment, intervention, and evaluation.* (pp. 9–11).

Exercise 1.2 allows the students to apply the problem-solving approach to challenges or problems they faced.

EP 2.1.10a *Substantively and affectively prepare for action with individuals, families, groups, organizations, and communities.* (pp. 11–16).

EP 2.1.10b *Use empathy and other interpersonal skills.*

EP 2.1.10c *Develop a mutually agreed-on focus of work and desired outcomes.*

EP 2.1.10d *Collect, organize, and interpret client data.*

EP 2.1.10e *Assess client strengths and limitations.*

EP 2.1.10f *Develop mutually agreed-on intervention goals and objectives.*

EP 2.1.10g *Select appropriate intervention strategies.*

EP 2.1.10h *Initiate actions to achieve organizational goals.*

EP 2.1.10i *Implement prevention interventions that enhance client capacities.*

EP 2.1.10j *Help clients resolve problems.*

EP 2.1.10k *Negotiate, mediate, and advocate for clients.*

EP 2.1.10l *Facilitate transitions and endings.*

EP 2.1.10m *Critically analyze, monitor, and evaluate interventions.*

This material illustrates how the practice behaviors under this competency can be applied to working with clients.

EP 2.1.1c *Attend to professional roles and boundaries.* (pp. 16–18).

This material summarizes the roles that social workers engage in while working with individuals, groups, families, organizations, and communities.

EP 2.1.1b *Practice personal reflection and self-correction to assure continual professional development.*

EP 2.1.1c *Attend to professional roles and boundaries.* (pp. 18–19).

Exercise 1.3 allows students to reflect on the social work roles in which they want to engage.

EP 2.1.7a *Utilize conceptual frameworks to guide the process of assessment, intervention, and evaluation.* (pp. 22–26).

This material describes the medical model approach and the ecological model approach to assessing emotional and behavioral challenges that individuals face.

EP 2.1.7a *Utilize conceptual frameworks to guide the process of assessment, intervention, and evaluation.* (p. 22).

Exercise 1.4 is designed to have students apply the medical model approach to major mental disorders.

EP 2.1.7a *Utilize conceptual frameworks to guide the process of assessment, intervention, and evaluation.* (p. 27).

Exercise 1.5 is designed to have students examine the medical model and the ecological model in assessing dysfunctional behavior.

EP 2.1.7a *Utilize conceptual frameworks to guide the process of assessment, intervention, and evaluation.* (pp. 26–28).

Five goals of professional social work practice are conceptualized.

EP 2.1.1b *Practice personal reflection and self-correction to assure continual professional development.* (p. 28).

Exercise 1.6 is designed to have students reflect upon their interest in achieving each of the five goals of social work.

EP 2.1.7a *Utilize conceptual frameworks to guide the process of assessment, intervention, and evaluation.* (pp. 28–31).

This material conceptualizes specific activities performed by social workers.

EP 2.1.1b *Practice personal reflection and self-correction to assure continual professional development.* (pp. 31–32).

Exercise 1.7 is designed to have students reflect on the kinds of activities that they want to engage in as social workers.

EP 2.1.1 through 2.1.10m. *The 10 competencies and 41 practice behaviors of 2008* EPAS. (pp. 32–36).

This material reprints the competencies and practice behaviors of 2008 *EPAS*.

EP 2.1.7a *Utilize conceptual frameworks to guide the process of assessment, intervention, and evaluation.* (pp. 36–37).

This material lists numerous intervention strategies that social workers utilize in working with clients.

EP 2.1.10b *Use empathy and other interpersonal skills.* (p. 38).

This icebreaker facilitates student use of interpersonal skills in interacting with each other.

EP 2.1.10b *Use empathy and other interpersonal skills.* (p. 39).

This icebreaker facilitates student use of interpersonal skills in interacting with each other.

EP 2.1.1 through 2.1.10m. *The 10 competencies and 41 practice behaviors of 2008* EPAS. (pp. 39–42).

This exercise is designed to help students self-assess the extent to which they have acquired the core competencies and core practice behaviors in social work.

EP 2.1.1 through 2.1.10m. *The 10 competencies and 41 practice behaviors of 2008* EPAS. (pp. 42–50).

This exercise presents a framework for social work programs to assess the extent to which each social work student has attained the 10 competencies and 41 practice behaviors in in-class courses and in field placement.

CHAPTER 2

Social Work Values

EP 2.1.2a, b, c, d

Most people tend to believe that decisions rest primarily on objective facts and figures. But in fact, values form the bases of most decisions. For example, in the political arena in the United States, political decisions largely reflect which party controls the most votes—Republicans or Democrats. This chapter will:

A. Describe value dilemmas in social work
B. Discuss knowledge and values
C. Compare the value dilemmas of clients and the value dilemmas of social workers
D. Describe respect for the dignity and uniqueness of individuals
E. Describe the client's right to self-determination
F. Distinguish between confidentiality and privileged communication
G. Contrast the residual and the institutional views of social welfare
H. Discuss the establishing of professional boundaries with clients
I. Discuss the worker's obligation to promote social and economic justice and to safeguard human rights

VALUE DILEMMAS IN SOCIAL WORK

Let's assume that you are a social worker and are assigned the following case. What would you do to help this family?

Mrs. Kehl is 2 months pregnant. She works part-time in a shoe factory and is paid the minimum wage. Her husband is a janitor in a business office and earns only slightly more. They already have seven children and are living in substandard poverty conditions. They do not wish to have additional children; this pregnancy resulted from a failure of the birth control method they were using. The family is Catholic and attends church regularly. On the one hand, they want to have an abortion; they feel their family is already being hurt because of a lack of money. On the other hand, they believe having an abortion is immoral.

This case raises a number of questions about values. As a social worker, how would you help this family weigh their views about abortion against their desire to limit their family size to improve their living conditions?

This case is not unique. Most situations that clients face involve, at least partially, value dilemmas. Here are a few more examples.

Mr. Ritter is 82 years old and has terminal cancer. He has lived a full life but now is in severe pain. He is rather depressed and is seriously considering taking his own life. Should he be allowed to?

Mr. and Mrs. Sinclair have a 2-year-old child who has a profound cognitive disability and who also needs extensive medical care. They have three older children. The family's emotional and physical resources are being severely drained, and family relationships are increasingly tense. Yet the family feels the child will develop at a faster pace in their home than in an institution or in a group home. What should they do?

Mr. and Mrs. Fedders have been married for 6 years and have two children. Their love for each other has been practically nonexistent for the past 3 years. Mr. Fedders recently discovered his wife has been having an affair. They both hold religious beliefs against divorce, but they are seriously considering terminating their marriage. How should a social worker help them?

Mr. Franzene is on probation for 2 years for theft. For the past 18 months he has stayed out of trouble. He inadvertently reveals to his probation officer that he took two pens from a discount store. Should his probation officer make a report on this?

LaVonne Hall recently left a mental hospital and was helped by her aftercare worker to obtain a filing job. While intoxicated and angry, Ms. Hall calls her worker and says that she has been fired. She then says that she is going to shoot her former employer and hangs up. What should the worker do?

Mr. Townsend's neighbors occasionally hear cries of anguish from Mr. Townsend's two children. The neighbors report this to protective services because they suspect abuse. A protective service worker investigates, and Mr. Townsend and the children state the cries are the result of spankings. How does the worker decide when harsh spanking should be considered abuse?

Mr. and Mrs. Stonek's only child was taken away 2 years ago and placed in a foster home because of neglect. The father drank excessively, and the mother was very depressed. Over the past 2 years, the Stoneks have occasionally made efforts to improve their lives but have always "slid back." For the past 2 months, Mr. Stonek has been involved in Alcoholics Anonymous and has only occasionally gotten drunk. Mrs. Stonek presently seems less depressed and feels having her son back would make her life more meaningful. The Stoneks ask to have their child returned. Should the child be returned? How would you as the worker arrive at a decision?

Mrs. Barta seeks counseling at a comprehensive mental health center. She states her husband is having intercourse with their 11-year-old daughter. The counselor arranges a joint meeting with the Bartas. Mr. Barta first denies the accusation but then admits it after being confronted with what his wife has seen and heard. How should the worker attempt to help this family?

Mrs. Johnson is a caseworker at a public welfare agency in a rural county. She observes and collects evidence that the director makes a range of decisions that deny migrant workers in the area (most of whom are Mexican Americans) public assistance benefits for which they are eligible. If she confronts the director with this evidence, Mrs. Johnson believes she will be fired or at least denied merit increases and promotions at work. What should she do?

Mrs. Gordon seeks counseling from a sex therapist. She indicates she is fairly content with her marriage and has an enjoyable sex life with her husband. Yet she feels substantial guilt about her desire and following through on her desire to masturbate. How can the therapist help her?

A community worker in an inner city is working with residents to organize a rent strike against a landlord who neglects making essential repairs. The building does not have adequate heat and is infested with rats and roaches. The organizer wonders whether she should fully inform the residents of the risks involved in a rent strike (such as being evicted). She fears that if she fully informs the tenants of the risks, they probably will decide not to strike, and essential improvements in living conditions will not be made. What should she do?

These examples highlight the fact that much of social work practice involves value dilemmas. Social work is both an art and a science. Because social work is partly an art, a worker must frequently make decisions based on values rather than on knowledge. It also means that the change techniques workers use are often based on theory and value assumptions rather than on proven intervention techniques.

One value assumption that is frequently useful in helping clients resolve value dilemmas is the principle of *self-determination*. According to this principle, clients have the right to hold and express their own opinions and to act on them, as long as in so doing they do not infringe on the rights of others. When clients face a dilemma, a worker can often proceed effectively by helping the clients first define their problems precisely and then examine fully the merits and shortcomings of the various alternatives to resolving the problem. After this is done, clients are then given the responsibility to decide which course of action they desire to pursue. This problem-solving format might be useful for many of the situations we listed. For example, the Kehls might list all their reasons for and against having an abortion and then make a decision. This same approach might also be useful in helping the Sinclairs decide whether to place their child with the profound cognitive disability in an institution or a group home and in helping the Fedders decide whether to terminate their marriage.

Although this self-determination principle can be useful, *there are no absolutes in social work practice.* Guidelines are simply guidelines. What works in one situation may not resolve problems in others. Suppose, for example, that Mr. Ritter makes a list of the reasons for and against taking his life and decides that there is no rational reason for him to endure further pain. Such a decision raises a value dilemma for the social worker regarding whether the worker should attempt to stop Mr. Ritter from taking his life. Or suppose the Bartas decide they do not want further counseling on the incestuous relationship between Mr. Barta and his daughter because they both conclude that delving into it further will break up their marriage and their family. What should the worker do then?

Much of social work practice depends on the worker's professional judgment. Directors of social welfare agencies frequently tell me that their best workers are those who have common sense and who are able to "trust their guts" (that is, trust their feelings, intuition, and perceptions). This chapter spells out value assumptions and principles of social work practice. These guidelines (and all other guidelines presented in this text) are to be applied not as absolutes but simply as concepts that may be useful in working with people. An effective worker understands and uses these guidelines to make a professional judgment on whether a guideline is, or is not, appropriate when working with particular people.

KNOWLEDGE AND VALUES

It is important for workers to be able to distinguish between values and knowledge and to be aware of the role each plays in social work practice. Pincus and Minahan (1973) concisely defined the difference between values and knowledge:

> Values are beliefs, preferences, or assumptions about what is desirable or good for man [humans]. An example is the belief that society has an obligation to help each individual realize his fullest potential. They are not assertions about how the world is and what we know about it, but how it *should* be. As such, value statements cannot be subjected to scientific investigation; they must be accepted on faith. Thus we can speak of a value as being right or wrong only in relation to the particular belief system or ethical code being used as a standard.
>
> What we will refer to as knowledge statements, on the other hand, are observations about the world and man [humans] which have been verified or are capable of verification. An example is that black people have a shorter life expectancy than white people in the United States. When we speak of a knowledge statement as being right or wrong, we are referring to the extent to which the assertion has been confirmed through objective empirical investigation. (p. 38)

The distinction between values and knowledge can be illustrated in some of the cases described earlier. First, let's look at the abortion question. Suppose a woman questions the abortion procedure because she feels it is immoral. She believes it means killing an unborn baby. Implicit in this value statement is the belief that life begins at or shortly after conception—a belief that is not verifiable.

Now suppose that a woman has qualms about abortion because she fears the risks of the medical procedure or fears there is a high probability of feeling remorseful after the abortion. Informational questions are raised, and knowledge, or empirical evidence, can be presented showing that the health risks of abortion are less than those of carrying the child to full term, and evidence can be presented showing that only a small percentage of women who have an abortion experience severe remorse (Hyde & DeLamater, 2011).

Mrs. Gordon's guilt over masturbating is also a useful illustration. If she feels guilty because she believes masturbating is immoral and sinful, then she obviously has a belief system that asserts it is wrong to masturbate. To resolve this value dilemma, she must decide either to change her belief system or to stop masturbating. However, if she feels guilty because she fears she is hurting herself physiologically or hindering her sex life with her husband, she could be shown that both of these beliefs are erroneous by pointing out that most married men and women masturbate, masturbation is highly recommended by sex therapists, and masturbation usually fosters rather than hinders a sexual relationship (Hyde & DeLamater, 2011).

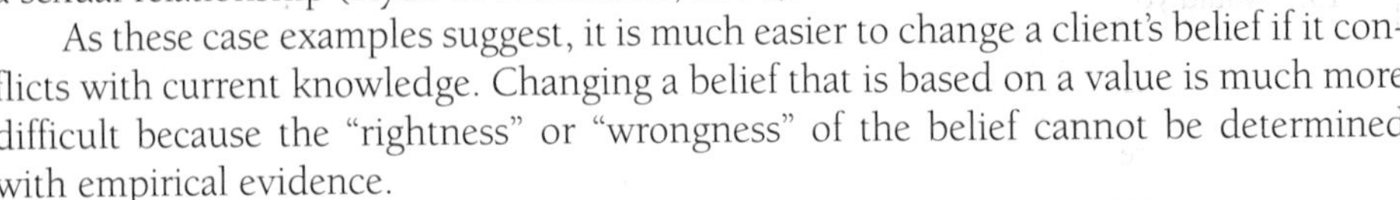

EP 2.1.2a

As these case examples suggest, it is much easier to change a client's belief if it conflicts with current knowledge. Changing a belief that is based on a value is much more difficult because the "rightness" or "wrongness" of the belief cannot be determined with empirical evidence.

Exercise 2.1: Clarifying My Values

Goal: This exercise is designed to help you identify and clarify your values on a number of prominent issues related to social work.

Step 1: It should be noted that for most of these questions there are no right or wrong answers. Each student should answer the following questions.

Values Questionnaire

	Yes	Uncertain	No
1. Assume you are single. Would you marry someone of a different race?			
2. If you were going to adopt a child, would you adopt a child of a different race?			
3. Are you in favor of a woman becoming president of the United States?			
4. Do you believe busing should be used to attempt to achieve racial integration in schools?			
5. Do you support affirmative action programs that assert that certain minority groups and women should be given preference in hiring over white males?			
6. Do you believe a father who commits incest with his 10-year-old daughter should be placed in jail?			
7. Do you believe prostitution should be legalized?			
8. If you or your partner were pregnant and in a situation where it would be very difficult to raise a child, would you seriously consider abortion?			
9. Do you support a constitutional amendment to make abortion illegal?			
10. Would you be willing to be a surrogate mother? If you are male, would you be willing to have your wife or future wife become a surrogate mother?			

Values Questionnaire (*continued*)

11. Do you believe that the death penalty should be used for certain crimes?			
12. Do you believe that the United States should support an extensive program to develop the capacity to clone human beings?			
13. Do you support artificial insemination for humans?			
14. Do you believe people should remain virgins until they marry?			
15. Would you vote for an African American candidate for president of the United States?			
16. If you were married, would you seriously consider having an extramarital affair?			
17. Do you believe that persons who have a profound cognitive disability (so severe that they are functioning at less than a 6-month intellectual level) should be kept alive indefinitely at taxpayers' expense?			
18. Do you believe that marijuana should be legalized?			
19. Would you be upset if a son or daughter of yours were gay/lesbian?			
20. Do you believe you could objectively counsel someone who had brutally raped four women?			
21. Do you think people should limit the size of their families to two children?			
22. Do you favor a law to limit families to two children?			
23. Do you think a person who is gay/lesbian should be allowed to teach in elementary and secondary schools?			
24. Do you approve of a young couple trying out marriage by living together before actually getting married?			
25. Would you be in favor of a group home for drug addicts being located in your neighborhood?			
26. Do you think the government should help support day-care centers for working mothers?			
27. Do you think women in the military service should take part in active combat?			
28. Do you think the United States should build more nuclear power plants to generate electricity?			
29. Would you encourage your son to have premarital sex?			
30. Would you encourage your daughter to have premarital sex?			

(*continues*)

Values Questionnaire (*continued*)

31. When you become an older person and unable to care for your needs, would you be willing to be placed in a nursing home?			
32. Do you support physician-assisted suicide when the victim is terminally ill and in intense pain?			
33. Would you consider marrying someone who is divorced and has two children? (Assume you are single in answering this question.)			
34. Do you believe you would enjoy being a social worker at a group home for persons with severe cognitive disability?			
35. Do you believe the legal drinking age should be less than 21 years?			
36. Would you marry someone who is of a different religion than you?			
37. Do you believe there are circumstances that justify a person taking his or her own life?			
38. Would you divorce your spouse if you found out he or she had had an extramarital affair?			
39. Would you allow a child of yours to play frequently with a child who has AIDS?			
40. Do you believe that most welfare recipients are able-bodied loafers?			
41. Do you believe you would be comfortable in hugging a person who has AIDS?			
42. Do you believe you would be comfortable rooming with a person who has AIDS?			
43. Do you think social workers should inform a client's current sexual partners that the client is HIV positive if the client refuses to do so?			
44. Are you supportive of same-sex marriages?			

Step 2: This an optional step. The instructor collects the questionnaires so that anonymity is assured and lists the question numbers on the blackboard. After tallying the results (with the help of volunteers), the instructor seeks to open a discussion. For example, if most students indicate that they would not marry someone of a different race, the instructor asks, "Does this suggest that most of you have some racial prejudices?"

VALUE DILEMMAS OF CLIENTS AND SOCIAL WORKERS

It is important for social workers to recognize exactly who is confronting a value dilemma. (This will be discussed in more detail later.) An important guideline in social work practice is not to become overly emotionally involved in a client's case. (If you find yourself frequently taking clients' problems home with you so that your dwelling on their problems interferes with your life, then you are overly involved.) If a client faces a dilemma about whether to obtain a divorce, or have an abortion, or place a member of the family in an institution, it is important for you to be aware that the dilemma is the *client's*, not yours. This awareness will help you to remain objective and thereby be most helpful to your client. If, however, you feel strongly that a client is doing something immoral (for example, if you believe abortion is murder), then *you* face a value dilemma. In such a situation it will be very difficult for you to remain objective.

When you face a dilemma about a client's actions or plans, the following guidelines are sometimes helpful:

1. The first step in resolving such a question is to recognize its existence. Such self-awareness is often difficult to attain. Ethical questions are often ambiguous and make us feel uncomfortable. Therefore, we like to avoid them.
2. Self-awareness is not enough unless it is put to use with clients. Kelman (1965) recommended that workers should "label" their values for the client and allow the client to "talk back" in a sort of mutual influence situation. Such an approach *may* be useful in working with clients who are involved with drugs, or are having extramarital affairs, or have been arrested for stealing, and so forth. However, there is a danger to this approach. The worker's values may not be in the client's best interest. When the workers share their values, they are influencing (and perhaps also manipulating) the client. For example, if a worker is morally opposed to abortion, sharing those values with a young unmarried and pregnant woman probably will influence her not to have an abortion, which may or may not be in this woman's best interest. In deciding whether to share values, that worker has to make a professional judgment about what will be most constructive and helpful for the client.
3. When a worker's personal values conflict with the values of the social work profession (for example, in the area of sexual orientation), it is generally advisable for the worker to adhere to the values of the profession when providing services to clients. The Code of Ethics of the National Association of Social Workers is a useful guide to the values of the social work profession. (A copy of this code appears at www.naswdc.org.)
4. Clients should be encouraged to explore their own values and to relate alternative actions to their own value systems. Clients need protection against manipulation that would encroach on their freedom of choice. For example, if a worker is morally opposed to abortion, clients might well be encouraged to see (and referral arrangements be made to see) someone who views abortion as a viable alternative.
5. A useful moral code advanced by Glasser (1965) allows clients to fulfill their needs and to do what they want to do, as long as by doing so they do not deprive others of the ability to fulfill their needs. I have found this code very useful in counseling people considering abortion and in a wide variety of other situations—-counseling gays and lesbians, people involved in premarital relationships, and so forth. The code is also useful in working with adults involved in child abuse, incest, and extramarital affairs because those involved need to examine the effects of their actions on others. There is no one right moral code—what works for one person may not work for another because of differences in lifestyles, life goals, and personal values.
6. Loewenberg and Dolgoff (2004) have developed a rank order of ethical priorities. They suggest that social work practitioners can use these prioritized values when making ethical decisions. In the event that two values are competing, the social worker should abide by the one higher in the order. For instance, if the worker is debating between value 1 (protection of life) and value 2 (right to equality), the worker should act in accordance with value 1. Likewise, value 2 should take precedence over values 3–7, and so on.

Dolgoff, Loewenberg, and Harrington's (2009) prioritized values are as follows:

1. *Protection of life.* This might include provision of adequate food, shelter, clothing, or health care. It might concern acting in response to a person's suicide threat or threat of physically harming another.

2. *Right to equality.* This means that people should be treated fairly and equally. A social worker should seek to facilitate fairness and equality—except when there is a value conflict involving protection of life.
3. *Right to autonomy.* Persons should be allowed to make their own choices about their lives.
4. *Right to experience least harm.* People have the right to be protected from injury. If injury is unavoidable, they have the right to experience the least injury possible, the least lasting harm, or the most easily reversible harm.

EP 2.1.2d

5. *Right to a decent quality of life.* People have the right to seek and attain a "better quality of life" than they currently have.
6. *Right to privacy and confidentiality.* People have the right not to have their private information made public.
7. *Right to truth and all relevant information.* People have the right to know the truth and the right to receive accurate information.

Exercise 2.2: Applying Dolgoff, Loewenberg, and Harrington's Rank Order of Ethical Priorities

Goal: This exercise is designed to assist you in understanding Dolgoff et al.'s rank order of ethical priorities.

Step 1: You are a social worker for a county human services department. In a city neighborhood you encounter a group of African Americans in a heated conflict over a race-related issue with members of the Ku Klux Klan. There is imminent danger of physical violence erupting. Using Dolgoff et al.'s rank order of ethical priorities, which of the following values is the one that you need to first attend to? (circle this value)

a. Protect life.
b. Maintain autonomy, independence, and freedom.
c. Promote a better quality of life.
d. Strengthen every person's right to privacy/confidentiality.
e. Speak the truth and fully disclose all relevant information.
f. Practice in accord with rules and regulations voluntarily accepted.

Step 2: What action(s) would you take to seek to support the value you selected?

Elaine Congress (2000) has developed the following five-step ETHIC process model of decision makings:

EP 2.1.2d

- E Examine relevant personal, societal, agency, client, and professional values.
- T Think about what ethical standard of the NASW Code of Ethics applies, as well as relevant laws and case decisions.
- H Hypothesize about possible consequences of different decisions.
- I Identify who will benefit and who will be harmed in view of social work's commitment to the most vulnerable.
- C Consult with supervisor and colleagues about the most ethical choice.

Exercise 2.3: Applying Congress's ETHIC Process Model of Decision Making

Goal: This exercise is designed to assist you in applying the ETHIC process model.

Step 1: You are a social worker who works for a hospice organization in California. You have a client who has an advanced case of amyotrophic lateral sclerosis (also referred to as Lou Gehrig's disease, and also known as ALS). ALS is a progressive, fatal disease caused by the degeneration of the nerve cells in the central nervous system that control voluntary muscle movement. Affected individuals eventually lose the ability to initiate and control all voluntary movement.

Your client, John Hawkins, has lost control of most of his muscles. He has a prognosis of 4 months left to live. He and his wife ask you to find a state in which Mr. Hawkins could legally end his life through physician-assisted suicide. Physician-assisted suicide, at the time of this writing, is not legal in California, but is legal in Oregon, Washington, and Montana. Using the following ETHIC model, speculate how you would proceed in arriving at a decision of how to respond to the Hawkins' request.

Step 2: What do you see as the relevant personal, societal, client, and professional values in regard to the Hawkins' request?

Step 3: Are there ethical standards of the NASW Code of Ethics that apply, as well as relevant laws and case decisions?

Step 4: Hypothesize about possible consequences of different decisions.

Step 5: Identify who will benefit and who will be harmed in view of different decisions.

Step 6: Speculate what your supervisor and colleagues at hospice are apt to advise about the most ethical choice.

Step 7: What do you see as the strengths and shortcomings of using the ETHIC model?

RESPECT FOR THE DIGNITY AND UNIQUENESS OF INDIVIDUALS

Every human being is unique in a variety of ways—value system, personality, life goals, financial resources, emotional and physical strengths, personal concerns, past experiences, peer pressures, emotional reactions, self-identity, family relationships, and deviant behavioral patterns. In working with a client, a social worker needs to perceive and respect the uniqueness of the client's situation. *Individualization* is the ethical value in social work and other helping professions of viewing, and relating to, the client as a person or group rather than as one whose characteristics are simply typical of a class.

Individualization is relatively easy for a social worker to achieve when the worker is assisting clients who have values, goals, behavioral patterns, and personal characteristics similar to the worker's. Individualization is harder to achieve when a worker is assigned clients who have values or behavioral patterns that the worker views as disgusting. For example, a worker may have difficulty viewing a client with respect when that client has raped a young girl, or is involved in an incestuous relationship, or has killed a member of his family, or has severely abused a child. A general guideline in such situations is that the worker should accept and respect the client but not accept the deviant behavior that needs to be changed. If a worker is unable to convey acceptance of the client, a helping relationship will not be established. If such a relationship is not established, the worker will have practically no opportunity to help the client change deviant behaviors. A second guideline is that if a worker views a client as being disgusting and is unable to establish a working relationship, then the worker should transfer the case to another worker. There should be no disgrace or embarrassment in having to transfer a case for such reasons; it is irrational for a worker to expect to like every client or for every client to like the worker (Ellis & Harper, 1977).

EP 2.1.2a

Exercise 2.4: Clients I Would Be Uncomfortable Working With

Goal: This exercise is designed to assist you in identifying types of clients that you may be uncomfortable (and thereby not fully objective) in working with.

Step 1: Check from the following list those clients you believe you would experience discomfort in working with:

____ A serial rapist

____ A child molestor

____ Someone with intense body odor

____ Someone who has a profound cognitive disability

____ A hit man for the mafia

____ A pathological liar

____ A father who is sexually involved with his 11-year-old daughter

____ A member of the Ku Klux Klan

____ A bigamist

____ A terrorist who has killed several people

____ A young person who is suicidal

____ A 17-year-old who wants an abortion

____ A person who is gay or lesbian

____ A child-care provider who shook a baby to death

____ A person whose religious beliefs are sharply different from yours

____ A person who is severely addicted to alcohol or cocaine

____ Someone who is labeled schizophrenic

____ A husband who battered his wife on several occasions

____ A wife who has a history of extramarital affairs

Step 2: For the items that you checked, specify as precisely as you can why you believe you would be uncomfortable in working with such a client.

Step 3: Review the list of the clients you checked. Specify the types of clients with whom you believe you would have considerable difficulty in establishing a working relationship and therefore should transfer to another worker.

Social workers occasionally encounter "raw" situations. For a while I worked in a mental hospital for the criminally insane and had a variety of clients who had committed a wide range of asocial and bizarre acts, including incest, rape, decapitation of a girlfriend, sodomy, sexual exhibitionism, and removing corpses from graves. I've worked in a variety of other settings and encountered other raw situations. Achieving an attitude of respect for people who commit bizarre actions is difficult at times, but rehabilitation will not occur unless it is achieved.

EP 2.1.1b

Social psychologists have firmly established the theoretical principle that people's images of themselves develop largely out of their interactions and communications with others. A long time ago Charles Cooley (1902) called this process the *looking glass self-concept*. The looking glass says that people develop their self-concept in terms of how other people relate to them, as if others were a looking glass or mirror. For example, a person who receives respect from others and is praised for positive qualities is likely to feel good about himself or herself, will gradually develop a positive sense of worth, will be happier, and will seek responsible and socially acceptable ways to maintain the respect of others.

Exercise 2.5: Components of My Self-Concept That Contain Remnants from the Past

Goal: This exercise is designed to help you recognize that some "tapes in your head" about who you are have remnants from your past.

Step 1: Reflect back to when you were younger (perhaps in the age range from 4 to 12 years of age). Write down what people significant in your life (parents, teachers, siblings, peers, etc.) said about you:

____ Intelligence

____ Health

____ Looks

____ Worth as a person

____ Morals

____ Sexuality

____ Abilities

____ Friends

____ Future

Step 2: Reflect on your current self-concept. Specify all these views that remain as part of your current self-concept.

Step 3: Specify whether you believe your current self-concept was partly formed in terms of the "looking glass self-concept."

Conversely, if a person commits a deviant act and *then* is shunned by others, viewed as different, and treated with disrespect, that person will develop a *failure identity*. According to Glasser (1972), people with failure identities withdraw from society, become emotionally disturbed, or express their discontent in delinquent and deviant actions.

For example, if a neighborhood identifies a youth as being a troublemaker (a delinquent), the neighbors are likely to relate to the youth as if she were not to be trusted, may erroneously accuse her of delinquent acts, and will label her semidelinquent and aggressive behavior as being delinquent. In the absence of objective ways to gauge whether she is, in fact, a delinquent, she will rely on the subjective evaluations of others. Thus, gradually, as she is related to as being a delinquent, she is likely to perceive herself in that way and will begin to enact the delinquent role.

Compton and Galaway (1975) expanded on the importance of social workers' attending carefully to their communications with clients:

> Social workers and other professionals intervening in the lives of people are well advised to be constantly sensitive to the message they are extending to others about their worth. Do we, in the little things we do, communicate to the other person that he is a unique individual to be highly prized? What, for example, is the message communicated when we safeguard time and provide a client with a specific time to be seen as opposed to a catch-me-on-a-catch-as-catch-can basis for visits? Do appointments in advance communicate to the client a higher sense of respect than unannounced visits or hurriedly arranged telephone appointments? And, speaking of telephoning, how about the all too frequently overlooked return call? What message does the client get from the worker in terms of the client's worth when the worker does not have the courtesy or good sense to return telephone calls promptly? How about the ability to listen to clients, to secure from them their own account of their situation, and to avoid prejudgments? And does not privacy, both in terms of how the social worker conducts the interviews and how he treats the material gained from interviews, communicate something to clients about the esteem in which they are held? A worker attempting to operationalize the premise of individual uniqueness and dignity may find it useful to repeatedly inquire of himself, "What does this action on my part communicate to the client about my perception of his personhood?" (pp. 106–107)

The principle of individualization also plays a key role in social work treatment. Various problems, needs, goals, and values of clients involve different patterns of relationships with clients and different methods of helping. For example, consider the needs of a teenage male who is placed in a group home for being beyond parental control. At times he may need an understanding but firm counselor who sets and enforces strict limits. At times he may need encouragement and guidance in how to perform better at school. If conflicts develop between the youth and other boys at the group home, the counselor may need to play a mediating role. If the youth is shy, counseling on how to be more assertive may be needed. If his parents are fairly ineffective in their parenting role, the counselor may seek to have the parents enroll in a parent effectiveness training program (Gordon, 1970). If the youth is being treated unfairly at school or by the juvenile court, the counselor may play an advocate role and attempt to change the system. If the youth has behavior problems, the reasons need to be explored and an intervention program developed.

A thorny problem facing social workers involves striking an effective balance between classification and individualization. There is a need in all human service areas to generalize beyond individuals and to organize data on the basis of common characteristics. Classification is essential to make sense out of a mass of data and is an essential part of developing theories. The danger of putting people into a particular category is that such a classification may lead social workers to respond to people as objects rather than as individuals. Compton and Galaway (1975) commented about the labeling process:

> The pitfalls of this process are being documented in a growing body of literature from sociologists studying deviance from a labeling perspective. Not only does labeling or classification lead to a distortion of individual differences, but, as labeling theorists and their supporting research are noting, a person labeled deviant, those doing the labeling, and the surrounding audience frequently respond to the deviant on the basis of the label rather than on the basis of individual characteristics. This creates conditions for the development of a self-fulfilling prophecy in which the person becomes what he has been labeled. (p. 107)

In the same vein, Toch (1970) noted,

> Playing the classification game in the abstract, as is done in universities, is a joyful, exhilarating experience, harmless and inconsequential. Classifying people in life is a grim business which channelizes destinies and determines fate. A man becomes a category, he is processed as a category, plays his assigned role, lives up to the implications. Labeled irrational, he acts crazy; catalogued dangerous, he becomes dangerous or he stays behind bars. (p. 55)

EP 2.1.1b

This labeling process, most simply stated, occurs because of Cooley's *looking glass self* in which people define who and what they are by how others relate to them. A person labeled as mentally ill, or a delinquent, or an ex-con, or a welfare mother is then likely to define himself or herself by these labels and unfortunately begin playing these roles. Social workers have to continue to be alert to the dangers of labeling and should interact with each client (or judge, attorney, professor, and so forth) as a person rather than as a label.

Exercise 2.6: Labeling Becoming a Self-Fulfilling Prophecy

Goal: This exercise is designed to show you the powerful effects of labeling.

Step 1: Specify a situation in your life where someone conveyed something positive to you, and it was a factor in leading you to excel in that area. (Perhaps it was someone saying you were good at _____, and it led you to excel in that area.)

Step 2: Specify a situation in your life where someone conveyed something negative to you, and it was a factor in leading you to do something dysfunctional/deviant or to put forth minimal effort and you then failed. (Perhaps it was someone saying you were "stupid," or terrible at _____, and it led to you to failing or doing something you know you should not have done.)

Step 3: Comment on the following: "If, as social workers, we want clients to make positive changes, we first need to treat clients with respect and convey that we strongly believe they have the potential for making the kind of choices that will result in a better life for them."

THE CLIENT'S RIGHT TO SELF-DETERMINATION

Social workers believe that clients have the right to express their own opinions and to act on them, as long as by so doing clients do not infringe on the rights of others. This principle is in sharp contrast to the layperson's views that a social worker seeks to "remold" clients into a pattern chosen by the worker. Instead, the workers' efforts are geared to enhancing clients' abilities to help themselves. Client self-determination derives logically from belief in the inherent dignity of each person. If people have dignity, then it follows that they should be permitted to determine their own lifestyles as far as possible.

Social workers believe that making all decisions and doing everything for a client is self-defeating, because it leads to increased dependence rather than greater self-reliance and self-sufficiency. For people to grow, to mature, to become responsible, they need to make their own decisions and take responsibility for the consequences. Mistakes and emotional pain will occur. But that is part of life. We learn by our mistakes and by trial and error. Respect for the clients' ability to make their own decisions is associated with the principle that social work is a cooperative endeavor between clients and workers (client participation). Social work is done *with,* not *to,* a client. Plans imposed on people without their active involvement have a way of not turning out well.

Four points should be made in operationalizing the principle of *client self-determination*. First, self-determination implies that clients should be made aware that there are alternatives for resolving the personal or social problems they face. Self-determination involves having clients make decisions—that is, making a choice selected from several courses of action. If there were only one course of action, there would be no choice, and therefore clients would not have the right of self-determination. As will be discussed further in later chapters, the role of a social worker in helping clients involves (1) building a helping relationship, (2) exploring problems in depth with clients, and (3) exploring alternative solutions with clients, then choosing a course of action. This third step is the implementation of the principle of self-determination.

Second, self-determination means that the client, rather than the worker, is the chief problem solver. Workers need to recognize that the client *owns* the problem and therefore has the chief responsibility to resolve the problem. This is an area in which social work differs markedly from other professions. Most professionals, such as physicians and attorneys, advise clients about what they believe clients ought to do. Doctors, lawyers, and dentists are experts in advising clients. The client's decision making after receiving the expert's advice in such situations is generally limited to the choice of whether to accept the professional's advice.

In sharp contrast, social workers should seek to establish not an expert-inferior relationship but a relationship between equals. The worker's expertise does *not* lie in knowing or recommending what is best for the client. Rather, the expertise lies in assisting clients to define their problems, develop and examine the alternatives for resolving the problems, maximize their capacities and opportunities to make decisions for themselves, and implement the decisions they make. In conjunction with this principle, Dumont (1968) noted,

> The most destructive thing in psychotherapy is a "rescue fantasy" in the therapist—a feeling that the therapist is the divinely sent agent to pull a tormented soul from the pit of suffering and adversity and put him back on the road to happiness and glory. A major reason this fantasy is so destructive is that it carries the conviction that the patient will be saved only through and by the therapist. When such a conviction is communicated to the patient, verbally or otherwise, he has no choice other than to rebel and leave or become more helpless, dependent, and sick. (p. 60)

Third, self-determination does not prohibit or restrict social workers from offering an opinion or making a suggestion. In fact, social workers have an obligation to share their viewpoints with their clients. Compton and Galaway (1975) noted,

> Workers have the obligations of sharing with clients their own thinking, perhaps their own experiences, not as a way of directing the clients' lives but rather as an additional source of information and input for the clients to consider in their own decision making. It is imperative, however, that the social workers' input be recognized as information to be considered and not an edict to be followed. (p. 111)

The key to implementing this principle is for the social worker to phrase the alternative as a suggestion rather than as advice. For example, if a client is worried about how her elderly mother, who is living alone and whose physical and mental capacities are deteriorating, will be able to have her physical, emotional, and social needs met, the social worker should not advise: "The best thing for you to do is to place her in a nursing home." Instead the worker should offer a suggestion for the client to consider: "Have you thought about placing your mother in a nursing home?"

Fourth, client self-determination is possible and should be encouraged even in areas in which the social worker has the additional function to protect society. Three areas in social work for which the worker has this additional function are in protective services, in prisons, and in probation and parole. Compton and Galaway (1975) noted,

> A probation agency, for example, may enforce the legal requirement that the probationer must report to the probation officer; this is not a matter for client self-determination. But the sensitive officer can allow for considerable client self-determination in the frequency of reporting, the length of the interviews, the time of reporting, and the content to be discussed during the interviews. (p. 112)

Actually, probationers can also be informed that they even have a choice in reporting to the probation officer. In working with involuntary clients who are angry with the legal authority held by the social worker, it is often helpful for the worker to inform the clients that they do have a choice regarding whether they are willing to meet the minimum legal requirements. The consequences of not cooperating (such as being sent to prison or having their children taken away in the case of abusive parents) are also made clear to them. This approach appears to be useful because it reduces the clients' inclination to view the social worker as a parent or a cop. Instead of playing the game of how much they can get away with, this approach puts the responsibility for their future squarely on the clients. They are faced with the decision of reporting or suffering the consequences of not reporting; of deciding whether to stop abusing their children or of suffering the consequences of making no effort to refrain from abusing their children. In this connection O'Connor (1972) noted,

> The recognition of man's [a person's] right to free choice guarantees that he may choose to run his life as he sees fit. This choice may run counter to society's welfare and even his own, yet essentially it is his choice and his prerogative. Society may censure, but it cannot take from him his right; nor would society strip him of his dignity by a censure. The criminal then has a right to say "crime is my choice and I am willing to pay the price. If you send me to prison, I am paying my debt to society and refuse to submit to your attempts to reform me." The principle of self-determination makes it incumbent upon society to honor such a plea. (pp. 485–486)

In working with involuntary clients whose actions have adversely affected other people in the past (for example, abusive parents), the worker's obligation is to outline the minimum legal requirements (for example, no further incidents of abuse) and specify the consequences if these clients decide not to meet these requirements. Even in such situations, clients have a choice in deciding whether they will meet the requirements. If they are not met by a client, the worker must follow through and implement the consequences to maintain credibility with the client. Often the consequences have therapeutic shock value as clients learn they can no longer manipulate the system and are responsible for the consequences they suffer.

CONFIDENTIALITY

Confidentiality is an implicit or explicit agreement between a professional and a client that the professional will maintain the private nature of information about the client. An *absolute* implementation of confidentiality means that the professional will not share client disclosures with anyone, unless authorized by the client in writing or required by law. Because of the principle of confidentiality, professionals can be sued if they disclose information that the client is able to document has a damaging effect on him or her.

Confidentiality is important because clients may decide not to share their secrets, personal concerns, and asocial thoughts and actions with a professional if they believe the information will be revealed to others. A basic principle of counseling is that clients must feel comfortable in fully revealing themselves to the professional without fear that their secret revelations will be used against them.

Confidentiality is "absolute" when information revealed to a professional is *never* passed on to anyone in any form. Such information would never be shared with other agency staff, fed into a computer, or written in a case record. A student or beginning practitioner tends to think in absolutes and may naively promise clients absolute confidentiality. Absolute confidentiality, however, is seldom achieved.

Social workers today generally function as part of a larger agency. Much of the client's communication is written into case records and shared orally with staff in the system as part of the service-delivery process. Social workers share details with supervisors, and many work in teams and are expected to share information. Therefore, instead of absolute confidentiality, it is more precise to indicate that a system of *relative* confidentiality is being used in social work practice (Wilson, 1978, p. 3).

Confidentiality is a legal matter, and there is a fair amount of uncertainty about what is an unlawful violation. In addition, there have been few test cases in court to determine this issue. Let me provide a brief summary of how agencies handle issues related to confidentiality.

Practically all agencies allow (and in fact encourage) their workers to discuss a client's circumstances with other professionals employed at the same agency. At many agencies (such as a mental hospital) the input of many professionals (psychiatrist, psychologist, social workers, nurses, physical therapist, and so forth) is used in assessing a client and developing a treatment plan.

Many agencies feel it is inappropriate to share or discuss a client's case with a secretary. (Yet the secretary does the typing and usually knows as much about each client as the professional staff does.)

Most agencies believe it is inappropriate to discuss a client's case with professionals at another agency unless the client first signs a release-of-information form (see Figure 2.1). (Yet, informally, professionals employed by different agencies do at times share information about a client without the client's authorization.)

Nearly all agencies share case information with social work interns. (Whether it is legally permissible to share information with student interns has not been determined.)

It is certainly permissible to discuss a case with others for educational purposes if no identifying information about the client is given. But this too is a gray area because the person talking about the case will not be able to determine precisely when identifying information is being given. Let me give you an example.

Some years ago I was employed at a maximum-security hospital for the criminally insane and had on my caseload a young male who had decapitated his 17-year-old girlfriend. Such a criminal offense is indeed shocking and rare. People in the client's local area will never forget the offense. If I were to discuss this case in a class at a university (which I occasionally do), I would never be fully assured that no one would be able to identify the offender. There is always the chance that

Lakeview Counseling Center
Consent to Release Confidential Information to Another (third) Party

________________ at Lakeview Counseling Center requests permission from ________________
(Name of social worker)

________________ to release confidential information about ________________. This information will be released to:
(Name of client) (Name of client)

Name: ________________ Address: ________________

Position: ________________ ________________

Agency: ________________

Material to be released: ________________

____

____

The information will be used/disclosed for the following purposes: ________________

____

____

My signature verifies that I know what information is being disclosed. I am aware that this consent can be revoked (in writing) at any time. My questions about this form have been answered.

This consent form expires on ________________ unless revoked by me in writing prior to that date.
(Date)

________________ (Client's signature or "X") ________________ (Date signed) ________________ (Witness)

________________ (Client's guardian—if applicable) ________________ (Date signed) ________________ (Witness)

________________ (Lakeview Counseling Center representative) ________________ (Date signed)

Figure 2.1
Release-of-information form (sample copy of a suggested format).

one of the students may have lived in the client's home community and would recognize the offender.

A question that is sometimes raised in relation to confidentiality is whether clients have a right to see the agency's records on them. According to the 1974 Federal Privacy Act, any agency receiving federal funds must allow clients to see their records. Furthermore, if a client requests a copy of the record, the agency must provide one. If the client is a minor, both the child and the child's parents have the right of access to the client's records. (For individuals who are 18 years old or older or who attend postsecondary institutions, the access to educational records and the consent required before access by others resides with them rather than their parents.)

It is probably a good idea not to put anything into a client's record that you do not want the client to see. Numerous private agencies that receive no federal funds also now have policies to allow clients access to their records.

Another problematic area is the thorny question of when a professional should violate confidence and inform others. Again, many gray areas surround this question (Wilson, 1978). Most state statutes permit or require the professional to inform the appropriate people when a client admits to a past or intended *serious* criminal act. Yet the question of how serious a crime must be before there is an obligation to report it has not been resolved. On the extreme end of the severity continuum, it has been established that a professional *must* inform the appropriate people.

A precedent-setting case occurred in *Tarasoff v. Regents of the University of California, 1974 (University of Pittsburgh Law Review,* 1975). In this case a university student informed his psychiatrist that he was going to shoot his girlfriend. The psychiatrist informed the campus police of this threat but did not inform the intended victim or her parents. Campus security picked up and questioned the student and soon released him, concluding that he "appeared rational." Shortly afterward he murdered his girlfriend. Her parents sued the psychiatrist, and the U.S. Supreme Court ruled,

> When a doctor or a psychiatrist, in the exercise of his professional skills and knowledge, determines, or shall determine that a warning is essential to avert danger arising from a medical or psychological condition of his patient, he incurs a legal obligation to give that warning. (*University of Pittsburgh Law Review,* 1975, p. 159)

The Court also concluded,

> The public policy favoring protection of the confidential character of patient-psychotherapist communication must yield in instances in which disclosure is essential to avert danger to others. The protective privilege ends where the public peril begins. (p. 161)

Thus, the Court set a precedent holding that a professional is liable for failure to warn the intended victim. This precedent has continued to be upheld in court decisions involving a helping professional's obligation to inform the intended victim (Schwartz, 1989, pp. 225–226).

For what intended crimes must a helping professional inform the police and the intended victim? Do such crimes include embezzlement, pornography, and larceny? Apparently not. Schoener (2000) has reviewed court decisions in this area and concludes helping professionals are obligated to inform the intended victim (along with the police) only when a client threatens serious physical violence to a specific person. Student interns or beginning practitioners are advised to ask their supervisors when questions in this area arise.

Several years ago I was the faculty supervisor for a student in a field placement at a public assistance agency. The student intern had an unmarried mother on his caseload. A trusting, working relationship between the intern and the mother was developed. The mother then informed the student she was dating a person who was sometimes abusive to her when he was drunk. The mother further indicated there was a warrant for the boyfriend's arrest in another state for an armed robbery charge. The student intern contacted me inquiring whether it was his obligation to inform the police, thereby violating confidentiality. My response was that he should discuss this with his agency supervisor to find out the agency's policy in regard to this question.

Wilson (1978) further concluded,

> In summary, a professional whose client confesses an intended or past crime can find himself in a very delicate position, both legally and ethically. There are enough conflicting beliefs on how this should be handled, so that clear guidelines are lacking. Social workers who receive a communication about a serious criminal act by a client would be wise to consult an attorney for a detailed research of appropriate state statutes and a review of recent court rulings that might help determine the desired course of action. (p. 121)

In a number of other areas a professional is permitted, expected, or required to violate confidentiality.[1] These areas include the following:

When a client formally (usually in writing) authorizes the professional to release information.

[1]An extended discussion of these areas is contained in Suanna J. Wilson, *Confidentiality in Social Work: Issues and Principles* (New York: Free Press, 1978), and in Donald T. Dickson, *Confidentiality and Privacy in Social Work* (New York: Free Press, 1998).

When a professional is called to testify in a criminal case (state statutes vary regarding guidelines on what information may be kept confidential in such criminal proceedings, and therefore practitioners must research their own particular state statutes in this area).

When a client files a lawsuit against a professional (for example, for malpractice).

When a client threatens suicide and a professional may be forced to violate confidentiality to save the client's life. (The treating professional is encouraged to violate confidentiality in such circumstances, but there is not necessarily a legal requirement to do so.)

When a client threatens to harm his or her therapist.

When a professional becomes aware that a minor has committed a crime, when a minor is used by adults as an accessory in a crime, or when a minor is a victim of criminal actions. In such situations most states require that counselors inform the legal authorities. Again, the question arises of how serious the crime must be before it is reported.

When there is evidence of child abuse or neglect. Most states require professionals to report the evidence to the designated child-protection agency.

EP 2.1.2b, d

When a client's emotional or physical condition makes his or her employment a clear danger to self or others (for example, when a counselor discovers that a client who is an airplane pilot has a serious drinking problem).

In all these areas, professional judgment must be used in deciding when the circumstances justify violating confidentiality.

Exercise 2.7: Do You Violate Confidentiality to Blow the Whistle on Embezzling?

Goal: This exercise is designed to help you understand the complexities surrounding a potential whistle-blowing situation.

You are a social worker for the United Way. Tim Mehan, hired 4 years ago as director of United Way, is a charismatic, creative fund-raiser who in 4 years has doubled the amount of United Way money being raised in your community. United Way agencies are now being allocated significantly more funds, and more clients are being served. However, there is a major issue. Helen Jarvis, bookkeeper for United Way, shows you evidence that Mr. Mehan is systematically embezzling money—he apparently has a severe gambling addiction at a casino in the area. Ms. Jarvis asks you whether the two of you should "blow the whistle" on this embezzling. The United Way's books will be audited in the next 5 weeks by an accounting firm, and there is a high probability the missing funds will be noted. If this embezzlement becomes public knowledge, the resulting scandal will undoubtedly lead to a sharp reduction in contributions to United Way. Revealing this situation may also jeopardize your employment and that of Ms. Jarvis. What do you recommend that you and Ms. Jarvis should do?

Privacy and Confidentiality in the Computer Era

Protecting the confidentiality of files and records in human service organizations is becoming much more difficult as the technology of compiling, storing, and receiving information on clients expands exponentially. Vast amounts of data can be gathered, recorded, stored, and processed quickly, easily, and inexpensively. More than a decade ago, Dickson (1998) noted,

> At one time, a patient's or client's record might have consisted of some basic information on a single file card, or a number of pages of personal data, process notes, and observations. Today, such a record might consist of hundreds of pages of text along with still or moving visual images and recorded sound, all stored on tape, disk, hard drive, or

> CD-ROM as electronic/magnetic impulses. The record might be copied into a central database of case records, and could be linked with or contain cross-references to other databases containing other records for the same individual, family, or condition. The records could be accessed, sorted, merged, compiled, and transmitted. They could be downloaded and printed, instantly copied, and transmitted by fax or computer modem to numerous other locations, anywhere in the country or internationally. And with the appropriate linkages, the record could be accessed by other computers or other data systems near and far. Along with all this, the expansion of federal and state government and private third-party insurers in monitoring and reimbursing service delivery has greatly increased the potential for broad access to and dispersion of recorded information. (pp. 124–125)

It is possible (although some legislative acts prevent certain linkages) to link or combine a client's health, mental health, social service, juvenile court, adult court, education, and law-enforcement records. At times, individuals learn that inaccuracies in their records have found their way into computerized databases, with severe, adverse consequences.

The preservation of privacy and confidentiality is a major challenge. Faxed and computer-transmitted records and e-mails can be intercepted by third parties. Confidential information can be posted on the Internet, where it is seen and can be copied by millions of people anywhere around the world. Even the destruction of records is complicated. Records can be shredded and erased from computer files, but a record that was assumed to have been destroyed or have been deleted may exist in another location or under another name or identification number. Therefore, it is important for human service agencies to keep a log of what client information has been transmitted, when, to whom, and in what form.

Because of the potential for violations of privacy and confidentiality, social workers need in-depth understanding of the privacy rights and confidentiality rights of individuals and families. What information to gather, store, replicate, transmit, and who has access and for what purposes, are crucial issues.

Confidentiality and HIPAA Regulations

Congress recognized the need for national public record privacy standards in 1996 when it enacted the Health Insurance Portability and Accountability Act (HIPAA). The law included provisions designed to save money for health-care businesses by encouraging electronic transfers, but it also required new safeguards to protect the security and confidentiality of that information.

A major concern was the security and privacy of electronic health records and their transmission between health-care entities. The security standards HIPAA mandated are designed to establish industry "best practice." Health-care providers must have security policies that are documented and implemented. Health-care providers generally utilize a number of security mechanisms to permit only the sender, recipient, and authorized personnel to have access to data passing through electronic systems.

Most health-care providers require all employees to read and sign a confidentiality agreement, in which the employees agree not to directly or indirectly disclose confidential information in an inappropriate manner. Confidential or protected health-care information is information pertaining to the physical or mental health or condition of an individual, how health care is delivered to an individual, and the source of payment for an individual's health care.

Under HIPAA, patients

- Must be told (in writing) how their health-care information may be used
- Have a right to see their medical records
- Have a right to amend (change) incorrect or incomplete information in their records
- Must give authorization before information is released (with a few exceptions)
- Have a right to complain formally if they believe their privacy was not protected

HIPAA also requires health-care providers to observe all existing state and federal laws and regulations relating to the transmission and storage of, and access to, records and other health care data and to maintain the security and confidentiality of patient-specific information.

Privileged Communication

Privileged communication is closely related to confidentiality but is narrower in scope. *Privileged communication* is a legal term pertaining to the admission of evidence in a court; *confidentiality* refers to laws or rules of professional ethics that regulate the disclosure of information by a client to a professional. Bernstein (1975) defined *privileged communication* as follows:

> In states where certain professional groups are granted privileged communication, the client or his attorney has the privilege of preventing the professional from answering questions about their communication when called as a witness in court. (p. 521)

Privileged communication protects the client, and the right to exercise this privilege belongs to the client, not to the professional.

Four fundamental conditions are necessary to establish privilege against disclosure:

1. Communications must originate in the confidence that they will not be disclosed.
2. The element of confidentiality must be essential to the maintenance of the relationship between the parties.
3. The relationship is one which in the opinion of the community ought to be fostered.
4. The injury that would inure to the relationship as a result of disclosure must be greater than the benefit gained in regard to the correct disposal of litigation. (Wigmore, 1961, p. 52)

These conditions lay the foundation for the determination of privileged communication by the judiciary. Every case that raises the issue of privileged communication is evaluated by whether it meets these conditions.

Many state statutes contain exceptions to privileged communication whereby the professional must testify in court. A list of these exceptions is contained in Wilson (1978). Examples of such exceptions include the following:

- The client waives privilege.
- The client introduces privileged material into litigation.
- A communication does not meet Wigmore's four criteria.
- The social worker is called to testify in a criminal case.
- A client sues his or her counselor.
- A client commits or threatens a criminal act.
- A patient threatens suicide.
- A client threatens to harm his or her therapist.
- Physicians must report certain medical conditions and treatments.
- A minor is involved in criminal activity.
- Child abuse or neglect is suspected.
- A client is using certain types of drugs.
- A client's condition makes his or her employment hazardous to others.
- The court orders a professional examination.
- Involuntary hospitalization is needed for someone's protection.
- The client dies.
- A treating professional needs to collect fees for services rendered.
- Information is learned outside the professional treatment relationship.
- Information is shared in the presence of a third person.
- The federal government needs certain information.
- The right of privileged communication is not transferable from one state to another.
- Emergency action is needed to save a client's life.
- Legal action is needed for protection of a minor.

- A client engages in treasonous activities.
- A presentence investigation report is prepared.

In the past few decades, social workers have been successful in most states in attaining passage of state legislation that recognizes social worker–client privileged communication to avoid forced disclosures of confidential information in court. In states in which social workers are not granted privileged communication, they can be subpoenaed by any party to a court action and thereby forced to testify in court fully and under oath about all that transpired between the client and the social worker. If they fail to testify, they can be found in contempt of court by the judge and fined, sent to jail, or both. Such court appearances can be detrimental to the client-worker relationship and to future work with the client.

Social workers in recent years have been successful in all states in securing passage of legislation that licenses (or certifies) social workers. A section of such legislation usually contains a provision that recognizes social worker–client privileged communication. In various states a number of other professionals have been licensed and have secured recognition of privileged communication with clients. These professionals include attorneys, accountants, physicians, the clergy, guidance counselors, marriage counselors, nurses, psychiatrists, and psychologists.

Explaining Confidentiality to Clients

How should a worker respond to clients' questions about confidentiality? Clients often wonder when they seek services how the information they reveal will be used. Clients need to be assured that the information they divulge will be kept confidential; otherwise they are unlikely to share their secret concerns. Compare the following two responses to a question asked by a husband who is seeking marriage counseling for himself and his wife:

First response:
Husband: Will what we say here be told to others?
Worker: Our agency operates on a system of relative confidentiality. This means I may discuss certain aspects of your case with other staff members at this agency, but I will not discuss your case with anyone else outside the agency. There is one exception to this: if I am subpoenaed (which might happen if you decide to get a divorce and the divorce is contested), then I would have to reveal what we talked about. I guess there might be one additional exception. Should the need arise for me to talk with professionals at other agencies (for example, your doctor), then I would first ask you to sign a release-of-information form allowing me to discuss your case.

Second response:
Husband: Will what we say here be told to others?
Worker: No, what you say here will be kept within this agency. I know when clients first come to an agency they often wonder how the information they reveal will be used. I assure you that what we talk about will be kept confidential.

The second response is probably the most desirable at agencies where the chances of subpoenas are unlikely. The first response, though more thorough, is likely to suggest to clients that there is a moderate chance that information they reveal will be used against them at some future time, which will inhibit them from sharing their "secret" concerns.

However, if a worker is providing services in an area with a moderate or high chance of court action, then clients should be more fully informed about the limits of confidentiality. For example, a probation and parole officer should inform clients (early in the supervision period) about his or her obligations to the court if a client reveals a violation of the conditions of probation (for example, by committing another offense), as illustrated in this excerpt from an interview:

Probation Officer: I'm here to help you in any way I can. If you have personal concerns and want to talk to someone, I'd be happy to talk with you. If you choose to talk with someone else, that's certainly okay with me. The important thing is that when you have personal concerns, you get them worked out. We all have personal concerns at times. If you choose to talk to me, it will be kept confidential. The only information that will not be kept confidential is a violation by you of the conditions of probation, which we have discussed and which you have a copy of. If you violate the conditions of probation, and I find out, either by your telling me, or in some other way, I am required to make a report to the court of the violation. Do you have questions about this?

Probationee: No.

Probation Officer: All right, if you have some concerns now, or in the future, I'll be happy to talk with you.

Probationee: There is one concern I have. My girlfriend's parents as yet don't know I've been arrested and placed on probation. He's a minister, and his wife is a schoolteacher. I don't know what they will say when they find out I'm in trouble. How do you think I should handle this? [The interview continues—and a trusting, helping relationship begins to develop.]

Confidentiality and AIDS

The major social concerns and controversies encompassing AIDS are far too numerous to be addressed here, so the focus will be on confidentiality and AIDS. Once a person has been positively diagnosed as having antibodies to HIV and therefore is capable of transmitting the virus to others, who else should have access to this information? Do social workers have an obligation to help protect the public health that outweighs their clients' interests? Is it ethically permissible for social workers to notify identifiable partners who are in danger of contracting the AIDS virus, if their clients refuse to change high-risk behaviors or to warn their partners? Where does a social worker's obligation to preserve client confidentiality end and duty to protect or warn another person begin?

Clients who are HIV-positive may be reluctant to inform their sexual partners for a variety of reasons. They may be concerned about the possibility of being abandoned. They may be angry because they suspect their partners infected them. They may fear that their partners might tell others that they are HIV-positive.

The NASW's policy statement (Landers, 1993) on HIV/AIDS concerning whether there is a duty to inform is as follows:

> Practitioners and agencies may perceive a responsibility to warn third parties of their potential for infection if their spouses, other sexual partners, or partners in intravenous drug use are HIV-infected and the partners refuse to warn them. (p. 3)

In this HIV/AIDS policy statement, NASW refers to the "duty to warn" principle, which was established by the 1974 case *Tarasoff v. Regents of the University of California* (*University of Pittsburgh Law Review,* 1975). In this precedent-setting case, the California Supreme Court ruled that psychotherapists have a duty to warn a potential victim when the professional believes there is a clear danger, even if this means breaching confidentiality. The court concluded, "The protective privilege ends where the public peril begins." Whether *Tarasoff* applies to AIDS cases has not been tested. All *Tarasoff* cases tested in court have involved threats with weapons or arson, not sexually transmitted diseases.

In regard to the thorny issue of partner notification, Dickson (1998) states,

EP 2.1.2b, c, d

> For social workers—and other professionals—disclosure of a patient's or client's HIV/AIDS status to others presents significant ethical and perhaps legal problems. Ethically, a strong argument can be made that if the patient or client refuses to tell a spouse, sexual partner, or other who is in danger of exposure, the social worker should take steps to protect that individual.... However, there is often a conflicting state confidentiality statute, with penalties for unauthorized disclosure of HIV or AIDS. Until the case and statutory law are better harmonized, the best course for the social worker is to work with the patient or client to get him or her to notify those at risk or, failing that, to gain an informed consent for notification. If this is unsuccessful, a court-ordered release of the confidential information is possible. As always, consultation and careful documentation are called for. (p. 212)

Exercise 2.8: Do You Have a Duty to Inform a Person at Risk of Acquiring HIV?

Goal: This exercise is designed to better inform you of the complicated issues surrounding whether to violate confidentiality.

You are a social worker, and one of your clients informs you that he recently tested positive for HIV. You begin to assist him with his feelings and concerns and also give him the name of a physician who has expertise in medically treating HIV-positive individuals. The client further informs you that he has a female sexual partner who is unaware of his HIV status. You urge him to inform her so that precautions can be taken to prevent the transfer of the HIV virus to her—and to suggest it may be in her best interest to be tested to determine her HIV status. He refuses to inform her, saying she'll leave him if she finds out. Do you seek to get a court-ordered release of confidential information, which may (or may not) be attained over a period of weeks? Do you contact the girlfriend and violate confidentiality by revealing his HIV status—which in the long run may lengthen her life and her quality of life? What other options do you have? Please specify what you believe you would do.

OTHER VALUES

Additional values and principles of social work practice are briefly summarized in this section. You should also study the Code of Ethics of the National Association of Social Workers and the Canadian Association of Social Workers' Code of Ethics, which summarize important practice ethics for social workers. The NASW is the largest professional association representing the social work profession in the United States, and the Canadian Association of Social Workers is the largest professional association representing the social work profession in Canada. (The NASW Code of Ethics appears at www.naswdc.org. The Canadian Association of Social Workers' Code of Ethics and Guidelines for Ethical Practice appears at www.casw-acts.ca.)

Another important statement of ethics relevant to social work is the "Ethics in Social Work, Statement of Principles," developed jointly by the International Federation of Social Workers and the International Association of Schools of social work (2004). It can be accessed at http://www.ifsw.org.

Residual and Institutional Orientations toward Social Welfare

There are two conflicting views of the role of social welfare in our society (Wilensky & Lebeaux, 1965). The *residual* view promotes a gap-filling or first-aid role. This view holds that social welfare services should be provided only when an individual's needs are not properly met through other societal institutions, primarily the family and the market economy. Social services and financial aid should not be provided until all measures or efforts have failed (other efforts include the exhaustion of the individual's or the family's resources). In addition, the residual view asserts that funds and services should be provided on a short-term basis (primarily during emergencies) and withdrawn when the individual or the family again becomes self-sufficient.

EP 2.1.1b

The residual view has characterized social welfare as "charity for unfortunates" (Wilensky & Lebeaux, 1965, p. 14). Funds and services are seen not as a right (something to which one is entitled) but as a gift, with the receiver having certain obligations (for example, to receive financial aid the recipient may be required to perform certain low-grade work assignments). An associated belief holds that the causes of recipients' difficulties are rooted in their own malfunctioning (that is, recipients are brought to their predicament through their own fault because of some personal inadequacy, or ill-advised activity, or sin). Under the residual view, a stigma is usually attached to receiving services or funds.

Exercise 2.9: The Residual View Stigma

Goal: This exercise is designed to help you recognize the stigma about receiving social welfare funds or services that is associated with the residual view.

Reflect on a time when you were aware that you had intense unwanted emotions (such as depression, anger, or confusion) related to a personal situation or dilemma that you faced (please do not specify the dilemma or situation). Did you experience reluctance to seek counseling because you were wary of what others might think of you? If "yes," please specify your concerns related to this residual stigma. Also specify whether you did, or did not, seek counseling for this dilemma or situation.

The opposing point of view has been called the *institutional* view. According to this view, social welfare programs are to be "accepted as a proper, legitimate function of modern industrial society in helping individuals achieve self-fulfillment" (Wilensky & Lebeaux, 1965, p. 14). Under this view, there is no stigma attached to receiving funds or services; recipients are entitled to such help. Associated with this view is the belief that individuals' difficulties result from causes largely beyond their control (for example, a person is unemployed because of a lack of employment opportunities).

The residual approach characterized social welfare programs from our early history to the Depression of the 1930s. Since the Great Depression, both approaches have been applied to social welfare programs, with some programs being largely residual in nature while others are more institutional in design and implementation. Social workers generally believe in the institutional approach and strive to develop and provide programs with this orientation.

At the present time a so-called devolution revolution is occurring with regard to the provision of human services in our society. Decisions about the provision of key social welfare programs are being transferred from the federal government down to the state level. A major program affected by the devolution revolution was Aid to Families with Dependent Children (AFDC).

From 1935 to the middle 1990s, the federal government required all states to provide the AFDC program to eligible families. (The program was created by the 1935 Social Security Act.) This public assistance program provided monthly checks primarily to low-income mothers with children under age 18. The precise parameters of eligibility for AFDC varied from state to state. Payments were made for both the parent (or parents) and the children in eligible families. Financing and administration of the AFDC program was shared by federal and state governments. In many states, counties also participated in financing and administration. In 1996, federal legislation was enacted that dismantled the AFDC program. The entire concept that poor families are entitled to basic human and health services has now been questioned. As Chapter 13 indicates, many policy makers now believe that private charities can respond, at a lower cost, to local social problems than public services can. The 1996 Welfare Reform Act (the Personal Responsibility and Work Opportunity Reconciliation Act) called for the following: (1) Each state sets its own eligibility rules and amounts for financial assistance. The federal government provides block grants to states to assist in financing the programs that are developed. (2) Recipients of financial benefits receive no more than 2 years of assistance without working, and there is a 5-year lifetime limit of benefits for adults.

In 1935, when the AFDC program was enacted, it was thought best for single mothers to stay at home to raise their children. The 1996 welfare reform legislation asserts that single mothers (and fathers) have an obligation to work for a living. The safety net for poor families with young children now has some major holes. Clearly, the legislation marks a shift by our society to the residual approach. The profession of social work is being challenged to confront the devolution revolution and to respond to the needs of those who are falling through the holes in the safety net.

Establishing Professional Boundaries with Clients

Is it appropriate for a social worker to have lunch or dinner with a client? Is it appropriate to attend a party (where alcoholic drinks are being served) where clients may be present? Is it appropriate to hug a client who is experiencing emotional distress? These are examples of *boundary questions* that arise in interactions with clients.

As the years have passed, I have seen a variety of boundary problems. A well-meaning male psychotherapist was charged by a female client for unethical conduct because he occasionally gave her hugs and because he overstepped (according to her) the boundaries of a professional relationship by giving her his room air-conditioner after he had central air installed in his home. In another case, a man charged a female psychotherapist with alienation of affection after the psychotherapist and the man's wife, who was a client of the female therapist, had dinner a few times and the wife became attracted to the therapist. Some social work faculty members have dated social work students, and now universities across the country are questioning the propriety of such relationships. (A power differential exists between students and faculty, and many campuses now view such dating relationships as evidence that the involved students could use to prove sexual harassment.) A female social work intern at a group home for adolescent males was confronted by her agency supervisor because she sought to become friends with the residents. She frequently played pool with them and occasionally shared some of her "partying" stories, and one of the residents became infatuated with her. A male intern at a shelter for runaway youths occasionally related jokes that had some sexual connotations; one of the female residents charged that such behavior was evidence that the intern was making romantic advances toward her. A female intern was terminated at her field placement at a halfway house for chemically addicted correctional residents after she began dating one of the residents. A male intern at a shelter for battered women was confronted by his agency supervisor about the "provocative and revealing" clothes he tended to wear, which was a factor in some of the residents becoming infatuated with him.

Social workers have an obligation to establish appropriate boundaries in professional relationships with clients. The Canadian Association of Social Workers' Code of Ethics and Guidelines for Ethical Practice (2005) contains the following statements on these boundary issues:

> Dual or multiple relationships occur when social workers relate to clients in more than one relationship, whether professional, social or business. Dual or multiple relationships can occur simultaneously or consecutively. While having contact with clients in different life situations is not inherently harmful, it is the responsibility of the social worker to evaluate

> the nature of the various contacts to determine whether the social worker is in a position of power and/or authority that may unduly and/or negatively affect the decisions and actions of their client.
>
> Social workers avoid engaging in physical contact with clients when there is a possibility of harm to the client as a result of the contact. Social workers who engage in appropriate physical contact with clients are responsible for setting clear, appropriate and culturally sensitive boundaries to govern such physical contact.
>
> Social workers do not engage in romantic relationships, sexual activities or sexual contact with clients, even if such contact is sought by clients.
>
> Social workers who have provided psychotherapy or in-depth counselling do not engage in romantic relationships, sexual activities or sexual contact with former clients. It is the responsibility of the social worker to evaluate the nature of the professional relationship they had with a client and to determine whether the social worker is in a position of power and/or authority that may unduly and/or negatively affect the decisions and actions of their former client.
>
> Social workers do not engage in a romantic relationship, sexual activities or sexual contact with social work students whom they are supervising or teaching.

The NASW Code of Ethics (1996) contains these statements on boundary issues:

> Social workers should not take unfair advantage of any professional relationship or exploit others to further their personal, religious, political, or business interests.
>
> Social workers should not engage in dual or multiple relationships with clients or former clients in which there is a risk of exploitation or potential harm to the client. In instances when dual or multiple relationships are unavoidable, social workers should take steps to protect clients and are responsible for setting clear, appropriate, and culturally sensitive boundaries. (Dual or multiple relationships occur when social workers relate to clients in more than one relationship, whether professional, social, or business. Dual or multiple relationships can occur simultaneously or consecutively.)
>
> Social workers should under no circumstances engage in sexual activities or sexual contact with current clients, whether such contact is consensual or forced.
>
> Social workers should not engage in activities or sexual contact with clients' relatives or other individuals with whom clients maintain a close, personal relationship where there is a risk of exploitation or potential harm to the client. Sexual activity or sexual contact with clients' relatives or other individuals with whom clients maintain a personal relationship has the potential to be harmful to the client and may make it difficult for the social worker and client to maintain appropriate professional boundaries. Social workers—not their clients, their clients' relatives, or other individuals with whom the client maintains a professional relationship—assume the full burden for setting clear, appropriate, and culturally sensitive boundaries.
>
> Social workers should not engage in sexual activities or sexual contact with former clients because of the potential for harm to the client.
>
> Social workers should not provide clinical services to individuals with whom they have had a prior sexual relationship.
>
> Social workers should not engage in physical contact with clients where there is a possibility of psychological harm to the client as a result of the contact (such as cradling or caressing clients). Social workers who engage in appropriate physical contact with clients are responsible for setting clear, appropriate, and culturally sensitive boundaries that govern such physical contact.

EP 2.1.2b

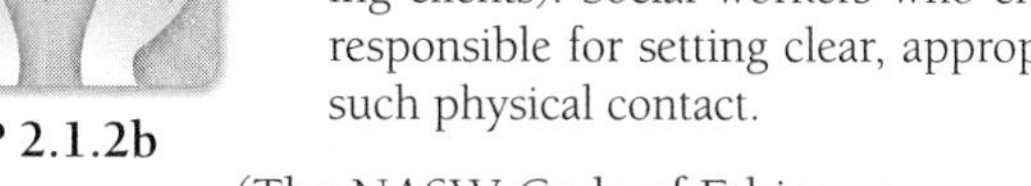

(The NASW Code of Ethics appears at www.naswdc.org.)

Exercise 2.10: Dual Relationships in Small Rural Communities

Goal: This exercise is designed to help you understand the complexities of avoiding dual relationships in small rural communities.

Step 1: In small rural communities, nearly everyone knows everyone else, and there is considerable social interaction. A dual relationship arises for a social worker when he or she provides professional services to a client and then enters into a social or business relationship with that client. Assume that you are a social worker in a rural community, that you are serving on a church committee, and that one of your clients joins this committee. What do you do?

Step 2: You are on a volleyball team in your community. The team has a ritual of having a few beers after playing volleyball. A client of yours joins the team. What do you do?

Step 3: One of your clients is the only cement contractor in your community. You own a house, and you need a new driveway. Are you going to contact this cement contractor to pour a new driveway for you? Give your rationale for what you will do.

Exercise 2.11: Hugging a Client and Going to Lunch with a Client

EP 2.1.2a, b, d

Goal: This exercise is designed to help you clarify when hugging and having lunch with a client may be appropriate.

Step 1: We all need positive physical contact with others. It may be constructive and desirable to ask a 7-year-old child whether she or he would like a hug when the child is experiencing emotional distress. But a hug may send the wrong message to a client. State your guidelines about when, and when not, to hug a client.

Step 2: Having lunch with a shy 8-year-old at a fast-food restaurant may have therapeutic value. But dining with a client, at times, may send the wrong message. State your guidelines on when, and when not, to have lunch with a client.

It is impossible to develop guidelines that answer every question that might arise when social workers set boundaries with clients, but the following guidelines may be useful in resolving some boundary dilemmas:

- In your professional *and* your personal life, try to be a role model for the values and principles of the social work profession.
- In relationships with clients, try to gain their respect and to exemplify the values and principles of the social work profession, rather than establish a friend-to-friend relationship.
- Never try to meet your personal needs or wants in relationships with clients.
- Try to increase your awareness of your own needs, feelings, values, and limitations so you become increasingly aware of how such factors may affect client relationships.

- When questions arise about the appropriateness of certain interactions with a client (such as whether to go to lunch), try to arrive at an answer by gauging whether the interaction will have a constructive impact on the client and your relationship. If a concrete, beneficial impact cannot be objectively specified, do not engage in the interaction.
- Constructive professional relationships with clients require a certain amount of distance. If you have questions about whether contemplated social interactions will interfere with the boundaries of a professional relationship, consult your supervisor or a respected colleague.
- In your professional social work role with clients, be aware of any inappropriate behavior, verbal communications, and dress on your part. For example, sharing details of your "wild" parties with clients is unprofessional.

Promoting Social and Economic Justice and Safeguarding Human Rights

Social workers have an obligation to promote social and economic justice for those who are oppressed or victimized by discrimination. According to the Council on Social Work Education, social work educational programs need to "*provide a learning environment in which respect for all persons and understanding of diversity and difference are practiced*" (Council on Social Work Education [CSWE], 2008). In *EPAS* (CSWE, 2008) social work educational programs are mandated to have a commitment to diversity, "including age, class, color, culture, disability, ethnicity, gender, gender identity and expression, immigration status, political ideology, race, religion, sex, and sexual orientation." According to the NASW Code of Ethics (1996, p. 27), "Social workers should act to prevent and eliminate domination of, exploitation of, and discrimination against any person, group, or class on the basis of race, ethnicity, national origin, color, sex, sexual orientation, age, marital status, political belief religion, or mental or physical disability."

The social work profession holds that society has a responsibility to all of its members to provide security, acceptance, and satisfaction of basic cultural, social, and biological needs. Only when basic needs are met is it possible for individuals to develop their maximum potentials. Therefore, social workers have a special responsibility to protect and secure civil rights based on democratic principles and a moral responsibility to work toward eradicating discrimination for any reason. Clients' civil rights need to be protected to preserve human dignity and self-respect.

In promoting social and economic justice for oppressed populations, social workers are expected to have an understanding of (1) the consequences and dynamics of social and economic injustice, including the forms of human oppression and discrimination, and (2) the impact of economic deprivation, discrimination, and oppression on populations-at-risk. Social workers have an ethical obligation to understand and appreciate human diversity. They are expected to have and use skills to promote social change that furthers the achievement of individual and collective social and economic justice.

In recent years the Council on Social Work Education has placed increased emphasis on human rights. For example, in the 2008 *EPAS* statement, Educational Policy 1.1 on values states: "service, social justice, the dignity and worth of the person, human rights, importance of human relationships, integrity, competence, and scientific inquiry are the core values of social work" (CSWE, 2008). The 2008 *EPAS* statement adds, "Each person, regardless of position in society, has basic human rights, such as freedom, safety, privacy, an adequate standard of living, health care, and education. Social workers recognize the global interconnections of oppression and are knowledgeable about theories of justice and strategies to promote human and civil rights."

Reichert (2007), however, has noted that "human rights" has received very limited attention in social work curricula and in social work course materials and lectures. Often, a human rights focus is "invisible" in social work curricula. Social work literature continually prefers the term *social justice* in analyzing core values relevant to the social work profession.

Barker (2003, pp. 404–405) defined *social justice* as

> An ideal condition in which all members of a society have the same basic rights, protection, opportunities, obligations, and social benefits. Implicit in this concept is the notion that historical inequalities should be acknowledged and remedied through specific measures. A key social work value, social justice entails advocacy to confront discrimination, oppression, and institutional inequities.

Barker (2003, p. 203) defined *human rights* as

> The opportunity to be accorded the same prerogatives and obligations in social fulfillment as are accorded to all others without distinction as to race, gender, language, or religion. In 1948, the U.N. Commission on Human Rights spelled out these opportunities. They include the basic *civil rights* recognized in democratic constitutions such as life, liberty, and personal security; freedom from arbitrary arrest, detention, or exile; the right to fair and public hearings by impartial tribunals; freedom of thought, conscience, and religion; and freedom of peaceful association. They also include economic, social, and cultural rights such as the right to work, education, and social security; to participate in the cultural life of the community; and to share in the benefits of scientific advancement and the arts.

Reichert (2007, p. 4) compares the concept of "human rights" to the concept of "social justice":

> Human rights provide the social work profession with a global and contemporary set of guidelines, whereas social justice tends to be defined in vague terminology such as fairness versus unfairness or equality versus inequality. . . . This distinction gives human rights an authority that social justice lacks. Human rights can elicit discussion of common issues by people from all walks of life and every corner of the world.

What are basic "human rights"? A clear specification of basic human rights has not been agreed upon. A key starting point in articulating such rights is the UN's *Universal Declaration of Human Rights* (United Nations, 1948). The following rights are identified in this document:

All humans are born free and equal in dignity and rights.
Everyone is entitled to all of the rights in the UNDR regardless of any distinction.
The right to life, liberty, and the security of the person.
Prohibition of slavery.
Prohibition of torture.
Right to recognition as a person before the law.
All must be treated equally under the law.
Right to a remedy of any violation of these rights.
Prohibition of arbitrary arrest, detention, or exile.
Right to a fair trial.
People shall be presumed innocent until proven guilty.
Right to freedom from arbitrary interference with private life.
Right to freedom of movement.
Right to seek asylum.
Right to a nationality.
Right to marry; marriage must be consented to by both parties; the family is entitled to protection from the state.
Right to property.
Right to freedom of thought, conscience, and religion.
Right to freedom of opinion and expression.
Right to freedom of assembly and association.
Right to participate in the government of one's country.
Right to economic, social, and cultural rights necessary for dignity and free development of personality.
Right to work and equitable compensation.
Right to rest and leisure from work.
Right to an adequate standard of living, including food, clothing, housing, and medical care.
Right to education.
Right to participate in cultural activities and to share in scientific achievements.
Right to a world order in which these rights can be realized.

Each has duties to their community; rights shall be limited only in regards to respecting the rights of others.

None of the rights may be interpreted as allowing any action to destroy these rights.

Every member nation of the UN has approved the *Universal Declaration*, but it is not legally binding on any nation. Because it articulates human rights in somewhat vague terms, determining when (or if) a country/government is violating basic human rights is sometimes difficult. Most countries recognize that the safeguarding of human rights has evolved into a major worldwide goal. Yet identifying violations is currently an imprecise science. It is common for a government to accuse other governments of violating human rights while at the same time "overlooking" its own violations. Reichert (2007, p. 8) states:

> The United States; compared to many other countries, fails to fulfill its obligation to promote human rights for all.... For instance, our failure to provide adequate health care for children and all expectant mothers violates the same Universal Declaration of Human Rights that U.S. political leaders continually call upon to denigrate China, Cuba, and Iraq, among other countries. The infant mortality rate is higher in the United States than in any other industrialized nation...and, within the U.S. itself, infant mortality rates are disparate among racial groups, with African-American infants suffering a mortality rate more than twice that of non-Hispanic whites.

It is hoped that greater attention to articulating basic human rights will lead countries to initiate programs that safeguard such rights for all citizens. Increased attention to articulating and protecting basic human rights has promise of being a key countervailing force to facilitate curbing discrimination against people of color, women, persons with a disability, gays and lesbians, and other groups who are currently victimized by discrimination.

Focus on Family

The focus of social work services is often on the family. A family is seen as an interacting independent system. The problems faced by any person are usually influenced by the dynamics within a family, as illustrated in the following example.

A schoolteacher became concerned when one of her pupils was consistently failing, and she referred the child for psychological testing. Testing revealed a normal IQ, but failure was found to be caused by a low self-concept (the girl was reluctant to do her academic work because she saw herself as being incapable of doing it). A school social worker met with the family and observed that the low self-concept was primarily a result of the parents' ridiculing and criticizing the child and seldom giving emotional support, encouragement, or compliments.

A family is an interacting system, and change in one member affects other members. For example, in some abusive families, the abused child is a scapegoat on which the parents vent their anger and hostility. If the abused child is removed from the home, another child within the family is at times selected to be the scapegoat (Leavitt, 1974).

EP 2.1.2b, d

Another reason for the focus on the family rather than on the individual is that the other family members are often needed in the treatment process. For example, other family members can put pressure on an alcoholic to have him or her acknowledge that a problem exists. The family members may also need counseling to help them cope with the person when he or she is drinking, and these family members may play important roles in providing emotional support for the alcoholic's efforts to stop drinking.

Exercise 2.12: When Rights of Family Members Clash

Goal: This exercise is designed to show you that a client's right to privacy sometimes clashes with the rights of others to be informed.

A client of yours, Kelly North, is married and wants to have children. She informs you that she is a carrier of Huntington's disease. As yet there is no cure for this disease, but there may be in 10 to 20 years. Ms. North is 26 years old. Huntington's disease is an inherited condition. It is transmitted by a dominant gene and affects half of the offspring of those who carry the gene. The symptoms include hallucinations, profound mood swings, dementia, and spasmodic movements of limbs and facial muscles. Symptoms generally begin to occur around age 30. Ms. North refuses to tell her husband about her condition, and she requests that you do not tell him—because she fears her husband would be unwilling to have children if he found out. When the well-being of other people is at risk, does their right to such information take precedence over your client's right to privacy? What are you going to do?

Accountability

Increasingly, federal and state governmental units and private funding sources are requiring that the effectiveness of service programs be measured. Gradually, programs found to be ineffective are being phased out. Although some social workers view accountability with trepidation and claim the paperwork involved interferes with serving clients, members of the social work profession have an obligation to funding sources to provide the highest-quality services. Two hundred years ago, bloodletting was thought to be an effective treatment technique. Only a few decades ago, lobotomies were erroneously thought to be effective. Now the value of electroshock therapy, psychoanalysis, and some other therapy techniques is being questioned. Program outcome studies have also demonstrated that orphanages are not the best place to raise homeless children; long-term hospitalization is not the best way to help those who are emotionally disturbed; probation generally has higher rehabilitative value than long-term confinement in prison; the Job Corps program of the 1960s was too expensive for the outcomes achieved; children with a cognitive disability can be better served in their home communities through local programs than by confinement in an institution; and so on.

Social workers need to become skilled at evaluating the extent to which they are being effective in providing services. Widely ranging evaluation techniques are now available to assess the effectiveness of current services and to identify unmet needs and service gaps. One of the most useful approaches is management by objectives (MBO). This technique involves specifying the objectives of a program, stating in measurable terms how and when these objectives are to be met, and then periodically measuring the extent to which the objectives are being met.

MBO is also one of the most useful approaches that social workers can use to assess their own effectiveness in providing services. Many agencies now require their workers, with the involvement of their clients, to (1) identify and specify what the goals will be for each client—generally this is done together with clients during the initial interviews; (2) write down in detail what the client and the worker will do to accomplish the goals—deadlines for accomplishing these tasks are also set; and (3) assess, when treatment is terminated (and perhaps periodically during the treatment process), the extent to which the goals have been achieved. (See the section on evidence-based practice in Chapter 11.)

If goals are generally not being achieved, the worker needs to identify and examine the underlying reasons. Perhaps unrealistic goals are being set. Perhaps the program or the treatment techniques are ineffective. Perhaps certain components of the treatment program are having an adverse effect. Perhaps other reasons account for the low success rate. Appropriate changes then need to be made.

Conversely, if the goals are generally being met, workers can use this information to document to funding sources and to supervisors that high-quality services are being provided.

SUMMARY

Several values underlying social work practice and their implications for practice were presented. Social work is both an art and a science. Because social work is partly an art, a worker frequently must make decisions based on values rather than on knowledge. Change techniques used by workers are often based on theory and value assumptions rather than on proven therapy techniques.

Values were distinguished from knowledge. Values are beliefs, preferences, or assumptions about what is desirable or good for people. Knowledge statements are observations about the world and people that have been verified or are capable of verification. It is much easier to change a client's belief that conflicts with current knowledge than it is to change a belief based on values. Guidelines were presented for how a worker should handle a value conflict between the worker and the client.

An important value of social work is respect for the dignity and uniqueness of the individual. The importance of individualizing each client was discussed, and guidelines were presented on how to relate to clients whose behavior is viewed as disgusting by the worker. Involved in individualization is the ability to accept clients but not the deviant behavior to be changed, careful attendance to clients' communications, and the discreet use of labeling.

Self-determination is the clients' right to express their own opinions and to act on them, as long as clients do not infringe on the rights of others. Clients should be made aware that there are alternatives for resolving the personal and social problems they face. Self-determination means that the client, not the worker, is the chief problem solver, although the worker has an obligation to suggest resolution approaches that the client may not be aware of.

Confidentiality is the implicit or explicit agreement between a professional and a client to maintain the private nature of information about the client. In professional practice, a system of relative confidentiality currently exists, rather than a system of absolute confidentiality. Numerous unresolved questions surrounding confidentiality were raised, and some guidelines on how beginning practitioners should handle these questions were presented. At times, circumstances arise in which a professional is permitted, expected, or required to violate confidentiality, and many of these circumstances were listed—for example, when a client admits to a past or intended serious criminal act. Protecting the confidentiality of clients' files and records in human service organizations is becoming much more difficult as information technology expands exponentially.

EP 2.1.2d

Other values of social work practice were summarized: belief in the institutional approach for the delivery of social services rather than the residual approach; establishment of professional boundaries with clients; promotion of social and economic justice for those being oppressed or discriminated against; focus on family instead of the individual in provision of services; and accountability.

In the overview of guidelines for social work practice, you were advised that such guidelines are to be applied not as absolutes but simply as concepts that *may* be useful in working with people.

EXERCISES

1. Confidentiality

Goal: To get a feel for when to uphold, and when to violate, confidentiality.

Step 1: Divide into groups of about five students. Each group answers the questions raised in the following vignettes.

a. You are a social worker at a public school, and you have been working with a family that has multiple problems. Two of the children are in special education programs for the emotionally disturbed. The mother has occasionally been hospitalized for emotional problems. The father has been investigated by protective services for child abuse in the past. Mother and father are having marital problems and are presently separated. The father comes to your office and demands to see the school's records on his children and his family. As a social worker, would you show him these records?

b. You are a social worker at a mental health center, and you are working with a client who appears to be emotionally upset. He states he has heard that his girlfriend is seeing someone else. While saying this, he becomes enraged and says he intends to shoot her. He asks you not to tell anyone what he has said. As you endeavor to discuss his threat, he becomes more upset and walks out, stating, "I'll make sure she doesn't cheat on me." Should you violate confidentiality and inform someone? If so, whom would you inform?

c. You are a social worker at a drug abuse treatment center, and you have been working with a 23-year-old female. You establish a good working relationship with her. She says something has been bothering her for a long time, but she states she won't discuss it unless you agree not to tell anyone. You assure her that what she reveals will be kept confidential. She then reveals that she had an incestuous relationship with her stepfather that started when she was 14 and lasted nearly 3 years. She believes her unresolved feeling about this experience is one of the reasons she sometimes drinks too much. In a staff meeting on this client, would you reveal to the other staff what she has said?

Step 2: Groups share their answers with the class. The instructor then summarizes the text's answers to the questions, which involve (a) the 1974 Federal Privacy Act, (b) the 1974 *Tarasoff v. Regents of the University of California* decision, and (c) guideline's about sharing information with other staff.

Step 3: Class discussion about how social work practice uses a system of relative, rather than absolute, confidentiality. Class review of chapter guidelines on when to uphold and when to violate confidentiality.

2. Clarifying Values

EP 2.1.2a, d

Goal: To clarify values on a number of prominent issues in social work.

Step 1: Class discussion of why social workers need to be aware of their personal values and aware of professional values, when workers should take a nonjudgmental position with clients, and when they should seek to sell to clients (or enforce to clients) a particular set of values.

In groups of three, develop answers, and reasons for your answers, to the following 10 questions.

a. You are a protective service worker and you have evidence that a father is committing incest with his 10-year-old daughter. Would you seek to end the incest by (1) providing counseling services to all family members to keep the family intact, (2) bringing legal charges against the father, or (3) seeking to do both at the same time?

b. Do you support a constitutional amendment to make abortion illegal?

c. Does a social worker have an obligation to preserve confidentiality if an HIV-infected client refuses to inform his or her sexual partner of the infection (while persisting in behavior that places the partner at risk), or does the social worker have an obligation to warn the partner about the peril?

d. Do you support affirmative action programs that assert that certain minority groups and women should be given preference in hiring over white males?

e. If an elderly person who is terminally ill and in intense pain wants to end his or her life, should physicians be allowed to provide assistance in helping this person die?

f. Do you believe the United States should support an extensive program to develop the capacity to clone human beings?

g. Do you believe in capital punishment for certain crimes?

h. Do you think a gay or lesbian teacher should be allowed to teach in elementary and secondary schools?

i. Do you think women in military service should fight in combat?

j. Should condoms and other contraceptives be provided to requesting students through health-care clinics located in middle schools and high schools?

Step 2: Groups present and discuss their answers. Each question is taken one at a time. (*Note:* The purpose of this exercise is to help you clarify your values and not to sell any particular value system.)

Step 3: Discuss how you felt when others in class expressed views that you strongly disagree with.

3. New Frontier to Rings of Fire

EP 2.1.5a, b, c

Goal: To help you clarify your values about humanity.

Step 1: Form groups of about five. Your instructor reads the following vignette to the students:

The United States has recently completed building a remarkable spaceship, named *New Frontier,* that is capable of carrying seven people to planets in other galaxies. *New Frontier* uses nuclear power and is guided by a new computer system that does not require a pilot to fly the spaceship.

Our government has recently discovered a new planet in a faraway galaxy that has an atmosphere very similar to Earth's atmosphere and appears capable of supporting life. This planet has been named Rings of Fire as it has a red hue and several rings around it, similar to those of Saturn.

Your group has been chosen by the president of the United States to select the seven people who will take the first flight. *New Frontier* is presently located on a remote Samoan island.

Suddedly a nuclear war breaks out in the Middle East, and the superpowers quickly enter the conflict. The bombs and the radioactive fallout will destroy civilization as we know it. The chief scientist frantically calls your group. She indicates your group has 15 minutes to select the seven people to go on *New Frontier* to Rings of Fire. A country we are fighting in this war has sent a nuclear missile to this Samoan island to destroy *New Frontier*. There are 13 people close enough to board *New Frontier*. The chief scientist wants your group to select the 7 people so that these 13 people do not begin fighting among themselves. If your group does not select seven people in 15 minutes; there is a danger the human race will cease to exist. The seven people selected may well be the only hope for continuing the human race. Your group has only the following information about the 13 people.

1. Chief scientist, 57 years old, has a husband and three children who live in Beaumont, Texas.
2. Male Korean medical student, 24 years old.
3. White male rabbi, 28 years old.
4. Female Samoan prostitute who has herpes, 35 years old.
5. White male professional baseball player, 26 years old and gay.
6. Protestant male child, 8 years old.
7. White female who has a cognitive disability from not having enough oxygen at birth, 10 years old.
8. White Catholic male who is unemployed and has cerebral palsy, 27 years old.
9. White male truck driver who has a history of not getting along with people and of getting into numerous fights, 34 years old.
10. Samoan farmer who has had a vasectomy, 22 years old.
11. Female Japanese stockbroker, 27 years old.
12. White female who is depressed and has a long history of being hospitalized for emotional problems, 35 years old.
13. White female who is a millionaire via inheritance and detests working, 26 years old.

Step 2: Distribute copies of this list to each group. Each group has 15 minutes to complete the task; your instructor will announce when 10, 5, 3, and 1 minute remain.

Step 3: Group presentation of its choices and the reasons for its selections. Class discussion of (a) the values underlying the selections and (b) the merits and shortcomings of this exercise.

COMPETENCY NOTES

The following identifies where Educational Policy (EP) competencies and practice behaviors are discussed in the chapter.

EP 2.1.2a *Recognize and manage personal values in a way that allows professional values to guide practice.*

EP 2.1.2b *Make ethical decisions by applying standards of the National Association of Social Workers Code of Ethics and, as applicable, of the International Federation of Social Workers/International Association of Schools of Social Work Ethics in Social Work, Statement of Principles.*

EP 2.1.2c *Tolerate ambiguity in resolving ethical conflicts.*

EP 2.1.2d *Apply strategies of ethical reasoning to arrive at principled decisions.* (Chapter 2).

This chapter describes social work values, including: value dilemmas; knowledge and values; dignity and uniqueness of individuals; client's right to self-determination; confidentiality and privileged communication; residual and institutional views of social welfare; professional boundaries with clients; and social workers' obligation to promote social and economic justice and to safeguard human rights.

EP 2.1.2a *Recognize and manage personal values in a way that allows professional values to guide practice.* (pp. 56–58).

Exercise 2.1 is designed to help students clarify their values on a number of prominent issues related to social work.

EP 2.1.2d *Apply strategies of ethical reasoning to arrive at principled decisions.* (p. 60).

Exercise 2.2 is designed to assist students in understanding Dolgoff et al.'s rank order of ethical priorities.

EP 2.1.2d *Apply strategies of ethical reasoning to arrive at principled decisions.* (pp. 60–61).

Exercise 2.3 is designed to assist students in applying the ETHIC process model.

EP 2.1.2a *Recognize and manage personal values in a way that allows professional values to guide practice.* (pp. 62–63).

Exercise 2.4 is designed to assist students in identifying types of clients with whom they may be uncomfortable working, and thereby not be fully objective.

EP 2.1.1b *Practice personal reflection and self-correction to assure continual professional development.* (pp. 63–64).

Exercise 2.5 is designed to have students reflect on components of their self-concept that contain remnants from the past.

EP 2.1.1b *Practice personal reflection and self-correction to assure continual professional development.* (p. 65).

Exercise 2.6 is designed to have students reflect on the powerful effects of labeling.

EP 2.1.2b *Make ethical decisions by applying standards of the National Association of Social Workers Code of Ethics and, as applicable, of the International Federation of Social Workers/International Association of Schools of Social Work Ethics in Social Work, Statement of Principles.*

EP 2.1.2d *Apply strategies of ethical reasoning to arrive at principled decisions.* (p. 71).

Exercise 2.7 is designed to help students understand the complexities surrounding a potential whistle-blowing situation.

EP 2.1.2b *Make ethical decisions by applying standards of the National Association of Social Workers Code of Ethics and, as applicable, of the International Federation of Social Workers/International Association of Schools of Social Work Ethics in Social Work, Statement of Principles.*

EP 2.1.2c *Tolerate ambiguity in resolving ethical conflicts.*

EP 2.1.2d *Apply strategies of ethical reasoning to arrive at principled decisions.* (p. 76).

Exercise 2.8 is designed to inform students of the complicated issues surrounding whether to violate confidentiality.

EP 2.1.1b *Practice personal reflection and self-correction to assure continual professional development.* (p. 77).

Exercise 2.9 is designed to have students reflect upon the stigma about receiving social welfare funds that is associated with the residual view.

EP 2.1.2b *Make ethical decisions by applying standards of the National Association of Social Workers Code of Ethics and, as applicable, of the International Federation of Social Workers/International Association of Schools of Social Work Ethics in Social Work, Statement of Principles.* (pp. 79–80).

Exercise 2.10 is designed to help students understand the complexities of avoiding dual relationships in small rural communities.

EP 2.1.2a *Recognize and manage personal values in a way that allows professional values to guide practice.*

EP 2.1.2b *Make ethical decisions by applying standards of the National Association of Social Workers Code of Ethics and, as applicable, of the International Federation of Social Workers/International Association of Schools of Social Work Ethics in Social Work, Statement of Principles.*

EP 2.1.2d *Apply strategies of ethical reasoning to arrive at principled decisions.* (p. 80).

Exercise 2.11 is designed to help students clarify when hugging and having lunch with a client may be appropriate.

EP 2.1.2b *Make ethical decisions by applying standards of the National Association of Social Workers Code of Ethics and, as applicable, of the International Federation of Social Workers/International Association of Schools of Social Work Ethics in Social Work, Statement of Principles.* (pp. 83–84).

EP 2.1.2d *Apply strategies of ethical reasoning to arrive at principled decisions.*

Exercise 2.12 is designed to show students that a client's right to privacy sometimes clashes with the rights of others to be informed.

EP 2.1.2d *Apply strategies of ethical reasoning to arrive at principled decisions.* (pp. 85–86).

This exercise is designed to help students better understand when to uphold, and when to violate, confidentiality.

EP 2.1.2a *Recognize and manage personal values in a way that allows professional values to guide practice.*

EP 2.1.2d *Apply strategies of ethical reasoning to arrive at principled decisions.* (pp. 86–87).

This exercise is designed to help students clarify a number of prominent issues in social work.

EP 2.1.5a *Understand forms and mechanisms of oppression and discrimination.*

EP 2.1.5b *Advocate for human rights and social and economic justice.* (p. 87).

EP 2.1.5c *Engage in practices that advance social and economic justice.* (p. 87).

This exercise is designed to help students clarify their values about humanity.

CHAPTER 3

Assessment

EAP 2.1.3b; 2.1.7a, 2.1.10e

Here is a simplified paradigm of the problem-solving process in social work:

Assessment → Intervention → Termination and Evaluation

In this chapter, we discuss the first element: assessment. This chapter will:

A. Identify the components of an assessment
B. Describe the strengths perspective
C. Identify sources of information for an assessment
D. Specify the knowledge used in making an assessment
E. Describe the environmental systems emphasis in conducting an assessment
F. Describe bio-psycho-social and cultural components in assessment
G. Identify guides for assessing problem systems

COMPONENTS OF AN ASSESSMENT

Assessment is a critical process in social work practice. The selection of goals and interventions depends largely on what is being assessed. An inaccurate or incomplete assessment can lead to inappropriate goals and inappropriate interventions. When an inaccurate or incomplete assessment is made, positive changes are unlikely to occur.

Hepworth and Larsen (1986) defined *assessment* as follows:

> Assessment is the process of gathering, analyzing, and synthesizing salient data into a formulation that encompasses the following vital dimensions: (1) the nature of clients' problems, including special attention to the roles that clients and significant others play in the difficulties; (2) the functioning (strengths, limitations, personality assets, and deficiencies) of clients and significant others; (3) motivation of clients to work on the problems; (4) relevant environmental factors that contribute to the problems; and (5) resources that are available or are needed to ameliorate the clients' difficulties. (p. 165)

Assessment has sometimes been referred to as *psychosocial diagnosis* (Hollis, 1972). But the term *diagnosis* focuses on what is wrong with the client, family, or group being diagnosed—such as having a disease, dysfunction, or mental problem. Because diagnosis has a negative connotation, many other social work educators, myself included, prefer *assessment*. Assessment includes not only what is wrong with the client[1] but also the resources, strengths, motivations, functional components, and other positive factors that can be used to resolve difficulties, to enhance functioning, and to promote

[1]In this chapter the term *client* is often used in a generic sense to refer to an individual, family, group, organization, or community that a practitioner is working with.

growth. Actually, assessment in its broadest sense is the base for the development of an intervention plan.

The *nature* of the assessment task varies significantly with the setting in which the social worker practices, but the *process* is similar in all settings. A social worker in a nursing home who is assessing an applicant for potential placement will look at variables that are radically different from those examined by a social worker in a protective service setting who is assessing an allegation of child abuse.

In some settings (as in many protective services programs), the social worker makes an independent assessment. With independent assessments, the social worker may consult with colleagues or professionals in other disciplines on complicated cases. In other settings (for example, mental health clinics, schools, and medical hospitals), the social worker is likely to be a member of a clinical team that makes an assessment. Other team members may include a psychologist, psychiatrist, nurse, and perhaps professionals from other disciplines. Team members have specific roles in the assessment process—roles based on their special professional expertise. The psychologist, for example, focuses primarily on psychological functioning and would probably administer a variety of psychological tests (including personality and intelligence tests). The social worker compiles a social history to assess family background, marital dynamics, environmental factors, and employment and educational background. In settings in which the social worker is the primary assessor, the assessment is generally completed in one to three sessions. With a clinical team approach, the case is usually more complicated, and assessment by the various professionals may take a few weeks.

Assessment is sometimes a product and sometimes an ongoing process. As a product, an assessment is a formulation at a point in time regarding the nature of a client's difficulties and resources. An example is a mental status assessment at a psychiatric hospital. Such an assessment is first focused on determining whether the client is sane or psychotic. If the client is assessed as psychotic, a psychiatric label is assigned and a recommended treatment approach is then stated. A product assessment usually has to be updated and revised months or sometimes years later. Such an assessment is, in essence, a working hypothesis of a client's difficulties and resources based on current data. As time passes, the client may change and so will environmental factors. Such changes require the assessment to be updated and revised periodically.

Assessment can also be an ongoing process, from the initial interview to the termination of the case. The length of time a client receives services may be weeks, months, or even years. During this period, the professionals working with the case are continually receiving and analyzing new information. In the early stages of client contact, the focus is primarily on gathering information to assess the client's problems and resources. Once these are tentatively specified, problem solving is emphasized. Resolution strategies are suggested and analyzed, and then one or more strategies are selected and implemented. But even in the problem-solving phase, new information related to the client's difficulties and resources is likely to emerge, necessitating a revision of the assessment. In fact, as contact between the professional and client continues, the client may disclose additional problems that need to be assessed and then resolved. It is common in initial contact for a client to withhold vital information for fear of condemnation. For example, a parent who is abusing a child may initially deny that the abuse is occurring. As time passes, if the parent comes to trust the worker, the parent may disclose that she at times loses control and then hits the child. As new information is provided, the initial assessment needs to be revised.

Hepworth and Larsen (1986) noted that assessment continues to occur even during the termination phase:

> The process of assessment continues even during the terminal phase of service. During the final interviews, the practitioner carefully evaluates the client's readiness to terminate, assesses the presence of residual difficulties that may cause future difficulties, and identifies

> possible emotional reactions to termination. The practitioner also considers possible strategies to assist the client to maintain improved functioning or to achieve additional progress after formal social work service is concluded. (p. 166)

THE STRENGTHS PERSPECTIVE

For most of the past several decades, social work and the other helping professions focused primarily on diagnosing the pathology, shortcomings, and dysfunctions of clients. One reason may be that Freudian psychology was the primary theory used in analyzing human behavior. Freudian psychology is based on a medical model, and its concepts are therefore geared to identify illness or pathology. It has very few concepts for identifying strengths. As described in Chapter 1, social work is now shifting to a systems model in assessing human behavior. This model focuses on identifying both strengths and weaknesses.

It is essential that social workers include clients' strengths in the assessment process. Today, social workers routinely focus on the strengths and resources of clients to help them resolve their difficulties. To use a client's strengths effectively, social workers must first identify those strengths, but, unfortunately, Maluccio (1979) found that many social workers focus too much on clients' perceived weaknesses and underestimate or are blind to their strengths. Maluccio concluded, "There is a need to shift the focus on social work education and practice from problems or pathology to strengths, resources, and potentialities in human beings and their environments" (p. 401).

A primary focus on weaknesses can impair a worker's capacity to identify a client's growth potential. Social workers strongly believe that clients have the right (and should be encouraged) to develop their potential fully. Focusing on pathology undermines this commitment.

Another reason for attending to clients' strengths is that many clients need help in enhancing their self-esteem. Many have feelings of worthlessness, feelings of inadequacy, a sense of being a failure, and a lack of self-confidence and self-respect. Glasser (1972) noted that low self-esteem often leads to emotional difficulties, withdrawal, or criminal activity. To help clients view themselves more positively, social workers must first view their clients as having considerable strengths and competencies. Berwick (1980) underscored this point in working with neglectful parents of children who fail to thrive:

> Self-esteem is already at a low ebb in many of the parents of these children, and the success of the hospital in nourishing a child when the mother has failed only serves to accentuate the pain of failure. . . . Even in the few cases that require foster care, the health care team's task is to seek strengths and to develop a sense of competence in both the parents and the child that will permit a synchronous nurturant relationship to emerge. (p. 270)

The strengths perspective is closely related to the concept of empowerment. Barker (2003) defined *empowerment* as "the process of helping individuals, families, groups, and communities to increase their personal, interpersonal, socioeconomic, and political strength and to develop influence toward improving their circumstances" (p. 142). The strengths perspective seeks to identify, use, build, and reinforce the strengths and abilities people already have. This is in contrast to the pathological perspective, which focuses on deficiencies and inabilities. The strengths perspective is useful across the life cycle and throughout all stages of the helping process—assessment, intervention, and evaluation. It emphasizes people's abilities, values, "interests, beliefs, resources, accomplishments, and aspirations" (Weick, Rapp, Sullivan, & Kisthardt, 1989).

According to Saleebey (1997, pp. 12–15), five principles underlie the guiding assumptions of the strengths perspective:

1. *Every individual, group, family, and community has strengths.* The strengths perspective is about discerning these resources. Saleebey notes,

> In the end, clients want to know that you actually care about them, that how they fare makes a difference to you, that you will listen to them, that you will respect them no matter what their history, and that you believe that they can build something of value with the resources within and around them. But most of all, clients want to know that you believe they can surmount adversity and begin the climb toward transformation and growth. (p. 12)

2. *Trauma, abuse, illness, and struggle can be injurious, but they also can be sources of challenge and opportunity*. Clients who have been victimized are seen as active and developing individuals who, through their traumas, learn skills and develop personal attributes that help them cope with future struggles. There is dignity to be found in having prevailed over obstacles. We often grow more from crises in which we find ways to handle situations effectively than from periods in our lives when we are content and comfortable.
3. *Assume that you do not know the upper limits of the capacity to grow and change, and take individual, group, and community aspirations seriously*. This principle means workers need to hold high expectations of clients and to form alliances with their visions, hopes, and values. Individuals, families, and communities have the capacity for restoration and rebounding. When workers connect with the hopes and dreams of clients, clients are likely to have greater faith in themselves. Then they are able to put forth the effort needed for their hopes and dreams to become self-fulfilling prophecies.
4. *We best serve clients by collaborating with them*. A worker is more effective when seen by the client as a collaborator or consultant rather than as an expert or a professional. A collaborative stance by a worker makes her or him less vulnerable to many of the adverse effects of an expert-inferior relationship, including paternalism, victim-blaming, and preemption of client views.
5. *Every environment is full of resources*. In every environment (no matter how harsh), there are individuals, groups, associations, and institutions with something to give, and with something that others may desperately need. The strengths perspective seeks to identify these resources and make them available to benefit individuals, families, and groups in a community.

EAP 2.1.10e

With the strengths perspective, a client's current problems and challenges are identified, along with the strengths and resources.

Exercise 3.1: Assessing an Individual

Goal: This exercise is designed to assist you in learning how to write an assessment of an individual. (Please code the name of the individual for confidentiality reasons.)

Step 1: Briefly describe the individual—including coded name, age, gender, height, weight, occupation or school grade level, family information, overall health, financial resources, religion, race or ethnic background, personality characteristics, school performance, health status, arrests and convictions, marital or dating status, hobbies, special interests, outside systems impacting this individual, and so on.

Step 2: Describe the current problems and challenges this person has.

Step 3: Specify the strengths or resources this person has for meeting his or her problems and challenges.

Step 4: Specify the recommended courses of action you believe this person should take to better handle his or her problems and challenges.

SOURCES OF INFORMATION

Information used in making an assessment comes from a variety of sources. The following are the principal sources.

The Client's Verbal Report

A client's verbal report is often the primary source and in some cases the only source of information. (For example, social workers in private practice sometimes obtain information only from the client.) A variety of information can be obtained in this way: description of the problems; feelings about the problems; views of the client's personal resources to combat the problems; motivations to make efforts to resolve the problems; the history of the problems; views of the causes; a description of what has already been done in attempting to resolve the problems.

Although clients are often fairly accurate in describing their difficulties and resources, workers should be aware that verbal reports are sometimes distorted by embarrassment, bias, distorted perceptions, and strong emotions. For example, a married woman whose husband left her for someone else may be so immersed in her emotional reactions that she cannot be objective about the role she played in the breakup of her marriage. In some settings, clients deliberately try to conceal, or even distort, information. Abusive parents, for example, may deny they have abused their children. Alcoholics, because of the nature of the addictive process, are likely to deny they have a drinking problem. Correctional clients may try to conceal some of their illegal activities.

A client's verbal report should be respected as valid until additional information indicates otherwise. In some settings, as in protective services, it is often necessary to verify a client's denial that a problem exists by checking with other sources, such as neighbors, relatives, and school personnel.

Assessment Forms

Many agencies, before or after the first interview, ask clients to supply such information as name, address, telephone number, employer, years of school completed, marital status, description of problem, and names of family members. Such information is most efficiently collected by having the client fill out a form.

Self-report forms can also be used in the assessment process. Some clients, particularly adolescents, may be more relaxed and more truthful if they can answer questions on a form, while being assured that only helping professionals at the agency will see the answers. Sources such as Fischer and Corcoran (2006), Thyer and Wodarski (2004), and Bloom, Fischer, and Orme (2006) can acquaint social workers with available assessment forms and their proper use.

A worker who chooses to use a self-report instrument should be knowledgeable about the instrument and guidelines for its use. Research on its reliability and validity should be carefully studied to evaluate its usefulness. Also, the worker needs to use common sense in interpreting the results. Like so many other parts of the assessment process, a test result is a starting point, rather than an end product.

Computer-Assisted Assessment Forms

Nurius and Hudson (1993) developed a computer-based evaluation tool that includes the Walmyr Assessment Scales. These scales were developed by Hudson (1992) and include scales that measure self-esteem, depression, anxiety, clinical stress, peer relations, homophobia, sexual attitudes, alcohol involvement, marital satisfaction, sexual satisfaction, physical abuse of partner, nonphysical abuse of partner, parental attitude toward children, children's attitudes toward father and mother, family relations, sibling relations, children's behavior, and a general screening inventory. Clients can complete the scales manually or on a personal computer.

Computer programs accommodate different types of scales, including self-anchored, single-item, multiple-item, checklists, and multidimensional rating scales. Hepworth, Rooney, and Larsen (1997) note,

> Computer-aided assessment deserves the attention of practitioners. Clients reportedly respond well to this technology. The greatest potential for use of this tool derives from the computer's ability to process, integrate, and synthesize data from expanded sources of information. The computer's objectivity also reduces evaluative errors caused by subjective interpretations of data by practitioners. (p. 202)

Collateral Sources

Information is sometimes collected from collateral sources: friends, relatives, neighbors, physicians, other social agencies, teachers, and others who may be able to provide relevant information. In some cases, clients have received social services from a number of other agencies. Summary information about such clients is often obtained from these agencies.

Some workers overlook collateral sources; as a result, potentially valuable information is not collected. Less frequently, workers spend too much time gathering collateral information. In social work practice, a practitioner needs to exercise prudence in deciding what information is needed. In many circumstances, it is essential to get the client's verbal consent and have the client sign release-of-information forms before contacting collateral sources. (See Chapter 2 for a description of confidentiality and release-of-information forms.)

Psychological Tests

There are a variety of personality and intelligence tests. Most psychological tests are designed to be administered by psychologists. The tests that Hudson (1992) developed for clinical social workers, however, are an exception.

Caution should be used with psychological tests, because most are not designed to be administered or interpreted by social workers. Such administration and interpretation is the responsibility of psychologists. In addition, most personality tests have low validity and reliability and should be used with extreme caution, if at all.

Nonverbal Behavior

Clients' nonverbal behavior provides a valuable source of information. As practitioners become more experienced, they give greater attention to, and become more competent at, identifying and interpreting nonverbal cues. These cues are invaluable in identifying what clients are actually thinking and feeling. Nonverbal cues include gestures, posture, breathing patterns, tension in facial and neck muscles, facial color, eye movements, choice of clothes, physical appearance, eye contact, and tone of voice. Such cues give information about stress levels, kinds of feelings being experienced, and whether the client is telling the truth. For example, a client who folds his arms over his chest and frowns every time a worker brings up a particular topic is conveying valuable information about his feelings related to that topic.

Interactions with Significant Others and Home Visits

Observing a client interacting with people who are important in her life reveals a lot of information. These significant others include family members, other close relatives, peers, friends, and neighbors. The way a client presents herself in an office may differ dramatically from the way she interacts at home. In an office setting, a client may present an image that is atypical for her. A home visit provides information not only about how a client interacts with significant others but also about environmental factors. For example, a home visit investigating a charge that a single mother is neglecting her children will reveal information about home cleanliness, available food and diet, presence of animals (including pets and rats), presence of cockroaches and insects, available clothing, possible drug abuse by the parent, home interactions between mother and children, interactions between the mother and neighbors, type of neighborhood, and financial circumstances.

Social work emphasizes the importance of assessing the person-in-environment, and home visits by the social worker are an integral part of assessing the environmental factors that affect a client. Remember that an office setting is an unnatural arena for family interaction. In an unnatural setting, families are less likely to interact as they do at home. Most people are more relaxed in their own homes, and a home visit can help clients feel more accepted and less anxious.

Nevertheless, like conclusions drawn from any source of information, conclusions drawn from observed interaction, even at the client's home, can be erroneous. The way family members interact while being observed may be atypical of how they interact when they know they are not being observed. In addition, many clients feel some discomfort if the worker is better educated than they and has a higher societal status.

Worker's Conclusions from Direct Interactions

Clients often manifest similar interactional patterns in their social relationships. The way clients interact with a worker therefore provides clues to their difficulties or successes in interactions with others. Some of the many ways in which a worker may experience clients include their being nonassertive, passive, submissive, aggressive, withdrawn, passive-aggressive, personable, caring, manipulative, highly motivated, insecure, or dependent. Such observations can provide valuable information about a client's problematic behavior.

I once counseled a 22-year-old college student who complained that her roommates used her as a "doormat." They frequently borrowed her car, failed to pay for gas, wore her clothes without asking, and ate the food she bought without asking. In the interview she came across as nonassertive (in her verbal and nonverbal communication) and as making extraordinary efforts to please me. I pointed out these specific behaviors to her and asked whether she might be inadvertently communicating through these behaviors that she would not object to her roommates "using her things." She thought about it for awhile and acknowledged that my assessment was probably accurate. She was then instructed in how to express her concerns assertively to her roommates. With role-playing, she gradually acquired the confidence to confront her roommates about these concerns.

There are cautions and limitations to using your personal conclusions to assess a client's interactions with others. A client may interact atypically with a social worker because she or he wants to convey an atypical image. Just as some people change their patterns when interacting with a police officer, some clients seek to convey an atypical image when interacting with a worker. Also, the worker's personality may lead clients to interact atypically. For example, if a worker comes across as aggressive and highly confrontative, the client is likely to become either passive and submissive or aggressive. Therefore, to use observations effectively in assessing clients' behaviors, the worker must have substantial awareness of self and of how he or she tends to affect others during interactions. The worker also must convey a nonjudgmental attitude. For lasting change to occur, most clients need to feel competent. To feel competent, most clients need to value and believe in themselves.

EAP 2.1.10e

Exercise 3.2: Assessing a Family

Goal: This exercise is designed to assist you in learning how to write an assessment of a family. (Please code the names of the family members for confidentiality reasons.)

Step 1: Briefly describe a family—including coded names of the members, ages, gender of each member, race or ethnic background, occupations of members, educational levels achieved by each, religion, relationships among family members, health issues, arrests and convictions, important personality characteristics of members, special interests of members, political orientations, family values, family activities, other systems affecting this family, and so forth.

Step 2: Describe the current problems and challenges this family has.

Step 3: Specify the strengths or resources this family has for meeting its problems and challenges.

Step 4: Specify the recommended courses of action you believe this family should take to better handle its problems and challenges.

KNOWLEDGE USED IN MAKING AN ASSESSMENT

Extensive knowledge of human behavior and the social environment is needed for a high degree of accuracy when assessing the problems of a client system. As Hepworth and Larsen (1986) noted,

> To assess the problems of a client system (individual, couple, or family) . . . requires extensive knowledge about that system as well as careful consideration of the multifarious systems (e.g., economic, legal, educational, medical, religious, social, interpersonal) that impinge upon the client system. Moreover, to assess the functioning of an individual entails

> evaluating various aspects of that person's functioning. For example, one must consider dynamic interactions among the biophysical, cognitive, emotional, cultural, behavioral, and motivational subsystems and the relationships of those interactions to problematic situations. (p. 172)

At first glance, learning about all the factors that Hepworth and Larsen mention seems overwhelming, but such knowledge is obtained in college from a variety of social work courses. A key course or courses in most social work programs is human behavior and the social environment. Practice and policy courses also cover some of these areas. Other disciplines that provide background information are sociology, psychology, anthropology, biology, political science, women's studies, ethnic studies, history, communication, philosophy, religious studies, and economics.

In addition, the overall purpose of an assessment gives considerable focus to what knowledge is needed. For example, a social worker assessing an older adult applicant for placement in a nursing home would first need to know the nursing home's criteria for accepting applicants. Such criteria may include financial resources, medical conditions, physical strengths and impairments, emotional and behavioral patterns, special needs, level of cognitive functioning, and degree of willingness to enter a nursing home. Based on the nursing home's criteria, the social worker would then obtain information from the client, family members, physicians, and other relevant sources to determine the extent to which the client meets the criteria.

A careful assessment sharpens the focus on what factors should be examined. For example, for a fourth-grade child who is performing considerably below his grade level in schoolwork, the following variables might be examined: Does he have a learning disability? What is his IQ? Is he having emotional difficulties? Does he have low self-esteem? Is low self-esteem contributing to his low level of performance? Does he have a visual or hearing impairment or other medical problems? Are factors in his home and family life influencing his school performance? What specific educational subjects and tasks is he doing fairly well at, and which is he having the most trouble with? How does he interact with peers and with teachers? Has he experienced significant traumas in the past that may still be affecting him? Is he involved in using and perhaps abusing drugs? Is he motivated to do his best in school? How does he feel about his school performance?[2]

The theory or theories a practitioner uses have a major influence on what is examined during an assessment. For example, Freudian psychology focuses on pathology, or unconscious processes, on fixations during a child's development, on sexuality, and on traumatic experiences during childhood. In contrast, rational therapy asserts that thinking patterns determine emotions and actions, and therefore the focus is on identifying client self-talk that leads to unwanted emotions and dysfunctional behaviors. (Module 1 summarizes rational therapy.) What workers look for in their analysis has a big effect on the outcome. For example, practically everyone has traumatic early childhood experiences—so it is not surprising that an adherent of Freudian psychology doing an assessment would identify some traumatic early childhood experiences and then hypothesize them as causes of the client's current problems. Similarly, all individuals talk to themselves in negative ways at times, so it is not surprising that a rational therapist would find evidence to support his or her theory in an assessment.

The worker's favorite theories of assessment and intervention can have enormous consequences for the client. For example, adherents of Freudian psychology are much

---

[2]Additional material elsewhere in this text may be valuable in conducting an assessment: Chapter 4, how to write a social history; Chapters 4 and 5, interviewing and counseling (helpful when gathering information from clients and from collateral resources); Chapters 6 and 7, group dynamics; Chapter 8, family functioning and family systems (useful in assessing families); Chapter 9, how to analyze social welfare organizations; Chapter 10, how to assess community needs and how to conduct a community needs assessment; Chapter 12, diversity and populations-at-risk; Chapter 13, spirituality.

more inclined to assess a person as psychotic (because they believe mental illness exists) than are adherents of reality therapy, who believe that mental illness is a myth. (Module 3 describes reality therapy.)

EAP 2.1.10e

Most theories of human behavior have not been proven. Many practitioners make the mistake of assuming that their favorite theory or theories are factual. When an assessment is based on a theory of human behavior, the practitioner should be aware that the results of the assessment rest on the accuracy of the theory. Practitioners need to realize that their assessment of someone is not "gospel" but only a hypothesis. (See the section on evidence-based practice in Chapter 11.)

Exercise 3.3: Assessing a Group

Goal: This exercise is designed to assist you in learning how to assess a group. (In writing this assessment, it may be valuable to read Chapters 6 and 7.)

Step 1: Briefly describe a group you have participated in—such as a student social work club, a church group, or a group in high school. In your description, cover the following:

- Goals of the group
- Characteristics of members
- When the group was formed
- How decisions are made
- Who has the most power in making decisions
- Group norms
- Group activities and projects
- Hidden agendas of some group members
- Level of cohesiveness of group
- Disruptive behavior displayed by some members
- Roles of officers in the group
- Outside systems affecting this group

Step 2: Describe the current problems and challenges this group has.

Step 3: Specify the strengths or resources this group has for meeting its problems and challenges.

Step 4: Specify the recommended courses of action that you believe this group should take to better handle its problems and challenges.

ENVIRONMENTAL SYSTEMS EMPHASIS

As described in Chapter 1, social work is increasingly using an ecological perspective in assessing human behavior. The ecological perspective involves considering the adaptive fit of human beings and their environments—that is, the ecology of people in their "life space," which includes all the components of the social and physical environments that affect them. The ecological perspective stresses the importance of assessing the person in the environment. Such an assessment therefore focuses not only on the person but also on environmental systems.

When assessing environment, the worker should limit his or her attention to those elements that are affecting (positively or negatively) the problem situation. In some cases the elements may be obvious (for example, substandard housing and serious financial problems). In other cases the elements may be subtle (for instance, having aloof parents who give little encouragement).

Although the assessment of environmental factors should be limited to those that affect the client's problematic situations, certain basic environmental needs are universal. A partial list of these includes the following:

- Adequate housing
- Safety from hazards and safety from air, noise, and water pollution
- Opportunities for a quality education
- Adequate social support systems (for example, family and relatives, neighbors, friends, and organized groups)
- Access to quality health care
- Access to recreational facilities
- Adequate police and fire protection
- Adequate financial resources to purchase essential items for an acceptable standard of living
- Sufficient food and opportunities for a nutritional diet
- Adequate clothing
- Emotional support from significant others
- Support from significant others to be drug free

Some students majoring in social work have the misconception that social workers sit in offices and counsel clients. True, counseling is a function, but workers have many more responsibilities. They work with families, of course, but they also work with organizations and a variety of other groups to assess community needs and to meet unmet needs. For most social workers, in-office counseling is only a small fraction of the total services provided. A major part of their work involves assessing environmental systems and then endeavoring to change those systems that have a negative impact on clients. To change the environment, a worker may use a variety of skills, such as brokering, advocacy, program development, mediation, research, enabling, and case management. Here are a few examples:

- A protective services worker removes a child from a family in which she is being sexually abused and places her in a foster home.
- A worker arranges for visiting nurses and Meals on Wheels (home-delivered hot meals for homebound persons) to serve an elderly couple so they can continue to live independently.
- A worker arranges for homemaker services for a single mother with three young children; such services involve shopping, cleaning, budgeting, preparing balanced meals, doing the laundry, and teaching these skills to the mother.
- A worker works with a women's group to develop a shelter for battered women and their children in the community.
- A worker helps a community develop local chapters of needed self-help groups, such as Alcoholics Anonymous, Narcotics Anonymous, and Parents Anonymous.

EAP 2.1.10e

- A worker refers a family with a terminally ill member to a hospice program.
- A practitioner works with parents of children with special needs to establish closer collaboration with schoolteachers to enhance the children's functioning in school.
- A worker joins with other health professionals in seeking to raise the state's licensing standards for residential treatment centers, nursing homes, or day-care centers.

Exercise 3.4: Assessing an Organization

Goal: This exercise is designed to assist you in learning how to assess an organization. (In writing this assessment, it may be valuable to read Chapter 9.)

Step 1: Briefly describe an organization. This may be an organization you have participated in, such as the department in which your social work program is located. It may be a sorority or a fraternity, a church you attend, and so on. In your description, cover the following:

- The mission and goals
- Services provided
- Organizational structure
- Funding sources
- Eligibility criteria for clients and customers
- Characteristics of clients and customers
- Number of members and employees
- Characteristics of members and employees
- Morale of members and employees
- Public image of organization
- Your overall impression of the organization

Step 2: Describe the current problems and challenges this organization has.

Step 3: Specify the strengths or resources this organization has for meeting its problems and challenges.

Step 4: Specify the recommended courses of action that you believe this organization should take to better handle its problems and challenges.

ATTENDING TO BIO-PSYCHO-SOCIAL AND CULTURAL COMPONENTS IN ASSESSMENT

As indicated earlier in this chapter, social work is increasingly using an ecological perspective in assessing human behavior, with such an emphasis, social workers need to attend to biological, psychological, sociological and cultural variables in doing an assessment. In using this conceptualization it is important to recognize that there is sometimes overlap between some of these variables. For example, the favorite leisure patterns of a family (such as practicing tai chi) can be considered to be both a sociological and a cultural factor. For another example, a person's IQ score can be considered to be both a biological and a psychological variable. To illustrate assessing a family in terms of bio-psycho-social and cultural variables, we will examine the Gomez family.

Maria Gomez came into the office of Concetta Martinez, a county protective services worker. Ms. Gomez had two black-and-blue, swollen eyes, and a cast on her wrist and lower forearm. She stated her husband had beuten her while intoxicated the previous day. She added he had also hit her two older children yesterday.

Ms. Gomez gave the following additional information. Her husband, Carlos, is generally a good husband, except when he is intoxicated—which occurs once or twice a week. Carlos and Maria have been married for the past 4 years. They have a 3-year-old daughter, Carla, Ms. Gomez has a son, Santos, 9 years old, who has a mild cognitive disability from lack of oxygen at birth. She has a daughter, 7 years old, Karina, who has been diagnosed with Asperger's syndrome. Carlos Gomez is not the biological father of both Santos and Karina.

Ms. Gomez indicated the first few months of her marriage to Carlos were wonderful. However, after the birth of Carla, Ms. Gomez saw a side of Carlos that she had never witnessed before. Instead of coming directly home from work as a roofer, he would occasionally stop at a tavern, with some of his fellow workers, and sometimes become intoxicated. Carlos also began neglecting Maria's two older children and would become irate with Maria when she was attentive to them. Carlos also began to abuse both Maria and her two older children. Carlos would sometimes tell Maria that he was the "boss" of the family, and would not allow Maria to work outside the home—even though the family's income was below the poverty line.

The protective services agency became involved with the family after the social worker at Santos's school questioned him about his bruises. The school social worker than reported the case to the county protective services agency.

Ms. Gomez indicated her Catholic, upbringing has led her to believe it would be a sin to divorce her husband.

POSSIBLE BIOLOGICAL VARIABLES IN THIS CASE

- A genetic component to Carlos Gomez's drinking behavior
- A genetic component to Karina Gomez having Asperger's syndrome
- Santos Gomez having a cognitive disability

POSSIBLE PSYCHOLOGICAL VARIABLES IN THIS CASE

- Carlos Gomez having anger—management issues
- Carlos Gomez's drinking behavior (perhaps he is drinking due to certain unidentified psychological needs)
- The lower IQ of Santos Gomez as a result of his cognitive disability
- The learning challenges faced by Karina Gomez due to having Asperger's syndrome

POSSIBLE SOCIOLOGICAL VARIABLES IN THIS CASE

- The family being a blended family
- Carlos Gomez's drinking behavior may partially involve the socialization patterns and expectations of his fellow workers

- The perspective of Ms. Gomez that he has to be the "boss" of his family, that he has a right to physically hit his wife and children, and that his wife should not work outside the home
- The belief of Mrs. Gomez that getting a divorce is a sin
- The family living below the poverty line
- The family facing a domestic abuse crisis, which may result in a divorce

POSSIBLE CULTURAL VARIABLES

- The perspective of Mr. Gomez that he has to be the boss of his family, and that his wife should not work outside the home
- The belief of Mrs. Gomez that her church believes it is a sin for her to divorce her husband

GUIDES FOR ASSESSING PROBLEM SYSTEMS

Assessments focus on evaluating clients' needs and problems, and the concept of "problem system" is helpful. Hepworth and Larsen (1986) defined *problem system:*

> The configuration of the client(s), other people, and elements of the environment that interact to produce the problematic situation are designated as the problem system. The problem system revolves around the client's concerns and is limited to those persons and factors directly involved in the client's ecological context. (p. 174)

The following 16 questions are useful guides for assessing problem systems.

1. What specifically are the problems? Many problems have several dimensions. It is crucial in an assessment to articulate the subproblems and dimensions of the problem as specifically and accurately as possible. For example, a 27-year-old wife with two children whose husband is killed in a traffic accident caused by a drunk driver may have a variety of needs and problems. She will probably undergo several emotional reactions to the death (including denial of the tragedy, depression, anger at the drunk driver, possible guilt over unresolved conflicts she had with her husband, anger that the husband left her with two children to raise alone) and nightmares. Because intensive grieving is highly stressful, she may come down with one or more stress-related illnesses (such as skin rashes, ulcers, or hypertension). She may seek to escape her problems by using drugs. She is likely to have financial difficulties caused by loss of her husband's income. She will need companionship and emotional support. Her children may have a variety of emotional reactions to the death, which they will need help in handling. She may need help in learning to take on the child-care responsibilities previously performed by her husband. She may face a sharp reduction in her standard of living with the loss of her husband's income. She may be forced to seek a job (if she is not working) or to seek a higher-paying job. She may be forced to apply for public assistance benefits and have to cope with the embarrassment she may feel about being on welfare. She may need legal help to receive any death benefits she is entitled to. At some point in the future, she may have to decide whether to begin dating again. To do an accurate assessment, the social worker must identify, prioritize, and specify these problems and subproblems. Subproblems not identified in an assessment will not be combated in the problem-solving phase.

2. How does the client view the problems? The meanings that clients assign to negative events in their lives are often as important as, or more important than, the events themselves. For example, a woman may end a relationship with a man she has been engaged to for over a year. The man's view of the breakup will largely determine the problems he faces.

Let's assume he tells himself the following: "Life is not worth living. My life is ruined forever. I might just as well end it right now." Such a person is very depressed and perhaps suicidal. These are the problems he then needs help with. In contrast, let's assume he tells himself the following: "I'll miss her somewhat, but it's probably best we end it now. The last 3 or 4 months we apparently grew in different directions. I'm somewhat relieved she broke up with me, as I was thinking about ending the relationship myself. It's easier with both of us wanting out of the relationship. I'll soon find someone else to date." In this case, the man will probably be somewhat sad but also relieved that the relationship is over. With such views, he may have little need for social services.

3. Who is involved in the problem system? The problem system includes all the people who are involved in producing the problematic situation. In the example in which the husband was killed in a traffic accident, the problem system would definitely include the surviving wife and her two children. The problem system also may include others who are highly involved with this family, such as in-laws, other relatives, neighbors, friends, or employers. Such people may need help for the grief they are experiencing, and some may be part of the intervention process by becoming a social support system for the wife and her children. Another problem system that may or may not be identified is the drunk driver and his close family members. The drunk driver and his family may need help for the guilt and remorse they are experiencing, and the driver is probably also in need of help for his drinking problem.

4. How are the participants involved? In this aspect of the assessment process, the focus is on identifying the roles that each person plays in the problem system. Some systems become very complex. For example, a multiproblem family will require considerable analysis to determine the roles played by each member. In a multiproblem family, several problems need to be identified. For each problem, each family member may be playing one or more roles. Detailed information is needed about how each person affects and is affected by others.

5. What are the causes of the problems? Frequently, identifying the causes of problems will suggest ways to intervene. If a husband abuses his wife when he is angry, then helping him learn alternative ways to vent his anger (such as jogging or expressing his feelings in an assertive rather than an aggressive manner) may be constructive. If he abuses his wife when under stress, then instructing him in stress management techniques (such as relaxation techniques) may be useful. If he abuses his wife only when intoxicated, he may benefit from an alcohol treatment program.

When making an assessment, remember that all human behavior is purposeful. A powerful way of analyzing human behavior is as follows:

Antecedents → Thought Processes → Behavior → Consequences

The following is an example:

Antecedent: Jim Schroeder, age 20, is raised in a family and peer culture that glorifies sexual conquests. He is on his second date with a woman and is alone with her late in the evening in her apartment.

Thought Processes: "She is really sexy. Since I've wined and dined her twice, it's time for her to show her appreciation. She wants it as much as I do. I'll show her what a great lover I am. She may protest a little, but I can overcome that. Once we get involved sexually, she'll be emotionally committed to me."

Behavior: Date rape.

Consequences: The woman is traumatized. She calls the police after Mr. Schroeder leaves. He is arrested and charged with first-degree sexual assault. The police also immediately refer the victim to a rape crisis center, and she receives medical services and extensive counseling.

Why did Mr. Schroeder commit date rape? Analyzing behavior through this model identifies the antecedents and the thought processes that led to the date rape. Once these antecedents and thought processes have been identified, interventions can be made to prevent and deter such victimization in the future. For example, Mr. Schroeder might have benefited from educational programs in middle school and high school that emphasize (a) communication about sexual interest between people who are dating rather than aggressive behavior, (b) the rights of women in our society, and (c) the consequences of date rape and the long-term effects on victims. Current interventions for Mr. Schroeder may include (a) individual counseling, (b) correctional time for having committed a serious offense, (c) probation, (d) community service, and (e) group therapy for sexual offenders—perhaps with a component that has victims of sexual assaults describe the long-term adverse effects that they experience. The only way to prevent Mr. Schroeder from committing sexual assaults in the future is to change his thought processes.

6. Where does the problematic behavior occur? Problematic behavior tends to occur in certain locations and not in others. A child may throw temper tantrums at home but not at school or when visiting relatives. Perhaps the child has learned that having a tantrum at home manipulates his parents into giving him what he wants; perhaps he has also learned that throwing a tantrum elsewhere results in ridicule instead of getting what he wants. Identifying where problematic behavior does *not* occur is as important as identifying where it does occur. Both may provide clues to factors that trigger the behavior and factors that prevent it from occurring. For example, a married couple may get into heated arguments when they visit the wife's parents but not when they visit the husband's parents. Perhaps certain factors lead to increased tension when the couple visits the wife's parents—such as the husband's feeling he is being put down and not accepted by the wife's parents. An excellent way to determine why arguments occur at the wife's parents' home is to ask each spouse what the arguments were about and why they occurred.

7. When does the problematic behavior occur? Closely related to *where* the problematic behavior occurs is the question of *when* it occurs. The process of identifying when problematic behavior occurs and when it does not occur frequently reveals valuable clues to factors that trigger the behavior. A client who frequently becomes depressed at a certain time of the year may be grieving about a serious loss that occurred at that time some years ago—such as the death of a loved one or a divorce—or the client may be suffering from seasonal affective disorder (SAD). Identifying when serious arguments occur for a married couple may suggest factors that trigger the conflict: one or both drinking at a party, one having contact with someone she or he dated in the past, one spouse participating in activities that the other is excluded from, or a misbehaving child (the parents may disagree about discipline). A child may feign a headache or throw a temper tantrum when she has to go someplace she does not want to go or when she is told to do something (such as studying her spelling words) that she views as unpleasant. A male in a romantic relationship may start talking about taking his life whenever his woman friend suggests they stop dating. A person with a drinking problem may drink to excess whenever she has intense unwanted emotions, such as anger, frustration, depression, and feelings of insecurity. Once the antecedents that trigger the problematic behavior are identified, the intervention phase can then focus on making the kinds of changes that will reduce the frequency of the behavior.

8. What are the frequency, intensity, and duration of the problematic behavior? Someone who becomes intoxicated once or twice a year may not have a drinking problem, whereas someone who becomes intoxicated once or twice a week probably does. Someone who becomes depressed for a day or two every 3 months probably does not have a serious problem with depression, but someone who is depressed daily certainly does.

Closely related to the frequency of the problematic behavior is its intensity. Someone who is mildly depressed is much more functional than someone who is so severely depressed that he sleeps 15 hours a day, cries frequently during his waking hours, and cannot think rationally. Many other problematic behaviors have varying degrees of intensity, such as extent of intoxication, extent of violent behavior when angry, intensity of family arguments, and extent of overeating.

The duration of the behavior is also an important assessment variable. For example, when someone is intoxicated, how long does she continue to drink to maintain the intoxication? Or, if he is angry or depressed or under high stress, what is the typical duration of the problem behavior? A marital disagreement that lasts 3 weeks is obviously much more serious than one that lasts 20 minutes.

An assessment of the frequency, intensity, and duration of the behavior helps specify its severity and clarify its impact on the client and members of the family.

9. What is the history of the problematic behavior? Examining the history of a problem often identifies the events that triggered the dysfunctional behavior. For example, if an eighth-grade child develops a school phobia, looking into the history of the problem would first seek to identify when the phobia began to occur. Then what was happening in the child's life at this time could be identified. What made her fear going to school? Perhaps she was not getting the grades she desired. Perhaps her classmates were making her life miserable. Perhaps her parents were having severe marital conflict, and she erroneously believed that by staying home she could help ease the marital conflict. Perhaps it is part of a larger anxiety-related problem that has been developing for years. Identifying the antecedents or triggers will help in designing an intervention plan to reduce the frequency and severity of the behavior.

However, identifying the antecedents that initially caused the dysfunctional behavior may not fully isolate the current factors that are maintaining the behavior. For example, a child may have developed a school phobia because two of his classmates were bullying him; but they moved to another city, so other factors are probably causing the child to want to stay home, such as being able to watch television or play all day and not having any schoolwork to do.

For voluntary clients, it is also often revealing to seek out the *precipitating events* that led them to seek help. Often, their problems have existed for months, even years, and identifying the precipitating events yields valuable information. For example, a person who has been bulimic for 2½ years seeks help after she notices blood in her vomit. She believes she might have internal bleeding; she is referred to a physician who finds that her esophagus is severely damaged. A married couple who have been arguing periodically for 3 years seek counseling after they have their first serious physical fight; both are fearful their feuding has entered a new phase that could potentially be life threatening to both. Precipitating events can usually be identified by the practitioner's asking (and probing) clients to identify the reasons for seeking help at this time.

Involuntary clients usually have a crisis or a series of crises that result in their being seen by a practitioner. A practitioner needs to obtain as much information about these crises as possible (often from collateral sources) to determine why an involuntary client is being referred and what his or her problems are. Such information is also useful in confronting the involuntary client. (Many involuntary clients deny they have a problem.)

10. What does the client want? A key social work value is to start where the client is. In an initial interview with a client, whether voluntary or involuntary, it is crucial to address any problems that the client identifies. Failure to do so may leave the client feeling helpless or annoyed, either of which interferes with the eventual intervention effort. In addition, too often assessment is made from the practitioner's perspective rather than from the client's. An adult services worker for a public welfare department was assigned the following case. A 78-year-old man was living alone in a house on a farm where he had been born and raised. The house was in a shambles; it was filthy and had no running water or toilet facilities. Dishes were washed (when they were washed) in rainwater. A small wood-burning stove in the kitchen was used to heat the house. The elderly man was mentally alert but suffered from a variety of minor medical problems: He was overweight and had gout and hypertension. He drank to excess and also rolled and smoked his own cigarettes, which was a potential fire hazard especially when he was intoxicated. The worker decided it would be best for the man to be placed in a nursing home where adequate care could be given. To the worker's surprise, the man refused and bluntly stated, "I was born and raised here, and I'm going to die here. If you would get a court order to place me in a nursing home, which I don't believe you will be able to get, I'll give up the will to live, and die quickly there." The worker was shocked. She discussed the case with her supervisor, and her supervisor pointed out that she may have been viewing the situation from what she wanted rather than what the client wanted. The worker agreed.

This example points out that what a worker views as being a problem may not be viewed as a problem by a client. If the client chooses to live in a substandard living situation, that is *his* choice—and he has a right to do so, *as long as he is not hurting anyone else in the process*. If, however, young children were living with this elderly man, then child neglect would need to be considered. Should that be the case, changes in living conditions would need to be made, or the children might need to be removed from the home.

In any assessment, it is crucial to accurately obtain the client's view of the problem and what the client wants. If the client's desires are realistic and obtainable, satisfying them should generally be a major goal of the helping process. If what the client wants is not realistic, the reasons that his or her desires cannot be fulfilled need to be tactfully explained.

11. How has the client attempted to handle the problem? The ways in which clients have attempted to cope with their problems provide valuable information during an assessment. Clients may have tried ways of resolving their problems that did not work. Those strategies can be then eliminated from consideration in the problem-solving phase.

Suppose a client has tried strategies that were partially successful. Perhaps with increased effort or some modifications, they will work. For example, a client suffering from a high level of stress learned to relax using imagery relaxation. However, she did not think to use the technique when she was highly anxious or frustrated. She was then instructed to set aside 15 minutes every morning before going to work and 15 minutes in the evening to practice the technique. Structuring imagery relaxation into daily activities proved to be a useful way of helping her combat the stress.

Examining the strategies that clients have used to try to resolve their problems can reveal valuable information about their coping and problem-solving skills. If clients have marked deficits in problem solving, it may be helpful to instruct them in the problem-solving approach (see Chapter 7 for a description).

Some clients respond to interpersonal difficulties by becoming passive or nonassertive. Others become aggressive. If either is the case, it may be desirable to instruct clients in using assertiveness to handle interpersonal conflict (see Module 2 for a description of assertiveness training).

Often, clients have good problem-solving and interpersonal skills in some situations but not in others. For example, a schoolteacher was able to handle disruptive students in his classroom but was ineffective in dealing with his own children. A closer examination revealed that he was divorced and was fearful that if he disciplined his children they would want to live with his ex-wife. Through counseling, he came to realize that his children would respect him more if he more clearly specified and enforced behavioral limits. Once this was accomplished, he was able to use the same child management skills he used in the classroom with his own children.

12. What skills does the client need to combat the problem? An assessment of a problematic situation should also identify the skills that clients need to resolve their difficulties. If a parent is having difficulties with a child, needed skills may include listening, negotiating, setting limits, following through on consequences, and nurturing. If a couple is having marital conflicts, they may need problem-solving, communication, listening, and conflict management skills. (Sometimes helping a couple learn these skills is more productive in the long run than helping them resolve their present conflicts.) If a client frequently loses considerable sums of money while gambling, he may need to learn how to say no assertively when his friends ask him to play poker or go to the racetrack. If a client is depressed, she may need to learn what she can do to counter the depression (see Module 1 for some strategies).

13. What are the bio-psycho-social and cultural components of the problem? See a discussion and illustration in the prior section in this chapter.

14. What external resources are needed to combat the problem? An assessment should identify not only the skills that clients need to combat their problems but also the external resources they need. A single mother on public assistance may need day-care services, transportation, and job training to help her become employable. Someone addicted to gambling may need a self-help group, such as Gamblers Anonymous, to give him the emotional support and guidance he needs to combat his addiction. A bulimic may need medical attention to assess and treat physical damage from binging and purging, one-to-one counseling to stop the binge-purge cycle, support from a self-help eating disorders group, and instruction in what is a nutritious and well-balanced diet. Once an assessment is made, a social worker often acts as a broker or case manager in connecting clients with needed services and resources. Frequently, some or all of the needed services are not provided by the practitioner's agency, and arrangements need to be made for the services to be provided by other agencies, organizations, self-help groups, and natural support systems (such as neighbors, family members, fellow workers, church groups, and social groups).

15. What are the client's resources, skills, and strengths? A quality assessment also identifies the resources, strengths, and skills that clients already possess to combat their problems. The importance of identifying such strengths has been described. Sometimes problems are resolved by empowering clients to use resources and skills they already have to mitigate their problematic behavior. Through counseling, clients who have frequent stress-related illnesses may learn that applying the following techniques will help them relax and reduce their high stress levels: positive thinking, problem solving rather than "awfulizing" about their problems, using social support systems, and being more assertive with significant others in expressing their feelings and concerns. A couple with marital problems may find their relationship improving when they treat each other with the same kind of respect that they give to strangers and acquaintances; many spouses use tact in communicating with acquaintances but not in communicating with each other. A person who is grieving about the death of a loved one may find that discussing her grief with friends and relatives not only helps ventilate her grief but also helps her develop a social support system for putting her life back together.

16. What are the recommended courses of action? The recommended courses of action are also called the *treatment plan* and the *intervention plan*. Once a client's difficulties and strengths have been assessed, the next step is to set goals and arrive at a course of action to accomplish the goals. Some authorities conceptualize goal setting and specifying recommended courses of action as a process that follows an assessment. However, in social work practice, most assessments contain a recommended course of action; therefore, this process is discussed briefly here.

Goals should be jointly agreed to by the client and the worker and should be realistic and obtainable. Goals should be geared to resolving the identified problems and should be stated in such a way that they are operational and measurable. An *operational goal* is a goal that can be directly translated into a course of action so it can be accomplished. For example, an operational goal for a nonassertive client might be to learn to be assertive with significant others, and assertiveness training might be the course of action to accomplish this goal. A *measurable goal* is a goal that is stated in such a way that the extent of progress toward attaining the goal can be measured. For example, one way to measure whether a client is making progress in becoming more assertive is for the client to record for 2 weeks the number of times he is assertive and nonassertive in interactions with significant others. The client is then given training in being assertive. Afterward, he keeps records for another 2 weeks. If the number of assertive behaviors after treatment is higher, measurable progress has occurred.

The stated courses of action should be realistic and obtainable. Generally they also should be agreed to by the client. A client who disagrees with these courses of action is unlikely to carry them out. (With some involuntary clients, there are exceptions to this guideline that the recommended courses of actions should be agreed to by the client. For example, a battering husband may not agree with his probation officer's presentence recommendation to the court that he have no contact with his abused wife, who has filed for a divorce.)

The stated courses of action should usually be selected through the following process. After a goal is set, the client and the worker generate a list of feasible courses of action to accomplish the goal. The strengths and shortcomings of each alternative are considered. Then the client and the worker together select the course of action.

EAP 2.1.10e

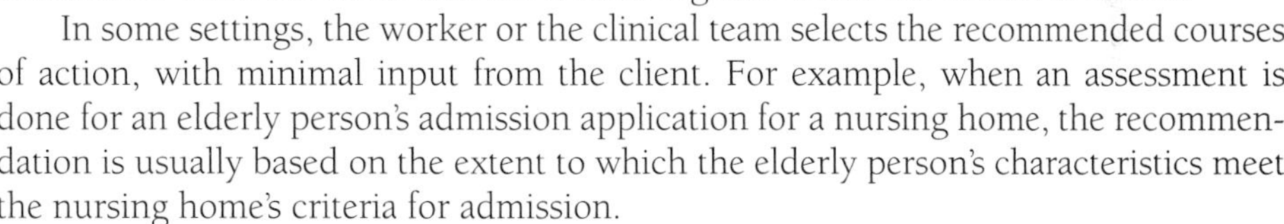

In some settings, the worker or the clinical team selects the recommended courses of action, with minimal input from the client. For example, when an assessment is done for an elderly person's admission application for a nursing home, the recommendation is usually based on the extent to which the elderly person's characteristics meet the nursing home's criteria for admission.

Exercise 3.5: Assessing a Community

Goal: This exercise is designed to assist you in learning how to assess a community. (In writing this assessment, it may be valuable to read Chapter 10.)

Step 1: Briefly describe a community. (This may be a community you've lived in or a community you visited. It may be a community that you viewed in a movie, such as *Boyz N the Hood*. It may be your college community.) In your description, cover the following:

- Population size
- Racial and ethnic characteristics of the population
- Major industries
- Financial circumstances of population
- Unemployment rate
- Housing patterns (homes, condos, apartments, deteriorating units, etc.)
- Major religions of the population
- Governing structure
- Who the main decision makers are
- Human services that are provided
- Transportation systems
- Climate and geography
- Self-help groups
- Community values
- Significant community activities

Step 2: Describe the current problems and challenges this community has.

Step 3: Specify the strengths or resources this community has for meeting its problems and challenges.

Step 4: Specify the recommended courses of action that you believe this community should take to better handle its problems and challenges.

Step 5: (Optional) The instructor may have each student present his or her assessment to the class, with a discussion after each presentation.

SUMMARY

Assessment is a critical process in social work practice. The selection of goals and interventions largely depends on the assessment. An assessment should include not only what is wrong with a client but also the client's resources, skills, and strengths that can be used in resolving difficulties and promoting growth. Too often in the past, assessments focused only on clients' shortcomings and pathology.

The nature of the assessment process varies significantly with the type of setting in which the social worker practices. In some settings the social worker makes an independent assessment, and in other settings the social worker is a member of a clinical team that makes an assessment. An assessment is, in essence, a working hypothesis of a client's difficulties and resources based on current data. As time passes, assessments have to be revised and updated as changes occur in the client and in his or her environment.

Data used in making an assessment are derived from various sources: the client's verbal report, assessment forms, computer-assisted assessment forms, collateral sources, psychological tests, the client's nonverbal behavior, home visits, observation of the client interacting with significant others, and the worker's intuition after interacting with the client.

To do a quality assessment, a worker needs extensive knowledge of human behavior and the social environment. An assessment may require knowledge about multifarious systems, biophysical factors, behavioral factors, motivational factors, family systems, and environmental factors. Such knowledge is obtained from a variety of courses that social work majors typically take in college. The purpose of an assessment is to give focus to the kinds of factors that are examined.

The theory or theories of human behavior that a practitioner subscribes to will have a major influence on what is examined during the assessment. What a worker examines when conducting an assessment has a large effect on the outcome. Most theories of human behavior have not been proven; therefore, practitioners need to be aware that their assessment of someone is only a hypothesis.

Social work is increasingly using an ecological perspective to assess human behavior. An ecological perspective asserts that it is important to assess the person-in—environment. This chapter presented 16 questions that serve as guides for what to examine in conducting an assessment.

EXERCISES

1. Writing an Assessment

EAP 2.1.10e

Goal: To give you experience in writing an assessment.

Step 1: Your instructor explains the purpose of the exercise and then summarizes the 16 key questions for writing assessments. (Alternatively, you can read these questions in the text.)

Step 2: A volunteer constructs a *contrived* problem prior to the next class period. At the next class period, your instructor interviews the volunteer about the contrived problem. The other students in the class then independently write up an assessment that covers the following topics:

a. Specific problems
b. Client's views of problems
c. People involved in the problem system
d. Roles of participants in problem system
e. Causes of problems
f. Where the problematic behavior occurs
g. When the behavior occurs
h. Frequency, intensity, and duration of the behavior
i. History of the behavior
j. Client's goals regarding this behavior
k. Strategies client has used to handle the problem
I. Skills client needs to resolve the problem
m. External resources needed to combat the problem
n. Client's resources, skills, and strengths
o. Recommended courses of action

During the interview your instructor will ask questions that provide you with the data for topics a–n. A significant percentage (40%) of your grade will be based on the quality of your response to "Recommend courses of action."

Step 3: Write up your assessment and turn it in on the designated date. Before returning the graded papers, your instructor will read one or two high-quality recommended courses of action.

Step 4: Student discussion of the merits and shortcomings of this assignment.

2. Assessing Bio-Psycho-Social and Cultural Components

EAP 2.1.7a.b

Goal: To learn to have a bio-psycho-social and cultural perspective in assessing clients.

Step 1: Resend the material in this chapter on bio-psycho-social and cultural assessment.

Step 2: Answer the following questions about this case.

William Weatherford is a social worker, employed as a parole officer. He is assigned the case of Jim Mills, a man who has recently been paroled. The following is background information.

> When Jim Mills was 2 years old his mother remarried. His stepfather beat him with 2×4's when he did not eat his food fast enough or when he did not finish what was put on his plate. He was tied with ropes and locked in closets. When Jim turned 5 he was not allowed in the house during the day. If he wet his pants he was made to were those clothes unwashed the next day. Covered with bruises, dried urine, and feces, Jim was put outside and told to behave himself. School was another torment. He was placed in the "slow" class and labeled as antisocial when he did not play with the other children. By this time Jim recoiled if anyone came too close to him or tried to touch him.
>
> Eventually, relatives, who believed he would soon be killed, talked his mother into allowing them to adopt him. The short, skinny child was moved from a deteriorated inner-city neighborhood to middle-class suburb. He was given tutors to help him catch up with his schoolwork. He joined cub scouts and had his own body-building equipment. It sounds like a happy ending—it wasn't.
>
> One snowy winter evening his family went out to dinner with the next-door neighbors. Jim, now a teenager, walked over to talk to that neighbor's daughter, a friend who attended the same high school. They drank some Coke and watched television. They snacked on some pizza. The girl told Jim to leave because their parents would soon be getting home. Jim did something entirely different. He picked up a knife and stabbed her over 50 times. Knife in hand, he walked home, leaving a trail of blood in the sparkling snow. He climbed into bed without changing his bloody clothes and went to sleep. Police found him there within the hour.

The girl's family was well known in the community. The press had a heyday. Jim answered any question he was asked, except for questions about the night of the murder. The court showed some leniency. Jim was sentenced to 25 years of prison. His survivor instinct intact, he learned many things in prison, some good and some bad. He became the prison Brewmeister when he found out that drinking would take away some of the pain. He discovered drugs. He found out they would take away some of the pain. He found out he was not "slow," but had an exceptionally high IQ. He found the prison library, where he devoured books on philosophy, religion, history, and metaphysics. He was initiated into the Native American Sweat Lodge. The Sweat Lodge is a ceremonial saunce and is an important event in many Native American cultures. It represents acceptance and respect from fellow Native Americans.

When Jim had done a little over 15 years of his time, he was paroled. The family that adopted him had stayed in touch but did not want him to return to their neighborhood. So he returned to the first neighborhood in the inner city to live with his aunt.

a. What are the possible biological variables in this case?

b. What are the possible psychological variables in this case?

c. What are the possible sociological variables in this case?

d. What are possible cultural variables in this case?

Step 3: The leader asks for volunteers to share with the class what they wrote. The class then discusses the usefulness of identifying these variables when conducting an assessment.

COMPETENCY NOTES

The following identifies where Educational Policy (EP) competencies and practice behaviors are discussed in the chapter.

EP 2.1.3b *Analyze models of assessment, prevention, intervention, and evaluation.*

EP 2.1.7a *Utilize conceptual frameworks to guide the process of assessment, intervention, and evaluation.*

EP 2.1.10e *Assess client strengths and limitations.* (Chapter 3).

This chapter presents models and conceptual frameworks to guide the process of assessment.

EP 2.1.10e *Assess client strengths and limitations.* (pp. 93–94).

Exercise 3.1 is designed to assist students in learning how to write an assessment of an individual.

EP 2.1.10e *Assess client strengths and limitations.* (p. 97).

Exercise 3.2 is designed to assist students in learning how to write an assessment of a family.

EP 2.1.10e *Assess client strengths and limitations.* (p. 99).

Exercise 3.3 is designed to assist students in learning how to write an assessment of a group.

EP 2.1.10e *Assess client strengths and limitations.* (p. 101).

Exercise 3.4 is designed to assist students in learning how to assess on organization.

EP 2.1.10e *Assess client strengths and limitations.* (pp. 109–110).

Exercise 3.5 is designed to assist students in learning how to assess a community.

EP 2.1.10e *Assess client strengths and limitations.* (p. 111).

This exercise is designed to give students experience in writing an assessment.

EP 2.1.7a *Utilize conceptual frameworks to guide the process of assessment, intervention, and evaluation.*

EP 2.1.7b *Critique and apply knowledge to understand person and environment.* (pp. 111–112).

This exercise is designed to assist students in having a bio-psycho-social and cultural perspective in assessing clients.

CHAPTER 4

Social Work with Individuals: Interviewing

EP 2.1.3c; 2.1.10d

Social work practice with individuals is aimed at helping them on a one-to-one basis to resolve personal and social problems. Perhaps the two most essential skills social workers need in working with individuals are interviewing and counseling skills. This chapter presents material on how to interview; the next chapter focuses on how to counsel. This chapter will:

A. Describe three types of social work interviews
B. Suggest how to begin and close interviews
C. Describe how to phrase effective questions
D. Provide guidelines on note taking during interviews
E. Discuss the tape recording and videotaping of interviews

THREE TYPES OF SOCIAL WORK INTERVIEWS

Most social work interviews can be classified as informational (to obtain data for a social study or for a social history), assessment (to arrive at an appraisal), or intervention (to help clients change). Often, the three types overlap. For example, a protective services worker in the initial interview with a couple suspected of child abuse will often obtain background information about the family members and seek to arrive at an appraisal of whether child abuse has occurred. If abuse is occurring, the worker may also begin helping the family make changes to end further abuse. Despite overlap, the three types of interviews differ in the way they are structured and conducted.

Informational or Social History Interviews

Informational interviews are designed to obtain background or life history material related to the client's personal or social problem. The purpose is not to learn all there is to know about the person's background but to seek information that will enable the worker (or agency) to better understand the client so that decisions can be made regarding the kinds of services that should be provided. Such information includes both objective facts and subjective feelings and attitudes. In addition to the client, others interviewed or contacted may include parents, friends, other relatives, employers, and other agencies having contact with the client (such as social service agencies, police departments, and schools).

The specific information desired in a social history varies somewhat from agency to agency. An adoption agency, for example, is interested in information about the child-rearing philosophies of potential adoptive parents, whereas a sheltered workshop is interested in the specific work capacities of potential clients. As the social history example in Exhibit 4.1 shows, a social history usually has fact sheet information

Exhibit 4.1 Example of a Social History

WISCONSIN STATE HOSPITAL
SOCIAL HISTORY
Donald Cooper*

Birth date: June 30, 1982

Occupation: Accountant

Race: White

Religion: Unaffiliated

Marital status: Divorced, and currently engaged

Height: 5′10″

Weight: 180

Home Address: 2030 Lincoln Drive
Milwaukee, Wisconsin

Phone: (414) 726-4567

PRESENTING PROBLEMS: Mr. Cooper was committed to this hospital by Judge Chewenka of Washington County for a 60-day observation period. Mr. Cooper was arrested on August 1 on the charge of sexually molesting a minor earlier in the day. The reported victim was an 8-year-old girl whom Mr. Cooper reportedly enticed into his car at the girl's school, and then fondled her genitals after driving to a secluded area.

Mr. Cooper has been arrested on three previous occasions for fondling young girls; each time the charges were dropped after Mr. Cooper consented to receiving psychiatric care. Besides minor traffic violations, he has no other arrest record.

FAMILY BACKGROUND AND EARLY HISTORY: Mr. Cooper's father, Dave Cooper, has been a dairy farmer near Stevens Point all his life. His income has been marginal through the years. Dave Cooper gives the impression of being a meek, submissive person who reportedly has a drinking problem. Dave Cooper indicated he has no idea why his son would become involved in his current difficulties.

Dave Cooper's wife died when Donald was 8 years old, after being ill with cancer for a relatively short time. Dave Cooper mentioned this was a substantial blow to the children and to himself. He added that he has not as yet fully adjusted to his wife's death.

Donald has one sibling, Mary, who is 1 year older. She is currently married to a serviceman, and they are now stationed in San Diego.

Dave Cooper reported his son's developmental milestones were normal, except he sometimes was enuretic until age 5. Dave Cooper reported Donald had a very close relationship with his mother but seemed to adjust satisfactorily to her death. Dave Cooper continued to provide and care for the two children after his wife died.

SCHOOL PERFORMANCE: Mr. Cooper received slightly above-average grades in elementary and high school and received a 2-year associate degree in accounting from Portage County Vocational School. Mr. Cooper reported he neither disliked nor liked school and that he was somewhat of a loner during his school years.

GENERAL HEALTH: Mr. Cooper reports his health has been good. He had a hernia operation at age 20 with no lingering complications.

MARITAL HISTORY: Mr. Cooper was married at age 19 to Nancy Riehle, whom he met in high school. It was a forced marriage and ended after 1 year because of "incompatibility." His ex-wife was interviewed and had no explanation for his involvement in his current difficulties. She is currently receiving $400 per month in child support, and is currently a typist and caring for their 10-year-old daughter. The daughter has not been informed of her father's current confinement; she seldom has contact with her father. The ex-wife appeared to be very dominating and overly critical of Donald, whom she views as "morally immature."

Mr. Cooper is currently engaged to Mary Gautier, and the marriage was planned for December 2 of this year. Miss Gautier indicated she is now reconsidering the upcoming marriage. She is a charming, attractive, petite person currently employed at Jones High School as a secretary. She mentioned she was shocked on being informed of her fiancé's arrest, and had not previously known about his prior arrests. She mentioned she still loves Donald, but feels that unless his reported involvement with young girls is discontinued, it would be better for them to break their engagement. She mentioned she has had sexual relations with Mr. Cooper about twice a week for the past 6 months, which she described as "satisfying" for her, and she also thought for her fiancé.

EMPLOYMENT HISTORY: Mr. Cooper has been employed as an accountant at Paul Realty Company for the past 5 years. His supervisor, John Namman, reported his work is reliable, that he associates well with other employees, but is sometimes "moody." Mr. Cooper

*Name and other identifying information have been changed in this social history.

(continued)

Exhibit 4.1 *(continued)*

reported he likes his current job and hopes he can return after his confinement.

Prior to this position, Mr. Cooper worked as an accountant for two other firms where his work was also reported as acceptable. While in high school and in vocational school, he helped his father on the farm.

PRIOR CONTACT WITH SOCIAL AGENCIES: Since Mr. Cooper's first arrest for fondling young girls 6 years ago, he has been seeing Dr. Timmer at Midwest Psychiatric Center occasionally.

Dr. Timmer reported Mr. Cooper's difficulty is due to the following past history. (Mr. Cooper also related these events in an interview.)

Mr. Cooper mentioned his family life was fairly normal until his mother died when he was 8 years old. His father then began drinking. When sober, his father was considerate, quiet, and an adequate family provider. However, when intoxicated, he was verbally, and sometimes physically, abusive to the children. The children became terrified when they knew their father was drinking. Therefore, when they heard him coming home, they learned to hide by crawling under a blanket. While under the blanket, in fear, they began fondling each other, which seemed to make them feel better. Now, Mr. Cooper mentioned that when he feels "moody" or depressed, he seeks young girls to fondle, hoping to feel better again.

In treating Mr. Cooper, Dr. Timmer has been using a modified psychoanalytic approach, but he admits the therapy has apparently not yet curbed Mr. Cooper's involvement with young girls.

GENERAL IMPRESSIONS: In the interviews, Mr. Cooper appeared to be very concerned about his fondling behaviors with young girls and displayed motivation to curb the deviant behavior. He appears to have traditional middle-class values. He is fairly attractive, and has a pleasant personality.

Mr. Cooper, however, has had repeated incidents of involvement with young girls, even while under psychiatric care. The latest incident occurred at a time when Mr. Cooper is engaged, and as his fiancée reported, when he is having satisfying relations with her. His deviant behavior is apparently deeply entrenched. Sexual activities such as Mr. Cooper's are difficult to change. Perhaps rational therapy (see Module 1) might be used to teach him other ways of handling his emotions of depression and moodiness, instead of through seeking to fondle young girls. Also, an arrangement might be made with the local mental health center to have Mr. Cooper call and receive immediate counseling (perhaps staying overnight at the center) whenever he has a strong urge to fondle young girls.

(name, age, occupation, and so on), plus information about the presenting question or problem, early childhood experiences and development, family background, school performance, dating and marital history, employment history, contact with other agencies, and general impressions. The desired objectives and formats of social histories vary greatly from agency to agency.

Here are a few examples of informational interviews: A social worker at a mental hospital seeks background information to better understand the problems and social functioning of an inpatient. A probation officer conducts a social investigation to guide the court in dealing with someone charged with a felony. A worker for a community welfare council interviews people in a multiproblem neighborhood to identify what they view as their most urgent unmet needs. A worker at a nursing home does a social history on a new resident to obtain information about current social and personal problems and about special interests, which will help determine the kinds of services and activities that are needed to meet the resident's needs and interests.

Assessment Interviews

Assessment or decision-making interviews are more focused in purpose than informational interviews. The questions asked in assessment interviews are aimed at making *specific* decisions involving human services. For example, a protective services worker investigates a child abuse complaint to determine whether abuse is occurring. A public assistance worker interviews an unmarried woman who is pregnant to determine eligibility for financial assistance. A vocational rehabilitation counselor interviews a client with a developmental disability to determine eligibility for a range of services, including financial assistance, vocational training, and sheltered workshop participation. A social worker at a residential facility for persons with developmental disabilities interviews the parents of a child with a severe cognitive disability to obtain information that will be used by the admissions committee to determine whether the child should be admitted. A director of a group home for adolescent boys interviews a youth on juvenile probation who is having severe conflict with his parents to determine whether he would benefit from the group home or whether a correctional school would be more appropriate.

Intervention Interviews

The purpose of intervention interviews is to help clients make changes, or to change the social environment to help clients function better, or both. A shy parent is counseled on how to be more assertive. A depressed, lonely, or suicidal client is counseled on how to handle such problems better. A client on probation is counseled on how to apply for and find a job. A couple having marital problems are counseled on how to communicate and handle their problems better. A newly married couple distressed by the husband's premature ejaculation are counseled on how to resolve such a dysfunction (Hyde & DeLamater, 2006). A couple with problems disciplining their children might be given instructional sessions in parent effectiveness training techniques (Gordon, 1970). These are all examples of helping clients make changes.

Other intervention interviews are geared to changing the social environment to facilitate a client's social functioning. For example, the spouse of a client with a drinking problem is counseled on how to help the spouse stop drinking and develop a meaningful life separate from alcohol. Interviews may have an intervention goal without the person for whom the change is sought being present. Kadushin (1972) gives some examples:

> These include interviews with persons important in the client's life, where the social worker acts as a broker or advocate in the client's behalf. The social worker engaged in brokerage or advocacy may interview people in strategic positions in an attempt to influence them on behalf of the client. The purpose of the interview is to change the balance of forces in the social environment in the client's favor. The school social worker may interview a teacher in order to influence her to show more accepting understanding of a client. The social worker at the neighborhood service center may interview a worker at the housing authority or at the local department of public welfare in order to obtain for his client full entitlement to housing rights or to assistance. Or a social worker may accompany an inarticulate client to an employment interview in an effort to influence the decision in the client's favor. In each instance the scheduled interview has a definite, and in these cases, therapeutic purpose on behalf of the client. (p. 19)[1]

Intervention interviews are the most common in social work, and therefore this text focuses mainly on this type.

THE PLACE OF THE INTERVIEW

Social work interviews can take place anywhere—in the office, in the client's home, on street corners, in restaurants, in institutions. Office interviews permit control of the physical setting, usually make the interviewer comfortable, and usually can be arranged to ensure privacy. Office interviews also reduce the worker's travel time between interviews.

Home visits have an advantage in helping the interviewer better understand the living conditions of the interviewee. Family interactions can also be observed. Some clients, such as those with severe disabilities, find it difficult or impossible to travel to

[1]Alfred Kadushin, *The Social Work Interview*. Copyright © 1972, Columbia University Press, New York. This and all other quotations from the same source are used with permission.

an office; therefore, home visits are common in social work. Other clients find an office "foreign" to them and are more comfortable in their home or in other settings.

The home visit also offers opportunities for the worker to enter the life of the interviewee as a participant—opening a stuck door, moving furniture, holding a crying baby. However, there is also the chance that the interviewer may have to respond to conflict between family members if it occurs, and some clients may feel that a home visit suggests that the worker is spying on them. Distractions are also more likely to occur—for example, phone calls, TV programs that other family members want to watch, friends dropping by to visit.

In practice I have found that although the physical setting may have an effect on the start of an interview, the effect can almost always be handled by a skillful interviewer. For example, on a home visit where a number of other people are present, the worker can suggest to the client that they go to a restaurant where they can have a soda and talk without interruptions from other family members. The interviewer's skills are almost always more important than the setting in determining the productivity of an interview.

OPENING THE FIRST INTERVIEW

When Interviewee Initiated

If someone has asked to see a social worker and has come to the appointment, it is best to let that person state exactly what he or she is concerned about. The counselor should, of course, greet the client with something like "Hi, I'm Jane Bernes, and I'm a counselor at this agency." After the client has been seated, the client often begins indicating his or her concerns. If this does not happen, the worker should say something brief and neutral (not to sidetrack the client) to help the client get started, such as: "You came in here to see me about something today."

Openings that are *not* as desirable include the following: (1) "I'm glad you came in this afternoon." The client may know that you are being superficial and may not in fact be glad to hear what he or she has to say. (2) "In what way can I help you?" The worker should not erroneously convey that he or she is the chief problem solver. The client owns the problem and is the primary problem solver. (3) "You have a problem?" The word *problem* in a counseling situation may suggest to the client that the worker is viewing the client as a psychiatric case.

Benjamin (1974) recommended the following about small talk at the beginning of an interview:

> Sometimes at the outset there is room or need for small talk on the interviewer's part, something to help the interviewee get started. But we should attempt this only when we truly feel that it will be helpful. Brief statements such as the following may break the ice: "With traffic the way it is around here, you must have found it hard to get a parking place" or "It's nice to have a sunny day after all that rain, isn't it?" (p. 13)[2]

Kadushin (1972) gave these suggestions on how to start an interview:

> It is helpful if the interviewer can greet the interviewee by name. She invites her in, goes through the familiar social amenities—taking her coat, offering her a chair, and demonstrating her concern that she is reasonably comfortable. The interviewer gives the interviewee a chance to get settled—to compose herself, to absorb first impressions, to get her bearings, to catch her breath. She needs a little time to get used to the room and the interviewer. . . .

---

[2]Alfred Benjamin, *Helping Interview: With Case Illustrations*, 3E. © 1987 Wadsworth, a part of Cengage Learning, Inc. Reproduced by permission. www.cengage.com/permissions.

EP. 2.1.3c

It is helpful, particularly at the beginning and the end of the contact, to make general conversation rather than engage in an interview. . . .The preliminary chit-chat may be about the weather, parking problems, cooking, baseball, or the high cost of living.

This socializing is not a waste of time. It eases the client's transition from the familiar mode of conversational interaction into a new and unfamiliar role which demands responses for which he has little experience. The conversation has the additional and very important advantage of permitting the interviewee to become acquainted with and size up the interviewer as a person. (pp. 130–131)

Exercise 4.1: Introducing Yourself When the Interview Is Interviewee Initiated

Goal: This exercise is designed to give you the opportunity to practice the skill of introducing yourself.

You are a social worker at a nursing home. A family member (whom you have not previously met) of a resident wants to discuss something with you. Write the words you would say to introduce yourself—using some small talk and also inviting the family member to have a seat in your office.

When Interviewer Initiated

EP 2.1.3c

Whether talking to a client, to a client's relative, or to professionals at other agencies, the worker should indicate his or her role or position at the agency and then state the purpose of the interview. Thus, a school counselor may say to a student who is receiving failing grades, "Hi, John. I'm Mr. Roberts, a social worker at this school. I asked that you see me today because I was looking at your grade report. It looks as if you are having difficulty in some of your courses. Perhaps we can talk about the reasons." A protective services worker might say, "Hi, I'm Mary Seely, a protective services worker with Rock County Social Services. Information that raises questions about the care your child is receiving has come to our attention. I realize there are always two sides to any such report, and therefore I would like to talk with you about this."

Exercise 4.2: Introducing Yourself When the Interview Is Interviewer Initiated

Goal: This exercise is designed to give you the opportunity to practice the skill of introducing yourself while stating the purpose of the interview.

You are a juvenile probation officer for Wood County Human Services Department. Amy Harper, age 15, has recently been arrested by the police for shoplifting, Ms. Harper has not yet appeared in juvenile court. This is your first meeting with Ms. Harper. The purpose of your meeting is to begin to get information from Ms. Harper regarding her views of what happened and background information about her and her family. This information is needed so you can begin to compile your recommendation to the juvenile court about whether Ms. Harper should be placed on juvenile probation or should be offered an opportunity to attend a juvenile diversion program (which consists of 1-hour group meetings each week for 10 weeks with other first-time juvenile offenders). Write the words you would say to introduce yourself, to invite Ms. Harper to have a seat in your office, and to state the purpose of this first meeting.

CLOSING AN INTERVIEW

Closing is not always easy. Ideally, both the interviewer and the interviewee would accept the fact that the interview is ending, and the subjects being discussed would not be left hanging. Saying something like "Well, you really have serious problems, but I've got to catch my ride. When can we talk further?" would be abrupt and unprofessional. Such abrupt endings are likely to be perceived by the interviewee as being discourteous and uncaring.

There are some useful guidelines on how to terminate an interview. Kadushin (1972) recommended the following:

> Preparation for termination begins with the very beginning of the interview. The interviewee should be informed explicitly at the beginning that a definite period of time has been allotted for the interview, that she is free to use some, or all, of this time but that going beyond the time limit is clearly discouraged. Unless an unusual situation develops, it is understood that the interview will terminate at the end of the allotted time. (p. 207)

When the allotted time is nearly up, the interviewer may inform the interviewee by saying something like this: "Well, our time is just about up. Is there anything you'd like to add before we look at where we have arrived and where we now go from here?" At the end of the interview, it is often helpful to summarize what was discussed. If the interview focused only on exploring the client's problems, another interview should be set up for fuller exploration and to begin looking at alternatives.

I find it helpful to give clients "homework" assignments between interviews. A couple who are having trouble communicating with each other, for example, might be encouraged to set aside a certain amount of time each evening to discuss their personal thoughts with each other. At the next interview, this "homework" assignment is reviewed.

Reid and Shyne (1969) found that if an agency establishes a set, limited period for contact with the client (including both the number of interviews and the length of each interview), both worker and client make more productive use of the time as they mobilize their efforts to accomplish the tasks within the designated time.

Ideally, the interviewee would be emotionally at ease when the interview ends. Therefore, the interviewer should not introduce emotionally charged content at the end but should seek a reduction in intensity of emotion.

If an interviewee displays reluctance to end the interview, it is sometimes helpful to confront this directly by saying, "It appears to me that you wish we had more time." The reasons for the interviewee's reluctance can then be discussed, and perhaps another appointment can be made.

Just as it is sometimes advisable to begin an interview with small talk, a short social conversation at the end can be useful because it provides a transition out of the interview. There are many styles of closing. The style used will depend on the interviewer, the interviewee, and what was said during the interview.

At times, an interview can be closed with a restatement of the way the interviewer and interviewee agreed to proceed. Here is an example: "I'm glad you have decided to have the pregnancy test. If it's positive, give me a call so we can arrange another time to further discuss the options we briefly talked about here."

At times, the interviewer may make a more explicit summation of what was discussed, what decisions were arrived at, what questions remain to be resolved, and what actions will be taken. A somewhat different approach is to ask the interviewee to summarize the decisions he arrived at during the interview and what actions he now intends to take.

Sometimes as an interview is closing, concerns that were alluded to but not fully discussed might be mentioned as topics to be discussed at the next interview. I find that some clients first reveal their most serious concerns at the end of the interview, perhaps because they needed time to become comfortable and to gain confidence that the interviewer is a competent person who may have some useful suggestions. In such instances, the interviewer has to decide whether to extend the interview beyond the allotted time or to set up another appointment to discuss these concerns.

EP 2.1.3c

Benjamin (1974) observed:

> Closing is especially important because what occurs during this last stage is likely to determine the interviewee's impression of the interview as a whole. We must make certain that we have given him full opportunity to express himself, or, alternatively, we must set a mutually convenient time for this purpose. We should leave enough time for closing so that we are not rushed, since this might create the impression that we are evicting the interviewee. (p. 32)

Exercise 4.3: Closing an Interview

Goal: This exercise is designed to give you the opportunity to practice the skill of closing an interview.

You are a social worker for a hospice program. Dr. Richard Miller has referred Karen Meersman, age 83, to your hospice services. Ms. Meersman is in an advanced stage of ovarian cancer. She has received both chemotherapy and radiation therapy, and the cancer has not gone into remission. Ms. Meersman refuses to have additional chemotherapy, as research indicates the side effects would be more adverse than the potential benefits. It is estimated by Dr. Miller that Ms. Meersman has less than 6 months left to live.

You have your first meeting with Ms. Meersman and her 57-year-old daughter, Helen Kraft, at an assisted living facility. You are compassionate and empathetic. You listen to the mother and daughter briefly trace the struggles they have had with Ms. Meersman having ovarian cancer. You seek to lighten the tone of the interview, at times, by asking Ms. Meersman questions such as "Tell me about some of your most memorable occasions in your life" and "Tell me about your son and two daughters." You then explain that Ms. Meersman meets the eligibility criteria for hospice services. You also summarize the services that hospice is able to provide, including medication for pain relief, emotional support for Ms. Meersman and close family members, nursing care assistance at this assisted living facility, assistance with helping Ms. Meersman get her financial circumstances in order, being available during crises, assisting with funeral arrangements, and providing bereavement services for close family members. You indicate tomorrow at a certain time you will return with a hospice nurse, whom you will introduce.

There are several acceptable ways to close the interview. Write the words you would say to close it. Then summarize your rationale for choosing this approach.

QUESTIONING

Questions are asked for a variety of purposes: to obtain information, to help clients tell their stories, to build a relationship, to help clients look at alternative strategies, and to help clients select solutions. The tone in which the question is asked is often as important as the question itself. For a client who is depressed, an appropriate tone should indicate caring and understanding. For someone who is angry, the tone should imply recognition of the anger and willingness to examine the anger. For someone who is anxious, the tone should convey reassurance.

In exploring clients' problems and alternative solutions, a series of questions with an increasingly specific focus is usually advisable. Kadushin (1972) expanded on this point:

> The successive questions should act as a funnel, moving from general to more specific aspects of the content being discussed. As discussion of one area is completed at the mor specific end of the funnel, the new content area introduced for discussion should start w another general, open-ended question. (p. 149)

"How do you feel about that?" is a common question that I find useful for a var situations—for example, when a client is pregnant or is involved in a failing r Another common question that I ask when a client has a problem that involve else is "Could you describe what kind of a person *(name)* is?" Such questic getting a rapid impression of the client's thoughts and feelings about the

Skilled interviewers use probing questions to help clients elaborate on the specific details of their concerns and to help clients look in greater detail at the merits, shortcomings, and consequences of possible resolution strategies. Probing questions with a client who feels her husband drinks too much might include the following: "How much does he drink?" "How often does he drink?" "How does he act when intoxicated?" "What concerns you most about his drinking?" The concerns she mentions also need to be explored in depth, using probing questions such as the following: "Given his drinking, how do you now feel about him?" "Does he recognize that he has a drinking problem?" "Do you think he would be willing to come in to talk about these concerns?" Probes should be used not in a cross-examinating fashion but in a manner that gradually permits the interviewer and the interviewee to see the situations more clearly.

EP 2.1.3c

Various errors should generally be avoided in phrasing questions. Some of these are shown in Exhibit 4.2. The questions classified there as "errors" should not be used unless a worker has a *specific, constructive* purpose for phrasing the question in that way.

Exercise 4.4: Phrasing Questions

Goal: This exercise is designed to assist you in learning to phrase questions professionally and constructively.

1. You are a social worker at a high school, and you have had several meetings with Kara Whitford about dating issues she has and about her future (which she is confused about) when she graduates in 3½ months. You are informed by one of her teachers that her parents have recently decided to get a divorce and that this has been very upsetting to Kara. You meet with Kara. Write the words you would say to her to express your compassion and to encourage her to share her concerns related to the divorce of her parents. Summarize your rationale for your phrasing of this question.

2. You are a child protective services worker for Lincoln County Human Services. A school system reports that 7-year-old John Komarek has several bruises on his arms, legs, back, and face. You meet with John at school, and he informs you that his dad hit him several times last night. You call the Komareks to make an appointment to discuss this. Mr. Komarek answers the phone. Write the words you would say to him to arrange a time for you to go on a home visit (taking another worker along) to discuss this incident. Summarize your rationale for phrasing your approach this way.

3. You are a social worker at a Temporary Assistance for Needy Families (TANF) agency. You have assisted Ms. Marcella Gomez (a single mother with two young children) in receiving job training for a secretarial position and in making child-care arrangements. Although Ms. Gomez is one of your most competent clients, she was not hired for any of the six positions she applied for. You note that Ms. Gomez is untidy in her personal appearance and usually has an unpleasant body odor. Write the words you would say to her that will tactfully assist her in examining whether her personal appearance and lack of showering may be a factor in

Exhibit 4.2 Phrasing Questions

Errors in Phrasing Questions	A Desirable Neutral Formulation
THE LOADED QUESTION: This question assumes an unknown action is occurring.	
"When did you last hit your wife?"	"Have you ever hit your wife?"
"What are you going to do when John breaks up with you?"	"Do you think John is considering breaking up with you?"
THE SUGGESTIVE, OR LEADING, QUESTION: The interviewer suggests a "desired" answer.	
"Don't you think it's high time you stop drinking and shape up?"	"Do you think you have a drinking problem?"
"You're really making good progress—aren't you?"	"What progress do you think you're making?"
YES-NO QUESTION: Such questions do not encourage elaboration.	
"Do you ever do anything together with your husband?"	"What kinds of things do you and your husband do together?"
"You really don't like Mary—do you?"	"How do you feel toward Mary?"
EITHER-OR QUESTION: The interviewee might prefer both or neither or a third.	
"Would you like to talk about your marriage or your job this morning?"	"What would you like to talk about this morning?"
"Have you and Tim decided to get married or to have an abortion?"	"What alternatives have you and Tim talked about?"
BOMBARDING: The interviewer asks two or more questions at the same time.	
"How are you feeling today, and did you and your husband get a chance to further discuss what we talked about last week?" "What were your parents' reactions when you told them you were pregnant? Did they suggest getting an abortion? How do you feel about having an abortion?" "Since graduating from high school have you found a job, a place to live, and are you still dating the same person?"	Such questions should be asked separately.
GARBLED QUESTION: Such questions usually occur when the interviewer is unclear about what he or she wants to ask.	
"You've been considering, uh, what was it, oh yeah, something about what we talked about last time—now how do you feel about that?" "Have you thought about—no, that wouldn't work, another possible thing you could do is—I don't know. What were we talking about?"	Interviewers need to be clear about what they want to ask before speaking. Pauses are better than asking garbled questions.

her not being successful in attaining a position. Summarize your rationale for phrasing your question this way.

4. You are a social worker at an adoption agency. A couple (both in their early 30s), Harold and Emily Nolan, have applied to adopt a child. This is your third meeting for the adoption study. You visit the Nolans at their home. It is 10 a.m. When you arrive for the appointment, you are surprised when you detect the odor of alcohol on Mrs. Nolan's breath. Write the words you would say to her that will tactfully assist in exploring why it appears she may have had one (or more) alcoholic beverages this early in the morning. Summarize your rationale for your phrasing of this question.

5. You are a social worker at a Planned Parenthood clinic. Ms. Roberta Greene has been a client for the past several months. She is 16 years old, has been on a birth control pill, but has a history of skipping 3 or 4 days in taking the pill. She fears she may be pregnant. The clinic performs a pregnancy test, and the result is "positive." You meet with her to give her the result. Write the words you would say in informing her of the result—and write the words you would say to her to encourage her to share her feelings, concerns, and questions about being pregnant. Summarize your rationale for phrasing what you say this way.

NOTE TAKING

Note taking is an integral part of counseling. Workers need notes to refresh their memory of past interviews, to record the contracts made with clients, to record information for social histories, to share important facts with colleagues, and to record what has been done or left undone. Benjamin (1974) observed,

> In our culture, when note taking is discriminately handled, it is not resented. On the contrary, its absence may be looked upon as negligence or lack of respect. Usually no explanation of our recording practice is required. However, should an explanation be requisite because of the needs of either or both partners in the interview, it can be easily provided. (p. 58)

Note taking should be subordinate to interviewing. Don't let note taking interfere with the flow of the interview. For example, avoid saying or conveying, "I wish you would talk slower, I can't write that fast." Don't turn note taking into cross-examination—for example, "Let's see if I got it right, you state you sometimes think about getting a divorce because you find marriage confining." Convey that you are relaxed and comfortable with note taking. Don't be secretive about taking notes; otherwise, the client may become suspicious or anxious. At times, it is important for a worker to record certain kinds of information to demonstrate an interest in the client. Such expected information includes certain addresses, names, telephone numbers, contract goals, and tasks.

Note taking presents a possible distraction to interview interaction. When a worker breaks eye contact to make notes, the focus may shift from what *is being* said to what *has been* said. Ideally, workers should acquire the capacity to take notes unobtrusively without seeming to shift their attention from the client to what is being written. Kadushin (1972) advised,

> The effect of note taking needs to be assessed periodically during the interview. If at any point the interviewee appears to be upset or made hesitant by note taking, this should be raised for explicit discussion. If, despite the interviewee's stated assent, note taking appears to be a disruptive tactic, one might best forget it. (p. 206)

Note taking generally decreases in quantity as a worker gains experience. When recording, don't emphasize the importance of note taking by, for example, sitting with a pen and paper between you and the client or by recording most of what a client says. Most experienced interviewers find they often don't need to make notes during the interview. Frequently, writing down a few key phrases and points afterward enables the worker to recall important points. Benjamin (1974) stressed honesty in taking notes:

EP 2.1.3c

> I am certain of one thing: we must be honest. If the notes taken are to be used for the purpose of research, we should state this at the outset. In the event that the information gathered cannot be kept confidential, we should frankly indicate this, too. Above all, we should not promise confidentiality if we are not certain that we can provide it. (p. 60)

Exercise 4.5: Explaining Note Taking to a Client

Goal: This exercise is designed to give you the opportunity to practice the skill of explaining why you are taking notes during an interview.

You are an adult probation and parole officer. Mr. Rodney Wyler has been convicted of embezzling more than $200,000 from his employer. You meet with Mr. Wyler, introduce yourself, and indicate that one of your first responsibilities is to write a presentencing report, which the judge will review before determining the sentence that she will impose. (A presentencing report is similar to the social history in Exhibit 4.1). You ask Mr. Wyler if he has any questions at this time. He indicates he does not have any. You start asking Mr. Wyler questions to obtain background information about him. How do you briefly explain to him the necessity for you to take notes? Write the words you would use. Also summarize your rationale for phrasing what you say this way.

TAPE RECORDING AND VIDEOTAPING

Audio and video recording of interviews are increasingly being used. Both have advantages over note taking because they provide a full record of what was said. However, a worker cannot refer to tapes as readily as to written notes. Tapes can be transcribed, but this is expensive.

Tape recordings and note taking are generally used for different purposes. Tape recordings are used as a mirror to reflect to interviewer or to interviewee exactly what was said and how. As such they have a *self-confrontation* or *sensitivity* value, because they reflect how a person interacts with others. Playing back tapes can show clients where they have interactional problems (for example, shyness). For interviewers, the tapes can improve counseling and interviewing skills.

An initial concern of interviewers in deciding whether to use tape recordings is how the interviewee will react to being taped. I have used both audiotaping and videotaping extensively and find that clients soon forget the interview is being taped. A number of other authorities agree. Benjamin (1974), for example, said:

> I am firmly convinced that after the first few minutes he will not react to it at all for he will no longer notice it. It is my belief that, as a matter of ethics, the fact that the interview is being taped should not be concealed. If I tell him that it is my custom to record interviews to learn from them afterwards and that the tape will be kept confidential, he will usually not object. He will not be uneasy unless he feels that I am. If I can say that he, too, may listen to the tapes to learn, so much the better. If after all this the interviewee still objects, it is probably best to respect his feelings. Some people are simply afraid or suspicious. In areas or cultures in which the tape recorder is seldom used or seen, for the interviewer to insist might prove harmful indeed. When one finds he is working with suspicious people, the wise thing to do is to get at the suspiciousness and leave the tape recorder alone for the time being. (p. 62)

Some counselors routinely videotape interviews. When clients review the tape, they can more fully grasp what was said and gain valuable feedback about how they interact. Videotaping allows both interviewer and interviewee to study their verbal and nonverbal communication simultaneously.

VIDEOTAPING FOR TRAINING PURPOSES

Most educational programs in social work and counseling use videotaping of simulated counseling situations to help students develop and assess their interviewing and counseling skills. Growing numbers of programs use videotaping as one approach to assess students' aptitude for social work. An essential capacity of social work is the ability to counsel and relate to people. This capacity is necessary in social work practice with individuals, groups, families, organizations, and communities, and for performing competently in micro, mezzo, and macro practice.

In many undergraduate and graduate programs in social work, students must now demonstrate, usually in a practice course, that they have a sufficient level of counseling and interviewing skills that will give field placement agencies substantial assurance that they will be able to counsel clients. One way of helping students to develop their interviewing and counseling skills is by videotaped role-playing. Each student in the class is videotaped (usually in a video lab) in the role of a counselor while counseling someone else about a contrived problem. This videotape is later reviewed jointly by student and instructor. Students are usually graded on a pass/fail basis on this videotaped role-play. They are permitted to videotape a role-playing situation as many times as they want. If they fail to make an acceptable tape, they are not allowed to pass the course and are encouraged to transfer to another major. This course, therefore, serves as a first step in screening out students from the program. The emphasis of this requirement, however, is not on culling students from the program but on helping them develop their interviewing and counseling techniques. If a student feels the instructor's review of the tape is unfair, an appeal process is available in which the student can take the tape to other social work faculty members for their review.

When Zastrow and Navarre (1979) studied the effectiveness of videotapes as a training tool, they found that students are initially apprehensive about the videotaped role-playing. This apprehensiveness is partially reduced by lecture material and class discussions on "how to counsel" and by role-playing counseling situations in class (generally two students counseling two other students about a contrived problem). Following the videotaped role-playing, most students express considerable increased confidence in their capacities to counsel and a substantial reduction in their apprehensiveness about being videotaped in the future. These student responses of how videotaping is helpful are typical (Zastrow & Navarre, 1979):

> It helped make me comfortable in a counseling situation. I was able to test out different ways in helping a client and when reviewing the tape I saw what things I did well, and what I need to work on to become a better counselor.

> I became aware of my own voice, posture, and gestures and the importance they play in counseling.
>
> I was able to see an actual picture of myself, not what I thought I looked like, and was able to see where I made my mistakes and could have done something different.
>
> I feel that the best way to learn something is to actually do it, instead of just talking about it. I also thought it was useful to watch the tape and look for your mistakes. This is the best way to correct them.
>
> I became aware of exactly how I came across to the client and I noticed that I was suggesting things to him—which I didn't even realize before reviewing the tape.
>
> Made me more aware of my self-presence (mannerisms). Gave me the opportunity early in my academic career to have a slight taste of what counseling is about and what I might be in store for!
>
> I was not confident in my counseling skills at first. But after seeing the videotape I saw that I could do it. Videotaping is a good confidence builder. (pp. 201–202)

The benefits of using videotaped role-playing to assess and develop counseling skills include the following:

1. Students report it is a valuable tool in learning how to counsel.
2. Difficulties that a student has in counseling and relating to people can be identified and shown to the student; then efforts can be made to make improvements.
3. Students whose capacities lie elsewhere can be identified early in their college career and counseled into some other major.
4. Videotaping links theory with practice and thereby makes the course more meaningful and relevant.
5. Students report that videotaping provides considerable feedback about themselves and about how they relate to others.
6. Students report that videotaping builds their confidence for counseling "real" clients in the future and gives them an opportunity to test their skills and interpersonal behaviors in a safe setting.
7. This laboratory approach helps students make the transition from theory to real practice.
8. The approach provides assurance to field placement agencies that student interns will have an acceptable level of counseling expertise.

Zastrow and Navarre (1979) also found that almost all students are able (sometimes after three or four attempts) to develop their interviewing and counseling skills to an acceptable level. It is interesting that most of the few students identified with this approach as not having an aptitude for social work voluntarily decided to switch to another major. They also concluded after viewing their videotapes that they didn't have the capabilities to be a social worker.

SUMMARY

Most social work interviews are for information (to obtain data for a social study or for writing a social history), assessment (to arrive at an appraisal), or intervention (to help clients change). Often, the three types overlap. Intervention interviews are the most common in social work. Their purpose is to help clients make changes or to change the social environment to help clients function better, or both.

Social work interviews can take place anywhere. Most commonly, they occur in the interviewer's office or in the client's home. Although location does affect an interview, the interviewer's skills are almost always more important in obtaining a productive interview.

Material about how to begin and how to end interviews is presented. In interviewee-initiated interviews, the initial focus is on helping clients become comfortable and start relating their concerns. In interviewer-initiated interviews, the initial focus, after the introductions, is for the interviewer to state the purpose concisely and then begin the dialogue. There are a variety of ways to close interviews. The style used depends on the interviewer, the interviewee, and what was said during the interview. Ideally, both interviewer and interviewee should accept the fact that the interview is ending. Topics being discussed should not be left hanging. Most interviews end with either the interviewer or the interviewee summarizing what was said or summarizing what courses of action are now planned.

Questions in interviews are used for a variety of purposes—to gather information, to help clients tell their stories, to help them look at alternative solutions, and to help them select a strategy. The tone in which a question is asked is often as important as the question itself. Probing questions are common in social work practice. Several types of questions should usually be avoided: loaded questions, suggestive questions, yes-no questions, either-or questions, clustered questions (bombarding), and garbled questions.

Note taking is an integral part of counseling and should be unobtrusive so it does not interfere with the flow of the interview.

EP 2.1.3c

Audiotape and videotape recordings are increasingly used to provide a full record of what was said. They are generally used for different purposes than note taking. Reviewing tapes helps clients grasp more fully what was said and gives them valuable feedback on how they interact. Reviewing tapes is particularly valuable for counselors, helping them assess and hone their interviewing skills.

EXERCISE

Writing a Social History

Goal: The purpose of this exercise is to give students practice in writing a social history.

Step 1: At an earlier class session, the instructor informs the class there will be an exercise in a future session designed to teach them how to write a social history. Students read the material in this chapter on how to write a social history. The instructor informs the students they may use the format and subheadings in the example of a social history presented in this chapter (see Exhibit 4.1) or an adaptation of it. The instructor asks for a volunteer to develop (1) a contrived story about some unusual incident that has led him or her to become a client of an agency and (2) background information covering the following material:

- Birth date
- Religion
- Occupation
- Marital status
- Height
- Weight
- Address
- Home phone
- Why referred
  - By whom
- Early developmental history
  - Toilet trained (what age)
  - First walked (what age)
  - First talked (what age)
  - Relationship to parents, brothers, sisters
- Education*
  - Kindergarten
  - Grades school
  - Junior high
  - High school
  - College
- Employment history
  - Where worked
  - How long
- Health
- Family life
  - Dating
  - Courtship
- Prior contact with other social agencies

*Places, grades, relationships to other students, and attitudes about these schools

The instructor informs the class that at a future session she or he will interview the "client" and that each student will have to write a social history based on this interview. (The volunteer may be excused from having to write the social history.) The instructor informs the students that a significant part of their grade for this project will depend on their *realistic* recommendations on how to intervene effectively to help this "client." The instructor indicates that bringing tape recorders to the interview for the write-ups is acceptable.

Step 2: The instructor interviews the "client" during a future class session, covering the information contained in step 1. In this interview the instructor explores problems but ends the interview before the client chooses specific courses of action to resolve the situation. A major focus of this exercise is to give students practice in arriving at recommendations for how to intervene. The instructor sets a deadline for when students are to hand in their social histories. After grading them, the instructor reads to the class one or two (without naming the writers) that were particularly well done.

COMPETENCY NOTES

The following identifies where Educational Policy (EP) competencies and practice behaviors are discussed in the chapter.

EP 2.1.3c *Demonstrate effective oral and written communication in working with individuals, families, groups, organizations, communities, and colleagues.*

EP 2.1.10d *Collect, organize, and interpret client data.* (Chapter 5).

This chapter focuses on interviewing. Oral and written communication are discussed, along with collecting, organizing, and interpreting client data.

EP 2.1.3c *Demonstrate effective oral and written communication in working with individuals, families, groups, organizations, communities, and colleagues.* (p. 119).

Exercise 4.1 is designed to give students practice in introducing themselves to clients.

EP 2.1.3c *Demonstrate effective oral and written communication in working with individuals, families, groups, organizations, communities, and colleagues.* (p. 119).

Exercise 4.2 is designed to give students practice in introducing themselves to clients, while also stating the purpose of the interview.

EP 2.1.3c *Demonstrate effective oral and written communication in working with individuals, families, groups, organizations, communities, and colleagues.* (p. 121).

Exercise 4.3 is designed to give students practice in closing an interview.

EP 2.1.3c *Demonstrate effective oral and written communication in working with individuals, families, groups, organizations, communities, and colleagues.* (p. 122 and 124).

Exercise 4.4 is designed to give students practice in phrasing questions professionally and constructively.

EP 2.1.3c *Demonstrate effective oral and written communication in working with individuals, families, groups, organizations, communities, and colleagues.* (p. 125).

Exercise 4.5 is designed to give students practice in explaining to clients why they are taking notes during an interview.

EP 2.1.3c *Demonstrate effective oral and written communication in working with individuals, families, groups, organizations, communities, and colleagues.* (pp. 128–129).

This exercise is designed to give students practice in writing a social history.

CHAPTER 5

Social Work with Individuals: Counseling

EP 2.1.3c; 2.1.10a,b,c,d, e,f,g,j,l

Counseling someone with personal problems requires neither magic nor mysticism.[1] Training and experience in counseling are beneficial, but everyone has the potential to help others by listening and talking through their difficulties. Counseling with a beneficial outcome can be done by a friend, neighbor, or relative; the local barber, hairdresser, banker, and bartender; as well as by social workers, psychiatrists, psychologists, guidance counselors, and the clergy. This is not to say that everyone is effective at counseling. Professional people, because of their training and experience, have a higher probability of being effective, but competence and rapport, rather than degrees or certificates, are the keys to desirable outcomes. All of us at one time or another counsel others; the closer that counseling (including friend-to-friend counseling) approaches professional counseling, the higher is the probability of a successful outcome. This chapter will:

A. Describe how professional counseling should be done
B. Describe counseling from the worker's perspective
C. Provide guidelines on counseling clients
D. Describe counseling from the client's perspective
E. Describe clients' reactions to having a personal problem

COUNSELING FROM THE WORKER'S PERSPECTIVE

Simply stated, counseling consists of three phases: (1) building a relationship, (2) exploring problems in depth, and (3) exploring alternative solutions with the client and selecting a course of action. (These phases are components of the problem-solving approach, described in Chapter 1.) Successful counseling gradually proceeds from one phase to the next, with some overlap. While problems are explored, the relationship between counselor and client continues to develop in many cases, and problems are generally being examined in greater depth even as alternative solutions/strategies are explored. At the end of a series of counseling interviews, there is often the fourth phase of termination and evaluation. (Guidelines on the counselor's role in each of these phases are presented in the next section.)

---

[1]This chapter is adapted from three other chapters written by this author: (1) "How to Counsel," in *The Personal Problem Solver,* edited by Charles Zastrow and Dae H. Chang, © 1977, pp. 267–274. Adapted by permission of Prentice Hall, Inc., Englewood Cliffs, New Jersey. (2) "Self-Talk in Counseling," in *Talk to Yourself: Using the Power of Self-Talk,* © 1979, pp. 266–279. Adapted by permission of Prentice Hall, Inc., Englewood Cliffs, New Jersey. (3) "The Counseling Process," in *Introduction to Social Work and Social Welfare,* 7th ed. (Pacific Grove: Brooks/Cole, 2000), pp. 185–189.

Exhibit 5.1 Summary of Key Guidelines in Counseling Clients

1. Establish a working relationship:
   a. Introduce yourself and begin with a little small talk.
   b. Have client talk about his or her concerns by saying something like "Do you have some concerns you'd like to talk about today?"
   c. After the client discusses his or her concerns for 3 or 4 minutes, "connect" with the feelings by saying something like the following: "How are you feeling about this?" "This must really be difficult for you." "I sense you're feeling (such and such) about this."
2. Explore the client's concerns in depth.
3. Explore alternative solutions to the concerns with the client:
   a. In doing this, *first* ask the client what he or she has tried and what he or she is thinking about trying.
   b. Don't give advice. Instead, phrase your resolution options as suggestions, such as "Have you thought about trying ______?"

Before the initial interview, a counselor is often unaware of the concerns (or problems) new clients have. What should be the counselor's objective in the first interview? Simply put, to build a helping relationship and to begin exploring the client's problems. The third phase—examining alternative solutions—may or may not be arrived at in the initial interview. Every interview has a goal or an objective, and the counselor should use this goal to give focus to the interview.

On many occasions the first problem that clients present may not be the one that they are most concerned about. Clients sometimes initially present problems that they believe are more socially acceptable to test how objective, accepting, and helpful the counselor will be. I once had a client who mentioned six "presenting" problems before sharing the one she was most concerned about, which was the guilt she experienced over masturbating.

A format for workers to use when counseling others is presented in Exhibit 5.1.

COUNSELING FROM THE CLIENT'S PERSPECTIVE

The counseling process also can be conceptualized from the client's point of view. For counseling to be successful, clients must arrive at a progressive series of "self-talk" statements (that is, clients must arrive at having certain thoughts and beliefs). These self-talk stages are the following:

Stage 1 *Problem awareness:* "I have a problem."

Stage 2 *Relationship to counselor:* "I think this counselor has what it takes to help me."

Stage 3 *Motivation:* "I want to improve my situation and am willing to put forth the effort to do so."

Stage 4 *Conceptualizing the problem:* "My problem is not overwhelming but has specific components that can be changed."

Stage 5 *Exploration of resolution strategies:* "I see there are several courses of action that I might try in order to do something about my situation."

Stage 6 *Selection of a strategy:* "I think this approach might help, and I am willing to try it."

Stage 7 *Implementation:* "This approach is helping me."

Stage 8 *Termination and evaluation:* "Although this approach takes a lot of my time and effort, it's worth it."

This conceptualization of the counseling process presents a framework for assessing and improving the effectiveness of counseling. When counseling is not producing positive changes in clients, this framework helps identify reasons for the lack of progress. Once reasons are identified, changes can be made.

Exhibit 5.2 Strategies for Working with Hostile, Involuntary Clients

Significant numbers of involuntary clients are openly hostile in initial (and sometimes later) contacts with their assigned workers. What strategies can workers use to develop rapport with such clients and to motivate them to make positive changes? Six strategies are summarized here.

1. Treat such clients with respect. Workers need to understand that such clients probably do not want to discuss their situation with a social worker. Modeling respect can help calm clients and may then lead clients to show respect for the worker.
2. Allow clients to vent their unhappiness over being forced to see a worker. In many cases, it is useful to indicate, "It is understandable that you are upset about having to be here. If the tables were turned and I was in your situation, I wouldn't want to be here either. It may help us to begin by you summarizing your concerns about being forced to be here." Venting concerns can have a calming effect.
3. Allowing clients to vent concerns may also generate goals that the worker can help clients work toward. For example, if a client is seeing a child welfare worker because he physically abused his son while disciplining him, the worker can say, "I know you disciplined your child because you want the best for him—however, hurting a child is not acceptable. I wonder if we could explore some alternatives, like timeouts for Timmy and anger management techniques?" *A key ingredient in working with involuntary clients is establishing goals that are personally meaningful to them.* Workers should seek to limit involuntary goals to legal mandates and then seek to add realistic goals that clients desire. The strategy here is to search for common ground between the legal mandates and clients' personal goals. Often, redefining the problem in a way that adequately addresses the concerns of both client and referral source reduces the client's resistance and makes a workable agreement possible.
4. Use the "disarming" technique (described in greater detail in Chapter 7), which involves finding some truth in what involuntary clients are saying even when workers believe they are largely wrong, irrational, unfair, or unreasonable. There is always a grain of truth to be found. When workers disarm clients with this technique, clients may recognize that workers are offering respect; this may make them more cooperative. This technique also facilitates open (rather than defensive) communication.
5. Do not subject yourself to extensive verbal abuse. If hostile clients become overly verbally abusive, postpone the contact with something like "Sir, I'm treating you with respect, and in exchange I also have a right to be treated with respect. I see we presently are not getting anywhere. I will contact you tomorrow—by that time we will hopefully be better able to more calmly discuss this."
6. If clients continue to be verbally abusive in subsequent meetings, workers should meet with their immediate supervisor to discuss available options—such as referring the involuntary client back to the original referral source or transferring the case to another worker.

Stage 1: Problem Awareness

At this initial stage, clients must say to themselves, "I have a problem—I need to do something about my situation." If clients refuse to acknowledge that they have problems, they will not be motivated to change. In some areas of counseling (for example, working with problem drinkers), people have difficulty acknowledging that they have a problem. Involuntary clients (those forced to seek counseling) frequently deny that a problem exists. Social workers encounter involuntary clients in a variety of settings: protective services, corrections, certain public school settings, group homes, mental health facilities, nursing homes, and hospitals.

For people in denial, constructive changes are not likely to occur unless counselors find a way to convince them that there is a problem. Counselors focus on the denial by exploring why clients believe the problem doesn't exist and by gathering evidence to document the existence of the problem. Clients then need to be confronted (in a tactful manner) with this evidence. If after such a confrontation they are still in denial, counselors must accept that the client *owns* the problem, and there is little more that counselors can do constructively at this time, except perhaps to indicate they will be available in the future if the client wants to talk. (For additional strategies on how to work with hostile, involuntary clients, see Exhibit 5.2.)

EP 2.1.3c

At times someone who acknowledges a problem may prefer to try to resolve it without help from others. The person "owns" the problem and therefore has a right to decide how to handle it. If the person decides to work on it alone, the counselor should respect this decision but also indicate that he or she will be available in the future by saying something like "If you do decide later that you'd like to talk about it, my door is always open."

Exercise 5.1: Stating Goals for Involuntary Clients in Terms of Legal Mandates

Goal: This exercise gives you an opportunity to practice phrasing goals for involuntary clients in terms of legal mandates.

You are the facilitator for a group dynamics group. Group members are individuals who were arrested and convicted for driving while intoxicated. (The group has 2-hour meetings each week, for a period of 8 weeks.) Before the start of the first meeting, Mr. Ron Lewis comes to you and says he does not want to be here, that he will not participate in saying anything at the meetings, and that he does not have a drinking problem. He indicates his arrest occurred the first time he ever drove after having too much to drink.

You are aware that when the group sessions end you need to make a report (to the court) on each member who was ordered to attend. The minimal legal mandates for "passing" this group are as follows: (1) attendance at each meeting—unless a medical excuse is provided in writing, (2) staying awake during sessions, and (3) not interfering with the educational experiences of the other members. If any member fails to meet these minimal requirements, the court has the right to review the case of that person and impose a harsher sentence.

Write the exact words you would use to tell Mr. Lewis what he needs to do to "pass" this course. In your statement to him, you may want to add that he has the option not to attend but that if he exercises that option you will inform the court, and the court is likely to impose an even harsher sentence.

Stage 2: Relationship to Counselor

The client–counselor relationship operates in every stage of the counseling process. For counseling to be effective, clients must arrive at the point where their self-talk is, "I think this counselor has what it takes to help me." If clients think, "This counselor can't help me. I don't need a head shrinker. I don't trust this counselor," counseling will fail unless a more positive relationship is established. Throughout counseling, and especially in the initial meetings, counselors must be aware of and give attention to the kind of relationship that is developing with each client. Eriksen (1979) emphasized the importance of a helping relationship being formed with clients:

EP 2.1.3c

> The relationship that develops between worker and client is the very cornerstone of helping. Through the helping relationship, the client and worker come together to unblock communication that is preventing problem solving. . . .
>
> Through the vehicle of the helping relationship, the client can communicate to the worker what she thinks, knows and feels about her problem. This kind of in-depth communication, when reinforced by effective responses by her worker, will strengthen the helping relationship itself and will soon open the door to problem solving. (p. 54)

Exercise 5.2: Identifying a Client's Concerns about a Counselor

Goal: This exercise is designed to have you identify the concerns of a client about seeing a counselor and to then have you speculate about what the counselor needs to do to alleviate these concerns.

Step 1: Imagine that you are a client going to a counselor. What concerns would you have about the counselor? Consider such factors as level of expertise, empathy, arrogance, confidentiality, personal appearance, verbal communication, nonverbal communication, problem-solving skills, being nonjudgmental, and capacity to relate to you.

Step 2: Specify the qualities and characteristics that you would like your counselor to have.

Step 3: Specify what you would want your counselor to do to alleviate the concerns that you identified in step 1.

The following guidelines can help build a constructive relationship.

1. Try to establish a nonthreatening, comfortable atmosphere where clients feel safe to communicate fully their troubles while feeling accepted as individuals.
2. In initial contacts with clients, you need to "sell" yourself, not arrogantly but as a knowledgeable, understanding person who may be able to help and who wants to try.
3. Be calm. Do not laugh or express shock when clients begin to open up about their problems. Even subtle responses can lead clients to believe that you are not going to understand their difficulties, and they usually will stop discussing them. Remaining calm is not always easy. I remember one interview with a client who had brutally murdered his estranged partner by decapitating her. It took 45 minutes for the client to explain his reasons for killing her and to recount how he had planned and carried out this murder. The details were shocking, but I had to continue to take a professional approach, to remain calm, and to continue to maintain a nonthreatening atmosphere so that he would feel free to relate what occurred.
4. Be nonjudgmental, not moralistic. Show respect for clients' values and do not try to sell your own. Values that work for you may not be best for someone else in a different situation. For example, if a single client is pregnant, do not attempt to force your values on adoption or abortion on her. Let her decide on the course of action after a full examination of the problem and an exploration of alternative solutions.
5. View clients as equals. Rookie counselors sometimes make the mistake of thinking that because clients are sharing intimate secrets the counselor must be very important, and they end up constructing a superior-inferior relationship. If clients feel they are being treated as inferiors, they will be less motivated to reveal and discuss personal difficulties.
6. Use a shared vocabulary. This does not mean using the same slang words and the same accent as clients. If clients see counselors as artificial in their use of slang or accent, they may be seriously offended. Use words that clients understand and that are not offensive.

7. Your tone of voice should convey that you empathetically understand and care about the client's feelings.
8. Keep what clients say confidential. People unfortunately have nearly irresistible urges to share juicy secrets. If clients discover that their confidentiality has been violated, a working relationship can be quickly destroyed. (See the material on confidentiality in Chapter 2.)
9. If you counsel a relative or a friend, you are probably emotionally involved, and you may get upset or begin to argue. If that happens, it is almost always best to drop the subject immediately, as tactfully as possible. Perhaps after tempers cool, the subject can be brought up again, or perhaps you should refer the individual to someone else. When you find yourself becoming upset, further discussion will not be productive. Many professional counselors refuse to counsel friends or relatives because of the emotional involvement. A calm, detached perspective is needed to help clients objectively explore problems and alternative solutions.

Stage 3: Motivation

EP 2.1.10e

For counseling to be effective, clients must (sooner or later) conclude, "I want to improve my situation and am willing to put forth the effort to do so." Unless clients become motivated to change, constructive changes are not likely to occur. In counseling, the key variable in determining whether clients will improve their circumstances is their motivation to want to improve and put forth the necessary effort (Losoncy, 1977).

Exercise 5.3: Understanding Lack of Motivation

Goal: This exercise is designed to help you understand some of the reasons why certain people are not motivated to improve their life circumstances.

Step 1: Briefly summarize (using a coded name) three or four people you know who are making little effort to improve their life circumstances. An example is the following. Barth is 26 years old and very healthy, yet he has not worked for the last 18 months in a community that has a very low unemployment rate.

Step 2: Speculate about the reasons why these people are displaying little motivation to improve their life circumstances.

Step 3: If you were the counselor for these people, what would you do to seek to motivate these people to put forth effort to improve their life circumstances?

Counselors can best motivate discouraged or apathetic people by being encouraging. According to Losoncy (1977), encouraging people have the following characteristics:

1. Complete acceptance of the discouraged person, but not of the dysfunctional behavior that has to be changed. Convey "I accept you exactly as you are, with no conditions attached."
2. A nonblaming attitude, so the discouraged person no longer feels a need to lie, pretend, or wear a mask.
3. Empathy. Be aware of and to some extent feel what the discouraged person is feeling. Empathy occurs, as described by Kadushin (1972), when a counselor

   > *feels* with the client rather than for him. Feeling *for* the client would be a sympathetic rather than an empathic response. Somebody once said that if you have a capacity for empathy you feel squat when you see a squat vase and feel tall when you look at a tall vase. Empathy is entering imaginatively into the inner life of someone else. It is not enough simply to be empathically understanding; one needs to communicate to the client that one accurately perceives and feels his situation. (, 52)

4. Genuine interest in the client's progress; convey that the client is an important, worthwhile person.
5. Confidence in the capacity of the discouraged person to improve.
6. Sincere enthusiasm about the discouraged person's interests, ideas, and risk-taking actions. Discouraged people need to believe in themselves, and they also need an encouraging person who conveys that they are important, worthwhile persons.
7. Nonjudgmental listening, so the discouraged person's real thoughts and feelings can be expressed freely, without fear of censure.
8. The ability to notice (reward) every small instance of progress (particularly during the beginning of the relationship) and to notice (reward) positives about the client. Even small compliments about something unrelated to the counseling goals go a long way toward motivating clients.
9. The ability to motivate. Motivating a discouraged person takes a long, long time. Discouraged people often have a long history of failures. Reversing this trend requires time. Listen to and understand this person as fully as possible.
10. A sincere belief in the discouraged person's ability to find a purpose in life.
11. The ability to allow the person to take risks without passing judgment.
12. The ability to reinforce the person's *efforts*. The important thing is that people try, not that they necessarily succeed. As long as they are making efforts to improve, there is hope.
13. The ability to help the discouraged person see the falseness and negative consequences of self-defeating statements (such as "I'm a failure"). Every person has skills and deficiencies, and every person should be encouraged to build strengths and lessen weaknesses.
14. The capacity to recognize that all that you can do is give your best effort in trying to motivate the person. Success is not guaranteed. A counselor with no hope of motivating is no longer effective.
15. The skill to look for the client's uniquenesses and strengths. These should be communicated so that clients begin to realize they are special and worthwhile. This process leads to a sense of improved self-worth and gives them courage to take risks and change.
16. Awareness of the negative consequences of overdependency. As clients begin to take risks and make constructive changes, counselors should start to help them develop self-encouragement, in which they are encouraged to make and trust their own decisions and to take more risks.

(*Note:* These guidelines on motivating clients are also useful in building counseling relationships with them.)

Exhibit 5.3 Motivational Interviewing

Admitting the existence of a problem is difficult because clients often (erroneously) perceive themselves as weak, sinful, or irresponsible. Also, recognition brings with it an acknowledgment that change is inevitable. Clients often mourn the loss of that which must be changed. For example, alcoholics mourn the loss of their drinking because their social activities are centered around it. Alcohol has become their "best Friend," which they do not want to give up. Denial of a drinking problem helps them to "keep their best friend." Constructive changes are not apt to occur for people in denial, unless counselors find a way to convince them that the problem exists.

Researchers have found that people go through a process when they make positive changes, and this process can be conceptualized in a series of steps or stages. The Stages of Change Model, part of the Transtheoretical Model of Change, outlines the process of change that individuals go through when they successfully make changes in their lives (Prochaska & DiClemente, 1982).

Brief Definition of Each Stage of Change

Stage	Basic Definition
1. PRECONTEMPLATION	A person is not seeing a need for a lifestyle change.
2. CONTEMPLATION	A person is considering making a change but has not decided yet.
3. PREPARATION	A person has decided to make changes and is considering how to make them.
4. ACTION	A person is actively doing something to change.
5. MAINTENANCE	A person is working to maintain the change or new lifestyle. There may be some temptations to return to the former behavior or even small relapses.

Motivational interviewing is designed to help clients in stages 1, 2, or 3 to move toward stages 4 and 5. The Stages of Change are dynamic—a person may move through them once or recycle through them several times before reaching success and maintaining a behavior change over time. Individuals may move back and forth between stages on any single issue or may simultaneously be in different stages of change for two or more behaviors.

Motivational interviewing is not technique but rather a style, a facilitative way of being with people. This facilitative style encourages self-motivation for positive change within individuals. The development of motivational interviewing in the early 1980s by William R. Miller and Stephen Rollnick (1981) was out of response to substance abusers in treatment who had high dropout rates, high relapse rates, and poor outcomes overall in treatment. This lack of progress in treatment portrayed the individuals as resistant and unmotivated to change. The question of why people *do* change became the foundation of developing motivational interviewing. Instead of dismissing challenging clients as unmotivated and unable to change, motivational interviewing skills allow social workers to become equipped with the skills to enhance motivation and to help clients become active in the change process. Motivational interviewing is now used with a variety of clients who are in the precontemplation stage or in the contemplation stage—such as clients who deny they have such problems as an eating disorder, a gambling addiction, a dysfunctional sexual addiction, an anger management challenge, or interpersonal difficulties.

The principles of motivational interviewing include the following:

- **Express Empathy:** Empathy involves seeing the world through the client's eyes, thinking about things as the client thinks about things, feeling things as the client feels them, and sharing in the client's experiences. Expression of empathy is critical to the motivational interviewing process. When clients feel that they are understood, they are more apt to open up and share their own experiences. Having clients share experiences in depth allows the social worker to assess when and where they need support and what barriers there may be to the change-planning process. When clients perceive the social worker as empathetic, they become more open to gentle challenges by the social worker about lifestyle changes. Clients become more comfortable openly examining their ambivalence about change and less likely to defend their ideas of possible denial. The social worker's accurate understanding of the client's experience facilitates change. The following is an example of an empathic statement to a client who acknowledges he has a challenge, at times, of getting into trouble associated with his drinking: "I applaud you for looking at whether you need to make some changes about your drinking patterns. Looking at how much one drinks can be very scary."
- **Roll with Resistance:** In motivational interviewing, the social worker does not fight resistance but "rolls with it." Statements made by the client demonstrating resistance are not challenged. Instead, the social worker uses the client's momentum to further explore the client's views. Using this approach, resistance tends to be decreased rather than increased, as the client is not being reinforced for being argumentative to the social worker's statement. Motivational interviewing encourages clients to develop their own solutions to problems that they themselves have defined. Thus, there is no real power in the client–social worker

(continued)

Exhibit 5.3 *(continued)*

relationship for the client to challenge. In exploring client concerns, social workers invite new ways of thinking about things, but do not impose their ways of thinking onto the clients.

A useful technique when a client is resisting change is using a reflection, where the social worker is responding to resistance with nonresistance by repeating the client's statement in a neutral form. An example of this would be if a social worker says to a client, "I would like to talk about when you spent a night in jail after receiving a citation for driving while intoxicated." The client responds, "What's to talk about? The police and you have already made your mind up that it was my fault." The social worker would respond with the reflection, "So you feel like your opinion doesn't matter?" instead of responding with a statement reflecting the facts documented in the police report. Rolling with resistance avoids confrontations with clients on issues they have.

- **Develop Discrepancy:** Motivation for change occurs when people perceive a discrepancy between where they are and where they want to be, Social workers help clients examine the discrepancies between where their current behavior is at and what they have identified as their future goals. When clients perceive that their current behaviors are not leading toward some important future goal, they become more motivated to make life changes. Social workers respectfully and gently help clients gain insight that some of their current ways of living may lead them away from, instead of toward, their goals.

  If a client states he has a problem with drinking alcoholic beverages but is uncertain if he is ready to commit to no longer drinking, the social worker can create a gap between where he is currently at and where he wants to be by the following types of statements/questions:

  "What will your life be like 10 years from now if you continue to use?

  "How do you believe your life will improve if you stop drinking?"

  "Tell me some of the good things, and less good things, about your drinking."

  "What was your life like before you started having problems with drinking?"

Support Self-Efficacy: Self-efficacy is the belief that one is capable of performing in a certain manner to attain certain goals. A client's belief that change is possible is an important motivator to succeeding in making a change. As clients are held responsible for choosing and carrying out actions to change in the motivational interviewing approach, the social worker focuses his or her effort on helping the clients stay motivated. Supporting client's sense of self-efficacy is a great way of helping individuals stay motivated. The belief that there is no right way to change can help develop a belief within an individual that he or she can make a change. The social worker wants the client to develop the argument for change. Change should be derived from the individual not from outside the individual. One technique for helping a client assess his or her willingness to change is the following "Readiness to Change Ruler."

On the following scale (show client) from 1 to 5, what number best reflects how ready you are <u>at the present time</u> to change your (the behavior)?

Circle One

Not Ready to Change	Thinking of Changing	Undecided/ Uncertain	Somewhat Ready	Very Ready to Change
1	2	3	4	5

The social worker needs to operate at the same level of change where the client is, in order to minimize resistance and gain cooperation.

For example, if a client states he is "Somewhat Ready" to give up drinking alcoholic beverages, the social worker may gently inquire, "What will it take for you to be ready to give up drinking?"

- Conveying Hope: Finding and nurturing hope with a client is a key to recovering. Conveying hope includes not just optimism, but also conveying the belief that the client has the capacity to conquer his or her challenges.
- Supportive Relationships: A common component of recovery is the presence of others who believe in the person's potential to recover. Therefore, the social worker seeks to foster supportive relationships for the client with friends, family, and others in the community. For many alcoholics, Alcoholics Anonymous (AA) assists in being a critical source of support. AA members have experienced similar difficulties, and are on a similar journey of recovery. Reciprocal relationships and mutual support networks enhance the alcoholic's self-esteem and recovery journey.
- Empowerment: The social worker seeks to convey to the client that he or she has the resources (internal strengths and social support networks) to conquer his or her challenges.
- Coping Strategies: The social worker facilitates the client in developing coping and problem-solving skills to resolve other personal and family challenges that the client is facing.
- Meaning in Life: Developing a sense of meaning and overall purpose is important for sustaining the recovery process. The social worker facilitates the client in setting (and achieving) short and long-term goals that are personally meaningful and gratifying to him or her.

EP 2.1.1b

Stage 4: Conceptualizing the Problem

For counseling to be effective, clients need to say to themselves, "My problem is not overwhelming but has specific components that can be changed." Many clients view their situation as so complex that they become highly anxious and emotional and cannot see that their problem is solvable.

Exercise 5.4: Understanding the Tendency to Awfulize

Goal: This exercise is designed to show you that most of us have a tendency to awfulize when bad events happen to us.

Step 1: Specify your awfulizing thoughts when a bad event happened to you, such as getting a traffic ticket, someone breaking up with you, a pet dying, or failing a test. For example, when someone ends a romantic relationship, we may awfulize by telling ourselves such things as the following: "That jerk—he/she just used me!" "My life is ruined—I'll never find anyone else as special to love me again." "That jerk—s/he probably found someone else to love—I'll find out who it is, and make both their lives miserable." "This is absolutely the worst thing that could happen to me—life is no longer worth living."

Step 2: Awfulizing thoughts lead us to feel bad, hurt, or angry. When we have severe negative emotions, we focus on our emotions, preventing ourselves from focusing on realistically problem-solving our issues or challenges. Specify how your awfulizing thoughts in step 1 interfered with your capacities to problem-solve your issues or challenges.

Several years ago I counseled a teenager who had missed her menstrual period for 3 months and was so overwhelmingly afraid of being pregnant that she was unable to figure out on her own that the first step was to have a pregnancy test. (When she finally took the test, the results showed she was not pregnant.) To help clients conceptualize their problems, counselors need to explore the problems together in depth with clients. The following guidelines focus on how to explore problems in depth:

1. Many rookie counselors suggest solutions as soon as a problem is identified, without exploring the problem area in depth. For example, an advocate of abortion may advise this solution as soon as a single female reveals that she is pregnant, without taking the time to discover whether she is strongly opposed to abortion, really wants a baby, or intends to marry soon.
2. In exploring problems in depth, counselor and client need to examine the severity of the problem, how long the problem has existed, its causes, how the client feels about the problem, and the client's physical and mental coping capacities and strengths before exploring alternative solutions. For example, the counselor and a single pregnant client need to explore the following: How does she feel about being pregnant? Has she seen a doctor? About how long has she been pregnant? Do her parents know? What are their feelings and concerns if they know? Has she informed her sexual partner? What are his feelings and concerns if he knows? What does she feel is the most urgent situation to deal with first? Answers to such questions will determine the future direction of counseling.

3. Once a problem area is identified, usually a number of subproblems can be identified. Explore all of them—for example, deciding how to tell the father, obtaining medical care, obtaining funds for medical expenses, deciding where to live, deciding whether to leave school or stop working during the pregnancy, deciding whether to terminate the pregnancy, and making plans for after the child is delivered or the pregnancy is terminated.
4. In a multiproblem situation, the best way to decide which problem to handle first is to ask clients which problem they perceive as most pressing. If that problem can be solved, explore it in depth and together develop a solution strategy. Problem-solving success will increase clients' confidence in the counselor and thereby further solidify the relationship.
5. Convey empathy, not sympathy. Empathy is the capacity to show that you are aware of and can to some extent feel what the client is saying. Sympathy is also a sharing of feelings, but it offers pity. The difference is subtle. Empathy facilitates problem solving; sympathy is often problem prolonging. Giving sympathy usually causes clients to dwell on their emotions without taking action to improve the situation.

   Benjamin (1974) further described how to be empathic:

   > The empathic interviewer tries as much as he possibly can to feel his way into the internal frame of reference of the interviewee and to see the world through the latter's eyes as if that world were his own world. The words "as if" are crucial for although the interviewer is empathic, he never loses sight of the fact that he remains his own self. Knowing all the time that he is distinct from the interviewee, he tries to feel his way about in the internal world of thought and feeling of the other in order to come as close to him as possible, to understand with him as much as possible. (p. 47)[2]

   The difference between sympathy and empathy is apparent in responses to the following statement by a client whose male friend recently ended their 3-year relationship: "How could he do this to me, after all I've done for him? He's hurt me so much."

   Sympathetic response: "He's such a schnook! I don't see how you can ever face the world. You're probably going to be miserable for a long, long time."

   Empathic response: "I know ending this relationship hurts deeply. Part of your emotional pain appears to be related to your confusion as to why he wants to end the relationship. Have you discussed this with him?"

   Keith-Lucas (1972) gave a cogent example separating sympathy, pity, and empathy:

   > Consider three reactions to someone who has told us that he strongly dislikes his wife. The sympathetic person would say, "Oh, I know exactly how you feel. I can't bear mine, either." The two of them would comfort each other but nothing would come of it. The pitying person would commiserate but add that he himself was most happily married. Why doesn't the other come to dinner sometime and see what married life could be like? This, in most cases, would only increase the frustration of the unhappy husband and help him to put his problem further outside himself, on to his wife or his lack of good fortune. The empathetic person might say something like, "That must be terribly difficult for you. What do you think might possibly help?" and only the empathetic person, of the three, would have said anything that would lead to some change in the situation. (pp. 80–81)

6. "Trust your guts." The most important tool counselors have is their feelings and perceptions. Counselors should continually strive to place themselves in their client's situation (with the client's values and pressures). To use the earlier example,

[2]Alfred Benjamin, *Helping Interview: With Case Illustrations,* 3E. © 1987 Wadsworth, a part of Cengage Learning, Inc. Reproduced by permission. www.cengage.com/permissions

if the client is 17 years old, single, and pregnant, and has parents who are very critical of the situation and who want her to have an abortion, a competent counselor will continually strive to feel what the client is feeling and to perceive the world from her perspective, with her goals, difficulties, pressures, and values. We are never 100% accurate in placing ourselves in our client's situation, but 70 to 80% is usually sufficient to gain an awareness of the client's pressures, problems, and perspectives. This information is very useful in determining what additional areas need to be explored, what she should say to her parents, and what might be possible solutions. Stated somewhat differently, counselors should wonder, "What is this person trying to tell me, and how can I make it clear that I understand not only intellectually but empathically?"

7. When you believe that the client has touched on an important area of concern, further communication can be encouraged in the following ways:
   - Show interest nonverbally.
   - Pause. Rookie counselors usually become anxious when there is a pause and hasten to say something, anything, to have conversation continue. This is usually a mistake, especially when it leads to a change in an important topic. Pauses give clients time to think about the important area of concern, so they can explore it thoughtfully.
   - Probe neutrally. "Could you tell me more about it?" "How do you feel about that?" "I'm not sure I understand what you have in mind."
   - Summarize what the client is saying. "During this past hour you made a number of critical comments about your spouse; it sounds as if some things about your marriage are making you unhappy."
   - Reflect feelings. "You seem angry," or "You appear to be depressed about that."

EP 2.1.10b

Exercise 5.5: Reflecting Feelings and Meanings

Goal: This exercise is designed to give you the opportunity to practice the skill of reflecting feelings and meanings.

1. You are a social worker at a social service agency. Ann Marie Caleb states, "My life is ruined. John broke up with me 2 days ago. I'll never find anyone else as good for me as him. I am so confused as to why he broke up. I guess I'm not a lovable person. I thought we would get married in a couple of years. Life is no longer worth living." Write the words you would say in reflecting the feelings and meanings in what Ms. Caleb has said.

2. You are a counselor at a campus counseling center. A 20-year-old female student, Ellen Megan states, "I'm flunking biology. It is a required course that I must pass. I'm so stupid. I study and study for that course, but just can't get a passing grade. I should drop out of college right now—at least that way I'd save my parents a lot of money. Nothing is going well for me. No one wants to date me. I have no money, and now I'm flunking out of college." Write the words you would say in reflecting the feelings and meanings in what Ms. Megan has said.

3. You are a social worker at a Planned Parenthood clinic. You have just informed a client, Peggy Putnam, that she has a positive test for being pregnant. Ms. Putnam begins to cry, and says, "My life plans just went 'poof.' I don't want an abortion as it is immoral. I'm no longer dating the guy who is the father of this child—he's now dating my former best friend. The worst of it is I'll never be able to go to college. How could I be so stupid to get pregnant! I don't know how to take care of a baby. No one will ever want to date a single mother with a young child." Write the words you would say in reflecting the feelings and meanings in what Ms. Putnam has said.

4. You are a social worker for a social service agency. A 52-year-old client, Tom Cherwenka, states, "I have really screwed up. Last week I got arrested for drunk driving. When my wife found out, she said it was the 'last straw' and she has now contacted an attorney to draw up divorce papers. My two adult sons have told me they are really embarrassed about what I did. Life without my wife will really be empty and lonely. I'm so confused about what I can now do to put my life back together. I'm a real 'loser'!" Write the words you would say in reflecting the feeling and meaning in what Mr. Cherwenka has said.

5. You are a social worker at a hospice program. A 22-year-old male, Gregorio Maldonado, is reflecting on his loss: "My mother was my best friend. I so wanted to make her proud of me. When she was killed in that car accident, part of me also died. My upcoming graduation from college now seems insignificant. I'm without a job, have little money, and have no one to share my thoughts and feelings with. You will never know how much her death has affected me. I can hardly sleep at night." Write the words you would say in reflecting the feelings and meanings in what Mr. Maldonado has said.

8. Approach socially unacceptable topics tactfully. Tact is an essential quality of competent counselors. Try not to ask a question in such a way that the answer puts the respondent in an embarrassing position. Suppose you have good relationship with a teenage client and you have reason to suspect that this person has concerns about masturbating. How would you tactfully bring up the subject? One possible approach is "When I was your age, I had a number of concerns about masturbating. That was unfortunate. Most teenagers masturbate, and many have strong feelings of guilt or shame about it. Although masturbation has been stigmatized, it is a natural outlet for sexual feelings and is not harmful. In fact, most sex therapists recommend masturbating as a way to release sexual tensions. I'm wondering if you have some questions or concerns about masturbation that would be helpful for us to discuss?" Informing the youth that you also had concerns about this subject personalizes it and informs the teenager that you successfully dealt with concerns similar to those he or she is currently facing. This self-disclosing process fosters communication and relationship building.

EP 2.1.3c

Exercise 5.6: Exploring a Socially Unacceptable Topic with Tact

Goal: This exercise is designed to give you an opportunity to phrase tactfully a question that is designed to have a client give you information about a socially unacceptable topic.

1. You are a social worker at a social service agency. A client has told you that he has been unemployed for the past 6 months, that his girlfriend recently broke up with him (the loss of whom he deeply regrets), and that he is so depressed that he sometimes sleeps 12 to 13 hours a night. He also says that he drinks too much and that his future looks really bleak. Write the words you would use in inquiring whether he sometimes thinks about ending his life.

2. You are a social worker at a social service agency. You have a client who rather frequently expels intestinal gas. You and the other staff at the agency find such behavior to be obnoxious. The person has been unemployed for the past 3 months, and in the past 14 years (the client is age 34), he has frequently been fired from janitorial jobs. You wonder if his frequent expulsion of intestinal gas may be a factor in causing his spotty work history. Write the words you would use in having him look at whether his obnoxious habit is a reason for his being discharged from jobs and a reason he has difficulty in now being hired.

A question occasionally arises about when counselors should self-disclose by sharing past experiences. An advantage of self-disclosure is that the client will then think you have expertise on the issue (because you have dealt with an issue similar to what the client is dealing with). The client is also likely to feel that you will be understanding of his or her feelings and concerns about the issue—because you too have "lived" the issue. A disadvantage of self-disclosing is that the client may come to view the counselor as needing counseling. (The client is particularly likely to reach this conclusion if counselors reveal, by nonverbal and verbal communication, that they still have unresolved issues surrounding these experiences.) Also, when working in certain settings (for example, drug treatment centers), a statement that the counselor continues to engage in behaviors that the client needs to change (such as getting drunk or smoking pot) may be used as an excuse for the client to continue problematic behaviors. A good rule to follow in deciding whether to self-disclose is to first ask yourself, "If I share these personal experiences, are they likely to have a constructive effect?" If you are unable to objectively specify a possibly beneficial effect, you should not self-disclose the experience.

9. When pointing out clients' limitations, mention and compliment them on their assets. Mentioning a limitation causes clients to feel that something is being laid bare or taken away. A compliment in another area gives something back.
10. Watch for nonverbal cues. Competent counselors generally use such cues to identify when a sensitive subject is being touched on because clients display their anxiety by changes in tone of voice, fidgeting, tightening facial or neck muscles, yawning, assuming a stiff posture, or flushing. Some counselors even claim they can tell when clients become anxious by observing when their pupils dilate.
11. Be honest. An untruth always runs the risk of being discovered. If that happens, your client's confidence in you will be seriously damaged, and your relationship may be seriously jeopardized. If a client asks an important question that you cannot answer, it is usually best to say, "Unfortunately I don't know the answer, but let me check into it and I'll let you know by ___ (a specified time)." Being honest goes

beyond not telling lies. Counselors should always tactfully inform clients of shortcomings that they really need to attend to. For example, if an individual is being fired from jobs because of poor grooming habits, this fact needs to be brought to his or her attention. Or if a trainee's relationship skills and intervention capacities are not suited for the helping profession, that person needs to be "counseled out" in the interest of clients and in the trainee's own best interests.

12. Listen attentively. View clients' words from their perspective, not from yours. Unfortunately, some counselors, caught up in their own interests and concerns, don't always tune out these personal thoughts while clients are speaking. This guideline seems simple, but it is not always easy to follow. Kadushin (1972) expanded on why listening attentively is difficult:

> The nature of spoken communication presents a special hazard, seducing the interviewer into an easy nonlistening. The hazard lies in the great discrepancy between the number of words that are normally spoken in one minute and the number of words that can be absorbed in that time. Thought is much more rapid than speech. The average rate of spoken speech is about 125 words per minute. We can read and understand an average of 300–500 words per minute. There is, then, a considerable amount of dead time in spoken communication, during which the listener's mind can easily become distracted. The listener starts talking internally to take up the slack in time. Listening to the internal monologue may go on side by side with listening to the external dialogue. More often, however, it goes on at the expense of listening to the external dialogue. The interviewer becomes lost in some private reverie—planning, musing, dreaming. (p. 188)[3]

Kadushin (1972) gave the following suggestions on how to listen effectively:

> Rather than becoming preoccupied as a consequence of the availability of the spare time between the slow spoken words, the good interviewer exploits this time in the service of more effective listening. The listener keeps focused on the interviewee but uses the time made available to the mind by slowness of speech to move rapidly back and forth along the path of the interview, testing, connecting, questioning: How does what I am hearing now relate to what I heard before? How does it modify what I heard before? How does it conflict with it, support it, make it more understandable? What can I anticipate hearing next? What do I miss hearing that needs asking about? What is he trying to tell me? What other meanings can the message have? What are his motives in telling me this? (p. 190)[4]

Stage 5: Exploration of Resolution Strategies

After (or sometimes while) a problem is explored in depth, the next step is to consider alternative solutions. In exploring solutions, it is almost always best for counselors to begin by asking something like "Have you thought about ways to resolve this?" Clients generally have been aware for some time that they have a problem. In most cases, they have already tried to resolve the problem. Therefore, this question often elicits alternatives that the client has tried but that have not worked. They can then be discarded. In addition, this question can elicit from the client high-quality alternatives that the counselor has not thought of and that may well work for the client. Merits, shortcomings, and consequences of the client's alternatives should be tactfully and thoroughly examined. Counselors should then mention other potential solutions, and their merits and shortcomings should also be examined.

---

[3]Alfred Kadushin, *The Social Work Interview*. Copyright © 1972 Columbia University Press, New York. Reprinted by permission.

[4]Alfred Kadushin, *The Social Work Interview*. Copyright © 1972 Columbia University Press, New York. Reprinted by permission.

EP 2.1.10j

Each client is unique, and so are his or her problems. What works for one client may not work for another. Abortion, for example, may be compatible with one client's values and circumstances but undesirable for another client. If counseling is going to be effective, the client needs to say, "I see there are several courses of action that I might take to try to do something about my situation." Unless clients realize that resolution strategies exist, counseling is likely to fail.

Exercise 5.7: Generating Options and Resolution Strategies

Goal: This exercise is designed to give you practice in generating options and resolution strategies.

(The more options we can generate and the more creative we can be in generating options, the higher is the probability of high-quality options being available for the client to consider.) You are a social worker at a social service agency. A 28-year-old woman has arrangements made to be married in 5 weeks. She now has "cold feet at the altar," as she indicates she is confused about whether (1) she really loves the person she is engaged to, (2) she should call off the wedding, and (3) she ever wants to be married. Write down all the options that would be worthwhile for this woman to consider regarding this dilemma.

Stage 6: Selection of a Strategy

After counselor and client discuss the probable effects and consequences of possible resolution strategies, it is essential that the client conclude, "I think this approach might help me, and I am willing to try it." If a client is indecisive or refuses to commit to a course of action, constructive change will not occur. For example, if a client says, "I know I have a drinking problem, but I am unwilling to take any action to cut down on my drinking," counseling probably will not be successful.

Clients usually have the right to self-determination—that is, to choose the course of action they want to take. The counselor's role is to help clients clarify and understand the likely consequences of each alternative. It is generally not the counselor's role to give advice or choose the alternative. If the counselor selects the alternative, there are two possible outcomes: (1) The alternative may prove to be undesirable, in which case the client will blame the counselor for the advice and the future relationship will be seriously hampered. (2) The alternative may prove to be beneficial. This immediate outcome is desirable, but clients will not "own" the result—*they* didn't make the outcome happen, the counselor did. The client will then become overly dependent on the counselor, seeking his or her advice far too often and becoming reluctant to make decisions on his or her own. In practice, most courses of action have both desirable and undesirable consequences. An unmarried mother who keeps her child may receive considerable gratification from being with and raising the child, but she may also blame the counselor for her long-term financial hardship and isolated social life.

Not giving advice does not mean that counselors should not suggest alternatives. On the contrary, it is the counselor's responsibility to suggest and explore all viable alternatives with clients. A good rule to follow is that when you believe a client should take a certain course of action, phrase it as a suggestion, "Have you thought about . . .?" rather than as advice, "I think you should . . ."

Clients' rights to self-determination should be taken away only if the selected course of action will seriously hurt others or themselves. For example, if it is highly probable that a parent will continue to abuse a child or if the client attempts to take her own life, counselor intervention is suggested. For most situations, however, clients have the right to select their resolutions, even when counselors believe that another alternative would be a better course of action. Frequently, clients are in a better position to know what is best for their situation, and if it doesn't work out, they should not be deprived of the opportunity to learn from the mistake.

Stage 7: Implementation

Counseling will be successful only if clients follow through on their commitment to try a resolution approach and then conclude, "This approach is beginning to help me." If clients follow through on the commitment but instead conclude, "I don't believe this approach is helping me," counseling is again failing. If this occurs, counselor and client need to examine the reasons for no gain and perhaps try another strategy. Here are some guidelines for implementing a resolution approach:

1. Attempt to form an explicit, realistic "contract" with clients. When clients do select an alternative, they should clearly understand the goals, what tasks need to be carried out, how to do the tasks, and who will carry out each task. Frequently, it is desirable to write a "contract" for future reference, with a time limit set for accomplishing each task. For example, if an unmarried mother decides to keep her child and now needs to make long-range financial plans, this goal should be understood and specific courses of action decided on—seeking public assistance, seeking support from the alleged father, securing an apartment within her budget, and so on. Furthermore, who will do what task within a set time limit should be specified.

   Negotiating a contract (and perhaps renegotiating it in future interviews) brings a focus to the interview. Client and counselor are less likely to get sidetracked by extraneous issues, and the interview's productivity can be sustained.

   If the client and the counselor differ in their expectations of desired goals or in their expectations of who will do what tasks, the contract negotiation process forces client and counselor to discuss and, one hopes, resolve their differences. For additional material on contracts, see Exhibit 5.4.
2. Counseling is done *with* clients, not *to* or *for* them. Clients should have the responsibility of doing many of the tasks necessary to improve the situation. Here is a good rule to follow: Clients should take responsibility for those tasks that they can carry out, and counselors should attempt to do only those that are beyond the clients' capacities. Doing things *for* clients, such as giving advice, risks creating a dependency relationship. Furthermore, succeeding at tasks leads to personal growth and prepares clients for future responsibilities.

EP 2.1.3c

3. Role-play certain tasks that clients lack confidence or experience in carrying out. For example, if a pregnant single woman wants help in telling her male friend about the pregnancy, role-playing will assist her in selecting words and the strategy for informing him. The counselor can first play the woman's role and model an approach, with the woman playing the male role. Then the roles are reversed so the woman can practice telling her male friend.

Exercise 5.8: Contracting

Goal: This exercise is designed to assist you in learning how to write behavioral contracts.

Step 1: Specify a behavior of yours that you know you should change, such as drinking to excess, procrastinating in writing papers, or lack of exercising.

Exhibit 5.4 Guidelines for Formulating a Contract

Contracts in social work practice specify goals and the tasks to be performed to accomplish them. In addition, contracts set deadlines for completing tasks and identify rewards for successful task completion. Contracts also specify consequences for unsuccessful completion of tasks. A contract is, therefore, an agreement between a social worker and one or more clients in their joint efforts to achieve specified outcomes. Formulating an explicit contract is directly related to a positive outcome for clients (Hepworth & Larsen, 1993, p. 365).

A contract, in outline format, should contain the following components:

1. Goals to be accomplished (ranked in order of priority)
2. Tasks to be accomplished by the client and by the worker (These tasks must be directly related to accomplishing the goals, so that accomplishing the tasks results in successfully meeting the goals.)
3. Time frame for completing the tasks
4. Means of monitoring progress in task completion and goal accomplishment
5. Rewards for the client if the terms of the contract are met
6. Adverse consequences to the client upon nonfulfillment of the terms of the contract

Some workers prefer written contracts, and others prefer oral contracts. A written contract has the advantage of emphasizing the commitment to the contract by both worker and client, and it also minimizes the risks of misunderstandings. An oral contract avoids the sterility of a written contract. Research comparing the effectiveness of written versus oral contracts shows that oral contracts are generally as effective as written contracts with regard to meeting goals (Hepworth & Larsen, 1993, p. 381). If workers use an oral contract, they should still record the essential elements of the contract in their notes for future reference.

The most difficult element in an effective contract is formulating goals. Goals specify what the client wishes to accomplish and should directly relate to the needs, wants, or problems being encountered by the client. Goals serve the following important functions:

1. Goals ensure that workers and clients are in agreement about the objectives to be accomplished.
2. Goals provide direction to the helping process and thereby reduce needless wandering.
3. Goals guide selection of appropriate tasks (and interventions) to achieve the objectives.
4. Goals serve as outcome criteria in evaluating the extent to which the tasks (and interventions) are succeeding.

Useful guidelines when setting goals include the following:

1. *Goals must relate to the desired end results sought by the client.* Clients must believe that accomplishing the selected goals will enhance their well-being. Therefore, workers need to integrally involve clients in selecting and specifying the goals.
2. *Goals should be stated in specific and measurable terms.* Nebulous goals (such as "Client gaining increased control over his emotions") are not sufficient and often lead the client to "drift" or wander in the helping process. A specific goal (such as "The client will express his angry feelings with his mother in an assertive rather than an aggressive manner when they are having conflicts") is more effective. In addition, it is also measurable, whereas a nebulous goal is not. The client's mother (and others) can monitor the number of times, over a specified period, that the client expresses his angry feelings assertively rather than aggressively. Clients tend to define goals nebulously, so it is important for workers to help clients state goals that are both specific and measurable.
3. *Goals should be feasible.* Unachievable goals set clients up for failure, which then leads to disappointment, disillusionment, and a sense of defeat. It is vital that the goals chosen can be accomplished. For clients with grandiose tendencies, it is important for workers to assist them (tactfully) in lowering their expectations to what can reasonably be attained.

   When arriving at feasible goal statements with clients, workers should agree only to assist them in working toward goals for which the workers have the requisite skills and knowledge. If the goal is beyond the worker's competence (for example, assisting the client in overcoming a complex sexual dysfunction), the worker should refer the client to a more appropriate resource.

Once clients settle on their goals, the final step in negotiating goal statements is to assign priorities to the goals. This ensures that the initial change efforts are directed to the goal that is most important to the client.

The following scenario provides an example. First, background information: Ray and Klareen Norwood have been married for 3 years. They seek counseling because Klareen is increasingly afraid of Ray's angry outbursts. Ray is physically and verbally abusive to her when he is angry. He has not hit Klareen yet, but she is afraid that Ray's escalating aggressiveness will lead to her being battered. Klareen is seriously considering separating from Ray. She has already contacted an attorney to discuss divorce proceedings. Both partners, however, state that they want to maintain the marriage.

(continued)

Exhibit 5.4 *(continued)*

At the end of the second meeting with the Norwoods, this contract is prepared:

Goals: (a) Ray will cease being physically abusive to Klareen and will reduce by at least two-thirds his verbal abuse incidents over the next 30 days. (This goal is rated number one.) (b) The Norwoods will begin discussing, at some future date, raising a family. (This goal is rated number two.) The Norwoods both agree to put off further discussion at this time because Klareen says she first needs to decide whether she wants to remain in the marriage.

Tasks of the participants: Worker: The social worker will instruct Ray in the following anger control techniques: (1) Expressing his angry feelings to Klareen in an assertive rather than aggressive manner (see Module 2). (2) Reducing the intensity and frequency of his outbursts by countering his negative and irrational self-talk with rational and positive self-talk (Module 1). (3) Countering his feelings of anger with deep-breathing relaxation (Chapter 14). And (4) learning to blow off steam nondestructively through such physical activities as jogging or hitting a pillow (Chapter 14).

Mr. Norwood: Ray will attend weekly counseling sessions to learn and practice anger control techniques. His main task is to use these techniques to cease his physical abuse of Klareen and to substantially reduce his verbal abuse of Klareen. After 30 days, if Ray succeeds, a renegotiation of the terms of the contract will occur.

Mrs. Norwood: Klareen will attend weekly counseling sessions with Ray. In addition, she will seek to calmly discuss issues she has with Ray (in and outside the counseling sessions) to avoid provoking Ray's anger. Klareen also has the responsibility to record any incidents in which Ray is physically or verbally abusive to her in the next 30 days.

Duration of contract: 30 days

Means of monitoring progress: Klareen will record incidents where Ray expresses his anger toward her in assertive or nondestructive ways. (This measures the positive ways in which Ray is learning to express his anger.) Klareen will also record any incidents in which Ray is verbally or physically abusive to her.

Rewards for Ray and Klareen if contract is met: They will continue their marriage, which is what both partners want.

Consequences for Ray and Klareen if contract is not met: If Ray hits Klareen one time in the next 30 days, she will separate. If Ray does not reduce by two-thirds the number of times he is verbally abusive in the next month, she will separate. (To get baseline information, Klareen is asked to identify in the past week—taking each day at a time—the number of times Ray was verbally abusive. Nine incidents are identified. As a result, Ray agrees he will, at most, be verbally aggressive to Klareen no more than 12 times in the next 28 days. If he exceeds this limit, it is agreed that Klareen will move in with her parents.)

Step 2: Prepare a contract, answering the following:

a. What behavior do you want to change? Be as specific as possible.

b. What is your goal?

c. What will you do to achieve this goal?

d. How will you reward yourself for achieving the goal and adhering to your contract?

e. If you fail to adhere to the contract, what adverse consequences will you give yourself (such as donating $10 to a charity each time you "screw up")?

Stage 8: Termination and Evaluation

If constructive change is to be long lasting or permanent, clients must conclude, "Although this approach takes a lot of my time and effort, it's worth it." If they conclude, "This approach has helped a little, but it's really not worth what I'm sacrificing for it," then an alternative course of action needs to be developed and implemented.

When clients meet commitments, reward them orally or in other ways. Rewarding clients increases their self-esteem and self-respect and motivates them to continue working to improve their circumstances.

One of the biggest reality shocks of new trainees entering the helping professions is that many clients, even after making commitments to improve their situations, do not carry out the steps outlined. If clients fail to meet the terms of the contract, effective workers generally do not punish. Punishment usually increases hostility without producing positive lasting changes. Also, don't accept excuses when commitments are not met. Excuses let people off the hook; they provide temporary relief, but they eventually lead to more failure and to a failure identity. Simply ask, "Do you still wish to try to fulfill your commitment?" If clients answer affirmatively, another time deadline acceptable to the client should be set.

Whether or not clients reach all their goals, careful attention should be given to terminating the relationship. If clients still have unresolved problems, a referral should be made to an appropriate agency or professional. Care should be taken in terminating the contact so that clients do not erroneously conclude that the counselor is rejecting them. Also, clients should be asked whether there are additional concerns that they would like help with.

The nature and intensity of the feelings clients experience as they end a relationship with a counselor vary according to a number of factors, including their personal characteristics, the progress they made, the nature of the relationship with the counselor, and the issues worked on. Because ending is an important event in the lives of most clients, the counselor should give them an opportunity to express feelings related to the ending of the counseling.

Clients may experience a variety of emotions about the ending, such as gratitude, ambivalence, anger, sadness, guilt, and fear. If they conclude the relationship without sharing their feelings, they may experience a sense of incompleteness. Therefore, the counselor should encourage clients to express their feelings about ending. The counselor may say something like the following to encourage the expression of feelings about ending: "In the weeks we met we discussed the following issues: ______. You have stated you have made progress on ______. We as yet have not shared our feelings about ending the relationship with one another. Since this is our final meeting with one another, what emotions are you now feeling?" After the client expresses his or her feelings, it is appropriate for the counselor to express

EP 2.1.10l

those feelings that would add to a pleasant and appropriate ending. (It perhaps is best for the counselor to choose which feelings are most constructive to express. For example, it probably would be counterproductive to express feelings of annoyance that the counselor has about the client.)

Often, when the counselor shares his or her feelings about the ending, clients may respond by sharing additional emotions of their own. The counselor may reflect their feelings and perhaps share more of his or her own. It then is time for the counselor and the client to complete the ending process by saying goodbye.

Exercise 5.9: Terminating and Encouraging Clients to Share Their Ending Feelings

Goal: This exercise is designed to give you an opportunity to practice the skills of terminating and encouraging clients to share their feelings about ending.

Step 1: You are a social worker at a social service agency. You have worked with Andy Morrissey for the past 2 ½ months. Andy is a 28-year-old computer programmer. You have helped him with several issues, including the recent death of his mother whom he was very close to, his girlfriend of 7 years breaking up with him (he is now beginning to date again), his struggling to keep his job as he mourned the loss of his mother and his girlfriend, and his drinking to excess (he now limits himself to two drinks when he goes out). You believe he no longer has acute issues that need to be worked on. Write the words that you would say to Mr. Morrissey to suggest that it now may be time to terminate his coming to see you.

Step 2: Assume you and Mr. Morrissey agree to terminate. Write the words that you would use in encouraging Mr. Morrissey to express his feelings about ending.

At the final interview or a few weeks after termination, it is usually beneficial to ask clients (orally or with a brief questionnaire) the following questions:

- Did the counseling help you? If "yes," how? If "no," why did it not help?
- What did the counselor do well?
- What were the shortcomings of the counseling that was received?
- What suggestions do you have for improving counseling services at this agency?
- Do you have some concerns for which you desire additional counseling?

This information is very useful in improving the counseling process and in determining whether the client needs additional help.

These guidelines on counseling should not be followed dogmatically because they will probably work only 70 to 80% of the time. The most important tools counselors have are their feelings, perceptions, relationship capacities, and interviewing skills.

One final important guideline: Counselors should refer a client to someone else, or at least discuss the case with another professional counselor, in any of the following situations: (1) if counselors are unable to empathize with the client, (2) if they feel the client is choosing unethical alternatives (such as seeking an abortion) that conflict with the counselor's basic value system, (3) if they feel the problem is of such a nature that they will not be able to help, or (4) if a working relationship is not established. Competent and secure counselors know that it is possible to work with and help some people but not all and that it is in the client's and the counselor's best interests to refer clients they cannot help to others who may be able to provide the counseling needed.

Counseling Skills at Work in Generalist Practice As you read the Case Example "Counseling Mrs. H: Principles in Action," (pp. 152–154), notice that the social work intern uses the following roles, which, as described in Chapter 1, are components of generalist social work practice: brokering Mrs. H to enroll in a work-training program; facilitating Mrs. H to receive employment; educating Mrs. H to understand she needed to seek employment; brokering Mrs. H to receive dental care; helping Mrs. H to problem-solve; and being an encouraging role model.

CLIENTS' REACTIONS TO HAVING A PERSONAL PROBLEM

In counseling clients, a crucial area that counselors need to be aware of and learn to handle effectively is clients' emotional reactions to having a personal problem. Lee Askew's example underscores the importance of this area. Mr. Askew has been an alcoholic for many years, and for most of these years he has been in denial. Why? First seen in counseling nearly 3 years ago, Mr. Askew has experienced a variety of problems related to his drinking. The following is a summary of Mr. Askew's social history:

> Lee Askew is 43 years old and has been drinking heavily since he was 16 years of age. For the past several years, he has drunk an average of a quart of vodka each day. His second marriage is in trouble because his wife, Callie, claims their money is spent on alcohol rather than on paying bills. Also, his wife has informed him she can no longer tolerate his drunken behavior—nearly every evening he is in a drunken stupor and rambles on, repeating himself until he finally falls asleep, often by passing out. Mr. Askew's first wife divorced him because of his drinking. When he is sober, he is friendly and enjoyable to be with. But as the day moves along, he increasingly becomes intoxicated, and his behavior becomes intolerable. Five years ago he had a serious automobile accident while intoxicated and was nearly killed. Three and one-half years ago he was again arrested for drunken driving. In the past 10 years he has held a variety of sales jobs and has been fired from three of these jobs for being intoxicated. Last night Mr. Askew physically abused his wife for the first time. This morning Mrs. Askew informed Lee that he must either seek help for his drinking or she will leave. Mr. Askew apologized for hitting his wife, claming he had had a bad day at work. Lee, however, refuses to acknowledge he has a drinking problem.

Mr. Askew's denial of his drinking problem is not unique. Clients display a variety of emotional reactions when confronted with evidence of a personal problem. The effectiveness of counseling frequently depends on counselors understanding such emotional reactions so they can help clients recognize that they do have a personal problem and need certain services.

An important contribution in this area has been made by Elisabeth Kübler-Ross. In *On Death and Dying,* Kübler-Ross (1969) describes five stages of dying that terminally ill people typically experience. These stages are not absolute, and not everyone goes through each one. But helping professionals who counsel the terminally ill have found this paradigm, when used in a flexible, insight-producing way, to be valuable in explaining why patients behave the way they do. The five stages also typify individual's reactions when confronted with serious personal problems.

Kübler-Ross's Five Stages of Dying

Mauksch (1975, p. 10) provided a concise summary of Kübler-Ross's five stages of dying:

1. *Denial:* "No, not me." This is a typical reaction when patients learn that they are terminally ill. Denial, says Dr. Ross, is important and necessary. It helps cushion the impact of the patient's awareness that death is inevitable.

(Text continues on p. 154)

CASE EXAMPLE Counseling Mrs. H: Principles in Action

Our social work program (similar to social work programs at other universities) places students in social service agencies for internships. As social work interns, students observe, and soon begin to do, the kind of work that social workers do. A frequent "reality shock" reported by interns is that many clients are apathetic, discouraged, and simply not motivated to improve. Often, the result is that clients do not follow through on commitments made during counseling sessions to improve their circumstances.

Last year at a county social services agency, I was supervising an intern who was surprised and frustrated when clients failed to follow through on commitments. The intern was working with a small caseload of Temporary Assistance to Needy Families (TANF) mothers. The intern commented, "The case examples discussed in textbooks are always successes, and I have not yet seen improvement in my cases." I reassured her that she was not at fault and that lack of improvement is more often the rule than the exception. I added that textbooks are very selective in that they usually present success cases, rather than typical cases, to illustrate theory. I cautioned that if she became discouraged and gave up being an "encouraging person," she had *no* hope of being effective. After further discussion, she developed an approach in which she used the counseling principles presented in this chapter. At the end of her internship, not all of the TANF mothers she was working with showed substantial improvement. Yet she had formed a respectful working relationship with each client, and some were making significant efforts to improve their circumstances. At the end of the semester, she wrote the following summary about her contacts with one client:

I was assigned the case of Mrs. H. She was 33 years of age and had three children, ages 15, 11, and 7. She had been receiving TANF assistance for the past 6 years, ever since her husband deserted her. During the past 4 years, the agency had made several efforts to get her a job, without success. The records showed Mrs. H did not want a full-time job, because she felt she was too busy taking care of her children. She applied for several part-time jobs but was not hired. Mrs. H felt she did not have any marketable skills, as she had never worked outside of her home.

I was assigned Mrs. H's case when she requested a social worker's help with a problem she was having with her 15-year-old son. Mrs. H had found some pot in her son's clothes drawer and didn't know how to handle the situation. I met with Mrs. H. Her home had a general unclean appearance. Mrs. H's physical appearance gave the impression she had been through a war. Her clothes were wrinkled and had what appeared to be food stains on several places. Her hair was greasy, she was quite obese, and she had few teeth left in her mouth. Dark circles were under her eyes, suggesting a great deal of fatigue and stress.

We met for about an hour and a half, and Mrs. H related much of her life history. She had never held a full-time job and had a "forced marriage" (due to becoming pregnant) shortly after she graduated from high school. Her husband had been a road construction worker and had a drinking problem. She had not heard from him in the previous year. She felt if he did come back, she would not even want to see him. She had heard also that when he left he moved to a distant state with another woman.

My aim in the first interview was to build a working relationship, obtain Mrs. H's trust, and help her explore what she saw as her problems. Her immediate problem appeared to be what to do about her discovery of pot. We discussed to some extent the legalities of smoking marijuana and the effects and consequences of the drug. I also said I could bring over some brief reading material on the drug the next day, and she responded by saying she would very much appreciate receiving such material.

We then role-played how she might bring up the subject of smoking marijuana with her son. First I played her role to model a possible approach, and she played her son. Then we reversed roles to give her practice in trying out an approach. Before discussing the subject with her son, she mentioned she wanted to look at the reading material I had promised her. I dropped off this material the next day. We also set another meeting for the following week.

At our next appointment, Mrs. H indicated she had discussed smoking marijuana with her son. Her son responded first with some surprise and some displeasure that Mrs. H had gone through his clothes drawer. The son, Jerry, indicated he had tried smoking marijuana only twice and was not that interested in smoking in the future. Mrs. H added that another related concern she had about Jerry was his interest in occasionally drinking beer with some of his friends. She indicated that she and Jerry had had some moderate disagreements in this area, and they were working on it.

I asked if she felt she needed help from our agency for this issue. She responded, "No, not at this time." I then asked if she needed any other additional help from our agency. She thanked me for the help I had given and said she was not aware of other areas where she needed help. I could have left, but I thought that as I had a good relationship established with her and had been of some prior help this might be an opportunity to have her take a look at her future.

I began by asking her what she would like to see herself doing 10 years from now. She responded by saying, "I haven't given that much thought. I probably will be doing what I'm doing now." I asked if she was satisfied with her current life. She rather firmly said no

CASE EXAMPLE *(continued)*

and went on at length about how difficult it is to live on an inadequate TANF budget and to raise three children by herself. She was also critical of her husband, who placed her in this situation by deserting her.

I conveyed an understanding of her concerns and mentioned that it was certainly true that past events had led to her current circumstances. But I added that what she wanted for the present and the future was largely up to her. She asked what I meant.

I said, "Take your financial situation, for example. You have a choice between staying home or seeking a job. Now, I know at the present time that working would not improve your finances very much. But if you don't begin learning an employable skill now and gradually working your way up in a job, what's going to happen when, in a year, your TANF benefits expire?" I explained to her that under the TANF program current (and future) single parents can only receive financial assistance for a maximum of 2 years. During that 2-year period, they need to prepare themselves for holding a job and then find a job. I added, "There are also other areas that we could work on, for example, dental care. But the choice is totally up to you. If you want to work on some of these areas, I'm very interested in working with you. If you aren't interested at the present time, there's little I can do."

Mrs. H responded by indicating she was aware that her teeth needed attention but added she didn't have the money to pay a dentist. I indicated the expenses were covered under her medical card (Medicaid program). She expressed surprise and indicated she would make an appointment with a dentist. She thanked me for the information, and I noted her face showed a spark of interest.

I then asked if she had thought about obtaining a job. She mentioned that would be nice but then started citing a number of reasons she thought that it would not be possible. Many of these appeared to me to be "self-defeating self-talk." The material below contains a summary of her negative self-talk, along with a more positive view for each reason that I suggested to her.

At this point I asked her to think over what we had talked about and indicated that I would ask Mrs. S to contact her.

A week later I stopped by to see Mrs. H. She mentioned that she had had an "inspirational" talk with Mrs. S. At that point she asked to be enrolled in our work-training program. I praised her decision. Within 3 months, she had obtained a receptionist job for a new car dealer. Equally important, she appeared to have a renewed interest in living and had improved her personal appearance with increased grooming attention, some new clothes, and a set of dentures. For me, as a student social work intern, this turned out to be a deeply rewarding, gratifying person to work with.

Mrs. H's Reasons for Not Seeking a Job	A More Positive View
1. "I've tried finding a job several times in the past and was not able to obtain one."	1. "Having tried in the past and failed does not mean you can't obtain a job at this time. We could provide you with work training in an area that you are interested in and also help you obtain a job after the training. You need to start thinking about your future, because in a year you will no longer be eligible for TANF assistance. Having a job now will help you prepare for the future. Also, there are other benefits in working, such as the opportunity to get to know other people."
2. "I'm really not skilled at any job. Frankly, it is very embarrassing to be turned down when I apply."	2. "Nothing ventured, nothing gained. As far as not having a skill, we can enroll you in a work-training program. We can also help you find a job. You are not alone in being turned down for a job. I have a friend who applied to 67 teaching positions before being hired. This person was becoming quite discouraged but kept on trying. She finally found one and really liked it. The key is to keep on trying and hoping."
3. "I won't be able to work and also take care of my home and family."	3. "A working mother does have a lot to do and limited time to get it all done. However, many mothers are able to do both." (At this point I asked if she

(continued)

CASE EXAMPLE (continued)

Mrs. H's Reasons for Not Seeking a Job	A More Positive View
	would be interested in discussing this area with a friend of mine, Mrs. S. has four children and used to receive financial assistance but now works full-time as a secretary. Mrs. S is an "encouraging" person. She got her job by first having work training, then volunteering at an agency to do clerical work. By volunteering, she developed her typing skills, and after a year the agency hired her. Mrs. H indicated she would be interested in talking with Mrs. S.)
4. "Frankly, my personal appearance is such that I don't think that anyone would hire me."	4. "You're selling yourself short. Our agency can help you with dental care and in getting some new clothes. When you meet with Mrs. S, you will see she probably will not win a beauty contest but has an inner beauty (personality) that helped her get a job. I think with a more positive attitude, people would note an inner beauty on your part."
5. "I wouldn't, if I worked, be able to watch some of my favorite game shows and soap operas during the day. My present daily routine would be greatly altered."	5. "This is true. But you would be able to meet more people if you worked and perhaps grow more as a person. Also, wouldn't your children be prouder of you if you worked? Are you really satisfied and contented with your present circumstances and current daily routine?"
6. "I don't own a car, and therefore don't have a way to get to a job even if I did get one."	6. "We can help you here by paying the cost of transportation and by helping you arrange for transportation. For example, we have volunteer drivers who would be able to provide transportation when you go for job interviews."

2. *Rage and anger:* "Why me?" Patients resent the fact that others will remain healthy and alive while they die. God is a special target for anger, since He is regarded as imposing, arbitrarily, the death sentence.
3. *Bargaining:* "Yes, me, but . . ." Patients accept the fact of death but strike bargains for more time. Mostly they bargain with God—"even among people who never talked with God before." They promise to be good or to do something in exchange for another week or month or year of life. Notes Dr. Ross, "What they promise is totally irrelevant, because they don't keep their promises anyway."
4. *Depression:* "Yes, me." First, people mourn past losses, things not done, wrongs committed. But then they enter a state of "preparatory grief," getting ready for the arrival of death. Patients grow quiet and don't want visitors. "A dying patient who doesn't want to see you anymore," says Dr. Ross, "is signaling he has finished his unfinished business with you, and it is a blessing. He can now let go peacefully."
5. *Acceptance:* "My time is very close now and it's all right." Dr. Ross describes this final stage as "not a happy stage, but neither is it unhappy. It's devoid of feelings but it's not resignation, it's really a victory."

In presenting these five stages, Kübler-Ross (1969) warns it is a mistake to expect that all terminally ill patients methodically pass through all five. Some never reach the fifth stage of acceptance. Others display reactions from two stages at the same time—for example, anger and denial. Still others waver between stages—reaching the depressed stage, then returning to an earlier stage of denial or anger.

Kübler-Ross's Five Stages as Emotional Reactions

Kübler-Ross's five stages also typify clients' emotional reactions when they are confronted with evidence of their personal problem. Denial, rage and anger, bargaining, depression, and acceptance are, in my experience, common reactions in numerous situations: A husband is informed his wife is having an affair; a single teenager is informed she is pregnant; an employee is fired for incompetence; a woman is informed she has a malignant tumor in her breast; a woman informs her fiancé she is ending their engagement. This list could be expanded infinitely, because we are all likely to have these emotional reactions. When clients recognize they have a personal problem, they experience a sense of loss, and Kübler-Ross's five stages are emotional reactions to loss. Lee Askew's case illustrates each stage.

Stage 1: Denial ("Not me.") Admitting the existence of a problem is difficult because clients often then (erroneously) perceive themselves as weak, sinful, or irresponsible. Also, recognition brings with it an acknowledgment that change is inevitable. Clients often mourn the loss of that which must be changed. Alcoholics thus mourn the loss of their drinking because their social activities are centered around it. Unless clients already have an openness or reaching-out pattern with others, it can be very difficult for them to share a new problem openly. Denial helps cushion the impact of the client's awareness that change is inevitable.

Constructive changes are not likely to occur for people in denial unless counselors find a way to convince them that the problem exists. Counselors therefore need to focus on the denial and explore why the person believes there is no problem. They should gather evidence to document the existence of the problem. Clients can then be confronted with this evidence in a tactful manner.

For more than 20 years, Mr. Askew has denied that he has a drinking problem. He believes that he needs alcohol to get through each day. He feels such a strong need for alcohol that he allowed his drinking to end his first marriage, and he will not face the fact that drinking is ruining his second marriage. He will not acknowledge that he nearly lost his life while driving when intoxicated, nor will he acknowledge that he has lost several jobs because of his drinking.

Mrs. Askew gave her husband an ultimatum: Either he sees a counselor or she is leaving now. Mr. Askew reluctantly decided to see a counselor. In counseling, Mr. Askew denied he had a drinking problem. He had excuses for everything: His car accident resulted from slippery roads. He was fired because his employers didn't like his suggestions for increasing sales. He ended his first marriage because his wife was a "nag." He denied having more than a couple of drinks a day.

Stage 2: Rage and Anger ("Why me?") Clients resent the fact that they have to change while others do not. Old friends, relatives, or society at large are doing the things that the clients must change. Anyone can be the target for their anger. Sometimes the anger is used to avoid discussing the issue at hand. At other times the anger is directed at the counselor for confronting the client with reality.

The underlying reasons for this anger need to be remembered here. Certain therapeutic techniques are especially helpful during this stage. Allowing clients to vent their anger reduces its intensity; once this happens, they are better able to examine their difficulties realistically. Conveying empathy and emotional support creates an atmosphere in which clients feel more comfortable examining their difficulties. Clients often feel overwhelmed by their problems, which is a factor in their intensely felt "Why me?" They need to see that their problems are not overwhelming but can be broken down into subproblems that are resolvable in a step-by-step fashion. During this stage, it is helpful for counselors to realize that clients angrily attacking them should not be taken personally. Reacting personally or angrily to clients' anger will only prolong their hostile behavior.

Lee Askew at times displayed anger while in counseling with Paul Decker. As indicated earlier, Mr. Askew at first denied he had a drinking problem. He had excuses for all the problems that were being caused by drinking. Mr. Decker knew counseling would not be productive unless this denial was broken through. Mr. Decker suggested that at the next session the Askews meet jointly to get both their perceptions of their marital problems. Mr. Askew reacted angrily to this suggestion, castigating his wife for making up stories about him, particularly his drinking. The counselor allowed Mr. Askew to vent his anger and then asked, "Are you fearful of what your wife might say?" Mr. Askew stated "no" and agreed to a joint meeting.

Several joint meetings were held with the Askews. Mr. Askew continued to deny his drinking problem. These denials were countered by Mr. Decker asking him questions that served to confront Mr. Askew with his problem, including how much he drank each day, how he acted while drunk, how Mrs. Askew felt about seeing her husband intoxicated, and whether his drinking has gotten him in trouble at work and with the police. Mr. Askew used anger to avoid confronting his alcoholism. Mr. Decker let Mr. Askew "spit fire" and vent. On a few occasions after Mr. Askew calmed down, Mr. Decker asked, "I wonder why you are reacting angrily to what is being said?" or "It appears we are touching a sensitive chord with you." Such questions were designed to help Mr. Askew understand why he was reacting angrily.

At other times, Mr. Askew would go into a tirade about how many of his friends drank and had a good time. He fumed about his wife pressuring him to stop drinking. He was clearly going through the "Why me?" stage. After allowing Mr. Askew to vent, Mr. Decker pointed out that unlike the drinking of social drinkers, his drinking controlled him; he was not in control of his drinking. Specific incidents were tactfully mentioned.

On one occasion Mr. Askew, with his wife present, castigated Mr. Decker for meddling in his family affairs. The counselor calmly listened and then replied, "Are you feeling angry at me because I'm forcing you to see that you face a choice between giving up drinking or losing your wife?" Mr. Askew at first reacted angrily to this but later acknowledged the statement was true.

Stage 3: Bargaining ("Yes, me, but . . .") During this stage, clients are beginning to accept the problem but will bargain for "just one more time." They promise to be good or to do something in exchange for another week or month before they embrace change. During this stage, counselors should confront clients with the reality of their circumstances and their bargaining efforts. During the bargaining stage, clients usually try to change a few circumstances in their lives, and they generally believe that just a few changes will allow them to continue in their old ways. They tell themselves that "if such and such changes, I can still continue to . . ." Bargaining is a common reaction. People who are urged to lose weight bargain for "strawberry shortcake"; smokers who are urged to quit bargain to smoke when tense; some spouses seek to preserve a marriage that is in trouble by means of a pregnancy.

Mr. Askew tried several bargains. He asked if he continued in counseling whether he could continue to drink socially. Both the counselor and Mrs. Askew doubted that he could quit after a few drinks and expressed their misgivings. Social drinking was tried for a week, and Mr. Askew became intoxicated on three occasions. At the next session Mrs. Askew again stated her ultimatum: "Stop drinking, or I'm leaving." Efforts were then made to get Mr. Askew involved in Alcoholics Anonymous (AA) meetings. Initial results in AA were good. Then a wedding came up, and Mr. Askew bargained with his wife (outside of counseling) that he would continue in AA if he could socially drink at special occasions such as the wedding. His wife struck the bargain on the condition that he quit after a few drinks. Mr. Askew became intoxicated at the wedding, and his actions (including wetting his pants) were intensely embarrassing to Mrs. Askew. At the next counseling session, Mrs. Askew again stated her ultimatum: "Stop drinking completely, or else I'm leaving." After other similar bargaining efforts, Mr. Askew was confronted by Mr. Decker with the statement that it appeared he was not committed to giving up drinking but was striking bargains to continue his drinking. Mr. Askew at first reacted angrily (back to the anger stage) but gradually acknowledged he was bargaining.

Stage 4: Depression ("Yes, me.") Clients in the depression stage become very quiet. They have, by now, stopped denying their problem. Their anger has subsided, and they no longer try to bargain. They have gained insight into their particular problem and realize they must change. Alternatives, however, are not yet perceived as viable solutions. They blame themselves in a "self-downing" manner for their problems and frequently mourn what they will have to give up. During this stage, counselors need to convey empathy and help clients see that their problems are not overwhelming. Clients need hope; frequently this can be accomplished by helping them develop resolution strategies.

Mr. Askew and his wife had been coming to weekly counseling for 3 ½ months. During this time Mr. Askew made some efforts to give up drinking. At times he would go for a week or two without drinking, but he always returned to the bottle. In counseling sessions, he vacillated between making excuses for his drinking (denial) and displaying anger or bargaining when confronted with the need to stop drinking. At the counseling session following a drinking episode, he would usually be depressed, acknowledging he was ruining his life. He would deprecate himself and beg his wife to give him one more chance. When she did, a week or two later he would find an excuse to start drinking again.

Mr. Askew came into counseling one day a little hung over and very depressed. He indicated he had gotten drunk the day before, and he and his wife had argued. He wasn't certain, but he thought he may have slapped her a few times. He added that afterward she packed a bag, indicated she was going to file for divorce, and left. Mr. Askew stated that life was not worth living without his wife. He fully acknowledged he had a drinking problem and had to abstain completely. The counselor and Mr. Askew discussed various alternatives. Mr. Askew stated with emotion that he would never take another drink and that he would demonstrate this to his wife. He further decided to wait for 2 weeks before contacting her so that she could sort out her feelings and thoughts. Mr. Askew left the interview depressed, realizing that his drinking may have ruined his marriage forever.

Stage 5: Acceptance ("I have a problem, but it's all right." "I can.") Clients make a concentrated effort at this stage to work out alternatives, not only those suggested earlier in treatment but also some of their own. Their attitude is now one of "I can do it." There is hope. A plan for rehabilitation can be presented if one was lacking or dismissed in the earlier stages. Fear is still present but very much reduced.

After 2 weeks Mr. Askew called his wife. They talked, and she agreed to attend the next counseling session. At this session, Mrs. Askew indicated she was ambivalent about ending her marriage, but she had totally had it with her husband's drunken behavior. They agreed to live apart for the next 4 months. If Lee participated in AA meetings and did not drink at all, then they would live together again, on the condition that he would never drink again.

EP 2.1.1b

That was over 2 years ago. Lee Askew has not had a drink, and he is active in AA helping other problem drinkers. He is also active in a speaker's bureau in which he talks to high school students and businesses and organizations about the dangers of alcohol and about treatment programs. After 3 months of separation, his wife returned, and both report their marriage and their careers are going well.

Exercise 5.10: Understanding Clients' Emotional Reactions to Having a Problem

Goal: This exercise is designed to help you better understand the Kübler-Ross model of emotional reactions to a loss.

Step 1: Reflect on a significant loss that you had—such as the ending of a relationship, getting a speeding ticket, or a pet dying. Specify the loss.

Step 2: Specify the extent to which you experienced emotional reactions consistent with Kübler-Ross's five reactions.

a. Denial:

b. Rage and anger:

c. Bargaining:

d. Depression:

e. Acceptance:

SUMMARY

From the counselor's perspective, counseling can be divided into three phases: (1) building a relationship, (2) exploring problems in depth, and (3) exploring alternative solutions, with the client then selecting a course of action. Successful counseling proceeds gradually from one phase to the next, with some overlap of these stages. At the end of a series of counseling interviews, there is often a fourth phase: termination and evaluation.

From the client's perspective, for counseling to be successful, clients must give themselves progressive stages of "self-talk" (that is, they must arrive at having certain thoughts and beliefs). These self-talk stages are the following:

Stage 1	*Problem awareness:* "I have a problem."
Stage 2	*Relationship to counselor:* "I think this counselor has what it takes to help me."
Stage 3	*Motivation:* "I want to improve my situation and am willing to put forth the effort to do so."
Stage 4	*Conceptualizing the problem:* "My problem is not overwhelming but has specific components that can be changed."
Stage 5	*Exploration of resolution strategies:* "I see there are several courses of action that I might take to try to do something about my situation."
Stage 6	*Selection of a strategy:* "I think this approach might help and I am willing to try it."
Stage 7	*Implementation:* "This approach is helping me."
Stage 8	*Termination and evaluation:* "Although this approach takes a lot of my time and effort, it's worth it."

This conceptualization presents a framework for improving the effectiveness of counseling. This framework indicates when counseling is not helpful; the reasons for lack of progress can be identified by examining clients' self-talk. Once these reasons are identified, changes can be made in the counseling process.

EP 2.1.7a

Counselors need to be aware of and learn to handle clients' emotional reactions to having a personal problem. Kübler-Ross's five stages of emotional reactions to loss are not unique to the terminally ill but are also typical reactions that clients display when confronted with evidence of a personal problem. Any time clients first recognize that they have a personal problem, a sense of loss occurs. Kübler-Ross's five stages are denial, rage and anger, bargaining, depression, and acceptance. Only when clients reach the fifth stage of acceptance are they ready to work effectively on alternatives for resolving their problems. With a better understanding of these emotional reactions, counselors will be more effective in selecting appropriate intervention strategies.

EXERCISES

1. Understanding Clients' Reactions to Having a Personal Problem

Goal: This exercise is designed to help students understand clients' reactions to having a personal problem.

Step 1: The instructor explains the purpose of the exercise. The instructor indicates that when a person acknowledges he or she has a personal problem, almost always that person experiences a loss of some kind. The loss may involve giving up something one has had (such as an alcoholic giving up drinking). Or the loss may involve recognition that a desired goal is not obtainable (for example, parents who have a child with a cognitive disability may feel the loss of not having a child of normal intelligence). When a loss is experienced, the person almost always has the emotional reactions described by Kübler-Ross. The instructor describes the following reactions to students: denial, anger and rage, bargaining, depression, and acceptance.

Step 2: The instructor asks students to volunteer to describe a loss they have had and has them comment on whether they experienced the five reactions described by Kübler-Ross.

EP 2.1.10a,b, e,g,j

Step 3: The instructor explains that clients frequently are not ready emotionally to work on resolving a personal problem or a loss until they reach the fifth stage of acceptance. The instructor asks the students who describe a loss if, in fact, they had to reach the stage of accepting their loss before they were able to make a concentrated effort to work on alternatives for resolving the problems.

2. Learning How to Counsel through Role-Playing

Goal: The purpose of this exercise is to help students develop their counseling skills through role-playing counseling situations.

Step 1: The instructor describes the goal of the exercise. The instructor indicates that the counseling process from the counselor's view can be divided into five phases: (1) starting the interview; (2) building a relationship; (3) exploring problems in depth; (4) exploring alternative solutions with the client, then choosing one or more of the alternatives; and (5) ending the interview. (Material on these five phases is summarized in Chapters 4 and 5.) The instructor briefly summarizes guidelines on how a counselor should handle each of these phases.

Step 2: Two students volunteer to role-play being clients. The "clients" come up with their own contrived problems. Here are some examples of possible problems:

a. Two college students are roommates. One believes the other has a drinking problem, but the other refuses to acknowledge a problem exists.
b. Two siblings are concerned about their mother living alone. Her health is failing, and her husband recently died. The siblings also believe they are unable to care for their mother because each is married and has a family and the mother is not easy to live with.
c. A husband and wife both want children, but the husband is infertile. The wife wants to become pregnant through artificial insemination. The husband objects to his wife getting pregnant using this means.

Step 3: The instructor counsels the two students who have contrived problems to demonstrate the five phases of counseling. After the counseling is completed, the class discusses the strengths and shortcomings of the counseling that was given.

Step 4: The instructor asks four more students to volunteer—two as clients having contrived problems and two as counselors for the two "clients." (It is useful to have two people, at this early stage, volunteer to be counselors to offset the potential of one counselor becoming "stuck" by not knowing what to say.) Role-play the interview.

Step 5: As an additional step, the instructor requires each student in the class to role-play as counselor and also as client (for some other student who role-plays being a counselor). Ideally each student should be videotaped in the role of the counselor, and this videotape should then be played back so students can assess the interview. (As described in Chapter 4, the videotaping may be used not only to help students develop their counseling skills but also as a screening device to counsel out students from the social work major if they are unable, after several tries, to make an acceptable videotape.)

Step 6: The instructor shows each videotape to the class. A brief class discussion is held after each tape is shown. This discussion should review the strengths and shortcomings of the counseling and also look at what else might be done. If each tape is shown to the class, it is helpful for each student to fill out the "Interviewer Skills Rating Sheet" on the following page, which is then given to the "counselor" for feedback purposes. (One advantage of showing each tape to the class is that students learn what should, and should not, be done in counseling.)

Note: Role-playing contrived counseling situations (and also videotaping such situations) can be structured in a variety of ways. This exercise presents some ideas, but the instructor of course has the autonomy to structure the role-playing in ways that he or she believes will be most beneficial.

EP 2.1.3c

3. Responding Effectively to Critical Statements from Clients

Goal: This exercise is designed to help students learn how to respond more effectively to highly emotional and complex statements made by clients.

Step 1: The instructor explains the purpose of the exercise. The instructor then reads to the class the first of the client statements listed below and asks the class for suggestions on the most effective way for a counselor to respond. There are various effective responses. (One way of responding to each of these statements is presented in the Appendix.) A class discussion of the merits and shortcomings of some of the students' suggested responses is likely to be a productive learning experience.

Step 2: After the class responds to and discusses the first statement, the instructor reads the second statement and again seeks responses and discussion from the students. This process continues with the remaining statements.

Interviewer Skills Rating Sheet

Student ______________________________ **Date** ______________

Skills	Needs Improvement	Satisfactory	Excellent
1. Opening remarks			
2. Explanation of counselor role			
3. Voice quality and volume			
4. Body posture			
5. Eye contact			
6. Behavioral congruence/facial expression (therapist's words match his/her outward appearance)			
7. Frequency of open-ended questions (not yes-no or multiple-choice questions)			
8. Amount of therapist's verbal activity			
9. Verbal following behavior (sequencing questions with client's answers, preparing client for shift in subject matter)			
10. Clarity of questions			
11. Ability to confront client with inconsistencies			
12. Use of humor			
13. Warmth/ability to put client at ease			
14. Use of silence			
15. Ability to help client define problems			

(continued)

Interviewer Skills Rating Sheet ***(continued)***

Skills	Needs Improvement	Satisfactory	Excellent
16. Ability to have client specify goals			
17. Paraphrasing			
18. Reflection of client's feelings			
19. Summarization of client information			
20. Ability to answer client's questions—provide useful information			
21. Extent to which interviewer presented him-herself as a professional			
22. Extent to which necessary data about the problem was obtained			
23. Ending the interview/length of interview			
24. Completeness of interview			
25. Extent to which a helpful relationship was developed.			
26. Extent to which alternative solutions to the problem were begun to be explored			

Positive Comments about Strengths Demonstrated during the Interview:

Areas Needing Attention:

CLIENT STATEMENTS

1. *Male client* (fifth interview): "There's something that's been bothering me for the past few weeks (pause). I'm beginning to feel that you're not really interested in me as a person. I have the feeling that the only reason you're meeting with me is because you're getting paid to see me."

2. *Engaged female*, age 20: "I'm engaged to marry Kent. My uncle thinks he's terrific, but my parents are telling me I'm making the biggest mistake of my life to marry him. They dislike him and also think I'm too young to marry. I'm so confused about what I should do. Kent is putting a lot of pressure on me to elope."

3. *Juvenile probationee*, age 16—who is recognized as being a con artist—in required weekly visit with probation agent: "Your office is really cool. You've really got it made. I admire your taste in furnishing this office. You deserve what you've got in life. I admire you. Those are great photographs on the wall. Did you take them?" The probation officer is aware that students received their midterm grade reports this past week.

4. *Male client*, age 27 (fourth interview): "I'm feeling real tense today. I've got a lot on my mind (pause). I don't think we've made much progress in the last three meetings, although I am gradually coming to trust you (pause). I haven't been fully honest with you. You know the marital problems I've been having? Well, the main reason our marriage hasn't gone well, and Karen doesn't even know this, is because for the past few years I've been involved with someone else—who happens to be a male. Karen no longer turns me on because I guess I'm more attracted to males."

5. *African American client* from an inner city who has a white therapist: "You honkies don't know what life is really like for us who live in a ghetto. You say you want to help me, but I don't buy that jive. How can you possibly help me when you have no idea what it is like to be black and living in a ghetto?"

6. *Teenage male delinquent* caught with marijuana in his possession at a correctional institution: "Please don't report this. You know I've been doing really well here at school and have a clean record. If you report this, my stay will be extended. I was only holding the drugs for a friend here. I'm not using any of it myself. Give me a break—everyone needs one in life." The youth was involved with drugs when he committed the offenses for which he was sent to this correctional facility.

COMPETENCY NOTES

The following identifies where Educational Policy (EP) competencies and practice behaviors are discussed in the chapter.

EP 2.1.3c *Demonstrate effective oral and written communication in working with individuals, families, groups, organizations, communities, and colleagues.*

EP 2.1.10a *Substantively and affectively prepare for action with individuals, families, groups, organizations, and communities.*

EP 2.1.10b *Use empathy and other interpersonal skills.*

EP 2.1.10c *Develop a mutually agreed-on focus of work and desired outcomes.*

EP 2.1.10d *Collect, organize, and interpret client data.*

EP 2.1.10e *Assess client strengths and limitations.*

EP 2.1.10f *Develop mutually agreed-on intervention goals and objectives.*

EP 2.1.10g *Select appropriate intervention strategies.*

EP 2.1.10j *Help clients resolve problems.*

EP 2.1.10l *Facilitate transitions and endings.* (Chapter 5).

This chapter presents content on all the practice behaviors associated with counseling individuals.

EP 2.1.3c *Demonstrate effective oral and written communication in working with individuals, families, groups, organizations, communities, and colleagues.* (p. 133).

Exercise 5.1 gives students practice in phrasing goals for involuntary clients in terms of legal mandates.

EP 2.1.3c *Demonstrate effective oral and written communication in working with individuals, families, groups, organizations, communities, and colleagues.* (pp. 133–134).

Exercise 5.2 is designed to have students identify the concerns of a client about seeing a counselor and then have them speculate about what the counselor needs to do to alleviate these concerns.

EP 2.1.10e *Assess client strengths and limitations.* (p. 135).

Exercise 5.3 is designed to help students understand some of the reasons why some people are not motivated to improve their life circumstances.

EP 2.1.1b *Practice personal reflection and self-correction to assure continual professional development.* (p. 139).

Exercise 5.4 is designed to show that most of us have a tendency to awfulize when bad events happen to us.

EP 2.1.10b *Use empathy and other interpersonal skills.* (pp. 141–142).

Exercise 5.5 is designed to give students practice in reflecting feelings and in reflecting meanings of messages from clients.

EP 2.1.3c *Demonstrate effective oral and written communication in working with individuals, families, groups, organizations, communities, and colleagues* (pp. 142–143).

Exercise 5.6 is designed to give students an opportunity to tactfully phrase a question that is designed to have a client give information about a socially unacceptable topic.

EP 2.1.10j *Help clients resolve problems* (p. 145).

Exercise 5.7 is designed to give students practice in generating options and resolution strategies.

EP 2.1.3c *Demonstrate effective oral and written communication in working with individuals, families, groups, organizations, communities, and colleagues* (pp. 146, 148–149).

Exercise 5.8 is designed to assist students in learning how to write behavioral contracts.

EP 2.1.10l *Facilitate transitions and endings* (p. 150).

Exercise 5.9 is designed to give students an opportunity to practice the skills of terminating and encouraging clients to share their feelings about ending contact with their counselor.

EP 2.1.1b *Practice personal reflection and self-correction to assure continual professional development* (pp. 157–158).

Exercise 5.10 is designed to help students better understand the Kübler-Ross model of emotional reactions to a loss.

EP 2.1.7a *Utilize conceptual frameworks to guide the process of assessment, intervention, and evaluation.* (pp. 159–160).

This exercise is designed to help students conceptualize clients' reactions to having a personal problem.

EP 2.1.10a *Substantively and affectively prepare for action with individuals, families, groups, organizations, and communities.*

EP 2.1.10b *Use empathy and other interpersonal skills.*

EP 2.1.10e *Assess client strengths and limitations.*

EP 2.1.10g *Select appropriate intervention strategies.*

EP 2.1.10j *Help clients resolve problems* (p. 160).

This exercise is designed to help students develop their counseling skills (and learn the practice behaviors identified above) through role-playing counseling situations.

EP 2.1.3c *Demonstrate effective oral and written communication in working with individuals, families, groups, organizations, communities, and colleagues* (pp. 161–163).

This exercise is designed to help students learn how to respond more effectively to highly emotional and complex statements made by clients.

CHAPTER 6

Social Work with Groups: Types of Groups and Guidelines for Leading Them

EP 2.1.7a

The practice of social work in groups is not a new phenomenon.[1] The ideological roots of social work with groups can be traced most directly to the settlement houses, informal self-help recreational organizations (YMCA, YWCA), Jewish centers, and scouting, all of which developed during the first three decades of the twentieth century. During this period, many social workers found group-based methods of intervention effective and efficient for confronting a variety of personal and social problems. The last 75 years have witnessed progressive interest in, and expansion of, group services in our society. The involvement of the social work profession in groups has broadened accordingly. Today it is not uncommon to find social workers as both group leaders and participants in a myriad of settings, helping solve or ameliorate human or social problems and planning for and creating change. There are many reasons behind the attractiveness of groups for members and for practitioners.

Johnson and Johnson (2000) define a group as "two or more individuals in face-to-face interaction, each aware of his or her membership in the group, each aware of the others who belong to the group, and each aware of their positive interdependence as they strive to achieve mutual goals" (p. 20). From this description, we can see that the members of a group relate to one another within a context of sensing they form a distinct entity, that they share a common goal or purpose, and that they have confidence that together they can accomplish as much as or more than would be possible were they to work separately. This commonality is characteristic of a wide variety of groups dealing with a multitude of societal problems.

The beginning social worker is likely to be surprised at the diversity of groups in existence and excited by the challenge of practicing social work in groups. The period from 1960 to the present has witnessed an explosion in the number of groups and group-based techniques used by the social work profession. This chapter will:

A. Describe types of groups in which social workers become involved
B. Define groupthink
C. Provide guidelines on how to start, lead, evaluate, and terminate groups

[1]Material in this chapter is adapted from Charles Zastrow, *Social Work with Groups: Using the Class as a Group Leadership Laboratory*, 5th ed. © 2002 Cengage Learning.

TYPES OF GROUPS

This section describes a significant sample of the types of groups in which social workers may become involved. The following types of groups are briefly described: recreation groups, recreation-skill groups, educational groups, task groups, problem-solving and decision-making groups, focus groups, self-help groups, socialization groups, counseling groups, and encounter groups. This list is not exhaustive; only the creativity of the helping professional and the client group served will provide such limits. However, the groups discussed here are frequently encountered by social workers.

Recreation Groups

The objective of recreation groups is to provide activities for enjoyment and exercise. Often such activities are spontaneous, and the groups are practically leaderless. The group service agency (such as YMCA, YWCA, or neighborhood center) may offer little more than physical space and the use of some equipment. Spontaneous playground activities, informal athletic games, and an open game room are examples. Some group agencies providing such physical space claim that recreation and interaction with others help build character and prevent delinquency among youth by providing an alternative to the street.

Recreation-Skill Groups

The objective of a recreation-skill group is to improve a set of skills while providing enjoyment. In contrast to recreational groups, this group has an adviser, coach, or instructor; also, there is more of a task orientation. Examples of activities include golf, basketball, needlework, arts and crafts, and swimming. Competitive team sports and leagues may emerge. Frequently such groups are led by professionals with recreational training rather than social work training. Social service agencies providing such services include YMCA, YWCA, Boy Scouts, Girl Scouts, neighborhood centers, and school recreation departments.

Educational Groups

EP 2.1.1b

The focus of educational groups is to help members acquire knowledge and learn complex skills. The leader generally is a professional person with considerable training and expertise in the subject area. Examples of topics include child-rearing practices, assertiveness training, techniques for becoming a more effective parent, preparing to be an adoptive parent, and training volunteers to perform a specialized task for a social service agency. Educational group leaders often function in a didactic manner and frequently are social workers. These groups may resemble a class, with considerable group interaction and discussion being encouraged. The Case Example "Assertiveness Training—An Educational Group" (p. 167) shows how assertiveness training can be taught in an educational group.

Exercise 6.1: My Most Rewarding and Least Rewarding Educational Group

Goal: This exercise is designed to assist you in identifying the factors that lead to rewarding and unrewarding educational group experiences.

Step 1: Briefly describe an educational group in which you participated that you found to be highly rewarding. Indicate why this group was highly rewarding to you. (The group may be a class.)

CASE EXAMPLE Assertiveness Training—An Educational Group

There are several advantages of group assertiveness training. A group provides a "laboratory" for testing or experimenting with new assertive behaviors. A group has a broader base for social modeling because each member sees the other members trying out various assertive approaches. A wider variety of feedback is also offered. Furthermore, a group is generally understanding and supportive. Finally, group pressure and expectations motivate members to conscientiously develop and practice new assertive responses.

A typical format for an assertiveness training group is as follows: The size of such groups generally ranges from 5 to 20 members. The first session is devoted to a lecture presentation on differences between assertive, nonassertive, and aggressive behavior. The specific steps in assertive training are then summarized. (These steps are presented in Module 2.) Several examples of typical situations are given to illustrate that assertive responses are generally more effective than aggressive or nonassertive responses.

In later sessions, specific situations calling for assertive responses are examined. It may be desirable to begin with situations not brought forth by members of the group (group members may at first be reluctant to reveal personal situations they face). Alberti and Emmons (1975, pp. 183–184) suggested the following situations be practiced:

1. Starting a conversation with a small group of strangers who are already engaged in conversation at a party
2. Saying "no" assertively when a roommate or friend asks to borrow something that you do not want to lend
3. Returning faulty or defective items to a store
4. Asking someone next to you to extinguish a cigarette
5. Asking someone to turn down a television that is too loud or not talk so loudly in the library or theater
6. Asking for a date or refusing a date on the phone and face-to-face
7. Expressing positive feelings; "soft assertions"
8. Responding assertively to a date or spouse who is giving you put-down comments
9. Assertively refusing to take an alcoholic beverage from a friend when you prefer not to drink

For each situation the following steps are used: (1) Each member is asked to visualize (form a mental image of) his or her response. (2) One member is selected to role-play an assertive response. (3) The group briefly discusses the strategy after it is role-played. (4) If a more effective response is desired, a new assertive response is role-played by a member. (5) The group discusses the strategy.

After this exercise, group members are encouraged to bring to the group real-life situations that are troubling them. These are often complex situations involving close, intimate relationships. Such situations may not have pat, simple resolutions.

The following steps are recommended for group leaders trying to help members become more assertive:

1. Help each group member identify the situations and interactions in which it would be to his or her benefit to be more assertive. Usually group members will bring up these situations themselves. Some members, however, may be reluctant to reveal problem interactions, or they may be unaware they could handle certain situations better by being more assertive. Considerable tact and skill by the leader is necessary in initiating problem areas of the latter type. (One approach that usually works is to have the members anonymously write the situations they want role-played on a note card.)
2. When a problem interaction is identified, each member of the group is asked to visualize a response silently. For complicated situations with no simple solutions, considerable discussion may arise about possible ways of resolving the matter.
3. A member (often someone other than the person with the problem situation) is asked to role-play an assertive response. The member with the problem may be asked to play the role of the person with whom he or she is having difficulty. The situation is then role-played.
4. The group briefly discusses the merits of the assertive strategy that was modeled in step 3.

If the strategy is effective and the person with the problem is comfortable with it, that person is then asked to role-play the approach. If the group believes there may be a more effective approach, steps 3 and 4 are repeated. If the person with the problem is uncomfortable about using a strategy that is effective, the reasons for the discomfort are then explored. For example, for very shy people, certain attitudes, such as "don't make waves" or the "meek shall inherit the earth" may need to be dealt with.

5. The person with the problem is asked to rehearse an assertive strategy silently, thinking of what he or she will say and what the consequences may be.
6. The person with the problem is asked to role-play an assertive strategy.
7. The group gives feedback about the merits of the strategy. Generally the person is praised for the effective aspects and coached on how to improve other aspects. This approach is practiced via role-playing until it is perfected and the person has developed sufficient comfort and self-confidence for the "real event." For feedback purposes, if possible, the approach is recorded on audiotape or videotape.
8. The person tries out the new response pattern in an actual situation.
9. The person describes at the next group meeting how the real-life test went. The person is complimented on the degree of success attained, and assistance is given on aspects that could be improved.

Step 2: Briefly describe an educational group in which you participated that you found to be very unrewarding. Indicate why this group was not very rewarding for you.

Task Groups

Task groups are formed to achieve a specific set of tasks or objectives. Social workers are likely to interact with or become involved in a variety of task groups. A *board of directors* is an administrative group charged with responsibility for setting the policy governing agency programs. A *task force* is a group established for a special purpose and is usually disbanded after the task is completed. A *committee* of an agency or organization is a group formed to deal with specific tasks or matters. An *ad hoc committee,* like a task force, is set up for one purpose and usually ceases functioning after completion of its task.

Problem-Solving and Decision-Making Groups

Both providers and consumers of social services may become involved in groups concerned with problem solving and decision making. There is considerable overlap between task groups and these groups; thus, problem-solving and decision-making groups can be considered a subcategory of task groups.

Providers of services use group meetings for such objectives as developing a treatment plan for a client or a group of clients, deciding how to best allocate scarce resources, deciding how to improve the delivery of services to clients, arriving at policy decisions for the agency, deciding how to improve coordination efforts with other agencies, and so on. Potential *consumers* of services may form a group to study an unmet need in the community and to advocate for the development of new programs to meet the need. Data on the need may be gathered, and the group may be used as a vehicle either to develop a program or to influence existing agencies to provide services. Social workers may function as stimulators and organizers of such group efforts as well as participants (see Chapter 10 on social work community practice).

One type of problem-solving group is the *nominal group,* which can be helpful in identifying problems. The Case Example "Nominal-Group Approach—A Problem Identification Technique for Problem-Solving Groups" (p. 169) describes one such group.

In problem-solving and decision-making groups, each participant normally has some interest or stake in the process and may gain or lose, depending on the outcome. Usually, there is a formal leader of some sort, although other leaders sometimes emerge during the process. Three issues are of importance to problem-solving and decision-making groups: group versus individual decision making, groupthink, and decision by consensus versus decision by majority vote.

Group versus Individual Decision Making Is group decision making superior to individual decision making? Evidence indicates that group decision making usually is superior to individual decision making (Johnson & Johnson, 2000), even when an individual decision is made by an expert.

There appear to be several reasons why group decision making is generally superior. First, through group interaction, the knowledge, abilities, and resources of each member are pooled. An individual acting alone often lacks some of the information, skills, or resources needed to arrive at the highest-quality decision. Second, working in the presence of others motivates a person to put forth more effort, to be more

CASE EXAMPLE Nominal-Group Approach—A Problem Identification Technique for Problem-Solving Groups

The nominal-group approach was developed by Delbecq and Van de Ven (1971) as a problem identification technique in social program development efforts. The approach involves meeting with potential users of a service. A *nominal group* is defined as "a group in which individuals work in the presence of others but do not verbally interact" (Van de Ven & Delbecq, 1971, p. 205). This need-identification approach emphasizes the importance of understanding clearly the view of the population that the group is trying to serve and asserts that potential consumers of new services should articulate their needs, problems, and goals. The main orientation is to respond to consumers' needs rather than independently develop programs for them. To accomplish this objective, the nominal-group approach is designed to receive input from all group members rather than just the more vocal or aggressive ones, as often happens in conventional group discussions. This technique has successfully been used in such applications as determining the housing difficulties of college students, reasons that have led delinquent youth into difficulty with police (Zastrow, 1973), and specific course topics wanted by students enrolling in social work courses (Zastrow & Navarre, 1977).

Research indicates that the nominal-group approach is superior to brainstorming and other types of interaction in groups in generating information relevant to a problem situation. Both quantity and quality of suggestions are enhanced with this technique (Van de Ven & Delbecq, 1971). Several features appear to be involved in leading to this superiority. The approach has a game mystique that stimulates the interest of participants. Creative tension is stimulated by the presence of others, which fosters individual commitment to the task. Evaluation of items is avoided, which substantially reduces the pressure against expressing minority opinions or conventional ideas. Conflicting, incompatible ideas are tolerated. Furthermore, the approach appears to be "a time-saving process since it can be activated and concluded with greater rapidity than interacting group processes" (Van de Ven & Delbecq, 1971, p. 210).

The mechanics of conducting a nominal group are as follows:

1. Gather together a group of participants, any size, ranging up to about 100, and explain the nature of the study. Emphasize the importance of their ideas related to this topic. Care should be taken to obtain a representative cross-section of the populations of interest.
2. Randomly divide the participants into small groups ranging in size from five to eight. Seat each group around a separate table or in desks arranged in a circle.
3. Distribute to each participant a sheet of paper containing a question that must be answered. For example, the wording for determining what social work students in a class see as shortcomings in the social work program that should be addressed might be: "What do you see as shortcomings in our social work program?"

Please—No Talking

4. For 15 to 20 minutes, the participants privately list items they feel are in response to the question being asked; no talking is permitted during this period.
5. A round-robin listing technique is then used in which each individual in turn is given the opportunity to disclose one item at a time to the group. This listing is done separately for each group with one of the members acting as a recorder. Ideas may be recorded on flip-chart paper or on a chalkboard. This round-robin listing continues until all members indicate they have no further ideas to share. Until this point is reached, there is no discussion or evaluation of ideas presented.
6. Following the listing of all ideas, the flip-chart sheets are posted on the wall with masking tape. There is a brief, informal discussion of the items, which is focused on clarifying what the ideas mean. There are two different approaches to reviewing the items. Either (1) all items are made known to all participants, or (2) members of each group briefly review only the items recorded for their group. Both approaches appear to work. With smaller groups, the first is usually used. With larger groups, in which the total number of listed items becomes very large, the second approach is generally used.
7. Once the participants are familiar with the items listed, each is asked to write privately on index cards the five items he or she feels are the most important.
8. These selections are then tabulated and posted. The highest-ranked problems or topics represent those considered most important by the group members.

careful, and to increase the quality of the work. Third, having more people working on a problem increases the probability that someone in the group will suggest the highest-quality solution. Fourth, through group interaction the members can build on one another's ideas and develop a high-quality decision based on this building-block approach. Fifth, through group discussion there is a greater chance of identifying the positive and negative consequences of each alternative. Therefore, the negative consequences of an inferior decision are more likely to be identified. Sixth, it is easier to identify other people's mistakes than it is to identify your own. Through group interaction you are more likely to identify the problem areas in the favorite alternatives of others, and others are more likely to identify the problem areas in your favorite alternative.

In general, the effectiveness of group decision making is enhanced when there is high involvement by all group members. High involvement increases the willingness of members to share their information and abilities in making a decision, increases their allegiance to the group, increases their commitment to implementing the decision, and increases their commitment to working for the group in the future. Most groups can become more effective by seeking to increase the involvement of all group members in making decisions.

There are only a few situations in which decisions might best be made by one or a few individuals: (1) when a decision has to be made so quickly it is not possible to have a meeting; (2) when the decision is relatively unimportant and the person making the decision follows precedents previously set by the group; and (3) when the decision is relatively unimportant, does not require committed action by most members of a group, and there is no reason to believe the group will object to the decision.

But there are also problems with group decision making. At times a subgroup will seek to "railroad" a decision that benefits them but is counterproductive for the whole group or for certain people outside the group. (Hitler, for example, used many tactics to sway groups he worked with to begin World War II and to exterminate 6 million Jews.) Railroading tactics include pressuring a group to make a quick decision without giving members time to analyze all the consequences, withholding information that is adverse to the desired decision, buying votes with promises, and suggesting there may be negative consequences for members who do not vote for the desired decision.

Another problem in group decision making is that friendships and paybacks for past favors sometimes lead members to vote for "the person" rather than for a decision based on thorough analysis of the consequences of the alternatives. Republicans and Democrats in Congress, for example, largely vote along party lines.

Sometimes groups reach incorrect or ineffective decisions because of a phenomenon known as *groupthink*

Groupthink Irving Janis (1971) identified groupthink as an unusual condition that prevents effective problem solving. Janis studied groups that advised presidents of the United States and found that powerful social pressures were often exerted whenever a dissident began to voice objections to what otherwise appeared to be a group consensus. *Groupthink* is a problem-solving process in which proposals are accepted without a critical, careful review of the pros and cons of the alternatives and in which considerable social pressure is brought to bear against expressing opposing points of view. Groupthink occurs partially because the norms of the group hold that it is more important to bolster group morale than to evaluate all alternatives critically. Another group norm that increases groupthink is that members should remain loyal to the group by sticking with the policies to which the group has already committed itself, even if those policies are not having the intended effects or are having disturbing unintended consequences.

Janis (1971) listed a number of factors that promote groupthink, including the following:

- Members have an illusion of being invulnerable, which leads them to become overly optimistic about their selected courses of action, to take extraordinary risks, and to fail to respond to clear warnings of danger.

- Members have an unquestioning belief in the group's moral rightness, which leads them to ignore the ethical consequences of their decisions.
- The group applies social pressures of disapproval on any member who momentarily questions the basic policies or who raises questions about a policy alternative favored by the majority.
- The group constructs rationalizations to discount warnings and other forms of negative feedback that would, if taken seriously, lead the members to rethink basic assumptions about policies that are not working out well.
- Group members hold stereotyped views of the leaders of opposing groups. Either these leaders are viewed as either being so evil that it would be a mistake to try genuinely to negotiate differences, or they are viewed as so stupid or so weak that they will not be able to prevent the group from attaining its objectives.
- Members sometimes assume "mind guard" roles in which they attempt to protect their leader and the group from negative information that might lead them to question the morality and effectiveness of past decisions.
- Members keep quiet about their misgivings and even minimize to themselves the importance of these misgivings. Through self-censorship members avoid deviating from what appears to be group consensus.
- Members believe practically everyone in the group fully agrees with the policies and programs of the group.

Numerous poor decision-making practices result from groupthink. The group limits its discussion to only those courses of action that are consistent with past decisions and policies. As a result, divergent strategies (some of them viable) are not considered. The group fails to reexamine a selected course of action, even when it discovers risks, drawbacks, and unintended consequences not previously considered. The group makes little effort to get cost-benefit information on possible strategies from experts who might be able to supply more accurate information. Members seek primarily to obtain facts and listen to opinions that support their preferred policy and tend to ignore facts and opinions that do not. The group fails to work out contingency plans to cope with foreseeable setbacks, and it spends little time considering how the chosen strategy might be sabotaged by political opponents or hampered by bureaucratic red tape.

Groupthink apparently affected decision making prior to the 2003 invasion of Iraq. Yahoo News (2004) reported the following:

EP 2.1.7a

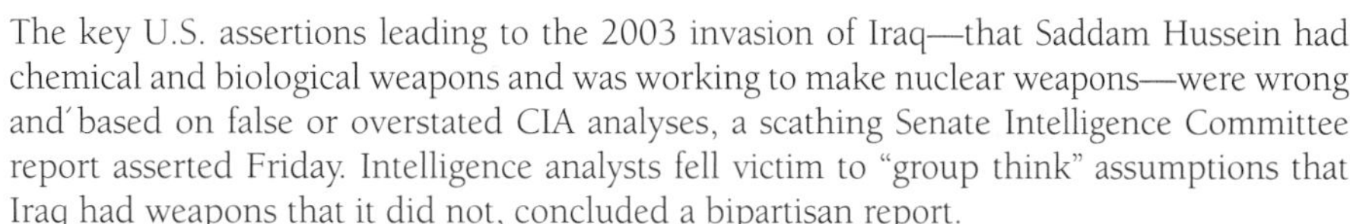
> The key U.S. assertions leading to the 2003 invasion of Iraq—that Saddam Hussein had chemical and biological weapons and was working to make nuclear weapons—were wrong and based on false or overstated CIA analyses, a scathing Senate Intelligence Committee report asserted Friday. Intelligence analysts fell victim to "group think" assumptions that Iraq had weapons that it did not, concluded a bipartisan report.

Exercise 6.2: My Groupthink Experience

Goal: This exercise is designed to assist you in understanding and applying the theoretical material on groupthink.

Step 1: Describe an experience in which you believed your group was going in the wrong direction yet you failed to express your thoughts or opinions.

Step 2: Specify why you failed to express your thoughts or opinions.

Step 3: Do you believe your reasons for not expressing your thoughts or opinions are consistent or inconsistent with groupthink? Explain your views.

Consensus versus Majority Voting Decision making by consensus is usually the most effective approach for getting all members to support and work for a decision. Consensus means that everyone is willing to go along with the decision, at least temporarily. This approach is also the most time-consuming because the concerns of each member need to be dealt with. For many decisions, consensus is difficult to achieve because members are likely to have diverse opinions about what should be done.

To use consensus effectively, group members need to have a certain mind-set, and the group has to have a trusting, cooperative atmosphere. For consensus to be arrived at, members need to feel free to present their views as clearly and logically as possible but to avoid blindly arguing their own individual views. They need to listen to and respect the views of other members. Members should *avoid* going along with the group if they believe the majority opinion is a mistake. It is a mistake to yield to the majority if the only reason is to avoid conflict and appear united. Members, however, might yield to the majority opinion if that position appears to have merit and is a position they believe has a fair chance of having positive outcomes.

To make consensus work effectively, differences of opinion are sought out and respectfully dealt with. Disagreements and divergent views are advantageous because they increase the chances that all crucial aspects will be reviewed, that members will build on the views of others, and that viable decisions will be made.

With consensus, the participation of all members is encouraged. The emphasis is on finding the best solution that everyone can agree on and support. If a group becomes stalemated between two possible alternatives, a vote is not taken to allow one subgroup to win while the other loses. Instead, a third alternative is sought to incorporate the major desires of both subgroups.

There are a number of benefits to consensus. Consensus resolves controversies and conflicts, so it increases the group's ability to make future high-quality decisions. If group members feel they have participated in the decision and support it, they are more likely to contribute their resources to implement the decision. Consensus is useful in making important, serious, and complex decisions in which the success of the decision depends on the commitment of all members.

There are some disadvantages to consensus. It takes a great deal of time and psychological energy. The pressure for group consensus can lead to groupthink. In this situation members go along with what they believe is the majority opinion, even when they have evidence or information (which they fail to share for fear of making waves) that the probable decision will be unproductive or even destructive. In addition, consensus will not work in many groups for a variety of reasons. A high level of trust may not exist in the group, thereby not allowing candor, honesty, and directness. Some members may try to dominate or manipulate the group rather than listen to and support one another as individuals. Some members may see the slow process required to arrive at consensus as painful, aggravating, and a waste of time.

Most groups make decisions by simple majority vote. With this approach, issues are discussed until they are clarified and a simple majority of the members has arrived at an alternative. A vote is then taken. There are several advantages to this type of decision making. Decisions are arrived at much faster than with the consensus approach. Most decisions in a group are not so important that full support of all members is necessary to achieve the objectives of the decision. Also, majority vote does not require, to as great an extent, the characteristics that are essential for consensus (such as trust, open communication, and willingness to give up one's favorite position).

There are also shortcomings of the simple majority approach. Minority opinions are not always safeguarded. Racial groups, women, certain ethnic groups, gay men and lesbians, and people with disabilities are minority groups that in the past have suffered from adverse decisions made by simple majority voting. Majority voting frequently splits a group into winners and losers, with the losers often becoming angry, frustrated, and apathetic. Sometimes the group of losers is nearly as large as the winners (such as having 49% of the vote), but they end up feeling their concerns are ignored. A large-size minority that feels it was outvoted may not lend its resources to implement the decision and may even work to subvert or overturn it. If the final vote alienates a minority, the group's future effectiveness is diminished. The majority rule approach may be interpreted by the minority as being an unfair means of control and manipulation by the majority. Therefore, to maintain effective group functioning, groups that use majority voting should seek to create a climate in which members feel they have "had their day in court" and have an obligation to go along with the group decision.

A compromise between consensus and simple majority is a high-percentage majority vote (such as two-thirds or three-fourths). This approach requires more time to arrive at a decision than a simple majority because more votes are needed. But it takes less time than consensus because not everyone has to be convinced or persuaded. A strong minority (such as 45%) can block a decision it dislikes, but a small majority cannot force its views on a strong minority. However, a small minority may still feel it is being controlled and manipulated by a high-percentage majority vote. A high-percentage majority vote will generally draw stronger support from group members than the simple majority approach, but it will not generate as much support as the consensus approach.

Focus Groups

Closely related to task groups and problem-solving and decision-making groups are focus groups. Focus groups are formed for a variety of purposes: to identify needs or issues, to generate proposals to resolve an identified issue, to test reactions to alternative approaches to an issue, and so forth. A focus group is a specially assembled collection of people who respond through a semistructured or structured discussion to the concerns and interests of the person, group, or organization that invited the participants. Members of the group are invited and encouraged to bring up their own ideas and views.

A *representative group* is a version of the focus group. Its strength is that its members have been selected specifically to represent different perspectives and points of view in a community. At its best, a representative group is a focus group that reflects the diversity in the community and seeks to bring these diverse views to the table; at its worst, it is a front group manipulated by schemers to make the community think that it has been involved.

Self-Help Groups

Self-help groups are increasingly popular and often successful in helping individuals with certain social or personal problems. Katz and Bender (1976) provided a comprehensive definition of *self-help groups:*

> Self-help groups are voluntary, small group structures for mutual aid and the accomplishment of a special purpose. They are usually formed by peers who have come together

CASE EXAMPLE Parents Anonymous—A Self-Help Group*

Parents Anonymous (PA) is a national self-help organization for parents who have abused or neglected their children. PA was originally established in 1970 by Jolly K in California, who was desperate to find help to meet her needs. For 4 years prior to this time, she struggled with an uncontrollable urge to severely punish her daughter. One afternoon she attempted to strangle her daughter. Desperate, she sought help from the local child-guidance clinic. She was placed in therapy. When asked by her therapist what she could do about this situation, she developed an idea; as she explained (Zauner, 1974, p. 247), "if alcoholics could stop drinking by getting together, and gamblers could stop gambling, maybe the same principle would work for abusers, too." With her therapist's encouragement, she formed "Mothers Anonymous" in 1970, and started a few local chapters in California. Nearly every major city in the United States and Canada now has a chapter, and the name has been changed to Parents Anonymous (because fathers who abuse their children are also eligible to join).

PA uses some of the basic therapeutic concepts of Alcoholics Anonymous. PA is a crisis intervention program that offers two main forms of help: (1) a weekly group meeting in which members share experiences and feelings and learn better control of their emotions and (2) personal and telephone contact among members during periods of crisis, particularly when a member feels a nearly uncontrollable desire to take his or her anger or frustration out on a child. Parents may be referred to PA by a social agency (including protective services) or may be self-referrals of parents who are aware they need help.

Starkweather and Turner (1975) described why some parents who abuse their children would rather participate in a self-help group than receive professional counseling:

> It has been our experience that most (abusive) parents judge themselves more harshly than other more objective people tend to judge them. The fear of losing their children frequently diminishes with reassurance from other members that they are not the monsters they think they are.
>
> Generally speaking, PA members are so afraid they are going to be judged by others as harshly as they judge themselves that they are afraid to go out and seek help. Frequently our members express fears of dealing with a professional person, seeing differences in education, sex, or social status as basic differences that would prevent easy communication or mutual understanding.
>
> Members express feelings of gratification at finding that other parents are "in the same boat." They contrast this with their feelings about professionals who, they often assume, have not taken out the time from their training and current job responsibilities to raise families of their own. (p. 151)

PA emphasizes honesty and directness. In the outside world, parents who are prone to abuse their children learn to hide this problem because society finds it difficult to stomach. In contrast, the goal of PA is to help parents admit and accept the fact that they are abusive. The term *abuse* is used liberally at meetings. PA has found that this insistence on frankness has a healthy effect. Parents are relieved because they've finally found a group of people who are able to accept abusive parents for what they really are. Furthermore, only when they are able to admit they are abusive can they begin to find ways to cope with this problem.

During PA meetings parents are expected actually to say they are beating their child or engaging in other forms of abuse, and the members challenge each other to find ways to curb such activities. Members also share constructive approaches that each has found useful, and efforts are made to help one another develop specific plans for dealing with situations that have in the past resulted in abusive episodes. Members learn to recognize danger signs and to then take necessary action to curb the potential abuse.

Leadership in the group is provided by a group member selected by the parents themselves. The leader, called a "chairperson," is normally assisted by a professional sponsor who serves as resource and backup person to the chair and the group members. The social worker who becomes the sponsor must be prepared to perform a variety of roles, including teacher-trainer, broker of community services needed by parents, advocate, consultant, and, in some instances, behavior changer (Hull, 1978).

*This description of Parents Anonymous is adapted from Charles Zastrow, "Parents Anonyumous," in *Social Work with Groups: Using the Class as a Group Leadership Laboratory*, 5th ed. © 2002 Cengage Learning, pp. 159-161.

for mutual assistance in satisfying a common need, overcoming a common handicap or life-disrupting problem, and bringing about desired social, and/or personal change. The initiators and members of such groups perceive that their needs are not, or cannot be, met by or through existing social institutions. Self-help groups emphasize face-to-face social interactions and the assumption of personal responsibility by members. They often provide material assistance as well as emotional support; they are frequently cause-oriented, and

Exhibit 6.1 Examples of Self-Help Groups

Organization	Service Focus
Abused Parents of America	For parents who are abused by their adult children
Adoptees' Liberty Movement Association	For adoptees searching for their natural parents
Alcoholics Anonymous	For adult alcoholics
American Diabetes Association	Clubs for diabetics, their families, and friends
American Sleep Apnea Association	For persons with sleep apnea and their families
Burns United Support Group	For burn victims
Candlelighters Childhood Cancer Foundation	For parents of young children with cancer
Conjoined Twins International	For families of conjoined twins
CROHNS	For persons with Crohns disease and their families
CUB (Concerned United Birthparents)	For adoption-affected people in coping with adoption, including assistance for locating family members
Depressed Anonymous	For depressed persons
Divorce Care	For divorced persons
Emotions Anonymous	For persons with emotional problems
Encephalitis Support Group	For those with encephalitis and their families
Families Anonymous	For relatives and friends of drug abusers
Fortune Society	For ex-offenders and their families
Gam-Anon	For families of gamblers
Gray Panthers	An intergenerational group
Herpes Anonymous	For persons with herpes and their families and friends
High Risk Moms, Inc.	For women experiencing a high-risk or problem pregnancy
Impotents World Association	For impotent men and their partners
Make Today Count	For persons with cancer and their families
Molesters Anonymous	For men who molest children
National Organization for Women	For women's rights
Overeaters Anonymous	For overweight persons
Parents Anonymous	For parents of abused children
Sexaholics Anonymous	For those with sexually self-destructive behavior
WINGS Foundation, Inc.	For men and women traumatized by incest

promulgate an ideology or values through which members may attain an enhanced sense of personal identity. (p. 9)

To convey the varieties and focuses of self-help groups that now exist (see Exhibit 6.1), two different classifications of these groups are summarized in the following paragraphs. Katz and Bender (1976) classified self-help groups into the following five categories:

1. Groups that focus on self-fulfillment or personal growth. Examples include Alcoholics Anonymous, Recovery Inc. (for former mental patients), Gamblers Anonymous, and Weight Watchers.

2. Groups that focus on social advocacy. Examples include Welfare Rights Organizations, MADD (Mothers Against Drunken Drivers), and the Committee for the Rights of the Disabled. Katz and Bender (1976) noted that the advocacy "can be both on behalf of broad issues, such as legislation, the creation of new services, change in the policies of existing institutions and so on, or it can be on behalf of individuals, families, or other small groups" (p. 38).
3. Groups that focus on creating alternative patterns for living. Examples include Gay Liberation and certain religious cults such as the Moonies.
4. *Outcast haven* or *rock-bottom* groups. Katz and Bender (1976) defined this type as follows:

   > These groups provide a refuge for the desperate, who are attempting to secure personal protection from the pressures of life and society, or to save themselves from mental or physical decline. This type of group usually involves a total commitment, a living-in arrangement or sheltered environment, with close supervision by peers or persons who have successfully grappled with similar problems of their own. (p. 38)

   Examples include ex-drug addict organizations.

5. Groups of mixed types that have characteristics of two or more categories. One such group is Parents Without Partners, which promotes personal growth, advocacy, and social events for its members.

Powell (1987) classified self-help groups into these five categories:

1. *Habit-disturbance organizations:* These organizations focus on a problem that is specific and concrete. Examples include Alcoholics Anonymous, Smokestoppers, Overeaters Anonymous, Gamblers Anonymous, Take Off Pounds Sensibly (TOPS), Women for Sobriety, Narcotics Anonymous, and Weight Watchers.
2. *General-purpose organizations:* These organizations address a wide range of problems and predicaments. Examples are Parents Anonymous (for parents of abused children), Emotions Anonymous (for persons with emotional problems), Compassionate Friends (for persons who have experienced a loss through death), and GROW, an organization that works to prevent hospitalization of mental patients through a comprehensive program of mutual aid. In contrast to habit-disturbance organizations, general-purpose organizations address a wider range of problems and predicaments.
3. *Lifestyle organizations:* These organizations seek to provide support for, and advocate for, the lifestyles of people whose members are viewed by society as being different (the dominant groups in society are generally indifferent or hostile to that difference). Examples of this category include Widow-to-Widow programs, Parents Without Partners, ALMA society (Adoptees' Liberty Movement Association), PFLAG (Parents, Families, and Friends of Lesbians and Gays), National Gay and Lesbian Task Force, and Gray Panthers, an intergenerational group that advocates for the elderly.
4. *Physical handicap organizations:* These organizations focus on major chronic diseases and conditions. Some are for people with conditions that are relatively stable, some for conditions that are likely to get worse, and some for terminal illnesses. Examples of this category include Make Today Count (for the terminally ill and their families), Emphysema Anonymous, Lost Chord clubs (for those who have had laryngectomies), stroke clubs, Mended Hearts, the Spina Bifida Association, and Self-Help for Hard of Hearing People.
5. *Significant-other organizations:* The members of these organizations are parents, spouses, and close relatives of troubled and troubling persons. Very often, members of significant-other groups are last-resort caregivers. Significant others contend with dysfunctional behavior. Through sharing their feelings, they obtain a measure of relief. In the course of sharing, they may also learn about new resources or new approaches. Examples of such organizations include Al-Anon, Gam-Anon, Toughlove, and the National Alliance for the Mentally Ill.

Why are self-help groups successful? Many self-help groups stress (1) members admitting to the group that they have a problem, (2) members recounting to the group their past experiences with their problem and their plans for handling the problem in the future, and (3) support from members (for example, a member who feels an intense urge to drink or to abuse a child is encouraged to call another member of the group to come over to stay with the person until the urge subsides).

Members of self-help groups have visceral understanding of one another's problems, which helps them help others. Having experienced the misery and consequences of the problem, they are highly motivated and dedicated to finding ways to help themselves and their fellow sufferers. The participants also benefit from the *helper therapy principle:* A helper gains psychological rewards by helping others (Riessman, 1965). Helping others makes a person feel good and worthwhile; it also enables the helpers to put their own problems into perspective as they see that others' problems may be as serious as, or even more serious than, their own.

When people help each other in self-help groups, they tend to feel empowered because they are able to control important aspects of their lives. When help is given from the outside (from an expert or a professional), there is a danger that dependency may develop, which is the opposite effect of empowerment. Empowerment increases motivation, energy, personal growth, and an ability to help that goes beyond helping oneself or receiving help.

Some self-help groups advocate for the rights and lifestyles of people whose members are viewed by society as being different. One such group is the National Gay and Lesbian Task Force. Some self-help groups (such as the National Association for Retarded Citizens) raise funds and operate community programs. Many people with a personal problem use self-help groups in the same way others use social agencies. An additional advantage is that self-help groups generally are able to operate with a minimal budget. Hundreds of these groups are in existence. Social workers often act as brokers in linking clients to appropriate self-help groups.

Riessman (1987, pp. ix–x) summarizes the distinctive characteristics of self-help groups as follows:

- A noncompetitive, cooperative orientation
- An anti-elite, antibureaucratic focus
- An emphasis on the indigenous—people who have the problem and know a lot about it from the inside, from experiencing it
- An attitude of do what you can, one day at a time (you can't solve everything at once)
- A shared, often revolving leadership
- An attitude of being helped through helping (the helper-therapy principle)...
- An understanding that helping is not a commodity to be bought and sold
- A strong optimism regarding the ability to change
- An understanding that although small may not necessarily be beautiful, it is a place to begin and the unit to build on
- A critical stance toward professionalism, which is often seen as pretentious, purist, distant, and mystifying. Self-helpers like simplicity and informality
- An emphasis on the consumer....The consumer is a producer of help and services
- An understanding that helping is at the center—knowing how to receive help, give help, and help yourself...
- An emphasis on empowerment

EP 2.1.10e

Exercise 6.3: Merits and Shortcomings of a Self-Help Group

Goal: This exercise is designed to assist you in having a better understanding of the merits and shortcomings of self-help groups.

Step 1: Interview someone who has participated in a self-help group. (If you have participated yourself, you may answer the questions in this exercise by sharing your personal experiences.) Most colleges have several self-help groups on campus—such as an eating disorder group, a gay and lesbian group, and groups combating substance abuse. The student counseling center is usually a good resource for identifying contact persons for the available self-help groups. Describe the goals of the self-help group that you gather information on.

Step 2: Describe the activities of this self-help group.

Step 3: Ask the person you interview to summarize the merits and shortcomings of this self-help group, and then record this information here.

EP 2.1.7a

The American Self-Help Group Clearinghouse is a web-based database of over 1,100 national and international self-help support groups for health, mental health, addictions, abuse, disabilities, parenting, caregiver concerns, and other stressful life situations. It is compiled and edited by Barbara Jo White and Edward J. Madara, with the web version updated by Nicole Klem. To access any self-help group contained in the database, type in a keyword on the website. The website can be easily accessed by typing "American Self-Help Group Clearinghouse," into your web browser.

Exercise 6.4: Checking Out Online Self-Help Groups

Goal: This exercise is designed to familiarize you with online self-help groups.

Using the Internet, check out the web pages of three online self-help groups. Some suggested websites are the following:

Alcoholics Anonymous: www.alcoholicsanonymous.org

Adult Children of Alcoholics: www.adultchildren.org

American Foundation for Suicide Prevention: www.afsp.org

Gamblers Anonymous: www.gamblersanonymous.org

Overeaters Anonymous: www.overeatersanonymous.org

Sexaholics Anonymous: www.sa.org

(You can locate over 1,100 additional self-help groups by typing "American Self-Help Group Clearinghouse" into your web browser. When this website is accessed, type in a keyword of the support group that you want.)

Summarize the information you find about the three online self-help groups.

Socialization Groups

The objective of socialization groups generally is to develop or change the attitudes and behaviors of group members to make members more socially acceptable. Developing social skills, increasing self-confidence, and planning for the future are other goals.

CASE EXAMPLE Socialization—Group at an Assisted Living Facility

Winterhaven is an assisted living facility that has 32 beds for mostly elderly residents. All the residents have either beginning-stage dementia issues or mobility issues—such as difficulty in walking because of medical conditions such as severe arthritis or stroke. The facility is staffed with nurses, nursing assistants, food preparation personnel, and one social worker, Jean Schible.

Every weekday evening at 7 p.m. a group meeting is held. All the residents are invited, but usually only about half of them attend. Some are too ill, some have visitors, and a few may be away on an outing.

This group meeting has three main objectives. One is to serve as a vehicle for residents to express their satisfactions and dissatisfactions with the facility and its programs. Sometimes the group meeting appears to be primarily a gripe session, but the social worker (who leads the meetings) makes sure the staff make conscientious efforts at improvement when the residents' concerns are legitimate. A frequent request is for greater variation in the meals that are served.

Another objective is to provide interesting lectures and activities. Speakers from the surrounding community are invited to talk about topics of interest to the residents. Often the speakers encourage residents to engage in discussions. Winterhaven is near a university, so faculty members are sometimes invited to talk. If there are no speakers, the social worker may lead the group in playing a game—such as a card game. At other times, musicians are invited to play for an hour or an hour and a half. Speakers and these activities have the benefit of giving residents something to look forward to. Many of them spend hours and hours in their own rooms—which can lead to melancholy and a sense of isolation. The group meeting helps to combat loneliness and melancholy.

The third objective of the group meeting is to convey information about planned daily activities and changes in the overall program at Winterhaven.

Illustrations include working with the following: a group of predelinquent youth in group activities to curb delinquency trends, a youth group of diverse racial backgrounds to reduce racial tensions, a group of elderly residents at a nursing home to remotivate them and get them involved in various activities, and a group of boys at a correctional school to help them make plans for returning to their home community. Leadership of such groups requires considerable skill and knowledge in using the group to foster individual growth and change. These leadership roles are frequently filled by social workers. (See the Case Example "Socialization—A Group at an Assisted Living Facility.")

Counseling Groups

Counseling groups are generally composed of members with rather severe emotional or personal problems. Leadership of such groups requires considerable skill, perceptiveness, knowledge of human behavior and group dynamics, group counseling capacities, and ability to use the group to bring about behavioral changes. Among other skills, the group leader needs to be highly perceptive regarding how each member is being affected by what is being communicated. Considerable competence is needed to develop and maintain a constructive atmosphere within the group. Like the goal of one-to-one counseling, the goal of counseling groups is generally to have members explore their problems in depth and then to develop one or more strategies for resolving them. The group facilitator generally uses one or more therapy approaches as a guide for changing attitudes and behaviors. These approaches include reality therapy, learning theory, rational therapy, and psychodrama.

Group counseling is being used increasingly in social work. It has several advantages over one-to-one counseling. The *helper therapy principle* (in which members interchange roles and sometimes become the helper for someone else's problems) is generally operative. In such roles, members receive psychological rewards for helping others. Groups also help members put their problems into perspective as they realize others have equally serious problems. Groups also help members who are having interaction problems test out new interaction approaches. Research has shown that it is generally easier to change the attitudes of an individual in a group

CASE EXAMPLE Counseling Group for Spouses of Adults with Cancer

Eight years ago Linda Sonsthagen's husband was diagnosed with cancer. Linda was a social worker, and her husband was a successful life insurance agent. They had two sons in grade school. Mr. Sonsthagen died 4 1/2 years ago, after having gone through a variety of treatment programs and experiencing considerable pain. He lost weight and his hair fell out. These years were extremely difficult for the Sonsthagens. Linda had to take a larger role in raising the children and was the primary caregiver to both her husband and the children. During these years, the Sonsthagens found that relatives and friends shied away from them. It took several months before they became aware that the reason was that friends and relatives saw cancer as something they didn't understand and wanted to avoid. Even more difficult was dealing emotionally with not knowing the course of the disorder, going through cycles of hope and then disappointment as different treatment approaches were tried. As her husband became more incapacitated, Linda found she had to assume more of his tasks—for example, home repairs, maintaining their two cars, disciplining the children, and other daily household tasks.

After her husband's death, Linda and the two children went through several months of mourning and grief. Linda discovered it was somewhat awkward to go to social functions alone. Fortunately, she had two single female friends with whom she increasingly socialized. These were very difficult years for Linda. She needed more than 2 years after her husband's death to rebuild her life in such a way that she was again comfortable. During these years, she received some financial help from the local chapter of the American Cancer Society. Through this organization, she met another woman whose husband was dying of cancer. They gave each other emotional support and shared useful ideas for handling problems.

Eighteen months ago Linda told the local chapter of the American Cancer Society that she was willing to volunteer her time to start a group for spouses of people with cancer and for spouses adjusting to a recent cancer death. The Cancer Society gave its approval and endorsement.

Linda started with nine members. The objectives were to give emotional support, to help members handle the new responsibilities they had to take on, and to help them deal with their emotional reactions. Linda used primarily a combination of rational therapy and reality therapy (see Modules 1 and 3). Reality therapy helped group members better understand and make decisions and plans for the problems they faced. For example, for members whose spouses had cancer, one focus was how to inform and handle their friends' and relatives' reactions to the illness. Survivors focused on rebuilding their lives. Rational therapy countered unwanted emotions. Common emotions included depression, guilt, anxiety, the feeling of being overwhelmed, and anger (particularly resulting from "Why does this have to happen to me?"). Members were instructed on how to do a rational self-analysis (see Module 1) of their unwanted emotions, and members often shared and discussed their analyses at group meetings.

On several occasions group members stated that the group was very helpful. They mentioned that knowing others faced similar plights was beneficial in and of itself. Seeing how others handled difficult decisions inspired them and gave them useful ideas on how to handle crises they faced. When a member suffered a serious crisis (for example, a spouse hospitalized for a serious operation), other members were available for phone contact and to lend physical assistance.

After 8 months, the local chapter of the American Cancer Society was so encouraged by the results that it offered Linda a full-time position to run additional groups and to be available for individual counseling for people with cancer and for their relatives. Linda gave up her part-time job as a counselor at the YWCA and took this position. Her first effort was to divide her group, which was growing, into two groups. The definition of eligible membership was expanded: One group was for adults who have a family member with cancer, the other for survivors. At this time, Linda is leading one group of the first type and two groups of the second type.

than in one-on-one counseling (Johnson & Johnson, 2009). Research on conformity has found that group pressure can have a substantial effect on changing attitudes and beliefs (Johnson & Johnson, 2009). Furthermore, group counseling permits the social worker to help more than one person at a time, with potential savings in the use of professional effort.

In essence a group facilitator uses the principles of one-to-one counseling (discussed in Chapter 5) and of group dynamics (see Chapter 7) to work with clients to change dysfunctional attitudes and behavior. Generally the group facilitator also uses the principles of certain treatment techniques (such as reality therapy, rational therapy, parent effectiveness training, and assertiveness training) to help clients resolve personal and emotional problems. The selection of the techniques to use should be based on the nature of the problems presented.

Encounter Groups

Encounter groups and sensitivity training groups (these terms are used somewhat synonymously) are groups in which members relate to each other in a close interpersonal manner and self-disclosure is required. The goal is to improve interpersonal awareness. An *encounter group* is a typically unstructured group in which participants seek to increase their sensitivity, reponsiveness, and emotional expressiveness, as by freely verbalizing and responding to emotions. It is designed to promote the personal growth of the participants.

A *sensitivity group* is a nonclinical group (not intended for persons with severe emotional problems), which focuses on interpersonal interactions and on self-awareness and self-understanding in an effort to help them become more aware of their own feelings and behaviors, and of the feelings and behaviors of others.

Sensitivity groups usually generate an outpouring of emotion rarely found in other groups.

An encounter group may meet for a few hours or for a few days. Once increased interpersonal awareness is achieved, it is anticipated that attitudes and behaviors will change. For these changes to occur, a three-phase process generally takes place: unfreezing, change, and refreezing.

Unfreezing occurs through a deliberate process of interacting in nontraditional ways. Our attitudes and behavior patterns have been developed through years of social experiences, experimentation, and refinement. Such patterns have now become nearly automatic. Our interpersonal style generally has considerable utility in our everyday interactions. Deep down, however, we may recognize a need for improvement but are reluctant to make the effort, partly because our present style is somewhat functional and partly because we are afraid to reveal things about ourselves. Unfreezing occurs when we decide certain patterns of our present behavior need to be changed and we are psychologically ready to explore ways to make changes.

Tubbs and Baird (1976) described the unfreezing process in sensitivity groups:

> Unfreezing occurs when our expectations are violated. We become less sure of ourselves when traditional ways of doing things are not followed. In the encounter group, the leader usually does not act like a leader. He or she frequently starts with a brief statement encouraging the group members to participate, to be open and honest, and to expect things to be different. Group members may begin by taking off their shoes, sitting in a circle on the floor, and holding hands with their eyes closed. The leader then encourages them to feel intensely the sensations they are experiencing, the size and texture of the hands they are holding and so forth.
>
> Other structured exercises or experiences may be planned to help the group focus on the "here-and-now" experience. Pairs may go for "trust walks" in which each person alternatively is led around with his eyes closed. Sitting face-to-face and conducting a hand dialogue, or a silent facial mirroring often helps to break the initial barriers to change. Other techniques may involve the "pass around" in which a person in the center of a tight circle relaxes and is physically passed around the circle. Those who have trouble feeling a part of the group are encouraged to break into or out of the circle of people whose hands are tightly held. With these experiences, most participants begin to feel more open to conversation about what they have experienced. This sharing of experiences or self-disclosure about the here and now provides more data for the group to discuss. (p. 48)

The second phase of the process is *change*. In sensitivity groups, change is facilitated by spontaneous reactions or feedback to how a person "comes across" to others. In everyday interaction we almost never get spontaneous feedback, and we tend to repeat ineffective interaction patterns because we lack knowledge of our effect on others. But in sensitivity groups, such feedback is strongly encouraged. The following set of interactions illustrates such feedback:

Carl: All right (in a sharp tone), let's get this trust walk over with, and stop dilly-dallying around. I'll lead the first person around—who wants to be blindfolded first?
Judy: Your statement makes me feel uncomfortable. I feel you're saying this group is a waste of your time. Also, it's the third time tonight you've ordered us around.
Jim: I feel the same way, like you're trying to tell us peons what to do. Even the tone of your voice sounds autocratic, and I get the message you're really down on this group.
Carl: I'm sorry, I didn't mean it to sound like that. I wonder if I do that outside the group too?

Such feedback provides new insights on how we affect others. Once problem interactions are identified, members are encouraged to try out new response patterns in the relative safety of the group.

The third and final phase is *refreezing*. Unfortunately, this term is not the most descriptive because it implies rigidity with a new set of response patterns. The goal in this phase is to experiment with new sets of behaviors so that members become growing, continually changing people who increasingly become more effective in their interactions with others. In terminating a sensitivity group, the leader may alert the participants to be on guard because former dysfunctional behavior patterns tend to creep back in.

The goal of sensitivity groups provides an interesting contrast to that of most counseling groups (see Exhibit 6.2). In counseling groups, the goal is for all members to explore their personal or emotional problems and develop a strategy to resolve the problems. In comparison, sensitivity groups foster increased personal and interpersonal awareness and then develop more effective interaction patterns. Sensitivity groups generally do not attempt to identify and change specific emotional or personal problems (drinking problems, feelings of depression, sexual dysfunctions, and so on). The philosophy behind sensitivity groups is that with increased personal and interpersonal awareness, people will be better able to avoid, cope with, and handle specific personal problems that arise.

Sensitivity groups are used for a wide variety of purposes: to train professional counselors to be more perceptive and effective in interpersonal interactions with clients and with other professionals, to train managers to be more effective in their business interactions, to help clients with overt relationship problems become more aware of how they affect others and to help them develop more effective interaction patterns, and to train interested citizens in becoming more aware and effective in their interactions.

Despite their popularity, sensitivity groups remain controversial. In some cases, inadequately trained and incompetent individuals have become self-proclaimed leaders and have enticed people to join through sensational advertising. If handled poorly, the short duration of some groups can intensify personal problems—for example, when

Exhibit 6.2 Contrasting Goals of Counseling Groups and Sensitivity Groups

Counseling Groups		Sensitivity Groups	
Step 1	**Step 2**	**Step 1**	**Step 2**
Examine problems in depth.	Develop and select from various resolution approaches a strategy to resolve the problem.	Help each person become more aware of self and how she or he affects others in inter-personal interactions.	Help person develop more effective interaction patterns.

a person's defense mechanisms are stripped away without developing adaptive coping patterns. Many authorities on sensitivity training disclaim the use of encounter groups as a form of psychotherapy and discourage those with serious personal problems from joining such groups. Carl Rogers (1970), in reviewing his own extensive experience as leader/participant, echoed these concerns:

> Frequently the behavior changes that occur, if any, are not lasting. In addition, the individual may become deeply involved in revealing himself and then be left with problems which are not worked through. Less common, but still noteworthy, there are also very occasional accounts of an individual having a psychotic episode during or immediately following an intensive group experience. We must keep in mind that not all people are suited for groups. (pp. 40–41)

In some cases, the popularity of sensitivity groups has led individuals to enter harmful groups with incompetent leaders where normal ethical standards have been abused. Shostrom (1969, pp. 38–39) has identified means by which those interested in encounter groups can prevent exploitation: (1) Never participate in a group of fewer than a half-dozen members. The necessary and valuable candor generated by an effective group cannot be dissipated, shared, or examined by too small a group, and scapegoating or purely vicious ganging up can develop. (2) Never join an encounter group on impulse—as a fling, binge, or surrender to the unplanned. (3) Never stay with a group that has a behavioral ax to grind. (4) Never participate in a group that lacks formal connection with a professional on whom you can check.

After reviewing the research on the outcome of sensitivity groups, Lieberman, Yalom, and Miles (1973) provided an appropriate perspective for those interested in the intensive group experience:

> Encounter groups present a clear and evident danger if they are used for radical surgery to produce a new man [person]. The danger is even greater when the leader and the participants share this misconception. If we no longer expect groups to produce magical, lasting change and if we stop seeing them as panaceas, we can regard them as useful, socially sanctioned opportunities for human beings to explore and to express themselves. Then we can begin to work on ways to improve them so that they may make a meaningful contribution toward solving human problems. (p. 73)

HOW TO START, LEAD, TERMINATE, AND EVALUATE GROUPS

In the remainder of this chapter we focus on guidelines for starting, running, and terminating groups. This section covers homework, session planning, relaxing before a meeting, cues on entering the meeting room, seating arrangements, introductions, role clarification, agendas, additional guidelines for leading a group, terminating a group, and evaluating a group. Many students fear taking a leadership role in groups. They are uncertain about what leaders do, and they fear they do not have the qualities or traits to be a leader. Amazingly, the truth is that even the most fearful and anxious students have already taken leadership roles in many groups. Every student has in the past been a member of several groups and has performed some essential tasks for these groups. As we shall see in Chapter 7, performing an essential task is simultaneously an effective leadership action.

Homework

Extensive preparation is the key to a successful experience for group members (including yourself). Even experienced leaders prepare carefully for each group and for each meeting.

When planning a new group, be sure to answer the following questions: What are the group's overall purpose and goals? What possible ways can these general goals be accomplished? What are the characteristics of the members? Do some members have unique, individual goals or needs? What resources do members need to accomplish the general goals? What should the agenda be for the first meeting? Group members should have considerable input in suggesting and deciding on the specific goals of the group. How can this best be accomplished? When the group first meets, should an icebreaker exercise be used—if so, what? Should refreshments be provided? How should the chairs be arranged? What type of group atmosphere will best help the group accomplish its tasks? What is the best available meeting place? Why have you been selected to lead the group? What do the members expect you to do?

As you plan for the first meeting, it is helpful to view the group as a new member would view it. Here are some questions and concerns that a new member might have: What are the goals of this group? Why am I joining? Will my personal goals be met in this group? Will I feel comfortable in this group? Will I be accepted by other members? Will the other members be radically different from me in backgrounds and interests? If I do not like this group, can I get out of attending meetings? Will other members respect what I have to say, or will they laugh and make fun of me? By considering such concerns, the leader can plan the first meeting in a way that helps members feel comfortable and will clarify their questions about the group's goals and activities.

EP 2.1.16b

Exercise 6.5: My Concerns about Joining a Group

Goal: This exercise is designed to help you identify (a) the concerns that you would have about joining a group and (b) what you want the leader to do to make you feel comfortable.

Step 1: Assume the dean of your college has invited you to be a member of the newly formed Dean's Student Advisory Council. Specify your concerns and reservations about joining this group. (The dean will be leading the group.)

Step 2: What would you like to see the dean say and do to meet your concerns and reservations and to help you feel comfortable?

Step 3: Do you believe your concerns and reservations are unique or similar to those that other members would have? Explain your reasons.

Step 4: If you stated in step 3 that your concerns and reservations are similar to those of other new members, does this exercise help you identify what you would need to say and do to help members feel comfortable if you were leading a group? Please explain.

It is *absolutely essential* for a group leader to identify needs and expectations before the first meeting. The quickest way to fail as a leader is to try to lead a group in a direction different from what the members want. For example, I once attended a workshop with other counselors titled "Grief, Death, and Dying." The counselors expected material on how to counsel clients who were grieving about the death of a loved one. The presenter instead gave a historical review of how present-day funeral rituals evolved since the Middle Ages. The audience was very disappointed.

There are various ways to identify what members want. Before the first meeting, try to ask at least some members about their expectations. If you are asked by someone to lead the group, it is essential to ask that person about the expectations for the group. At the first meeting, ask members to give their views about what they desire from the group. Another way (which needs to be done for preparatory reasons anyway) is to "scout" the following about the members:

1. How many members are expected?
2. What are their characteristics—ages, socioeconomic status, racial and ethnic backgrounds, gender mix, educational and professional backgrounds, and so on?
3. How knowledgeable and informed are members about the topics that will be dealt with?
4. What are likely personal goals and agendas of the various members?
5. How motivated are members to accomplish the group purposes? This can partly be determined by examining how voluntary the membership is. Groups composed of involuntary members (for example, a person who is court ordered to attend because of conviction for driving while intoxicated) may have little motivation and may even be hostile because they are being forced to attend.
6. What are the underlying value systems of members? A group of teenagers on juvenile probation will differ significantly from a group of retired priests. (That said, take care to view the members as unique persons rather than by stereotypes.)

When planning for the first meeting (and additional meetings), visualize in great detail how you, as leader, want the meeting to go. Here is an example:

> The members will arrive at various times. I will be there early to greet them, introduce myself, help them feel comfortable, and engage in small talk. Small talk likely to be of interest to these new members: ____, ____, and ____.
>
> I will begin the meeting by introducing myself and stating the overall purpose of the group. As an icebreaker exercise, I will ask the group to give me a list of four or five facts they would like to know about other members and then have members introduce themselves and give these facts about themselves. I will also briefly summarize my professional experience and encourage members to ask questions about me and the group.
>
> After the icebreaker exercise, I will again briefly state the group's overall purpose and ask if members have questions about this. Possible questions that may arise are ____. If such questions arise, my answers will be ____.
>
> We will then proceed to items on the agenda (which I previously mailed to the members). During the discussion of these items, the questions that may arise are ____. My answers to such questions, should they arise, are ____.
>
> The kind of group atmosphere I will seek to create is democratic. Such an atmosphere is best suited for encouraging all members to participate in formulating the group goals and then to contribute their time and resources toward accomplishing them. I will seek to do this by arranging the chairs in a circle, by drawing out through questions those who are silent, by using humor, and by making sure that I don't dominate the conversation.
>
> I will end the meeting by summarizing what has been covered and the decisions that have been made. We will set a time for the next meeting. Finally, I will ask if anyone has additional comments or questions. Throughout the meeting I will encourage a positive atmosphere, partly by complimenting the members on the contributions they make.

After a group has met for one or more times, the leader should review these questions: Have our overall goals been sufficiently clarified? If not, what needs to be done in this clarification process? Are we making adequate progress in accomplishing its goals? If not, what obstacles that we need to confront are slowing us down? Have we selected adequate courses of action to reach our goals, or are there more effective courses of action that we could consider? What items should be on the agenda for our next meeting? What activities should we plan? Will successful completion of these activities move us toward accomplishing our overall goals? If not, perhaps other activities need to be selected. Does each member seem sufficiently interested and motivated to help us accomplish its goals, or do some members appear to be disinterested? If so, why do they appear to be disinterested, and what could we try to stimulate their interests?

Session Planning

In planning a session, it is essential to be fully aware of the group's overall goals. It is also essential to identify specific goals for each session. Know *exactly* what you want to accomplish in each session and make sure that all the items on the agenda relate to these goals. Here are some suggestions.

1. *Select content that is relevant.* The material should be relevant not only to the specific goals for the session but also to the backgrounds and interests of participants. For example, in a time management presentation, the time-saver tips you give to college students probably will be quite different from those for business executives. An excellent way to evaluate the relevance of your material is to define precisely how it will be valuable to members. Ask yourself, "If a group member asks why should I know this, can I give a valid reason?" If you are unable to come up with more than a vague answer, consider discarding that material and selecting more relevant material.
2. *Use a number of examples.* Examples illustrate key concepts. They also stimulate interest. People remember examples much more than statistics. Thus, in a presentation on spouse abuse, vivid real-life stories of the drastic effects of battering will stay with members much longer than statistics on spouse abuse.
3. *Present materials in a logical order.* It is generally a good idea to begin by summarizing the agenda for the session. Ideally, one topic will blend into the next. If group exercises are used, place them next to the related theoretical material.
4. *Plan the time.* Once you have the content of the session fairly well organized, estimate how long each segment will take. Accurate estimations will help you determine if you have too much or too little material planned for the allotted time. Plan what you will do if the content is covered faster or slower than what you are estimating. Always be prepared to cover extra material should the anticipated content be covered more quickly than you estimated. If you are showing a videotape or have a guest speaker, have appropriate substitute material in case something goes awry.
5. *Be flexible with your agenda.* A variety of events can make it desirable to change the agenda during a session. The material may be covered much faster than anticipated, or interpersonal conflict may erupt that may take considerable time to process. Some members may bring up subjects related to the group's overall purpose that are valuable for the group to focus on at the moment.
6. *Change pace occasionally.* People pay attention for longer periods if there is an occasional change of pace. Long, long lectures or discussions are boring. Change pace in a variety of ways: Use a group exercise, show a film, invite a guest speaker, take a break, have a debate, make a PowerPoint presentation, change topics, and so on. In group counseling sessions, change pace by switching from one member's problems to another's concerns. If you are presenting a lecture, you can increase attention in several ways:

   - Speak extemporaneously rather than read the material.
   - Occasionally walk around the room rather than stand or sit in one place.
   - Draw out the participants by asking questions.

(An excellent way to learn how to give more stimulating presentations is to observe the nonverbal and verbal communication patterns of dynamic speakers.) Remember to use appropriate transitions so the topics blend into one another rather than becoming choppy and confusing. As you select methods, be aware that people remember information better if they receive it actively (such as through an exercise) than if they receive it passively (through listening).

Relaxing before a Meeting

Before a meeting, you may be nervous about how it will go. Some anxiety is helpful; you will be mentally alert, and you will attend more carefully to what is being communicated. Some leaders, however, have an excessively high level of anxiety that reduces their effectiveness. If your anxiety is too high, you can reduce it by engaging in relaxing activities. Relaxation techniques are highly recommended and are described in Chapter 14. Other suggestions include taking a walk, jogging, listening to relaxing music, and finding a place where you can be alone to clear your mind. Effective group leaders learn they can reduce their level of anxiety by using one or more of these techniques. Practice in leading groups will also build your confidence.

Cues on Entering the Meeting Room

It is important for you, as leader, to be on time, and perhaps a little early. Being early allows you to see that everything is arranged as you planned. You'll be able to do what needs to be done—seeing that the refreshments are available, erasing the chalkboard, arranging the chairs, and so on. It also allows you to observe the moods of the members. If you have not previously met the group, arriving early gives you an opportunity to gain information about the participants' interests by observing their age, gender, clothes and personal appearance, small talk, and the way they interact with one another. Effective leaders notice such cues and generally find ways to "join" the participants.

I was once asked to give a workshop on suicide prevention to a high school class. On arriving, I was informed by the teacher that a classmate had recently taken his life. Instead of beginning with my planned presentation, I acknowledged that I had just been informed about their former classmate, and I asked each of them anonymously to jot down one or two concerns or questions. We then proceeded to have a lively discussion related to these. This discussion was no doubt more valuable than the formal presentation I planned to give because it zeroed in on their immediate concerns.

Seating Arrangements

Seating arrangements are important. They affect who talks to whom and influence who plays leadership roles. As a result, they can affect group cohesion and morale.

It is important in most groups for members to have eye contact with one another. It is even more important for the group leader to be able to make eye contact with everyone to obtain nonverbal feedback about what members are thinking and feeling.

A circle is ideal for generating discussion, for encouraging a sense of equal status, and for promoting openness and cohesion. The traditional classroom arrangement (with the leader in front and everyone facing that person while sitting in rows) has the effect of placing the leader in a position of authority. It also tends to inhibit communication because members can make eye contact only with those closest to them.

Tables have advantages and disadvantages. They provide a place to write and to put work materials. Some members feel more comfortable at a table because it gives them something to lean on. However, tables also restrict movement and can serve as a barrier. Carefully consider whether tables are desirable or undesirable for your group. If members are to sift through papers or are expected to take notes, tables are useful. In counseling groups, tables are seldom used because they act as a barrier. In many settings, tables can be arranged to best meet the goals of the meeting. For example, arranging small tables in a circle facilitates communication.

Tables influence how group members interact with each other. If the table is rectangular, it is customary for the leader to sit at one end, at the "head" of the table. This positioning creates an "authority" dynamic wherein the "head" does more talking and has a greater influence on the discussion. If an egalitarian atmosphere is desired, use a round or square table. The "head of the table" effect can also be reduced by placing two rectangular tables together to make a square.

Tables also influence interactions by where people sit. People are most likely to talk to those sitting at right angles to them and then to those next to them. People sitting directly across receive less communication, and those sitting anywhere else are even less likely to be addressed.

When a group meets for the first time (and often later), members are most likely to sit next to friends. If it is important for everyone in the group to interact, it may be desirable to ask people to sit next to people they don't know to counteract potential cliquishness and to encourage members to get to know each other.

Introductions

During the introduction, summarize your credentials in such a way that members gain a sense of confidence that you as the leader can fulfill their expectations. If you are being introduced by someone else, a brief and concise summary of your credentials *for the expected role* is desirable. If you are introducing yourself, summarize your important credentials in a nonarrogant fashion. Deliver your summary in a way that creates the desired atmosphere—whether it is informal or formal, fun or serious, and so on. An excellent way to handle the introduction is to use an icebreaker exercise (described in Chapter 1).

In meeting with a group, it is highly desirable to learn members' names as quickly as possible. This requires extra attention by you. Name tags facilitate this process for everyone. Members appreciate being called by name—it conveys that they have importance.

If the group is small, it is generally advantageous for members to introduce themselves—perhaps by using an icebreaker. This is also a good time for members to state their expectations for the group. This helps uncover hidden agendas. If a stated expectation is beyond the scope of the group, you should tactfully state this and discuss it to prevent unrealistic expectations from becoming a source of frustration or dissatisfaction.

Role Clarification

As the leader of the group, you should be clear about your roles and responsibilities. If you are unclear, discuss with the group their expectations about the appropriate roles for the leader and members. One way of doing this is for the group to select goals and then decide which tasks and responsibilities each member will have in achieving those goals. In most situations, it is clearly a mistake for the leader to do most of the work. Groups are most productive if all members make substantial contributions. The more members contribute to the group, the more they will feel a part of the group psychologically.

Even if you are fairly clear about what you would like your role to be, other members may be confused about your role or may have different expectations of you. If there is a realistic chance that the other members are unclear about your role, explain carefully what you perceive your role to be. If members indicate they have different expectations, take time here to decide who will do what. In explaining what you perceive your role to be, be humble about your skills and resources. You want to come across as a knowledgeable "human" rather than as an authority figure who has all the answers.

Always be prepared to explain the reasoning behind the things you do. If you are leading an exercise, inform the group about its goals or objectives. If questions arise about whether its goals are consistent with the group's overall goals, be prepared to provide an explanation.

The role that leaders assume in groups varies from situation to situation. For example, there are marked differences in responsibilities of the leader of a therapy group and those of a committee assessing the social service needs of a community.

Agendas

Most meetings have agendas. Ideally, all group members should have an opportunity to suggest items for the agenda. If possible, send the agenda to members several days before the meeting to give them an opportunity to prepare.

Agenda items should be briefly reviewed at the start of the meeting, before consideration of the first item. This review gives members a chance to suggest additions, deletions, or other changes. In some meetings it may be appropriate for the group to discuss, and perhaps vote on, the suggested changes in the agenda.

Additional Guidelines for Leading a Group

1. Remember that leadership is a shared responsibility. Every member at times will take on leadership roles. Designated leaders should not dominate a group, nor should they believe they are responsible for directing the group in all of its task functions and group maintenance functions (these functions are described in Chapter 7). Actually, productivity and group cohesion are substantially increased when everyone contributes.
2. Use decision-making procedures that are best suited for the issues facing the group. (The merits and shortcomings of decision making by consensus and by majority voting were discussed earlier in this chapter.)
3. Create a cooperative group atmosphere rather than a competitive one (see Chapter 7).
4. View controversy and conflict as natural and desirable for resolving issues and furthering discussion. In resolving conflicts and in handling the issues and problems facing the group, use a problem-solving approach rather than a win-lose approach (see Chapter 7).
5. Try to create an atmosphere of open and honest communication.
6. Give attention to how you end a session. A few minutes before the session is scheduled to end or when it appears the group has exhausted a subject, conclude with a brief summary of the key points made in the meeting. This helps members remember major points, and it leaves them with a sense of achievement. Closing also helps members transition to the outside world.

Terminating a Group

Termination is about separating from the group and from group members. Separation typically generates mixed feelings that vary in intensity according to a number of factors. The greater the members' emotional closeness and investment in a group, the greater is their feeling of loss. The greater the feeling of success in accomplishing group goals, the greater is the feeling of "sweetness and sorrow"—sweetness from feeling that they have grown and had success and sorrow from separating from the group that has come to be an important and meaningful part of their lives. The more emotionally dependent members become on a group, the more likely they are to feel anger, rejection, and depression over termination. The more they have experienced difficulties in separating in the past from significant others, the more likely they are to experience group separation as difficult.

There are several types of termination: (1) termination of a successful group, (2) termination of an unsuccessful group, (3) a member dropping out, (4) transfer of a member, and (5) departure of the leader.

Termination of a Successful Group In a successful group, members have generally accomplished their goals. Termination of such a group can generate the "sweetness and sorrow" reaction. They are delighted with their accomplishments, which are increasing their self-confidence and self-esteem. But they may also experience varying levels of loss because they are emotionally invested in the group. Such groups may decide to have dinner together or have some other ceremony to commemorate and recognize the group's accomplishments.

In terminating a successful group, it is essential that formal termination begin one or more meetings before the final meeting. Ideally, the date of the last meeting should be discussed and agreed on well in advance. (The final meeting of some groups is scheduled even before the group begins to meet.) Sufficient time has to be allowed in terminating successful groups so that (1) group progress can be evaluated; (2) plans can be made for continued work; (3) work can be done on unresolved, last-minute issues; (4) emotional reactions to terminating can be handled; and (5) members can discuss whether they want to plan a special social event for the group's ending.

Good-byes are often sad, but negative feelings can be offset by emphasizing what members have given and received, the ways they have grown, the skills they have learned, and the accomplishments of the group. In some cases, an extra session is held to complete unfinished business items. The members may decide to have periodic "class reunions" or social get-togethers.

Termination of an Unsuccessful Group In an unsuccessful group, most or all of the group's goals are largely unmet. Members' reactions to the lack of progress will vary considerably: anger, frustration, disappointment, despair, guilt (for unproductive efforts or lack of effort), scapegoating, blaming, and apathy. In rare cases, it is possible for an unsuccessful group to be fairly pleased and accepting of its efforts. For example, a group formed to write a grant (when there was limited hope of funding from the federal government) may be pleased with its efforts and with the new relationships formed and only mildly disappointed by the failure of the group's objective.

Terminating an unsuccessful group is as important as terminating a successful one. As with all groups, plans for termination should be made well in advance. The date of the last meeting should be discussed and agreed on by the members long before the final meeting. Sufficient time should be allowed so that (1) the reasons for the lack of progress of the group can be assessed and analyzed; (2) alternatives for achieving the goals can be discussed (these may involve changing the format of the present group, referral of members to other groups, and alternatives involving individual actions rather than group efforts); (3) emotional reactions to terminating and to the lack of progress can be handled; (4) members can work on unresolved, last-minute issues; and (5) members can discuss whether they want to plan for the group's ending.

At times, ending an unsuccessful group is chaotic and abrupt. A group appointed to write a grant may be nearly finished when they are informed the funding organization has a financial shortfall and is therefore withdrawing its request for funding proposals. This group may end abruptly in despair. Or, in a group of involuntary members (such as at a prison or at an adolescent residential treatment facility), the leader may decide that continuing the group is counterproductive because members are continually goofing off and are not putting effort into achieving the group goals. In any case, the reasons for the group's ending should be fully explained and time given to handle members' reactions to the closing. If there is insufficient time at the last meeting to deal with these tasks, it is sometimes advisable

EP 2.1.1b

either to have another session or for the leader to meet individually with members to discuss their reactions to the group's failure, alternatives for reaching goals, reactions to the group's ending, and unresolved concerns. When an unsuccessful group ends abruptly, some group members may be highly critical of the leader, of other members, or of group experiences. If the leader contracts members to learn their thoughts about the group, he or she should be prepared to respond to highly critical feedback. To prepare, the leader can "visualize" possible criticisms and then formulate positive and realistic responses.

Exercise 6.6: Successful and Unsuccessful Group Experiences

Goal: This exercise is designed to have you reflect about how you felt when you participated in a successful group and when you participated in an unsuccessful group.

Step 1: Describe a successful group in which you participated. Indicate why you defined this group to be successful. Perhaps the goals were accomplished, or perhaps you enjoyed the camaraderie.

Step 2: What feelings did you experience about participating in this group?

Step 3: Describe an unsuccessful group in which you participated. Indicate why you defined this group to be unsuccessful. Perhaps the goals were not accomplished, or you disliked certain members, or you were asked to leave.

Step 4: What feelings did you experience about participating in this group?

Dropping Out When a member drops out, that member terminates even though the group continues on. A member drops out for a variety of reasons. She becomes disenchanted with the group and feels that neither she nor the group will accomplish the goals. He disagrees with or dislikes another group member. She is a parent who must now provide child care at the time the group meets or has begun a new job whose work hours conflict with meeting times. There are numerous reasons.

When a member drops out without informing the group of his or her reasons, you as leader should contact the individual to learn why he or she decided to terminate. In some instances, it is desirable for you to explain that leaving is a major decision that should not be made abruptly and that you would like an opportunity to explore the reasons that led to the decision. If the reason is conflict with another member, perhaps the conflict can be resolved. Perhaps other actions can be taken that will enable the member to return.

If the member decides not to return after being contacted and encouraged to return, the reasons for leaving should be attended to. The member may be raising legitimate concerns that need to be dealt with so that other members do not become discouraged and leave. If a person drops out of a counseling group, a sensitivity group, or an educational group and still has unresolved personal concerns, referral to another group or to one-to-one professional help may be advisable.

Whenever members drop out, you need to inform them of their positive contributions to the group. Dropping out is often viewed as a personal failure, and therefore you need to thank the person for any positive contributions to help dispel any sense of personal failure.

Don't neglect remaining members; they too experience a variety of emotions. Some will feel they failed this person. Some will feel guilt for what they said or did—or for failing to do or say what they believe would have led the member to stay. Some will feel relief or joy; perhaps they view the member as unworthy of the group or as an obstacle in the group's efforts to accomplish its goals. Others will feel sadness and be concerned that something tragic has happened to that member. Some will be angry, feeling the person is abandoning the group. Still others will feel personally rejected. Often rumors begin to circulate about the person's reasons for leaving. Therefore it is essential that the group be informed of the reasons. A member's leaving can be devastating to group morale. And if other members have also recently left, the group's survival can be jeopardized.

Ideally, members leaving should inform the group of their reasons, either in person or in writing. If they do not, you or another member should contact them to ascertain their reasons for leaving and inform the group.

Transfer of a Member Transfer of a group member to another group or to some other type of professional services generally involves a planned arrangement between the group leader and the member. The transfer can occur for a variety of reasons. In a problem-solving group, the employing agency may decide that the member's talents and skills could be better used in another capacity. In a counseling group, the leader and person leaving may jointly decide that the transferee will be served better by receiving more specialized services with a somewhat different intervention. A member may be transferred because of a conflict that cannot be resolved, especially when the conflict is severely interfering with group goals. For example, a serious and insurmountable gap in mutual understanding and communication caused by differences in religious beliefs, values, or language may exist.

When a transfer occurs, you as leader should do everything possible to prevent it from being unexpected or abrupt. The member being transferred should clearly understand the reasons for the transfer and ideally should be accepting of it. Be sure to explain to the group why the person is transferring. Ideally, the member should explain his or her reasons to the group; this gives other members an opportunity to wish the person well and to gain a sense of closure.

Departure of the Leader Sometimes you must terminate your work with a group. This termination is often difficult for both you and the members. Emotional reactions can be intense, and adequate time for working through them may not be available. You may experience intense emotions, including guilt, for not being able to follow through on your commitment to lead the group until its goals are accomplished. Members who feel vulnerable and depend on you may be devastated. Some may erroneously personalize your leaving as resulting from something they said or did. Some may feel anger and betrayal; they made a commitment to the group, confided and trusted in you, and now feel rejected.

When you leave, you should encourage members to express their feelings. You may want to initiate this expression by explaining fully why you are leaving, giving members positive comments about the group, and stating your feelings of sadness and guilt over leaving. Before leaving, you or the group should select a new leader. If the new leader is not a member of the group, you should inform the new leader (privately) about the goals, member characteristics, current tasks and difficulties in the group, and progress toward group goals. The new leader should be introduced to the group by you; your goal is a smooth transition shifting your responsibilities to the new leader.

Evaluating a Group

In the past few decades, accountability has become a major emphasis in social welfare. Funding sources demand research evidence that allocated funds are having a beneficial effect. An essential component of accountability is evaluation.

In broad terms, evaluation is designed to assess whether the services provided were effective and efficient. When the services provided by a group are evaluated, there are two dimensions of evaluation: process evaluation and outcome evaluation.

Process Evaluation *Process evaluation* is an assessment, generally by group members, of the aspects of the process that were useful or detrimental. Feedback about techniques and incidents that blocked or enhanced process is of immense value to you as group leader. With this information, you can hone certain skills, eliminate materials, and give direction for approaches and materials to add. Positive feedback generally helps build your confidence. Feedback that is highly critical can be humbling and even devastating. It is far better to make changes suggested by the evaluation than to reject and "deny" the feedback and repeat the same mistakes in future groups. You need to welcome criticism and be prepared to respond to it constructively. After all, this is the way social workers expect clients to respond to constructive criticism.

Process evaluation can be conducted orally by asking group members to discuss the aspects, techniques, materials, and incidents that were constructive and those that were counterproductive. An advantage of oral evaluation is that most members enjoy a spoken discussion. A disadvantage is that some members may not give constructive negative feedback verbally because the social norm in such situations is to focus on the positives.

Process evaluation also can be accomplished by means of a brief questionnaire in which members address three key areas:

1. The group's strengths. (Cite specific materials and incidents. Also cite skills and techniques used by the leader.)
2. The group's shortcomings. (Cite specific materials and incidents. Also cite skills and techniques used by the leader.)
3. Specific suggestions for changes.

In process evaluations, group members typically cite positive factors more than negative ones (Hepworth & Larsen, 1986, p. 590). Such positive feedback not only has a "stroking value" but also enables leaders to be more aware of their strengths, so they can increase the use of these strengths in the future. Nevertheless, negative feedback is as valuable as, and often more valuable than, positive feedback. It informs you of aspects that need improvement, which you can then attend to.

Another way of evaluating process is by *peer review*. Peer review is conducted by having one or more "peers" (usually other group leaders) periodically sit in on your group. (Some agencies have one-way mirrors so the group can be unobtrusively observed.) Before a peer review, the agency or organization should agree on a set of principles or criteria that reflect quality group leadership. A peer review is a review of a small portion of the total functioning of the group. That small portion may be typical, or atypical, of the total functioning of the group. (Many colleges and universities use a peer review process in which tenured faculty in a department sit in on classes of recently hired faculty.)

In a variation of the peer-review process, meetings may be taped (either audio or video). The tape is played back and reviewed by you and a peer (or by your supervisor). Before taping a meeting, you should explain to the members the reasons for taping, indicate who will view the tape, and then ask members for their permission to tape the session.

Outcome Evaluation *Outcome evaluation* assesses the extent to which the goals formulated when the group began have been accomplished. Specific approaches to measure goal attainment are single-subject design, task achievement scaling, and satisfaction questionnaire.

Single-Subject Design Single-subject design has become increasingly popular in the helping professions in the past several decades. There are more than a dozen variations of single-subject design, some of them complex and rigorous. Fortunately, the simpler designs can be used by entry-level social workers in many situations. Single-subject design is described in considerable detail in Chapter 11.

Task Achievement Scaling The objective of this approach is to gauge the degree to which group members and the leader have completed agreed-on tasks. Work toward member and group goals is broken into many separate actions or tasks. Tasks are selected by mutual agreement, and members are assigned or select specific tasks to reach their personal goal and the group's overall goal. Usually, a deadline is set for completing each task. *Task achievement scaling* rates the degree to which each agreed-on task has, in fact, been achieved.

Reid and Epstein (1972) used a 4-point scale to record progress on each task: 4 = completely achieved; 3 = substantially achieved, action is still necessary; 2 = partially achieved, considerable work remains to be done; and 1 = minimally achieved or not achieved. Where appropriate, they have a fifth rating, "no," for "no opportunity to work on task." With this approach, only results are rated—not effort, motivation, or good intentions. The appealing features of task achievement scaling are its simplicity and the fact that it can be used when more rigorous procedures are not feasible because of insufficient time or data, or difficulties in finding a suitable way to measure changes in the target behavior.

Task achievement scaling has some limitations. For example, if the tasks were incorrectly conceptualized as being constructive in meeting the goals of the group, then completing the tasks will have little effect on accomplishing group goals.

Satisfaction Questionnaire Another way to assess a group outcome is to have members fill out a questionnaire that measures satisfaction. An example is the "Group Member Satisfaction Questionnaire" shown in Exhibit 6.3. Such questionnaires are a relatively simple and inexpensive way to measure members' satisfaction with the group. The questionnaire can be filled out at the last meeting or mailed to members some time later. Questions that evaluate process (described in this chapter) can also be included.

Satisfaction questionnaires have some limitations. Responses are affected by the respondent's mood. In addition, dissatisfied members are less likely to fill out the questionnaire, particularly if it is administered by mail (Sheafor, Horejsi, & Horejsi, 1988, p. 390).

A few concluding comments are in order about the personal benefits you will receive in leading groups. Through learning how to lead effectively, you will grow as a person, become more self-confident, feel good about yourself, develop highly marketable skills, improve interpersonal relationships, and help yourself and other members accomplish important tasks. Leaders are not born. They are trained. We all have the potential to become effective group leaders. You can do it!

Exhibit 6.3 Group Member Satisfaction Questionnaire

Thank you for taking a few minutes to evaluate your experiences in our group. Your answers to this brief questionnaire will help us improve future groups. Feel free to offer your comments. To ensure anonymity, please do not sign your name.

1. Did you accomplish what you expected when you joined the group?
   ___ Yes, completely
   ___ Mostly
   ___ No real progress
   ___ Worse off now than before
   Comments ______________________

2. Do you feel the group accomplished its goals?
   ___ Yes, completely
   ___ Mostly
   ___ No real progress
   ___ The group was an utter failure
   Comments ______________________

3. How do you feel about the group leader?
   ___ Very satisfied
   ___ Satisfied
   ___ No feelings one way or another
   ___ Dissatisfied
   ___ Very dissatisfied
   Comments ______________________

4. How do you feel about the other members in the group?
   ___ Satisfied with everyone
   ___ Satisfied with some and dissatisfied with others
   ___ No feelings one way or another
   ___ Dissatisfied with most of the other members
   ___ Dissatisfied with all of the other members
   ___ Very dissatisfied with all of the other members
   Comments ______________________

SUMMARY

The historical roots of social group work lie in informal recreational organizations such as the YWCA and YMCA, scouting, Jewish centers, settlement houses, and 4-H Clubs. Today almost every social service agency provides some group services. Most undergraduate and graduate social work programs provide practice courses to train students to lead groups, particularly socialization, educational, and therapeutic groups. Groups frequently encountered in social work practice include recreation, recreation-skill, educational, task, problem-solving and decision-making, focus, self-help, socialization, counseling, and encounter groups.

Group decision making in problem-solving and decision-making groups is usually superior to individual decision making. Problem-solving groups sometimes fall victim to groupthink, which can lead a group to make ineffective and even destructive decisions. Decisions made by consensus have the best chance of gaining members' support. Decisions made by simple majority voting are arrived at much faster than those made by consensus. The decision-making technique a group uses will depend on many factors.

Socialization groups generally endeavor to develop or change attitudes and behaviors of group members in some socially accepted direction. Social skill development, increasing self-confidence, and planning for the future are other objectives.

Counseling groups generally strive to help members explore personal or emotional problems and then develop strategies to resolve the problems. Group facilitators use principles of one-to-one intervention and group dynamics to assist members in achieving positive changes in attitudes and behaviors. In contrast, sensitivity groups foster increased personal and interpersonal awareness and develop more effective interaction patterns.

The chapter concluded with guidelines for starting, leading, terminating, and evaluating groups. Topics included homework, planning a session, relaxing before starting a meeting, cues on entering the meeting room, seating arrangements, introductions, clarifying roles, agenda, terminating a group, and evaluating a group.

EXERCISES

1. Assertiveness Training

EP 2.1.10J

Goal: Demonstrate to the class how to run an educational group by illustrating how to run an assertiveness training group.

Step 1: The instructor indicates the purpose of this exercise. The instructor describes nonassertive, aggressive, and assertive behaviors (see Module 2 for descriptions).

Step 2: The instructor distributes a handout that describes the 12 steps of assertiveness training (contained in Module 2). The instructor summarizes these steps.

Step 3: The instructor asks for volunteers (two for each situation) to role-play assertively the situations that the instructor gives them, such as

a. Asking someone who is smoking next to you to put out a cigarette
b. Asking for a date and refusing a date
c. Indicating to your objecting father that you want to live with the person you are dating

After a situation is role-played, the class discusses the assertiveness strategy.

EP 2.1.7a

Step 4: Students write anonymously on a note card one or two situations involving assertiveness that they are struggling with and that they would like others in the class to role-play.

Step 5: The instructor collects these note cards and selects some situations for volunteers to role-play. After a situation is role-played, the class discusses the merits and shortcomings of the assertiveness strategy that was used.

2. The Nominal Group

EP 2.1.1b

Goal: This exercise is designed to have the class learn how a nominal group is conducted.

The instructor asks a question for the nominal group to consider, such as "What do you see as the shortcomings of our social work program?" (Do not mention the names of faculty members.) The class follows the steps for conducting a nominal group as described in this chapter.

3. Trust Walk

Goal: This exercise is designed to demonstrate an approach—the trust walk—that is frequently used in sensitivity groups. A trust walk helps students get in touch with aspects of themselves that they are unaware of.

Step 1: The instructor informs the class of the purpose of the exercise. The students form groups of two. (If a member is without a partner, the instructor can be a partner.) A member of each subgroup closes his or her eyes and keeps them closed during the first part of this exercise. The "seeing" partner is instructed to lead the "blind" partner down corridors, around the room, and perhaps outside. The "seeing" partner can lead the "blind" partner with spoken directions and by taking a hand. The "seeing" person has the responsibility to watch that the "blind" partner does not run into objects, fall, stumble, or get hurt in any way. (The instructor tells students to be very careful going up and down stairs.)

Step 2: After 8 to 10 minutes, the partners reverse roles and continue the exercise for another 8 to 10 minutes.

Step 3: The students then discuss their feelings about the trust walk. The instructor asks questions such as the following: Did you occasionally open your eyes when you were the "nonseeing" partner? Did you have trust in your partner? Did you feel you would run into objects and hurt yourself? Were you afraid? If yes, how did you handle these fears? Did you become aware of feelings or thoughts about yourself that you previously were unaware of? If yes, what thoughts and feelings?

COMPETENCY NOTES

The following identifies where Educational Policy (EP) competencies and practice behaviors are discussed in the chapter.

EP 2.1.7a *Utilize conceptual frameworks to guide the process of assessment, intervention, and evaluation.* (pp. 165–183).

This material conceptualizes the types of groups in which social workers become involved.

EP 2.1.1b *Practice personal reflection and self-correction to assure continual professional development.* (pp. 166 and 168).

Exercise 6.1 is designed to have students reflect upon the factors that lead to rewarding and unrewarding educational group experiences.

EP 2.1.7a *Utilize conceptual frameworks to guide the process of assessment, intervention, and evaluation.* (pp. 171–172).

Exercise 6.2 is designed to assist students in understanding and applying the conceptual material on groupthink.

EP 2.1.10e *Assess client strengths and limitations.* (pp. 177–178).

Exercise 6.3 is designed to assist students in having a better understanding of the merits and shortcomings of self-help groups.

EP 2.1.7a *Utilize conceptual frameworks to guide the process of assessment, intervention, and evaluation.* (p. 178).

Exercise 6.4 is designed to introduce students to the vast number of online self-help groups that have been conceptualized and developed.

EP 2.1.10a *Substantively and affectively prepare for action with individuals, families, groups, organizations, and communities.*

EP 2.1.10l *Facilitate transitions and endings.*

EP 2.1.10m *Critically analyze, monitor, and evaluate interventions.* (pp. 183–195).

This material provides guidelines on how to start, lead, terminate, and evaluate groups.

EP 2.1.1b *Practice personal reflection and self-correction to assure continual professional development* (p. 184).

Exercise 6.5 is designed to have students reflect upon: (a) the concerns that they would have about joining a group, and (b) what they would want the leader to do to make them feel more comfortable.

EP 2.1.1b *Practice personal reflection and self-correction to assure continual professional development.* (p. 191).

Exercise 6.6 is designed to have students reflect upon how they felt when they participated in a successful group, and when they participated in an unsuccessful group.

EP 2.1.10j *Help clients resolve problems.* (p. 191).

This exercise is designed to help students learn assertiveness training, which then can be used to help clients learn to be more assertive in interactions with others.

EP 2.1.7a *Utilize conceptual frameworks to guide the process of assessment, intervention, and evaluation.* (p. 196).

This nominal group exercise is designed to demonstrate to students how the nominal group approach can be utilized in assessment, intervention, and evaluation.

EP 2.1.1b *Practice personal reflection and self-correction to assure continual professional development.* (p. 196).

This exercise is designed to demonstrate an approach—the trust walk—that is frequently used in sensitivity groups. A trust walk helps students get in touch with aspects of themselves that they are unaware of.

CHAPTER 7

Social Work with Groups: Concepts and Skills

EP 2.1.7a

Effective groups are exhilarating and exciting for both the group leader and the members.[1] This chapter will:

A. Present key group dynamic concepts: membership groups and reference groups, stages in group development, task roles and maintenance roles, leadership theory, social power bases in groups, and group norms
B. Describe conflict resolution strategies
C. Provide guidelines for leading counseling groups

MEMBERSHIP GROUPS AND REFERENCE GROUPS

A *membership group* is any group we belong to. Membership in a group is clearly defined—either we belong or we don't. Membership is thus a boundary condition.

Some people are marginal members of a group. For example, Tim Kelly attends classes, works evenings, and doesn't live on campus. He likes his coworkers but knows very few students. He comes to campus only for classes and leaves immediately afterward. Tim is a marginal member of the student body.

Full psychological membership in a group occurs only when a person is positively attracted to being a member and is positively accepted as a member. Tim Kelly has limited psychological membership with the student body because he has only a slight identification with the campus. The more a person is attracted to a group, the greater is that person's commitment to accomplishing the goals of the group.

Aspiring members include those who are seeking admission to a group but have not yet been admitted. They are not members but act as if they are. For example, students who want to join a fraternity or sorority will act like members to increase their chances of being admitted. Aspiring members identify psychologically with the group even though they are not as yet formally admitted.

There is also a difference between voluntary membership and involuntary membership. Individuals who deliberately choose to belong to a group, such as a fraternity or athletic team, are voluntary members. In many situations, people have little or no choice about becoming a group member. Social workers routinely work with groups

[1]Material in this chapter is adapted from Charles Zastrow, "Parents Anonymous," in *Social Work with Groups: Using the Class as a Group Leadership Laboratory*, 5th ed. © 2002 Cengage Learning, pp. 13–22, 56–65, 81–85, 92–102, 175–185. Grafton H. Hull, Jr., was a contributing author to this chapter.

whose membership is involuntary—for example, in prison settings, mental hospitals, and residential treatment facilities. Involuntary group members may initially be uninterested in participating and are sometimes hostile and disruptive.

Reference groups are groups whose influence we are willing to accept. We closely identify with these groups. Tim Kelly's work group is his reference group; the student body, for all practical purposes, is not.

Reference groups have two distinct functions. First, members' behavior, attitudes, and other characteristics become standards we use to judge and evaluate ourselves and others. Second, reference groups have a normative function in that we seek to conform to their standards.

EP 2.1.7a

In a given group, only some members are referents for us. Referents are people who influence us and whom we, in turn, seek to influence. In a large group, we normally have only a small subgroup of referents. These referents may be selected because they have ideas, values, or beliefs similar to ours, because we can easily identify with them, or just because we enjoy associating with them. Referents may or may not be in positions of power. For example, some adolescents reject the norms of their parents and other adults and become members of Goth groups that dress and act differently from the norm. Others join gangs that offer acceptance and friendship despite their location on the margins of society. Still others are drawn toward athletes and other student leaders because they are perceived as being influential or powerful members of the student body. We tend to tune out and interact with others who do not belong to our reference group.

Exercise 7.1: Understanding Membership Groups and Reference Groups

Goal: This exercise is designed to help you understand the concepts of reference groups and membership groups.

Step 1: Identify a group that you are a member of that is not a reference group for you. Explain why it is not a reference group for you.

Step 2: Identify a group that you are a member of that is a reference group for you. Explain why you identify with this reference group.

GROUP DEVELOPMENT

Groups change over time. Numerous models or frameworks describe group change. In this section we examine two sequential-stage models and one recurring-phase model.

The Garland, Jones, and Kolodny Model

Garland, Jones, and Kolodny (1965) identified five sequential stages of development in social work groups. Their model describes problems that commonly arise as groups form and develop. Understanding these problems, it is theorized, enables leaders to anticipate and respond to member reactions more effectively. The conceptualization of Garland and his colleagues is particularly applicable to socialization groups and counseling groups. To a lesser extent, the model also applies to self-help groups, problem-solving and decision-making groups, educational groups, recreation-skill groups, and some task groups.

Closeness (how emotionally close members will allow themselves to become) is the central focus of this model. Degrees of closeness are reflected in *struggles* that occur at the five stages of group growth identified by Garland, Jones, and Kolodny: preaffiliation, power and control, intimacy, differentiation, and separation.

In the first stage, *preaffiliation,* members are ambivalent about joining the group. Interaction is guarded. Members test, often through approach and avoidance behavior, whether they really want to belong to the group. New situations are frightening, and members try to protect themselves from being hurt or taken advantage of. They attempt to maintain a certain amount of distance and to get what they can from the group without risking much. Individuals are aware that group involvement will make demands that may be frustrating or even painful. However, they are attracted to the group because they have had satisfying experiences in other groups and membership in this group offers similar rewards.

In the first stage, the leader seeks to increase members' attraction to the group. The leader accomplishes this by explaining the purpose of the group, inviting members' input, explaining the importance of confidentiality, and helping members feel that they are important to the group. Group activities may be used to enhance member participation. The first stage gradually ends as members come to feel fairly safe and comfortable and view the rewards as worth a tentative emotional commitment.

The second stage, *power and control,* emerges as group characteristics begin to develop. Patterns of communication emerge, alliances and subgroups begin to appear, members take on certain roles and responsibilities, norms and methods for handling tasks develop, and membership questions arise. Such processes are necessary for the group to conduct its business. However, these processes lead to struggle as the members establish their places in the group. Each member seeks power, partly for self-protection and partly to gain greater control over the gratifications and rewards to be received from the group. In this struggle, the group leader is a major source of gratification. The leader is perceived as having the greatest power to influence the group's direction and to give or to withhold emotional and material rewards. At this point, members realize that the group is becoming important to them.

The second stage is a transitional stage wherein certain basic issues need to be resolved. Who has primary control over the group's affairs—the group or its leader? Limits of power for the leader and group are questioned. This uncertainty results in anxiety among, and considerable testing by, members as they gauge the limits and seek to establish norms for power and authority. Rebellion is not uncommon, and dropout rates are often highest at this stage. During this struggle, leaders should (1) help members understand the nature of the power struggle, (2) give emotional support to weather the discomfort of uncertainty, and (3) help the group establish norms to resolve the uncertainty. It is very important that group members develop trust in the leader so that the leader can maintain a safe balance of shared power and control. When trust is achieved, members make a major commitment to become involved in the group.

In the third stage, *intimacy,* likes and dislikes are expressed. The group becomes a "family," with "sibling rivalry" arising between members and the leader sometimes even referred to as a parent. Feelings about the group at this stage are more openly expressed and discussed. The group is now viewed as a place where growth and change take place. Individuals examine and make efforts to change personal attitudes, concerns, and problems. Group tasks are worked on, and there is a feeling of "oneness" or cohesiveness. Struggle or turmoil during this stage leads members to explore and make changes in their personal lives and to examine what the group is all about.

During the fourth stage, *differentiation,* members increasingly experiment with new and alternative behavior patterns. There is a recognition of individual rights and needs and a high level of communication among members. The group is able to organize itself more efficiently. Leadership is shared, and roles are more functional. Power problems are now minimal, and decisions are made and carried out with less emotion and on a more objective basis.

During the differentiation stage, the group is analogous to a high-functioning family in which the children have reached adulthood and are pursuing their own lives successfully. Relationships are between equals, members are mutually supportive, and members relate to each other in ways that are rational and objective. Members value each other and the group as a whole. The leader encourages the group to run itself and helps members begin to evaluate what they have accomplished with respect to their individual and group goals.

EP 2.1.7a

The final stage is *separation*. The purposes of the group have been achieved, and members have learned new behavioral patterns that enable them to move on to other social experiences. Termination is not always easy. Members are sometimes reluctant to move on and may even display regressive behavior in an effort to prolong the safety of the group. They also may express anger over ending the group or even psychologically deny the end is near. The leader's (or worker's) role in termination is to help members separate from the group by emphasizing activities that increase their connection with others outside the group and reduce those connections that have helped pull members together. The focus is on evaluation of accomplishments, acknowledgment of feelings about ending, and providing support as the group ends.

Exercise 7.2: The Garland, Jones, and Kolodny Model

Goal: This exercise is designed to help you use the Garland, Jones, and Kolodny model to analyze groups.

Write a description of a group that you have participated in that has at least some of the group development stages identified by the Garland, Jones, and Kolodny model. Identify the stages of your group that are consistent with the model. Describe any developmental stages of your group that are inconsistent with this model.

The Tuckman Model

Tuckman (1965) reviewed more than 50 studies of counseling and sensitivity groups with limited duration and concluded that groups go through the following predictable stages:

1. *Forming:* Members become oriented toward each other, work on being accepted, and learn more about the group. A period of uncertainty ensues in which members try to determine their place in the group and the rules and procedures of the group.
2. *Storming:* Conflicts begin to arise as members resist the influence of the group and rebel against accomplishing the tasks. Members often confront their various differences, and management of conflict becomes the focus of attention.
3. *Norming:* The group establishes cohesiveness and commitment, and in the process group members discover new ways to work together. Norms are set for appropriate behavior.
4. *Performing:* The group works as a unit to achieve the group's goals. The group gains proficiency in achieving its goals and becomes more flexible in its patterns of working together.
5. *Adjourning:* The group disbands. The feelings that members experience are similar to those in the "separation stage" of the Garland, Jones, and Kolodny model.

EP 2.1.7a

Exercise 7.3: The Tuckman Model

Goal: This exercise is designed to help you use the Tuckman model to analyze groups.

Write a description of a group that you have participated in that has at least some of the group development stages identified by the Tuckman model. Identify the stages of your group that are consistent with the model. Describe any developmental stages of your group that are inconsistent with this model.

The Bales Model

The Garland, Jones, and Kolodny model and the Tuckman model are sequential-stage models—that is, they specify sequential stages of group development. In contrast, Bales (1965) developed a recurring-phase model. He hypothesized that groups continuously strive to achieve equilibrium between task-oriented work and emotional expressions, in order to build better relationships among group members. (Task roles and social/emotional roles are described in the next section.) According to Bales, groups tend to oscillate between these two concerns—sometimes focusing on identifying and performing work tasks that must be conducted to achieve goals and at other times focusing on building morale and improving the social and emotional atmosphere.

Note that the sequential-stage and recurring-phase perspectives are not necessarily contradictory. Both are useful for understanding group development. The sequential-stage perspective assumes that groups move through various stages while dealing with basic themes that surface as they become relevant to the group's work. The recurring-phase perspective assumes that the issues underlying the basic themes are never completely resolved and tend to recur.

It is common for leaders just beginning their work with groups to expect a smooth transition between stages, and they are often disappointed if this transition doesn't occur. In addition, many new practitioners, lacking experience and trust in the group process, tend to prematurely force the group out of certain stages—that is, they rush the process of group development. Experience will demonstrate the futility of such efforts. Barring unforeseen circumstances, groups move at their own pace and eventually arrive at the same destination. Groups that skip stages or groups whose development is otherwise thwarted often return to a stage with "unfinished business." Good leaders recognize this and allow natural group processes to evolve. Although groups sometimes do get mired in one stage, this happens less often than neophyte leaders fear it will.

TASK ROLES AND MAINTENANCE ROLES

All groups (whether organized for therapeutic reasons, for problem solving, or for other objectives) rely on members performing a variety of roles. Group needs require that both task roles and group-building roles be performed satisfactorily. *Task roles* are roles needed to accomplish specific group goals; *maintenance roles* are roles that strengthen the social and emotional aspects of group life (Pfeiffer & Jones, 1976).

Johnson and Johnson (1975, p. 26) summarized *task roles* as follows:

Information and opinion giver: Offers facts, opinions, ideas, suggestions, and relevant information to help group discussion.

Information and opinion seeker: Asks for facts, information, opinions, ideas, and feelings from other members to help group discussion.

Starter: Proposes goals and tasks to initiate action within the group.

Direction giver: Develops plans on how to proceed, and focuses attention on the task to be done.

Summarizer: Pulls together related ideas or suggestions, and restates and summarizes major points discussed.

Coordinator: Shows relationships among various ideas by pulling them together, and harmonizes activities of various subgroups and members.

Diagnoser: Figures out sources of difficulties the group has in working effectively and obstacles to progress in accomplishing the group's goals.

Energizer: Stimulates a higher quality of work from the group.

Reality tester: Examines the practicality and workability of ideas, evaluates alternative solutions, and applies them to real situations to see how they will work.

Evaluator: Compares group decisions and accomplishments with group standards and goals.

The Johnsons (1975, p. 27) also identified *group maintenance roles,* which strengthen social and emotional bonds within the group:

Encourager of participation: Warmly encourages everyone to participate, gives recognition for contributions, demonstrates acceptance and openness to ideas of others, and is friendly and responsive to group members.

Harmonizer and compromiser: Persuades members to analyze constructively their differences in opinions, searches for common elements in conflicts, and tries to reconcile disagreements.

Tension reliever: Eases tensions and increases the enjoyment of group members by joking, suggesting breaks, and proposing fun approaches to group work.

Communication helper: Shows good communication skills, and makes sure that each group member understands what other members are saying.

Evaluator of emotional climate: Asks members how they feel about the way in which the group is working and about each other, and shares own feelings about both.

Process observer: Watches the process by which the group is working, and uses the observations to help examine group effectiveness.

Standard setter: Expresses group standards and goals to make members aware of the direction of the work and the progress being made toward the goal and to get open acceptance of group norms and procedures.

Active listener: Listens and serves as an interested audience for other members, is receptive to others' ideas, goes along with the group when not in disagreement.

Trust builder: Accepts and supports openness of other group members, reinforcing risk taking and encouraging individuality.

Interpersonal problem solver: Promotes open discussion of conflicts between group members to resolve conflicts and increase group togetherness.

Hersey and Blanchard (1977) developed a situational theory of leadership that serves as a guideline for when leaders should focus on task behaviors, on maintenance behaviors, or on both. In essence, the theory asserts that when members have low maturity for accomplishing a specific task, leaders should engage in high-task and low-maintenance behaviors. Hersey and Blanchard refer to this situation as *telling,* because leader behaviors are most effective when leaders define members' roles and tell them how, when, and where to do needed tasks. The task maturity of members increases as their experience and understanding of the task increases. For moderately mature members, leaders should engage in high-task and high-maintenance behaviors. This combination of behaviors is referred to as *selling,* because leaders should not only provide clear direction for role and task responsibilities but should also use maintenance behaviors to get members to "buy into" decisions.

EP 2.1.7a

Also, according to Hersey and Blanchard, when group members' commitment to the task increases, so does their maturity. When members are committed to accomplishing the task and have the ability and knowledge to complete the task, leaders should engage in low-task and high-maintenance behaviors, referred to as *participating*. Finally, for groups in which members are both willing and able to take responsibility for directing their own task behavior, leaders should engage in low-task and low-maintenance behaviors, referred to as *delegating*. Delegating allows members considerable autonomy.

Exercise 7.4: Your Task and Maintenance Contributions to a Group

Goal: This exercise is designed to assist you in understanding your task and maintenance contributions to a group.

Step 1: Identify a group you are currently participating in or participated in in the past. Briefly describe this group, including its goals.

Step 2: Review the list of task roles, and then describe your task contributions to this group.

Step 3: Review the list of maintenance roles, and then describe your maintenance contributions to this group.

LEADERSHIP THEORY

Four approaches to leadership theory are discussed in this section: trait, position, style, and distributed functions.

The Trait Approach

Aristotle observed, "From the hour of their birth some are marked for subjugation, and others for command" (Johnson & Johnson, 2000, p. 186). As implied by this comment, the trait approach to leadership has existed for millennia. This approach assumes that leaders have personal characteristics or traits that make them different from followers. It also implies that leaders are born, not made, and that leaders emerge naturally rather than being trained. The trait approach has been called the *great person* theory of leadership.

Krech, Crutchfield, and Ballachey (1962) reviewed research studies on leadership traits. Their results suggested leaders need to be perceived as (1) being a member of the group they are attempting to lead, (2) embodying to a special degree the norms and values that are central to the group, (3) being the most qualified group member for the task at hand, and (4) fitting members' expectations about how the leader should behave and what functions he or she should serve.

Research on personality traits indicates that leaders, compared with followers, tend to be better adjusted, more dominant, more extroverted, and more assertive; they often have greater interpersonal sensitivity. Other traits, such as intelligence, enthusiasm, self-confidence, and equalitarianism, also frequently characterize leaders (Hare, 1962).

Although potential leaders tend to have more of all positive attributes than other members have, they cannot be so extreme that they become deviates. In a classic study, for example, Davie and Hare (1956) found that B students were the campus leaders and A students were sometimes treated as outcasts for being "curve wreckers." Also, people who do most of the talking often win most of the decisions and become leaders, unless they talk *too* much and antagonize the other members (March, 1956).

Two leadership traits that have received considerable attention are charisma and Machiavellianism.

Charisma Johnson and Johnson (2000, p. 189) defined *charisma* as "an extraordinary power, as of working miracles." Johnson and Johnson (1987) gave the following definition of a *charismatic leader*:

> A charismatic leader has (1) an extraordinary power or vision and is able to communicate it to others or (2) unusual powers of practical leadership that will enable him or her to achieve the goals that will alleviate followers' distress. The charismatic leader has a sense of mission, a belief in the social-change movement he or she leads, and confidence in himself or herself as the chosen instrument to lead the movement to its destination. The leader appears extremely self-confident in order to inspire others with the faith that the movement he or she leads will prevail and ultimately reduce their distress. (p. 190)

Some charismatic leaders inspire their followers to adore and be extraordinarily committed to them. Others offer members hope and promise of deliverance from distress.

EP 2.1.7a

Charisma has proven difficult to define precisely. Qualities and characteristics of charismatic leaders differ dramatically. Consider, for example, the characteristics of these charismatic leaders: Martin Luther King, Jr., General George Patton, Gandhi, and Hitler.

One difficulty with quantifying charismatic leadership is that charismatics express this quality in numerous ways. A second difficulty is that many leaders do very well without being charismatic.

Exercise 7.5: The Charismatic Leader

Goal: This exercise is designed to assist you in identifying charismatic people and to understand the various characteristics that lead to charisma.

Step 1: Write the names of three people you identify as being charismatic—presidents, political leaders, religious leaders, teachers, acquaintances of yours, and so on. For each person you identify, list the characteristics that make this person (in your view) charismatic.

Step 2: For the three persons you wrote about, identify the charismatic characteristics that all three appear to have.

Step 3: Do any of these persons have unique charismatic characteristics (that is, characteristics that are not held by the other two)? If "yes," identify the person, and state his or her unique characteristics.

Machiavellianism Niccolò Machiavelli (1469–1527) was an Italian statesman who advocated that rulers use cunning, craft, deceit, and duplicity to increase their power and control. (Machiavelli was not the originator of this approach; earlier theorists also conceptualized leadership as manipulation for self-enhancement. However, the term *Machiavellianism* is now synonymous with the notion that politics is amoral and that unscrupulous means can therefore justifiably be used to achieve political power.) Machiavellian leadership is based on the concepts that followers (1) are basically fallible, gullible, untrustworthy, and weak; (2) are impersonal objects; and (3) should be manipulated for leaders to achieve their goals.

Christie and Geis (1970) concluded that Machiavellian leaders have four characteristics: (1) They have little emotional involvement in interpersonal relationships because it is easier emotionally to manipulate others if they are seen as "impersonal objects." (2) They are not concerned with conventional morality and take a utilitarian view (what they can get out of it) rather than a moral view of their interactions. (3) They have a fairly accurate perception of the needs of their followers, which facilitates their capacity to manipulate them. (4) They have a low degree of ideological commitment; they manipulate others for personal benefit rather than for achieving ideological goals.

Although some leaders have Machiavellian characteristics, most do not. Groups simply do not function effectively or efficiently with Machiavellian leaders.

EP 2.1.7a

In recent years, the trait theory of leadership has declined in popularity, partly because research results raise questions about its validity. For example, different leadership positions often require different leadership traits. The characteristics of a good military leader differ markedly from those of a good group therapy leader. Moreover, traits found in leaders are also found in followers. Qualities such as intelligence and a well-adjusted personality have some correlation with strong leadership, but many intelligent, well-adjusted people never get top leadership positions. The best rule for selecting leaders involves choosing people with the necessary skills, qualities, and motivation to help a group accomplish its goals.

Exercise 7.6: Machiavellian Leaders

Goal: This exercise is designed to assist you in understanding the characteristics of Machiavellian leaders.

Some authorities view Joseph Stalin, Adolf Hitler, and Saddam Hussein as being Machiavellian leaders. Identify three persons you view as being Machiavellian leaders. (These persons may include one or more of the leaders just mentioned.) For each person you list, write the characteristics he or she had (or has) that are Machiavellian.

The Position Approach

Large organizations have several levels of leadership. The position approach defines leadership in terms of the authority associated with a particular position and focuses on the behavior of people in high-level positions. Training and personal background of leaders have also been examined.

Studies using the position approach, however, reveal little consistency in how people assume leadership positions. Individuals with little training become leaders; others spend years developing their skills. Also, individuals in different leadership positions display a variety of appropriate behaviors. A drill sergeant is not expected to be empathetic, but a therapy group leader is. It is difficult to compile a list of leadership traits using this approach. Not surprisingly, the position approach has shown that what constitutes leadership behavior depends on the particular requirements of the position.

It is also difficult to define which behaviors are leadership behavior and which are not. Certainly not all the behavior of designated authority figures is leadership behavior. Also, leadership behavior among group members who are not designated leaders is often difficult to clarify. An experienced supervisor who joins a new firm, for example, may categorize her staff members according to guidelines set by her former employer. If the positions she uses are not interchangeable with those already in use at her new place of employment, communication problems may develop, and her leadership abilities or the ability of her staff will be questioned.

The Style Approach

Because research on the trait approach was turning out contradictory results, Lewin, Lippitt, and White (1939) focused on leadership *styles*. These researchers described three leadership styles: authoritarian, democratic, and laissez-faire.

Authoritarian leaders have more absolute power than democratic leaders. They alone set goals and policies, dictate the activities of members, and set major plans. They alone reward and punish, and they alone know the succession of future steps in the group's activities. In contrast, democratic leaders seek maximum involvement and participation of members in all decisions affecting the group. They spread responsibility rather than concentrate it.

Authoritarian leadership can be efficient and decisive. One hazard, however, is that group members often do what they are told out of necessity and not because of their commitment to group goals. The authoritarian leader who anticipates approval from subordinates for accomplishments achieved may be surprised to find backbiting and bickering common in the group. Unsuccessful authoritarian leadership generates factionalism and behind-the-scenes jockeying and maneuvering for position among members, and it leads to a decline in morale.

Democratic leadership, in contrast, is slow in decision making and sometimes confusing but is frequently more effective because strong cooperation emerges when members participate in decision making. With democratic leadership, interpersonal hostilities between members, dissatisfactions with the leader, and concern for personal advancement are discussed and acted on. The danger is that the private, behind-the-scenes complaining that can happen in the authoritarian approach becomes public conflict in a democratic approach. However, once the public conflict is resolved, strong personal commitments develop that motivate members to implement group decisions rather than to subvert them. The potential for sabotage in authoritarian groups is high, and therein lies the advantage of the democratic style.

Democratic leaders know that mistakes are inevitable and that the group will suffer from them. Yet such mistakes require that leaders stand by without interfering because to do otherwise harms the democratic process and impedes group progress.

In certain situations, authoritarian leadership is most effective, whereas in others democratic leadership is most effective (Hare, 1962). As in any situation, groups are more effective when members' expectations about behavior are met. When group members anticipate a democratic style, as they do in educational settings, classrooms, and discussion groups, the democratic style produces the most effective groups. When members anticipate forceful leadership, as in industry or military service, authoritarian leadership results in more effective groups.

In the *laissez-faire* style, there is very little participation by the leader. Group members function (or flounder) with little input by the designated leader. There are a few conditions in which group members function best under laissez-faire leadership (when the members are committed to a course of action, have the resources to implement it, and need a minimum of designated leader influence to work effectively).

EP 2.1.7a

Because different leadership styles are required in different situations (even within the same group), research interest in recent years has switched to the distributed-functions approach.

Exercise 7.7: Authoritarian, Democratic, and Laissez-Faire Leaders

Goal: This exercise is designed to help you understand these three types of leadership styles.

Step 1: Identify someone who used an authoritarian style in leading a group. State what the leader did that led you to conclude his or her style was authoritarian. Also state what the reactions of the other group members were to this authoritarian style.

Step 2: Identify someone who used a democratic style in leading a group. State what the leader did that led you to conclude his or her style was democratic. Also state what the reactions of the other group members were to this democratic style.

Step 3: Identify someone who used a laissez-faire style in leading a group. State what the leader did that led you to conclude his or her style was laissez-faire. Also state what the reactions of the other group members were to this laissez-faire style.

The Distributed-Functions Approach

This approach defines *leadership* as the performance of acts that help the group reach its goals and maintain itself in good working order (Johnson & Johnson, 1975). Leadership functions include setting group goals, selecting and implementing tasks to achieve goals, and providing resources to accomplish goals. Leadership functions also include the group maintenance tasks of improving group cohesion and seeking to ensure that individual members are satisfied. This approach seeks to discover what tasks are essential to achieve group goals under various circumstances and how different group members take part in these actions.

The distributed-functions approach stands in direct contrast to the great person theory of leadership. It asserts that at times any group member may be a leader by taking actions that serve group functions. Leadership is viewed as specific to a particular group in a particular situation. Telling a joke, for example, may relieve tension in some situations and thus may be leadership behavior. According to the functional approach, leadership occurs whenever any member influences other members to help the group reach its goals. Because at times all group members influence other members, each member leads.

The functional approach asserts that leadership is a learned set of skills that anyone with certain minimal requirements can acquire. Responsible membership is the same thing as responsible leadership; both involve doing what needs to be done to help the group maintain itself and accomplish its goals. This approach asserts that people can be taught the skills and behaviors that help the group accomplish its tasks and maintain good working relationships. The implication for a social work practice course is that practically everyone can learn to be an effective leader. However, being a *designated leader* and engaging in leadership behavior are different. A designated leader has responsibilities that continue for the duration of the group, whereas members who engage in leadership behaviors do so temporarily—this leadership role shifts from member to member.

Like any member of the group, the designated leader may need to adopt one or more of the task roles or maintenance roles discussed earlier in this chapter. Indeed, designated leaders have a special obligation to be alert for such occasions and to assume or assist others to assume whichever roles are timely and appropriate. The designated leader's contribution to the group is not limited, however, by assuming specified roles. He or she is responsible for functions that range from performing intake to planning for termination. The needs and developmental stage of a group will require a leader who can at different times assume the previously described roles and also the following ones:

- Executive (the top coordinator of group activities)
- Policymaker (establishing group goals and policies)
- Planner (deciding the means by which the group will achieve its goals)
- Expert (source of readily available information and skills)
- External group representative (the official spokesperson for the group)
- Controller of internal relations (managing the structure as a way to control in-group relations)
- Purveyor of rewards and punishments (promotions, demotions, and pleasant and unpleasant tasks)
- Arbitrator and mediator (both judge and conciliator with the power to reduce or to increase factionalism within the group)
- Exemplar (shows what members should be and do)
- Ideologist (the source of the group's beliefs and values)
- Scapegoat (the target for members' frustrations and disappointments)

EP 2.1.7a

Exercise 7.8: Applying the Distributed-Functions Approach

Goal: This exercise is designed to show you that you already have taken on leadership functions in a group.

The distributed-functions approach asserts that every member of a group will be a leader at times by taking actions that serve group functions. Identify a group that you are currently in or that you were a member of in the past. Describe actions that you took that were useful to the group. (When you made positive contributions to this group, you were taking on leadership responsibilities.)

SOCIAL POWER BASES IN GROUPS

French and Raven (1968) developed a framework for understanding the extent to which group members have influence or power over each other. They identified five types of power: reward, coercive, legitimate, referent, and expert. This framework allows group leaders to analyze the source of their power and also suggests when, and when not, to use their power.

Power is often viewed negatively. But *every* interaction involves power. In groups, it is natural and generally desirable that every member seeks to influence other members—this is how personal goals and group goals are accomplished.

Reward power is based on the perception of B (one member) that A (another member or the entire group) has the capacity to dispense rewards or remove negative consequences in response to B's behavior. A's power will be greater the more group members value the reward and the more they believe they cannot get the reward from anyone else. Rewards include such things as promotions, pay increases, days off, and praise. Group members often work hard for someone who has high reward power, will usually like the person, and will communicate effectively with him or her. But reward power can backfire if members feel they are being conned or bribed into going along, which can lead to dislike of the high-reward person. If A uses reward power in a conflict situation with B, B may feel he is being bribed and controlled.

Coercive power is based on B's perception that A can dispense adverse consequences or remove positive consequences. Coercive power stems from B's expectation that she will be punished by A if she fails to conform to A's wishes. The ability to fire workers if they fall below a given level of production is a common example of coercive power. The distinction between reward and coercive power is important. French and Raven noted that reward power tends to increase the attraction of B toward A, whereas coercive power decreases this attraction. If A uses coercive power to settle a conflict, it increases B's hostility, resentment, and anger. Threats often lead to aggression and counterthreats. Thus, coercive power can exacerbate the conflict by leading both A and B to distrust each other and to retaliate. Therefore, whenever possible, coercive power should not be used in a conflict situation. (Unfortunately, it often is, with the result that conflict is exacerbated. For example, military threats often increase conflict between rival countries.)

Legitimate power is based on B's perception that A has a legitimate right to prescribe behavior for him and that B has an obligation to accept this influence. Legitimate power is the most complex of the five power bases and is based on some internalized value or norm. Cultural values constitute one common basis for legitimate power and include such things as intelligence, age, caste, and physical characteristics. For example, in some cultures the elderly are highly respected and granted the right to prescribe behavior for others. Acceptance of a social structure is another basis; legitimate power in a formal organization is largely a relationship between positions rather than between people (such as the perceived right of supervisors to assign work). A third basis is a legitimizing agent; the process of electing a group leader is a common way to legitimize a person's right to a position that has legitimate power associated with it.

The areas in which legitimate power may be used are generally specified (for example, in a job description). The attempted use of power outside the prescribed range decreases the legitimate power and attractiveness of the authority figure.

Referent power is based on B's identification with A. Identification in this context means either a feeling of oneness with A or a desire for such an identity. The stronger B's identification with A, the greater is B's attraction to A and the greater A's referent power: "I am like A, and therefore I will believe or behave as A does," or "I want to be like A, and I will be more like A if I believe or behave as A does." In ambiguous situations, B will evaluate his thoughts, beliefs, and values in terms of what A thinks, believes, and values. In ambiguous situations, B is likely to adopt the thoughts, beliefs, and values of the individual or group with which he identifies. French and Raven noted that B is often not consciously aware of the referent power that A exerts.

Expert power is based on the perception that A has some special knowledge or expertise. Accepting a physician's advice in medical matters is a common example. Another is accepting directions from a service station owner when in a strange city. For expert influence to occur, it is necessary for B to think that A has the right answer and for B to trust that A is telling the truth. A client accepting a counselor's suggestion exemplifies the effect of expert power. Expert power is more limited than referent power because the expert is seen as having superior knowledge or ability only in specific areas. French and Raven (1968) noted that the attempted exertion of expert power outside the perceived range of that power will reduce it—that is, an undermining of confidence will take place.

EP 2.1.7a

French and Raven (1968) theorized that for all five types, the stronger the basis of power, the greater will be the power. Referent power is thought to have the broadest range of power. Attempts to use power outside the prescribed range may reduce the power.

Exercise 7.9: The Power Bases in This Class

Goal: This exercise is designed to assist you in understanding and applying the power bases identified by French and Raven.

This class can be viewed as being a group. For each of the following types of power, please write the following: Who in this class has this type of power? Has the person (or persons) engaged in actions that demonstrated this type of power? If "yes," describe these actions.

Reward power:

Coercive power:

Legitimate power:

Referent power:

Expert power:

PERSONAL GOALS AND GROUP GOALS

A *goal* is an end toward which an individual or a group of people are working. It is an ideal or a desired end point that people value. A personal goal is a goal held by a member. A group goal is a goal held by enough members that the group can be said to be working toward its achievement. All groups have goals, and every person who joins a group has personal goals. Groups have both short- and long-range goals. The short-range goals are stepping-stones to reaching the long-range goals.

It is very important to set group goals. The effectiveness and efficiency of the group can be measured by the extent to which its goals are achieved. Goals give direction to groups and to their members. They direct the group's programs and efforts. Conflicts of opinion between members are often resolved by deciding which opinion is most helpful in achieving group goals. Group goals are a motivating force. Once members commit to achieving a certain goal, they feel an obligation to put forth their abilities, efforts, and resources to attain this end.

Members' motivation to work to accomplish group goals is increased by involving members in setting the goals. Through involvement, members (1) have a greater chance of having their personal goals for joining the group become a component of the group goals, (2) have an increased awareness of the importance of choosing these goals, and (3) feel a greater commitment to providing their resources to achieve the goals.

The more congruence there is between members' personal goals and the group's goals, the more attracted to the group the members will be and the more willing to provide their resources and energies to the group. Members' personal goals can be heterogeneous (different) or homogeneous (alike). The more homogeneous personal goals are, the more likely are members to agree on group goals and work together to achieve them. They also tend to be happier with the group when personal goals are homogeneous.

When members have heterogeneous personal goals, hidden agendas can develop. A *hidden agenda* is a personal goal held by a member that is unknown to the other group members and that interferes with group goals. Hidden agendas can be very destructive. I have participated in groups where an individual observed the comments and actions of others to obtain evidence to bring legal harassment charges. Usually, however, hidden agendas are less destructive. For example, a lonely person who enjoys talking may slow a group down by monopolizing meetings with irrelevant small talk.

Because hidden agendas can severely hamper group processes, it is important that groups set goals that incorporate members' personal goals. With such a focus, hidden agendas are likely to be minimized.

Note, however, that *all* groups operate on two levels: the surface task and the hidden needs and motivations. Although hidden agendas siphon energy, they also reflect individual needs and may or may not be known to the person who holds them. All members join groups with the intention of meeting their personal needs. Sometimes after initial needs are met, other, less obvious ones surface. Such needs are normal and expected. The real issue is the effect these needs have on the group. The important question is whether meeting A's needs will prevent B (or the group) from satisfying needs. The goal is to find a means to legitimize individual needs in ways that allow for effective problem solving.

EP 2.1.7a

Managing hidden agendas requires that members and leaders be on the lookout for them and support members who try to bring hidden agendas to the surface. One such approach might involve saying, "I wonder if we've said all that we feel about this idea. Perhaps we should go around the room once more and see whether anyone has anything to add." At the same time, leaders and members should be aware that some hidden agendas are best left hidden. Criticizing a member for a hidden agenda can create defensiveness and inhibit problem solving.

Exercise 7.10: Group Goals, Personal Goals, and Hidden Agendas in This Class

Goal: This exercise is designed to assist you in understanding the dynamics between group goals, personal goals, and hidden agendas.

Step 1: Specify the group goals that the instructor wants for this class. (Usually the "course objectives" section of the syllabus will specify the group goals desired by the instructor.) In his or her lectures, the instructor may have identified additional desired group goals.

Step 2: Have all the students in the class "accepted" the desired group goals of the class? If "no," describe why you believe some students have not accepted the instructor's group goals.

Step 3: Did the instructor ask the students for additional group goals that they desired for the class? If "yes," did the students suggest additional group goals? If "yes" to the latter question, what were the additional group goals that were suggested—and then were they adopted for this class?

Step 4: Specify the personal goals that you have for this class. Are they consistent with the group goals?

Step 5: Do you believe some members of the class have "personal goals" or "hidden agendas" that are inconsistent with the group goals? (These personal goals or hidden agendas may include "not wanting to study very much" or "wanting help in resolving a personal dilemma.") If "yes," specify these inconsistent personal goals or hidden agendas.

GROUP NORMS

Group norms are rules that specify proper group behavior. To be a norm, a rule must be accepted by a majority of the group. If a person recognizes a norm and believes the benefits of conforming outweigh the consequences of deviating, the norm can influence that person's behavior. At first, members may conform because of pressures from the group. As time passes, though, members generally internalize norms and conform automatically. Norms provide one of the most important mechanisms of social control over members of groups and over society as a whole.

Every group has norms. If you frequently socialize with a certain group of students, for example, your group will gradually set norms as to what is acceptable and unacceptable behavior at gatherings. Your classes will have certain norms covering smoking, arriving late, absences, meeting deadlines, raising a hand before speaking, and cheating on exams.

Some norms are set formally—bylaws and constitutions of organizations, for instance, specify responsibilities for the officers. Other norms are set informally. During a department meeting, the department chair may frown at a faculty member who is reading his mail. If that faculty member responds to the nonverbal communication and puts aside his mail, other faculty members may observe the nonverbal interaction and decide never to read their mail during meetings. Through this process, a norm against reading mail has informally been established.

Norms have an "ought to" or "must" quality, and they vary in importance. There are strong pressures to obey and, in some cases, severe penalties for violating *important* norms—confidentiality in counseling groups, for example. If a member violates confidentiality by revealing personal information about another member to others outside the group, he may be penalized by expulsion from the group. Failure to obey less important norms, such as not belching at meetings, generates only mild disapproval and little or no penalty.

Members are often only subconsciously aware of many of the norms that are guiding their behavior. If one were to ask a group member to define her group's norms, she would probably be able to list only a few because many norms are taken for granted. Norms relating to dress, promptness, or foul language are often given little thought by group members.

When a person enters a new group, he generally feels strange and uncomfortable because he is unaware of the norms. So he searches for clues to norms, asking himself such questions as these: What is appropriate to disclose, and what is not? Who is in the in-group, and who is left out? Is smoking permissible? Can I tell a joke? Do members raise their hands before speaking? What role does each member play? Is the group competitive or cooperative? Are there hidden agendas? Are there coalitions? Which members are more powerful?

Some group norms are fairly universal, so new members who have worked in groups before will be aware of many norms that are likely to be operating. For example, an individual who joins a counseling group will expect other members to be honest, open, and self-disclosing. Many groups have norms such as reciprocity (if someone does something kind or helpful for you, you should do something kind or helpful in return); fair play (don't lie or cheat to get what you want); social responsibility (you should help those who need help); and shared air time (everyone should have a chance to talk, and no one should monopolize the conversation).

New members may learn norms by talking privately with a group member they trust. They may ask questions such as the following: Who has the power? Is it acceptable to say or do such and such? Are there coalitions in the group? Do some members have hidden agendas? Are there personal matters that some members are sensitive about? Someone who is overweight, for example, may express discomfort with comments on dieting, and other members may individually decide not to mention dieting when the overweight person is present.

Although norms are learned in a variety of ways, the most common way is through positive and negative reinforcement. Through a process of trial and error, members identify which of their behaviors are accepted and rewarded by the group and which are judged inappropriate or destructive. Another way members identify norms is through "modeling," which involves learning through observing another member's behavior.

Some norms are in the bylaws, constitution, minutes, or other documents of a group or organization. For example, there may be guidelines for placing an item on the agenda, the duties and responsibilities of the officers, and the decision-making procedures for resolving crucial issues. Furthermore, norms can take the form of role expectations that can be official or unofficial. Officially, the chair of a group is expected to call and run meetings; the secretary keeps minutes. Unofficially, a wealthy member is expected to make donations when the group needs funds. Likewise, a member who is skilled at reducing tension is expected to ease the tension level when it gets too high.

Some norms develop less formally through nonverbal communications. For example, the leader of a counseling group may shake his head in disapproval of one member mimicking another. The other members note the gesture and then individually (without discussion) decide not to mimic anyone in the group in the future.

EP 2.1.7a

New norms may develop from suggestions on group policy or procedures made by group members. For example, a member may suggest, "For an item to be placed on the agenda, the members must be informed of it at least forty-eight hours before the meeting to give them an opportunity to think about it." If the group approves of the suggestion, it becomes a policy and a norm.

Exercise 7.11: Group Norms in This Class

Goal: This exercise is designed to assist you in identifying group norms and to understand the processes that led to their development.

Step 1: Specify the group norms that exist for proper behavior in this class.

Step 2: Identify the processes that occurred that led to these group norms. (For example, the department may have standards for acceptable behavior in a class. The NASW Code of Ethics has statements on confidentiality, honesty, and opposition to making racist and sexist remarks. The CSWE's *Educational Policy and Accreditation Standards* has statements on diversity, populations at risk, and promoting social and economic justice. The instructor may have made statements about proper behavior in this class. Some students may have made statements about what they view as offensive remarks and behaviors.)

CONFORMITY

Some classic studies have examined conforming behavior. Sherif (1936) examined the "autokinetic effect." In this experiment, subjects were placed in a darkened room and asked to judge how far a dot of light moves. Although the light appeared to move (the autokinetic effect), it actually did not. Each subject saw the dot of light and made a

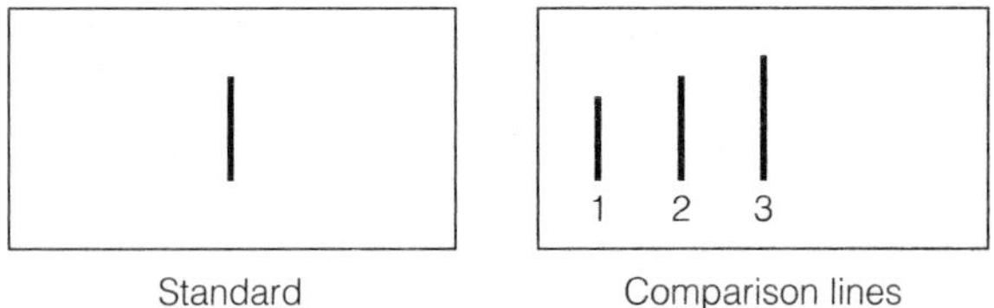

Figure 7.1
Cards used in Asch's conformity studies.

Source: © Cengage Learning, 2013.

series of individual judgments about how far the light moved. The subjects were then brought together in groups of three to judge again how far the light moved. In this situation, their judgments tended to converge to a group standard. Later, when they again viewed the light alone, they often retained the group standard and gave that answer. The key finding from this study and many after it is that when a situation is ambiguous and there is no objective way to determine the "right" answer, members rely on the group to define "reality." This means membership in a group determines for individuals many of the things they will see, learn, think about, and do.

Asch (1955) also examined conforming behavior. Asch investigated what happens when an individual's judgment conflicts with the judgments of other group members. The experiments were designed as follows. There were two sets of cards, as shown in Figure 7.1. Subjects were arranged in groups of seven to nine, seated at a table, and asked to state in turn which line was closest in length to the standard. In the control groups, practically all subjects chose line 2. Now, here is where things get interesting: In the experimental groups, all members, except for one subject, were accomplices of the experimenter. The subject was seated at or near the end of the line for giving his or her judgment. Accomplices all chose the same *incorrect* line. When it came to the subject's turn, he or she was then faced with relying on individual judgment or conforming to the group judgment. In a variety of similar studies, Asch found that more than one-third of the subjects conformed to the group judgment. Such a large percentage is amazing because there was no overt group pressure to conform, the situation was not ambiguous, and the subjects did not know each other. In addition, there were neither promises of future favor or advancement, nor threats of ostracism or punishment.

Conformity is the yielding to group pressure. For there to be conformity, there must be conflict—conflict between the influences exerted by the group and those forces in individuals that tend to lead them to value, believe, and act in some other way. For members experiencing such conflict, there are two available options: Announce an independent decision, or conform with the group's position. Conforming takes two forms: (1) The expedient conformer outwardly agrees but inwardly disagrees. (2) The true conformer both outwardly and inwardly comes to agree with the group.

A number of conclusions have arisen from conformity research (Krech et al., 1962, pp. 509–512):

1. Considerable amounts of yielding are produced by group pressure, even when the bogus group consensus is obviously wrong. In one study, 50 military officers were asked to indicate which of two figures, a star and a circle presented side by side, was larger in an area. The circle was clearly about one-third larger, but under group pressure 46 percent of the men agreed with the bogus group consensus.
2. Many people can be pressured into yielding on attitude and opinion items, even those with significant personal implications. For example, 50 military officers were asked privately and under bogus group consensus to state their opinion on the following: "I doubt whether I would make a good leader." In private, none of the officers expressed agreement, but under unanimous group pressure, 37 percent expressed agreement.
3. Yielding is far greater on difficult, subjective items than on easy, objective ones.

4. Individual differences in yielding are extremely large. A few people yield on almost all items; a few yield on none; most people yield on some and not on others.
5. When people are retested individually and privately on the same items some time later, the yielding effect mostly disappears as they tend to revert to their own unchanged private judgment. But a small part of the yielding effect remains, indicating group pressure has a lasting effect on changing attitudes.
6. As a group increases in size, the pressure for yielding increases, and more yielding occurs. When a person is opposed by a single other person, there is very little yielding.
7. Yielding is markedly reduced when a person has the support of one other person (a partner) in the group. Apparently, a dissident opinion has a tremendous effect in strengthening the independence of like-minded people.

In a dramatic series of studies, Milgram (1963) demonstrated that subjects in an experimental situation would administer electric shocks of dangerous strength to another person when instructed to do so by the experimenter. (Unknown to the subject, the person did not actually receive the electrical shocks.) Most subjects complied with the experimenter's commands, even when instructed to give increasingly strong shocks to the victim, and despite the victim's protests and cries of anguish. These studies demonstrated that people will yield to "authoritative" commands even when the behavior is incompatible with their own moral, normal standards of conduct. Milgram suggested his studies help us understand why the German people complied with the unethical commands of Hitler. Group pressures, especially when viewed as authoritative, have a tremendous effect on our actions, attitudes, and beliefs.

EP 2.1.7a

Schachter (1959) developed a theory of social comparison. Schachter assumed that we all have a need to evaluate the "rightness" of our feelings, opinions, values, and attitudes. He also assumed that we all have a need to evaluate the extent of our abilities. Schachter then theorized and conducted studies to demonstrate that in the absence of objective, nonsocial means of evaluation, a person will rely on other people as comparison points of reference. To a large extent, the groups we belong to define social reality for us. For most of our opinions, values, beliefs, and abilities, there is no objective, nonsocial way to evaluate ourselves, so we rely on others.

Exercise 7.12: Your Yielding to Group Pressure

Goal: This exercise is designed to help you understand that all of us have yielded (at one time or another) to group pressure. The exercise also helps you understand your feelings about yielding.

Step 1: Describe a group that you participated in, in which you yielded to group pressure. Specify the issue or action that you yielded to. (If you have difficulty in identifying a time when you yielded, feel free to identify an issue in which you yielded to pressure from your parents.)

Step 2: Specify your thoughts and feelings during the time when you yielded. Also specify your thoughts and feelings after you yielded.

Step 3: If you had to do it over, would you still yield? Why, or why not?

IDIOSYNCRATIC CREDITS

Every member of a group gains credits (and status) by showing competence and by conforming to expectations at that time. Eventually these credits allow a person to break the group's norms and rules without being chastised. To some extent, after credits accumulate, nonconformity to general procedures or expectations serves as a confirming feature of one's status. Yet there is a limit on the number of earned idiosyncratic credits. Nonconformity beyond this limit can result in a dramatic decrease in status and even rejection by other group members.

COMPETITIVE GROUPS AND COOPERATIVE GROUPS

Groups basically have either a cooperative or a competitive group atmosphere. In a cooperative group, open and honest communication, trust, pooling of resources, and cohesion prevail. Research has found a number of positive consequences for a cooperative group atmosphere in problem-solving groups. Cooperation among members increases creativity, coordination of effort, division of labor, emotional involvement in group accomplishment, helping and sharing, interpersonal skills, cooperative attitudes and values, positive self-attitudes, liking among group members, positive attitudes toward the group and tasks, divergent thinking, acceptance of individual and cultural differences, and problem-solving skills.

Cooperative group atmospheres result when members' personal goals are perceived as compatible, identical, or complementary. An example of a highly cooperative group is a successful basketball team in which the main goal of each member is to win and the main goal of the team is to win. In a cooperative group, members seek to coordinate their efforts with those of other members to achieve the goals of the group. To establish a cooperative atmosphere, rewards to members must be based on the quantity and quality of group performance rather than on individual performance.

In contrast, competitive atmospheres can be detrimental and destructive. Competitive atmospheres exist when members perceive their personal goals as incompatible, different, conflicting, or mutually exclusive. In highly competitive groups, a member achieves his or her goal only if other members fail to obtain their goals. An example is a job group interview held for several job applicants. The consequences of competition in problem-solving groups are numerous. Competition decreases creativity, coordination of effort, division of labor, helping and sharing, and cohesion. Competition promotes ineffective communication, suspicion and mistrust, high anxiety, competitive values and attitudes, negative self-attitudes, dislike among group members, and negative attitudes toward the group and its tasks. Competition encourages rejection of differences of opinion, divergent thinking, and cultural and individual differences. A competitive atmosphere often leads to low effectiveness in solving complex problems.

Kelly and Stahelski (1970) examined the question of what happens when a competitive person joins a group that has a cooperative atmosphere. Because cooperative groups are much more effective in problem solving than competitive groups are, the question is significant. Three consequences were found to occur: (1) The competitive behavior of the new member leads other members to behave competitively. (2) The competitive person views the former cooperative members as having always been competitive. (3) The former cooperative members are generally aware that their competitive behavior is largely a consequence of the new member's competitiveness. Thus, it appears that one competitive person can change a cooperative group into a competitive group. Why does a competitive person have such a strong, destructive effect? Apparently, the cooperative members realize the competitive person, if given a chance, will take advantage of their cooperativeness and use it to his or her own advantage. In many situations, their only recourse to prevent exploitation is to also become competitive. If a cooperative group is to survive, it is important that new members have an orientation compatible with that of the other members.

CONFLICT AND CREATIVITY

Conflict is an antagonistic state of action involving divergent ideas or interests and is inevitable in groups. Johnson and Johnson (1975) summarize the potential merits and dangers of a conflict in a group:

> A conflict among group members is a moment of truth in group effectiveness, a test of the group's health, a crisis that can weaken or strengthen the group, a critical event that may bring creative insight and closer relationships among members—or lasting resentment, smoldering hostility, and psychological scars. Conflicts can push members away from one another or pull them into closer and more cooperative relationships. Conflicts may contain the seeds of group destruction or the seeds of a more unified and cooperative unit.... They have the potential for producing both highly constructive and highly destructive consequences for group functioning. (p. 139)

Many people in our society erroneously believe that conflicts produce only negative results and should be avoided. Conflict is seen as a cause of divorce, low work morale, deterioration of friendships, psychological trauma, violence, and social disorder. In reality, the cause of these destructive events is the ineffective and harmful management of conflicts. People have divergent interests, beliefs, values, and goals, so it is inevitable that conflicts will occur in interpersonal relationships.

Conflicts are a natural part of any relationship within a group, and they are desirable because, when handled effectively, they have a number of payoffs. Without conflict, members may become bored; disagreements often spark the interest and curiosity of group members and produce lively discussions. Conflicts motivate members to define issues more sharply, search harder for resolution strategies, and work harder in implementing solutions. Conflicts also can lead to greater commitment, cohesion, communication, and cooperation and can revitalize stagnant groups. By expressing and working out their dissatisfactions, group members can assess their beliefs, values, and opinions. Therefore, verbal conflicts can lead to personal growth and encourage innovation and creativity.

EP 2.1.1b

Exercise 7.13: My Tolerance for Conflicts

Goal: This exercise is designed to assist you in assessing whether you need to become more assertive in confronting interpersonal conflicts.

Step 1: Do you shy away (by usually giving in) from interpersonal conflicts? If "yes," explain your reasons.

Step 2: If you shy away from interpersonal conflicts, do you feel when you give in that the other person is "trodding" on your personal rights?

Step 3: Do you believe that you need to more assertively confront your interpersonal conflicts? If "yes," what do you intend to do to become more assertive in confronting conflicts?

STRATEGIES FOR RESOLVING CONFLICTS

There are a variety of strategies for resolving conflicts. Among them are the win-lose approach, no-lose problem solving, role reversal, empathy, inquiry, I-messages, disarming, stroking, mediation, letting go or forgiving, and the law of requisite variety.

Win-Lose Approach

In ineffective groups, resolutions of conflict between opposing positions become win-lose situations. In many competitive fields, such as sports, business, and politics, individuals or teams are pitted against each other. In groups, conflicts are often cast in the same competitive mold. Because each side denies the legitimacy of the other's interests and concerns, members attempt to sell their position without really listening to the other side. Power blocks are formed to support one position against another. The original goals and objectives of the group may fade into the background as only a "win" on issues becomes the objective of the warring sides.

In win-lose situations, the group as a whole loses because it fails to achieve its long-range goals and objectives. The losing side is not motivated to carry out the winning decision. The losers resent the winners and may attempt to reverse the decision or impede its implementation. In such an atmosphere, distrust increases between opposing sides, communication becomes more limited and inaccurate, and group cohesion decreases. Members' unresolved feelings often result in biased judgments and actions; members will frequently refuse to vote for a good idea simply because they dislike the person who suggested it.

Communication is severely hampered in groups that handle conflict in a win-lose fashion. Conflict in win-lose situations leads to the denial or distortion of unpleasant facts and information, as each side is likely to deny, hide, or distort information inconsistent with its position in an effort to win. Members misinterpret the ideas and actions of those perceived as opponents, causing "blind spots" in communication. A win-lose approach leads to deceitful expression of ideas and feelings because winning sometimes receives higher priority than honesty. Disagreement tends to be interpreted as personal rejection by opposing group members, and the group's future decisions are generally poor.

No-Lose Problem Solving

The no-lose problem-solving approach asserts that it is almost always possible for both sides to have their needs met in a conflict situation. This approach, a variation of the problem-solving approach described earlier in this chapter, was developed by Thomas Gordon (1970) and is based on two basic premises: (1) All persons have the right to have their needs met. (2) What is in conflict between the two sides is almost never their *needs* but their *solutions* to those needs.

The distinction between needs and solutions is all-important. Assume that a student social work club is arguing over whether to fund a graduation party for seniors or a campus day-care center is in danger of being closed. An analysis of needs and solutions in this discussion would reveal that the club is arguing over solutions rather than needs. There is a need to honor the graduating seniors and a need for the day-care center to receive operating funds. However, there are a variety of ways of meeting both needs. The club may spend its current funds on a graduation party and then hold a fund-raiser for the day-care center; or fund the center and hold a graduation party by having members donate food, refreshments, and a few dollars at the party. Half of the club's funds could go to the center, the remainder to a reduced-cost graduation party. In addition, many other solutions could be generated to meet these needs.

The six steps to the *no-lose problem-solving approach,* as described by Gordon (1970), are the following:

1. Identify and define the needs of each opposing side.
2. Generate possible alternative solutions.
3. Evaluate the alternative solutions.
4. Decide on the best acceptable solution.
5. Work out ways of implementing the solution.
6. Evaluate how the solution worked.

The first step is by far the most difficult because group members often view conflicts in terms of win-lose and attempt to identify and meet primarily their own needs. When each side's needs in a conflict are identified, however, what usually is in conflict are not the *needs* of each side but their *solutions*. No-lose problem solving will generally lead to creative solutions, after all six steps are followed. (Readers will note the "no-lose problem-solving process" is identical to the "problem-solving process" described in Chapter 1.)

The advantages of this no-lose approach are that both sides fulfill their needs and group harmony and cohesion are increased. Also, the resentment, hostility, and subversive actions of a win-lose situation are eliminated. Actually, it is in each group member's best interest to resolve conflicts in a way that will help all members achieve their short-term goals and needs and increase the long-term effectiveness of the group, so that the long-term goals and needs of all members have a better chance of being achieved. Frequently, when groups function through win-lose, the winning side may win some battles, but the effectiveness of the group may diminish. All members may thus fail to accomplish their long-term goals and satisfy their needs.

With a problem-solving approach, members tend to listen to one another, recognize the legitimacy of one another's interests, and influence one another with rational arguments. Instead of a competitive environment, problem solving encourages an atmosphere of cooperation.

The differences between a win-lose strategy and a problem-solving strategy are summarized in Exhibit 7.1.

Role Reversal

A useful strategy for resolving both intragroup and intergroup conflict is role reversal. Here is the basic rule for role reversal: *Each person expresses his or her opinions or views only after restating the ideas and feelings of the opposing person*. These ideas and feelings should be restated in your own words rather than parroted or mimicked in the exact words of the other person. It is advisable to begin your restatement with "Your position is...," "You seem to be saying...," or "You apparently feel...." Approval or disapproval, blaming, giving advice, interpreting, or persuading should be avoided.

 **Exhibit 7.1 Differences Between Strategies**

Win-Lose Strategy	Problem-Solving Strategy
The conflict is defined as a win-lose situation.	The conflict is viewed as a problem.
Each side seeks solutions to meet only its needs.	Each person seeks to find solutions to meet the needs of all members.
Each side attempts to force the other side into submission.	Each person cooperates with others to find mutually acceptable compromises.
Each side increases its power by emphasizing its independence from the other and the other's dependence on itself.	Each person equalizes power by emphasizing interdependence.
Each side inaccurately, deceitfully, and misleadingly communicates its goals, needs, and ideas; information inconsistent or harmful to one's position is not shared.	Each person honestly and openly communicates goals, needs, and ideas.
No expression of empathy or understanding is made of the views, values, and opinions of the other side.	Efforts are made to convey empathy and understanding of the views, values, and opinions of others.
Threats are used to attempt to force the other side into submission.	Threats are avoided to reduce the defensiveness of others.
Rigid adherence to one's position is expressed.	A willingness to be flexible is expressed.
Changes in position are made very slowly, in an effort to force concessions from the other side.	Positions are changed readily to help in problem solving.
No suggestions are sought from third parties because the focus is on forcing the other side to give in.	Third parties are sought to help in problem solving

In addition, nonverbal messages should be consistent with the verbal paraphrasing and convey interest, openness, and attentiveness to the opposition's ideas and feelings. Above all, role reversal should be the expression of a sincere interest in understanding the other person's feelings, ideas, and position.

Role reversal can result in a reevaluation and a change of attitude concerning the issue by both parties, for the group members involved are likely to be perceived as people who are understanding, willing to compromise, cooperative, and trustworthy. The approach has also been found to increase cooperative behavior between role reversers, to clarify misunderstandings, to change win-lose situations into problem-solving situations, and, most important, to allow the issue to be perceived from the opponent's frame of reference.

Empathy

A technique closely related to role reversal is the expression of empathy. Empathy is putting yourself in the shoes of the person you are in conflict with and expressing your understanding of what the person is thinking and saying. Here are some phrases that help you get started:

"What you seem to be saying is..."

"I take it that you think..."

"I sense you feel ___ about this issue."

When you express empathy, it is essential to mirror what was said in a nonjudgmental way and to grasp the essence of what the other person is thinking or feeling. Similar to role reversal, the use of empathy facilitates open communication, assists in clarifying misunderstandings, increases cooperative behavior, and facilitates the process of no-lose problem solving.

Inquiry

If you are in conflict with someone and are confused about his or her thoughts and feelings, the inquiry technique is often useful. This technique involves using gentle, probing questions to learn more about what the other person is thinking and feeling. Tone of voice is crucial in this technique; asking a question sarcastically or defensively is likely to result in defensive responses.

I-Messages

Most of us are raised to respond to conflict with "you-messages." There are two types of you-messages: a *solution* message and a *put-down* message. A solution message orders, directs, commands, warns, threatens, preaches, moralizes, or advises. A put-down message blames, judges, criticizes, ridicules, or name-calls. Examples of you-messages include "You stop that," "Don't do that," "I hate you," and "You should know better." You-messages tend to inhibit open communication. You-messages are generally counterproductive because people do not like to be ordered or criticized. You-messages frequently result in an ongoing struggle between the two people involved.

In contrast, I-messages foster open communication. They are nonblaming messages that communicate how the sender of the message believes the receiver is affecting the sender. I-messages do not provide solutions, and they do not criticize. It is possible to send an I-message without using the word *I*.

I-messages communicate much more honestly the effect of behavior, and they help the other person to assume responsibility for his or her behavior. An I-message conveys to the person you are in conflict with that you trust him or her to respect your needs and to handle the conflict constructively. I-messages are much less likely to provoke an argument. They facilitate honesty, openness, and more cordial relationships. (I-messages and you-messages are described in Module 4.)

Disarming

When you are in conflict with someone, the disarming technique is an effective way to move toward resolution. This technique involves finding some truth in what the other person (or side) is saying and then expressing this "agreement"—even if you feel that what the other person is saying is largely wrong, unreasonable, irrational, or unfair. When using the disarming technique, it is important for you to be genuine in what you say and express your agreement in a sincere way.

There is always a grain of truth in what someone else is saying, even if it sounds obnoxious and insulting. When you disarm the other side with this technique, those disagreeing with you will recognize that you respect them. As a result, they won't feel so dogmatic and will have less of an urge to insist that they are right and you are wrong. They are then likely to be more willing to examine the merits of your point of view. If you want respect, you have to give respect first. If you want to be listened to, this technique helps you listen to the other person first and avoids defensive communication. Friendly responses facilitate open communication; hostile responses usually result in defensive communication.

Stroking

Stroking is closely related to disarming. When using this technique, you say something genuinely positive to the person (or side) you are in conflict with, even in the heat of (verbal) battle. Stroking is a sign of respect. During an argument or conflict, we have a tendency to reject the other person before we get rejected (so we can save face). Often we overreact, and differences of opinion blow out of proportion. To prevent this, let those with whom you disagree know that although you are at odds with them you still think highly of them. This strategy makes it easier for them to open up and to listen.

Mediation

Mediation is increasingly used to resolve conflicts. Mediation involves intervention by an acceptable, impartial, and neutral third party, who has no decision-making power, to assist contending parties in voluntarily reaching their own mutually acceptable settlement of issues in dispute. Mediation leaves decision making in the hands of the people in conflict. It is a voluntary process: The participants must be willing to accept the assistance of the mediator. Mediation is usually initiated when the parties no longer believe they can resolve the conflict on their own and when the only means of resolution appears to be impartial third-party assistance. (Mediation is described more fully in Module 4.)

Letting Go or Forgiving

If we hold long-term grudges against others, the primary people we are hurting, (both emotionally and health-wise) are ourselves. Emotionally we hurt ourselves by being in a state of periodic anger (which occurs when we think about the perceived "wrong"). By holding a grudge, we also raise our level of stress, which (as described in Chapter 14) often leads to a variety of stress-related illnesses. Mentally nursing a grudge puts your body through the same strains as a major stressful event: muscles tense, blood pressure rises, and sweating increases.

Two strategies to get rid of holding a long-term grudge are "letting go" and forgiving. With the letting-go strategy, we reframe our thinking so that we no longer dwell on the perceived wrong. One way of reframing our thinking is to do a rational self-analysis (described in Module 1). If there is no way to change a perceived "wrong," the best thing we can do for our mental and physical well-being is to "let go" of it.

Forgiveness is actually another strategy for letting go. When you forgive someone who has hurt you, you make yourself—rather than the person who hurt you—responsible for your happiness.

The Law of Requisite Variety

If used appropriately, the strategies described so far will help resolve interpersonal conflicts in most cases. If these strategies fail, you can probably correctly conclude that the person you are in conflict with does not want to resolve the conflict. Perhaps, for reasons beyond your control, the person is very hostile and wants to generate conflicts to meet personal needs. Or perhaps he or she wants to make your life uncomfortable!

What can you do when you realize that another person really wants to sustain a conflict? The law of requisite variety provides one option. According to this law, if you continue to come up with creative new ways of responding to the daggers being thrown at you, eventually the other person will tire of the turmoil and decide to "bury the hatchet." Here is an example:

Janice and Pete Palmer were married about a year ago. Unknown to Janice, Pete was having lunch about once a month with a former partner (Paula) whom he dated over a 3-year period. Seven months ago Janice walked into a restaurant at noon and saw her husband with Paula. In a fit of rage, Janice stomped out. That evening she and Pete had a major blowup. Pete claimed that Paula was just a friend and that nothing romantic was occurring. Janice yelled and screamed. Pete indicated he would stop having lunch with Paula. But he didn't keep his promise. About once a month he continued to see her, and when Janice found out, they again had a major argument. Janice suggested a number of resolution options, including marriage counseling. Pete refused to go to counseling and also indicated (the win-lose approach) that he was going to continue having lunch with Paula. Then one day Janice ran into one of her former partners—Dave. Dave invited Janice for lunch or dinner. A light bulb went on for Janice—she accepted the invitation. Later she gleefully told Pete (Pete knew Dave had dated Janice in the past).

EP 2.1.7a

Pete became jealous and tried to talk Janice out of the dinner. Janice of course said "No way." This threw Pete into fits of anguish. When Janice came home, Pete politely said he had called Paula that evening to inform her he was canceling their next scheduled lunch, and that he felt it was best that they no longer meet for lunch. Pete then asked Janice if she also would no longer get together with Dave. She indicated "Yes." Through this experience, Pete and Janice learned to respect and appreciate each other to a greater extent.

Exercise 7.14: Resolving Your Conflicts Effectively

Goal: This exercise is designed to inform you about how to resolve interpersonal conflicts more effectively.

Step 1: Describe a serious interpersonal conflict that you had with someone who was important to you.

Step 2: What conflict resolution strategies did you use to attempt to resolve the conflict?

Step 3: What conflict resolution strategies did the other person seek to use?

Step 4: Was the conflict successfully resolved? If "yes," describe what led to the resolution. If "no," specify why it was not resolved.

Step 5: Review the conflict resolution techniques described in this chapter. Specify those that you believe might have been effective in more rapidly resolving the conflict. Provide an explanation for your views.

Step 6: Which of the conflict resolution techniques do you intend to use in the future?

HANDLING DISRUPTIVE BEHAVIOR

There may be hostile or disruptive members in any group, even in groups whose members come voluntarily. However, they are more likely to be found in involuntary groups. Involuntary members often (at least at the initial meetings of the group) wish they were a thousand other places rather than in the group. They are often angry because they are forced to come, and they may believe that the group will be a "complete waste of time."

Social workers encounter involuntary clients in various settings: corrections, protective services, mental health facilities, certain public school settings, group homes, residential treatment facilities, nursing homes, and hospitals. In such settings, groups are often established that unwilling clients are required to attend and social workers are expected to lead. Disruptive behavior includes being aggressive, competing, fooling around, sympathy seeking, and failing to finish tasks on time. To more vividly describe these disruptive behaviors, I will ascribe "personalities" to the behaviors.

Bears openly express anger, rage, frustration, resentment, and hostility, They are unhappy as members of the group or with what is happening in the group. They express discontent in a variety of ways: verbally, by attacking other members; nonverbally, by facial expressions; or physically, by aggressively pushing and shoving other members.

Bears who directly express unhappiness in an active fashion can also express unhappiness in passive-aggressive ways through indirect aggression. Bach and Wyden (1981) have called indirect aggression "crazy-making." Indirect aggressors maintain a front of kindness but find subtle, indirect ways to express their anger, rage, or frustrations. Bach and Wyden label direct aggression "clean fighting" because feelings are expressed openly and can be identified and resolved. "Dirty fighters" use indirect tricks and never clearly express their feelings, which often causes a great deal of pain and can destroy effective communication. Most disruptive behaviors involve an element of indirect aggression.

If you have a relationship with a "dirty fighter," he or she will identify what will "press your buttons." Dirty fighters casually and subtly press these buttons to get you going.

Eager beavers volunteer to do crucial tasks but have little intention of completing them; they seduce other members into believing they are willing contributors. They may partially perform some tasks to show good faith but then employ a variety of excuses to explain why the tasks can't be completed on time.

Clowns are disrupters who are rarely serious. They are always joking and clowning around, even when other members want to be serious. A clown inhibits other members from expressing their thoughts and feelings because they fear they will be ridiculed.

Psychoanalyzers continually analyze what other members do and say. They often use psychological terms and delight in analyzing what others really mean and what's wrong with them. The psychoanalyzer often slows a group by getting members to engage in mind reading rather than task completion. Other members are inhibited from expressing their thoughts and feelings; they don't want to be analyzed.

Withholders have important information or resources that would help the group accomplish its task, but they intentionally withhold assistance. They are more interested in watching the group struggle and spin its wheels.

Beltliners are dirty fighters. Everyone has a psychological "beltline" under which lie subjects that we are extremely sensitive about. Beltline items include physical characteristics, intelligence, past behavior, past unhappy events, or personality characteristics. An overweight person, for example, may be highly sensitive about comments related to obesity. Beltliners make subtle negative comments about sensitive areas to threaten group cohesion and morale.

Guiltmakers attempt to control others by making them feel guilty. They trap the group into helping them with personal needs and goals, rather than working toward group goals. Guiltmakers use common expressions such as "You never do anything for me" and "All I've done for you and this is the thanks I get" to trigger the guilt response.

Catastrophe criers, by exaggerating the seriousness of a problem, would have group members believe that consequences will be not minor but disastrous. "Catastrophiers" focus only on examining the severity of the problem and not on developing and implementing problem-solving approaches, so they exacerbate problems.

Subject changers do not want the group to deal with crucial issues or with controversy and conflict. When difficult situations arise, they change the subject. They prevent the group from dealing with crucial topics. There are a variety of reasons for seeking to change a subject; for example, changers may detest heated debates or may fear the debate will reveal something they wish to keep hidden.

Whiners continually complain about one thing or another without taking action to resolve the problem. Because they seek attention and sympathy, they slow group progress.

If a group is competing with another group, a betrayer, or **Benedict Arnold,** supplies confidential information to the other group. The betrayer encourages people outside the group to ridicule or disregard it or slyly arranges to have the group's funding cut back. Within a group, Benedict Arnolds attempt to prevent the group from accomplishing its goals.

Instead of honestly sharing concerns, frustrations, and discontent, **trivial tyrannizers** annoy the group with constant interruptions and digressions. They arrive late and leave early, fail to show up for crucial meetings, or bring up concerns the group has already acted on. Besides raising unnecessary questions about the wording of the minutes, for instance, trivial tyrannizers may yawn or read something when other members are speaking.

Shirkers are disruptive simply by failing to do anything for the group. When assigned certain tasks, shirkers will evade these responsibilities by using a variety of excuses.

Power grabbers attempt to become the group leader or the power behind the leader by convincing other members that they have more expertise than anyone else in the group or by buying the support of others with money, favors, or promises. Power grabbers create conflicts that make the leader look bad, and sabotage the efforts of the leader, even though they may not assume leadership power.

Because **paranoiacs** are excessively or irrationally suspicious and distrustful of others in the group, they always feel picked on. Much of their time is spent defending themselves and finding fault with other members. Paranoiac individuals often feel that other members must be discredited before they can amass enough evidence to discredit the paranoiacs.

Note that disrupters are often intentionally aware of the effects of their behavior. Most of these examples are of this type. However, some disrupters act out of unconscious personal needs and may not be aware that their behavior is disruptive. The following suggestions for handling disruptive behavior apply whether disrupters are aware or unaware of the effects of their behavior.

There are three main ways leaders can handle hostile and disruptive behavior. The approach you choose should be based on your judgment about which will be most helpful to the group:

1. *Allow the member to continue to express the disruptive behavior.* Such expression has a vent effect, so the member may become less disruptive as time goes on. It is often helpful to tactfully ask disruptive members to express their concerns.

   Tactfully asking the member probing questions about his concerns and modeling good listening skills while reflecting his feelings often helps defuse a disruptive situation. In certain instances there may be benefit in using a role reversal: Ask the disrupter to argue the alternate point of view while you take the disrupter's position. Whenever possible, disruption should be dealt with as a group issue, and the group may, in fact, decide to deal with at least some of the disrupter's concerns, especially those that are legitimate. Through resolution of some of these concerns, the disruptive member may become less unhappy and begin to see that the group has some payoffs.

2. *Assertively confront the member about how her behavior is disrupting the group.* This confrontation can take place with other group members present, or leaders can meet privately with the person. (When confronting a disruptive member, it is helpful to use one or more of the conflict resolution strategies described in the previous section.) Whether you confront privately or publicly should be based on your judgment of which will be most beneficial. If other members are present, they may be able to help by elaborating on the ways in which the behavior is disruptive. Also, having others present emphasizes the seriousness of the problem. A disadvantage of confrontation when others are present is that hostile members may feel ganged up on and may be more inhibited in fully expressing what they are unhappy about. In some instances, simply indicating to the members in private that you are concerned about their behavior and are considering opening it up as a matter of discussion for the entire group will help them reconsider whether the disruptions are accomplishing the desired purpose.
3. *Have other members do the confronting.* Certain situations are best handled by someone other than the leader. Another member may have better rapport with the person, and the disruptive member may be more responsive if the confrontation comes from the neutral member.

EP 2.1.7a

Any of these approaches may prove fruitful. It is important to realize that conflict and differences in opinion are not uncommon or unnatural in groups and in fact may be healthy.

Exercise 7.15: Handling the Disruptive Behavior of a Group Member

Goal: This exercise is designed to help you handle the disruptive behavior of a group member.

Step 1: Describe the disruptive behavior of someone who was also a member of a group that you were involved in.

Step 2: How did the disruptive behavior affect the group?

Step 3: What actions (if any) did the other group members take to attempt to minimize the effects of the disruptive behavior? Were these actions effective?

Step 4: If the actions were not very effective, review the material on handling disruptive behavior in this chapter. What actions might have been taken by you (or by other group members) to more effectively handle the disruptive behavior?

GROUP SIZE

The size of a group affects members' satisfactions, interactions, and output. Smaller groups often rate more favorably in these aspects (Toseland & Rivas, 2007). Larger groups tend to create more stress, have more communication difficulties, and, though successful in some tasks because of the greater number of skills available, be generally less efficient or productive. In larger groups, each person has less opportunity to talk, and some people feel inhibited and reluctant to talk. In discussion groups, it has been shown that as the size of the group increases, the most frequent contributor assumes an increasingly prominent role in the discussion. The bigger the group, the greater is the gap in participation between the most frequent contributor and other members of a group.

In one classic study, Slater (1958) found that groups of five persons were considered most satisfactory by members. Observations of the interactions of groups smaller than five indicated the members were inhibited from expressing their ideas through fear of alienating one another and thereby destroying the group. With more than five, members felt restrictions on participating.

Groups of two tend to avoid expressing disagreement and antagonism. This size also has high tension levels because each member is "on the spot," as each is forced to react to what the other says. In disputes, deadlock often arises because there is no majority and the group then breaks up.

EP 2.1.10a, l, & m

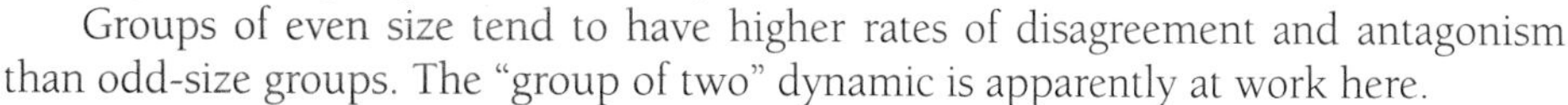

Groups of even size tend to have higher rates of disagreement and antagonism than odd-size groups. The "group of two" dynamic is apparently at work here.

Groups of three have majority-over-minority problems. A two-to-one split leaves the minority feeling isolated.

To sum up, for any given task there is an optimal group size. The more complex the task, the larger is the optimal size to ensure the greatest number of needed abilities and skills.

STARTING, LEADING, AND ENDING COUNSELING GROUPS[2]

Extensive preparation is needed for leading counseling groups. Leaders should have considerable training in (1) assessing human behavior and human problems; (2) comprehensive intervention approaches—such as reality therapy, behavior therapy, and rational therapy (see Modules 1–3); (3) specialized intervention techniques—such as assertiveness training (Module 2) and relaxation techniques (Chapter 14); (4) interviewing and counseling; and (5) principles of group dynamics—such as cohesion, task roles, social and emotional roles, and effects of authoritarian versus democratic styles

---

[2] Material in this section is adapted from Charles Zastrow, "Starting and Leading Therapy Groups: A Beginner's Guide," *Journal of Independent Social Work,* 4, no. 4, 1990, pp. 7–26. Republished by permission of Taylor & Francis, http://www.tandfonline.com.

of leadership. Baccalaureate and master's programs in social work generally provide considerable material on these areas. For any counseling group, leaders also need to study the literature on the causes of the problems that members are experiencing, the most effective intervention strategies, the prognosis for positive changes, and expectations about the length of time intervention strategies need to be applied to induce positive changes.

In this section I summarize a number of guidelines for starting, leading, and ending counseling groups. Chapter 6 covered substantial material on preparation and homework, relaxing before starting a session, cues on entering the meeting room, seating arrangements, introductions, and clarifying roles. This material is directly applicable to counseling groups and will not be repeated here. (Students studying how to lead counseling groups should review this material.) In this section we focus on building rapport, exploring problems in depth, exploring alternative solutions, ending a session, and ending a group.

Building Rapport

In group counseling, as in individual counseling, there are two types of members: voluntary and involuntary. In *voluntary* groups, group facilitators can take a more casual, less directive approach to begin with. In such groups facilitators may begin by involving members in small talk. This preliminary chitchat may be about the weather, parking problems, baseball, something currently in the news, and so on. Such casual conversation lets group members get acquainted with the facilitator and other members. In *involuntary* groups, facilitators often begin by introducing themselves and making a formal statement about the purpose of the group. Then members may be asked to introduce themselves. Generally, in involuntary groups, less is left up to the members themselves because they have less motivation for being there and less commitment to the group itself.

Sometimes, with both voluntary and involuntary clients, it is helpful (after introductions) to begin a session by providing some factual information. You as group leader can do this in a brief presentation or by showing a short film or videotape. For example, if your group comprises involuntary clients who have been convicted of driving while intoxicated, you might show a film that vividly demonstrates that as alcohol consumption increases, reaction times slow and the chances of serious accidents occurring dramatically increase. Factual information provides educational material and triggers discussion. Sometimes after factual information is presented, it is useful to involve members in an exercise related to the material.

When members are forced to attend a group they do not want to attend, as is the case with involuntary clients, you may begin by saying something like "I know most of you really don't want to be here, and I wouldn't either if I were forced to come. I wonder if we might begin by talking about your anger and unhappiness about being here." Then you can convey the purposes of the group, what is going to happen, and how the members can satisfy the minimal requirements of "passing." Mention that each member can (1) choose to participate actively and get as much out of the group as possible, (2) remain silent and listen to what others have to say, (3) vent anger and unhappiness in disruptive ways (which will probably anger and alienate others in the group), or (4) refuse to come, which will have certain consequences. You can then indicate that you can in no way control their behavior, so the choice is up to them. Such an approach almost always leads involuntary clients to choose either the first or second alternative, perhaps because they conclude that you understand their anger. They then focus on fulfilling the requirements of their forced attendance in the least painful way.

If the group has met previously, you may choose to begin by bringing up for discussion a topic that was not fully discussed at the last meeting. Or, if homework assignments were given out, you may begin with "Jim, at the last meeting you indicated you were going to do (such and such). How did that work out?"

Try to establish a nonthreatening group atmosphere in which members feel accepted and safe enough to communicate their troubles fully. During the initial contacts, you need to "sell" yourself (but not arrogantly) as a knowledgeable, understanding person who may be able to help and who wants to try. Your tone of voice should convey the message that you understand and care about group members' feelings. Be calm and never laugh or express shock when members begin to open up about problems. Emotional outbursts, even if subtle, will lead group members to believe that you are not going to understand or accept their difficulties, and so they will usually stop discussing them.

View group members as equals. Inexperienced facilitators sometimes make the mistake of thinking that because someone is sharing intimate secrets with them, they must be very important, and they end up assuming a superior position relative to their clients. If members feel that they are being treated as inferiors, they will be less motivated to reveal and discuss personal issues.

Use a "shared vocabulary" with members. This does not mean that you should use the same slang and the same accent as group members. If clients perceive you are mimicking their speech patterns, they may be seriously offended. To communicate effectively, use words that members understand and do not find offensive.

You (and other members) need to keep what members say confidential. Unfortunately, many people have nearly irresistible urges to share secrets with someone else. If a group member discovers that confidentiality has been violated, that member's trust in the group will be quickly destroyed. It is essential that you underscore the importance of "what is said in the group, remains in the group."

Exploring Problems in Depth

In exploring a member's problems in depth, you and group members need to examine such areas as the extent of the problem, how long the problem has existed, its causes, how the member feels about the problem, and what physical and mental capacities and strengths the individual has to cope with the difficulty, before exploring alternative solutions.

A problem area is often multidimensional—that is, numerous problems are usually involved. Explore all of these. A good way to decide which problem to handle first is to ask members which problems they feel are most pressing. If a problem can be solved, start by exploring that problem in depth and develop a solution together. Success in solving one problem will increase members' confidence in you and thereby further solidify rapport.

Convey empathy, not sympathy, and encourage group members to do so, too. Empathy is the capacity to understand and to share in another person's feelings. Sympathy also involves sharing feelings, but it results in offering pity. The difference is subtle, but empathy encourages problem solving, whereas sympathy encourages members to dwell on their problems without taking action to improve the situation. For example, if you offer sympathy to a person who is frustrated and angry about someone ending a romantic relationship with him, that person will keep telling his sad story over and over, each time having an emotional outpouring reinforced by your sympathy, without taking any action to improve the situation. Telling the story over and over only reopens old wounds and prolongs the anger and frustration.

"Trust your guts." Your most important resources are your own feelings and perceptions. Continually strive to place yourself in members' shoes, understanding that their values and pressures may be different from your own. You will probably never be 100% on target in your appraisal of a client's pressures, problems, and perspectives, but 70 to 80% percent is usually sufficient to be helpful. Empathizing is very useful in helping you determine what additional areas need to be explored, what you should say, and what the possible solutions are.

When you believe that a client has touched on an important area of concern, further communication can be encouraged in a number of ways. Show interest nonverbally (by making and continuing eye contact, leaning forward, and raising eyebrows slightly); this encourages further sharing. Allow for pauses. Inexperienced facilitators usually become anxious during pauses and hasten to say something—anything—to have conversation continue. This is usually a mistake, especially when it leads to a change in the topic. Although a pause may make members anxious, it gives them time to think about what areas of concern are most important and then usually motivates them to continue conversation in that area.

Neutral probes that do not control the direction of conversation but encourage further communication are helpful. For example, "Could you tell me more about it?" "Why do you feel that way?" and "I'm not sure I understand what you have in mind" all ask for further information, but just what kind is left up to the member. Reflecting feelings—for example, "You seem angry" or "You appear to be depressed about that"—works the same way. Summarizing what a group member is saying shows that you are listening and that you have received the same message he or she sent. An example is, "During this past hour, you made a number of critical comments about your spouse; it sounds like you're fairly unhappy about certain aspects of your marriage."

Approach socially unacceptable topics tactfully. Tact is an essential quality of a competent facilitator. Try not to ask a question in such a way that the answer will put the respondent in an embarrassing position.

When pointing out a member's limitation, mention and compliment the person on any assets. When a limitation is mentioned, he or she will figuratively feel naked, as if something has been taken away. Therefore, compliment the person in another area to give something back.

Watch for nonverbal cues and use them to identify sensitive subjects. Clients generally display anxiety by a changing tone of voice, fidgeting, yawning, stiff posture, or a flushed face.

Be honest. An untruth always runs the risk of being discovered. If that happens, the group member's confidence in you will be damaged and the relationship seriously jeopardized. But being honest goes beyond not telling lies. Always point out shortcomings that are in the group member's best interest to correct. For example, if a father's negative comments to his son are a factor in the son developing a negative self-concept (which is partly responsible for the son receiving failing grades at school), bring this to the father's attention.

Exploring Alternative Solutions

After a problem is explored in depth, the next step is for you and group members to consider alternative solutions. Your role is generally to begin by asking something like "Have you thought about ways to resolve this?" The merits, shortcomings, and consequences of the alternatives thought of by the member should then be tactfully and thoroughly examined. Next, involve other members by asking them if they are aware of other alternatives that might work for this situation. Those who suggest alternatives temporarily assume a "helper" role. In such a role, the helper therapy principle is operating as a member receives psychological rewards from helping others. If you have additional viable alternatives to suggest, mention them at this time. The merits, shortcomings, and consequences of the alternatives suggested by group members and by you should then be thoroughly explored.

Group members usually have the right to self-determination—that is, to choose a course of action among possible alternatives. Your role is to help each individual clarify and understand the likely consequences of each available alternative but generally not to give advice or choose the alternative. If *you* select the alternative, either of two outcomes is possible: (1) The alternative proves undesirable for the person, in which case he or she probably will blame you for the advice and your future relationship will be seriously hampered. Or (2) the alternative proves desirable for the person, which is advantageous, but the person then becomes overly dependent on you, seeking your advice for nearly every decision and generally being reluctant to make decisions on his or her own.

The warning about giving advice does *not* mean that you should not suggest alternatives that your client hasn't considered. On the contrary, it is your responsibility to suggest and explore all viable alternatives with a client. Here is a good rule to follow: When you believe a client should take a certain course of action, phrase it as a suggestion, "Have you thought about . . .?" rather than an opinion, "I think you should . . ."

Group counseling is done *with* group members, not *to* or *for* them. Each member should have responsibility for doing many of the tasks necessary to improve a situation. Another good rule to follow is that members should take responsibility for the tasks that they have the capacity to do. Like giving advice, doing things *for* group members brings with it the risk of a dependent relationship. Furthermore, success leads to personal growth and better prepares clients to take on future responsibilities.

A group member's right to self-determination should be taken away only if the selected course of action has a high probability of seriously hurting the client or others. For example, if it is highly probable that a member will attempt to take his life, you must intervene (make arrangements for the member to receive inpatient psychiatric care) even if the intervention is a course of action that he or she objects to. In most situations, however, members should have the right to select an alternative, even when you believe that another course of action would be better. Frequently, clients are in a better position to know what is best for themselves, and if it doesn't turn out—well, they then get to learn from their mistake.

When members select an alternative, they should clearly understand the goals, what tasks need to be carried out, how to accomplish the tasks, and who will do them. Frequently, it is desirable to write a "contract" for future reference, with a time limit set for accomplishment of each task. If group members fail to meet the terms of a contract, do not criticize them or accept excuses. Excuses let people off the hook; they provide temporary relief, but they eventually lead to more failure and to a failure identity. Simply ask, "Do you still wish to try to fulfill your commitment?" If the person answers affirmatively, another time deadline acceptable to the member should be set.

Perhaps the biggest single factor in determining whether a member's situation will improve is his or her motivation to carry out essential tasks. Try to motivate apathetic members. One way to increase motivation is to clarify what will be gained by meeting a goal. When individuals meet commitments, reward them, verbally or in other ways. Never criticize members for failing. Criticism usually increases hostility and rarely leads to positive, lasting change. It serves only as a temporary means of obtaining different behavior; when people no longer believe they are under surveillance, they usually return to their dysfunctional behavior.

If a group member lacks confidence or experience, role-play the task before the member attempts it. For example, if a member wants help in telling his partner that he wants to end the relationship, role-playing the situation in the group will help him select words and an appropriate strategy. You or a group member can play his role and model an approach, letting him play his partner's role. Then reverse the roles so that he can practice telling his partner.

Ending a Session

Ending is not easy. Ideally, you and the group members accept that the session is ending and that subjects being discussed should not be left hanging. Abrupt endings can be perceived as discourteous and rejecting.

There are some useful guidelines on how to terminate a therapy session. Preparation for ending the session should be initiated at the very beginning of the session. Members should be explicitly informed about when the session will end. Unless an unusual situation develops, assertively seek to terminate at the scheduled time.

When the allotted time is nearly up, inform members by saying something like "I see our time is just about up. Is there anything you'd like to add before we look at where we've arrived and where we go from here?" At the end of the session, it is often helpful to summarize what was discussed. If this session focused only on exploring problems, another one should be set up for fuller exploration and to begin looking at alternatives for resolving the problems.

Give members "homework" assignments between sessions. For example, a couple who is having trouble communicating with each other might be encouraged to set aside a certain amount of time each evening to discuss their personal thoughts with each other. At the next session this assignment would be reviewed.

Ideally, group members should be emotionally at ease when the session ends. Therefore, don't introduce emotionally charged content at the end but instead start to reduce the intensity of emotion. Just as it is sometimes advisable to begin a session with small talk, a short social conversation at the end can provide transition. If a member displays reluctance to end a session, it is sometimes helpful to confront this directly by saying, "It appears to me that you wished we had more time." The reasons for the person's reluctance can then be discussed.

At times a session can be ended by restating the way you and the group agreed to proceed. Or you may undertake a more explicit summation of what was discussed, what decisions were arrived at, what questions remain to be resolved, and what actions will be taken.

A somewhat different approach is to ask each member to state one item that was discussed or learned from the session, and what he or she now plans to do. Some counseling groups end by having members state a "bad" feeling they now intend to get rid of and then state a good feeling that will replace the bad one.

Sometimes concerns that were alluded to but not fully discussed are mentioned in closing as topics that will be taken up at the next session. Some members will reveal their most serious concerns for the first time at the end of a session, perhaps because they are ambivalent about whether they are ready to explore these concerns fully with the group. In these instances, you must make a professional judgment about whether to extend the session beyond the allotted time, to set up an appointment to discuss these concerns privately, or to wait until the next group session.

Sometimes it is helpful to end a group session by leading the group in a relaxation exercise. (Relaxation exercises are described in Chapter 14.) A relaxation exercise not only helps members relax but also reduces their level of stress so they can view their problems more objectively and work on resolving them after they leave.

Closing is especially important because what occurs during this last phase is likely to determine members' impressions of the session as a whole. Leave enough time for closing so the members don't feel rushed, which can create the impression that they are being "evicted."

Ending a Group

The ending phase of a group frequently offers the highest potential for powerful, important work. Group members often feel a sense of urgency as they realize there is little time left; this can lead them to reveal their most sensitive and personal concerns. Because the work remaining to be done is usually clearly identified at this point, members can focus on completing it. However, the relationship dynamics are also heightened in this phase as the members prepare to move away from each other. The termination of the group can evoke powerful feelings.

If group members have grown emotionally close, the ending of the group will be viewed as a loss and will produce a variety of emotions. Kübler-Ross's (1969) stages of dying can also be used to describe other important losses, including the ending of a successful and cohesive group. Members may display denial (by ignoring the imminent end of the group), anger and rage, or sadness and depression. They may bargain for an extension of the group in various ways, such as urging that the group deal with additional problems. Ideally, members will vent and work through such feelings and gradually come to accept the ending of the group. (Kübler-Ross's stages are more fully described in Chapter 5.)

Other emotions may also be displayed. Some members may feel guilty because of adverse comments they made or because they believe they failed to take certain actions that would have benefited themselves or other members of the group. If a member left prematurely, some members may feel that the group let that person down. Members may want to share their feelings about the support system they will lose when the group ends. Members who want the group to continue may interpret the ending as a personal rejection. Conversely, members who feel that the group was very successful may want to have a celebration to give recognition to the successes and to say good-bye.

Concluding sessions are in many ways the most difficult. Strong emotions are often generated and should be worked through. It is painful to terminate a group when members have shared their most personal and important concerns and feelings. Our society has done little to train us to handle such separations; many of us adhere to the norm of being "strong" and not expressing feelings.

You can help members accept the ending of the group in a number of ways, and the process of terminating a group should, in fact, begin during the early stages of the group. This guideline is particularly relevant for time-limited groups. Attempt to prevent dependency between members and you. The goal is independence and better functioning; reiterate this whenever appropriate during group sessions.

Summarize the emotional reactions that people have to group endings. An appropriate point for a discussion may occur when some members display denial, anger, guilt, bargaining, or sadness. When discussing these feelings, share your personal feelings and recollections, for the ending of the group has meaning for you as well. You, in effect, provide a model that can help members express their concerns about ending the group. Use a problem-solving approach to alleviate concerns; for example, if a member is apprehensive about future problems, suggest several other counseling resources.

The ending process should provide enough time for you and the members to sort out feelings and use the ending productively. A sudden ending cuts short necessary work and may not allow enough time to work through feelings and complete the remaining tasks. Sometimes, members indirectly express their anger by being late, appearing apathetic, being sarcastic, or battling over minor issues. In these situations, respond directly to the indirect cues by saying something like "I wonder if your recent critical remarks are related to your anger that this group is ending? I know you have invested a lot in this group and may dislike the idea that our meetings are coming to an end." By helping members recognize and articulate their feelings, you can help them express and work through those feelings. Once such feelings are dealt with, members will be more productive during the remaining time.

At or near the end of some groups, members may test new skills and do things independently. They may report having tackled a tough problem or dealt with an issue by themselves. Acknowledge their independence and make positive remarks about the members' ability to "go it alone."

At times, you may be the person leaving the group, perhaps to take a job elsewhere. In these situations, try to create a smooth transition and, if appropriate, involve members in selecting the new leader. At times it is helpful for you and the new leader to be coleaders for a brief period.

The ending of a group is always a transition to something else. The important element during the ending phase is to work with all members to help them develop a game plan so that the transition will enable them to work toward higher goals. The transition should work not to stifle members but to help them progress. Life is full of transitions and passages: from childhood to puberty, from school to the work world, from being single to being married, from working to retirement, and so on. In a transition phase, we have the potential to control our future; the choices we make and the efforts we put forth will determine whether the transition will be constructive or destructive for us. Helping each member make productive, realistic plans for the future is a key goal of the ending phase.

During the process of terminating a group, obtain feedback about how to improve future groups by having members fill out a brief evaluation at the last (or next-to-last) session. This evaluation should be done anonymously. The following questions apply to a variety of therapy groups. For the first seven questions, use the following scale: (1) strongly disagree, (2) disagree, (3) neutral or uncertain, (4) agree, (5) strongly agree.

1. I am very satisfied with what this group accomplished.
   1 2 3 4 5
2. My personal goals in this group have been attained.
   1 2 3 4 5
3. I truly enjoyed being a member of this group.
   1 2 3 4 5
4. The facilitator has done a superb job in leading the group.
   1 2 3 4 5
5. This has been one of the most rewarding groups I have participated in.
   1 2 3 4 5
6. I have grown extensively as a person through participating in this group.
   1 2 3 4 5
7. I have made substantial progress in resolving the personal problems that led me to join this group.
   1 2 3 4 5

The next three questions are open-ended.

8. The strengths of this group are . . .
9. The shortcomings of this group are . . .
10. My suggestions for changes in this group are . . .

At the final session it is also desirable for members to discuss what they got out of the group, the merits of the group, and suggestions for improving it. They should be given a chance to bring up unfinished business. In some cases, an extra session may be held to complete unfinished business items.

COFACILITATING GROUPS

Even though many settings do not have the resources for two leaders facilitating a single group, some programs do allow for this type of group facilitation. Also, many students in internships are given opportunities to cofacilitate groups with either their field instructor or some other professional at their agency. The cofacilitator approach has the following advantages:

- Each facilitator can grow from working with, observing, and learning from the other.
- Group members can benefit from the different life experiences, insights, and perspectives of the two facilitators.
- The two facilitators can complement each other, with the group thereby benefiting.
- The two facilitators can provide valuable feedback to each other by discussing what happened in a session and how to approach a complex issue.
- The two facilitators can serve as models for the members in how they relate to and communicate with each other and with the group.
- If one of the leaders is female and the other is male, barriers that some members have involving gender can be effectively confronted, explored, and resolved.
- While one facilitator is working with a particular member, the other facilitator can scan the group to get a sense of how the other members are reacting.
- Coleading offers a certain safety, especially when practitioners are leading a group for the first time. Beginning group facilitators often experience self-doubt and anxiety. Facing a group for the first time with a cofacilitator whom you respect and trust can make what initially seems a frightening task a delightful learning experience.

The major disadvantages of two facilitators leading a group occur when the facilitators fail to develop and maintain an effective working relationship. To develop a good working relationship, it is essential that they respect each other. Facilitators will have differences in leadership style and will not always agree or share the same perceptions and interpretations; this is normal and healthy. However, when there is mutual respect, they generally will be able to communicate and discuss these differences, trust each other, and work cooperatively instead of competitively. If trust and respect between the facilitators is lacking, the group is bound to sense the disharmony and be negatively affected. Power struggles between incompatible cofacilitators can divide the group. Friction between facilitators can serve as a model for members to focus on negatives within the group and to subtly or overtly verbally hurt one another.

It is important for group facilitators to learn whom they can and cannot cofacilitate with. Even secure, competent, and experienced facilitators who respect one another don't always work effectively together. A facilitator who leads by giving suggestions aimed at providing quick answers for every problem will have trouble working with a facilitator who believes members grow by struggling and arriving at their own answers to their personal issues. If two facilitators discover that they can't work together effectively, it doesn't necessarily mean that one is right and the other wrong or that one or both are incompetent. It simply means that their styles clash and that each would be better off making arrangements to work with someone with a more compatible style.

It is important for cofacilitators to get together regularly (ideally shortly after the end of each session) to discuss where the group is and where it needs to go. Additional areas to discuss include how the facilitators view the group and individual members, how they feel about working with each other, and how to approach complex issues. They also need to make plans for the next session.

LEGAL SAFEGUARDS FOR GROUP FACILITATORS

EP 2.1.2d

Unfortunately, filing lawsuits has become a national pastime. The key way group facilitators can avoid malpractice suits (or provide a defense if one arises) is to maintain reasonable, ordinary, and prudent (wise and judicious) practices. The following guidelines translate the terms *reasonable, ordinary,* and *prudent* into concrete actions:

- Screen candidates carefully for a group experience. Many potential problems can be avoided with effective screening practices. Select group members whose needs and goals are compatible with the goals of the group, who will not impede the group process, and whose well-being will not be jeopardized by the group experience.
- Adequately inform members about the group process. Entrance procedures, time parameters of the group experience, expectations of group participation, goals of the group, intervention methods that will be used, rights of members, responsibilities of members and facilitator, methods of payment (where appropriate), and termination procedures should be explained at the outset of the group.
- Obtain written parental consent for all minors who are attending a counseling group.
- Obtain written informed consent contracts at the outset of a group. Barker (2003) defines informed consent as follows:

> The granting of permission by the client to the social worker and agency or other professional person to use specific *intervention,* including diagnosis, treatment, follow-up, and research. This permission must be based on full disclosure of the facts needed to make the decision intelligently. Informed consent must be based on knowledge of the risks and alternatives. (p. 217)

- Have a clear rationale for the techniques and exercises you use in group sessions. Be prepared to concisely explain and defend the theoretical underpinnings of your techniques and exercises.

- Consult with your supervisor or an attorney on issues involving complex legal and ethical matters.
- Avoid becoming entangled in a social relationship with group participants.
- Be aware of those situations in which you legally are required to break confidentiality. (See the section on confidentiality in Chapter 2.)
- Carry malpractice insurance.
- Keep up with theoretical and research developments that apply to group therapy.
- Be knowledgeable about, and abide by, the codes of ethics for social workers. In the United States, refer to the NASW Code of Ethics (1996), which appears at www.naswdc.org. In Canada, refer to the Canadian Association of Social Workers' *Code of Ethics and Guidelines for Ethical Practice* (2005), which appears at www.casw-acts.ca.
- Be aware of when it is appropriate to refer a group member for another form of treatment, and also be aware of when group counseling might be inadvisable.
- Instruct members in how to evaluate their progress toward their individual goals. Also, routinely assess the general progress of the group.
- Write and maintain adequate records on the needs and goals of each member and the progress (or lack thereof) made by each member in the group.
- Do not promise magical cures. Create reasonable expectations about what the group can and cannot achieve.
- Practice within the boundaries of your state and local laws.
- If you work for an agency, have a contract that specifies the agency's legal liability for your professional functioning.
- Abide by the policies of the agency that employs you. If you strongly disagree with agency policies and if they interfere with your ability to do your job, seek first to change these policies. If the policies cannot be changed, consider resigning.
- Define clearly to members what confidentiality means, why it is important, and that what the members disclose should be kept confidential—even though the members should be aware that confidentiality cannot be guaranteed because some members may intentionally or unintentionally breach confidentiality.

SUMMARY

A membership group is a group a person belongs to; a reference group is one whose influence a person is willing to accept. This chapter summarizes key group dynamic concepts and presents guidelines for leading counseling groups.

Three models of group development are presented. The Garland, Jones, and Kolodny model hypothesizes five sequential stages: preaffiliation, power and control, intimacy, differentiation, and separation. The Tuckman model also hypothesizes five sequential stages: forming, storming, norming, performing, and adjourning. Bales developed a recurring-phase model. According to Bales, groups continuously seek equilibrium between task-oriented work and emotional expressions, in order to build better relationships among group members.

All groups have task roles and maintenance roles to be performed by members. Task roles are needed to accomplish the specific goals set by the group. Maintenance roles strengthen the social and emotional aspects of group life.

The theory of leadership highlighted in this chapter is the distributed-functions approach. According to this approach, leadership is the performance of acts that help the group reach its goals and maintain itself in good working order, and leadership occurs when any member influences other members to help the group reach its goals. Because all group members at times influence other group members, each member in a group exerts leadership.

French and Raven identified five types of power that group members can use to influence each other: reward, coercive, legitimate, referent, and expert. Each type has different effects on those being influenced.

Personal goals and group goals should be identified soon after a group is formed. The more congruent personal goals are with group goals, the more effective the group is likely to be. Conformity studies have found that a group has considerable influence on members' opinions and attitudes.

Groups often function more effectively in an atmosphere of cooperation than in a competitive atmosphere. If handled constructively, conflict and controversy can have numerous beneficial effects on a group, including increasing creativity. The no-lose problem-solving approach is much more effective in resolving conflict than is the win-lose approach. Additional strategies for resolving conflicts include role reversal, empathy, inquiry, I-messages, disarming, stroking, mediation, and the law of requisite variety. Hostile or disruptive members should generally be confronted by the leader or by other group members.

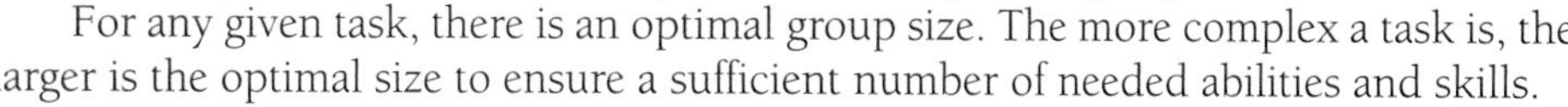

For any given task, there is an optimal group size. The more complex a task is, the larger is the optimal size to ensure a sufficient number of needed abilities and skills.

This chapter concludes with guidelines for leading counseling groups. Aspects discussed include building rapport, exploring problems in depth, exploring alternative solutions, ending a session, and ending a group. Guidelines are also presented on how to cofacilitate counseling groups and on establishing legal safeguards for group facilitators.

EP 2.1.10a

EXERCISES

1. Group Therapy in Action

Goal: To give class members an experiential awareness of being in a group therapy session.

Step 1: The instructor indicates that at the next class period a simulated group therapy session will be conducted. Each student is given the "homework" assignment of identifying one or two personal problems that a friend or relative currently has. Students are told that they should not reveal the identity of the person having the problem and that the personal problem should be that of a friend or relative (and not their own).

Step 2: At the next class period, the instructor begins by stating the following ground rules. "Today we will have a simulated group therapy session to give you an experiential awareness of being in group therapy. Because this is a class, I strongly request that you do not reveal any personal information about any dilemmas or difficulties you are experiencing. Instead, I ask you to describe one or two complicated personal dilemmas that a friend or relative is currently facing. For confidentiality reasons, please do not reveal the identity of the person whose problems you talk about. Remember, for reasons of confidentiality, what is said here stays here. Are there any questions about what we are going to do or about the ground rules?"

Step 3: The instructor asks students to begin sharing the concerns. If the class is reluctant, the instructor may initiate the process by asking a normally vocal student to begin. When a student is sharing, the instructor should encourage other students to probe with questions to explore the problem further and suggest realistic and creative courses of action to resolve the problem. (In group therapy sessions, each member at times takes on the role of a therapist.)

Step 4: After the dilemma revealed by one student is fully discussed and problem-solved, other students share the dilemmas they've brought. Continue until the end of the class period or until no one has anything further to share. At the end of the exercise, the instructor asks students their thoughts about the benefits and shortcomings of the exercise and their suggestions for changes in the format of the exercise when it is again used.

Comment: During the exercise, one or more of the students may begin talking about a personal problem. At this point the instructor needs to make a judgment about whether to let the student continue. The instructor should not allow any students to divulge personal information that they are apt to regret later.

EP 2.1.10a

2. Facilitating an Intervention Group

Goal: To develop skills at leading intervention groups.

Step 1: The instructor states the purpose of the exercise and indicates that a component of most class sessions will be for the students to take turns in facilitating an intervention group. The instructor demonstrates how to do this: The instructor shares a personal issue that she or he is currently dealing with or has dealt with in the past. Possible topics include depression, grief management, ending a relationship, creative financing, stress management, assertiveness, and resolving an interpersonal dispute. The instructor asks if anyone in the group has experienced a similar issue and encourages volunteers to share. The instructor then asks the group for ideas (strategies) on how to seek to resolve dilemmas that have been raised. The merits and shortcomings of these strategies are discussed. The instructor ends the exercise by summarizing important points that were made during the exercise.

Step 2: The instructor passes out a sign-up sheet, and each student selects a date in class to lead the group as described in step 1. Each student should take 15 to 20 minutes to lead the group. Each student is graded on a pass/fail basis by the instructor. Students who do not "pass" at first are given additional opportunities to lead a group in later class sessions. The instructor should inform those students who have to lead another session about what they need to work on to improve. When students are facilitating such intervention groups, it is advisable for the instructor to sit outside the circle of students, so that the students attend to the facilitator rather than to the instructor. When sitting outside the circle, the instructor should evaluate the facilitator on such areas as facilitation strengths demonstrated, areas needing attention, and suggestions for changes. The instructor also notes to the facilitator whether she or he has "passed" or whether another session has to be led. If someone continues to not receive a "pass" after several tries, the student and the instructor should meet privately to explore options of what to do. (Because of the importance of social work students being able to facilitate intervention groups, the instructor may choose to set the grading requirement that a passing grade on this exercise is needed in order for students to receive a passing grade in the class.)

EP 2.1.7a; 2.1.10j

Note: During these intervention exercises, these two ground rules must be strictly followed:

1. *Confidentiality.* "What is said here stays here" and should not be revealed outside the class.
2. *Emotional safety.* If a student begins to share and then feels that his or her disclosure is becoming too personal, the student should say, "This is becoming too personal," and there should be no group pressure for that person to say more.

3. Resolving Interpersonal Conflicts

Goal: To understand conflict resolution strategies and to become more skillful in resolving future interpersonal conflicts.

Step 1: Students write down on a sheet of paper a summary of a recent interpersonal conflict that they had—perhaps involving a friend, a relative, another student, or a faculty member. The summary should include who the conflict was with, what was at issue, and how it was resolved. (If the issue has not been resolved, the summary should contain a description of the current status of the conflict.)

Step 2: The instructor describes the following conflict resolution strategies: the win-lose approach, the problem-solving approach, role reversal, empathy, inquiry, being assertive, I-messages, disarming, stroking, mediation, and the law of requisite variety. (These strategies should be written on the chalkboard so students can refer to them later.)

Step 3: The class forms groups of three students each. The subgroups share with each other the nature of the interpersonal conflict that they wrote on a sheet of paper. (Students have a right not to reveal what they wrote.) For each conflict that is shared in the subgroup, the students explore whether *needs* or *solutions* of the people involved in the conflict were primarily at issue. The subgroups identify whether any of these strategies were used (or would have been helpful to use) in resolving the conflict: the problem-solving approach, role reversal, empathy, inquiry, being assertive, I-messages, disarming, stroking, mediation, and the law of requisite variety.

Step 4: When the class re-forms, students have an opportunity to ask questions about conflict resolution. Some students may want to share a complicated unresolved conflict situation they are now experiencing to obtain feedback on how it may be effectively resolved.

COMPETENCY NOTES

The following identifies where Educational Policy (EP) competencies and practice behaviors are discussed in the chapter.

EP 2.1.7a *Utilize conceptual frameworks to guide the process of assessment, intervention, and evaluation*. (Chapter 7).

This material conceptualizes key group dynamic concepts, including handling the disruptive behavior of members, membership groups and reference groups, stages in group development, task roles and maintenance roles, leadership theory, social power bases in groups, group norms, and conflict resolution strategies.

EP 2.1.7a *Utilize conceptual frameworks to guide the process of assessment, intervention, and evaluation*. (p. 199).

Exercise 7.1 is designed to help students understand the concepts of reference groups and membership groups.

EP 2.1.7a *Utilize conceptual frameworks to guide the process of assessment, intervention, and evaluation*. (p. 201).

Exercise 7.2 is designed to help students use the Garland, Jones, and Kolodny model to analyze groups.

EP 2.1.7a *Utilize conceptual frameworks to guide the process of assessment, intervention, and evaluation*. (pp. 201–202).

Exercise 7.3 is designed to help students use the Tuckman model to analyze groups.

EP 2.1.7a *Utilize conceptual frameworks to guide the process of assessment, intervention, and evaluation*. (p. 204).

Exercise 7.4 is designed to help students understand task contributions and maintenance contributions in groups.

EP 2.1.7a *Utilize conceptual frameworks to guide the process of assessment, intervention, and evaluation*. (pp. 205–206).

Exercise 7.5 is designed to assist students in identifying charismatic people and to understand various characteristics that lead to charisma.

EP 2.1.7a *Utilize conceptual frameworks to guide the process of assessment, intervention, and evaluation*. (p. 206).

Exercise 7.6 is designed to assist students in understanding the characteristics of Machiavellian leaders.

EP 2.1.7a *Utilize conceptual frameworks to guide the process of assessment, intervention, and evaluation*. (p. 208).

Exercise 7.7 is designed to help students understand authoritarian, democratic, and laissez-faire leaders.

EP 2.1.7a *Utilize conceptual frameworks to guide the process of assessment, intervention, and evaluation*. (p. 209).

Exercise 7.8 is designed to show students that they already have taken on leadership functions in groups.

EP 2.1.7a *Utilize conceptual frameworks to guide the process of assessment, intervention, and evaluation.* (p. 211).

Exercise 7.9 is designed to help students understand and apply the power bases in groups identified by French and Raven.

EP 2.1.7a *Utilize conceptual frameworks to guide the process of assessment, intervention, and evaluation.* (pp. 212–213).

Exercise 7.10 is designed to assist students in understanding the dynamics between group goals, personal goals, and hidden agendas.

EP 2.1.7a *Utilize conceptual frameworks to guide the process of assessment, intervention, and evaluation.* (p. 215).

Exercise 7.11 is designed to assist students in identifying group norms and to understand the processes that led to their development.

EP 2.1.7a *Utilize conceptual frameworks to guide the process of assessment, intervention, and evaluation.* (pp. 217–218).

Exercise 7.12 is designed to help students understand that everyone has yielded to group pressure. The exercise also allows students to reflect on their feelings about yielding.

EP 2.1.1b *Practice personal reflection and self-correction to assure continual professional development.* (pp. 219–220).

Exercise 7.13 is designed to have students reflect upon whether they need to become more assertive in confronting interpersonal conflicts.

EP 2.1.7a *Utilize conceptual frameworks to guide the process of assessment, intervention, and evaluation.* (p. 225).

Exercise 7.14 is designed to inform students about how to resolve interpersonal conflicts more effectively.

EP 2.1.7a *Utilize conceptual frameworks to guide the process of assessment, intervention, and evaluation.* (pp. 228–229).

Exercise 7.15 is designed to help students handle the disruptive behavior of a group member.

EP 2.1.10a *Substantively and affectively prepare for action with individuals, families, groups, organizations, and communities.*

EP 2.1.10l *Facilitate transitions and endings.*

EP 2.1.10m *Critically analyze, monitor, and evaluate interventions.* (pp. 229–237).

This material provides guidelines on starting, leading, and ending counseling groups.

EP 2.1.2d *Apply strategies of ethical reasoning to arrive at principled decisions.* (pp. 237–238).

This material summarizes legal safeguards for group facilitators.

EP 2.1.10a *Substantively and affectively prepare for action with individuals, families, groups, organizations, and communities.* (p. 239).

This exercise gives students an experiential awareness of being in a group therapy session.

EP 2.1.10a *Substantively and affectively prepare for action with individuals, families, groups, organizations, and communities.* (pp. 239–240).

This exercise is designed to help students develop skills at leading intervention groups.

EP 2.1.7a *Utilize conceptual frameworks to guide the process of assessment, intervention, and evaluation.*

EP 2.1.10 *Help clients resolve problems.* (pp. 240–241).

This exercise is designed to assist students in understanding conflict resolution strategies and to become more skillful in resolving future interpersonal conflicts.

CHAPTER 8

Social Work with Families

EP 2.1.7a; 2.1.10a, b, c, d, e, f, g, j, l

The focus of social work services is often the family, which is an interacting, interdependent system. The problems that people face are usually influenced by dynamics within the family, and dynamics within the family are, in turn, influenced by the wider social and cultural environment. Because a family is an interacting system, change in any member will affect all other members. Tensions between husband and wife, for example, will be felt by their children, who may respond with disturbed behavior. Treating the children's behavior alone would not get to the root of the family problem (Compton & Galaway, 1999).

Another reason for the focus on the family as a whole rather than on certain individuals is that the participation of other family members is often needed in the treatment process. They can help identify family patterns. In addition, the whole family, once members perceive the relationships among their various behaviors, can form a powerful team in reestablishing healthier patterns (Wells, 1998). For example, family members can pressure their alcoholic mother to acknowledge her problem. They may provide important emotional support for her efforts to stop drinking. They may also need counseling themselves (or support from a self-help group) to assist in coping with her when she is drinking.

This chapter will:

A. Describe the diversity of family forms
B. Describe the societal functions of families
C. Describe family problems and the social work services available to families
D. Present two family assessment techniques
E. Present three approaches to family counseling

DIVERSITY OF FAMILY FORMS

The family is a social institution that is found in every culture and has been defined by Coleman and Cressey (1995, p. 124) as "a group of people related by marriage, ancestry, or adoption who live together in a common household." This definition does not cover a number of living arrangements whose members consider themselves a family, such as

- A husband and wife raising two foster children who have been in the household for several years
- Two women, lesbians in a loving relationship, raising children born to one of the partners while in a heterosexual marriage that ended in divorce
- Grandparents raising grandchildren because of illness or addiction of the parents
- Where one spouse lives away from home—perhaps because of military service in a foreign country or because of incarceration

- Where one child who has a severe and profound cognitive disability lives in a residential treatment facility
- A man and a woman who have been living together for years in a loving relationship but never legally married

A wide diversity of family patterns exists in the world (see the Case Example, "Sex-Role Expectations Are Culturally Determined" on page 245). Families in different cultures take a variety of forms. In some societies, husband and wife live in separate buildings. In others, they live apart for several years after the birth of a child. In some societies, husbands are permitted to have more than one wife. In a few countries, wives are allowed to have more than one husband. Some cultures permit (and a few encourage) premarital and extramarital intercourse.

Some societies have large communes where adults and children live together. There are communes in which the children are raised separately from adults. In some cultures, surrogate parents (rather than the natural parents) raise the children. Some societies encourage certain types of homosexual relationships, and a few recognize homosexual as well as heterosexual marriages.

In many cultures, marriages are still arranged by the parents. In a few societies, an infant may be "married" before birth (if the baby is of the wrong sex, the marriage is dissolved). Some societies do not recognize romantic love. Some cultures expect older men to marry young girls. Others expect older women to marry young boys. Most societies prohibit the marriage of close relatives, but a few subcultures encourage marriage between brothers and sisters or between first cousins. Some expect a man to marry his father's brother's daughter, whereas others insist that he marry his mother's sister's daughter. In some societies, a man, on marrying, makes a substantial gift to the bride's father, whereas in others the bride's father gives a substantial gift to the new husband.

These are indeed substantial variations in family patterns. People in each of these societies feel strongly that their particular pattern is normal and proper, and many feel the pattern is divinely ordained. Suggested changes in their particular form are viewed with suspicion and defensiveness and are often sharply criticized as being unnatural, immoral, and a threat to the survival of the family.

Despite these variations, sociologists note that most family systems can be classified into two basic forms: the extended family and the nuclear family. An *extended family* consists of a number of relatives living together, such as parents, children, grandparents, great-grandparents, aunts, uncles, in-laws, and cousins. The extended family is the predominant pattern in preindustrial societies. The members divide various agricultural, domestic, and other duties among themselves.

A *nuclear family* consists of a married couple and their children living together. The nuclear family type emerged from the extended family. Extended families tend to be more functional in agricultural societies where many "hands" are needed; the nuclear family is more suited to the demands of complex, industrialized societies, because its smaller size and potential geographic mobility enable it to adapt more easily to changing conditions—such as the need to relocate to obtain a better job.

Although the nuclear family is still the predominant family form in the United States, Canada, and many other industrialized countries, it is a serious mistake for social workers and other helping professionals to use the nuclear family as the ideal model that individuals in our society should strive to form. Many other family forms are functioning in our society, such as the following:

- A married couple without children who are the primary caregivers for the wife's mother, who has Alzheimer's disease and resides with the couple
- Two gay men in a committed relationship, each of whom has joint custody of two children with his former wife
- A childless married couple who have decided not to conceive children
- A single parent with three young children

CASE EXAMPLE Sex-Role Expectations Are Culturally Determined

In the classic study *Sex and Temperament in Three Primitive Societies,* Margaret Mead (1935) demonstrated that sex-role expectations are culturally rather than biologically determined. The study further showed that family socialization patterns are immensely influenced by the larger culture. The study was conducted with three tribes in New Guinea in the early 1930s. Mead found that many characteristics that Americans classify as typically feminine or masculine are classified differently in these tribes.

Both sexes among the Arapesh would seem feminine to us. Both men and women are gentle, nurturant, and compliant. The personalities of males and females in this society are not sharply differentiated by sex. Both girls and boys learn to be unaggressive, cooperative, and responsive to the needs and wants of others. Relations between husband and wife parallel the traditional mother-child relations in our society, with the Arapesh husband often seeing his role as providing training to his much younger wife.

In contrast, among the Mundugamors, both sexes would seem masculine to us. Both are headhunters and cannibals, are nonnurturant and aggressive, and actively initiate sexual involvement.

The most interesting society that Mead studied was the Tchambuli. This society virtually reverses our traditional sex-role expectations and stereotypes. The men spend much more time than the women in grooming and decorating themselves. Also, the men spend much of their time painting, carving, and practicing dance steps. In contrast, the women are efficient, impersonal, unadorned, managerial, and brisk. The women are the traders and have most of the economic power.

- A blended family in which the husband and wife have children in the current marriage, plus children from earlier marriages, all of whom live in the household
- An unmarried young couple living together in what amounts to a trial marriage

In the past few decades, there has been a trend in the United States for greater diversity in marital arrangements and family forms. There are increasing numbers of transracial marriages, marriages between spouses of diverse ages and cultural backgrounds, transracial adoptions, single-parent families, and blended families. Although some social workers may personally judge a few of these types to be "wrong," it is essential that they not allow their personal beliefs to reduce the quality or quantity of professional services that are provided to these family units. It is also essential that social workers who work with families of diverse cultural backgrounds learn about those backgrounds and understand the customary norms for family functioning.

EP. 2.1.1b

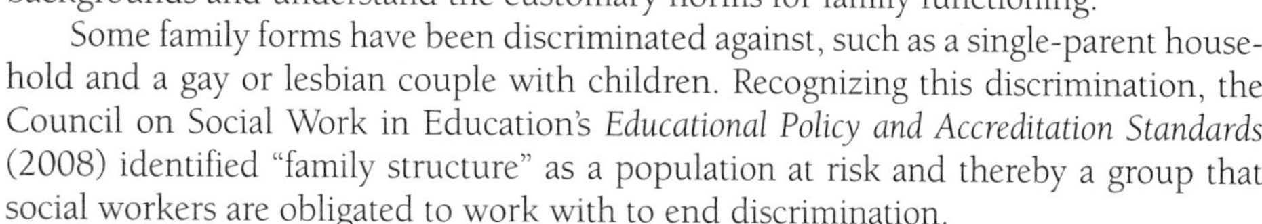

Some family forms have been discriminated against, such as a single-parent household and a gay or lesbian couple with children. Recognizing this discrimination, the Council on Social Work in Education's *Educational Policy and Accreditation Standards* (2008) identified "family structure" as a population at risk and thereby a group that social workers are obligated to work with to end discrimination.

Exercise 8.1: Description of My Family

Goal: This exercise is designed to assist you in better understanding your family dynamics.

Write a description of your family. Provide information on who is a member (may include aunts, uncles, grandparents, foster children, etc.), ages and gender of members, occupation or professions of members, religious orientations, political orientations, family values, educational levels attained by members, significant qualities or characteristics of members, hobbies or interests of members, significant family activities, current stresses or challenges faced by members or by the family, significant resources and strengths of the family, and past family crises.

SOCIETAL FUNCTIONS OF FAMILIES

Families in modern industrial societies perform the following essential functions that help maintain the continuity and stability of society:

1. *Replacement of the population.* Every society has some system for replacing its members. Practically all societies consider the family as the unit in which children are to be produced. Societies define the rights and responsibilities of the reproductive partners within the family unit. These rights and responsibilities help maintain the stability of society, although they are defined differently from one society to another.
2. *Care of the young.* Children require care and protection until at least the age of puberty. The family is a primary institution for the rearing of children. Modern societies have generally developed supportive institutions to help in caring for the young—for example, medical services, day-care centers, parent training programs, and residential treatment centers.
3. *Socialization of new members.* To become productive members of society, children have to be socialized into the culture. Children are expected to acquire a language, learn social values and mores, and dress and behave within the norms of society. The family plays a major role in this socialization process. In modern societies, as numerous other groups and resources are involved in this socialization process. Schools, the mass media, peer groups, the police, movies, and books and other written material are important influences. (Sometimes these different influences clash by advocating opposing values and attitudes.)
4. *Regulation of sexual behavior.* Failure to regulate sexual behavior results in clashes between individuals because of jealousy and exploitation. Every society has rules that regulate sexual behavior within family units. Most societies, for example, have incest taboos, and most disapprove of extramarital sex.
5. *Source of affection.* Humans need affection, emotional support, and positive recognition from others (including approval, smiles, encouragement, and reinforcement for accomplishments). Without such affection and recognition, our emotional, intellectual, physical, and social growth would be stunted. The family is an important source for obtaining affection and recognition, because family members generally regard each other as among the most important people in their lives and gain emotional and social satisfaction from family relationships.

FAMILY PROBLEMS AND THE NATURE OF SOCIAL WORK

An infinite number of problems occurs in families. Exhibit 8.1 lists a few of them. When problems arise in a family, social services are often needed. The types and forms of services that social workers provide to troubled families are extremely varied. We can group them into two major categories: in-home services and out-of-home services.

In-home services are preventive. Although not all are offered literally within the home itself, they are specifically designed to help families stay together. They include financial aid, protective services (services to safeguard children or frail older adults from abuse and neglect), family preservation services (intensive crisis intervention within the home setting where children are so seriously at risk that removal to foster care would otherwise be required), family therapy (intensive counseling to improve family relationships), day care (caretaking services for children or older adults to provide respite for caregivers who might otherwise be overwhelmed or to permit them to work outside the home), homemaker services (for the same purpose), and family-life education (classes, often offered at traditional family service agencies, that cover such topics as child development, parenting skills, and communication issues). Not all of these services can be provided by social workers, but workers must know where to find them and how to help the family obtain them when needed (Suppes & Wells, 2003).

Out-of-home services are services that must be operationalized when the family can no longer remain intact. They are a manifestation that something has gone seriously

Exhibit 8.1 A Sampling of Family Problems

Divorce
Alcohol or drug abuse
Unwanted pregnancy
Bankruptcy
Poverty
Terminal illness
Chronic illness
Death
Desertion
"Empty-shell" marriage
Emotional problems of one or more members
Behavioral problems of one or more members
Child abuse
Child neglect
Sexual abuse
Spouse abuse
Elder abuse
Unemployment of wage earners
Money management difficulties
Injury from serious automobile accident involving one or more members
A child with a severe cognitive disability
Incarceration or institutionalization of one or more members
Compulsive gambling by one or more members
Victim of a crime
Forced retirement of a wage earner
Caregiver for an elderly relative
Involvement of a child in delinquent and criminal activities
Illness of a member who acquires AIDS
A runaway teenager
Sexual dysfunctions of one or more members
Infidelity
Infertility

wrong, because the breakup of any family amounts to a tragedy that will have ramifications beyond family boundaries. Although family members usually receive the blame, the larger system (social environment and the level of support it provides to troubled families) may be called into question. Out-of-home services include foster care, adoption, group homes, institutional care (for example, residential treatment centers), and the judicial system (which provides a different kind of institutional care, prison, or jail, for family members who have run into difficulty with the law).

To perform these services, social workers engage in a variety of roles (for example, broker, educator, advocate, supporter, mediator). The following examples illustrate many common services and important roles.

- Mark Schwanke, age 32, has AIDS. Ms. Seely, a social worker with the AIDS Support Network in the community, serves as a case manager in providing a variety of services to Mark, his wife (who is HIV-positive), and their two children. These services include medical information and care, housing, counseling, emotional support services, and financial assistance. Because of frequent discrimination against persons with AIDS and persons with the AIDS virus, Ms. Seely often must advocate on the family's behalf to ensure that they receive the services they need.
- Beth Roessler, age 15, has been convicted of committing six burglaries. Steve Padek, a juvenile probation officer and social worker, is her juvenile probation officer. Mr. Padek provides the following services to Beth and her mother, who is divorced: He holds weekly supervision meetings with Beth to monitor her school performance and leisure activities, links Beth's mother with a Parents Without Partners group, and conducts several counseling sessions with Beth and her mother to mediate conflicts in their relationship.
- The aunt of Amy Sund, a 3-year-old child, has contacted Protective Services about Amy's mother (Pat) and her lover's physical abuse of Amy. Investigators confirm the abuse; Amy has bruises and rope burns on her body. Instead of referring the case to court, Protective Services refers the case to Family Preservation for services. Maria Gomez, social worker at Family Preservation, meets with Pat Sund and Amy a total of 37 times over the next 90 days. Pat Sund terminates her relationship with her abusive lover, is accepted into a financial assistance program through the Social Services Department for a 2-year period, and enrolls in a job training program. Ms. Gomez arranges for child care for Amy when Ms. Sund is attending the job training program. Ms. Gomez also arranges for a temporary housekeeper who provides training in cleaning the

apartment and in making meals. Ms. Gomez encourages Ms. Sund to join the local chapter of Parents Anonymous, which she does. (Parents Anonymous is described in Chapter 6.) Had family preservation services been unavailable or unsuccessful, Amy would have had to be placed in a foster home.

- Cindy Rogerson, age 27, has three young children. She is badly battered by her husband and contacts the House of Hope, a shelter for battered women and their children. Sue Frank, a social worker at the shelter, makes arrangements for shelter for Mrs. Rogerson and her children. The oldest child is attending school, so Ms. Frank arranges for him to continue attending school. Ms. Frank provides one-to-one counseling to Mrs. Rogerson at the shelter to help her explore her options and to inform her of potential resources that she may not be aware of. Ms. Frank also leads groups at the shelter for residents and nonresidents, which Mrs. Rogerson is required to attend while at the shelter. After 2½ weeks, Mrs. Rogerson decides she wants to return to her husband. Ms. Frank convinces Mrs. Rogerson to give her husband an ultimatum prior to returning—he must receive family counseling together with her from the Family Service agency in the community and must attend a group for batterers in the community. Mrs. Rogerson reluctantly agrees. Mrs. Rogerson, at the urging of Ms. Frank, only then returns to live with her husband, with the understanding that she will leave immediately if he hits her again or if he drops out of either family counseling or the group for batterers.
- Katy Hynek, age 76, has Alzheimer's disease. She has been living alone in her house since her husband died 3 years ago. Her physician contacts Adult Services of the Department of Social Services and requests that an assessment of living arrangements be conducted. Linda Sutton, social worker, does an assessment and determines that Katy Hynek can no longer live alone. Katy's son Mark and his wife Annette agree to have Katy move in with them. During the next 19 months, Ms. Sutton has periodic contact with the Hyneks. As is common with this disease, Katy Hynek's physical and mental condition continues to deteriorate. Ms. Sutton listens to Mark and Annette's concerns and seeks to answer their questions about the disease. She also provides suggestions to help them cope with the changes in Katy's condition. As Katy's condition deteriorates, Ms. Sutton makes arrangements for Katy to attend an adult day-care center during the daytime, partly for respite care for Mark and Annette. At the end of 19 months, Mark and Annette request a meeting with Ms. Sutton to discuss the possibility of placing Katy in a nursing home as her condition has so deteriorated that she now needs 24-hour care. (For example, she gets up in the middle of the night and gets lost in closets; she is also now incontinent.) The pros and cons of placing Katy in a nursing home are identified and discussed. Making the decision is exceedingly emotional and agonizing for Mark and Annette. With a careful discussion of the entire situation with Ms. Sutton, Mark and Annette decide they have no choice but to seek a nursing home placement. Ms. Sutton gives them the names of three nursing homes, which they visit, and then they select one.

EP 2.1.7a

FAMILY ASSESSMENT

The two areas in family social work practice that have received the most attention are family assessment and family therapy. In this section, we focus on family assessment.

There are a variety of ways to assess families. Conducting a social history of a family and its members is a widely used approach (see Chapter 4). With regard to family assessment, however, two techniques have received considerable discussion in recent years: eco-maps and genograms.

Eco-Maps

The eco-map is a paper-and-pencil assessment tool used to assess specific troubles and plan interventions for clients. The eco-map, a drawing of the client family in its social

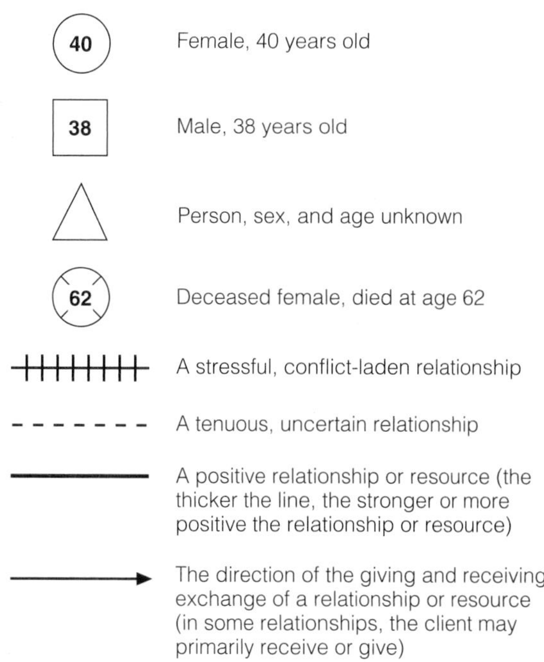

Figure 8.1
Symbols commonly used in an eco-map.

Source: © Cengage Learning, 2013.

environment, is usually drawn jointly by the social worker and the client. It helps both parties achieve a holistic or ecological view of the client's family life and the nature of the family's relationships with groups, associations, organizations, and other families and individuals. The eco-map has been used in a variety of situations, including marriage and family counseling and adoption and foster-care home studies. It has also been used to supplement traditional social histories and case records. The eco-map is a shorthand method for recording basic social information. The technique helps clients and workers gain insight into the clients' problems by providing a "snapshot view" of important interactions at a particular point in time. Ann Hartman (1978) is the primary developer of this tool.

A typical eco-map consists of a family diagram surrounded by a set of circles and lines used to describe the family within an environmental context. Eco-map users can create their own abbreviations and symbols, but the most commonly used symbols are shown in Figure 8.1.

First, a circle (representing the client's family) is drawn in the center of a large blank sheet of paper (see Figure 8.2 on page 250). The composition of the family is indicated in the circle. Other circles are then drawn around the family circle. These circles represent other systems—that is, the groups, other families, individuals, and organizations—with which the family ordinarily interacts. Lines are drawn to describe the relationships that members of the client family have with these systems. Arrows show the flow of energy (giving or receiving resources and communication between family members and significant systems). Figure 8.3 on page 250 shows the eco-map for the family, described in the Case Example "Using an Eco-Map: The Wilbur Family."

An eco-map helps both worker and client view the client's family from a systems and ecological perspective. Sometimes, as happened in the Wilbur case example, clients and workers gain greater insight into the social dynamics of a problematic situation. For the worker, a completed eco-map graphically displays important interactions of a client family with other systems (that is, the groups, other families, individuals, and organizations) that the family ordinarily interacts with at a particular point in time. Such a diagram allows the worker to better understand the environmental factors affecting the family. It thus helps the worker generate hypotheses of problematic dynamics in the family-environmental system, which the worker can then further explore

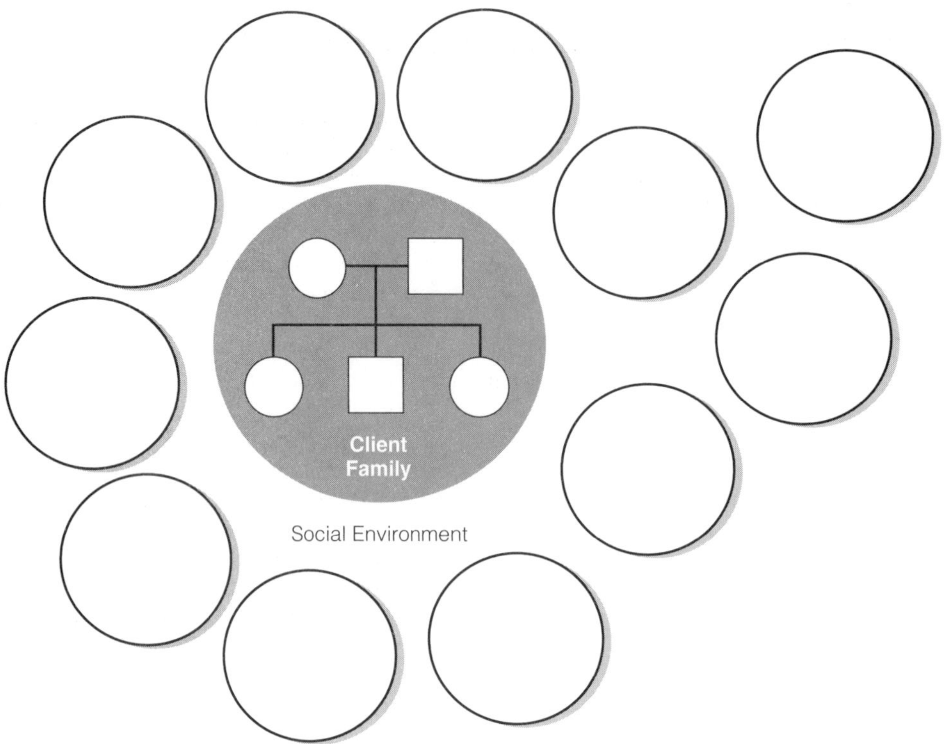

Figure 8.2
Setting up an eco-map.
Source: © Cengage Learning, 2013.

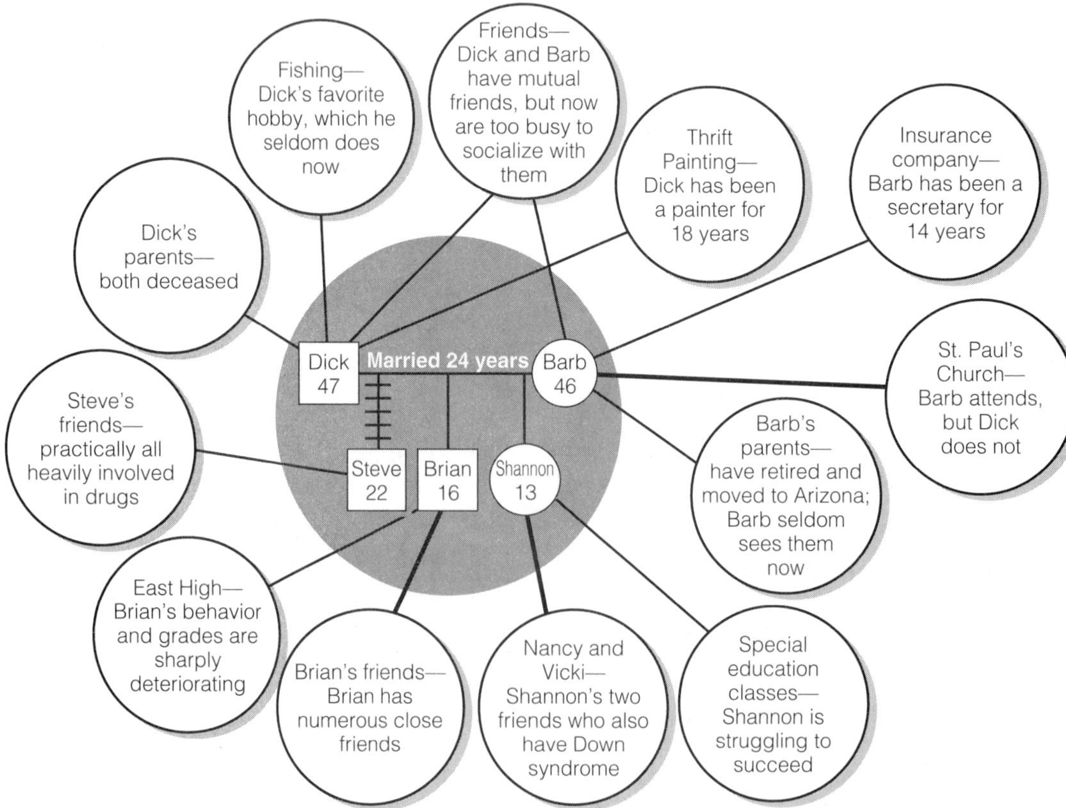

Figure 8.3
Sample eco-map: The Wilbur family.
Source: © Cengage Learning, 2013.

CASE EXAMPLE Using an Eco-Map: The Wilbur Family

Barb and Dick Wilbur are contacted by Mary Timm, school social worker at East High School. The Wilburs' second-oldest son, Brian (age 16), had a knife in his jacket at school and liquor on his breath. The Wilburs are shocked. They agree to meet with Ms. Timm the next day to discuss these incidents. Brian will also be present.

At the meeting, Ms. Timm asks Brian why he brought a knife to school. At first, he refuses to respond. Ms. Timm also notes that records show he used to receive mainly B's, but now his grades are primarily D's and F's. Mr. and Mrs. Wilbur also sternly ask Brian what is happening. They add that the school system has informed them that he apparently has been drinking during school hours. Gradually tears come to Brian's eyes. He says no one cares about him. He asserts his parents are too busy at work and too busy looking after his older brother, Steve, and his younger sister, Shannon.

At first, Mr. and Mrs. Wilbur are surprised. They indicate they love Brian very much. Gradually they disclose they have been so involved with the demands of their other two children that they may have been "shortchanging" Brian in recent months. Shannon, age 13, has Down syndrome and requires considerable individual attention, especially with her coursework. (Shannon is enrolled in special education courses.)

Brian is asked where he obtained the knife. He hesitantly indicates his older brother, Steve, gave it to him for "protection." Brian adds that he sees nothing wrong with carrying a knife; Steve frequently carries a pistol. In addition, Brian says Steve urged him to take the knife to school because some people who are unhappy with Steve have said they may come after Brian. Ms. Timm asks Mr. and Mrs. Wilbur if they know anything about this. Barb and Dick suggest it may be best if Brian is excused at this point. Ms. Timm sets up a later meeting with Brian, and he leaves.

Both Barb and Dick then become teary-eyed. They indicate they are nearing their wit's end. Both work full-time, and in recent years Steve and Shannon have required so much of their attention that they now no longer are able to spend any time with their former friends. In addition, they have been arguing more and more. They feel that their family is disintegrating and that they are "failing" as parents. They also disclose that Steve is addicted to both alcohol and cocaine and has been for several years. He has been in for inpatient treatment three times but always goes back to using soon after leaving treatment. They don't know where Steve is getting the money for his cocaine habit. They fear he may be dealing. He hasn't been able to hold a full-time job. He is usually terminated because he shows up for work while under the influence. Currently, he is working part-time as a bartender.

Mr. and Mrs. Wilbur fear that unless something is done soon, Brian may follow in Steve's footsteps. They add they have contemplated asking Steve to leave but are reluctant to do so, because they feel it is their parental obligation to provide a house for their children as long as the children want to stay.

At this point, Ms. Timm suggests it may be helpful to diagram their present dilemma. Together the Wilburs and Ms. Timm draw the eco-map shown in Figure 8.3.

While drawing the map, Ms. Timm asks whether providing housing for Steve is helping him or whether it may be a factor in enabling him to continue his drug use and his irresponsible behavior. The eco-map helps the Wilburs see that as a result of working full-time and spending the remainder of their waking hours caring for Shannon, Steve, and Brian, they are gradually becoming too emotionally and physically exhausted to cope. During the past few years, they have stopped socializing.

The Wilburs ask Ms. Timm to explain what she means by "enabling" Steve to continue his drug use and his irresponsible behavior. Ms. Timm explains enabling and indicates that a "tough love" approach may be an option. (In this case, a tough love approach would involve the Wilburs' demanding that Steve live elsewhere if he continues to abuse alcohol and cocaine.) Ms. Timm also gives them pamphlets that describe enabling and tough love. They make an appointment for the next week.

For the next several weeks, Ms. Timm continues to meet weekly with the Wilburs and individually with Brian. The Wilburs eventually decide to use a tough love approach with Steve. Steve leaves but continues to use alcohol and cocaine. However, living on his own does appear to be somewhat beneficial as he now works full-time at a maintenance job to pay his bills. With Steve out of the house, Barb and Dick Wilbur are able to spend more time with Brian and Shannon, and they begin to socialize again with some of their former friends.

Counseling Skills at Work in Generalist Practice

In the Wilbur case example, the social worker used the following roles that, as described in Chapter 1, are components of generalist social work practice: family counselor, educator (helping Mr. and Mrs. Wilbur realize they needed to use a tough love approach with Steve), broker (encouraging the Wilburs to again socialize with their friends), and problem-solver.

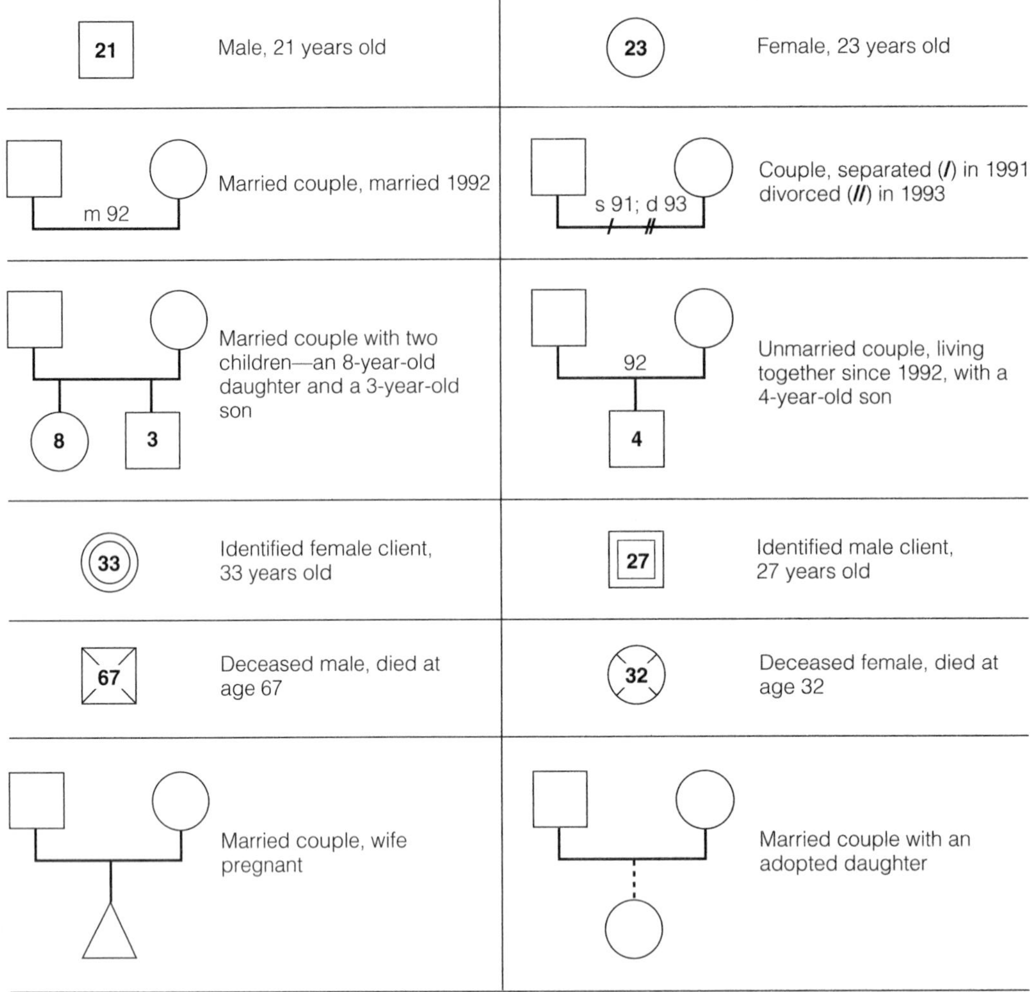

Figure 8.4
Symbols commonly used in a genogram.

Source: © Cengage Learning, 2013.

by questioning the family members. Once problematic dynamics are identified, the worker can focus attention on helping family members generate strategies to resolve the problematic dynamics.

Similarly, an eco-map helps client family members identify and understand problematic dynamics in their family-environmental system. Once these dynamics are identified, family members are in a position to generate strategies (together with their worker) to resolve problems.

Genograms

The genogram is a graphic way of investigating the origins of a client's or client family's presenting problem by diagramming the family over at least three generations. The client and worker usually jointly construct the family genogram, which is essentially a family tree. Murray Bowen is the primary developer of this technique (Kerr & Bowen, 1988). The genogram helps the worker and family members examine problematic emotional and behavioral patterns in an intergenerational context. Patterns tend to repeat themselves; what happens in one generation often occurs in the next. Genograms help family members identify and understand family relationship patterns.

Commonly used genogram symbols are shown in Figure 8.4. Together, the symbols provide a visual picture of a family tree, for at least three generations, including

CASE EXAMPLE Using a Genogram: The Kull Family

Jim Kull is referred by Rock County District Attorney's Office to the Rock County Domestic Violence Program. He was arrested two nights ago for an incident in which his wife, Diane, received several severe bruises on her body and her face. Kris Koeffler, a social worker, has an intake interview with Mr. Kull. Mr. Kull is an involuntary client and is reluctant to discuss the incident. Ms. Koeffler informs Mr. Kull he has a right not to discuss it, but if he chooses not to, she is obligated to inform the district attorney that he refused services. She adds that in such cases the district attorney usually files a battery charge with the court, which may lead to jail time.

Mr. Kull reluctantly states he and his wife had a disagreement, which ended with her slapping him and him defending himself by throwing a few punches. He adds that yesterday, when he was in jail, he was informed she left home with the children and is now staying at a women's shelter. He is worried she may contact an attorney and seek a divorce.

Ms. Koeffler inquires about the specifics of the "disagreement." Mr. Kull indicates he came home after having a few beers, his dinner was cold, and he "got on" Mrs. Kull for not cleaning the house. He adds that Mrs. Kull then started "mouthing off," which eventually escalated into them pushing and hitting each other. Ms. Koeffler then inquires whether such incidents had occurred in the past. Mr. Kull indicates "a few times" and then adds that getting physical with his wife is the only way for him to "make her shape up." He indicates he works all day long as a carpenter while his wife sits home watching soap operas. He feels she is not doing her "fair share"; he states the house usually looks like a "pigpen."

Ms. Koeffler asks Mr. Kull if he feels getting physical with his wife is justifiable. He responds with "sure" and adds that his dad frequently told him "spare the rod, and spoil both the wife and the kids." Ms. Koeffler asks if his father was at times abusive to him when he was a child. He indicates that he was and adds that to this day he detests his dad for being abusive to him and to his mother.

Ms. Koeffler then suggests that together they draw a "family tree," focusing on three areas: episodes of heavy drinking, episodes of physical abuse, and traditional versus modern gender stereotypes. Ms. Koeffler explains that a traditional gender stereotype includes the husband as the primary decision maker and the wife as submissive to him and primarily responsible for domestic tasks. The modern gender stereotype involves an equalitarian relationship between husband and wife. After an initial reluctance (related to his expressing confusion as to how such a "tree" would help get his wife back), Mr. Kull agrees to cooperate in drawing such a "tree." The resulting genogram is presented in Figure 8.5.

The genogram helps Mr. Kull see that he and his wife are products of family systems that have strikingly different values and customs. In his family the males drink heavily, have a traditional view of marriage, and use physical force in interactions with their spouses. (Mr. Kull further adds his father also physically abused his brother and sister when they were younger.) On questioning, Mr. Kull mentions he frequently spanks his children and has struck them "once or twice." Ms. Koeffler asks Mr. Kull how he feels about repeating the same patterns of abuse with his wife and children that he despises his father for using. Tears come to his eyes, and he says "not good."

Ms. Koeffler and Mr. Kull then discuss courses of action that he might take to change his family interactions and how he might best approach his wife in requesting that she and the children return. Mr. Kull agrees to attend Alcoholics Anonymous (AA) meetings as well as a therapy group for batterers. After a month of attending these weekly meetings, he contacts his wife and asks her to return. Mrs. Kull agrees to return *if* he stops drinking (since most of the abuse occurred when he was intoxicated), *if* he agrees to continue to attend group intervention and AA meetings, and *if* he agrees to go to counseling with her. Mr. Kull readily agrees. (Mrs. Kull's parents, who have never liked her husband, express their disapproval.)

For the first few months, Mr. Kull is on his best behavior, and there is considerable harmony in the family. Then one day, on his birthday, he decides to stop for a few beers after work. He drinks until he is intoxicated. When he finally arrives home, he starts to verbally and physically abuse Mrs. Kull and the children. For Mrs. Kull, this is the last straw. She takes the children to her parents' house, where they stay for several days, until they are able to find and move into an apartment. She also files for divorce and follows through in obtaining one.

At first glance, this case is not a "success." In reality, many social work cases are not successful. However, Mr. Kull now realizes that he has acquired, and acts out, certain dysfunctional family patterns. Unfortunately, he is not ready to make lasting changes. Perhaps in the future he will be more committed. At the present time he has returned to drinking heavily. Mrs. Kull and the children are safer and can now start to break the cycle of abuse.

Counseling Skills at Work in Generalist Practice

In the Kull family case example, the social worker used the following roles that, as described in Chapter 1, are components of generalist social work practice: brokering Mr. Kull to participate in AA meetings, educating Mrs. Kull to understand she needs to take action to stop the physical abuse, and brokering Mr. Kull to attend an intervention group for batterers.

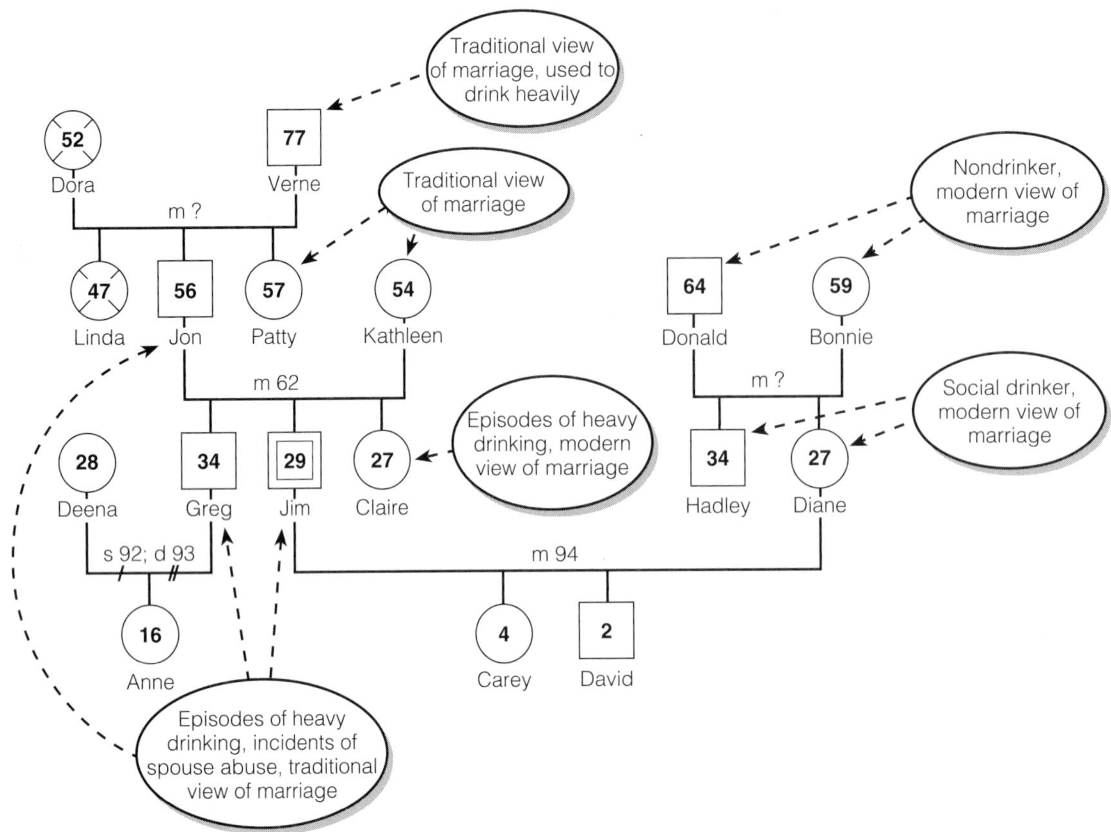

Figure 8.5
Sample genogram: The Jim and Diane Kull family.

the following: who the members are; their names, ages, and gender; marital status; and sibling positions. When relevant, additional items of information are included, such as emotional difficulties, behavioral problems, religious affiliation, ethnic origins, geographic locations, occupations, socioeconomic status, and significant life events. The use of the genogram is illustrated in the Kull family case example on page 253.

In summary, genograms are useful to both worker and clients. For the worker, a completed genogram graphically points out intergenerational family dynamics. Such a diagram allows the worker to better understand the intergenerational patterns affecting a client family. It then helps the worker generate hypotheses of problematic patterns from prior generations, which the worker can further explore by questioning family members. Once problematic dynamics are identified, the worker can then focus attention on helping family members generate strategies to resolve the patterns. A strengths perspective should also be used by workers—that is, they should also focus on helping family members identify intergenerational patterns that are *resources* that will help the family confront challenges. (Such resources include longevity, high educational achievement levels, valuing and practicing good health patterns, low rates of divorce, and high levels of constructive community participation.)

Similarly, for the client family, a genogram helps family members identify and understand problematic intergenerational problem patterns and resources. Once such patterns are identified, family members can begin to generate strategies (together with their worker) to break these patterns.

The genogram and the eco-map have a number of similarities. With both techniques, users gain insight into family dynamics. Some of the symbols used in the two approaches are identical. There are differences, however. The eco-map focuses attention on the family's interactions with groups, resources, organizations, associations, other families, and other individuals. The genogram focuses attention on intergenerational patterns, particularly those that are problematic or dysfunctional.

FAMILY COUNSELING IN SYSTEMS PERSPECTIVE

Levels of Family Need

Families are important social systems, and because they are systems, the actions of any family member will affect the lives of every other member in some way.[1] For that reason, social workers who counsel families must consider the effects of their interventions on the family as a whole as well as on individual members. Due to the complexity of family practice, a substantial amount of literature has been developed in the social work profession to assist the family counselor to assess and intervene with family systems. Several examples of social work with families have been described previously in this chapter.

Family work is not a "one size fits all" endeavor, because families come with very different levels of need. Social workers must assess these different levels carefully in order to determine the most effective intervention in any given circumstance. To assist family counselors in their work, Kilpatrick and Holland (2003) described four distinct levels of family need. Families at Level I lack the requirements for basic survival, such as food and shelter. Because of the stress of such difficult circumstances, nurturance in these families is often minimal, and violence may be ongoing. Social workers who assess a family at Level I will need to mobilize many in-home services, especially financial aid, food, and shelter. If violence is present, protective services will need to be mobilized, and mother and children may need temporary respite at a domestic violence shelter. Out-of-home services may need to be mobilized as well, such as the judicial system to restrain a batterer. But the social worker's primary goal is to prevent the family from falling apart, and if the family survives the immediate crises, additional counseling will be offered to help improve the family's internal relationships.

The Kull family, described in the genogram case example (p. 253), is a family that could be classified at Level I because of the ongoing violence. At the time of referral, Mrs. Kull and the children lacked a secure home because of Mr. Kull's violence and were staying at a shelter. The social worker's initial intervention focused on safety issues. Even though the marriage of Mr. and Mrs. Kull ultimately fell apart, the intervention was successful in terms of achieving safety for Mrs. Kull and the children.

Level II families, according to Kilpatrick and Holland's classification, are those where basic needs for safety, stability, and nurturance have been met but the family lacks an effective authority structure. Children are frequently out of control, and substance abuse is often a serious issue. Violence may be a threat, but family members do not appear to be in immediate danger. In families such as these, parents need assistance in setting limits for their children and in maintaining appropriate authority. The Wilbur family, discussed in this chapter's illustration of the eco-map (see Figure 8.3), is a good example of a Level II family.

Level III families are not in immediate danger of homelessness or violence, the children are basically under control, but there are important issues involving how members of the family relate to one another. The parents may have control of the children, but the children may not be respected enough, or allowed enough autonomy, to grow into confident adults. If two parents are present, one may totally dominate the other. Level III families, in fact, tend to suffer from *too much* control. Appropriate personal space is lacking, and subsystems boundaries (discussed later in the chapter) are enmeshed. At the same time, paradoxically, members of these families feel distant and isolated from one another.

Level IV families are functioning effectively according to everyday measures, but their members wish to develop greater self-realization, resolve some kind of inner

---

[1]The remainder of this chapter was especially written for this edition by Carolyn Wells, PhD. Dr. Wells is Professor Emeritus at the University of Wisconsin—Oshkosh Department of Social Work and has been a practicing family counselor.

conflict, or explore spiritual yearnings. Level IV families hope to increase to the fullness, richness, and quality of their lives. These families are indeed fortunate.

Kilpatrick and Holland employ an unusual but helpful architectural metaphor to distinguish the four levels of need: that of a house. Level I is represented by the basement of the house (basic survival). Level II is represented by the outer walls and roof of the house (structure and organization). Level III is represented by the inner walls and door of the house (personal space and boundaries). Level IV is represented by the "decorations and furnishings."

The Whitlock Family

This chapter continues with a detailed description of family treatment with a family functioning at Level III, the Whitlocks. Working with Level III families is a complex process requiring advanced knowledge and skill and is usually conducted in a professional office setting by a licensed clinical social worker (minimum of an MSW with a clinical specialization plus supervised experience) or by some other licensed professional such as a psychologist.

The treatment scenario begins as follows: The Whitlock family walks into the social worker's office in an orderly fashion, the oldest son looking annoyed and bored, the younger children looking scared. Mrs. Whitlock introduces the group to the counselor immediately, saying that she is sure nothing is wrong with her family, although the younger daughter Susan has been crying all the time lately, has been doing poorly in school, and is obese. The mother says she is sure Susan will grow out of these problems, but when the little girl's teacher called and said Susan was talking about suicide, the mother decided she had to seek help for the girl. The only reason the rest of the family is here, she announces, is because the social worker requested that everyone be present at the first interview.

The father stands by the door while the mother talks, and no one sits down. The social worker notes that the older daughter stands close to the father and the younger son looks at the floor. The older son moves to the window and looks out, whistling to himself. When the mother, holding Susan's hand, finishes her rapid-fire introductory speech, the counselor takes advantage of the pause to invite the family to be seated. She asks each person present to introduce himself or herself. She notes that the older daughter has difficulty with that request; she stutters badly and can't utter the first sound of her name.

Let's leave the Whitlocks for a moment and discuss a few basic ideas important to family counseling. When any family consults a social worker for help in reducing family pain, there is hope. The act of seeking help is a positive indication that the family is capable of constructive change. However, families often consult a worker with the intention to have the counselor "fix" a particular member, such as Susan Whitlock. The member whom the family wants "fixed" is commonly called the *identified client.*

The goal of the family system is to go on as it was before the problematic behavior became noticeable. Given that families are social systems, however, and that the behavior of any one member of a system affects (and is affected by) all other members, the counselor will suspect that something going on in the family as a whole may be prompting the particular behavior of concern. In other words, the behavior of the identified client may be a symptom of a broader family problem. For that reason, although the counselor will assist in dealing with the presenting issue, he or she will work to involve all family members in the counseling process, even young children. The worker will want to assess from direct observation and careful questioning whether the problematic behavior of the identified client may play an important function in maintaining the family system or may be the result of some stress in the family system. Careful assessment is important because the identified client may be responding to stress *within* the family. But stress also may come from a system other than the family as a whole. It may come instead from a subsystem. For example, the identified client may have a

CASE EXAMPLE School Phobia

A system inherently attempts to maintain a dynamic balance, or homeostasis, to maintain the particular arrangement or ordering of parts that was successful in the past and resulted in establishment of the system. As an example of how problematic behavior in a family member may help maintain the family homeostasis (balance of the system so the system can continue), let us discuss a school phobia that arose in a little girl in a Jefferson County, Wisconsin, elementary school. The school phobia arose apparently spontaneously, but the school social worker discovered on her first home visit that the little girl was almost mute with strangers (at least with the social worker herself) and in fact ran out to the yard rather than cope with a new person. The mother would not fetch the daughter ("she's too frightened of strangers") and offered only the most broad and general information about the child's development. However, the mother did want to talk about herself; she listed a variety of stresses in her life unrelated to the daughter, in particular her aloof husband and her boring job. It became increasingly clear that this mother resented the time and attention her daughter was receiving; she wanted some attention herself. Yet the only reason she was receiving any attention from her husband was because of the daughter's phobia. The husband had to talk to the lonely woman fairly often because of the little girl's problematic behaviors (in the home the child would often stay in her room, or refuse her supper, and so forth). Because of the girl's school phobia, the mother got to stay home from her disliked job and to talk with her husband.

A combination of family counseling to help create a genuine relationship between the marital pair without the assistance of the daughter's problematic behaviors, plus reduction in the mother's work hours, helped reduce this family's need for a problematic daughter. At school, during the initial stages of the family counseling, the little girl was placed in a special class with an empathic and firm teacher. The father was assigned the task of taking his daughter to school. The mother was to accompany them but not take responsibility. Fortunately, the father was a well-meaning person and faithfully carried out his responsibility, which strengthened his relationship with the child and thus his investment in the family system as a whole. After successfully getting the child to school, the father and the mother would discuss their success, strengthening their own communication and increasing their appreciation of one another. The school phobia disappeared within a few weeks.

biological imbalance such as a metabolic disorder. Or significant stress may originate in a larger or suprasystem, such as the identified client's school—there may be some bullying going on there, teasing, or some other disturbing problem.

EP 2.1.7a

In the early days of systems-oriented family therapy, many social workers would agree to provide services only if every family member participated. Today, however, it is recognized that working with a subgroup of the family, even with an individual alone if that is the only family member willing or able to come for counseling, can be helpful. But working with families as wholes is often the most productive way to proceed. A brief example of systems-oriented family treatment is presented in the Case Example "School Phobia."

THREE APPROACHES TO FAMILY COUNSELING

Several noted family counselors have contributed to the growing theory and practice of family counseling. Here we briefly describe three approaches: a communication pattern approach, a family subsystem approach, and a cognitive behavioral approach.

A Communication Pattern Approach

Virginia Satir (deceased social work pioneer in family therapy) stressed clarification of family communication patterns in her work. Her ideas were so insightful that they strongly influence family counseling theory and practice today. She noted that communication patterns among troubled families tend to be vague and indirect. In other words, rather than speaking clearly for themselves, the marital pair avoid talking with each other about their needs and desires; or they talk to each other through their children. Children are thus maneuvered into the stressful position of speaking for, and therefore allying with, one parent or another, precipitating fear of loss of the other.[2]

In Satir's view, indirect communication in the troubled family begins with the courtship process (if not before) because of the low self-esteem of the individuals involved. Each potential partner feels worthless but hides the feeling of worthlessness by acting confident and strong. Neither person talks about these feelings of worthlessness for fear of driving the potential mate away. So each sees in the other a strong person who will take care of him or her and essentially becomes part of a couple to gain an extension of the self, but a stronger self who will be able to meet all felt needs; in other words, each marries (or commits) to "get" (Satir, 1967, pp. 8–10).

Unfortunately, after marriage some of the illusions must fall away. Each partner realizes at some level that the other is not just an extension of the self. One insists on using a separate toothbrush, for example, and the other wants to share the same one. Such incidents force perceptions of difference, and difference is experienced as bad because it leads to arguments. A desire for fusion and to be cared for conflicts with the other's different felt needs. Facing difference feels frightening—it might lead to arguments, and that could result in the other's leaving.

Hence, each frightened partner with low self-esteem and high need for the other masks differences as much as possible, attempting to please the other on one level to keep him or her, while fearing and resenting expressed needs from the other that may be experienced as undesirable. Because both partners are in the same uncomfortable position of resenting differences yet needing the other, interpersonal communication gradually becomes more and more indirect. Rather than risk a clear statement, such as "I'd like to get a dog," the partner desiring a pet might state something like "Aunt Matilda likes dogs." The hope is that the other will mind-read the intended message and then spontaneously agree to get a dog for the family. However, the receiver of this particular message will more likely communicate a return response dealing with Aunt Matilda, bringing disappointment to the speaker. The speaker isn't able to negotiate the desired dog with this type of communication and is left with angry feelings and a sense of unfulfilled needs, but this state of affairs is experienced as being preferable to risking a point-blank denial. Meanwhile, the receiver of the message becomes aware of the disappointment or anger of the speaker through nonverbal channels but has no idea what caused it. If the partner is also afraid to deal with conflict, he or she will not ask the reason for the apparent upset. So the misunderstanding and tension build.

Satir also notes that communicating involves far more than the literal meaning of the words used. First, she notes that much communication is nonverbal—gestures, facial expressions, voice tone, posture, and the like. If nonverbal communication matches the meaning of the words used (if, for example, "I am sad" is accompanied by tears and a downturned mouth), then Satir considers the communication *congruent*. The receiver is not likely to misunderstand the meaning of this message because the verbal and nonverbal components agree. However, messages sent are often *incongruent*. For example, "I am sad" may be accompanied by a grin. Which message should the receiver believe—the words or the facial expression? The receiver is likely to make a mistaken interpretation unless he or she explicitly asks the sender to explain. But the person who feels safe only with indirect communication is not likely to ask. Moreover, the sender who becomes skilled at sending incongruent communication for self-protection may even be unaware of the action and will be unable to explain if asked. Satir believes that incongruent communication leads to misunderstanding in troubled families. Mother, for example, says to her spouse, "I am angry with you." However, because she fears rejection if she sends this message too forcefully, she smiles sweetly as she says it. The spouse chooses to believe the smile, not to take his spouse's words seriously, and continues the very behavior that made

---

[2]Traditional terms such as marital pair, spouse, or partner are used in this chapter for convenience but should be understood to include other adult partners in committed relationships involving children (gay couples, stepparents, etc.).

her use the word *angry*. This makes her angrier, but she doesn't feel safe enough to express the feeling more congruently, and the communication driving the spouses apart goes on.

Incongruent communication is one example of a double message; another type of double message places the receiver in a *double bind,* where no matter how he or she responds, the sender will criticize. This situation can occur when Father says, on the one hand, that all good children pick up their toys, yet on the other hand tells his son that all "real" boys are messy. The boy who receives these two messages will be unable to please his father whether he keeps his toys neat or messy. He may solve the problem by refusing to listen at all. At the extreme, he may pull away from reality to such a degree that he develops a severe emotional disturbance.

Satir's intervention goals and techniques are based on her assumption that people have the inherent ability (even drive) to grow and to mature. She felt that people can choose to take responsibility for their own lives and actions and that mature individuals will

1. Manifest themselves clearly to others
2. Be in touch with signals from their internal selves, thus letting themselves know openly what they think and feel
3. Be able to see and hear what is outside themselves as differentiated from themselves and as different from anything else
4. Behave toward another person as someone who is separate and unique
5. Treat the presence of differentness as an opportunity to learn and explore rather than as a threat or signal of conflict. (Satir, 1967, p. 92)

To help members of a troubled family differentiate from one another and learn to "own" their special unique beings, Satir patiently taught each person to speak for himself or herself and to send I-messages.[3] She served as an active, directive, loving role model. She taught that differentness is normal and should be viewed as a catalyst for growth. She pointed out incongruent messages and double binds and taught family members to send clear, congruent messages. She used touch and other nonverbal means, such as family sculpting, to illustrate to families the unverbalized assumptions they operate by, and in this way she took the burden of labeling off identified clients and revealed their symptomatic behavior as a product of the family system as a whole.

Family sculpting is used for both assessment and treatment purposes. It is a physical arrangement of the members of a family in space, with the placement of each person determined by an individual family member acting as "director." The resulting tableau represents that person's symbolic view of family relationships. Goldenberg and Goldenberg (1991) describe family sculpting as follows:

> The procedure calls for each member to arrange the bodies of all the other family members in a defined space, according to his or her perception of their relationships either at present or at a specific point in the past. Who the sculptor designates as domineering, meek and submissive, loving and touching, belligerent, benevolent, clinging, and so on, and how those people relate to each other becomes apparent to all who witness the tableau. The sculptor is invited to explain the creation, and a lively debate between members may follow. The adolescent boy who places his parents at opposite ends of the family group while he and his brothers and sisters are huddled together in the center conveys a great deal more about his views of the workings of the family system than he would probably be able to state in words. By the same token, his father's sculpture—placing himself apart from all others, including his wife—may reveal his sense of loneliness, isolation, and rejection by his family. The mother may present herself as a confidante of her daughter but ignored by the males in the family, and so forth. (p. 242)

Satir also analyzed rules in the family and helped clarify them in the context that some rules may be bad but the people setting the rules or bound by them are not. She taught that bad rules can be changed, and she had the family members negotiate new ones as she insisted that each member be heard in her presence, thus teaching respect for each person and point of view.

---

[3]I-messages are described in Chapter 7 and in Module 4.

EP 2.1.7a

Clearly, then, Satir viewed the family as a system and worked with the family as a whole as the means of relieving the distress of the identified client or of the family itself because of the previous dysfunctional behavior of the identified client. Her major emphasis in intervention with the family as a system was to clarify the family's communication patterns and to help them become direct and congruent. Her techniques work particularly well with Level III families where self-expression and self-esteem need nurturing and development (Kilpatrick & Holland, 2003).

Exercise 8.2: Analyzing My Family through Satir's Concepts

Goal: This exercise is designed to assist you in understanding and applying Satir's concepts.

Step 1: Satir focuses on communication patterns in troubled families being vague and indirect, considerable communication being nonverbal in troubled families, incongruent messages being used, double-bind messages being sent, and the low self-esteem of some members needing to be improved. Are some members of your family communicating in ways identified by Satir? If "yes," please describe. Do some members of your family have low self-esteem? If "yes," code the name (for confidentiality reasons) and briefly describe why you believe this member (or members) has low self-esteem.

Step 2: Briefly describe your thoughts on the merits and shortcomings of Satir's approach.

A Family Subsystem Approach

Like Satir, Salvador Minuchin is a pioneer in family counseling who operates from a systems perspective. In short, this means that if a particular person is referred for counseling because of certain undesirable symptoms, Minuchin assumes that this behavior is generated and maintained by needs of the family as a whole and that intervention with the family will be necessary for effective alleviation of the problems of the identified client.

Unlike Satir, however, Minuchin's major emphasis in counseling is not clarification of communication patterns per se but restructuring of the major subsystems within the family (spouse, parental, sibling) so each can accomplish its appropriate functions.[4] Because of this emphasis, Minuchin is considered to be a member of the *structural* school of family counselors. In restructuring the family, Minuchin works with communication patterns in the family, just as in clarifying communication patterns, Satir restructured the family subsystems into a more functional relationship. However, Minuchin's theoretical perspective on the importance of clear, direct communication versus a functional family structure is clearly different. Minuchin, for example, bypasses direct cognitive understanding by a family of its communication patterns to restructure the family subsystems. For example, he may use a paradoxical suggestion

[4]This approach works particularly well with Level II families who need to develop effective authority structures and with Level III families who need to establish appropriate subsystem boundaries (Kilpatrick & Holland, 2003).

in working with a resistant family. However, he does so only in highly selected circumstances where direct explorations and clarifications of family communication patterns and behavior in counseling failed to change the dysfunctional aspects.

Paradoxical suggestion is a technique in which the counselor tells the family members to continue their symptomatic behavior and sometimes to "improve on it." This technique makes members more aware of the existence of the dysfunctional behavior and the dysfunctional consequences they derive from it. The ultimate goal of a paradoxical suggestion is to subtly encourage one or more family members to terminate engaging in the dysfunctional behavior. Minuchin provided the following illustration of the use of a paradoxical suggestion:

> A systemic paradox is used in treatment of the Allen family, in which an eight-year-old boy is failing in school. The therapist determines that the symptom serves the function of keeping the mother's disappointment focused on her son, Billy, rather than her husband. The husband is failing in business and, rather than redoubling his efforts, is sinking into apathy, leaving the mother to shoulder much of the financial burden. He gives off signals that he would collapse if confronted openly with this issue and the mother collaborates in protecting him. Whenever she becomes angry at his lack of ambition, she nags Billy to straighten out and make something of himself, do his homework, practice his violin, or clean up his room. The mother and Billy end up fighting, and the father retires to the den to watch television. Both parents deny there is a marital problem, the wife stating, "My husband doesn't like to fight and I've accepted this."
>
> The therapist tells the mother it is important for her to continue to express her disappointment in Billy, because otherwise she might begin to express her dissatisfaction with her husband. This would be risky, as her husband might become depressed, and since Billy is younger and more resilient than her husband, he can take it better. Billy is advised to continue to protect his father by keeping the mother's disappointment focused on him, and the father is commended for his cooperation. The mother has an immediate recoil, saying, "You're suggesting I fight with my eight-year-old son instead of my husband, a grown man? Why should I damage my son to protect my husband?" thus defining her own predicament. The husband supports the therapist, saying he thinks her suggestion is a good one "because Billy bounces right back. With him it doesn't last for a long period of time, and he doesn't get depressed as I do. Besides, we can't know for sure if it's doing him any damage." The mother is outraged at her husband and proceeds to fight with him. The conflict is refocused onto the parents, and Billy is released from his middle position. Defining and prescribing their system in a way that is both accurate and unacceptable makes it impossible for them to continue it. (Minuchin & Fishman, 1981, p. 247)

In this example, by the use of paradoxical suggestion Minuchin clarified the boundaries around the spouse subsystem in such a way that the son is appropriately excluded. Solving the problems of the spouse subsystem is squarely placed back within the boundaries of the spouse subsystem. The wife's disappointment with her husband is not "cured," nor is the apathetic behavior of the husband toward his failing business, but the wife's dissatisfaction with her spouse is now appropriately expressed within the boundaries of the spouse dyad, where it can be dealt with directly. Before use of this intervention technique, 8-year-old Billy was being pulled in between the spouses to divert them from fighting. Billy's inappropriate inclusion by the parents in their spouse subsystem might temporarily work to keep the family together for a longer period, but the cost to Billy is unacceptable. In the long run, using Billy this way will not work for the spouses either, for their problems obviously cannot be solved by Billy's failing in school.

In Minuchin's structural perspective, every family contains multiple interacting systems, including each particular individual and the various dyads, but three major subsystems are of particular importance in families with children: the spouse, the parental, and the sibling subsystems. Each has different major functions that must be fulfilled if the family is to survive as a healthy unit. The *spouse* subsystem must be able to protect itself as a unique entity with clear boundaries if the spouses' long-term psychological needs are to be met. This will involve certain rules of interaction with other significant subsystems, such as in-laws or children, that reinforce rather than interfere with the rights and needs of the spouses to interact as spouses. Once children are born, a *parental* subsystem then comes into being. The parental subsystem is likely to interfere with the spouse subsystem, because when one parent bonds closely with a newborn child, the primacy of the relationship with the other spouse is threatened. Moreover, in-laws may demand parental rights that conflict with the wants and needs of the biological parents. Later on, older children may be asked to take on parental functions that interfere with their own needs to be nurtured and protected as they learn and grow. Finally, the *sibling* subsystem is of particular importance because this is the context in which children first learn what the world is all about for them: initially, how to interact and deal with peers and hierarchies. Minuchin points out that families continue to develop and change as children are added, grow, and leave home, so constant adaptational changes are required for every family. The family has both to maintain itself and to change with the changing conditions. Sometimes professional intervention is required to help troubled families cope successfully.

In working with a given family, Minuchin analyzes its structure to determine whether the boundaries of the major subsystems are clear and defined, or too enmeshed (too close, as when a parent and a child are emotionally closer than the two members of the spouse subsystem), or too disengaged (as when two spouses communicate with each other only through their children). Minuchin diagrams a hypothetical structure of the family, noting positions and types of boundaries as they exist when the family is referred. He then rediagrams the subsystem boundaries as new information emerges or as they change throughout the treatment process. His goal is to restructure the family so there is (1) a functioning spouse subsystem with a clear boundary differentiating it from other subsystems; (2) a parental subsystem with clear executive functions that may or may not involve other persons besides the spouses, but where at any rate the channels of authority are clear; and (3) a sibling subsystem that is free from enmeshment with both the spouse and the parental subsystems so the siblings may develop and grow under the protection, guidance, and appropriate authority of the parents.

To achieve these objectives, Minuchin developed a creative variety of techniques ranging from direct education of the family members all the way to the occasional use of paradoxical suggestion, where the family interactional patterns are restructured within appropriate subsystem boundaries without the members' conscious understanding of how it happened. Minuchin uses himself actively and directly within the counseling sessions according to his assessment of the requirements of the situation. He moves people physically around his office or out of the office, and himself physically as well, to demonstrate and enact appropriate and inappropriate subsystem boundaries.

EP 2.1.7a

Minuchin cautions against preoccupation with counseling techniques. He believes that they should be studied with care and then consciously forgotten, so the educated counselor can spontaneously meet the requirements of each unique therapeutic situation. He describes his own restructuring techniques in family counseling as belonging to three major categories: boundary making, unbalancing the current dysfunctional family structure, and complementarity (changing perceptions of hierarchical relationships within the family) (Minuchin & Fishman, 1981, p. 145).

Exercise 8.3: Analyzing My Family through Minuchin's Concepts

Goal: This exercise is designed to assist you in understanding and applying Minuchin's concepts.

Step 1: Describe the functional and dysfunctional components of the spouse subsystem in your family.

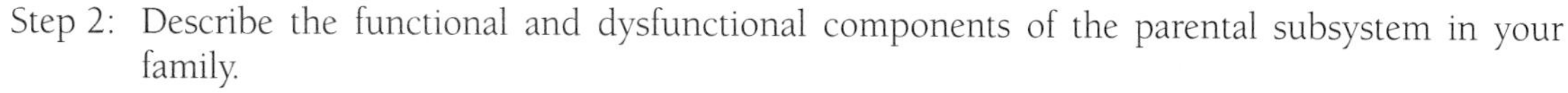

Step 2: Describe the functional and dysfunctional components of the parental subsystem in your family.

Step 3: Describe the functional and dysfunctional components of the sibling subsystem in your family.

Step 4: Briefly describe your thoughts on the merits and shortcomings of Minuchin's approach.

A Cognitive-Behavioral Approach

Cognitive-behavioral therapy has been developed by a variety of theorists, including Albert Ellis (2000), Aaron Beck (1976), Richard Stuart (1976), Gerald Patterson (1971), and Robert Liberman (1971). Cognitive-behavioral therapy is further described in this text in Modules 1 and 2. Cognitive-behavioral theorists have developed a number of intervention strategies, which are described in Modules 1 and 2.

Cognitive-behavioral theorists assert that cognitive factors (thoughts, attitudes, beliefs, expectations) are the primary determinants of all of our emotions and behaviors. They assert that negative and irrational thoughts are the primary determinants of unwanted emotions and dysfunctional behaviors. They further assert that changing negative and irrational thoughts in a positive and rational direction is the primary strategy to alleviate unwanted emotions and dysfunctional behaviors. (See Modules 1 and 2 for a further explanation of this theoretical perspective.) Three intervention strategies that have been applied to family therapy are cognitive restructuring, contingency contracting, and family management skills.

Cognitive Restructuring Cognitive restructuring is directed at restructuring distorted beliefs (schemas) in marriage counseling in order to change a couple's dysfunctional interactions. Such marital schemas are likely to contain thoughts and attitudes about how spousal relationships should work, how different marital problems should be handled, what's involved in building a happy family, what responsibilities each partners should assume, and so forth.

There are an infinite number of schemas (distorted beliefs). A few of these are presented for illustrative purposes:

A wife stops after work to shop, and the husband thinks, "She's late from work. She must be having an affair."

A husband gets up in the morning and realizes he is late for a meeting, so he rushes and leaves. The wife thinks, "He didn't kiss me good-bye. He must be angry."

A husband wants a traditional marital relationship, but the wife wants an equalitarian relationship including a career. The husband thinks, "My wife is ruining our marriage by not staying at home and letting me financially take care of us." The wife thinks, "My husband is ruining our marriage by trying to control me and by stifling me."

A wife drops a potted plant and thinks, "I'm not good at anything."

A husband prides himself at mind reading and erroneously draws conclusions without asking. For example, his wife is silent because of an upset stomach, and the husband erroneously concludes, "She is in mental discomfort—she must be contemplating dumping me."

Cognitive restructuring can also be used in family therapy. Often children and parents have schemas (distorted beliefs) about one another. The following are some illustrations:

A mother may think, "In order for my 14-year-old son to get into college and be a success in this world, he must get at least a 3.5 average in high school."

A 15-year-old daughter may think, "It is cool to experiment with using cocaine and LSD."

A 13-year-old son may think, "It is exciting to touch the breasts of girls in this neighborhood and fondle their private areas."

A 16-year-old daughter may think, "The way I can get noticed by boys is by being pencil thin—so I will eat practically nothing."

A father may think, "It is my job to educate my 14-year-old daughter about sex, so I will seduce her when my wife is out shopping."

A 9-year-old depressed son may think, "Life is so miserable—school is going awful, my parents don't love me, I have no friends. Perhaps I should end it with by taking a bunch of my dad's sleeping pills."

In marital therapy and in family therapy it is the focus of the therapist to have family members recognize these distorted belief systems and then to replace these distorted beliefs with more rational and positive thought patterns. The process is often time-consuming. Let us take the example of the 9-year-old depressed son who is contemplating suicide. Let us assume he and his parents are in family therapy. The therapist has a number of different options for seeking to restructure the negative cognitions of the youth. The therapist can help the youth to understand that suicide is a permanent solution to a temporary life situation; the therapist can help the youth to understand that changes can be made to improve his current life situation.

Some of the ways to improve his current life situation are as follows: The youth thinks, "My parents don't love me." In family therapy, his parents have the opportunity to dispute this belief by expressing their love for him. Other ways of improving his life situation are to find meaningful activities at school and in the community for him to get involved in—perhaps a sport activity, a music program, computer involvement, and so on. A mentor might be identified to become involved with him. His parents may be encouraged to spend more time with him—and to get involved in activities that all members of the family find meaningful and enjoyable. The focus of seeking to change his life situation, which he views as "miserable and not worth living," is to restructure his cognitions (by making changes in his living environment) so that he concludes "living is often filled with activities/events that are well-worth staying alive for and enjoying." An additional life-changing focus might be to examine his grade challenges in school and problem-solve how to improve these—such as through a tutor. (If the youth has extensive suicidal ideation, hospitalization for a brief time period may be considered in order to prevent a serious suicide attempt.)

Contingency Contracting Family members often want something from each other. For example, a child may want a higher weekly allowance. Parents may want a child to study more and attain higher grades. A teenager may want his father to give up smoking. A mother may want her daughter to be more respectful. A husband may want more attention and intimacy from his wife. A wife may want her husband to do more of the domestic chores around the house. Parents may want their 14-year-old son to stop experimenting with using alcohol and to clean his room weekly.

Therapists in marital or family therapy can assist family members to form contingency contracts with one another so that each family member gets more of what he or she wants. A contingency contract in family therapy is usually bilateral and specifies the obligations and the mutual reinforcements for each of the parties. Contingency contracts specify goals to be accomplished and the tasks to be performed to accomplish them. Contracts set deadlines for completion of the specified tasks and identify rewards for successful completion of tasks. Contracts also specify consequences for unsuccessful completion of tasks.

A contingency contract can be fairly simple. For example, a 15-year-old will receive an allowance of $30 per week if she satisfactorily completes all of the following tasks: cleaning her room once a week, taking out the garbage, and getting up and getting dressed each school day by 7:15 a.m. Failure to successfully complete these tasks for any week will result in an allowance of only $15.

A contingency contract can also be fairly complex. For example, a husband and wife may arrive at a contract involving a variety of areas: doing domestic tasks, intimacy issues, paying bills, parenting time for each of them with the children, nights to visit friends, and so on.

Family Management Skills All children will, at times, be disruptive in families. Behavioral therapists can instruct parents in a standardized package of skills using behavioral management practices to increase prosocial behavior and decrease problematic behavior in their children. This approach has been called *behavioral parent training* (BPT).

> Goldenberg and Goldenberg (2004, p. 306) note that BPT assumes a faulty parent-child interaction pattern has probably developed and been maintained through *reciprocity* (a child responding negatively to a negative parental input) and *coercion* (parents influencing behavior through the use of punishment). BPT intervention aims to change this mutually destructive pattern of interaction usually by training parents to observe and measure the child's problematic behavior and then to apply social learning techniques for accelerating desirable behavior, decelerating undesirable behavior, and maintaining the consequent cognitive and behavioral changes.
>
> As is true of all cognitive or behavioral interventions, parent training begins with an extensive assessment procedure. Before teaching parenting skills, the behavioral therapist relies on interviews, questionnaires, behavioral checklists, and naturalistic observations of parent-child interactions in order to identify the specific problem behavior along with its antecendent and consequent events. Through such a behavioral analysis, the therapist is able to pinpoint the problem more exactly; evaluate the form, frequency, and extent of its impact on the family; and systematically train parents to use social learning principles to replace the targeted behavior with more positive, mutually reinforcing interaction.

Parents can be taught a variety of behavioral techniques to more effectively change a child's disruptive behavior—after a *baseline* of all of the problematic behaviors has been determined. Some of these interventions are listed below:

1. *Time-out:* A technique that removes the child when he or she is disruptive from an activity or discussion and requires the child to sit, calmly detached from others, until he or she is able to participate with the group more appropriately.
2. *Reinforcement:* A procedure that strengthens the tendency of a desired response to occur. If a reinforcer (such as attention for a child who wants attention) is arranged to follow a desired behavior, there is increased probability that that desired behavior will be repeated. This approach has been called "Catch 'em being good."

3. *Punishment:* A procedure in which a disruptive child is presented with an unpleasant or undesired event following a disruptive behavior—the consequence of which is that there is decreased probability that the disruptive behavior will be repeated.
4. *Shaping:* A technique using reinforcement and punishment in which desired new patterns of behavior are fashioned by reinforcing progressively closer approximations of the desired behaviors and not reinforcing the disruptive behaviors.
5. *Modeling desired behaviors:* Parents model the desired behaviors (for example, when interpersonal conflicts occur) that they want their disruptive child to learn. Parents can model constructive ways to handle interpersonal conflicts and constructive ways to express their discontent when they are upset.
6. *Token economy:* Parents can be instructed to set up a token economy with their disruptive child. With this approach, the child is given tokens, or slips of paper, when he or she fulfills specified tasks or behaves according to some specified standard. Tokens may be taken away when the child displays disruptive behavior. The tokens can then be redeemed by the child for his or her choice of certain goods or privileges. (Token economies are more fully described in Module 2.)

EP 2.1.7a

Exercise 8.4: Applying Cognitive-Behavioral Concepts to My Family

Goal: This exercise is designed to assist you in applying cognitive-behavioral concepts to your family.

Step 1: Without identifying who the person is, describe someone in your family who has an unwanted emotion, such as someone who is depressed.

Step 2: Describe whether you believe applying cognitive-behavioral techniques (name the technique or techniques) would assist in alleviating the unwanted emotion.

Step 3: Without identifying who the person is, describe someone in your family who is displaying a dysfunctional behavior.

Step 4: Describe whether you believe applying cognitive-behavioral techniques (name the technique or techniques) would assist in alleviating the dysfunctional behavior.

FAMILY WORK IN THE TWENTY-FIRST CENTURY

In the developing years of family counseling, theoretical schools developed that viewed each other as rivals. Clear distinctions were maintained among them, and students tended to remain loyal to the theories under which they were trained. However, complex cases have a wicked tendency to refuse to resolve using one approach alone, so over time, experienced practitioners began to borrow across boundaries. Today, most counselors recognize that no single approach can resolve all family problems, so they tailor their interventions according to the unique characteristics of each case. At the same time, counselors are beginning to believe that family members themselves may be the best experts on resolving their own issues. Hence, many practitioners view their role today as one of *partner* with the families with whom they work, rather than as expert (Nichols & Schwartz, 2005). Counselors tend to consciously share more of their internal thought processes with the family and today use fewer paradoxical interventions that may work only on an unconscious level. Overall, the intervention process has become more democratic.

Gradually, also, the field as a whole is becoming more aware of the impact of biology on behavior. The old "nature-nurture" debate has been resolved in the sense that scientists have proven that the interactions between environmental, behavioral, and biological processes are ongoing and reciprocal. Neither nature nor nurture can be documented as determining behavior—both are important and are constantly affecting each other. Hormones and genetics strongly affect behavior, but social environments affect the production of hormones, the expression of genes, and thus behavior. For example, a high level of conflict in a home is associated with higher-than-normal cortisol levels in the children who live there (cortisol is a secretion of the adrenal glands); children with high levels of cortisol tend to experience a high incidence of anxiety disorders and social difficulties (Booth, Carver, & Granger, 2005).

Despite the theoretical advances in private practice counseling with American families, the driving force with respect to treatment in the early twenty-first century is increasingly economic. Families who are fortunate enough to have health insurance tend to be insured through managed care companies today. To receive enough clients to remain in the profession, private practice counselors must contract with these companies. Managed care companies, to increase profits, severely limit the number of counseling sessions they will authorize for a given family, and they also pay much less per session than does traditional insurance. Thus for a significantly reduced income, private practice counselors must engage in time-consuming paperwork and frustrating phone calls to try to authorize a small number of sessions. The decision regarding whether the managed care company will pay is made by a stranger who frequently has no training in family counseling. This situation is so frustrating that many private practice counselors have left the profession. An emerging form of managed care involves a "capitated" contract, where the counselor agrees to provide services for a specific managed care group for a set annual fee. This discourages counselors from offering numerous sessions to any given family, but at least the decision is theirs (Nichols & Schwartz, 2005).

Many intractable family problems in the twenty-first century (as, of course, in every other century) are not the result of faulty internal family dynamics but, rather, a result of social and economic forces beyond the family's control (or the counselor's, for that matter). Today unemployment, widespread lack of health care coverage, and an inhumanly low minimum wage create serious problems for many families. These issues lie in the area of public policy, so social work counselors are urged to become involved in working for social change.

BEGINNING THE COUNSELING PROCESS: THE WHITLOCK FAMILY

Let's return to the family system and to systems-oriented family work. We left the Whitlocks as they were entering their counselor's office.

From nonverbal cues of spatial position in the office, the family counselor has already formulated some initial hunches about family alliances. These hunches are based on visual data and hence are worth investigating, although only some will prove true. For example, the physical separation of the husband and wife, with the husband barely in the office and the wife well inside, might indicate an emotional distance between the two as well as the relative positions of the marital pair within the family, one at the center and one on the edge, so to speak. The location of the older daughter (Pat, 14), close to the father and also near the door, might indicate that they form a coalition of some sort. The mother's holding the younger daughter's hand (Susan, 10) might indicate a similar close bond. Both sons maintain positions alone, and each further separates himself from family contact in a physical way—the younger son (George, 7) by staring at the floor and the older son (Lacey, 16) by looking out the window and whistling. These cues also signal family pain, felt in different ways and probably to different degrees by each member. It is likely that this family does not experience much closeness as a group; however, it is also possible that anxiety relating to this interview alone is precipitating the separation of various members of this family system.

When the counselor seats the family and asks the members to introduce themselves, even though Mrs. Whitlock has already taken charge and done so for everyone, the counselor is structuring a new communication style that is important in family counseling to break old and unsatisfying patterns. Each family member needs to learn how to speak for himself or herself to minimize the amount of mind reading the other family members must do (and often inaccurately). In this way, also, the counselor can learn each family member's version of his or her own story.

When Pat Whitlock attempted to introduce herself, she found *p* a difficult sound to pronounce. After a second or two of stuttering, Mrs. Whitlock broke in in a loud, impatient voice. "Now Pat, take a deep breath and speak slowly, or you'll never learn to stop stuttering." She turned to the counselor and explained, "Pat doesn't need to stutter. She never stutters when she takes a deep breath first and slows down. She just tries to say everything so fast." "We'll come back to Pat when she's ready," the counselor commented. "Pat, you tell me when you are ready," the counselor continued. And then the counselor went around to each member of the family and asked for names. The counselor checked with Pat visually and observed that Pat was not yet ready to speak. She had a hunch that Pat needed to feel safe. The counselor then turned to Mr. Whitlock. "Mr. Whitlock, I'm wondering what it is that you hope will change for you and your family." This statement contains an embedded question that assumes that the father has hopes for change that may not necessarily be the same as the mother's. The question is aimed intentionally at Mr. Whitlock because all too often in the American family the male is excluded from important family transactions, partly because his primary work is considered to take place outside the home. Mrs. Whitlock has already demonstrated dominance in the family arena through her verbal intrusiveness, so the counselor feels it is important to bring the father into the conversation.

Mr. Whitlock responded that the problem as he saw it was out of the province of the counselor to help. His daughter was having problems in school as his wife said, but he knew that she was an intelligent girl and she was just a little lazy this year. Lots of children go through periods of being lazy. That was the same reason she was fat—she lacked self-discipline. She'd outgrow it. He wasn't concerned. What did bother him was his health. His stomach constantly bothered him. But, he repeated, he certainly didn't expect a family counselor to be much help with that. Moreover, he hated his job, and the counselor couldn't do anything about that either. These children all had to get to college, and the first one would start in 2 years. Time was passing fast, and the savings account looked pretty inadequate to put four children through college. However, if his wife thought that counseling was important for Susan and the agency asked him to come too, he wouldn't object. But he sure was upset about the cost. (Mr. Whitlock was already demonstrating potential for change—he was unhappy, he knew it, and when given an opportunity to express himself, words came flooding out. But his attitude, while overtly cooperative, came across like that of a self-perceived martyr, who was good enough to sacrifice himself but who would let his family know subtly that he was being wronged.)

"Now, Sam," interrupts Mrs. Whitlock, "you know you're just being a hypochondriac about your stomach. The doctor says there's nothing wrong with you. And you've got a good job. You always find something wrong with your boss, no matter who he is. And we're lucky all our children are bright and college material."

Mr. Whitlock spills out his words when elicited, the counselor notes, but Mrs. Whitlock has just cut him off. Is this by coincidence, or is it an ongoing pattern? This is something to check out over time.

The counselor now asks the oldest son, Lacey, what he experiences as a problem in the family. "We're okay," he responds, "only Dad's always afraid I'm going to screw my girlfriend, and Mom doesn't like her because of her religion . . ."

"And," interrupts Mrs. Whitlock, "she's skinny and she'll grow up to look worse. You can tell by what her own mother looks like. I can't imagine marrying a woman like that—that's why I keep my figure, so that the boys who date my girls can see that I'm . . ."

"But Mother," interrupts her son, "who says I'm going to marry her?"

"It's not a matter of wanting to marry her," Mrs. Whitlock retorts. "She's just the kind of girl who would try to trap you, just trap you—you're too young to understand . . ."

"I understand exactly what you mean," Lacey replies angrily. "You think she's going to get pregnant. That's crazy. I know what I'm doing!"

"Well," says Mother, looking vacant. Silence ensues.

The oldest son can stop Mother, the counselor notes. Father is silent and fidgeting.

Both parents are apparently worried about their older son's sexuality. How satisfactory is their own sexual relationship?

"How do you feel about Susan's problem?" the counselor asks Lacey. "She's okay, just a little too fat," he replies. "She'll be a knockout someday." "Anything else?" probes the counselor. "Nope," responds Lacey.

The counselor turns to Pat and asks how she feels about the family situation. Pat begins to respond, "Susan isn't v-very happy when k-k-kids t-tease her. K-kids are mean, and I tr-try to k-k- . . ."

"Now Pat, take a deep breath . . ." says Mother.

The counselor intervenes, "Let Pat keep going. I'm interested in what she has to say. You find that kids are mean sometimes, Pat, and what do you try to do about it?" "Tr-try to k-k-keep to myself a lot. The gym t-t-teacher lets me run on th-the t-track by m-m-my-self whenever I want t-t-to, and I run alone during study halls and by m-myself a lot after school. I hate school." Pat has said that she hates school clearly and effectively.

"You hate school, but you stay there when school is out in the afternoon?"

"Well, M-M-Mom w-w-won't let us stay in the house . . ."

Mrs. Whitlock breaks in. "She drives me crazy when she's home. All she does is sit in her room with the door closed and the radio blaring. Children need fresh air to stay healthy. I make her go out in the afternoon for her own good. All of the children have to get fresh air after school. That's my job, to keep them healthy until they know better. They'll thank me someday. A woman's place is in the home."

"I see," responds the counselor, noting to herself that Mother apparently holds a very traditional view of marriage. "But I don't believe that Pat is finished. Pat, go on."

"W-W-Well," says Pat, "th-th-that's ab-b-bout i-i-it."

Pat has been effectively silenced by Mother, notes the counselor. And she seems to stutter a little worse after each interruption.

"George," says the counselor, "please feel free to share with us what you think hurts in your family."

"Aw," says George looking at his toes, and then he starts to cry. "George," says Mr. Whitlock, "don't act like a baby." George drops his head and shoulders further.

Father has not scolded Pat, his apparent ally, for her stuttering. Mother has. But Father has ordered his youngest son to hide his feelings, just as Mother ordered Father to hide his feelings. Is it possible that Father tries to maintain his self-esteem by putting down his youngest son?

"He-he-he-he's n-n-not acting l-l-like a b-baby," says Pat. Interestingly, Pat, although apparently part of a coalition with the father, is now allying herself with George, with considerable personal effort.

George stops crying but continues to look at his toes with a theatrically tragic look on his face. Even with encouragement by the counselor, he won't say a word. He does look up at the counselor once or twice with big moist eyes, a pathetic, almost doglike expression warping his features.

"Susan," asks the counselor, "what makes you feel unhappy at times? I understand that sometimes you talk about being very unhappy, and that is why the family came here tonight." "Oh, not at home," states Susan firmly. "I never say anything at home. My teacher told on me. I thought she wouldn't tell, but she went and called Mom and she must have told her everything I said. I'm not going to talk to anybody anymore. Nothing's the matter with me except I wish I weren't so fat. But Mom says sometimes she's so upset she might as well commit suicide, and nobody cares."

At this point Mrs. Whitlock begins to cry loudly and insistently. "Now everybody's going to blame me," she sobs, "and I'm only trying to help as best I know how. Here I work hard trying to get everybody in here for this appointment, and nobody has even asked me what I think the problem is even though I tried to explain right when I got here. Just listen to her, saying that I've threatened to commit suicide, like it was all my idea. Susan, you know I never meant it, and you are a very naughty child for talking about that here." (The session is overtaken by several minutes of loud sobbing by Mother. The counselor gets a box of tissues.)

Mother has now effectively shut off Susan, as she has shut off Father, George, and Pat. Only Lacey has been able to gain the upper hand with her in this session, but Lacey's life is clearly far from his own. Now is not the time to bring this communication pattern to the attention of Mother and the family. Mother, although she is effectively manipulating (controlling everyone's attention and silencing others), is genuinely hurting.

The usual introductory social phase of an initial interview has been almost omitted in this particular session, because Mother immediately attempted to control the input of information to the counselor. The counselor has had to intervene immediately to model and elicit new communication patterns, asking for information from each family member directly rather than permitting that information to come through Mother. Now, of course, the counselor must intervene again. Any suicide threat in a counseling session must be addressed. "Mrs. Whitlock," the social worker begins, "suicide is always a worrisome threat. "I must ask you now: do you have any plans to carry out this threat?"

"Of course not," Mrs. Whitlock replies through angry tears. "I'm just trying to get people to do what I tell them."

"Let me ask again, to be sure," the counselor continues. "Have you ever made a plan to commit suicide? Have you thought of any means to do it?"

"I told you before," retorted the mother. "Of course I haven't."

"How about you, Susan?" asked the counselor. "Have you ever made a real plan to commit suicide?"

Susan looks startled "Oh no," she said, "it's just something you say when you get mad."

"I'm glad to hear that neither one of you intends to hurt yourself," the counselor replies, "and I'm sure your family is glad to hear this too."

The problem exploration phase of this interview has yielded rich data for the counselor. The family as a whole reveals itself as a system under considerable stress. Once the counselor has determined that the suicide threats are threats only (neither Mrs. Whitlock nor Susan actually intends to carry out such an act; neither has identified a means to do so), the social worker will work toward decreasing the immediate stress caused by the counseling session itself. Her goal at this point is to enable the family to decide to return for additional sessions.

Kleenex tissues and reassurance of the mother that she is capable and admirable, having produced four fine children, will mollify her and reestablish her position of family dominance, which will return the family to its normal homeostasis. In future interviews, the task will be to upset this same homeostasis because it manifestly inhibits self-expression and personal growth in every member of the family. The intervention goal for the future will be to restructure the rules and interactional patterns of the family system into a more satisfying and growth-enhancing system, with high rather than low morale or self-esteem among the members.

The basic purpose of an initial session is beginning problem definition, at least to the stage of the presenting problem; basic fact-finding related to the presenting problems, which one hopes will reveal clues about contributing underlying systemic factors; and helping the family to begin to trust the counselor. The counselor and family also need to work out a tentative initial contract, defining the initial "problem for work," the respective roles of the counselor and family, specification of who will be included in the interviews, fees, places of meeting, frequency and time of appointments, and so forth.

In the latter part of this initial interview, the counselor will endeavor to reduce the family's (particularly the mother's) fear of family counseling by helping them see the counselor's role as that of partner in problem solving, rather than judge. She can reassure the family that when pain is present, it is reasonable and normal to seek outside consultation to gain relief. The counselor will list several family strengths: intelligence, caring, ability to work hard, sense of responsibility, ability to present thoughts verbally (and the clear potential for those less comfortable with speaking, Pat and George, to develop the ability to do so).

The counselor will then help the family develop an initial commitment to counseling. Is the family willing to invest the time and effort necessary to make their family circumstances better? Can the family afford the fee (perhaps a sliding scale is available to alleviate worries about cost)? If the family is willing to enter into a contract to meet with the counselor for general improvement of family functioning, this is a useful and open-ended agreement. If the family is willing to meet with the counselor only on the more limited problem of learning how to help Susan, this is a valid contract also. If the entire family will agree to meet together regarding how to help Susan, then Susan becomes the key to working with the family. Later, the counselor may recontract with the parents: "It is becoming clearer that Susan's unhappiness has something to do with the fact that you, Mr. Whitlock, and you, Mrs. Whitlock, are not very happy yourselves, and that you sometimes are not happy about certain things concerning each other. I think it would be a good idea to talk about you and your relationship together. How about it?" When Mr. and Mrs. Whitlock have come to trust the counselor and her concern for them, they will more likely be willing to admit that they have a problem between themselves.

CONTINUING THE COUNSELING PROCESS: THE WHITLOCK FAMILY

For a counselor to work effectively with the Whitlocks (or any family), he or she will have to create a safe setting for interaction, a setting in which all members reduce their fearfulness and recognize that their attempts at communication will be received empathetically and nonjudgmentally. Reducing fear reduces the need for defensiveness. The counselor will need to structure the interviews with certain rules that help decrease the threat for all members, from very basic ones such as "no hitting," to more complex ones such as "each person here speaks for herself or himself."

The counselor needs to know how to ask for information in such a way that the person is enabled to answer. Questions that a family member may not feel safe to answer early in counseling may be necessary and possible later when trust is firmer. Techniques such as the use of embedded questions, which clearly verbalize the counselor's question without demanding or otherwise putting the client on the spot, are helpful, as are questions that ask for a description or clarification rather than a simple yes or no answer.

A feeling of safety in the counseling setting can also be enhanced by counselors' demonstrating that they are not afraid to discuss or observe issues that are emotion laden and by offering support as family members experience the fears, stresses, and strains of life itself and of the experience of counseling. Counselors also must be able to demonstrate that they will not be sucked into the family system with its destructive operational patterns. Use of a cocounselor on occasion can be very helpful in avoiding the pitfall of becoming too intimate a part of the family system rather than a change agent for the system. Also useful is a one-way mirror through which another team member can watch the session; this person can then enter the counseling room to discuss his or her observations. Also, the interview can be taped or videotaped so that the counselor, the family, or both can study it later.

Family interactional patterns and rules resist change. Merely "diagnosing" the nonfunctional behavior patterns and communication systems and telling family members about them will not be sufficient to create change. Family members need more than an intellectual grasp of their respective roles in maintaining dysfunctional family patterns. However, counselors must understand the patterns and rules of the ongoing family system if they are to select appropriate intervention techniques to change the system. Hence, counselors need to observe how the family interacts, so they will insist that family members talk with each other in the sessions. Where an identified client or scapegoat is present, counselors will try to understand the function of that individual in maintaining the system.

Often, the term *scapegoat* is used in a more limited sense than the term *identified client*. A child identified as a scapegoat is usually a child *blamed* by the rest of family for a series of misdemeanors that make the family angry at him or her: bad behavior, instigating family arguments, and so forth. The term *identified client* includes the scapegoat but can also include children whom other family members apparently do not blame for creating problems for anybody except themselves. They merely see the child as having embarrassing or self-destructive problems, such as obesity, suicidal tendencies, or anorexia nervosa.

In the Whitlock family, Susan is clearly the identified client, but why Susan, and what function does she perform? Other persons in the family could have been presented as the identified client: Pat, for one, because of her stuttering and extreme social discomfort, and Father, for another, because of his feelings of hopelessness and his physical problems, which appear to be psychosomatic in origin (that is, largely caused by stress). It is probable that Susan became the identified client in this case because she is manifesting Mother's own fantasies, "committing suicide."

The Whitlocks' counselor chooses to begin with a structural approach, combined with techniques derived from a communication model. She studies patterns of interaction in the family as a whole to determine what factors maintain Susan's symptomatic behavior. Further interviews reveal that Mother feels stressed and unappreciated, even though she is clearly the dominant parent and in that role is key to the family pain. Mother makes the decisions in this family. But what factors led to this situation? First, Mrs. Whitlock is at home all day every day, often alone, and Mr. Whitlock, who has a difficult job away from home, expects her to manage the household (chores and children) all by herself. In addition, Mrs. Whitlock, the only child of an elderly parent, learned when she was young that she could get anything she wanted by displaying fits of temper. Mr. Whitlock, however, was a middle child in a large family controlled by a very dominant male parent. No matter what he did, he didn't get the material things or the affection he wanted, so he withdrew and felt hopeless during much of his childhood. Mr. Whitlock feels he was shortchanged as a child, deprived of appreciation and nurturing, and that these are now owed him. Because they are not forthcoming from either his parents or his wife, he plays the martyr role.

The combination of an aggressive wife and a withdrawn, placating husband developed into an increasingly rigid behavioral pattern. On the surface of things, Mrs. Whitlock got everything she wanted, and Mr. Whitlock did her bidding. However, he was able to send effective messages to his wife that he did not appreciate how he was treated. Mr. Whitlock feels used and unappreciated; Mrs. Whitlock feels lonely and misunderstood. The spousal subsystem is clearly stressed.

A family pattern has developed in which everyone's self-esteem remains low and rules are rigid (set by the mother). Everything goes through Mother and must be approved by her before communication is considered valid. All males in the Whitlock family, at the time of entrance to counseling, respond by withdrawing in one way or another, and Pat also withdraws, through her stuttering. Only Susan is emotionally bonded with Mrs. Whitlock.

It is interesting to note how cultural norms for male and female gender roles affect the Whitlocks' life and emotions, helping produce some of the unhappiness and confusion of various family members. Mrs. Whitlock isn't happy, but she cannot openly admit her unhappiness to herself and thus examine the causes because she is doing exactly what she has been taught she should want to do: be a wife and a mother.

She thinks she ought to feel happy and spends a lot of energy telling herself and everybody else how happy she is and what a fine family she has. However, when her husband or children try to defy her strong will, she feels desperate and deserted and breaks into tears, threatening to commit suicide because "nobody cares about me around here." Because four children and one husband add up to five against one, incidents of defiance do occur with reasonable regularity, even with Mother the very dominant and controlling personality. However, Mother's tears, angry words, and accusations usually bring her the desired results. She wins each battle at the price of standing alone. Nobody dares to get emotionally close to her. All defend themselves against her.

Mother's closest emotional bond is with her 10-year-old daughter, Susan, who feels her mother's loneliness. Susan becomes fearful of leaving Mother (does poorly in school, stays home from school a lot), talks about suicide with her teacher when she does attend school (the environment in which she consciously feels the most stressed), and overeats. Susan's problem then has the function of manifesting Mother's unhappiness as well as her own.

Susan's problems are the ones recognized by the family quite simply because Mother is the parent with the power to recognize them. She is the dominant parent and thus can make the decision to take Susan to therapy when almost nobody else wants to go. Mother will want to help Susan because she feels a bond with Susan. She will not necessarily recognize that Susan's problems reveal her own distress, although this realization comes very close to the surface in the first interview.

Further interviews reveal that Mr. Whitlock feels alienated from and angry with his wife. He feels she has put him in an impossible position. He hates his work but believes he has to work to support his family. His gender-role norm dictates that monetary support of the family is up to him, or he is a failure. He feels responsible to support his children, but he sometimes wishes they hadn't been born. He feels stuck, and because Mrs. Whitlock "made" him have a large family, everything is her fault. To do his duty to his family, he will have to continue to do work he dislikes forever. He is extremely resentful. He can't express his resentment toward his wife overtly because she is too powerful. She verbally puts him down whenever he expresses resentment, or she bursts into tears and threatens suicide. Besides, she can make him feel very guilty about his wish to have had fewer children. How can he not want George and Susan? Sometimes Mr. Whitlock expresses his resentment toward his children in subtle ways—by criticizing Lacey's relationship with his girlfriend or George's hypersensitivity. Mr. Whitlock is also developing somatic problems—taking out on his own body what he cannot express against the significant others in his life. This happens because his constant tension affects his body chemistry.

Continued counseling sessions reveal clear coalitions or subsystems within the family: Father and Pat, Mother and Susan, Mother and Lacey (not as strong), Pat and George, which occasionally conflicts with Pat and Father. Father has little or no relationship with Lacey because of competition for influence with the mother. Lacey can get his way with Mother more than Father can. Mother respects Lacey more than she respects Father, for Lacey is a successful leader at school and a social success, although she disapproves of all the girls he dates. Father avoids George and Susan. He feels too tired to play with them when he comes home from work, although they are still little enough that at times they ask for his attention. Mother has little or no relationship with Pat, except to criticize her social awkwardness, her stuttering, and her appearance. Mother does not think Pat is a very good family showpiece. She is obviously awkward.

The normal *natural* subsystems do not manifest themselves in this family. The husband-wife, or spouse, subsystem exists only minimally: Father brings home the income, and Mother takes care of the housework and the children. Emotionally they do not satisfy each other's basic needs, and each feels resentful about what he or she is not getting (appreciation, love, and so forth). Each feels unjustly treated. However, Mr. and Mrs. Whitlock are also both fearful of completely losing each other, the only scrap of adult sustenance they have. Once Mother did run off with Susan to her father's home, terrifying Mr. Whitlock that he would be left having to hire a baby-sitter to take care of

George. She came home, however, and no one spoke of the incident thereafter until it finally came up in counseling. Mrs. Whitlock had hoped that her leaving would make Mr. Whitlock more attentive, but after the first stir, nothing changed. Mr. Whitlock felt he was already doing more than could be reasonably expected of him in holding up his end of the family bargain. Only Mr. Whitlock's fear of the unknown and his strong conservative values keep him from leaving his family. He feels he doesn't love Mrs. Whitlock any longer, although he doesn't admit it to her. He hasn't attempted a sexual relationship for years; she demeans him as being impotent. In fact, anger and fear of another pregnancy have created Mr. Whitlock's main sexual problem. Being ignored sexually, of course, effectively communicated to Mrs. Whitlock her husband's displeasure with her.

The children do not form a normal subsystem, either. Only Pat and George have even a minimal bond between them, and this is actually a substitute parent bond. Neither Mr. nor Mrs. Whitlock feels close to George—each has other favorites. George is alone except for Pat; their relationship has to be parental in nature as Pat is 7 years older. However, she cannot provide George with much protection because no one can stand up to Mother's anger except Lacey. The isolation is frightening for the little boy, and when he begins counseling he is effectively speechless. Mother's dominance has, in fact, kept all the children separate. She doesn't permit the children any sort of conflict in her presence, which creates an emotional separation among the children. Rather than help them solve problems of conflict together, so they can learn how to communicate and to resolve their differences constructively, she separates them and punishes them individually for quarreling. She also doesn't permit the children to stay inside the house during the day except to do chores, because they irritate her. The children actually don't have much time together. Mr. Whitlock, although he often disapproves of his wife's parenting when he is present to observe it, rarely offers any parenting of his own, corrective or otherwise. Lacey has no strong relationship with any sibling, nor does Susan. It is every child for himself or herself.

Contributions from Cognitive-Behavioral Theory

Thus far the social worker assisting the Whitlocks has been analyzing the family system using perspectives derived from communication and structural approaches. However, cognitive-behavioral theory also provides important insights. For example, much of the pain in this family derives from negative and/or irrational thoughts. Among these:

Mrs. Whitlock thinks that it is acceptable to model uncontrolled rage.

Mrs. Whitlock thinks that it is acceptable to utter suicidal thoughts out loud to help control her family members.

Mrs. Whitlock thinks that a woman's place is (only) in the home.

Mr. Whitlock thinks it is hopeless to confront his wife, that she is invincible just as his parents were when he was a little boy.

Both parents think it is Mr. Whitlock's responsibility to financially support the family on his own.

Both parents think that all four children must go to college right after high school.

Everyone in the family thinks he/she is unloved (misunderstood; unappreciated).

Part of the work of counselor is to confront these and other negative or irrational thoughts.

RESTRUCTURING THE FAMILY SYSTEM: THE WHITLOCK FAMILY

In this household of isolated individuals, it is clear that the family subsystems need to be restructured. First and foremost, the husband-wife bond needs to be strengthened and made primary to provide the protection and nurturance the children need.

For this to be achieved, however, the lopsided dominance relationship between Mr. and Mrs. Whitlock needs to be altered. The goal is not to switch dominance roles but rather to achieve a relationship in which each partner develops new respect and care for the other. Ideally, the relationship between the spouses will become egalitarian.

How might such a goal be achieved? Family counselors today often borrow from a wide variety of theoretical perspectives as needed. The Whitlocks' counselor, while primarily utilizing perspectives from communication and structural theories, decides to use tools from cognitive-behavioral theory. She recognizes that cognitive restructuring could be helpful for this family, beginning with Mrs. Whitlock's belief that it is acceptable for her to model threats of suicide and also to model uncontrolled rage. The counselor suspects that these practices of Mrs. Whitlock are not only harmful for the children but also block the development of a close relationship with her husband, who resents these practices.

It will be recalled that the social worker determined in the first counseling session that Mrs. Whitlock's threats of suicide are only that, threats; she has no actual plans or means to carry out such an action. Mrs. Whitlock uses these threats as her habitual response to frustration. Susan, copying her mother, has learned to threaten suicide when she encounters disappointment or upset (in her case, at school).

To help alter these dysfunctional behaviors, the social worker asks Mrs. Whitlock directly if she has any idea how Susan might have learned to threaten suicide. Mrs. Whitlock first looks uncomfortable, and then becomes very still. Her eyes fill with tears. She does not break into strategic sobbing as she did in the first session, however. Finally she says softly, "I guess she learned it from me."

The counselor nods soberly, and then asks, "Is this the kind of behavior you really want to model for your daughter, what you really want to teach Susan by your example?"

"No, of course not," the mother replies thoughtfully.

"Then I believe it is time for you to talk with Susan about threatening suicide," the counselor continues. "What do you want to say about that habit as you think about it here?"

A serious conversation ensues with Susan that spreads to the entire family. Finally, Mrs. Whitlock promises to stop her suicide threats, and urges Susan to do the same. As the counselor begins to praise this decision, however, Mrs. Whitlock asks what she should do now when her children do not obey her. The counselor validates Mrs. Whitlock by saying that every mother does need to manage her children. She asks the family to discuss what types of family management techniques might be effective in the family if suicide threats are no longer to be used. After much debate, an agreement is reached that both parents consider using timeouts with the younger children, rational discussion and contingency contracting with the older, and rewards for desired behaviors for all.

In the next session, the counselor again focuses on cognitive restructuring. She helps Mrs. Whitlock to think about her use of rage as a family management technique. The counselor points out that while Mrs. Whitlock's eruptions of rage may get her what she wants in the short run, they isolate her from the rest of her family in the long run. The counselor directs Mr. Whitlock to examine his own irrational thoughts also: he is no longer a small boy. He does have the power to stand up to his wife now that he is an adult, and, moreover, at times his children need him to protect them from their mother's rage. Mr. Whitlock can model self-control by refusing to withdraw in the face of his wife's anger and by remaining calm but firm. Regarding discipline of the children, both parents are counseled to experiment with the family management techniques suggested in the previous session.

Now that some of the Whitlocks' irrational thoughts and behaviors affecting family function have been brought to the light of day, the counselor senses that the time has come to work toward restructuring the subsystems in the family. Although the parental subsystem has been truncated to date so that it effectively consists of Mother only, Father may be ready to step in and take his rightful (and badly needed) place.

Moreover, the boundary between the spouse subsystem and the sibling subsystem is enmeshed. Mrs. Whitlock and Lacey, and Mr. Whitlock and Pat, are more involved emotionally than the two spouses are with each other. Such a lack of boundary between the spouse subsystem and the sibling subsystem can only be frightening and confusing to the children and to the marital pair as well.

The children could benefit by a strengthening of their subsystem as well. If the bonds among the children were stronger or their bonds with peers outside the family were stronger, their dependence on the emotional situation between their parents would not be so profound.

Restructuring a family system and creating a fulfilling family theme are difficult tasks. Certain techniques can help a family prepare for change, however. Family members can watch themselves interact on videotape, which can sensitize them to how they come across to each other. Even an audiotape recording can be very helpful for this purpose. Family members can also be separated from the rest of the family and allowed to observe family interaction patterns from behind a one-way mirror. Or a subgroup in the role of observers can sit behind the rest of the family as they interact. At the end of the specified interaction, the people in the subgroup can provide feedback to the rest of the family on the communication patterns they observe.

The counselor can have various members of the family group reenact conflicts through role-play. Role-play brings the conflicts right into the therapy room. But in role-play situations, there is opportunity to reconstruct the scenes. The counselor may choose to model more constructive ways of handling conflict or may instruct family members to reenact the scene but perform different or reversed roles. The counselor may have a child play the role of a parent in instances where discipline is an issue, may have the respective parent play the child, and so forth. Role-play offers the possibility of practicing new and more constructive methods of conflict resolution and of developing empathy for the other person's point of view.

In the counseling sessions, the counselor may choose to escalate stress to break a nonproductive stalemate in a family conflict. Escalation of stress can temporarily break an unhealthy pattern of interaction. For example, in the Whitlock family situation, the counselor might side with Father on every issue until Mother explodes; the counselor can then deal with the function of tears and threats and discuss and demonstrate other means of conflict resolution. Or the counselor may side with the mother on every issue until the father is goaded into changing his habitual pattern of placation and martyrdom and finally becomes angry enough to defend himself. The counselor can then observe his method of expressing angry feelings and learn why they are normally so ineffective in this particular family. New methods of self-assertion may be discussed, demonstrated, and practiced (Minuchin & Fishman, 1981, p. 179).

The counselor may take on an educator's role, explaining how apparent success at dominating and getting what a person wants in the short run can rob him or her of the goodwill of significant others, eventually resulting in isolation (no one left to dominate), as is happening between Mr. and Mrs. Whitlock. Development of a three-generational genogram can be helpful in exploring the genesis of these circumstances. To fortify the intellectual understanding, simulation and role-play games can also be used.

Satir (1972), for example, used family sculpting and communication games in which she had appropriate members of the family model the stance and nonverbal gestures of the placater, the blamer, the computer, and the distractor (Satir, 1972, pp. 59–79). Thus, Mrs. Whitlock would initially be assigned the role of the blamer. The counselor would help her position her body so that the nonverbal symbols of blaming would be highlighted and magnified—the pointed finger, twisted face, and so forth. Mr. Whitlock would be arranged as the placater, kneeling, open hand upward, and so forth. Lacey could be the distractor, looking off in an irrelevant direction, whistling, and so on, and Pat the computer (stiff body, upright spine). The next step is to act out the corresponding roles. Satir suggested role-playing the communication stereotypes in triads, keeping sessions to approximately 5 minutes in length. The family chooses the problem to communicate about, but each role player must stick to his or her role in a given role-play situation.

The very humor of some of the games and the surprises revealed through observing themselves on audiotape or videotape can loosen the rigid defenses of individual family members and break up the rigidity of the old communication patterns. Among the Whitlocks, a communication pattern exists in which Mrs. Whitlock plays blamer, Mr. Whitlock placater, and the children shift between the placater and the distractor roles in the real family situation. Through practice and demonstration, they can shift these patterns toward the more ideal interaction pattern that Satir called "leveling" or "telling it like it is."

Mrs. Whitlock also creates a typical double-bind situation for everyone. She insists that people shouldn't speak unless they have something pleasant to say. She also tells them people worth their salt are honest and should be frank, like herself. If she then asks a family member to express an opinion on something she has done (such as, "Look at the new dress I made, what do you think of it?") to get some attention that she craves, that family member will be in a double bind if he or she dislikes the dress. If the person lies and says the dress is lovely, that person will feel bad for lying. If the person is frank and honest, Mother feels unappreciated, becomes angry, and berates that family member. It is a "damned if you do, damned if you don't" communication system.

Because Mrs. Whitlock frequently places other family members in double-bind situations, they have learned to avoid real communication with her. They are experts at evasiveness ("I'm sure you must have worked hard on it, Mother") or at disappearing, either through silence, stuttering, or through activities away from home. Lacey generally chooses the last, by remaining as uninvolved as possible. The toll is great, even on Lacey, because he needs the nurturance and protection a family should provide. Moreover, Mrs. Whitlock is openly critical of all his friends, and Lacey can't always silence her. Mother recognizes that Lacey prefers his friends to her.

The toll is also great on Mrs. Whitlock, driving her to distress. Nobody levels with her, and she knows it. She has no idea that she creates double binds and thus has no idea of her own role in driving her family away. She can learn to identify the setup, however, through audiotapes, videotapes, and role-play, and she can then decide which she really wants most—a real relationship with her family or placation and rote obedience. She will need courage and persistence to break her patterns of relationship. It is hard to change, and besides, a dominant role provides a lot of immediate rewards.

The counselor identifies a destructive family communication "loop" involving Mother. Mother usually has to initiate verbal exchange if she wants verbal communication because of the various types of withdrawal of the rest of the family. But then when she succeeds in eliciting responses, she criticizes them, precipitating a new withdrawal response. The new withdrawal response angers her, and she criticizes further, usually in language conveying "I'm only telling you this because I love you." Her words are of love, but her voice tone and facial expression are of anger. Family members generally believe the visual communication cues rather than the verbal and respond as if attacked: Lacey by attacking in return, the others by further withdrawal, precipitating a new destructive communication loop, with Mother forcing a new response to try to maintain contact, being displeased with the response, and criticizing it. Pat and George effectively solve this problem by being unable to speak in their own various ways, so it is harder for Mother to "hook" them. Not surprisingly, Mrs. Whitlock feels closer to Lacey and Susan.

To break the loop, all family members have to recognize it intellectually. Then they have to practice new patterns of communication, using techniques of role-play and modeling by the counselor. Mrs. Whitlock's control of the communication process has to be blocked. The process will take a great deal of energy and commitment from the family. The person for whom new self-assertion will be hardest is Mr. Whitlock, because even though he has realized through previous cognitive restructuring work that he has the capability to stand up to his wife (he is no longer a small boy confronting big parents), to do so will involve determination and practice.

To help strengthen the marital bond, the counselor now assigns tasks to Mr. and Mrs. Whitlock that they are to do together without the children. Lacey is old enough to baby-sit, so the parents are instructed to go away together on several different weekends. Lacey agrees with enthusiasm to a contingency contract: in return for babysitting, Mr. Whitlock will teach him to drive. Like virtually all 16-year-olds, Lacey is eager to learn this new skill. Driving together, of course, will improve the relationship between Mr. Whitlock and Lacey.

The counselor engages the couple in a discussion of their lengthy sexual abstinence and brings the fear of pregnancy out into the open. Fear of pregnancy is discussed early in the counseling process, and Mr. and Mrs. Whitlock agree to share responsibility for birth control. Fortunately they don't have to cope with negative religious values in this area. Some sexual activity resumes. Later in the counseling process, as part of discussions of the functions of sex in the marriage as a means of communicating approval or disapproval, Mr. Whitlock will realize that he is equally responsible with his wife for procreating four children. Gradually he lets go of most of his resentment toward his wife for "insisting" on having the children. He begins to understand that his children crave his love and attention, which makes him feel more important in the family constellation.

Lacey's baby-sitting responsibilities will involve him more closely with the sibling system without bringing him in competition with Mrs. Whitlock. Attention from Lacey pleases all the children and helps strengthen the sibling system. Another related task the counselor assigns is for Mrs. Whitlock to take time outside of her family system without her children, leaving Mr. Whitlock in charge, strengthening his bond with the children and weakening her total dependence on child rearing as her only meaning in life. The counselor also meets with Susan and her teacher (as soon as possible after the commencement of the family counseling) to discuss ways to overcome her fear of school. A "big sister," who also acts as a tutor, is found for Susan. (A major and very important difference between social workers doing family counseling and professionals from other backgrounds such as psychology doing similar work is that social workers are much more likely to involve resources from the wider environment. That is because social workers are educated to use a "person-in-environment" perspective.)

An opening for working with another irrational family thought or belief arises. As mentioned earlier, Mrs. Whitlock openly verbalizes that "a woman's place is in the home." Her family has accepted this pronouncement without challenge, although such a role description is certainly very traditional and conservative. Because the mother repeats it often, however, it has become a virtual "family story."

The therapist decides to explore the belief. "Where did it come from?" she asks after repeating it during a session.

"Why, my mother told me," responds Mrs. Whitlock, obviously surprised at the question. "My mother always said a woman's place was in the home."

"Was your mother a full-time homemaker?"

"Yes, of course she was. In her generation everybody was."

"How happy was your mother as a full-time homemaker?"

"Very happy, of cour—" Mrs. Whitlock begins. And then she stops and begins to frown.

She continues slowly. "Actually, my mother had a beautiful contralto voice. She wanted to be a singer. She even began taking voice lessons, but her father made her stop. When I was a child Mother sang solos in church every Sunday, but I always knew she wanted to do more, to sing professionally. She died pretty young; her health was never very good, as I remember."

"Could your mother's health have been affected by frustration, perhaps frustration of her desire to be a singer?"

A vacant look comes over Mrs. Whitlock's face. This is difficult for her to think about. "I suppose so," she says at last.

After a lengthy pause, the counselor continues. "You know, times are changing. Many people today believe that a woman's place is anywhere she wants to be."

"But a mother must be available to supervise her children."

"Yes," agrees the counselor, validating the mother before challenging her. "That's a very important responsibility for any parent. But I'm not sure it's the sole responsibility of the mother. Today, fathers expect to pitch in, or other arrangements for child care can be made. People believe that women, like men, have dreams they wish to accomplish outside the home. I'm wondering if there's anything else you've wanted to do—a hobby, a profession, something like that."

"Oh," Mrs. Whitlock replies promptly. "I do have a hobby, right now. I love to sew, to make home decorations, curtains, draperies, that sort of thing."

"That's an impressive talent," responds the counselor seriously. "Have you ever thought of turning it into a paid profession?"

"But what about the children—"

"*Have* you ever thought of turning your talent at interior decoration into a paid profession? You know, that would relieve your husband from having to carry the entire burden of supporting this family. Your children are old enough now to spend some time by themselves."

Mr. Whitlock speaks without being specifically addressed, a rare offering. "I must admit, Elsie, it would be a relief to me. I might be able to look for a different job if we had another financial provider in the family."

Startled, Mrs. Whitlock asks her husband, "You mean, you would like me to work outside our home, Harry?"

While the counselor doesn't comment on it here, use of given names rather than titles such as "Mother" and "Daddy" indicate that these two are now functioning as members of a spousal subsystem, not just the parental subsystem.

"Yes," Mr. Whitlock replies simply. "If you would consider it and if you could find a job you liked, of course."

"Maybe it's time to change the family story," suggests the counselor. "By that, I mean that I think you have been using 'a woman's place is in the home' as a sort of family story, and I'm not sure it fits anymore. Can you think of something that might work better for you now?"

Again, it is Mr. Whitlock who speaks. "How about something like, 'a woman's place is anywhere in the human race.'?" He grins and continues, "and that might include the rat race they call the job market."

Mrs. Whitlock looks hard at her husband. The children are amazed; they've rarely heard their father speak so frankly.

"A woman's place is anywhere in the human race," Mrs. Whitlock repeats slowly. "What would my mother think?" Then she looks directly at her husband. "Why," she says with a smile that seems almost shy, "I think she would have liked it."

"Can we consider this your new family story?" asks the counselor. "A new story with an important new idea to think about?"

Both parents nod, and the children grin, pleased. "It's about time," says Lacey.

At this point, the counselor senses the entire family is ready to talk about change. In the next few sessions, she will invite each family member to discuss his or her hopes for the future. An eco-map may be helpful at this time to identify the family's relationship to external resources and to identify new resources that may be beneficial.

It becomes clear that Pat is not excited about going to college but would prefer to work in a music store for a while. She thinks she might want to go to college someday but is willing to save some money in advance for it. However, she is certain her parents would insist on college attendance right after high school and hence has resented rather than appreciated her parents' real financial sacrifice on her behalf as they tried to save for her college expenses. George and Susan are too young to know what they think about college, but Mr. and Mrs. Whitlock recognize that their preoccupation with college for their children is more their own expectation (reflecting a societal status symbol) than a necessity. Lacey does want to go to college right after high school but is willing to pay some of his own expenses.

None of the children want Mr. Whitlock to continue working at a job he hates. They feel responsible for his misery and helpless to change it. Mother also recognizes that Father's unhappiness more than cancels out the benefits of his reliable and adequate income. Moreover, Mrs. Whitlock recognizes that she doesn't enjoy being in the home all day herself, that maybe her place isn't totally in the home, and that perhaps she could better use her time and energy by providing part of the family income. Once Mrs. Whitlock recognizes her irritation with child rearing without guilt, the family can make some shifts in its linkage with the economic market.

However, finding new work will not be easy for either Mr. or Mrs. Whitlock. This is a time when nearly 10% of the population is unemployed, and many more people barely survive on part-time work only. In such hard times, Mr. and Mrs. Whitlock decide to attend local workshops together to develop new resumes and improve their interviewing skills. Mr. Whitlock, after a number of unsuccessful job applications, finally decides to ask his current employer if he can change positions within the company. He has been a bank auditor and feels like a "snoop" in this work. Fortunately, his employer allows him to change to a loan officer position; he begins to enjoy helping people with their financial needs. Mrs. Whitlock eventually finds a part-time job as an interior decorator through networking with members of her church.

Due to reduced stress on the job and help from his wife in providing financially for the family, Mr. Whitlock's stomach pains cease. Mrs. Whitlock finds that she enjoys her new job; her demands on the children taper off. The children are happy with the changes, and begin to understand that seemingly hopeless circumstances can be altered. They begin to believe that they can influence their own futures.

MAINTENANCE OF GAINS AND TERMINATION OF COUNSELING: THE WHITLOCK FAMILY

Family counseling can often be effectively completed in a few weeks, but the problems of the Whitlocks required a longer time to resolve. They were fortunate in that their insurance policy was unusually generous, although they ended up paying for the last several sessions out-of-pocket. Counseling for the family continued for approximately a year, until Mr. Whitlock was established in a new position and Mrs. Whitlock was working part-time and able to release her rigid control on the family system. Important changes have taken place and are being maintained. Lacey works part-time, saving for college, and Pat seriously visits music stores with an eye toward future employment. She still stutters somewhat but is no longer reprimanded for it. Susan attends school regularly, doing average work scholastically, and no longer talks of suicide. George talks, at least occasionally. Every family member pitches in with the household chores, although Mrs. Whitlock still does all the cooking, which she enjoys. Mr. and Mrs. Whitlock regularly take time to do things as a couple, and even though they still disagree with each other frequently, they can talk with each other about their feelings and work out compromise solutions. At this point, termination of counseling became appropriate.

Termination itself requires preparation so that the family system won't revert to its old patterns of interaction, which can be brought on by distress precipitated by the withdrawal of the person (the counselor) who has been actively intervening to restructure the system. Discussion of termination must begin well in advance of its occurrence. Mutual evaluations by family members of where they came from at the beginning of counseling, where they are now, and where they would like to go ideally can be helpful. Assurance by the counselor of continued availability should the family feel the need is also helpful. A gradual tapering off of interview sessions—for example, from once a week to once every 2 weeks, with a final meeting a month or so later—may help reduce regression. (For further information on termination and evaluation, see Chapters 6, 7, and 11.)

SUMMARY

This chapter describes social work practice with families. A wide diversity of family patterns exists in the world. Although the nuclear family is still the predominant family form in our society, it is a serious mistake for social workers to use the nuclear family as the ideal model that individuals should strive to form. Many other family forms also function well and deserve respect.

Family patterns and forms are substantially affected by the culture (larger system) in which they are located. Families in our society perform the following functions that help maintain continuity and stability in society: replacement of the population, care of the young, socialization of new members, regulation of sexual behavior, and provision of affection.

An infinite number of problems can occur in families. When there are problems in a family, social services are often needed. There is extensive variation in the types and forms of services that social workers provide to troubled families.

The two areas in social work practice with families that have received the most attention are family assessment and family counseling. Two assessment techniques are described: eco-maps and genograms. An eco-map provides a snapshot view of important family interactions at a particular point in time. A genogram, essentially a family tree, is a graphic way of investigating the origins of family problems over at least three generations.

One of the many social services provided to families is family counseling. In this chapter, family counseling is defined, and four levels of family need are described that can assist the family worker to determine effective interventions. Characteristics of open and closed family systems are described. Coalitions and alliances between subsystems and members of subsystems are discussed, as well as ideas about how and why certain subsystems are formed and how behaviors of particular subsystems affect behaviors in others. The role of the identified client or scapegoat in helping maintain unhealthy family homeostasis and in serving as somewhat socially acceptable tickets of admission to counseling is explored and discussed in detail.

Two system approaches to family counseling are described and compared: Satir's and Minuchin's. Satir stressed clarification of family communication patterns. Satir pointed out incongruent messages and double binds to family members and taught family members to send clear, congruent messages instead. She analyzed rules in the family and helped clarify them in the context that rules may be bad but the people setting or bound by them are not. She taught family members how to change bad rules and insisted each member be heard in her presence, thus teaching respect for each person and each point of view. She emphasized that differentness between family members should be openly acknowledged and used for growth.

Minuchin's major emphasis in counseling is restructuring the major subsystems (spouse, parental, and sibling) within the family so that each can accomplish its appropriate functions. Minuchin is considered to be a member of the structural approach to family counseling. According to Minuchin, the parental, the spouse, and the sibling subsystems have different major functions that must be fulfilled if the family is to survive as a healthy unit. In restructuring the family, Minuchin had members consciously understand and improve communication patterns. Or he bypassed direct cognitive understanding by a family of its communication patterns and instead used a paradoxical suggestion.

In addition to systems approaches to family counseling, the chapter introduces cognitive-behavioral theory, which can provide important tools for any approach to family work. The chapter illustrates how these tools can be used by the systems-oriented counselor. Changes in family work in the early twenty-first century are addressed, in particular the blurring of theoretical approaches to family counseling, the changing role of the counselor from expert to partner, and the impact of managed care on access to family counseling services. The chapter examines the role of the social worker as change agent in the guise of family counselor, using the perspective of family counseling as an example of the problem-solving process in systems perspective.

EXERCISES

EP 2.1.7a

1. An Eco-Map of My Family

Goal: To gain insight into the dynamics of families using eco-maps.

Step 1: Draw an eco-map of your family.

Step 2: Volunteers share and describe their eco-maps.

Step 3: Class discussion about problems encountered and the merits and shortcomings of eco-maps.

EP 2.1.7a

2. A Genogram of My Family

Goal: To gain insight into the dynamics of families using genograms.

Step 1: Draw a genogram of your family.

Step 2: Volunteers share and describe their genograms.

Step 3: Class discussion on the problems encountered and the merits and shortcomings of genograms.

EP 2.1.7a

3. The Application of Systems Theory Concepts to a Family's Interaction[5]

Goal: To explore systems theory principles. Student volunteers are asked to assume specific roles in a family. The family is presented with three situations, and family members are asked to describe their reactions. Following each situation is a brief class discussion focusing on the identification of various systems concepts to describe family interactions.

Step 1: Role-play. Three groups of volunteers are needed. You can opt to role-play the three situations extemporaneously or rehearse them for next class.

Step 2: Class presentations of the role-play.

Step 3: Class discussion of how the family system might be affected in each of the three situations.

Rob: husband and father; age 41; calm, level-headed; makes most of the family's decisions; works as an accountant; makes an upper-middle-class income

Laura: wife and mother; age 35; pleasant, attractive, warm; typically follows Rob's lead; does not work outside the home

Benji: 15-year-old son; quiet, private, likes to spend time alone; has a few friends who tend to have a history of minor delinquencies; maintains a B– average in school

Susie: 10-year-old daughter; outgoing, personable; has numerous friends and interests; maintains an A average in school

1. Rob loses his job and the family is in serious financial difficulty.

   FAMILY MEMBERS' REACTIONS

   a. Stress due to economic conditions may cause Rob and Laura to have marital conflict. The spouse subsystem may be weakened.

[5]This exercise was written by Karen K. Kirst-Ashman Professor Emeritus, PhD, in Social Work Department, University of Wisconsin—Whitewater.

b. Benji and Susie may be confused and worried about the future.

c. All family members might be angry at the lack of funds for personal use.

SYSTEMS THEORY APPLICATIONS

a. Homeostasis within the system is disrupted.

b. Change affecting Rob affects the entire family system.

c. The system may change from being an open system with easy interchange of information across system boundaries to a closed system under stress. New information and input may no longer be easily assimilated.

2. Rob finds another comparable job. However, Laura finds a full-time job as a receptionist at a law firm. She decides she likes the additional income and the feeling of competence and independence that the job provides.

FAMILY MEMBERS' REACTIONS

a. Rob may resent Laura's newfound sense of independence. The spouse subsystem may be further disrupted.

b. The children may resent not having a mother doing things for them at home more regularly.

c. All family members may feel more pressure to participate in household tasks when they are at home.

SYSTEMS THEORY APPLICATIONS

a. The parental subsystem may be disturbed as a result of the change in roles.

b. Boundaries within the system may change. Rob, Benji, and Susie may form a new subsystem in reaction to Laura's absence.

3. The school vice principal calls and complains that Benji has fallen asleep in his class several times and that a bottle of Southern Comfort was found in his school locker.

FAMILY MEMBERS' REACTIONS

a. Rob and Laura are shocked and worried about what to do.

b. Benji may feel isolated and become even more withdrawn.

c. Susie may become very worried about Benji and approach him to offer any help she can give.

SYSTEMS THEORY APPLICATIONS

a. Homeostasis within the family system has been disturbed.

b. The parental subsystem may be strengthened to combat this newly defined problem.

c. The sibling subsystem may be strengthened if Benji and Susie form an alliance.

d. The entire family system may have to become a more open system to work with outside resources to solve the problem. The schools, a counselor or therapist, or Alcoholics Anonymous may become involved in problem solving.

COMPETENCY NOTES

The following identifies where Educational Policy (EP) Competencies and practice behaviors are discussed in the chapter.

EP 2.1.7a *Utilize conceptual frameworks to guide the process of assessment, intervention, and evaluation.*

EP 2.1.10a *Substantively and affectively prepare for action with individuals, families, groups, organizations, and communities.*

EP 2.1.10b *Use empathy and other interpersonal skills.*

EP 2.1.10c *Develop a mutually agreed-on focus of work and desired outcomes.*

EP 2.1.10d *Collect, organize, and interpret client data.*

EP 2.1.10e *Assess client strengths and limitations.*

EP 2.1.10f *Develop mutually agreed-on intervention goals and objectives.*

EP 2.1.10g *Select appropriate intervention strategies.*

EP 2.1.10j *Help clients resolve problems.*

EP 2.1.10l *Facilitate transitions and endings.* (pp. 243–284).

This chapter presents content on all the practice behaviors associated with social work with families.

EP 2.1.1b *Practice personal reflection and self-correction to assure continual professional development.* (p. 245).

Exercise 8.1 is designed to assist students in better understanding their family dynamics.

EP 2.1.7a *Utilize conceptual frameworks to guide the process of assessment, intervention, and evaluation.* (pp. 248–254).

This section presents material on assessing families, using eco-maps and genograms.

EP 2.1.7a *Utilize conceptual frameworks to guide the process of assessment, intervention, and evaluation.* (pp. 257–266).

This section presents three conceptual frameworks to intervene in family therapy: a communication pattern approach, a family subsystem approach, and a cognitive-behavioral approach.

EP 2.1.7a *Utilize conceptual frameworks to guide the process of assessment, intervention, and evaluation.* (p. 260).

Exercise 8.2 is designed to assist students in understanding and applying Satir's concepts.

EP 2.1.7a *Utilize conceptual frameworks to guide the process of assessment, intervention, and evaluation.* (pp. 262–263).

Exercise 8.3 is designed to assist students in understanding and applying Minuchin's concepts.

EP 2.1.7a *Utilize conceptual frameworks to guide the process of assessment, intervention, and evaluation.* (p. 266).

Exercise 8.4 is designed to assist students in applying cognitive-behavioral concepts to their families.

EP 2.1.7a *Utilize conceptual frameworks to guide the process of assessment, intervention, and evaluation.* (p. 282).

This exercise is designed to assist students in gaining insight into their family dynamics, with the use of eco-maps.

EP 2.1.7a *Utilize conceptual frameworks to guide the process of assessment, intervention, and evaluation.* (p. 282).

This exercise is designed to assist students in gaining insight into their family dynamics, with the use of genograms.

EP 2.1.7a *Utilize conceptual frameworks to guide the process of assessment, intervention, and evaluation.* (pp. 282–283).

This exercise is designed to assist students in exploring family systems theory principles.

CHAPTER 9

Social Work with Organizations

EP 2.1.7a

The word *organization* as used here refers to a collectivity of individuals gathered together to serve a particular purpose. The purposes (or goals) that people organize to achieve are infinite in number, ranging from obtaining basic necessities to eliminating the threat of worldwide terrorism or attaining world peace. In each case, an organization exists because people working together can better accomplish tasks and achieve goals than one individual can. Etzioni (1964) described the importance of organizations in our lives:

> We are born in organizations, educated by organizations, and most of us spend much of our lives working for organizations. We spend much of our leisure time paying, playing, and praying in organizations. Most of us will die in an organization, and when the time comes for burial, the largest organization of all—the state—must grant official permission. (p. 1)

Netting, Kettner, and McMurtry (1998) summarized the importance of organizations for social work practice:

> As social workers, our roles within, interactions with, and attempts to manipulate organizations define much of what we do. Clients often come to us seeking help because they are not able to obtain help from organizations that are critical to their survival or quality of life. In turn, the resources we attempt to gain for these clients usually come from still other organizations. . . Social workers with little or no idea of how organizations operate, how they interact, or how they can be influenced and changed from both outside and inside are likely to be severely limited in their effectiveness. (pp. 193–194)

Although many disciplines (including business, psychology, political science, and sociology) have produced a prodigious amount of theory and research on organizations, the amount of social work literature devoted to organizations is limited, despite the importance of organizations to social work practice. One significant reference in this area is *Social Work Macro Practice,* 4th edition (Netting, Kettner, & McMurtry, 2007). Another is *Generalist Practice with Organizations and Communities* (Kirst-Ashman & Hull, 2009).

One subcategory of organizations that is particularly relevant to social work is social agencies. Most social workers are employed by social agencies.

This chapter provides an introduction to social work practice with organizations. This chapter will:

EP 2.1.1b

A. Present models of organizational behavior
B. Describe value orientations in organizational decision making
C. Compare liberalism and conservatism
D. Provide guidelines for thriving and surviving in a bureaucracy

Exercise 9.1: Appreciating Organizations

Goal: This exercise is designed to increase your interest in participating in organizations and to increase your interest in learning how to thrive in an organization.

Step 1: Many of my social work students tell me they want to work with individuals, families, and small groups. They also tell me they have little interest in learning about organizations. Please specify your interest (from 1 to 5, with 5 being high) in learning about organizations. Also, give a rationale for your rating.

Step 2: We have all participated in a number of organizations—schools, clubs at schools, business or social service agencies we have worked for, church organizations, boys and girls organizations (such as Boy Scouts and Girl Scouts). If you are studying to be a social worker, you will have a field placement at an agency and probably will be seeking a job at a social work agency (organization) after you graduate. List three organizations that you have enjoyed participating in, and also briefly describe why you enjoyed participating in each of these.

Step 3: You will probably be spending most of your career in working for a social work agency. Is it to your benefit to learn about organizations and to learn how to thrive in an organization?

___ Yes

___ No

MODELS OF ORGANIZATIONAL BEHAVIOR

The Autocratic Model

The autocratic model has existed for thousands of years. During the Industrial Revolution, it was the prominent model of organizational function. The model depends on *power*. Those who are in power act autocratically. The message to employees is "You do this—or else," meaning that employees who don't follow orders are penalized, often severely.

The autocratic model uses one-way communication—from the top down to workers. Management believes that it knows best. The employees' obligation is to follow orders. The thinking is that employees have to be persuaded, directed, and pushed into performance; this is management's task. Management does the thinking, and the workers obey the directives. Under autocratic conditions, the workers' role is *obedience* to management.

The autocratic model is very effective in some settings. Military organizations throughout the world are formulated on this model. The model was also used during the Industrial Revolution—for example, in building great railroad systems and in operating giant steel mills. Today, it is a legitimate question to wonder whether modern models of organizational behavior might not have worked better in these historic endeavors.

EP 2.1.1b

The autocratic model has a number of disadvantages. Workers are often in the best position to identify shortcomings in the structure and technology of the organizational system, but one-way communication prevents feedback to management. The model also fails to generate commitment among workers to accomplish organizational goals. Finally, the model fails to motivate workers to further develop their skills (skills that often would be highly beneficial to the employer).

Exercise 9.2: Working in an Autocratic Organization

Goal: This exercise is designed to assist you in understanding the merits and shortcomings of the autocratic model.

Step 1: Describe your experiences in working or participating in an organization in which your supervisor, coach, or teacher used the autocratic approach. (Perhaps it was a job where you waited tables; perhaps it was a team sport where you had an autocratic coach; perhaps it was a teacher or a member of the clergy.)

Step 2: Summarize your thoughts about the benefits and shortcomings of having an autocratic leader.

The Custodial Model

Many decades ago when the autocratic model was the predominant model of organizational behavior, some progressive managers began to study their employees and soon found that the autocratic model had disturbing side effects. Employees felt insecure about their continued employment, were frustrated, and had feelings of aggression toward management. They could not express their discontent directly, so they expressed it indirectly. Among other things, employees sabotaged production. Davis and Newstrom (1989) described sabotage in a wood-processing plant:

> Managers treated workers crudely, sometimes even to the point of physical abuse. Since employees could not strike back directly for fear of losing their jobs, they found another way to do it. They *symbolically* fed their supervisor to a log-shredding machine! They did this by purposely destroying good sheets of veneer, which made the supervisor look bad when monthly efficiency reports were prepared. (p. 31)

In the 1890s and 1900s, progressive employers thought that if these feelings could be alleviated, employees might work harder, which would increase productivity. To satisfy employees' security needs, a number of companies began to provide welfare programs, such as pension programs, child-care centers at the workplace, health insurance, and life insurance. However, researchers found that the custodial approach leads to dependence on the organization. According to Davis and Newstrom (1989, p. 31), "If employees have ten years of seniority under the union contract and a good pension program, they cannot afford to quit even if the grass looks greener somewhere else!"

Employees working under a custodial model tend to focus on economic rewards and benefits. They are happier and more content than under the autocratic model, but they don't have a high commitment to helping the organization accomplish its goals. They give *passive cooperation* to their employer. The model's most evident flaw is that most employees produce substantially below their capacities. They are not motivated to advance to higher capacities. Employees don't feel fulfilled or motivated. The point here is that contented employees are not necessarily the most productive employees.

The Scientific Management Model

One of the earliest and most important schools of thought on the management of workplace functions and tasks was based on the work of Frederick W. Taylor (1947). Taylor was a mechanical engineer, an American industrialist, and an educator. He focused primarily on management techniques that would increase productivity. He asserted that many organizational problems were the result of misunderstandings between managers and workers. Managers erroneously thought that workers were lazy and unemotional, and they mistakenly believed they understood workers' jobs. Workers mistakenly thought that managers only wanted to exploit them.

To solve these problems, Taylor developed the *scientific management model,* which focused on the need for managers to conduct scientific analyses of the workplace. One of the first steps was to conduct a careful study of how each job could best be accomplished. An excellent way to do this, according to Taylor, was to identify the best workers for each job and then carefully study how they effectively and efficiently did the work. The goal of this analysis was to discover the optimal way of doing the job—in Taylor's words, the "one best way." Once this best way was identified, tools could be modified to better complete the work, workers' abilities and interests could be fitted to particular job assignments, and the level of production that the average worker could sustain could be gauged.

Once the level of production for the average worker was determined, the next step was to provide incentives to increase productivity. Taylor's favorite strategy for doing this was the piece-rate wage: Workers were paid for each unit they produced. The goals of management were to produce more units, reduce unit cost, increase organizational productivity and profitability, and provide incentives for workers to produce more.

Taylor's work has been criticized as having a techniques bias because it tends to treat workers as little more than cogs in a wheel. No two workers are exactly alike, so the "one best way" of doing a job is often unique to the person doing it. Actually, forcing the same work approach on different workers may actually decrease both productivity and worker satisfaction. In addition, Taylor's approach has limited application to human services. Each client is unique—with unique needs, unique environmental impacting factors, and unique strengths and capacities—so each human services case has to be individualized, and therefore it is difficult (if not impossible) to specify the "one best way" to proceed.

The Human Relations Model

In 1927, the Hawthorne Works of the Western Electric Company in Chicago began a series of experiments designed to discover ways to increase worker satisfaction and worker productivity (Roethlisberger & Dickson, 1939). Hawthorne Works manufactured telephones on an assembly-line basis. Workers needed no special skills and performed simple, repetitive tasks. The workers were not unionized, and management sought to find ways to increase productivity. If job satisfaction could be increased, employees would work more efficiently, and productivity would then increase.

The company tested the effects on productivity of a number of factors: rest breaks, better lighting, changes in the number of work hours, changes in the wages paid, improved food facilities, and so on. The results were surprising. Productivity increased, as expected, with improved working conditions; but it also increased when working conditions worsened. This latter finding was unexpected and led to additional study.

The investigators discovered that participation in the experiments was extremely attractive to the workers. They felt they had been selected by management for their individual abilities, and so they worked harder even when working conditions became less favorable. In addition, the workers' morale and general attitude toward work improved because they felt they were receiving special attention. By participating in this study, the workers were able to work in smaller groups and became involved in making decisions. Working in smaller groups created a stronger sense of solidarity with their fellow workers. Being involved in decision making decreased their feelings of meaninglessness and powerlessness about their work.

In sociological and psychological research, the results of this study have become known as the *Hawthorne effect.* In essence, when subjects know they are participants in a study, this awareness leads them to behave differently and substantially influences the results.

The results of this study, and of other similar studies, led some researchers to conclude that the key variables affecting productivity are social factors. Etzioni (1964, pp. 34–35) summarized some of the basic tenets of the human relations approach:

- The level of production is set by social norms, not by physiological capacities.
- Noneconomic rewards and sanctions significantly affect the behavior of the workers and largely limit the effect of economic incentive plans.
- Workers do not act or react as individuals but as members of groups.
- The role of leadership is important in understanding social factors in organizations, and this leadership may be either formal or informal.

Numerous studies provide evidence to support these tenets (Netting, Kettner, & McMurtry, 2003).

Workers who are capable of greater productivity often will not excel because they are unwilling to exceed the "average" level set by the norms of the group, even if this means earning less. Studies have also found that attempts by management to influence workers' behaviors are often more successful if targeted at the group as a whole, rather than at individuals. Finally, studies have documented the importance of informal leadership in influencing workers' behavior in ways that can either amplify or negate formal leadership directives. This model asserts that managers who succeed in increasing productivity are most likely responsive to the workers' social needs.

One criticism of the human relations model is (surprisingly) that it tends to manipulate, dehumanize, oppress, and exploit workers. The model leads to the conclusion that management can increase productivity by helping workers become content rather than by increasing economic rewards for higher productivity. It concentrates power and decision making at the top. It is not intended to empower employees in the decision-making process or to assist them in acquiring genuine participation in running the organization. The practice of dealing with people on the basis of their perceived social relationships in the workplace may also be a factor in perpetuating the "good old boys" network; this network has disadvantaged women and people of color over the years. Another criticism of the human relations approach is that a happy workforce is not necessarily a productive workforce, because the norms for worker production may be set well below the workers' levels of capability.

Theory X and Theory Y

Douglas McGregor (1960) developed two theories of management. He theorized that management thinking and behavior are based on two different sets of assumptions, which he labeled Theory X and Theory Y.

Theory X managers view employees as incapable of much growth. Employees are perceived as having an inherent dislike for work and as attempting to evade work whenever possible. Therefore, X-type managers believe they must control, direct, force, or threaten employees to make them work. Employees are also viewed as having relatively little ambition, wishing to avoid responsibilities, and preferring to be directed. Theory X managers therefore spell out job responsibilities carefully, set work goals without employee input, use external rewards (such as money) to force employees to work, and punish those who deviate from established rules. Because Theory X managers reduce responsibilities to a level at which few mistakes can be made, work usually becomes so structured that it is monotonous and distasteful. These assumptions, of course, are inconsistent with what behavioral scientists assert are effective principles for directing, influencing, and motivating people. (Theory X managers are, in essence, adhering to an autocratic model of organizational behavior.)

In contrast, *Theory Y managers* view employees as wanting to grow and develop by exerting physical and mental effort to accomplish work objectives to which they are committed. These managers believe that the promise of internal rewards, such as self-respect and personal improvement, are stronger motivators than external rewards (money) and punishment. They also believe that under proper conditions, employees will not only accept responsibility but seek it. Most employees are assumed to have considerable ingenuity, creativity, and imagination for problem solving. Therefore, they are given considerable responsibility to test the limits of their capabilities. Mistakes and errors are viewed as necessary phases of the learning process, and work is structured so employees have a sense of accomplishment and growth.

EP 2.1.10e

Employees who work for Y-type managers are generally more creative and productive, experience greater work satisfaction, and are more highly motivated than employees who work for X-type managers. Under both management styles, expectations often become self-fulfilling prophecies.

Exercise 9.3: Theory X Managers versus Theory Y Managers

Goal: This exercise is designed to assist you in understanding the merits and shortcomings of these two styles of management.

Step 1: Describe someone you have interacted with who relates to others as depicted by Theory X. (This person may have been a manager, coach, teacher, or member of your family). Describe your reactions to interacting with this person.

Step 2: Describe someone you have interacted with who relates to others as depicted by Theory Y. Describe your reactions to interacting with this person.

Step 3: Summarize your views on the merits and shortcomings of relating to others according to Theory X.

Step 4: Summarize your views on the merits and shortcomings of relating to others according to Theory Y.

The Collegial Model

A useful extension of Theory Y, the *collegial model* emphasizes the team concept. It involves employees working closely together and feeling a commitment to achieve a common purpose. Some organizations—such as university departments, research laboratories, and most human services organizations—have a goal of creating a collegial atmosphere to facilitate achieving their purposes. (Sadly, many such organizations are unsuccessful in creating such an atmosphere.)

Creating a collegial atmosphere is highly dependent on management building a feeling of partnership with employees. When such a partnership develops, employees feel needed and useful. Managers are then viewed as joint contributors rather than as bosses. Management is the *coach* who builds a better team. Davis and Newstrom (1989) described some of the approaches to developing a team concept:

> The feeling of partnerships can be built in many ways. Some organizations have abolished the use of reserved parking spaces for executives, so every employee has an equal chance of finding one close to the workplace. Some firms have tried to eliminate the use of terms like "bosses" and "subordinates," feeling that those terms simply create perceptions of psychological distance between managers and nonmanagers. Other employers have removed time clocks, set up "fun committees," sponsored company canoe trips, or required managers to spend a week or two annually working in field or factory locations. All of these approaches are designed to build a spirit of mutuality, in which every person makes contributions and appreciates those of others. (p. 34)

If the sense of partnership is developed, employees produce quality work and seek to cooperate with coworkers, not because management directs them to do so but because they feel an internal obligation to produce high-quality work. The collegial approach thus leads to a sense of *self-discipline*. In this environment, employees are more likely to have a sense of fulfillment, to feel self-actualized, and to produce higher—quality work.

Theory Z

William Ouchi described the Japanese style of management in his 1981 best seller *Theory Z: How American Business Can Meet the Japanese Challenge*. In the late 1970s and early 1980s, the U.S. business world focused on the Japanese approach to management, as markets long dominated by American firms (such as the automobile industry) were taken over by Japanese industries. Japanese industrial organizations had rapidly overcome their earlier reputation for poor-quality work and were setting worldwide standards for quality and durability.

Ouchi asserted that *Theory Z*, the theoretical principles underlying the Japanese style of management, went beyond Theory Y. A business organization in Japan is more than the profitability-oriented entity that it is in the United States. It is a way of life. It provides lifetime employment. It is enmeshed with the nation's political, social, and economic network. Furthermore, its influence spills over into many other organizations, such as nursery schools, elementary and secondary schools, and universities.

The basic philosophy of Theory Z is that involved and committed workers are the key to increased productivity. Ideas and suggestions about how to improve the organization are routinely solicited and implemented, where feasible. One strategy for accomplishing this is the *quality circle,* where employees and management routinely meet to brainstorm about ways to improve productivity and quality.

In contrast to American organizations, Japanese organizations don't have written objectives or organizational charts. Most work is done in teams, and decisions are made by consensus. The teams tend to function without a designated leader. Cooperation within units, and between units, is emphasized. Loyalty to the organization is also emphasized, as is organizational loyalty to the employee.

EP 2.1.7a

Experiments designed to transplant Japanese-style management to the United States have met with mixed success. In most cases, American organizations have concluded that Theory Z probably works quite well in a homogeneous culture that has Japan's societal values, but some components do not fit well with the more heterogeneous and individualistic character of the United States. In addition, some firms in volatile industries (such as electronics) have difficulty balancing their desire to provide lifetime employment with the need to adjust their workforces to meet rapidly changing market demands.

Exercise 9.4: Understanding Theory Z

Goal: This exercise is designed to assist you in understanding Theory Z.

Step 1: Summarize the benefits or merits of a social agency using a Theory Z approach with its employees.

Step 2: Summarize the shortcomings of a social agency using a Theory Z approach with its employees.

Management by Objectives

Fundamental to the core of an organization is its purpose—that is, the commonly shared understanding of the reason for its existence. Management theorist Peter Drucker (1954) proposed a strategy for making organizational goals and objectives the central construct around which organizational life is designed to function. In other words, instead of focusing on employee needs and wants or on organizational structure as the ways to increase efficiency and productivity, Drucker proposed beginning with the desired outcome and working backward. The strategy is first to identify the organizational objectives or goals and then to adapt the organizational tasks, resources, and structure to meet those objectives. This *management by objectives* (MBO) approach is designed to focus the organization's efforts on meeting these objectives. Success is determined, then, by the degree to which stated objectives are reached.

This approach can be applied to the organization as a whole, as well as to internal divisions or departments. When the MBO approach is applied to internal divisions, the objectives set for each division should be consistent and supportive of the overall organizational objectives.

In many areas, including human services, the MBO approach can also be applied to the cases being serviced by each employee. Goals are set with each client, tasks to meet these goals are then determined, and deadlines are set for completion of these tasks. The degree of success of each case is then determined at a later date (often when a case is closed) by the extent to which stated goals were achieved.

An adaptation of the MBO approach, called *strategic planning and budgeting* (SPB), became popular in the 1990s and early 2000s. The process involves first specifying the overall vision or mission of an organization, then identifying a variety of more specific objectives or plans for achieving that vision, and finally adapting the resources to meet the specific high-priority objectives or plans. Organizations often hire outside consultants to oversee the SPB process.

One major advantage of the MBO approach for an organization (or its divisions) is that it produces clear statements (made available to all employees) about the objectives and the tasks that are expected to be accomplished in specified time periods. This type of activity tends to improve cooperation and collaboration. The MBO approach is also useful because it provides a guide for allocating resources and a focus for monitoring and evaluating organizational efforts.

EP 2.1.10e

An additional benefit of the MBO approach is in the area of diversity in the workplace. Before this approach, those responsible for hiring failed to employ women and people of color in significant numbers. As affirmative action programs were developed within organizations, the MBO approach was widely used to set specific hiring goals and objectives. The result was significant changes in recruitment approaches that enabled women and minorities to secure employment.

Exercise 9.5: Understanding Management by Objectives

Goal: This exercise is designed to assist you in understanding the MBO approach.

Step 1: Summarize the benefits or merits of a social agency using the MBO approach.

Step 2: Summarize the shortcomings of a social agency using the MBO approach.

Total Quality Management

The theorist most closely associated with developing the concept of total quality management (TQM) is W. Edwards Deming (1986). Deming formed many of his theories during World War II when he developed statistical methods to speed up military production. Deming taught the Japanese his theories of quality control and continuous improvement after World War II, and he is now recognized, along with J. Juran (1989) and others, for laying the groundwork for Japan's postwar industrial and economic boom.

Omachonu and Ross (1994) defined *total quality management* as follows: "The integration of all functions and processes within an organization in order to achieve continuous improvement of the quality of goods and services. The goal is customer satisfaction" (p. 1). TQM is based on a number of ideas. It means thinking about the quality of every function of the enterprise and is a start-to-finish process that integrates interrelated functions at all levels. It is a systems approach that considers every interaction between the various elements of the organization. TQM asserts that in many businesses and organizations, management makes the mistake of blaming what goes wrong on individual people, not on the system. TQM, instead, affirms the *85/15 rule:* In an organization, 85% of the problems can be corrected only by changing systems (structures, rules, practices, expectations, and traditions that are largely determined by management), and less than 15% can be resolved by correcting individual workers. When problems arise, TQM managers look for causes in the system and work to remove them before casting blame on workers.

TQM asserts that quality depends on continuous improvement of all of the organization's processes that lead to customer satisfaction. Customer satisfaction is the main objective of the organization. The customer is not merely the "point of sale"; the customer is part of the design and production process. Therefore, customers' needs must be monitored continuously.

Numerous organizations have adopted TQM to improve their goods and services. One reason for the emphasis on quality is that more and more consumers are shunning mass-produced, poorly made, disposable products. Companies are realizing that to remain competitive in global markets, high-quality products and services are essential.

There are a variety of approaches to TQM. For a summary of these approaches, see *Principles of Total Quality* (Omachonu & Ross, 1994). Hower (1994, p. 10) summarized many of the principles of TQM:

- Employees asking their external and internal customers what they need and providing more of it
- Instilling pride into every employee
- Concentrating on information and data (a common language) to solve problems, instead of concentrating on opinions and egos
- Developing leaders, not managers, and knowing the difference
- Improving every process (everyone is in a process), checking this improvement at predetermined times, then improving it again if necessary
- Helping every employee enjoy his or her work while the organization continues to become more productive
- Providing a forum or open atmosphere so that employees at all levels feel free to voice their opinions when they think they have good ideas
- Receiving a continuous increase in those suggestions and accepting and implementing the best ones
- Utilizing the teamwork concept, as teams often make better decisions than individuals
- Empowering these teams to implement their recommended solutions and learn from their failures
- Reducing the number of layers of authority to enhance this empowerment
- Recognizing complaints as opportunities for improvement

These principles give a "flavor" of TQM.

Summary Comments about Models of Organizational Behavior

The question of which model to apply to obtain the highest productivity depends on the tasks to be completed and on employee needs and expectations. For example, the autocratic model works well in military operations, where quick decisions are needed to respond to rapidly changing crises, but it does not work well in human services organizations in which employees expect Theory Y management style.

In addition, some of these models or approaches can be applied simultaneously. For example, management by objectives can be used at the same time that an organization is using any of the other models described here.

VALUE ORIENTATIONS IN ORGANIZATIONAL DECISION MAKING

In theory, decision making about organizational objectives and goals is a rational process, including identifying problems, specifying resource limitations, weighing advantages and disadvantages of proposed solutions, and selecting the resolution strategy with the fewest risks and the greatest chance of success. In practice, subjective influences (particularly value orientations) can derail the rational process. Most people tend to believe that decisions are made primarily on the basis of objective facts and figures. Decision makers, however, bring not only their objective knowledge and expertise to the decision-making process but also their value orientations, unique attitudes, feelings, biases, and vested interests. Values and assumptions form the bases of most decisions, and facts and figures are used to justify and reinforce these values and assumptions.

Consider the following questions pertinent to providing social services. What do they indicate about how we make our most important decisions?

Should abortion be permitted or prohibited during the first weeks following conception?

Should homosexuality be viewed as a natural expression of sexuality?

When does harsh discipline of a child become child abuse?

Should the primary objective of imprisonment be rehabilitation or retribution?

Answers to these questions usually are based not on data uncovered after careful research but on individual beliefs about the value of life, personal freedom, and protective social standards.

Even everyday decisions are based largely on values, and practically every decision also rests on assumptions. Without assumptions, nothing could be proved. Assumptions are made in every research study to test any hypothesis. For example, analysts conducting a market survey assume that the instruments they use (such as a questionnaire) will be valid and reliable. But it cannot even be proved that the sun will rise in the east tomorrow without assuming that history provides the proof.

The term *value orientation* refers to an individual's personal ideas about what is desirable and worthwhile. Most values are acquired through prior learning experiences in interactions with family, friends, educators, organizations such as churches, and anyone else who has made an impression on a person's thinking. The philosopher Edward Spranger (1928) believed that most people eventually come to rely on one of six value orientations:

1. *Theoretical:* A person with a theoretical orientation strives toward a rational, systematic ordering of knowledge. Personal preference does not count as much as being able to classify, compare, contrast, and interrelate various pieces of information. The theoretical person places value on simply knowing what is—and why.
2. *Economic:* An economic orientation places primary value on the utility of things, and practical uses of knowledge are given foremost attention. Proposed plans of action are assessed in terms of their costs and benefits. If the costs outweigh the benefits, the economic-oriented person is not likely to support the plan.
3. *Aesthetic:* An aesthetic orientation is grounded in an appreciation of artistic values, and personal preferences for form, harmony, and beauty are influential in making decisions. Because the experience of single events is considered an important end in itself, reactions to aesthetic qualities will frequently be expressed.
4. *Social:* A social orientation is an empathetic one that values other people as ends in themselves. Concern for the welfare of people pervades the behavior of the socially oriented decision maker, and primary consideration is given to the quality of human relationships.
5. *Political:* A political orientation involves a concern for identifying where power lies. Conflict and competition are seen as normal elements of group activity. Decisions and their outcomes are assessed in terms of how much power is obtained and by whom because influence over others is a valued goal.
6. *Religious:* A person with a religious orientation is directed by a desire to relate to the universe in some meaningful way. Personal beliefs about an "absolute good" or "higher order" are employed to determine the value of things, and decisions and their outcomes are placed into the context of such beliefs.

EP 2.1.7a

Although it is possible for a person to hold values in all six orientations, each person tends to favor one orientation when making decisions.

Exercise 9.6: Understanding Six Value Orientations

Goal: This exercise is designed to assist you in understanding which value orientations you tend to use in your decision making.

Step 1: Review the description of the theoretical, economic, aesthetic, social, political, and religious value orientations. Specify which orientations have the greatest effect on the major life decisions that you make.

Step 2: Indicate why you selected the value orientations that you identified in step 1.

LIBERALISM VERSUS CONSERVATISM

Two value orientations that have major impacts on human services organizations are liberalism and conservatism. The decisions that politicians and other decision makers make about human service issues often reflect their adherence to liberal or conservative principles.

Conservatives emphasize tradition and believe that rapid change usually results in more negative than positive consequences. Conservatives feel that government should not interfere with the workings of the marketplace. They encourage the government to support (for example, through tax incentives) rather than regulate business and industry. A free-market economy is thought to be the best way to ensure prosperity and fulfillment of individual needs. Conservatives embrace the adage "Government governs best which governs least." They believe that most government activities pose grave threats to individual liberty and to the smooth functioning of the free market.

Conservatives generally take a residual approach to social welfare programs (see Chapter 2 for a fuller description of the residual and institutional approaches to social welfare programs). They believe that dependency is a result of personal failure and that it is natural for inequality to exist among humans. They assert that the family, the church, and gainful employment should be the primary defenses against dependency. Social welfare should be a temporary function, they assert, that is used sparingly, because prolonged social welfare assistance leads recipients to become permanently dependent. Conservatives believe that charity is a moral virtue and that the "fortunate" are obligated to help the "less fortunate" become productive, contributing citizens in a society. If governmental funds are provided for health and social welfare services, conservatives advocate that such funding go to private organizations, which they believe are more effective and efficient than public agencies in providing services.

In contrast, liberals believe that change is generally good, as it brings progress, and that moderate change is best. They view society as needing regulation to ensure fair competition among various interests. In particular, a free-market economy is viewed as needing regulation to ensure fairness. Government programs, including social welfare programs, are viewed as necessary to help meet basic human needs. Liberals advocate government action to remedy social deficiencies and to improve human welfare. They feel that government regulation and intervention are often necessary to safeguard human rights, to control the excesses of capitalism, and to provide equal opportunities for success. They emphasize egalitarianism and the rights of minorities.

EP 2.1.7a

Liberals generally adhere to an institutional view of social welfare. They assert that because modern society has become so fragmented and complex and because traditional institutions (such as the family) have been unable to meet emerging human needs, few individuals can now function without the help of social services (including work training, job location services, child care, health care, and counseling).

Exercise 9.7: Understanding and Applying Liberalism and Conservatism

Goal: This exercise is designed to assist you in understanding your beliefs about liberalism and conservatism.

Step 1: Specify whether you tend in your political orientation to tilt toward liberalism or conservatism.

Step 2: Explain your rationale for the political orientation you selected in step 1.

THRIVING AND SURVIVING IN A BUREAUCRACY

Basic structural conflicts exist between helping professionals and the bureaucratic systems in which they work. Helping professionals place a high value on creativeness and changing the system to serve clients. Bureaucracies resist change and are most efficient when no one "rocks the boat." Helping professionals seek to personalize services by conveying to each client that "you count as a person." Bureaucracies are highly depersonalized, emotionally detached systems that view every employee and every client as a tiny component of a large system. In a large bureaucracy, employees count *not* as "persons" but only as functional parts of a system. Additional conflicting value orientations between helping professionals and bureaucratic systems are listed in Exhibit 9.1.

Any of these differences in value orientation can become an arena of conflict between helping professionals and the bureaucracies in which they function. Knopf (1979) summarized the potential areas of conflict between bureaucracies and helping professionals:

> The trademarks of a BS (bureaucratic system) are power, hierarchy, and specialization; that is, rules and roles. In essence, the result is depersonalization. The system itself is neither "good" nor "bad"; it is a system. I believe it to be amoral. It is efficient and effective, but in order to be so it must be impersonal in all of its functionings. This then is the location of the stress. The hallmark of the helping professional is a highly individualized, democratic, humanized, relationship-oriented service aimed at self-motivation. The hallmark of a bureaucratic system is a highly impersonalized, valueless (amoral), emotionally detached, hierarchical structure of organization. The dilemma of the HP (helping person) is how to give a personalized service to a client through a delivery system that is not set up in any way to do that. (pp. 21–22)

Exhibit 9.1 Value Conflicts Between Helping Professionals and Bureaucracies

Orientations of Helping Professionals	Orientations of Bureaucratic Systems
Desires democratic system for decision making.	Most decisions are made autocratically.
Desires that power be distributed equally among employees (horizontal structure).	Power is distributed vertically.
Desires that clients have considerable power in the system.	Power is held primarily by top executives.
Desires a flexible, changing system.	System is rigid and stable.
Desires that creativity and growth be emphasized.	Emphasis is on structure and the status quo.
Desires a client-oriented focus.	System is organization-centered.
Desires that communication be on a personalized level from person to person.	Communication is from level to level.
Desires shared decision making and shared responsibility structure.	A hierarchical decision-making structure and a hierarchical responsibility structure are characteristic.
Desires that decisions be made by those having the most knowledge.	Decisions are made by the decision-making authority assigned to each position in the hierarchy.
Desires shared leadership.	System uses autocratic leadership.
Believes feelings of clients and employees should be highly valued by the system.	Procedures and processes are highly valued.

Numerous helping professionals attribute a "personality" to the bureaucracy. They characterize the bureaucracy as "red tape," "officialism," "uncaring," "cruel," "the enemy." A negative personality is sometimes also attributed to officials, who are derided as "paper shufflers," "rigid," "deadwood," "inefficient," and "unproductive." Knopf (1979) cautioned against this tendency:

> The HP (helping person). . .may deal with the impersonal nature of the system by projecting values onto it and thereby give the BS (bureaucratic system) a "personality." In this way, we fool ourselves into thinking that we can deal with it in a personal way. Unfortunately, projection is almost always negative and reflects the dark or negative aspects of ourselves. The BS then becomes a screen onto which we vent our anger, sadness, or fright, and while a lot of energy is generated, very little is accomplished. Since the BS is amoral, it is unproductive to place a personality on it. (p. 25)

In other words, bureaucratic systems are neither good nor bad. They have neither a personality nor a value system. They are simply structures developed to carry out various tasks.

Helping professionals have various emotional responses to these conflicts in orientation with bureaucratic systems.[1] Common reactions are anger at the system, self-blame ("It's all my fault"), sadness and depression ("Poor me"; "Nobody appreciates all I've done"), and fright and paranoia ("They're out to get me"; "If I mess up I'm gone"). Knopf (1979) identified several roles that helping professionals assume in dealing with

[1]This description highlights a number of negatives about bureaucratic systems, particularly their impersonalization. In fairness, an advantage of being part of a large bureaucracy is that the potential is there for changing a powerful system to the clients' advantage. In tiny or nonbureaucratic systems, the social worker has lots of freedom but little opportunity or power to influence large systems or mobilize extensive resources on behalf of clients.

bureaucracies. **Warriors** lead open campaigns to destroy and malign the system. They discount the value of the system and often enter into a win-lose conflict. Warriors generally lose and are dismissed.

Gossips are covert warriors who complain to others (including clients, politicians, and the news media) about how terrible the system is. Gossips frequently single out a few officials for criticism. Bureaucratic systems often make life very difficult for gossips by assigning them distasteful tasks, refusing to promote them, giving very small salary increases, and perhaps even dismissing them.

Complainers resemble gossips but confine their complaints to other helping persons, to in-house staff, and to family members. Complainers want people to agree so they can find comfort in shared misery. They want to stay with the system and generally do.

Dancers are skillful at ignoring rules and procedures. They are frequently lonely, often reprimanded for incorrectly filling out forms, and have low investment in the system or in helping clients.

Defenders are scared, dislike conflict, and therefore defend the rules, the system, and bureaucratic officials. Defenders are often supervisors and are viewed by others as "bureaucrats."

Machines are "bureaucrats" who take on the orientation of the bureaucracy. Often a machine hasn't been involved in providing direct services for years. They are frequently named to head study committees and policy groups and to chair boards.

Executioners attack persons within an organization with enthusiasm and vigor. They usually have a high energy level and are impulsive. Executioners abuse power by indiscriminately attacking and dismissing not only employees but also services and programs. Executioners have power and are angry (although the anger is disguised and almost always denied). They are not committed to either the value orientation of helping professionals or to the bureaucracy.

Those roles won't get you very far and may destroy your career. There are alternatives, and they do work. Knopf (1979) listed 66 tips on how to survive in a bureaucracy. Some of the most useful suggestions are summarized here:

1. Whenever your needs or the needs of your clients are not met by the bureaucracy, use the following problem-solving approach: (a) Precisely identify your needs (or the needs of clients) that are in conflict with the bureaucracy; this step is defining the problem. (b) Generate a list of possible solutions. Be creative in generating a wide range of solutions. (c) Evaluate the merits and shortcomings of the possible solutions. (d) Select a solution. (e) Implement the solution. (f) Evaluate the solution.
2. Obtain knowledge of how your bureaucracy is structured and how it functions. This knowledge will reduce fear of the unknown, make the system more predictable, and help in identifying rational ways to best meet your needs and those of your clients.
3. Remember that bureaucrats are people who have feelings. Communication gaps are often most effectively reduced if you treat them with as much respect and interest as you treat your clients.
4. If you are at war with the bureaucracy, declare a truce. The system will find a way to dismiss you if you remain at war. With a truce, you can identify and use the strengths of the bureaucracy as an ally, rather than having the strengths being used against you as an enemy.
5. Know your work contract and job expectations. If the expectations are unclear, seek clarity.
6. Continue to develop your knowledge and awareness of specific helping skills. Take advantage of continuing education opportunities (for example, workshops, conferences, courses). Among other advantages, your continued professional development will assist you in being able to contract from a position of competency and skill.

7. Identify your professional strengths and limitations. Knowing your limitations will increase your ability to avoid undertaking responsibilities that are beyond your competencies.
8. Be aware that you can't change everything, so stop trying. In a bureaucracy, focus your change efforts on those aspects that most need change and that you have a fair chance of changing. Stop thinking and complaining about those aspects you cannot change. It is irrational to complain about things that you cannot change or to complain about those things that you do not intend to make an effort to change.
9. Learn how to control your emotions in your interactions with the bureaucracy. Emotions that are counterproductive (such as most angry outbursts) particularly need to be controlled. Doing a rational self-analysis on unwanted emotions (Module 1) is one way of gaining control of your unwanted emotions. Learning how to respond to stress in your personal life will also prepare you to handle stress at work better.
10. Develop and use a sense of humor. Humor takes the edge off adverse conditions and reduces negative feelings.
11. Learn to accept your mistakes and perhaps even to laugh at some of them. No one is perfect.
12. Take time to enjoy and develop a support system with your coworkers.
13. Acknowledge your mistakes and give in sometimes on minor matters. You may not be right, and giving in sometimes allows other people to do the same.
14. Keep yourself physically fit and mentally alert. Learn to use approaches that will reduce stress and prevent burnout (see Chapter 14).
15. Leave your work at the office. If you have urgent unfinished bureaucratic business, do it before leaving work or don't leave.
16. Occasionally take your supervisor and other administrators to lunch. Socializing prevents isolation and facilitates your involvement with and understanding of the system.
17. Do not seek self-actualization or ego satisfaction from the bureaucracy. A depersonalized system is incapable of providing this. Only you can satisfy your ego and become self-actualized.
18. Make speeches to community groups that accentuate the positives about your agency. Do not hesitate to ask after speeches that a thank-you letter be sent to your supervisor or agency director.
19. If you have a problem involving the bureaucracy, discuss it with other employees; focus on problem solving rather than on complaining. Groups are much more powerful and productive than an individual working alone to make changes in a system.
20. No matter how high you rise in a hierarchy, maintain direct service contact. Direct contact keeps you abreast of changing client needs, prevents you from getting stale, and keeps you attuned to the concerns of employees in lower levels of the hierarchy.
21. Do not try to change everything in the system at once. Attacking too much will overextend you and lead to burnout. Start small and be selective and specific. Double-check your facts to make certain they accurately prove your position before confronting bureaucratic officials.
22. Identify your career goals and determine whether they can be met in this system. If the answer is no, then (a) change your goals, (b) change the bureaucracy, or (c) seek a position elsewhere in which your goals can be met.

EP 2.1.7a

Exercise 9.8: Understanding the Orientations of Bureaucratic Systems

Goal: This exercise is designed to assist you in understanding the value conflicts between helping professionals and top management people in bureaucracies.

Step 1: Imagine yourself in the shoes of a top management person in a bureaucracy. Describe why such a person is likely to choose to adhere to the "orientations of bureaucratic systems."

Step 2: Imagine yourself in the shoes of a direct service social worker in an agency. Describe why this person is likely to adhere to the "orientations of helping professionals."

Step 3: Summarize the strategies that a direct service social worker should use to survive and thrive in an agency where top management adheres to the "orientations of bureaucratic systems."

SUMMARY

An organization is a collection of individuals gathered together to serve a particular purpose. This chapter surveys theories that provide a variety of perspectives for viewing and analyzing organizations. The theories covered include the autocratic model, the custodial model, the scientific management model, the human relations model, Theory X, Theory Y, the collegial model, Theory Z, management by objectives, and total quality management. These models are not exhaustive of the numerous models that have been developed. Any of these models can be applied successfully in some situations. Some of them can be applied to organizations while other models are being used.

Values and assumptions (rather than facts and figures) form the bases of most decisions in organizations. Spranger identified six value orientations that frequently have an impact on decision making: theoretical, economic, aesthetic, social, political, and religious.

Two diverse value orientations that have major impacts on human service organizations are liberalism and conservatism. Politicians and decision makers often base their decisions on human service issues on whether they adhere to a liberal or conservative philosophy. Conservatives generally advocate a residual approach to social welfare programs, whereas liberals generally take an institutional view of social welfare.

Knopf identified numerous potential areas of conflict between bureaucracies and helping professionals. Helping professionals want bureaucratic systems to individualize interactions with clients and employees, to be humanized, to be democratic in decision making, to be relationship oriented, and to quickly change to meet emerging needs. In contrast, bureaucratic systems are generally depersonalized, autocratic, procedures and process oriented, emotionally detached, and resistive of change. Such differences in orientations can become arenas of conflict between helping professionals and the systems in which they work. Suggestions are given for surviving in a bureaucracy.

EXERCISES

1. Hard Choices—Funding Social Programs

EP 2.1.10a

Goals: To help students understand that most decisions are based on values and assumptions and to realize that setting budgets for social programs involves hard choices because of scarce resources.

Step 1: The instructor explains that funding sources (such as the federal, state, and local governments and United Way) have to make difficult choices about how much money to allocate to diverse social programs. Financial resources to fund all social programs are simply unavailable, and some people suffer greatly because they do not receive needed services and funds.

Step 2: Students form subgroups of five or six members each. The instructor informs each subgroup that it is the funding source for human services in a local community and that it has $10 million to allocate for the following social programs, which need a total of $15 million. Each subgroup has the task of deciding how much money to allocate to each agency. No subgroup can spend more than $10 million. Read the following material:

The Center for Developmental Disabilities needs $1.5 million to care for adults who have severe or profound cognitive disabilities. These adults have such severe cognitive disabilities that most are unable to walk. It costs $75,000 a year to care for each adult. If the center does not receive its requested funds, some of these clients may not receive necessary medical care and may die.

The Anti-Poverty Agency needs $3.5 million to maintain families at an income level of only 80% of that defined as the poverty line. It costs $14,000 per year to maintain a family of three (generally a single parent with two children). If the agency does not receive its requested funds, many of these families will go hungry, have inadequate shelter, and lack essential clothing for winter.

Protective Services needs $1 million to combat abuse, neglect, and incest. If the agency does not receive all of its needed funds, a number of children will continue to be exposed to abuse, neglect, or incest, which could severely affect them for the rest of their lives.

The Mental Health Center needs $2.5 million to help clients with severe emotional problems, some of whom are so depressed they are suicidal. If the center does not receive all of its needed funds, inadequate services will be provided to clients, and the problems of many clients will intensify. A few may even take their own lives.

The Alcohol and Drug Abuse Treatment Center needs $2 million to help chemically dependent clients and their families. If the center does not receive all of its needed funds, inadequate services will mean that the problems experienced by clients and their families are likely to intensify. Because abuse of alcohol and drugs is a contributing factor to many other problem (such as poverty, mental illness, and family violence), these problems also will intensify.

The Shelter for Battered Women, which is located in a house in a residential area, is requesting $500,000. If funds are cut back, the shelter staff assert they will have to turn away some of the battered wives and their children who request shelter and other services.

Group Homes for Youths runs four group homes: two for young women and two for young men. It needs $500,000. If needed funds are cut back, this agency will have to reduce the number of youths it is serving. Some will be transferred to more expensive residential treatment programs, some will be returned to an unhealthy home environment, and some will simply run away.

The Red Cross needs $1 million for its blood bank and for disaster relief. If funds are cut back, there will be an insufficient supply of blood available for transfusions, and many of the families who are hit by disasters (such as tornadoes and floods) will not be served.

The Rehabilitation Center provides work training and sheltered work to clients with a variety of physical or mental disabilities. It needs $2 million, or it will be forced to turn away clients. If clients are turned away, they will lose hope of becoming productive and perhaps self-supporting. Some of these clients may also end up requesting assistance from the Mental Health Center and from the Anti-Poverty Agency.

Equal Rights is an agency providing a wide range of services to people of color in the area: work training, job placement, and housing location. It also investigates and takes legal action against employers and landlords charged with racial discrimination. The agency needs $500,000. If funds are cut back, discrimination against people of color will increase.

Step 3: Each subgroup shares with the class its decisions for allocating funds (The cuts that are made can be summarized on the chalkboard by having the instructor list the names of the agencies, and then having a representative from each subgroup list the amount of money that was cut—totaling $5 million—from the requested allocations.) Each subgroup states its reasons for making its cuts in funding. The instructor should help the students recognize that most of these reasons are based on values. The instructor asks the students to discuss how they felt making such funding decisions that would (in real life) have significant adverse impacts on potential recipients of services. The instructor asks the class if the exercise helps them understand that making funding decisions for human services involves hard choices caused by scarce resources.

EP 2.1.10a

2. Analyzing a Human Services Organization

Goal: To analyze a human services organization.

Visit (perhaps in groups of two or three) a human services agency and write a report covering the following information. (Some agencies may not have information or data on one or more questions. If the information is unavailable, indicate this in your reports.) Include in your report the name and telephone number of the person you met with.

a. What is the agency's mission statement?
b. What are its clients' major problems?
c. What services does the agency provide?
d. How are client needs determined?
e. What percentage of clients are people of color, women, gays or lesbians, elderly, or members of other at-risk populations?
f. What was the total cost of services for the past year?
g. How much money is spent on each program?
h. What are the agency's funding sources?
i. How much and what percentage of funds are received from each source?
j. What eligibility criteria must prospective clients meet before services will be provided?
k. What other agencies provide the same services in the community?
l. What is the organizational structure of the agency? For example, is there a formal chain of command?
m. Is there an informal organization (that is, people who exert a greater amount of influence on decision making than would be expected for their formal position in the bureaucracy)?
n. How much decision-making input do the direct service providers have on major policy decisions?
o. Does the agency have a board that oversees its operations? If yes, what are the backgrounds of the board members?
p. Do employees at every level feel valued?
q. What is the morale among employees?
r. What are the major unmet needs of the agency?
s. Does the agency have a handbook of personnel policies and procedures?
t. What is the public image of the agency in the community?
u. In recent years, what has been the rate of turnover among staff at the agency? What were the major reasons for leaving?
v. Does the agency have a process for evaluating the outcomes of its services? If yes, what is the process, and what are the outcome results?
w. What is your overall impression of the agency? For example, if you needed services that this agency provides, would you want to apply at this agency? Why, or why not?

COMPETENCY NOTES

The following identifies where Educational Policy (EP) competencies and practice behaviors are discussed in the chapter.

EP 2.1.7a *Utilize conceptual frameworks to guide the process of assessment, intervention, and evaluation.* (pp. 285–304).

This chapter conceptualizes models of organizational behavior, describes value orientations in organizational decision making, compares liberalism and conservatism, and provides guidelines for thriving and surviving in a bureaucracy.

EP 2.1.1b *Practice personal reflection and self-correction to assure continual professional development.* (p. 286).

Exercise 9.1 is designed to increase students' interest in participating in organizations, and to increase their interest in learning how to thrive in an organization.

EP 2.1.10e *Assess client strengths and limitations.* (p. 287).

Exercise 9.2 is designed to assist students in understanding the merits and shortcomings of the autocratic model.

EP 2.1.10e *Assess client strengths and limitations.* (pp. 290–291).

Exercise 9.3 is designed to assist students in understanding the merits and shortcomings of Theory X managers versus Theory Y managers.

EP 2.1.7a *Utilize conceptual frameworks to guide the process of assessment, intervention, and evaluation.* (p. 292).

Exercise 9.4 is designed to assist students in understanding Theory Z.

EP 2.1.10e *Assess client strengths and limitations.* (p. 293).

Exercise 9.5 is designed to assist students in understanding the strengths and shortcomings of the MBO approach.

EP 2.1.7a *Utilize conceptual frameworks to guide the process of assessment, intervention, and evaluation.* (pp. 295–296).

Exercise 9.6 is designed to assist students in understanding which value orientations they tend to use in making decisions.

EP 2.1.7a *Utilize conceptual frameworks to guide the process of assessment, intervention, and evaluation.* (p. 297).

Exercise 9.7 is designed to assist students in understanding their beliefs about liberalism and conservatism.

EP 2.1.7a *Utilize conceptual frameworks to guide the process of assessment, intervention, and evaluation.* (pp. 300–301).

Exercise 9.8 is designed to assist students in understanding the value conflicts between helping professionals and top management in bureaucracies.

EP 2.1.10a *Substantively and affectively prepare for action with individuals, families, groups, organizations, and communities.* (pp. 302–303).

This exercise helps students understand that most budget decisions are based on values and assumptions. The exercise also illustrates to students that setting budgets for social programs involves hard choices because of scarce resources.

EP 2.1.10a *Substantively and affectively prepare for action with individuals, families, groups, organizations, and communities.* (p. 303).

This exercise is designed to help students analyze a human services organization.

CHAPTER 10

Social Work Community Practice

EP 2.1.7a

Barker (2003) defined a *community* as "a group of individuals or families [who] share certain values, services, institutions, interests, or geographic proximity" (p. 83). He defined *community-based* practice as

> [the] integration of direct social work services with the skills traditionally associated with community organization and community development. For example, a social worker who provides some individual counseling or social group work in a neighborhood center might also facilitate efforts by community members to help improve their neighborhood, establish grassroots campaigns, and develop a community leadership group. (p. 84)

This chapter will:

A. Describe the impact of the changing technological landscape on community practice
B. Present three models of community practice
C. Identify macro-practice skills
D. Describe knowledge needed for macro practice
E. Describe the problem-solving process in community practice
F. Describe the community assets approach

The saying "May you live in interesting times" may or may not be an ancient Chinese curse, but it certainly is applicable to life and social work practice today. The pace of change continues to accelerate, and many current realities would have been unthinkable only a decade ago. According to a video "Did you Know" on http://futurestorm.blogspot.com:

- The country with the largest number of English-speaking individuals will soon be China.
- One out of eight marriages in 2007 was between couples who first met online.
- The number of text messages sent daily is greater than the number of persons alive worldwide.

Although technology is advancing, this has not been accompanied by an equivalent increase in the well-being of those living in the United States or other countries. The recession that started in the fall of 2008 pushed unemployment rates to levels not seen since 1982. In 2009, the percentage of Americans in poverty rose to 14.9%, the highest level since 1994 (U.S. Census Bureau, www.census.gov).

For those with jobs, there has not been an increase in inflation-adjusted income for essentially a decade. According to an analysis by the Economic Policy Institute a Washington think tank, inflation-adjusted median weekly wages dropped slightly for both high school and college graduates from 2000 to 2009 (www.epi.gov).

[1]This chapter was especially written for this text by James Winship, MSW, PhD. Dr. Winship is chair of and a professor in the social work department at the University of Wisconsin–Whitewater.

The economic situation impacts social welfare agencies and organizations in various ways. First, the stagnant economy leads to lower tax revenues, which leads to greater budget deficits at the federal level and lack of resources at the state and local levels. By law, states and local governments cannot have ongoing budget deficits.

Second, it increases the demand for services. By the fall of 2010, the poverty rate had risen to 14.3%, the highest level since 1994. The number of Americans without health insurance had reached 50 million, and 14% of the population relied on Food Stamps in 2010—an increase of 70% since 2007 (U.S. Census Bureau, www.census.gov).

Third, the budget deficits lead to an increased pressure to cut federal and state spending, and frequent targets are the programs that serve those experiencing poverty or other needs.

The response by social workers to these economic and social trends needs to be comprehensive. We need to plan effectively, so that existing resources are used as efficiently us possible. We need to educate the public on the real impacts of the changing economy and social conditions on those in need. And we need to advocate for legislation and programs that both meet human needs and promote social justice. The material is this chapter presents skills and knowledge that will assist social workers in these efforts.

It is clear that local communities will play an increasingly important role in developing programs and services for vulnerable populations, and social work will be one of the primary professions called upon in local communities to develop approaches to meet the needs of populations-at-risk. Social workers will be at the "front line" as they endeavor to respond to the needs of people in dire straits.

Social work practice will need to stress community building. This increased attention to community comes at a time when we are recognizing both the importance of community and the ways recent societal changes make it more difficult to strengthen communities. Churches, civic clubs, and other institutions in the local community are being asked to "take up the slack" created by the federal government downsizing it support for social welfare programs.

Healthy communities will be able to respond to social problems by providing a web of support for families individuals.

THE IMPACT OF THE CHANGING TECHNOLOGICAL LANDSCAPE ON COMMUNITY PRACTICE

In examining how technology can be useful in community practice, the increasing use of social media is the most prominent recent trend. In 2010, the number of users on Facebook reached 500 million, one-eighth of the world's population, and users spend 700 billion minutes a month on Facebook (U.S. Census Bureau, www.census.gov).

How can social media be used for community and society betterment? There is a debate on the efficacy for organizing through social media. There are certainly examples of the ripple effect through social media. As chronicled in the blog of the organization Dragonfly Effect (www.dragonflyeffect.com/blog), there are many examples of individual actions leading to change: "Friends of Sameer Bhatia recruited over 24,000 bone marrow donors in under 11 weeks through a well-executed social media campaign, resulting in an estimate 250+lives saved to date by bone marrow matches from those donors alone. More than 15,000 lemonade stands were opened to raise money for childhood cancer through Alex's Lemonade Stand, driven by Facebook messages, email and Tweets. More than $1,000,000 was raised in 2009 through Twitter by CharityWater, an organization that funds welt drilling to bring clean drinking water to Africa and has a strong and dynamic online presence. Each of these efforts began with a focused message and a powerful story, and was able to reach a wide audience and make a big impact amplified through the power of social technologies."

New techniques of advocacy and activism have emerged as the Internet and mobile communication have become integral parts of our lives. These are being used by non-geographical online communities as well as traditional communities. *Electronic advocacy* is the use of high technology in efforts to change public policy at the community, state, national, or international level. This includes a wide variety of strategies, tactics, and tools.

When most people think of social networking sites, well-publicized ones such as Facebook and MySpace come to mind. The largest growth in social networking, however, is in more specialized sites. For example, there are now very active sites for African American, Latino, and Asian American professionals. These sites include BlackPlanet, MiGente, and Asian Avenue. There are at least four sites for gay and lesbian professionals. In addition to taking advantage of opportunities for discussions on culture and pop culture as well as possible connections with others from similar backgrounds, members of the sites organize advocacy efforts affecting members of these online communities.

One extensive study of electronic activism (Earl, 2006) found that the most common uses of the Internet for protest tactics are these:

1. *Organizing online petitions*. Visitors to a site or responding to an e-mail sign a petition that is then forwarded to a government organization or company. One free petition hosting site, PetitionOnline.com, states that it has collected over 30 million cumulative signatures on thousands of petitions.
2. *Letter-writing and e-mailing campaigns*. Advocacy groups routinely use e-mail to advise members and supporters on pertinent legislative activities at the local, state, or national level. An e-mail is sent out alerting members and supporters of the proposed action or legislative deliberation, the significant issues, and the importance of calling, writing, or e-mailing elected representatives on the issue.

   This tactic is used on levels ranging from the national (advocacy groups such as the Children's Defense Fund, www.cdf.org) to social work student organizations on campus alerting members about legislation affecting the social work profession and marginalized groups.
3. *Boycott campaigns*. These target a company for issues such as environmental quality and poor treatment of workers and ask people participating in the boycott to keep a record of their activities related to the boycott and also to contact the company being boycotted.

John McNutt, a social work professor at the University of South Carolina, keeps an updated compendium of electronic advocacy sites at www.policymagic.org/electron.htm.

A second emerging use of technology is in the expanding number of Internet sites with state-level or community-level information on social indicators and trends for a number of different issues or age groups.

One example for those working with children and adolescents is Kids Count, a service of the Annie E. Casey Foundation (http://datacenter.kidscount.org). There are hundreds of measures of child well-being organized by state, county, and sometimes community. For example, a task force on preventing unwanted teen pregnancy in Charlotte compares with other similar cities in North Carolina could access that site to determine how teen pregnancy rates in that city have varied over a 5-year period, how Charlotte compares with other similar cities in North Carolina, and how North Carolina compares with other states.

The U.S. Census Bureau (www.census.gov) and the Center for Disease Control and Prevention (www.cdc.gov) contain valuable information on a state-by-state and county basis. Through a local municipality, social workers may get access to PolicyMap (www.Policymap.com), an online mapping tool that gives users access to over 10,000 indicators.

EP 2.1.1b

Community practice itself is changing to reflect the expanded definition of community in the early twenty-first century. Individuals can be members of online communities as well as geographical communities. An online community emerges when individuals with similar goals or interests connect and exchange information using web tools.

Exercise 10.1: My Use of the Internet and Social Media for Community Practice

Goal: This exercise is designed to increase your interest in using social media and the Internet to impact community practice.

Step 1: It should be noted that all of us have used the Internet to research information on social issues. Many of us have become involved in using the Internet to express our views to political decision makers on issues we feel strongly about. Summarize how you have used the Internet and social media to impact community practice.

Step 2: Summarize how you intend to use the Interest and social media to impact community practice in the future.

MODELS OF COMMUNITY PRACTICE

Several approaches have been developed to bring about community change. Rothman and Tropman (1995) categorized these approaches into three models: locality development, social planning, and social action. Real-world approaches to community change tend to have characteristics of all three types. Advocates of social planning, for example, at times use community change techniques such as extensive discussion and participation by a variety of groups, that are characteristic of the other two types. For analytical purposes, however, we'll view the three models as "pure" forms. (Examples of the three models are found in Exhibits 10.1, 10.2, and 10.3.)

Locality-Development Model

The locality-development (or community-development) model rests on the belief that community change can best be brought about through broad-based participation by a wide spectrum of people at the local community level. The model seeks to involve a cross section of individuals (including the disadvantaged and the power structure) in identifying and solving problems. Some themes emphasized in this model are democratic procedures, a consensus approach, voluntary cooperation, development of indigenous leadership, and self-help. For an example, read Exhibit 10.1.

Community practitioners of locality development function as enablers, catalysts, coordinators, and teachers of problem-solving skills and ethical values. It is assumed that conflicts among various groups can be creatively and constructively resolved. People are encouraged to express their differences freely but to put aside self-interests to further the interests of their community. The basic theme of this model is "Together we can figure out what to do and then do it." The locality-development model uses discussion and communication among different factions to reach consensus on which problems to focus on and which strategies and actions to use to resolve these problems.

Exhibit 10.1 The Locality Development Model

The Social Work Student Organization (SWSO) at the University of Wisconsin–Whitewater has been using a locality-development model for the past several years. Its method of proceeding, along with some of its activities, will be briefly described. The SWSO is a social work club; all majors in social work are invited to attend.

The social work program has averaged about 300 student majors for the past 5 years. Current members speak about SWSO in social work classes at the beginning of each semester, inviting nonmembers to join. SWSO also has a listserv of social work students who want to receive the weekly newsletter that SWSO sends out. The newsletter contains information about SWSO "socials," about volunteer opportunities, and about guest speakers at SWSO meetings. Meetings are held every Wednesday afternoon at 5 p.m.

Even though all social work majors are invited to join SWSO, on average about 40 to 60 students become active each semester.

SWSO elects a president, vice president, treasurer, secretary, two representatives to faculty meetings, and one representative to the Dean's Advisory Board (composed of one student representative from each department in the College of Letters and Sciences).

Decisions in SWSO meetings are made mostly by consensus. (When there is an issue where SWSO members are divided, a vote is taken.)

The social work program at this campus requires majors to become involved in 70 hours of community service activities before taking the 480-hour internship. (Students are eligible to take the internship after all other required social work courses are completed.) SWSO is highly involved in linking social work students with community service opportunities. Examples of opportunities include mentoring at-risk children at elementary schools in the community, visiting an elderly person in a nursing home on a weekly basis, tutoring adolescent males at a state correctional school, volunteering at a group home for youths and adults who have a cognitive disability, and volunteering at the campus day-care center.

One of the goals of SWSO is to provide community services to the local community. This goal enriches the community, allows student majors to test out whether they are truly interested in a career in social work, and helps student majors to develop their skills in providing social services. (Two faculty members serve as advisers to SWSO.)

SWSO also engages in several fund-raisers each year. The funds are donated to agencies that serve people in need—such as homeless shelters. One of the fund-raisers is a raffle for items donated by businesses in the community. Another popular fund-raiser is selling hot dogs several evenings a semester at a hot dog stand located in an area where several taverns serve primarily college students.

One of the annual projects of SWSO is "Pass It On." SWSO members notify students living in residence halls that at the end of the school year bins will be placed in the residence halls where students can place their unused canned food and discarded clothes. (All other students are also notified via the campus newspaper of the opportunity to donate their discarded clothes and unused canned goods.) The canned goods and clothes are then donated to food pantries and clothing pantries in the community.

Another activity of SWSO is to hold, once a year, an Employment Seeking Workshop for juniors and seniors majoring in social work. Four or five employers of social workers are invited to discuss the following:

- Where to look for jobs in social work
- What they like and do not like to see in cover letters and résumés
- Dressing and preparing for interviews
- Tips on what to say and what not to say in interviews
- Sending a thank-you letter after an interview, and how to tactfully inquire about the status of an application after an interview

This locality-development model for SWSO is beneficial to the community and develops the social work capacities of the students who actively become involved in SWSO.

Examples of such efforts include neighborhood work programs conducted by community-based agencies; Volunteers in Service to America; village-level work in some overseas community-development programs, including the Peace Corps; and activities performed by self-help groups. An analysis of locality-development efforts reveals that there is a greater likelihood of such efforts succeeding under the following conditions:

1. Leadership and organizational capacity within the community are sufficient.
2. Relatively simple tasks are adequate to accomplish the goal.
3. Small-scale projects will accomplish the goal.
4. The community is sufficiently committed to the project.

5. There is a common interest and people in the community believe that they will benefit from the project.
6. Benefits are tangible and not too far off in the future.
7. Predicted benefits outweigh the costs. (Rothman, 2000)

Community or locality development has expanded in recent years to include community economic development. One example is Chicanos por la Causa in Phoenix, Arizona (Weil & Gamble, 1995, p. 585). This organization received funding from corporations and development groups to improve services and resources to Hispanics in the following areas: job development and training, housing, day care, and educational and training services for adolescent parents and disadvantaged youths. Another example of this type of expansion is community gardening. Efforts to involve residents in urban neighborhoods in community gardens yield more than an increase in healthy foods. The benefits, according to the American Association of Community Gardens (2008), include underrepresented groups becoming more involved in their communities and developing a greater sense of community ownership and the building of community leaders. Also, because community gardeners become more aware of what is going in their neighborhoods, community gardening has been recognized by the Minneapolis police department and by police elsewhere as an effective crime prevention strategy.

EP 2.1.10e

Exercise 10.2: Analyzing the Locality-Development Model

Goal: This exercise is designed to help you recognize the merits and shortcomings of the locality-development model.

Step 1: Specify the merits of this approach.

Step 2: Specify the shortcomings of this approach.

Social Planning Model

The social planning model emphasizes problem solving. It assumes that community change in a complex environment requires highly trained and skilled planners who can guide complex change processes. The expert is crucial to identifying and resolving social problems. The expert, or planner, is generally employed by a segment of the power structure, such as an area planning agency, city or county planning department, mental health center, United Way board, or community welfare council. Because social planners are employed by the power structure, they tend to serve the interests of that structure. Marshaling community resources and facilitating radical social change are generally not emphasized in this approach.

In this model, planners gather facts, analyze data, and serve as program designers, implementors and facilitators. Exhibit 10.2 describes this process on a college campus. Community participation in social planning varies from little to substantial, depending on the community's attitudes toward the problems being addressed. For example, an effort to design and fund a community center for the elderly may or may not generate

Exhibit 10.2 The Social Planning Model

Emerald College has had an accredited baccalaureate social work program for the past 17 years. The program has an advisory board of 28 members, most of whom are agency practitioners in the community surrounding the college. The social work faculty consists of three people, all of whom have MSW degrees. The chair of the department is Dr. Julie Marzano. Dr. Marzano received her MSW and PhD in social welfare from the University of Wisconsin–Madison.

The advisory board recommends to the social work faculty that they should explore the feasibility of establishing an MSW program at Emerald College because the MSW program closest to Emerald College is 240 miles away.

Dr. Marzano first checks with the campus president and other administrators at the campus about doing a feasibility study for an MSW program. They approve the feasibility study. Dr. Marzano prepares a survey to be filled out by the directors of all the community service agencies in a 125-mile radius of the campus. The survey (among other questions) asks the directors to indicate how many of their social workers who have baccalaureate degrees would be interested in pursuing an MSW degree at Emerald College if the campus decided to offer such a degree. The survey finds overwhelming support for establishing an MSW program at Emerald College and indicates that 247 baccalaureate social workers would (sometime in the future) be interested in applying.

Dr. Marzano also surveys the 73 majors in the social work program to determine their interest in pursuing an MSW degree at this college if such a program were established. Thirty-seven indicate they would be very interested in applying if such a program were offered. Dr. Marzano concludes that the community desires an MSW program be established and that there appears to be a sufficient number of persons who would apply.

Dr. Marzano then checks with the Council on Social Work Education (CSWE) to identify the requirements for an accredited MSW program. An educational specialist at CSWE indicates the program needs to have a minimum of six full-time faculty and that the maximum recommended ratio of faculty to students is 1 to 12.

Dr. Marzano prepares a budget for six additional full-time faculty and for one full-time and one half-time administrative assistant. Dr. Marzano recommends in the budget that funds for the initial start-up costs for the program come from the endowment funds of the college. Dr. Marzano prepares a budget that estimates that an MSW program (charging $25,000 a year in tuition) would be self-sustaining if 70 students were annually enrolled. (The proposed MSW program has an advanced-standing component where as much as 20% of the student body would be given advanced-standing status. The eligibility criteria for advanced standing include the requirement that the student has graduated, in the past 5 years, from a CSWE-accredited baccalaureate program in social work. With advanced-standing status, as many as two semesters of the required four-semester program would be waived.)

Dr. Marzano first presents her MSW proposal (containing the budget) to the Social Work Advisory Board, which gives its approval. Dr. Marzano then presents the proposal to the campus president and other administrators. After raising several questions, these administrators give their approval. The campus president then presents the proposal for this MSW program to the Board of Regents for this campus. The Board, after reviewing it for 2½ months, gives its approval.

Dr. Marzano next prepares the necessary documents, which she submits to CSWE to begin the process of attaining accreditation for this new MSW program.

participation by interested community groups, depending on the politics surrounding such a center. Much of the focus of the social planning model is on identifying needs and on arranging and delivering goods and services to people who need them. In effect, the philosophy is "Let's get the facts and take the next rational steps."

EP 2.1.10e

Social planning approaches are receiving more and more attention as increasing numbers of people question the wisdom of spending an hour or two in traffic commuting each way to work, especially with the high price of gasoline, and express concern about pollution and the loss of open spaces, wetlands, farmland, and wildlife habitats. Advocates of what is described variously as "smart growth," "new urbanism," and "sustainable cities" hope to change current patterns of local land use and development (Banfield, Terris, & Vorsanger, 2001).

Exercise 10.3: Analyzing the Social Planning Model

Goal: This exercise is designed to help you comprehend the merits and shortcomings of the social planning model.

Step 1: Specify the merits of this approach.

Step 2: Specify the shortcomings of this approach.

Social-Action Model

The social-action model assumes that a disadvantaged (often oppressed) segment of the population needs to be organized, perhaps in alliance with others, to pressure the power structure to increase resources or for social justice. Social-action models seek basic changes in major institutions or in basic policies of formal organizations. The objective is the redistribution of power and resources. Whereas locality developers envision a unified community, social-action advocates see the power structure as the opposition—the target of action. Perhaps the best-known social activist was Saul Alinsky (1972, p. 130), who advised, "Pick the target, freeze it, personalize it, and polarize it."

In this model, community practitioners function as advocates, agitators, activists, partisans, brokers, and negotiators. Tactics used in social-action projects include protests, boycotts, confrontation, and negotiation. The change strategy is one of "Let's organize to overpower our oppressor" (Alinsky, 1969, p. 72). The client population is viewed as being "victimized" by the oppressive power structure. Examples of the social-action approach include boycotts during the civil rights movement of the 1960s, strikes by unions, protests by antiabortion groups, and protests by African American and Native American groups. Exhibit 10.3 describes social action at O' Hare airport in Chicago.

A valuable addition to the understanding of "what works?" in social action is Marshall Ganz's *Why David Sometimes Wins: Leadership, Organization, and Strategy in the California Farm Worker Movement* (2009). Ganz explains why Cesar Chavez's United Farm workers organization in California succeeded whereas earlier efforts by radicals and contemporaneous campaigns by the Agricultural Workers Organizing Committee (AWOC), sponsored by the AFL-CIO and by the Teamsters, failed. According to Ganz, there was greater motivation, deeper knowledge of the Mexican American culture of the Central Valley, and more open decision making in the United Farm Workers, coupled with an emphasis to learn from those one works with and from successes and mistakes.

Ganz applied his principles to training organizers for Barack Obama's 2008 presidential campaign. Campaign organizers learned to tell their own stories quickly and to form relationships with potential allies and volunteers. These precepts also can be applied to community practice outside of social action.

EP 2.1.10e

The social-action model is not widely used by social workers. Involvement in social action can lead employing agencies to penalize those social workers with unpleasant work assignments, low merit increases, and the withholding of promotions. Many agencies will accept minor and moderate changes in their service delivery systems but are threatened by the prospect of the radical changes often advocated by the social-action model.

Exhibit 10.4 on page 314 summarizes the three models.

Exhibit 10.3 The Social-Action Model

Saul Alinsky, one of the nation's most noted organizers, was working in the 1960s in the inner city of Chicago with a citizens' group known as the Woodlawn Ghetto Organization. City authorities had made commitments to this organization to improve several conditions in the neighborhood. However, it became clear that the commitments were not being met by the city. The question arose as how to find a tactic to pressure the city into meeting its commitments. An ingenious strategy was selected to pressure city officials by threatening to embarrass the city by tying up all the lavatories at O'Hare airport—the world's busiest airport. Alinsky (1972, pp. 143–144) describes this effort as follows:

> An intelligence study was launched to learn how many sit-down toilets for both men and women, as well as stand-up urinals, there were in the entire O'Hare Airport complex and how many men and women would be necessary for the nation's first "shit-in."
>
> The consequences of this kind of action would be catastrophic in many ways. People would be desperate for a place to relieve themselves. One can see children yelling at their parents, "Mommy, I've got to go," and desperate mothers surrendering, "All right—well, do it. Do it right here." O'Hare would soon become a shambles. The whole scene would become unbelievable and the laughter and ridicule would be nationwide. It would probably get a front page story in the London *Times*. It would be a source of great mortification and embarrassment to the city administration. It might even create the kind of emergency in which planes would have to be held up while passengers got back aboard to use the plane's toilet facilities.
>
> The threat of this tactic was leaked (again there may be a Freudian slip here, and again, so what?) back to the administration, and within 48 hours the Woodlawn Organization found itself in conference with the authorities who said they were certainly going to live up to their commitments and they could never understand where anyone got the idea that a promise made by Chicago's City Hall would not be observed.

Exercise 10.4: Analyzing the Social-Action Model

Goal: This exercise is designed to help you comprehend the merits and shortcomings of the social-action model.

Step 1: Specify the merits of this approach.

Step 2: Specify the shortcomings of this approach.

GENERALIST-PRACTICE SKILLS AND MACRO PRACTICE

Macro practice is an integral part of social work practice, and many of the skills and much of the training for micro and mezzo practice also apply to macro practice. Working on a scale larger than one-on-one or group still involves working with people, and the interpersonal and communication skills are indispensable in this area.

Especially in rural areas, the ability of social workers to communicate effectively with others and be accepted as a person can be as significant in getting approval or cooperation for a project as the worth of the project itself (Davenport & Davenport, 1982; Falck, 1966). Showing empathy and respect is not confined to counseling sessions.

Exhibit 10.4 Comparison of the Three Models of Community Practice

Characteristic	Locality Development	Social Planning	Social Action
1. Goals	Self-help; improve community living; emphasis on process goals	Using problem solving to resolve community problems; emphasis on task goals	Shifting of power relationships and resources to an oppressed group; basic institutional change; emphasis on task and process goals
2. Assumptions concerning community	Everyone wants community living to improve and is willing to contribute to the improvement	Social problems in the community can be resolved through the efforts of planning experts	The community has a power structure and one or more oppressed groups; social injustice is a major problem
3. Basic change strategy	Broad cross section of people involved in identifying and solving their problems	Experts using fact gathering and the problem-solving approach	Members of oppressed groups organizing to take action against the power structure, which is the enemy
4. Characteristic change tactics and techniques	Consensus: communication among community groups and interests; group discussion	Consensus or conflict	Conflict or contest: confrontation, direct action, negotiation
5. Practitioner roles	Catalyst, facilitator, coordinator, teacher of problem-solving skills	Expert planner, fact gatherer, analyst, program developer and implementer	Activist, advocate, agitator, broker, negotiator, partisan
6. Views about power structure	Members of power structure as collaborators in a common venture	Power structure as employers and sponsors	Power structure as external target of action, oppressors to be coerced or overturned
7. Views about client population	Citizens	Consumers	Victims
8. Views about client role	Participants in a problem-solving process	Consumers or recipients	Employers, constituents

In their article on planning in social work, Googins, Capoccia, and Kaufman (1983) also stressed the importance of the interactive aspects of planning as well as the analytic or cognitive dimensions. The interactive skills of social workers are crucial in facilitating and integrating the efforts of all the people involved in the planning process.

Problem-solving skills are also as appropriate on the macro level as they are at the micro and mezzo levels. The ability to help people clarify issues and problems, decide which issues are the most important, set feasible goals, evaluate options for action, decide on appropriate actions, and implement the plan and then evaluate it are as important in working with citizen groups and community projects as in individual work.

It has been my experience that well over half the attempts by groups to address community problems (for example, a group concerned about the lack of recreational facilities for youth) are not successful. In many cases, people who come to meetings with an interest in doing something are stymied by unorganized discussions or fragmented planning. Thirty-three people may come to the first meeting, 19 to the second, and only 5 to the third. Those 5 complain about apathy in the community, unaware that if someone had served as a facilitator in the meetings, the group might have made the kind of progress that would have maintained interest.

Related to this is the need for skills in working with groups. In working to help people form self-help groups, social workers use group work skills, including those of the enabler and catalyst. At the beginning, to attract potential members, social workers may use information networks as well as the media. As the group becomes established, workers begin to focus on process-oriented issues that help group members express themselves, work out differences, question the movement of the group, and so on (King & Meyers, 1981).

The skills of relationship formation and communication, problem solving, and working with groups are as important in macro practice as they are in working with individuals and groups. However, just as there are specific intervention techniques and knowledge appropriate for these levels, there also are specific skills and knowledge useful in macro practice. The following sections emphasize the importance of knowing your community.

KNOWLEDGE FOR MACRO PRACTICE

Know Your Community

Given your agency and client base, it is useful to know not only your community but also the community as it is perceived by newcomers to the area, by members of minority groups, by those with differing sexual orientations, and so on. Different groups have preferences for the kinds of help they seek or use. Farm families, according to one study, are more likely to turn to clergy, family, or friends when problems arise (Martinez-Brawley & Blundall, 1989). Pregnant teenagers in one urban area also demonstrated a preference for their informal supports (families and friends) over formal organizations (Bergman, 1989).

Too often social work educators talk in general terms about how social services and financial assistance programs meet human needs—for example, "Home health care services can be started in communities, which will be useful in helping the elderly stay in their homes." Although this statement is an accurate reflection of the worth of that service, it leaves the impression that all communities are essentially alike—that what will work in Midland, Texas, will work in Midland, Michigan. In actuality, characteristics of regions and communities work for and against the success of projects. For this reason, it is essential that you know the services, governmental structure, values, and other characteristics of the community you serve.

In localities that are ethnically diverse, you need to understand the values and economic and political realities of the various ethnic communities. A lack of understanding can lead to your identifying erroneous concerns that are inappropriate for members of these groups (Rivera & Erlich, 1992). This lack of understanding can also lead to the development of programs or approaches that are not culturally sensitive. One study on patterns of family intimacy yielded wide variations in bathing practices, sleeping arrangements (where children slept), and physical intimacy between African Americans, Cambodians, Caucasians, Hispanics, Koreans, and Vietnamese. The authors of the study fault sexual abuse prevention programs that are not sensitive to the values and customs of the groups with which they are working (Ahn & Gilbert, 1992).

How do local governments or departments therein really function today? Who is to blame when they don't function well? What are common long-range problems? What are common short-term problems? Does failure to resolve problems result from the lack of money and capable people? Or is it because of conflicting or overlapping responsibilities? Does the problem need to be handled by the city or be treated regionally or by the neighborhood? Is the system itself dysfunctional? Does it fail because of the people in charge or because it doesn't have enough people?

Average citizens (if unable to get help with a problem) may want to change the system. But they can't make much of a start without knowing something about "the system" or at least about the part that needs to change. A little digging may show that it isn't the system but the people in charge who are at fault. Or citizens may find that the local government wants to do certain things but can't—because the state constitution or the state legislature won't let it raise the money or provide the services.

Citizens who want to bring about change in community government should first analyze how the existing apparatus is meant to work, the departmental limits that concern them, who imposes limits, and how each part fits the system.

Beyond correcting particular problems, social workers and other citizens have a tremendous stake in finding workable solutions to the ever-increasing demands on governments. Future problems as well as current ones need to be considered. If we are to make intelligent proposals for change, we must first analyze our present government, its structure, its functions, what it can do now, and what it cannot do. We should also analyze our neighborhood governments and the more comprehensive systems of which our local government is a part, because the actions of these systems affect our local communities.

The questionnaire in Exhibit 10.5 is a useful tool for obtaining the kind of specific information that is invaluable in planning for services (or just functioning as a social worker in the community).

A recent development that can help you gain an understanding of your community is Geographic Information Systems (GIS) software. This software is used by social planners to present community or county data in a graphical format so that the data are more understandable. Community groups, too, are beginning to use these tools. For example, the New York Public Interest Group has a project that provides low-cost computer mapping services to grassroots organizations and nonprofit organizations (www.nypirg.org).

An even easier way to make community resources visible is through the creation of a customized Google Map of the community. Specific resources in an area (a food bank, a Boys and Girls Club) can be identified on a digital road or satellite map with placemarks. These can be combined with text, links to other websites, photos, and video (Google Maps User Guide, 2008).

Know the Organizations

Social workers who get involved in macro practice will need information about how organizations function in general and specific knowledge about their employing organizations. For example, if you work in protective services and are interested in starting a Parents Anonymous group for single mothers, one important issue is that of permission and approval. Does your supervisor approve of this involvement? Does this approval extend to your being involved in this undertaking on agency time? Are you acting as a representative for the agency or as an individual? Does your supervisor (or other administrator) see potential conflicts as a result of this activity? These questions are best answered before you become too involved. Otherwise, you may find yourself in a position not unlike the cartoon character who walks out on a tree limb and hears the sound of a saw.

I was once employed by a private social services agency in a midwestern city. Not long after I was hired, the director asked me to represent him at a meeting of people interested in expanding area mental health services. After the meeting, I enthusiastically reported to the director that I was serving on one of the task forces. He became irate, informing me that my purpose was to go and observe and not to become involved in a project about which he had reservations. What I didn't know how to do at that time was to get clarification on my purpose and ask what behaviors would be supported.

Another important concept is that of organizational memory. Individually, each of us may have positive or negative associations with a particular object or event because of past experiences. A friend of mine doesn't eat bananas because he once was violently ill after eating them. Even though he knows that the bananas didn't cause the flu, the association is too powerful.

Similarly, some organizations or governing bodies may be unwilling to become active in certain areas if past efforts were unsuccessful. If you and others are interested in starting a program that would provide jobs or job training for teenagers, you need

Exhibit 10.5 Your Community—Its Background

A. Community characteristics

1. What are the major population characteristics—for example, what percentage is white? Foreign-born? African American? Mexican American? Chinese American? Puerto Rican American? What are the principal ethnic and religious groups? What is the age composition? How do the population characteristics compare to state and national averages?
2. What are the principal economic characteristics of the community? Principal types of employment? Major industries? What other sources of wealth are there? Have there been recent changes in the economic life? (Moving in or out of industry? Substantial industrial or other expansions? Diversification?)
3. What is the unemployment rate? Its characteristics—that is, largely African American, Latino, young people, and so on? Have there been recent changes in this rate? If so, to what can the changes be attributed? Are there sections of your community where the rate is appreciably higher than the average?

   What is the median family income? If only average per capita income figures are available, assess using these questions: Is the average skewed because of large numbers of wealthy people? Large numbers of poor? How does it compare to the national average? (*Caution:* Even if it is lower or higher, it may not reflect, in either case, wide variations or a skewed range in your community.)
4. How affordable is the housing in your community? According to the National Low Income Housing Coalition (Pelletiere & Waltrip, 2007), housing is affordable if an individual or family is spending 30% of income on housing. An individual or family spending more than 50% is at risk of becoming homeless. In 2006, a wage earner on average needed to make $16.31 an hour to afford a standard two-bedroom apartment (or two wage earners in a family needed to make $16.31 an hour between them). One can find out how affordable housing is in your community by consulting the most recent *Out of Beach* report at www.nlihc.org.
5. To what degree are "outsiders" accepted by the "insiders" who have always lived there? To what degree do "newcomers" and "old-timers" use the same services and faculties?
6. What are the norms regarding the role of the church in helping? Do the churches help out their own members who are having difficulties or are in need? Do they help other community members who are not church members? If so, what kinds of persons are aided?
7. What are the norms on conformity to community values for individual conduct? Which norms seem to be strongest? How are people treated who violate these norms?

B. Community life

1. How many newspapers are there? (If more than one, are they independently owned?) Radio stations? Television stations? Are radio and television stations owned by newspapers? Is news of your community carried on a regular basis in a metropolitan newspaper? What are the principal out-of-town media influences? How does one learn about local government activities? Hearings? Meetings? Community cultural activities?
2. What are the voluntary welfare organizations? Is there a community welfare council? Joint fund-raising, such as United Way? If more than one overall fund-raising effort, why?
3. What are principal communitywide civic and service organizations? Fraternal groups? Labor organizations? Business organizations? Cultural groups? Do they work together on communitywide problems? Are there coalitions among these groups on common interests? Ad hoc? Of longer standing? Which groups are more likely to be aligned? On what kinds of issues? Are there neighborhood groups? If so, what are they organized around—cultural, school, political interests, other?
4. How successful is the community in resolving disputes among various groups or over issues such as schools and zoning? Is there high participation in local decision making (as measured by voter turnout)? Are the elected officials and local leaders committed to long-term local services, or are they "training" for statewide office?

Public Welfare/Social Services

A. Administration

1. What government agencies (town, county, state, federal) are involved in administration of public welfare or social services in your community?
2. Is there a public welfare board? If so, what is its composition? How are members selected? Are there legal requirements for their selection? What are the terms of office? Salaries? Duties?
3. What employees are engaged in public welfare or social service activities? How are they

(continued)

Exhibit 10.5 *(continued)*

selected? What qualifications are required? What are the salaries? Are any jobs available in public welfare or social service functions for those on public assistance?

B. Interagency cooperation
   1. What cooperative programs exist between public welfare agencies and the juvenile court, probation officers, schools, day-care centers, nursing homes, public health, other agencies?
   2. What cooperation is there with private social services agencies, if any exist? If there are any, what are they? Is there exchange of information? Joint planning?

C. Programs and facilities
   1. Noninstitutional care
      a. What agency or agencies administer services for children—neglected, abandoned children without parents or relatives to care for them? Are foster homes used? What is the rate of pay to foster homes? How are such homes chosen? Supervised?
      b. What money is available for aid to families with dependent children? General assistance? How much comes from state sources? Federal government? Local sources? What is the average amount available for each child? What is the caseload per worker? What type of care is provided? Are there efforts to help parents find jobs? If so, what kind? Are there adequate day-care centers?
      c. Is there an adoption service?
   2. Other public assistance programs
      a. What programs are there for needy blind persons? Permanently disabled? Partially disabled? Elderly who don't qualify for Social Security?
      b. What other assistance programs exist? Temporary assistance, special and corrective needs, exceptional needs (fares, emergencies, and so on), employment services, legal services, others? What money is available for such assistance? From what sources is it available? How do individuals apply for such assistance? How is information about such special assistance made available to the people?
      c. Are special assistance programs administered by a public department? If so, what agency or agencies?
   3. Institutional care
      a. Are there public institutions for individuals with a physical or mental disability? The elderly? Orphaned? Delinquent? Emotionally disturbed? Needy persons? If private institutions are used, how? On a contracting-for-services basis? Cost sharing? Are county, regional, or state institutions used? If so, on what basis?
      b. How are public institutions administered? What are the procedures and requirements for admission?
      c. What kind of services (educational, recreational, training, and so on) are provided in each public institution? Do any community groups or individuals provide services? If so, what kinds?
      d. What is the cost per resident per day? What is the average stay? Do any of the users pay? On what basis? Do these institutions operate on a budget or a given amount per day per patient?
      e. Are there standards for public institutions—inspections, licensing, state supervision, and so on?
      f. How many persons from your community are in state institutions? What is the cost to your local government per patient? What is the procedure for admission? Average length of stay by case type?
      g. Do any of the local institutions provide outpatient services? What kinds?
   4. Self-help groups and voluntary associations
      a. Are there self-help groups for persons seeking to work with others in similar situations? Are there local meetings of Alcoholics Anonymous, Narcotics Anonymous, and Recovery, Inc. (for persons with chronic mental illness), as well as of local (nonnationally affiliated) groups?
      b. Are there voluntary associations, such as churches and civic organizations, that are important sources of support and leadership, especially within neighborhoods or ethnic communities?

Source: This guide was adapted from League of Women Voters, *Know Your Community.* Copyright 1972, pp. 6, 7, 35–37. Adapted by permission of League of Women Voters of the United States.

to know whether anything in this area has been attempted before. It may be that 5 years ago a program was funded but was poorly supervised. Youths were paid for standing around and, in some instances, even when they weren't there. Armed with this knowledge, you will not be surprised when people have reservations about new youth employment programs and would thus take this into account in your effort to get approval.

Be cognizant about the realities of organizational change. As Pruger (1978) pointed out, much of the discussion of organizational change is not applicable or relevant to the situation of most social workers:

> Organizational change is an attractive subject to many students and faculty. Consequently, it is likely to come up in classroom discussions even where the formal curriculum seems to allow no place for any consideration of bureaucratic phenomena. The problem here is that most treatments are not helpful. They are ideological in character, rather than oriented to skill building. In class, as in the literature, the matter is too often addressed as if the central problem of change is to convince people to be for it. Though it is difficult to identify anyone who has directly opposed change, somehow there is an endless supply of able advocates seeking opportunities to cross swords with this invisible enemy. The results of these efforts are as morally satisfying as they are intellectually dulling. Through them, audiences regularly experience an invigorating, personal commitment to change. Unfortunately, such vicarious experience is no substitute for the patient observation, hard-headed analyses, and consistent behavior required to effect real change. (p. 161)

EP 2.1.7a

Exercise 10.5: Know Your Home Community

Goal: This exercise is designed to assist you in better understanding your home community.

Step 1: Specify the name and geographic location of your home community

Step 2: Using the questions in Exhibit 10.5 as a guide, write a description of your home community. (It is suggested that you do little or no research—simply write what you know about your home community. It is understood there will be a number of questions for which you do not know the answers. That is no problem.) Seek to provide a narrative description of what you know about your home community.

If you are interested in changing your employing organization or some other organization in the community, the following organizational characteristics are relevant:

1. All organizations change, just as individuals are not the same people they were a year ago, neither are organizations. Changes in funding or funding priorities, changes in societal values or trends, occurrences within the community, and changes in personnel all affect an organization's actions and policies.
2. The perceived risks and benefits of the proposed change to the organization need to be assessed and communicated to others in the organization as part of the change strategy. Identifying these can lead to understanding the sources of support and resistance to a proposed change (Frey, 1990).
3. Realize that change within an organization is a continuous process, and be prepared to attempt to influence organizational policies and politics when the opportunity arises. The juvenile probation worker who believes that his or her agency does an inadequate job of working with clients who are ethnic minority members can develop documentation to support this. If the present director and staff don't share the concern, the case can then be made if a new director is hired,

or new training funds become available, or if other changes in the organization or community occur that allow the issue to be raised again. To the organized go the spoils.

4. As change occurs slowly in organizations and communities, individuals who "stick around" are more likely to be able to contribute to change than are persons who "parachute" into a community and then leave a year or two later. The image of a community organizer that many people have is that of a social justice activist who comes into a community, helps people right wrongs, and then rides off like the Lone Ranger. Although outside organizers can be useful in winning battles, wars are won and lost by the people who have staying power in organizations and communities.

Know Funding Sources and Funding Cycles

Social workers often become involved in helping people or groups organize to develop services for unmet community needs. In some cases, such as self-help groups, money may not be needed. In many other cases, funds will be needed to put the ideas or plans into operation. Three questions are important in this area:

1. ***Where is the money?*** The person who has the gold rules. Many times organizations and communities are able to do only what the state or federal government is funding at that time. Knowledge of those funding sources is crucial, as is awareness of other sources of funding. In states where funding has been decentralized, county governments make most of the decisions about how mental health, mental retardation, and juvenile corrections services will be provided. In some areas, local foundations will provide "seed" money for services or organizations in their first year or two of operation. United Way or United Givers may be another source of funds for new or expanded services. Another option for securing money is fundraising, covered later in the chapter.
2. ***What is the funding cycle of the government unit or organization with the money?*** Every level of government—city, county, state, federal—and every formal organization has a defined fiscal year. For the federal government, it runs from October 1 to September 30. For many state and local governments, it runs from July 1 to June 30. Some organizations use the July 1 to June 30 fiscal year, and some use the standard calendar year. Depending on the fiscal year used, decisions on how money will be spent are made at different times by different government bodies. Suppose the fiscal year of a county government that might fund a Youth Diversion Project (to treat youthful offenders in their home community) runs from July 1 to June 30. Budget hearings and deliberations generally would be held in March and April for the coming year. By June 1 at the latest, all funding decisions for the coming year would be made. A community group that approached the county on that date would most likely be told "Maybe next year."
3. ***How "real" is the money?*** At times, the announcement of a new source of funds gets people excited about the prospect of doing something about unmet needs. Often, it turns out that the "new program" is simply a relabeling of an already-existing program that supports service programs and no additional money is available. I was working in Georgia in 1976 when Title XX funding for social services was introduced. Public hearings were held all over the state to help the state government decide how the $300 million-plus was to be spent. Hundreds of people came to hearings in rural counties, advocating their interest. (In reality, the hearings measured the effectiveness of individual agencies' transportation systems in busing their clients to the meetings rather than measuring community opinion!) What people discovered at the hearings was that there would be no additional money and if they wanted funding for new services, this would require reduced funding for the day-care centers, senior citizen programs, and so on that had been funded in the past years.

Social work students generally learn about governments and the mechanisms by which they fund programs in social welfare policy courses. This information may seem dry and somewhat irrelevant at the time, but it becomes extremely useful when they work in a community with unmet needs. When you and the people you work with are familiar with the political process, you are more likely to see political change as possible; when you are unfamiliar with change processes, you will tend to avoid them (Rubin & Rubin, 1992). Social workers who get involved in political processes also need to be aware of the informal as well as the formal political processes. Individuals with economic or other kinds of power can have great influence in local or statewide decision making, even though they never run for political office (Fellin, 1987).

SKILLS FOR MACRO PRACTICE: GROUP DECISION-MAKING TECHNIQUES

In addition to specific information and knowledge applicable to macro practice, numerous techniques are useful in certain situations. These techniques include brainstorming, nominal-group technique, and needs assessment.

Brainstorming

One excellent technique to use in groups that are looking for ways to accomplish a goal is brainstorming (Maier, 1970; Osborn, 1963). *Brainstorming* generates ideas about an issue. To use brainstorming effectively, people try to identify as many different ways of achieving a goal as possible. Developed by Osborn (1963), here are the ground rules:

1. Time: anywhere from about one minute to half an hour.
2. Brainstorm as long as ideas are being generated.
3. Be freewheeling and open.
4. The *quantity* of ideas counts, not the quality. A greater number of ideas increases the likelihood that usable ideas will be suggested.
5. Build on the ideas of other members whenever possible, so that thoughts are expanded and new combinations of ideas emerge.
6. Focus is on a single issue or problem. Don't skip from problem to problem, or try to brainstorm a multiproblem situation.
7. Create a relaxed, congenial, cooperative atmosphere.
8. Encourage every member (no matter how shy and reluctant to participate) to contribute.
9. Limit members to one idea at a time so that less-vocal individuals feel encouraged to say their ideas.
10. Explain the rationale and rules for brainstorming.
11. Seek members with some diversity of opinion and background.
12. After the brainstorming session is over, select the best ideas (or a synthesis of these ideas) related to the issue or problem.

Brainstorming has a number of advantages:

1. It increases involvement and participation by all members.
2. It reduces dependence on a single authority figure.
3. It provides a procedure for obtaining a large number of ideas in a relatively short period.
4. It reduces the pressure to say the "right things" to impress others in the group.
5. It makes the meeting more interesting, fun, and stimulating.
6. It encourages an open sharing of ideas.
7. It helps create a nonevaluative climate.
8. The ideas of one member can build on those of others so that creative and unique combinations are suggested.

Some shortcomings of brainstorming should be noted. For many people, brainstorming is a strange experience and can cause some initial discomfort. For a restricted, self-conscious group, brainstorming may actually hinder participation because it forces members into new patterns of behavior. That said, in some situations brainstorming can also be effective as an icebreaker that opens up a stuffy and inhibited group. Whether brainstorming will have an inhibiting effect or an opening-up effect will depend partially on the leader's skills and timing.

Here is one example of a situation in which brainstorming was useful. A group of residents in a part of a town where there were no recreational facilities for children negotiated with the city to turn a city-owned lot in the area into a park. The city council agreed to let the residents use the area indefinitely as a park and to have city maintenance personnel keep the area mowed. However, the residents would have to raise the money for the playground equipment.

A social worker met with the group and acted as facilitator for a brainstorming session. The 23 neighborhood residents were initially skeptical about the process but got into it as the ideas started proliferating. A total of 46 ideas were generated and then categorized. The two major categories were fund-raising and looking for playground equipment not presently being used. After some discussion, the residents decided to hold a carnival on the proposed site and to use that as a focus for the fund-raising effort. One group worked on that project. Another group made inquiries into locating unused playground equipment.

Nominal-Group Technique

The process for using this technique was explained in Chapter 6. It can be a useful approach to help groups reach consensus or at least to give group members information on the thoughts of the other members.

Several years ago I was asked *by* an interagency council in a medium-size southern county to help it define its priorities. The interagency council was well attended by representatives of health and social service agencies in that county, and the council leadership believed that the group could influence both United Way and the county commission if they were to speak with one voice. The problem, as always with service providers, was that members tended to think that their area of concern (the elderly, juveniles, people with developmental disabilities, and so on) was most deserving of support.

In a 1-day planning session, I met with 40 or more human services professionals representative of all the service providers. I asked the participants at each step to identify *two* groups that they considered to be especially in need of services and at a later stage in the process to list *two* specific kinds of services that should be started or strengthened. The use of the nominal-group technique canceled out the individual biases of the participants toward their own services. By the end of the day, participants had agreed on two specific service areas, which they later proposed to the funding bodies.

As this example indicates, nominal-group technique can provide members of a task force or planning group with information about their own priorities. As such, it can also be considered a needs assessment technique.

Needs Assessment

Needs assessment (NA) is a term that has acquired wide usage and a variety of meanings. It is used to refer to a statewide comprehensive appraisal of problems and needs. It also is used to refer to assessment of a community's needs or to an agency's assessment of its clients' needs. For example, a youth services agency in a community may conduct a needs assessment of its clientele. On a large or small scale, needs assessment refers to efforts to acquire and make sense of information so it can be used as an aid in decision making.

Defining Needs We can differentiate among four types of need: felt, expressed, proscribed, and comparative. *Felt needs* are needs that are perceived by the person with the need. For example, you perceive your need for water when you are thirsty or for shelter if you are homeless. However, we also use the same term to refer to *wants:* "I need a red Porsche so people will notice me." Egan (1985) pointed out that people can also have unfelt needs; for example, they may need medical care or dental care without realizing it. *Expressed needs* are the felt needs that are communicated to others because people don't automatically express the needs they feel. Part of the social worker's role is to help people voice their needs in such a way that others hear them.

Proscribed needs, or normative needs, are those that some expert or formal organization perceives to be needed in a given situation. A professor may write on a student's paper, "You need to write more clearly," although the student may not feel that this is a need or problem. In a family, a protective services agency may see a need for the parents to reduce the intensity and frequency of harsh disciplining of their children, even though the parents feel the discipline is justified and appropriate. Similarly, in a community, those outside the community may see that there is a need for youth programs or parenting classes, even though the residents don't feel that need. *Comparative needs* arise when we compare one area or community or part of town with another and notice a disparity. If one section of town receives few police patrols and a more affluent area has more police cars patrolling the streets, we can speak of a comparative need.

The capacity to distinguish among these four kinds of needs is essential for good community practice. We must be clear about who is defining the need so that one set of values is not blindly imposed on community residents by others (Egan, 1985).

Social workers involved in macro practice can find themselves in situations where they have no information for making decisions, or at other times they have an overabundance of data and have difficulty sorting out the pertinent information. When a needs assessment study is being designed, the following questions help sharpen its focus.

Why Do We Want the Information? A needs assessment (NA) is conducted for various reasons. A sponsoring group knows that a need exists, but without documentation it will be difficult to convince decision makers and others of the necessity for action. In the same vein, an NA can increase the visibility of an issue, condition, or subpopulation (Center for Social Research and Development, 1974).

An agency or organization may conduct an NA to determine whether its efforts are addressing the most critical needs. Especially when new money is involved, NAs can be used to gain information about problem areas to determine which area most needs attention.

Most funding organizations insist that funded projects and programs be evaluated to demonstrate that they are effective, and the information from a needs assessment can form the basis (or baseline) for a subsequent evaluation (National Highway Traffic Safety Administration, 2001). Various government and private funding organizations have policies that include a needs assessment as part of the proposal development process.

NAs can be used as consciousness-raising devices. Based on the work of Paolo Freire, who combined adult literacy with political action in working with the poor in Latin America, NAs designed with low-income community members in mind can become vehicles for discussing empowerment and community needs as well as for data collection and analysis (Marti-Costa & Serrano-Garcia, 1987).

One general rule: If you can't clearly answer the "why" question, you are probably better off not conducting a needs assessment at this time. Information collected without a clear purpose is rarely used.

Who Will Use the Data? In the early stages of drawing up an NA, it is essential to identify and involve the decision makers who will eventually use the data. Allowing the potential consumers of the data to define the NA's scope, focus, and content

Exhibit 10.6 Types of Information Used in Needs Assessments

A. *Profile of community characteristics:* A profile gives an overview of the demographic characteristics of a community—for example, age structure, ethnic and racial composition, length of residence, and so on.

B. *Profiles of domains of living:* These profiles provide data on the incidence of a problem and the social patterns of the population. This can include the following:
   1. Economic data, including income levels, expenditures analysis, money management, and credit patterns.
   2. Employment data, including occupational levels, work history, occupational aspiration levels, and vocational needs.
   3. Family patterns, such as parent-child relationships, adjustment problems of children, marriage problems, and divorce rate.
   4. Educational patterns, including educational attainment and needs of adults, school adjustment of children, school dropout rate, and educational attainment.
   5. Housing, such as density, condition of dwelling units, and overcrowding.
   6. Physical and mental health, including long-term disability, causes of death, incidence of diseases, and environment conditions.
   7. Home management, including housekeeping problems, nutrition, home maintenance, and child care.
   8. Recreational patterns, including leisure activities, sports and athletics, and cultural activities.
   9. Criminal justice, including adult crime and juvenile delinquency rates, fear of crimes, and so on.
   10. Life satisfaction, such as community solidarity and self-appraisal.

C. *Knowledge and utilization of services:* Persons needing a service often are unaware of existing services or resources. Before making decisions, it is important to discover whether this lack of knowledge among those needing services is one cause of the problem's persistence.

D. *Barriers to service utilization:* Individuals who need services may be aware of them and still not use the services because of barriers to utilization. The following types of barriers can be identified in a needs assessment:
   1. Physical barriers, such as inadequate transportation or distance of the agency from target population.
   2. Negative attitudes of the staff, as perceived by the clients or potential clients.
   3. Feelings that a social stigma is attached to service usage.
   4. Fee for usage, which is beyond the means of those needing services.
   5. Actual or perceived restrictive eligibility criteria.

E. *Existing community information system:* Before a service can be used, the potential service recipients must be aware of its existence. A needs assessment can identify the formal and informal channels by which a given group is most likely to be reached.

F. *Resource assessment:* Identification of existing and potential resources should occur before planning or allocating decisions are made.

G. *Political resources assessment:* Mobilizing of political and community leaders and the population at large may be necessary because decisions are generally made in the political arena.

is required if the findings are to have an impact on their concerns (Center for Social Research and Development, 1974, p. 58).

What Kind of Information Do We Want? Many different types of information can be appropriate for a given local needs assessment. Exhibit 10.6 summarizes some of the types of information used in needs assessments.

Where Do We Get the Data? Two broad categories of data are used in NAs: already-existing information and information that needs to be generated. Sources of existing information for every community include census records, state labor department and health department statistics, and agency records and reports. These data can serve as statistical indicators of the extent of problems or conditions. Studies conducted at some previous time for a different purpose are also potential sources of existing information.

Another good source of information is the regional planning commission that serves the given geographical area. In addition to possessing statistical information, individuals on planning commissions can direct you to other sources. City and county planning units also can be valuable sources of information.

Information that is not presently available may need to be generated. This can be done in many ways—for example, community forums or interviews with selected individuals, community leaders, frontline workers, or clients. One common tool for generating data is the survey. Three survey techniques often used are telephone interviews, mailed questionnaires, and person-to-person interviews.

Surveys have both advantages and disadvantages. A survey can yield useful information that cannot be obtained in other ways. Also, information that is directly relevant to the problem under consideration can be collected in a survey. The drawbacks are that surveys require substantial time, effort, expertise, and usually money. The way in which a survey is designed and conducted will influence the results. Thus, it is a good idea to bring in someone with expertise in surveys to assist with preparation and implementation. Potential sources of expertise are state human services departments, local colleges, and the business community.

If you are seeking information from individuals who have access to computers and the Internet, you may be able to use free online surveys to gather the information. Information generated by these can be downloaded to a spreadsheet for data analysis. Use a search engine to locate free online surveys.

Agency frontline workers are often an excellent source of information for determining needs, especially for expanded services. In Hamilton County, Ohio (which includes Cincinnati), 90 case managers were asked to review the records of more than 1,400 clients and report on the kinds of needs, met and unmet, their clients had. They determined that among the top priorities were unmet needs for ways to monitor medications and provide therapy, for socialization, and for subsidized apartments (Ford, Young, Perez, Obermeyer, & Rohmer, 1992).

Who Else Needs to Be Involved? In addition to potential users of the data, it may be appropriate to enlist the cooperation of other organizations, agencies, and prominent individuals in the needs assessment planning. This involvement may be advisable because the NA may reveal problem areas that the sponsoring agency is not involved in. Also, if other agencies help collect and prepare the data, they are more likely to use it in their own planning and decision making. A third reason is that at times information is more favorably received in a community if key individuals have been involved in the NA process.

What Information Is Necessary on an Ongoing Basis? Some of the NA information may become obsolete in a short time. One thing that agencies discover in conducting NAs is that certain types of information need to be updated periodically to be useful. Also, the NA process often indicates what information is not available; this in itself is an important finding.

EP 2.1.7a

An NA can be a long, complex, and costly process, or it may be relatively simple and straightforward. The process should mirror the NA's purpose and be designed to fully yield the information needed by those making decisions.

Exercise 10.6: Participating in a Needs Assessment

Goal: This exercise is designed to give you experience in participating in a needs assessment.

Step 1: Needs assessments usually seek to survey consumers of services about their views regarding gaps in services. Because you are a consumer of services at this campus, three questions will be asked. Specify what you see as the main areas that the social work program needs to improve on in providing educational services to students.

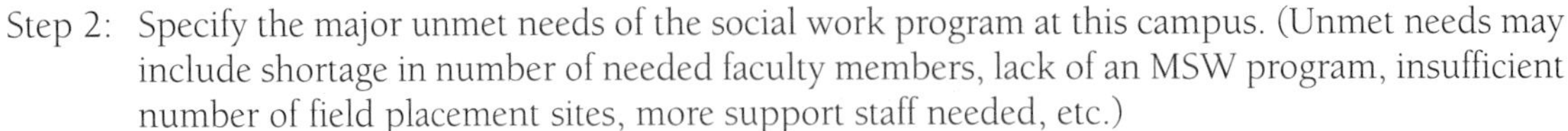

Step 2: Specify the major unmet needs of the social work program at this campus. (Unmet needs may include shortage in number of needed faculty members, lack of an MSW program, insufficient number of field placement sites, more support staff needed, etc.)

Step 3: Specify the major unmet needs of this college or university.

Step 4: (Optional) The instructor may choose to collect the information from each student and then compile it. This information should then be made available to the students in the class. The class may then brainstorm about how to meet the identified needs in these areas.

PUBLIC RELATIONS SKILLS

As social workers we are aware of the amount of misinformation out there about human services and the people who use them. We also are keenly aware of the power of the media. Yet we are often ill prepared to use the media to get our message across. Skills in public education and public relations are not generally a focus of social work curricula.

Brawley (1983) identified a number of barriers to effective use of the media:

> Many of the barriers that exist to the achievement of positive media treatment of human service topics are primarily psychological in nature. We think that the media are entirely out of sympathy with or disinterested in our causes; we drink that prevailing "news values" that stress conflict, immediacy, sensationalism, personalities, and the like present hopeless obstacles to the proper understanding and reporting of human service issues; or we view the domain of radio, television, and newspapers as alien territory that we enter only at considerable risk.
>
> Other barriers are more concrete. The typical human service practitioner simply does not know enough about the workings of the news media to know what opportunities exist for positive action and does not possess the tools needed to undertake activities in this area with confidence that his or her efforts will be productive. (p. 13)

Workers who want to use the media, either to publicize a new service on a one-time basis or to spotlight a community problem as part of a larger change process, must develop relationships with the media and acquire the skills to use the media.

Know Your Media

The first step in getting coverage for your program is to get to know, personally, the individuals who report the news in your community. Introduce yourself to the editor of a county weekly paper or the reporter for a daily paper that would cover your story. The persons in charge of news at local radio and television stations are also important to know.

When working with the media, you should follow some basic rules:

1. Be honest at all times. This means not only being truthful but also not leaving out important facts about a situation or issue. Media representatives will forgive mistakes if they trust you, so don't do anything to damage their trust.
2. Know the deadlines of newspapers and those of the radio and TV news shows. Nothing is as irritating for an editor as someone walking in with a news article 2 hours after the deadline or 5 minutes before the deadline.
3. Know the orientation of the newspaper. Are staff members pro–social services, or do they have axes to grind?
4. Know the staff of the newspaper. To whom do you address your story?
5. Don't complain about a story unless a serious error has been made, and then first call the reporter who handled the story. Don't go to his or her boss unless it is absolutely necessary.
6. Don't heckle newspeople by constantly asking them why a story you submitted wasn't used. It is all right to ask your contact if there was something wrong that you can correct next time. But there are many reasons your story might have been thrown out at the last minute to make room for something the editor considered more newsworthy.
7. Don't forget to say "thank you." Letting members of the press know you appreciate their efforts pays big dividends. When someone does a particularly good job of reporting about your program, a short, simple thank-you note will always be appreciated and remembered. And if you are thanking a reporter, write to the editor with a copy to the reporter.
8. Every newspaper is run differently. General rules of how newspapers operate are just that—general. To know the specifics of each paper, ask for a copy of its *style sheet*. This is a list of news article rules that editors give to beginning reporters. If a small newspaper doesn't have a style sheet, the editor will probably refer you to a sample article or articles as a guide to how articles should be written.
9. There are distinct differences in the editorial content of daily and weekly newspapers. Although a daily typically has a larger audience, a weekly places more stress on local issues and is therefore more closely targeted to the immediate needs of the readers. This is especially true in a rural area. Dailies usually have larger staffs than weeklies, so weekly editors may have a need for well-written news stories for their papers.

Use Media Skillfully

Familiarizing yourself with the rules of the media is one step toward getting good coverage, but this doesn't automatically get your story in print or on the air. If writing newspaper articles or public service announcements (PSAs) for the radio is not your forte, try one of these approaches:

1. *Find out whether the media will do the actual work.* Some newspapers do all of their own writing. If you want a feature on a client who has established a self-help program for others, a feature writer will come out and do the story. Similarly, some radio and television stations have people on staff who will develop public service information.
2. *Find community volunteers to do publicity.* People enjoy doing what they do well. In all communities, there are people with expertise in drawing, writing, design and layout, and so on. Some of these people will be interested in helping your agency, either for one project or on an ongoing basis. Journalism and public relations classes at nearby colleges and universities are also a good resource.
3. *Develop the skills.* Numerous excellent books on using the media have detailed explanations on writing news articles, getting your message on television, and so forth (Brawley 1995; Branston & Stafford, 2006). Writing or designing community

awareness materials is a skill. Like leading a group or interviewing, the more you do it, the better you get.

Supports for carrying out public relations and community awareness efforts are available on the Internet. A site that is particularly geared to people who work directly with homeless students but has broad application is the Community Awareness section of the website of the National Center for Homeless Education (www.serve.org/nche).

FUND-RAISING

People who help others are keenly aware of the limitations of government funding. There is rarely enough money, or money must be used for certain purposes but not for others. Regulations specifying how dollars are to be spent are intended to prevent waste and target the money, but they also limit flexibility.

For new or small agencies and community groups, it can be difficult to get any or sufficient government help. "New" money may not be available, or the agency or group may not have the expertise or time to write a complicated, 250-page grant proposal. In all these cases, fund-raising can be an answer.

In addition to the obvious benefit of obtaining money when you do fund-raising, there are other advantages:

1. You gain credibility when you can show that local people support you.

> When Kate Bradley was raising money for the Petros, Tennessee, health clinic, she learned the railroad was going to sell the land around its unused tracks. She wrote the president of the railroad and asked for the first option to buy the land for the clinic building. Then the politicians in Morgan County learned the land was for sale and tried to outbid her. It was clear they could double or triple her offer. Coal companies in Tennessee are used to getting their own way by using county and state politicians. Kate drove 175 miles to Nashville to meet with the railroad president and the representatives of the coal companies. When she walked into the meeting, she was the only woman in the room.
>
> The president said, "You must be Mrs. Bradley."
>
> "I am," she said, looking him straight in the eye. Without waiting to be asked, Kate Bradley spoke her piece to the older man:
>
> "Sir, I know you are going to honor your letter giving the health clinic the right to buy your land in Petros. I know these politicians can give you a lot more money. But I just want you to know that our money comes from cupcakes. We've had a rummage sale every Saturday, and held dinners and bake sales. Everyone in the community has given me a quilt, or a jar of beans, or put up some preserves to sell for the clinic. That's where my bid comes from."
>
> The railroad president sold her the land, and adjourned the meeting. (Flanagan, 1977, pp. 16–17)

2. It looks good to other funding sources if you have raised a significant amount of money. A women's center raised $2,500 its first year of operation through a raffle and solicitation of donations. The center was able to use this as a demonstration of public support when it went to United Way for support.
3. Fund-raising generates favorable publicity for the agency or group. When people buy tickets for a raffle, attend a benefit concert, or buy a cupcake, they have some contact with the sponsoring organization. This can be an opportunity to inform the public, one at a time, about the organization.

Numerous excellent books and pamphlets explain the how-to's of fund-raising (Clifton & Dahms, 1993; Flanagan, 1995; Keegan, 1994; Young, 1989). There are a variety of excellent sources on the Internet for learning how to raise money through fund-raising events and how to apply for grants. The library at Michigan State University, for example, has a listing of more than 400 websites with information on nonprofit fund-raising: www.lib.msu.edu/harris23/grants/4fcelec.htm.

When deciding what to do and carrying it out, you will find the following principles useful:

1. *Be creative*. One shelter for abused women in Wisconsin created and copyrighted a logo with the phrase "Women—You Can't Beat Them." They sell T-shirts, bags, and other items with that logo locally and nationally and support most of their activities with the proceeds.
2. *Work on your fears, and the fears of those working with you, of asking people for money*.

   Money is like sex. Everyone thinks about it, but no one is supposed to discuss it in polite company. Everyone has a lot of inhibitions about money, especially asking for money; think of all the cartoons of the office worker afraid to ask for a raise. In our society fears about money are normal.

   Most people are afraid to ask someone else for money. They are afraid they will fail and afraid they will lose face. A few admit they are afraid, but others will give a lot of excuses: I can't make calls at the office; I don't know anyone rich; I can't get a baby-sitter. Or they postpone forever: I can't do it until after the kids are back in school, the holidays, the election, the tennis season, the vacation, the promotion. Volunteers often make asking for money sound like a bothersome chore, like taking out the garbage. It is not a chore; it is a challenge. Asking for money is like going out to beat up a bear. The larger the amount, the more frightening it becomes because you have to beat up a bigger bear.

   One of the jobs of a good fund-raiser is to teach volunteers how to conquer their fear of the unknown. The first step is understanding that each person comes complete with his or her own set of fears and hang-ups, and the package of inhibitions usually includes a fear of asking for money. The second step is realizing this is normal and nothing to be ashamed of. The third step is working with the volunteers so they can get control of their own fears.

   It is imperative that you understand and appreciate your volunteers' real feelings, because when members succeed at fund-raising they do more than bring in money for the organization. They have also overcome their own fear. When they raise money, they have won a personal victory, they have conquered the bear. When people can raise money, they can do anything. (Flanagan, 1977, p. 38)

3. *Make the fund-raising activity appropriate for your community*. A benefit concert may not work in a small town where few people go out at night to hear music. Some churches have admonitions against gambling, which includes raffles. In a community where many people attend such churches, a raffle may not work.
4. *Depending on the nature of the project, look for an organization or a small group of individuals to support your project, rather than continually searching for funds*. One of the negatives of fund-raising is that it can take time, time that could be spent otherwise. Also, many foundations and funding sources want to fund only new projects and initiatives, not ongoing work. In some communities, social workers have persuaded a civic club or several high-income individuals to take on funding (or sometimes other responsibilities) for a recurring need, such as school supplies for low-income children.
5. *Make it fun*. When people work together on a project, they develop camaraderie and make friends. An atmosphere that allows the social as well as the work aspect of a fund-raising project (coffee, doughnuts, and fruit at work meetings, for example) helps people feel good about what they're doing. After a fund-raising effort is finished, celebrate what you have accomplished with a party.

POLITICAL ACTIVITY AND LOBBYING

Alexander (1982) stated, "the social work profession, from its inception, has had a love-hate relationship with politics" (p. 15). Partly because their interests and much of their interaction is on a one-to-one basis and partly because of a lack of political skills, social workers have shied away from the political arena. Yet because of their work "in the trenches," social workers have greater knowledge of inequities and inadequate legislation than most people.

In the social work profession there is growing acceptance of the need to understand the political process and to work with it. Social workers are now active in issues that affect the profession and that affect clients.

However, the extent of active political involvement by social workers is relatively low. In a recent survey of over a thousand randomly chosen National Association of Social Workers members, Rome and Hoehstetter (2010) found that although social workers vote in large numbers, less than 10% reported helping to organize or participate in political or cause-related rallies, only 4.3% reported testifying at a hearing on a bill or other action, and only 7% reported voicing opinions through the media—such as writing a letter to the editor.

The whole arena of social work and politics is too large to cover here. Examples of the ways social workers can be politically active include writing and introducing legislation, guiding it through the legislative process, and helping elect candidates. At various times, social workers will be involved in these activities. On a regular basis, however, social workers and human services agencies can attempt to influence local, state, and federal elected officials.

Attempting to influence elected officials—lobbying—is an activity that we usually associate with high-powered, high-paid lobbyists in expensive suits. But it is something that all social workers can do effectively. The following principles are useful:

1. Get to know your legislators. Agencies can invite elected officials to meet with staff to share information and concerns at a time when the legislature is not in session. My experience has been that breakfast is a good time for this. It's before the elected official's schedule is too busy, and it can be more relaxed than a meeting sandwiched between other appointments. Often, legislators don't know much about the nuts and bolts of what social workers and human services agencies do, and they appreciate the knowledge.
2. Contact your legislators not only when you want them to do something but also when you approve of what they've done. Elected officials don't get a lot of fan mail. They appreciate it and will remember it.
3. Never write anyone off. A lobbyist I know says, "There are no permanent friends or permanent enemies, only permanent issues." People who oppose your position may change eventually, especially if you don't treat them as the enemy. The social work value of treating people as individuals worthy of respect applies to people in public life as well as to clients.

EP 2.1.5b; 2.1.5c

Exercise 10.7: Getting Involved in Political Activity

Goal: This exercise is designed to show you that getting involved in political activity is remarkably easy to do.

Step 1: Identify a current political issue at the state or federal level that you feel strongly about. Specify this issue.

Step 2: Identify the e-mail address of one of your state or federal legislators (your instructor may be able to assist with this; state chapters of NASW are also a valuable resource in this area). Specify this e-mail address.

Step 3: Compose an e-mail that summarizes your views on the issue identified in step 1. (Write what you compose here.)

Step 4: Send the e-mail. Specify, here, the response that you receive from your legislator. (Remember: Do not be timid. Legislators want to hear from constituents.)

COMMUNITY PRACTICE: A PROBLEM-SOLVING PROCESS

One of the dilemmas of teaching social work practice is that reality is not always as sequential as we make it out to be. For example, in micro practice we talk of problem identification, then problem assessment or clarification, then goal setting. However, as you work with clients on one issue, they often reveal during goal setting that they have more urgent concerns. Similarly, in macro practice, things won't always go as smoothly as the following description of the process implies. Yet knowledge of the ideal is helpful. Therefore, in this section, we examine how the problem-solving process can be used in macro practice.[2]

Planning, according to Ruoss (1970), is organized foresight. From the time a problem or opportunity arises until some action is taken, the people involved in the decision making will in some manner gather information, look at alternatives, and make a decision. This may be done in an organized fashion, or the principals may just muddle through.

Many efforts, such as involving citizens in an advisory committee or designing a telephone reassurance system, seem overwhelming at first sight. A man was once invited to dinner, and when he arrived, he was seated at a table where an immense elephant, cooked in its entirety, was laid out before him. When he asked in shock how he was supposed to eat something so big, the host calmly replied, "One bite at a time."

In this section, we look at the planning process "one bite at a time." The various steps are grouped into three stages:

PREPLANNING: QUESTIONS TO ASK

- Why is the planning being done?
- Who is the sponsor?
- Who is to do the planning?
- Are varying points of view included?

PLANNING: PLANS TO MAKE

- Problem assessment
- Problem clarification
- Goal setting
- Objective setting

---

[2]This section is adapted from James R. Shimkus and James P. Winship, *Human Service Development: Working Together in the Community* (Athens: University of Georgia Printing Department, 1977), pp. 8–17. Adapted by permission of the copyright owners.

- Examination and decision among alternatives
- Determination of strategy

IMPACT: STEPS TO TAKE

- Implementation of strategy
- Monitoring
- Evaluation

Use this section as a guide for when you embark on a planning process. Be sure to consider all 13 steps; just be aware that the amount of time and effort you spend on each step will vary depending on the situation.

The agency setting, the time frame, the resources to be used, and other factors will (and should) determine how much effort you expend in each step. You don't call the Army Corps of Engineers to build a sandbox. Similarly, an extensive needs assessment or a prolonged search for all alternatives may be unnecessary if the outcome of the planning process is a relatively minor program change.

Preplanning: Questions to Ask

Preplanning includes all the activities that go on before a decision is made to confront actively a problem or opportunity. Answer "Why is the planning being done?" first. Generally, planning is done because someone perceives a problem or an opportunity. The existence of a problem or an opportunity, however, is not in itself sufficient reason to begin planning. Before you begin to plan, ask the following questions to check the validity of the problem and the assumptions on which it is based:

1. Is this concern *our* concern, or is it some other individual's or group's concern?
2. Is this concern our concern *alone*, or should it be shared with others?
3. Is this a concern that is important to us *now*, or would it be better to postpone consideration to a later time?
4. Is the apparent concern the *real concern*, or is it a symptom of a deeper underlying problem—or of a different but related problem? (DeBoer, 1970, p. 75)

Sometimes the "why" is answered for you. Legislation or administrative mandates may indicate that you must begin planning to comply with legislation or administrative policy by a certain date. Although there may be some latitude in these instances, thorough examination of those four questions is important before you move on to the issue of sponsorship.

From the beginning, the agency or organization sponsoring the human services development effort must be clearly identified. The organizational base often influences the nature of the effort. For example, a task force composed of professionals from many agencies and cities looking at the needs of youth will likely come up with a plan that differs from one developed by a single agency.

Another reason to clarify sponsorship is to identify those individuals who have responsibilities for working on the effort. Planning on the local level is linked to service delivery, and if the agency involved is to deliver the service, the administrator may be the person doing the planning. If the administrator is not the chief planner, the planning manager still needs to have the active support of the administrator to conduct the planning and to ensure that the results are implemented.

There may be times in a planning process when the administrator is the appropriate person to initiate contacts; if the administrator is not "on board" with the process and is not willing to take appropriate actions, planning may falter. At times, the administrator may also need to have the approval of his or her division or board before tackling a project.

The other component of the "who" question deals with the composition of the group doing the planning. A "planner" formulating a "plan" in an office separated from an agency's activities will produce a far different outcome than a task force composed of staff, representatives from other agencies, consumers, and other interested citizens.

Preplanning calls for persuasiveness. The project should be formulated with an eye toward the known philosophies of those who must approve what is to be done. Involving key persons who have differences at an early stage affords them the opportunity to voice their ideas, and the final product is less likely to be rejected by those who participated in it.

At times, influential individuals will register initial opposition to an effort and refuse to participate. In these situations, it is important that the planning group formulates its strategy in a way that recognizes and adjusts to the expected opposition.

Planning: Plans to Make

The first step in the planning sequence is problem assessment, which includes needs assessment, problem identification, problem causal analysis, and resource assessment.

Needs assessment involves the gathering, ordering, and analyzing of information pertinent to the problem.

Bernanos (1970) once stated that "the worst, the most corrupting of lies, are problems poorly stated." Problem identification is concerned with ascertaining whether the problem under consideration is the appropriate problem and how well the problem is stated.

The difficulty in problem identification lies in the subjective nature of "problems"—a problem is what somebody perceives as a problem. The nature of the problem is determined by the manner in which it is perceived (Cartwright, 1973). Perceptions of what a problem is are shaped by data, attitudes, and value judgments. A merchant and a juvenile court worker may interpret the same data on juvenile delinquency quite differently.

Because of the difficulty in defining a problem, determining who is to do the planning is very important. If the problem under consideration is a controversial one, such as juvenile delinquency, conflict about what the problem is and what the solution should be is inevitable. If the planning process is carried out by relatively few people, when the results are released or the program is to be implemented, there likely will be considerable conflict. The proposed program may be rejected or be so embroiled in controversy that it is not fully effective. This outcome may occur because the omission of certain persons from the planning process caused the planning group to overlook vital information about conditions, resources, or attitudes.

Whenever the problem under consideration is controversial or affects a large number of people, conflict will arise. It can be postponed; it cannot be avoided. What *can* be done is to attempt to involve the principals in the planning process, starting with problem identification. If people can agree on the problem, there is more likelihood that they will be able to agree on goals, objectives, alternatives, and strategies. If numerous people are involved, they are more likely to advocate the action or plan in the larger community.

As the dimensions of the problem are revealed, the next step is to clarify them. Three measures that are helpful in this process relate to the problem's identity (exactly what is it?), its location (where is the problem under consideration?), and its magnitude (what is the extent of the problem?). For example, a group working on housing might define the problem as deteriorating housing (what) in a 14-block neighborhood south of the downtown area (where), which has 37% substandard housing according to the last census, compared with 23% in the previous census (to what extent).

In clarifying a problem, it helps to identify what is *not* the problem. In the previous example, the problem is not the sidewalks, the streets, or the storm sewers.

After the problem is identified, the next component of problem assessment is to analyze its causes: the economic factors, political pressures, institutionalized values, and attitudes that contribute to the problem. A causal analysis may reveal that the problem under consideration is not the "real problem," and it may be necessary to backtrack and redefine the problem. Several decades ago, it was thought that people who committed crimes did so because they were mentally retarded. This theory led to the notion that the crime problem could be solved by developing approaches to prevent and treat mental retardation. Intelligence testing of prison inmates, however, found that most inmates were of normal intelligence. The mental retardation theory of criminal behavior was then discarded. Discarding this theory forced criminologists to change their conceptualizations of criminal behavior.

An integral part of problem assessment is resource assessment. This involves cataloging all actual and potential resources for dealing with the problem. It may include a compilation of agencies and community groups involved in or sympathetic to the problem, a listing of potential funding sources, and a determination of the amount of advocacy around this problem present in the community. In the case of funding sources, it is important to ascertain the limitations under which the money may be spent. In many instances, "form follows financing."

The next step in the planning process is to establish goals. Goals—the long-term aims of the project—may be expressed in general terms. They are statements about a desired condition, and they may not be attainable. In the neighborhood housing example, the goal might be to bring every housing unit in the neighborhood up to code-enforcement standards, even though the project planners know there is little likelihood of this occurring.

Whenever possible, it is helpful to express written goals in terms of generally accepted standards. In the housing example, the state or local housing code regulations serve as a standard. In other areas, such as child care or homemaker services, state agencies or private accrediting groups will have standards against which to measure the adequacy of a program.

After goals are established, the next step is to set specific objectives. These should relate directly to the goals, but they are different in that they describe outcomes that the planners realistically expect to meet instead of expressing an ideal condition.

Objectives are quantifiable. An objective is measurable in relation to what is to be done and within what time period it is to be done. The use of the standards and measures in the objectives should also reflect the quality desired. In the housing example, specific objectives might be the following:

1. Conducting a housing inspection of every house in the neighborhood within the first 3 months.
2. Rehabilitating 20 housing units in the first year that are structurally sound but do not presently meet code regulations.
3. Beginning proceedings to condemn and demolish all vacant houses judged not structurally sound.

There are two types of objectives: objectives that must be reached if the project is to be a success and objectives that are desirable but not essential. The three objectives listed above are essential objectives. A desirable objective might be as follows:

4. Planting trees along four residential streets.

Clear, specific objectives are necessary for several reasons. The consideration of alternatives and the selection of the strategy are based on the objectives. As computer operators say, "garbage in, garbage out." Furthermore, it is extremely difficult to evaluate a program if it does not have quantifiable objectives. Without good objectives, one can evaluate a program only by personal biases.

In the sport of archery there is one sure way for beginners to hit the bull's-eye on the side of the barn every time: Paint the bull's-eye after the arrow has landed! A program that is launched without a clear statement of goals is just such an arrow; though wide of the mark intended by its launchers long ago, it may be dubbed "on target" by anyone who can paint a convincing bull's-eye (DeBoer, 1970, p. 108).

After objectives are set, the next step is to examine and choose among alternative approaches. In most cases, there will be more than one way to meet the objectives.

The bases on which alternatives are judged will vary with the circumstances. Factors such as cost resources, technical feasibility, and political feasibility will be considered. The length of time in which a program has to prove itself is a consideration. If it is funded for only 1 year and then must find alternative sources of support, an approach that gives short-term results must be chosen. When selecting among alternatives, guard against the practice of selecting the approach that seems most manageable or most interesting or convenient for the staff rather than the one that best meets the objectives.

When the approach that best meets the objectives has been selected, the next step is to determine strategy. The process of identifying the problem, setting the goals and objectives, and choosing among alternatives has indicated *what* needs to be done. In determining the course of action, the questions of *how* it is to be done and *who* will do it are addressed.

In this step, you are packaging the plan of action. Parts of the strategy will have become apparent in the previous steps, but you can easily ignore some important factors unless a thorough examination of the proposed course of action is undertaken. Realism is imperative. Further refinements of the selected approach may be necessary. When considering who is to implement the plan and how it is to be done, the participants may discover that there are not sufficient resources to implement the approach fully, and some hard decisions about modifying the approach will need to be made.

In setting the strategy, you also need to build in procedures that facilitate implementation, monitoring, and evaluation. If money is to be secured for a new program and if there are civil service or state merit systems to work with, preparing the positions should be done before the money is received to cut down on the start-up time. Similarly, you can begin informally to look for staff before the hiring process officially begins.

The mechanisms for monitoring and evaluation need to be decided on at this time. If an evaluation of the effects of the actions on a target population is desired, then data on that population's characteristics need to be gathered before the program is implemented.

Impact: Steps to Take

The final stage of the planning process is the impact stage, which covers implementing the strategy, monitoring it, and evaluating it. In all these steps, especially implementation, the actual situation will determine what actions need to be taken.

The last two steps are too often left out. Planning is done, a program is launched, and then there is an inclination to neglect monitoring (that is, continually gaining information about the program's performance) and evaluation until a review is called for. The procedures and instruments for monitoring might include (1) reporting forms for fiscal transactions, personnel, training, and participant intake in a program; (2) site visits by appropriate persons; and (3) mechanisms for permitting client feedback.

Monitoring serves many important purposes. It provides information for guidance while the program is in operation. If the administrator receives up-to-date information, he or she can make adjustments and correct program flaws before they become major. Monitoring also provides information for periodic evaluations. Two requisites for effective evaluation are clear objectives against which to measure performance and accurate data that reflect the performance.

The importance of evaluation cannot be overstated. In the planning process itself, participants should continually check to see whether the objectives meet the problem and whether the strategy addresses the problem and objectives. Participants should also concern themselves with periodically evaluating how well they are working together.

VALUES AND MACRO PRACTICE

In Chapter 2, we discussed values in social work practice. In this section, we address values in macro practice. One of the values impacting macro practice involves the assertion at the start of the chapter that the client is the community and that the community benefits if human needs are met better than they were before. This assertion is a value statement that is not shared by everyone. Some people believe that social welfare benefits and services should be eliminated, or severely curtailed, either because they believe that people should "make it on their own" or because they do not want to support government helping programs with their taxes. Others may not share these values when it comes to particular actions or programs. Public or community education efforts in sex education are opposed by people who believe that information on sexuality leads to increased promiscuity among teenagers. Within their value framework, the community would be worse off if such community education efforts were carried out.

Another value issue that can be raised is whether social work and social welfare institutions are part of the problem or part of the solution. Galper (1980) stated, "Conventional social work community organization practice is as likely to serve a co-optive role, or to function as a commonly based approach to social control, as it is to operate as a vehicle for progressive change" (p. 151). From the perspective of Galper and other radicals, much of what is advocated in community organization and other macro-practice approaches has two basic aims. One is to give people who participate in planned change activities a sense of belonging, of not being powerless or isolated from society. Galper and others believe the sense of power may not reflect reality. The second goal is to make minor changes in programs or practices that do not have an impact on the major societal forces that oppress the poor, persons of color, and others (Galper, 1975).

An important value to consider in community, or macro, practice is *beneficence*. This can be defined as doing good for others and not doing harm (Netting, Kettner, & McMurty, 1998). It is essential that social workers in social planning and locality-development roles understand the life situations of those involved before setting up programs. For example, a group setting up a food pantry for low-income families needs to take into account the fact that most low-income adults work, and the hours of the food pantry need to accommodate the work schedules of both first- and second-shift workers. Otherwise, the service won't be of use to many people who could benefit from it.

All social workers in practice must question the goals of any effort they are involved in. They must also question the means they are using, especially in working with people who are culturally or ethnically different. It may be that what you envision as feasible may not seem so to the people you are working with.

A number of the activities previously discussed (lobbying, publicity, fund-raising, group decision making) may not be within the range of behaviors of many people. For example, many Asian Americans come from a culture in which authority is not questioned, so pressuring a local official is not an activity in which they feel comfortable. It has been my experience that Appalachian whites do not participate easily in community meetings in which a variety of persons are present. Their cultural values discourage "opening up," especially in front of strangers.

What social workers need to do, in Saul Alinsky's words, is to "never go outside the experience of your people. When an action or tactic is outside the experience of the people, the result is—confusion, fear, and ... a collapse of communication" (1972, p. 127). Social workers can look for culturally sensitive or culturally acceptable methods of achieving goals. For example, one traditional Native American ritual, the Talking Circle, has been used with a number of Northwest tribes in the United States as a means for group decision making and communication (Stephenson, 1983).

A FOCUS ON ASSETS

Paying attention to assets in a community is a new way of thinking about working with low-income communities or counties; its focus on resources rather than on problems has much in common with the strengths perspective in social work practice (Page-Adams & Sherraden, 1998). Traditional approaches to working with troubled neighborhoods and poor counties have focused on the deficits of the community—boarded-up houses, gang activity, lack of jobs—and have tried to "fix" these problems. An alternative approach is capacity-focused or asset-focused development. When the assets or strengths of a community are mapped, block by block or area by area, a surprising array of activities, strong groups, and talents is found. Citizens' associations and churches are found to be doing good work (although often not cooperating with each other). There are institutions in the community that are doing good work, with the capacity for doing more. The talents and abilities of individuals, often underutilized, are discovered (Kretzmann & McKnight, 1993).

Many communities have major social problems, such as high levels of poverty, homeless people, divorce, child abuse, battered spouses, unemployment, deteriorated housing, cancer and other health problems, crime, alcoholism and other drug abuse, school dropouts, and births outside of marriage. If we focus on these deficiencies and problems in a community, we are using the half-empty-glass approach. When we view the glass as half empty, we focus on the negative aspects of life, and we are likely to become consumed with negativity and overcome with despair. Furthermore, if the focus is on problems and deficiencies, most members of that community begin to despair. Despair becomes a self-fulfilling prophecy; members of the community put little effort into developing themselves and little effort into developing the community.

Of critical importance, therefore, is to see the glass as half full—that is, to focus on the positive elements in our lives and the positive elements in the community in which we live. Perception is reality. What we believe to be true often becomes the center of our thoughts so much that it really becomes true. By viewing the glass as half full, we see the depth of the human spirit and the richness of the creative potential that exists in every community. We identify people who are talented and experienced in a variety of areas. The rate of unemployment in some communities may be high. Let's say it's 17%—but that means 83% of able-bodied adults are employed! There are strong social networks and associations in every community. There are many successful people in every community. There are beautiful landscapes where nature can be enjoyed. There are people getting things done that need to be done by using what is available. In other words, a focus on strengths and assets leads to vitality and positive actions. Every citizen has capacities that can be tapped to make life in the community better.

Social work has had a long tradition of practice-focused strengths and assets. For example, Dennis Saleeby (2002) and his colleagues at the University of Kansas School of Social Welfare spent much of the last two decades developing, testing, and promoting a strengths perspective for social work practice. The strengths perspective provides an orientation to practice that seeks to uncover and reaffirm people's talents, abilities, survivor skills, and aspirations. A focus on the strengths found in individuals, families, groups, and communities increases the likelihood that people will reach the goals they set for themselves.

One approach to understanding the assets of a community is to map those assets. In talking with neighborhood residents, workers can ask the following questions:

- Name some individuals who in some way contribute something positive to this community. What is it that they do? What skills do they have?
- What organizations, including social organizations, are contributing something positive to this community? What is it that they do? Do they have any impacts on the community besides their stated goals?
- What churches, mosques, or synagogues are in the community? What do they presently do that contributes positively to the community? What other resources do they have that could potentially be of use to the community?
- What schools are located in the community? What do they presently do that benefits their students outside the school day/school calendar? What resources do they have that could potentially be of use to the community?

This format can be adapted to fit the specific context of the community. The information gathered can then be used to build on the assets of the neighborhood for community betterment (Dorfman, 1998).

The concept of social capital is also useful in thinking of the assets of individuals, especially those in distressed communities in inner cities or rural areas. Social capital can be thought of as the friends, colleagues, and more general contacts through whom you receive opportunities to use your financial and human capital (Johnson, 2003). In plainer language, individuals with a great deal of social capital will know much more about potential jobs, opportunities to make money, opportunities to get the most for their money, and ways to invest money wisely than will those with less social capital.

Social capital comes from social networks. A social network consists of any group of people linked through social connections ranging from casual acquaintance to close familial bonds. One way of differentiating social networks is through the distinction between "get by" and "get ahead" networks.

"Get by" networks are valuable in that an individual with pressing problems can receive assistance from others. If your car breaks down, whom do you know who can help you fix it so you do not have to pay an auto repair shop? If you are a working parent and your young child is sick, who can care for the child so that you do not have to lose a day's pay? "Get by" networks help with immediate needs, and there is reciprocity involved. There is an obligation to help the person who has helped you, and the obligation hinges on necessity to keep alive the possibility of asking for assistance at some time in the future.

"Get ahead" networks function to provide information about possibilities for advancement and about the way to reach these. Many jobs are secured through friends, business contacts, and relatives. Students living in middle-class/upper-middle-class suburbs are likely to have contacts through family and friends that can lead to part-time or summer employment, especially the kind of employment that can be useful in college admissions or deciding on career choice. An eighth grader in an affluent suburb who is considering medicine as a profession is likely to be able to talk with an older sibling or cousin of a friend or classmate in medical school, who can provide advice about the kinds of courses to take and appropriate summer experiences during the high school years, which could lead to the right college and then the right medical school. That kind of information is much less likely to be available to the student in a central city or severely distressed neighborhood (Winship & Hall, 2004). Efforts to expand the social capital of those living in isolated urban and rural neighborhoods include connecting owners of small businesses in these areas with their counterparts in more affluent communities and using the Internet to connect those with similar interests across economic lines.

Every person has assets of value to others. A strong community is a place that recognizes those assets and has relationships between people that facilitate the sharing of assets among residents. A weak community is one in which the assets of the residents are either not recognized or, if recognized, not shared with others.

Saleeby (2002) notes that an effective community practitioner must know how to do the following:

- Assess individuals' skills and strengths and then link them to the needs and aspirations of other residents or groups.
- Add up the cumulative resources of individuals and groups in the community and, with the residents, combine them in the development of programs and resources the community genuinely wants and needs (for example, a food pantry, or a child-care service).
- Ensure that all those who make a contribution to the human and resource capital of the community have the opportunity, through connection with others, to move toward achieving personal and familial goals, to create or develop an enterprise, or to solve problems.
- Help residents strengthen their sense of community through the development of activities that symbolically and practically cement ties between individuals and groups (for example, a street fair, a mini-grants program).

- Help ensure that individual well-being and resilience are a part of all community activities; that there is real work, real responsibility, real opportunity to produce income, and genuinely positive expectations of success and accomplishment. (p. 237)

EP 2.1.7a

For an excellent illustration of a successful asset-developing approach, see the section "Grassroots Approaches to Improving Deteriorating Neighborhoods" in Chapter 12 (p. 414). The section describes Bertha Gilkey's philosophy and strategies to develop a sense of community and to improve what was once a low-income, deteriorating housing project.

Exercise 10.8: The Assets of My Home Community

Goal: This exercise is designed to assist you in using a strengths-based approach to community practice.

Knowledge of community assets is as important as knowledge of community needs. Knowledge of assets provides hope of improving community life and often helps identify resources that may be used to improve identified community needs. Specify the assets and resources that exist in your home community. (Examples of assets include positive community values, financial resources, low unemployment rate, low crime rate, diversity in population, high educational levels achieved, existence of such clubs as Rotary, good transportation systems, a good public library system, and people having pride in their community.)

SUMMARY

Three models of community practice are the locality-development (also called community-development), social planning, and social-action models.

Community practice, also called *macro practice,* refers to social work activities in which the client is the community, where the focus of the change effort is larger than an individual, family, therapy group, or organization. Social workers are usually involved in community practice at some point in their careers.

There are similarities between community practice and work with individuals, families, groups, and organizations. Skills in communicating and forming relationships, skills in working with groups, and problem-solving skills are as applicable in this realm of practice as in the others. To be effective, however, social workers need to have knowledge of communities and organizations in general and of the specific community and organization(s) they work in. For some efforts, knowledge of funding sources and funding cycles is essential.

Depending on the kind of macro effort in which the social worker is involved, the following techniques can be used: group decision-making techniques, community awareness or publicity approaches, fund-raising techniques, and lobbying strategies.

The problem-solving model can also be used to address community problems. The various steps in a community problem-solving model were summarized in the following three stages: preplanning (questions to ask), planning (plans to make), and impact (steps to take). In using this or other macro approaches, value issues such as community values, the role of social welfare in society, and ethnic or cultural sensitivity have to be considered.

In the coming years, social workers interested in community practice and community well-being will increasingly find that the Internet and Social Media are valuable sources of knowledge and skill acquisition for their home communities. Paying attention to assets is a new way of thinking in building and sustaining a community.

EXERCISES

EP 2.1.7a

1. Community Needs Assessment

Goal: To conduct a community needs assessment.

Step 1: Form groups of five.

Step 2: Select a community and use the questions in Exhibit 10.5 to conduct a community needs assessment.

Note: Alternatively, the entire class can assess one community, with groups focusing on different topics.

EP 2.1.7a

2. Needs Assessment and Proposal Development

Goal: To conduct a needs assessment and develop proposals to meet the needs identified.

Step 1: Form groups of five or six. Your task will be to conduct a needs assessment of an issue on campus or in the surrounding community and then develop a proposal to meet the needs identified.

Note: This assignment may be a major course assignment. Alternatively, make as much progress as you can in a class period to conduct a needs assessment and develop a program proposal. For example, if the latter approach is used, ask the following questions:

a. What are the most urgent, unmet needs of our social work program?
b. What evidence or documentation is there that these are urgent, unmet needs?
c. What additional information needs to be sought to determine fully whether these needs are urgent and unmet?
d. What specific, realistic proposals do we have for meeting the needs that have been identified?

Step 2: The subgroups present their needs assessments and proposals in oral or written form. The instructor provides feedback to the subgroups.

EP 2.1.4a

3. Identifying Community Values

Goal: To examine the values of your home communities.

Note: Community values influence the types of services that are publicly available and supported by a community.

Break into groups of three or four. Discuss your home communities' reactions to the following community activities:

a. High school students seek to establish in their school a clinic that dispenses contraceptive materials.
b. An avowedly lesbian woman launches a campaign to seek election to a local political office (such as to the city council).
c. A group of working parents requests the local school system to establish an all-day kindergarten, partially to meet the needs of working parents.
d. An AIDS support group seeks authorization to use the public meeting room of the library for its weekly meetings.
e. A local organization seeks the establishment of an additional (or the first) shelter for the homeless in your neighborhood.

4. Analyzing Community Practice Efforts

Goal: To analyze community practice efforts.

Step 1: Form groups of three. Select a community change or community planning effort to report on to the class. An example of a planning effort is a project by the social work student organization

EP 2.1.7a

to arrange an educational conference or workshop on a topic such as AIDS. Another example is the efforts of a community group to establish a homeless shelter.

Step 2: Research information on the questions that follow on your selected community change effort. Try to interview at least one planner.

QUESTIONS

a. What are the goals of the planning effort? How many planners are involved? Who are the planners, and what are their planning credentials? Why is this planning effort being undertaken?
b. Which of the three community practice models is this planning group primarily using? What characteristics of this model are being displayed by the planners? Does this planning effort have some characteristics of the other models? If "yes," which models, and what characteristics of these models does it have?
c. What are the results of this planning effort—that is, to what extent are the goals being accomplished? What are the strengths and shortcomings of this planning effort?

COMPETENCY NOTES

The following identifies where Educational Policy (EP) competencies and practice behaviors are discussed in the chapter.

EP 2.1.7a *Utilize conceptual frameworks to guide the process of assessment, intervention, and evaluation,* (pp. 305–342).

This chapter conceptualizes three models of community practice, describes the impact of the changing technological landscape on community practice, identifies knowledge and skills for macro practice, describes the problem-solving process in community practice, and describes the community assets approach.

EP 2.1.1b *Practice personal reflection and self-correction to assure continual professional development.* (pp. 307–308).

Exercise 10.1 is designed to increase students' interest in using social media and the Internet to impact community practice.

EP 2.1.10e *Assess client strengths and limitations.* (p. 310).

Exercise 10.2 is designed to assist students in understanding the merits and shortcomings of the locality-development model.

EP 2.1.10e *Assess client strengths and limitations.* (pp. 311–312).

Exercise 10.3 is designed to assist students in understanding the merits and shortcomings of the social planning model.

EP 2.1.10e *Assess client strengths and limitations.* (pp. 312–313).

Exercise 10.4 is designed to assist students in understanding the merits and shortcomings of the social-action model.

EP 2.1.7a *Utilize conceptual frameworks to guide the process of assessment, intervention, and evaluation.* (p. 319).

Exercise 10.5 is designed to have students assess (using a conceptual framework in the chapter) their home community.

EP 2.1.7a *Utilize conceptual frameworks to guide the process of assessment, intervention, and evaluation.* (pp. 325–326).

Exercise 10.6 is designed to assist students in conceptualizing how to conduct a needs assessment.

EP 2.1.5b *Advocate for human rights and social and economic justice.*

EP 2.1.5c *Engage in practices that advance social and economic justice.* (pp. 330–331).

Exercise 10.7 is designed to show students that engaging in political activity is remarkably easy to do.

EP 2.1.7a *Utilize conceptual frameworks to guide the process of assessment, intervention, and evaluation.* (p. 339).

Exercise 10.8 is designed to assist students in using a strengths-based approach to community practice.

EP 2.1.7a *Utilize conceptual frameworks to guide the process of assessment, intervention, and evaluation.* (p. 340).

This exercise is designed to assist students in conceptualizing how to conduct a needs assessment.

EP 2.1.7a *Utilize conceptual frameworks to guide the process of assessment, intervention, and evaluation.* (p. 340).

This exercise is designed to assist students in understanding how to conduct a needs assessment and to develop proposals to meet the identified needs.

EP 2.1.4a *Recognize the extent to which a culture's structures and values may oppress, marginalize, alienate, or create or enhance privilege and power.* (p. 340).

This exercise is designed to have students examine the values of their home commumties.

EP 2.1.7a *Utilize conceptual frameworks to guide the process of assessment, intervention, and evaluation.* (pp. 340–341).

This exercise is designed to assist students in better understanding how to analyze community practice efforts.

CHAPTER 11

Evaluating Social Work Practice

EP 2.1.6a, b

Thus far in this course, you've learned about social work with individuals, families, groups, organizations, and communities.[1] You've studied systems analysis. You're no doubt eager to try out your new knowledge, confident that you can help your prospective clients. But wait! How will you know if your selected treatment approach is working?

As a professional social worker, you are accountable to your clients, to your agency, and to yourself. You'll want to know whether your clients achieve their goals and, if so, whether it is because of your interventions. In short, you'll want to evaluate your practice. That is what this chapter is all about.

Although most social workers evaluate their practice implicitly, few approach evaluation as systematically as they might. Systematic evaluation of your practice provides you with reliable information about the achievements of your clients and improves your practice (Slonim-Nevo & Anson, 1998). Good evaluation also helps you avoid jumping to unwarranted conclusions about your work.

This chapter will:

A. Describe outcome evaluation and evaluative research
B. Describe the single-system evaluation approach
C. Describe evidence-based practice
D. Describe program evaluation
E. Describe information technology in social work practice

WHAT IS EVALUATION?

Evaluation, as we shall use the term here, refers to the use of research techniques to assess the outcome of social work interventions. Thomas (1984) described two types of evaluation: outcome evaluation and evaluative research. As you will see, these two types of evaluation address different but related objectives.

Outcome evaluation asks whether the intended outcome occurred: Was the goal achieved? Outcome evaluation has a limited objective, and it is relatively easy to do. It requires minimal methodological know-how, and it doesn't impose rigid requirements on practice. Outcome evaluation should be part of normal practice. However, outcome evaluation does not provide a sound basis on which to conclude whether the intervention was effective.

---

[1]This chapter was specially written for this text by Wallace J. Gingerich, MSW, PhD. Dr. Gingerich is a professor in the Mandel School of Applied Social Sciences at Case Western Reserve University, Cleveland, Ohio.

EP 2.1.6a, b

Exercise 11.1: Understanding and Applying Outcome Evaluation

Goal: This exercise is designed to demonstrate the simplicity of outcome evaluation.

Step 1: State five goals that you have set for yourself in the past 5 years.

Goal 1:

Goal 2:

Goal 3:

Goal 4:

Goal 5:

Step 2: State the extent to which you have attained each goal and the instruments or criteria that you used to measure the extent to which each goal was attained.

Goal 1:

Goal 2:

Goal 3:

Goal 4:

Goal 5:

This exercise shows that you already have been involved, numerous times, in outcome evaluation.

Evaluative research also asks whether the intended outcome occurred, but in addition it seeks to determine if the outcome can be attributed to your intervention: Was treatment effective? Evaluative research is similar to traditional experimental research in that causal relationships are the focus of study. You might think of evaluative research as research applied to questions of practice effectiveness. Although it is relatively easy to determine whether the intended outcome was achieved (outcome evaluation), inferring that the outcome was the result of the intervention is considerably more difficult.

Evaluating the effectiveness of interventions is important. If we know that our intervention produced the outcome, we will want to continue using it. Conversely, if we know the intervention had little or no impact, we should stop using it and look for something better. Good evaluative research enables us to contribute to the knowledge base of our profession and is mandated by our professional code of ethics.

Although both types of evaluation are important for social work practice, the main focus of this chapter is on outcome evaluation. Outcome evaluation is an essential part of ordinary practice; you and your client will always want to know if the desired outcome was achieved. Outcome evaluation does not interfere with practice but can enhance and improve it (Gingerich, 1983). In contrast, the additional controls and measurements needed to conduct evaluative research may conflict with service objectives (Thomas, 1978). We are required as a profession to conduct scientific research to improve our knowledge of practice effectiveness; however, in many instances evaluative research is best left to trained researchers who can implement the rigorous controls and measurements required for inferring causality.

Just as social work practice is carried out at various levels of intervention (individuals, groups, families, organizations, and communities), evaluation is also carried out at different levels. Evaluation at the level of individuals, families, and groups is sometimes referred to as *clinical evaluation,* and evaluation at the level of program development and community practice is called *program evaluation*. The main focus of this chapter is on evaluation at the level of individuals, families, and groups. Many of the concepts and methods underlying clinical evaluation apply to program evaluation as well.

Until recently, evaluating practice usually meant using some form of experimental control group research design (Bloom, 1983). Such designs assign subjects randomly to two groups: One group gets the intervention, and the other does not (or gets a different intervention). After intervention, the groups are compared on some measure of the desired outcome. Assuming all else is equal, differences between the two groups are attributed to the intervention the experimental group received. Although experimental control group designs are a useful research strategy, they are often not practical for evaluating day-to-day social work practice.

During the 1970s a new approach to evaluating practice began to emerge, based on the earlier work of clinical psychologists who were trained in research (Bloom, 1983). This approach, known as *single-subject* or *single-system* research, took a rather different approach to evaluation, an approach much more compatible with clinical practice. Instead of comparing randomly assigned groups of clients on some outcome measure after intervention, the single-system approach observes a single client (or client system) repeatedly, before, during, and after intervention, and notes changes in the outcome measure that coincide with the intervention. In this way, it is possible to determine whether the outcome was achieved and, perhaps, whether the change was because of the intervention.

Single-system designs are not as rigorous methodologically as classical control group designs, but they are much more compatible with most social work practice. Furthermore, they are adequate in most instances for purposes of outcome evaluation. Thus, the single-system approach to evaluation is the one taken here.

THE SINGLE-SYSTEM EVALUATION APPROACH

Much has been written about how to evaluate practice (Alter & Evens, 1990; Barlow, Hayes, & Nelson, 1984; Barlow & Hersen, 1984; Bloom, Fischer, & Orme, 2009; Blythe & Tripodi, 1989; Jayaratne & Levy, 1979; Ogles, Lambert, & Fields, 2002; Thyer & Myers, 2007; Tripodi, 1994; Wiger & Solberg, 2001). As a result, the procedures for evaluating practice are well defined. They are generally described as follows:

1. Specify the goal.
2. Select suitable measures.
3. Record baseline data.
4. Select an evidence-informed intervention.
5. Implement the intervention and continue monitoring.
6. Assess change.
7. Infer effectiveness.
8. Assess threats to validity.

If these steps sound familiar, that is because they parallel very closely the steps you follow in social work practice (Jayaratne & Levy, 1979). Evaluation is based on the problem-solving process, just as social work practice is. The difference is one of emphasis, and it is a slight difference at that. Whereas the main purpose of practice is to produce a desired outcome, the main purpose of evaluation is to assess whether the outcome was in fact achieved.

Specify the Goal

The first step in single-system evaluation is to specify the goal of your work with your client. The goal should reflect the information obtained in the social work assessment and should state in concrete terms what will be different at the end of treatment. Usually the goal involves a change in behaviors, thoughts, or feelings or perhaps a change in social relationships or the environment. The goal should reflect the needs and wishes of your client and what is realistic to achieve, but it also must be an outcome that can be defined specifically and measured.

Specifying the goal is probably the single most important step in evaluating practice. It is essential that the behavior you select for the goal be the *same behavior* as the focus of intervention. Remember, when you evaluate your practice, you are evaluating whether the client changed and whether your intervention was successful. Your evaluation can show success only if it is focused on the actual changes the client is making. As you move ahead to the next step in evaluation and select a suitable measure, you can lose sight of your original goal, particularly if it is a difficult one to measure. After you have designed your measurement package, it's always a good idea to review your goal statement to be sure that both are focused on the same thing.

Select Suitable Measures

Evaluation requires that the desired outcome be measurable in some reliable way. To be measurable, the outcome must be quantifiable. At a minimum you must be able to tell whether it has occurred or not, but you may also be able to use a scale or some other procedure to rate the level of the outcome.

Although some outcomes seem to defy measurement, it would be irresponsible to intervene if you have no way to know if the outcome has occurred (Hudson, 1978). Neither you nor your client could tell if things were getting better. When workers say they cannot measure their clients' outcomes, they usually mean the outcomes are difficult to measure directly or they are too complicated and multifaceted to quantify. However, numerous advances have been made in the field of measurement in recent years, and many measuring instruments and procedures are available.

Measurement Methods The three main methods for measuring client outcomes are direct observation, self-anchored rating scales, and standardized measures (Bloom et al., 2009).

Direct Observation Many client outcomes are behavioral. Simply put, clients want to *do* something different. When the outcome can be stated in behavioral terms, direct observation by the client or by someone else is usually the measurement method of choice. Direct observation requires a clear, objective definition of the behavior. *Clear* means that two people using the definition agree on occurrences of the behavior. *Objective* means that the behavior is directly observable—that is, it requires little or no inference by the observer.

Examples of typical behavioral outcomes are playing cooperatively, completing assigned homework, having fewer headaches, or discussing disagreements calmly. Even some seemingly nonbehavioral outcomes, such as improved self-esteem or reduced depression, can be stated in behavioral terms. Clients can often give specific behavioral indicators of internal states when asked. For example, when asked what they will be doing (or not doing) when they have improved self-esteem, clients may indicate such behaviors as initiating conversations, making positive self-statements, or working more productively. Although it is not always possible to specify outcomes in behavioral terms, it is useful to attempt to do so. From a therapeutic standpoint, the client (and you) will have a more concrete idea of the actual desired outcome. From an evaluation standpoint, direct observation is generally considered the most reliable and direct measurement method. By the way, specifying behavioral outcomes does not imply that you must or even should use behaviorally based interventions. It simply means that the outcome you and the client are interested in is behavioral.

Various methods may be used to observe and count behaviors (Baer, Harrison, Fradenburg, Peterson, & Milla, 2005; Barlow et al., 1984). The most common method is a *frequency count*. Here, you simply record the number of times the behavior occurs during a specified time interval. For example, you might record the number of temper tantrums a child has each day or the number of problems a child solves correctly during math class. Frequency counts work well for discrete behaviors (behaviors that have clear beginnings and endings) that do not occur too frequently to make counting impractical.

A related method of observation is counting *discriminated operants*, which are behaviors that occur only in the presence of clearly specified antecedents. For example, a child can comply only when the parent makes a request, or a husband and wife can resolve differences only when they have a disagreement. In such cases, instead of reporting the absolute frequency of occurrence, you would report the percentage of times the desired behavior occurred following the antecedent.

Continuous behaviors (no clear beginnings or endings) or high-frequency behaviors can be observed by means of *time-sampling* methods. In time-sampling, the observation period is divided into short intervals (usually 5 to 15 seconds) during which you record the behavior as occurring or not. Usually this is done on an all-or-none basis, and the results are presented as a percentage. For example, you might observe whether a psychiatric patient attends to the therapy group discussion during a 10-minute period using 15-second intervals. If the patient was observed to attend in 35 of the 40 intervals, you would report that she or he attended 88% of the time.

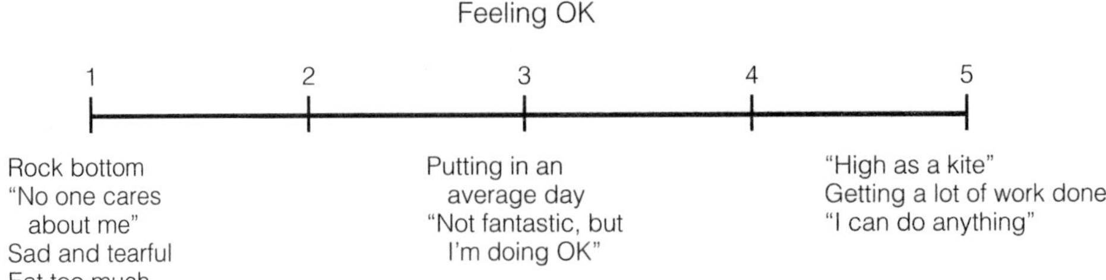

Figure 11.1
Self-anchored scale.

Source: © Cengage Learning, 2013.

Time-sampling is almost always done by someone other than the client, usually a staff member or perhaps a parent.

Several other observational methods are sometimes used. *Latency,* the elapsed time between a particular event and the behavior, can be measured—for example, the time it takes a child to get into bed after being told to do so. *Duration*, how long the behavior lasts, also can be measured—for example, how many minutes the child spends doing homework or how long a headache lasts.

General procedures for observing behaviors, as well as specific definitions, codes, and recording systems for observing many predetermined behaviors, are described in detail by Bellack and Hersen (1998) and Ciminero, Calhoun, and Adams (1986).

Self-Anchored Rating Scales Not all desired outcomes can be stated in behavioral terms. Sometimes the outcome is a change in an internal state (for example, thought, feeling, belief), such as becoming more self-confident, less anxious, or less depressed. In such cases, it would not make sense to try to define the outcome behaviorally if the client truly views the problem as an internal state. Accordingly, when the desired outcome is an internal state, the most direct method of measurement is of necessity some form of self-report.

One of the best methods of measuring internal states is to develop a self-anchored rating scale (Bloom, 1975). A self-anchored scale is a rating scale you and your client develop specifically to measure your client's outcome (Gingerich, 1979). To construct a self-anchored scale, begin with a 5- or 7-point rating scale (see Figure 11.1). Give the scale the name of the outcome you and your client have agreed on; for example, you might call it a "feeling good" scale.

Next, develop anchors for the low end of the scale by having your client imagine a recent time when she did not feel good at all. After she has begun to visualize the situation, ask her to recall (1) what she was doing, (2) any recurrent thoughts she was having, and (3) what she was feeling. Behaviors sometimes occur along with internal states; for example, your client may stay in bed all day, not answer the phone, cry frequently, and overeat on a bad day. Your client also may experience recurrent thoughts or self-statements such as "No one likes me," "I am ugly," or "Life is not worth living." Feelings are more difficult to elicit but often are expressed best in word pictures such as "feeling blue," "My stomach is tied up in knots," or "I'm down in the dumps." In any case, the behaviors, thoughts, and feelings the client experiences when at the low point on the scale become the anchors for that point.

Once you have anchored the low point, ask your client to imagine a recent time when she was feeling very good. This time you will elicit anchors for the high end of the scale. You should proceed to develop anchors for other points on the scale as well; ideally, at least alternate points of the scale should be anchored.

If you have developed the anchors carefully, the completed scale should be a sensitive measure of the client's outcome as she or he uniquely experiences it. Because self-anchored scales are client-specific, you must develop a new one for each new client and each new outcome.

Because self-anchored scales are subjective (they measure the client's internal state), they have sometimes been criticized on methodological grounds. Their reliability cannot be assessed directly, and they are always potentially reactive (more about these measurement issues later). However, self-report measures offer the most direct measure of internal states, and there is little evidence that self-reports are any less adequate methodologically than many other types of measures (Bloom et al., 2009). For purposes of outcome evaluation, self-anchored scales are often useful, and sometimes they are the only direct measure of the outcome.

Standardized Measures In most cases, the preferred method of tracking client change over time is direct observation of behavior or self-anchored ratings of internal states. That is because these methods are likely to provide the most direct and sensitive measures of outcome. Occasionally, however, standardized measures may exist that would provide a suitable measure of outcome. Furthermore, it is often a good idea to use standardized measures, in addition to behavioral and self-report measures, to provide a basis of comparison with known groups or to be sure that you are measuring what you think you are.

Standardized measures include tests, questionnaires, rating scales, inventories, and checklists. These measures have three characteristics. First, they have uniform procedures for administration and scoring, so everyone who uses the instrument uses it in the same way. Second, standardized measures must meet minimal standards of methodological adequacy (namely, reliability and validity). Third, most standardized measures have established norms—that is, they have guidelines for interpreting test scores based on the scores of known groups who have completed the measure or some independent standard of performance.

Standardized measures fall into two broad categories: published and unpublished. Published measures (commercially published) are described in *The Eighteenth Mental Measurements Yearbook* (Spies, Carlson & Geisinger, 2010). Published measures have met accepted standards of reliability and validity, so you can use them with assurance that they will in fact measure what you think they will. The publishers of these measures require a fee, however, and some of them are available only to psychologists or other qualified professionals.

Unpublished measures have been developed and used in research and practice situations but are not published commercially. There is no one source or listing of unpublished measures; however, several collections have particular value for social work practice. Hudson (1982) and Nurius and Hudson (1993) have developed more than 20 scales (known as the Walmyr scales) designed for use in social work practice. Sample scales include self-esteem, marital satisfaction, child's attitudes toward parents, and generalized contentment. Because all of these scales are scored and interpreted in the same way, they are easy to use in daily practice. Many of the most widely used Walmyr scales are reprinted in Fischer and Corcoran (2007), so you can review them and determine their suitability to your situation. The scales are copyrighted, however, which means you must purchase them from the publisher before using them in your work. Computerized versions of the scales are also available from the publisher.

Corcoran and Fischer (2007) have compiled a collection of several hundred measures that they refer to as *rapid assessment instruments*. Instruments are included for children, adults, and couples and cover a broad range of psychological, behavioral, and interpersonal problems. The sourcebook includes a description of each measure, its norms and scoring procedures, and reliability and validity data. In addition, each measure is reproduced in the book, so you can decide for yourself whether it would be suitable for your clinical application.

Ogles and colleagues (2002) have compiled a set of commercially published brief outcome measures that are widely used in mental health settings, including global measures such as the Hopkins Symptom Checklist (SCL-90-R) and the Outcome Questionnaire (OQ-45) as well as problem-specific measures such at the Beck Depression Inventory and Child Behavior Checklist.

In addition to those collections, a wide range of standardized measures may be found in Bellack and Hersen (1998); Ciminero et al., (1986); Freedman and Sherman (1987); Grotevant and Carlson (1987); Hersen and Bellack (1988); and Touliatos, Perlmutter, and Straus (1990).

General Issues in Measurement At times we refer to the reliability and validity of measurement. These terms describe the methodological adequacy of measures. *Validity* refers to what the measure measures, and *reliability* refers to how well it measures it. If a measure is not reliable, it will not give consistent and accurate readings. Thus, when observing behavior, for example, it is important that the description of the behavior be clear and objective so the observer will record it consistently from day to day. If a measure is not valid, it will not measure what you think it measures. That is why, when developing self-anchored scales, for example, you should be sure that the anchors the client gives are real indicators of the outcome for each scale point.

In addition to reliability and validity, you also want a measure to be *sensitive* to the changes you expect a client to make. Direct observation of client behavior and self-anchored rating scales are sensitive measures of most client outcomes. Standardized scales frequently are not as sensitive because these scales have been developed to measure personality traits that, by definition, are relatively fixed and are not likely to change significantly during intervention.

Another requirement of measurement in single-case evaluation is that the measure be suitable for *repeated use* (at least weekly) during treatment. This is true for most behavioral observation measures and self-anchored scales but is often not true for standardized scales. The rapid assessment scales described by Hudson (1982), Nurius and Hudson (1993), Corcoran and Fischer (2007), and Ogles et al. (2002) are exceptions.

Finally, it is important to consider the *reactivity* of your measure. In most instances, clients will be recording their own behavior, and the measurements process itself will likely have some impact on the behavior they are reporting. For example, if you ask a mother who complains of her child's temper tantrums to count the tantrums, it is likely that she will notice some new things about her child's behavior as well as her own, and her behavior and that of her child may change as a result.

Because reactivity influences the behavior the measure is meant to measure, it is difficult to sort out how much behavior change is due to the intervention and how much is due to reactivity. Researchers generally try to minimize this problem by using unobtrusive measures (having someone else observe the client, for example), so they can be more sure of the exact impact on the intervention. However, from a practice point of view, reactivity may actually benefit the client. This is especially true if you are helping someone learn problem-solving strategies in which observing and altering his or her own behavior are explicit goals of treatment.

Reactivity is a very complex process, and its effect is difficult to gauge. Generally, however, you should have your clients record *positive* behaviors or internal states rather than negative ones because the effect of reactivity (all else being equal) is likely to increase response rates rather than decrease them. For example, rather than recording an unwanted behavior, such as eating snacks between meals, you could have your clients record the number of times they thought of snacking but refrained. Koop (1988) provided an excellent discussion of the factors involved in estimating the reactivity of self-monitoring and how you can use it for your client's benefit.

Measurement of client outcomes is a crucial step in evaluating practice. Conclusions about whether the outcome has been achieved will be valid and trustworthy only if appropriate measures are used, so care and thoughtfulness are advised. You have also probably noticed the parallels between measurement as we have talked about it here and assessment as it was discussed in Chapter 3. We have been talking about the same process from different perspectives. In the present discussion of measurement, the emphasis has been on *how* to assess, whereas in Chapter 3 the emphasis was on *what* to assess. Clearly, you will want to pay careful attention to both aspects of assessment in your practice.

Record Baseline Data

After selection of the measure or measures, the next step is to collect data for a period of time before you implement the intervention. This is called *baselining,* meaning that you are establishing the rate of the outcome measure before intervention occurs and the expected change takes place. The main purpose for baselining is to provide a basis of comparison for data collected during and after treatment. If the treatment data show a different level or pattern from the baseline data, you may reasonably conclude there has been a change. If you collected data only after treatment, you would have no way of knowing whether there had been a change.

Because you may not implement treatment during the baseline period, an important question is, How long should you baseline? Barlow and colleagues (1984) made several recommendations. First, you should collect baseline data for a *minimum of three data points*. At least three points are required to begin to assess the level, trend, and stability of the data. (More about these properties later when we discuss assessing change.) Although three data points constitute a minimum, in normal practice baselines are often taken for a week or more. Some statistical aids for assessing change require a minimum of 10 baseline observations. Second, you should continue baselining until the data form a *stable pattern*. Frequently there is some fluctuation or trend in evidence during baseline; for example, there may be four or five tantrums one day and none the next or the number of tantrums may seem to be decreasing. The idea is to baseline long enough that the pattern of behaviors becomes clear and consistent and (ideally) there is no upward or downward trend.

To confirm the patterns contained in your data, you should always graph the data (see Figure 11.2). This is helpful for you, and graphs are a very effective way to provide feedback to your clients (and others such as parents and third-party funders). Using lined graph paper, begin by drawing a vertical line on the left side and a horizontal line at the bottom. The vertical axis is always used to represent the outcome, and the horizontal dimension represents time units. Thus, you might record self-anchored ratings of "feeling good" on the vertical axis and days on the horizontal axis. Drawn in this way, the pattern of the client outcome over time can readily be seen. Other considerations in graphing are discussed in more detail in Bloom et al. (2009) and Parsonson and Baer (1978).

Conceptually, baselining parallels the assessment phase of treatment, in which the worker gathers information about the level of the client's problem and when and where it happens. Seen in this way, baselining usually does not require you to delay the start of intervention any longer than you normally would. From a practice standpoint,

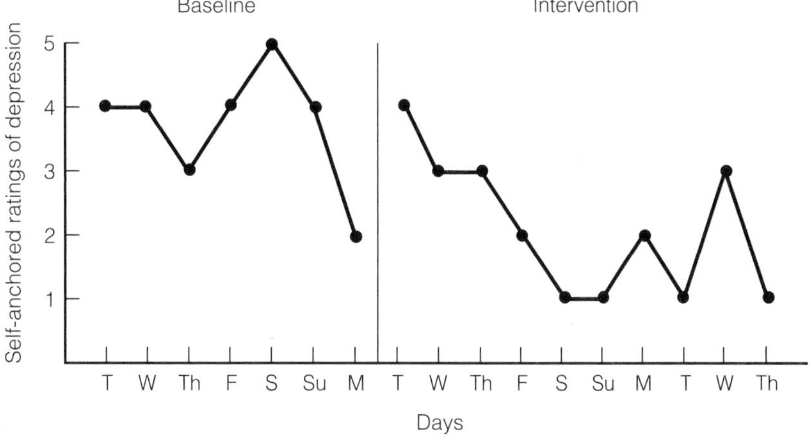

Figure 11.2
A simple graph.

Source: © Cengage Learning, 2013.

it is unwise to begin intervening until you have a clear description of the problem or desired outcome and have reliable information about its current level.

Occasionally you will find yourself in situations (crises, for example) in which you must intervene immediately—that is, you cannot delay introduction of treatment to gather baseline information. In these situations, you can gather baseline data *retrospectively* rather than *prospectively,* as has been described until now. To construct a baseline retrospectively, develop a measure of the goal behavior as usual; then ask clients to recall from memory how they would have rated themselves each day for the past week or so. This process is analogous to what workers often do during assessments when asking clients to give them a history of the target behavior; except here workers are getting the information in a more systematic way so it can be used as a basis for evaluation. Retrospective baselines are not as reliable as prospective baselines, but experience shows that they often yield useful information and, in any case, are better than having no information at all. Without any baseline data whatsoever, you will be severely hampered in determining whether there has been change in the goal behavior.

Select an Evidence-Informed Intervention

If you haven't already done so, now is the time to select the intervention you will use with your client. Selecting the best intervention is a critical step in effective social work practice. Increasingly, those who pay for social work services and the clients we serve expect us to use interventions that have been shown to be effective. Imagine yourself going to the doctor with symptoms of diabetes and the doctor prescribes an untested medication. You are not likely to benefit from the untested medication, and you would be forgoing a treatment (that is, insulin) that has been shown to be effective in controlling your disease. You would consider the doctor incompetent and engaging in unethical practice. The same holds true in social work practice.

Using known effective interventions is not just good practice; it is ethically required (see Exhibit 11.1). Consequently, among other things, your choice of intervention must reflect the degree to which there is evidence indicating that the intervention will be effective with your client. How can you find out if there is empirical support for the intervention you are considering or if there are interventions that have some evidence of effectiveness for the client problem you are working with? Follow the steps for locating practice-effectiveness evidence that have evolved over time, first in medical practice and more recently in social work practice (Cournoyer, 2004; Sackett, Straus, Richardson, Rosenberg, & Haynes, 2000). A thorough discussion of evidence-based social work practice is beyond the scope of this chapter, but here are the basic steps. *The Evidence-Based Social Work Skills Book* (Cournoyer, 2004) is highly recommended for more detailed guidance every step of the way.

Step 1. *Formulate your intervention question.* Your intervention question will usually consist of at least three components. You will want to know if *x intervention* has been shown to be effective for *y problem* with *z group* of clients. For example, have *family presentation services* been shown to be effective with *aggressive behavior* of *high school–age boys*? It is usually a good idea to start out with a specific question such as this, but if your search turns up little evidence you may want to come back and broaden your search. For example, you could leave off aggressive behavior to see if there is effectiveness evidence for any type of problem, or you could leave off the age or gender of the client group.

Step 2. *Search for evidence.* Usually, you will begin by consulting the bibliographic databases at your university or local public library, such as Social Work Abstracts, MEDLINE, or PsychInfo. Make sure you use search terms that the database will recognize. It is a good idea to use synonyms; for example, "home-based" and

Exhibit 11.1 Evidence-Based Practice

Basing one's practice on the best available evidence is often referred to as *evidence-based practice* (EBP). The concept of EBP evolved in the field of medicine in response to the realization that many patients did not receive the most effective treatments available, sometimes with unfortunate outcomes. The assumption was that practitioners were not informed about the best treatments or perhaps were influenced more by authority and tradition than by empirical evidence (Gambrill, 2006). The evolving paradigm of EBP not only emphasized the importance of empirical evidence in one's practice but also included skills for finding the best evidence and applying it to one's work. EBP is now well established in medical schools and is rapidly being adopted in social work programs as well (Rubin, 2007).

EBP is actually a broader concept than just using evidence-informed interventions. It incorporates using one's clinical expertise and the client's values and preferences when deciding what intervention to use (Sackett et al., 2000). Evidence-based intervention should be used only when you are competent to do the intervention and it is compatible with the client's wishes and situation. Evidence-based intervention is not only good practice; it is ethically required. As stated in the NASW *Code of Ethics,* competent social work practice requires that we base our practice "on recognized knowledge, including empirically based knowledge, relevant to social work and social work ethics" (National Association of Social Workers, 1996, 4.01c).

Although the term *evidence-based interventions* implies that some interventions are "evidence-based" and others are not, it is an oversimplification to think of EBP that way. There are many types of empirical evidence, ranging from the findings of randomized clinical trials (highly controlled control group studies), to simple follow-up studies, to descriptive studies and evolving best practices. EBP considers all of the evidence that is available and uses it to inform one's choice of intervention, consistent with one's professional competence and the client's preferences. For this reason it seems more accurate to describe this approach as "evidence-informed practice" than simply EBP (E. Gambrill, personal communication, September 2006).

Some EBP advocates argue that to treat anyone using treatments without known effectiveness is unethical. Also, some advocates assert that if one treatment program works better than other available treatment approaches, professionals have an ethical obligation to use it in order to best serve clients/patients. Advocates also have asserted that only interventions with demonstrated effectiveness should be supported financially. This assertion links demonstrations of effectiveness with funding through managed care systems (Gambrill, 1999).

There are seven steps in EBP:

Step 1. The professional first of all needs to be motivated to use EBP. A professional may be motivated to use EBP because the approach fosters using effective treatment strategies. However, if a managed care system mandates the use of EBP, the professional may resent forced use.

Step 2. The professional needs to formulate a clear and answerable question that is based on the client's problems and needs. The question should cover such aspects as diagnosis, likely results of various treatment strategies, side effects, prognosis, likely benefits, and costs. An example of a question is, "What are the most effective strategies to treat a 44-year-old recently divorced male who has a bipolar disorder?"

Step 3. Search the literature for relevant research that could help answer the question. EBP places greatest credibility on randomized control trials (RCTs). An RCT is an experiment in which participants are randomly assigned to either a treatment group or a control group. Ideally, neither the participant nor the treating professional knows which group is which. After a course of treatment (or control), improvement is measured by comparing pretreatment status with posttreatment status. If the treated group improves significantly more than the control group, the conclusion is that the treatment works (that is, it is better than no treatment).

Step 4. Carefully and critically appraise the research information for its validity and applicability to the client's needs and circumstances. Also to be considered in this appraisal process are (a) the client's wishes and needs (both stated and implicit) and (b) the professional's competencies to apply the various treatment strategies.

Step 5. Formulate and apply an intervention based on the appraisal in step 4. The selected intervention is based on what has been called the "best available evidence."

Step 6. Monitor the intervention (to verify that it was applied appropriately), and evaluate the benefits and side effects.

Step 7. The professional shares the results with others in order to add to the "best available evidence."

"multisystemic treatment" are often used interchangeably with "family preservation." A reference librarian who is familiar with the database you are using can often be helpful in selecting search terms. Another way to locate evidence is to consult the standard texts and manuals on the intervention you are considering to see if they cite any empirical support. Or you may want to do a general search of the Internet—sometimes pilot studies or studies in progress are reported on the web before they appear in the professional literature. You should also consult some of the evidence-based collaborations to see if someone has already done a systematic review. The Campbell Collaboration (www.campbellcollaboration.org) is one such source, but more are becoming available all the time (Cournoyer, 2004).

Step 3. *Evaluate the evidence.* When you finally locate some evidence, you must give some thought to its quality or validity. Some kinds of evidence are better than others. A scientific study provides more reliable evidence than a personal opinion. A rigorously controlled study provides better evidence than a simple case study. When possible you should focus on empirical studies of the intervention rather than professional opinion or authoritative statements. Use what you have learned in your research class to evaluate the quality of empirical data: Are the measures used reliable and valid, was the study design well controlled, were the subjects representative of your client group, and so forth? More and more, you will find systematic reviews (meta-analysis is one such type of review) of empirical support for interventions appearing in the professional literature and on collaborative sites. Reviews that have been published in respected scientific journals can usually be trusted to meet basic standards of scientific rigor and objectivity. Evidence you find on the Internet must be scrutinized carefully to determine the quality of the source and the reliability of the data.

Although this brief discussion has only scratched the surface of this important topic, you get the idea. When selecting an intervention, you need to consider whether it has empirical support. You find this by formulating your specific practice question, conducting a search of the databases and perhaps the Internet, and then evaluating the quality of the evidence and its applicability to your client.

Implement the Intervention and Continue Monitoring

Once you have selected an intervention, it is time to implement the intervention. The most important consideration from the point of view of evaluating practice is to specify and describe clearly and exactly what the intervention consists of. If your client improves, you will want to know what you did so you can do it again and describe it to other professionals as well.

This step sounds easy, but it is perhaps the most difficult aspect of evaluation. In fact, there is ongoing debate in the literature regarding the extent to which interventions can be described and replicated (Frank, 1973). The helping process is a complex, multifaceted activity that can probably never be described completely. The practical goal, however, is to describe the intervention with sufficient clarity and completeness that someone else can replicate it and obtain similar results (Blythe & Tripodi, 1989). Furthermore, it is assumed that although your actions from the start may be generally therapeutic, you will implement a *specific intervention* at the conclusion of baseline.

In addition to describing your intervention, you should verify that you have actually implemented it. Planning to do something does not necessarily mean it will happen. Occasionally, research studies on practice effectiveness have failed to produce positive results but on closer examination reveal that the intervention was never implemented as planned. This is important to know because it prevents you from mistakenly concluding that the intervention was unsuccessful when in fact it was never implemented.

Once you have implemented intervention, you should continue the same measurement procedure established during baseline (see Figure 11.2). It is important that there be no changes in the definitions, times of measurement, or measurement procedures because such changes could affect the data you obtain. If you keep the measurement procedure exactly the same as baseline, changes in the data during treatment will reflect changes in the outcome itself, not the measurement procedure.

Assess Change

After you have collected data on your outcome measure during the baseline and treatment phases, the next step is to assess whether there has been any change. Actually, the issue is whether any significant change has occurred from a statistical or clinical standpoint (Kazdin, 1977a). Statistical, or *experimental,* change is actual change in outcome between phases. It is assessed on purely statistical and logical grounds. Clinical, or *applied,* change is change that is sufficient, desirable, or meaningful from a clinical or practical standpoint.

The first task is to determine whether there has been experimental change—that is, whether there has been any real change in the outcome during intervention. This task is sometimes made difficult because of some of the unique characteristics of time-series data (Crosbie, 1993; Jones, Vaught, & Weinrott, 1977; Kratochwill, 1978; Rubin & Knox, 1996). Time-series data may be characterized by their level, trend, variability, and autocorrelation. *Level* refers to the central tendency, or location, of a set of data. When there is no trend, level is equivalent to the mean of observations in the baseline or treatment phase. *Trend* refers to a deterministic change in the level of the data over time—that is, a continuing upward or downward trend. *Variability* refers to the extent to which the data vary around the trend line. The more fluctuation around the trend line, the greater is the variability of the data. Finally, *autocorrelation* refers to the possibility that the value of one observation may be related to previous observations. This is a complicated statistical phenomenon, which in practical terms means that most of the usual statistical techniques (which assume independence of observations) may not be suitable for assessing change in time-series data.

There are two general approaches for assessing change in time-series data: visual analysis and statistical analysis. Visual analysis is emphasized here because it is fairly straightforward and easy and it is one procedure you should do routinely. The following discussion of visual analysis is based heavily on the work of Parsonson and Baer (1978).

Visual analysis simply means that you look at the graphed data and, applying rules of analysis, conclude whether there has been change in the client outcome from phase to phase. The standard of significance for visual analysis is "clearly evident and reliable"—that is, the change must be clear and unmistakable (Parsonson & Baer, 1978, p. 112).

The first step in visual analysis is to graph the baseline and treatment data following the suggestions noted earlier. The data within phases should be connected by a solid line, and the phases should be divided by a vertical line.

Ideally, in visual analysis you would want to see little or no overlap between phases and no clear trend in the data (see Figure 11.3a). In such cases, it is clear there has been a change. Also, the more immediate the change and the greater its magnitude, the easier it is to conclude there has been real change.

Sometimes the baseline data may contain a trend—that is, the outcome measure seems to be on a continuing increase or decrease. When this happens, you should make every effort to extend the period of baseline to see whether the trend tapers off and stabilizes around a constant level. If not, you must analyze change cautiously. If the trend is in the opposite direction of desired change, then it will have little impact on assessing change. However, if the trend is in the desired direction, assessment of change will be ambiguous (Figure 11.3b). From a practice standpoint, it may be wise not to intervene in such cases because the desired change appears to be happening already. If you must intervene and if intervention produces a large and immediate increase in outcome or a change in slope, you might cautiously conclude there has been change. However, in most situations where there is a trend in the desired direction, it will be difficult if not impossible to conclude reliably that there has been change.

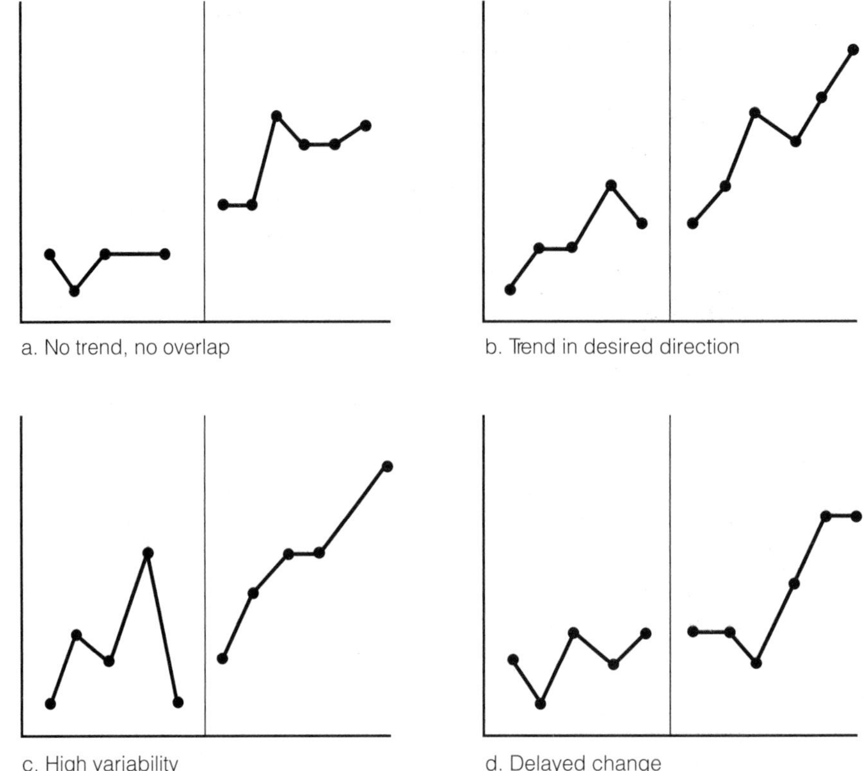

Figure 11.3
Visual analysis of graphed data.

Source: © Cengage Learning, 2013.

On occasion, the baseline data may be highly variable such that they overlap with the treatment data (Figure 11.3c). Again, your first strategy should be to try to reduce the variability by extending the baseline period or observing extraneous events affecting your client's responses that can be controlled. If not, it will be difficult to conclude unequivocally that there has been change. On rare occasions, the goal of intervention may be to increase or decrease the variability of a client's behavior (for example, to help a person with mood swings maintain a steadier state). Unfortunately, there are no readily available techniques for assessing change in variability of time-series data.

It is not uncommon in social work practice for client change to be delayed or gradual (Figure 11.3d). Because the change is not immediate and phases overlap, it is difficult to reach a reliable conclusion (Gibson & Ottenbacher, 1988). In such cases the best thing to do is continue the intervention and continue observing to see whether the behavior eventually stabilizes around a new level. If so, you can be relatively confident there has been change in the outcome.

Ideally, our interventions should be so effective that visual analysis of graphed data would be sufficient to reach reliable conclusions about change. Of course, we know that this doesn't always happen. Sometimes there appears to be some change, but the change doesn't strictly meet the criteria of "clearly evident and reliable." What then? Some writers suggest that if change is not clearly evident the intervention is simply not potent enough to be of interest, so we should abandon it altogether rather than try to sort out whether there was significant change. This argument is very persuasive from a practical standpoint. However, some of the outcomes we are interested in change slowly, and change may not be very immediate or dramatic. Furthermore, when we develop new interventions, it may be important to know whether there is even a small change, so we can improve and refine the intervention to the point that it may be of practical value. In cases such as these, statistical and quasi-statistical techniques may be needed to determine whether there has been a reliable change in outcome.

Although such techniques are beyond the scope of this text, good discussions are available in Bloom et al. (2009) and Briggs, Feyerherm, and Gingerich (2004).

In contrast to experimental significance, applied (clinical) significance compares the amount of change that has occurred with the amount of change thought necessary or desirable. This is often a difficult judgment to make because individuals disagree on what is necessary or desirable.

Kazdin (1977a) discussed a number of approaches for assessing applied significance. One of these, the *aim-star technique,* simply places an *aim-star* on the graph at the level and day that represent the desired outcome. You then graph the treatment data to see if they are moving in the direction of the aim-star. If the data coincide with the aim-star, you have achieved applied significance. *Goal attainment scaling* offers a similar approach conceptually (Kiresuk & Lund, 1978). Both procedures are admittedly subjective, although they probably better reflect what our clients consider significant change than does experimental significance.

Kazdin discussed several additional ways to evaluate applied significance. One of these, *social comparison,* compares the client's performance in the target area with that of "normal" peers. For example, you decide what a reasonable standard of cooperative play is by observing "normal" children in the natural setting. Another approach for assessing applied significance is called *subjective evaluation*. Here you would poll qualified individuals such as teachers, social workers, or probation officers to determine what a reasonable standard of performance would be. For a more detailed discussion of applied significance, see the articles by Kazdin (1977a) and Gingerich (1983).

In practice, you should always attempt to assess change using both experimental and applied criteria. At the minimum, you should perform visual analysis of graphed data and perhaps use some of the statistical techniques available if visual analysis is ambiguous. In addition, you should always specify before intervention what the goal of intervention is. You may express this verbally or graphically using the aim-star technique.

Those six procedures constitute the necessary steps for carrying out outcome evaluation as defined earlier. Your measure should indicate in quantitative terms what the desired outcome is; data should show what the baseline level was and whether there was change during intervention; and finally, your analysis should tell you whether the change was significant. Practice evaluation should be a regular part of normal social work practice.

You may have noticed that so far almost nothing has been said about intervention effectiveness—that is, whether the intervention was responsible for producing the change. The question of effectiveness leads us into evaluation research per se, in which we must use research designs to develop a logical and empirical basis for making inferences about treatment effectiveness. Although it is not the goal of this text to make you a skilled researcher, a brief review of research designs and design issues will help you begin to think about effectiveness and, perhaps more important, deter you from making assertions about effectiveness that go beyond your data.

Infer Effectiveness

To infer that your intervention was effective, you must show logically and empirically that the intervention is the only plausible explanation for the observed change in client outcome. In other words, you must rule out other possible explanations for the observed change.

The primary criterion for inferring causality is *concomitant variation*—that is, the observed change in client outcome must occur at (or soon after) the time the intervention is implemented. If change begins before intervention, logically we would have to conclude that something other than the intervention was responsible for the change. Likewise, if change occurs too long after intervention, other possible explanations take on more credence. (All of these steps are illustrated in the Case Example "Treatment of Obsessive-Compulsive Disorder.")

CASE EXAMPLE Treatment of Obsessive-Compulsive Disorder

This case example is based on a study by Cooper (1990), in which she used behavioral interventions to help a client reduce her ritualizing behavior. Cooper also noted improvement in depression and anxiety.

1. *Specify the goal*. This study involved a woman in her late 20s who displayed at intake pervasive ritualistic behavior, social isolation, depression, and anxiety. She had been in psychotherapy for the previous 5 years. The specific goals for this study were to reduce three behaviors: ritualistic opening and shutting of her makeup case, excessive rinsing in the shower, and ritualistic counting of belongings.
2. *Selecting suitable measures*. The measure used was client self-monitoring of the three behaviors on a 3 × 5 note card. The client recorded the number of times she opened and closed her makeup case, the minutes spent rinsing after soaping in the shower, and the percentage of time she counted her belongings when carrying them. In addition to these target behaviors, Cooper also asked her client to complete the Spielberger State-Trait Anxiety Inventory and the Beck Depression Inventory.
3. *Record baseline data*. Cooper implemented a modified form of the multiple baseline design in which each behavior was recorded for a variable period before the start of treatment. Baselines ranged from 13 days for opening and closing the makeup case to 6 weeks for counting belongings while carrying them.
4. *Select the intervention*. The selected intervention consisted of behavior modification techniques (including modeling and response prevention), which research had found to be effective for these problematic behaviors in women in their young adulthood.
5. *Implement intervention and continue monitoring*. The interventions were implemented, first toward the makeup case ritual, then the excessive rinsing, and finally the counting of belongings. The order of target behaviors was determined by client ratings of each on an anxiety hierarchy. Cooper continued to monitor each target behavior during the intervention period.
6. *Assess change*. Each target behavior was monitored during intervention (just as in baseline) and placed on a time-series graph. The results for the opening and closing of the makeup case are shown in Figure 11.4. It is clear from visual analysis that there was significant change during intervention—there was no overlap across phases, and behavior changed abruptly when treatment was started. Cooper did a celeration line test (that is, a trend-line test) that confirmed her visual analysis. The other two target behaviors showed similar reductions. Pre- and postmeasures on the State-Trait Anxiety Inventory and the Beck Depression Inventory showed no significant change. Anxiety scores began high and continued high, and depression scores began low and remained so throughout. Cooper did 3-month and 6-month follow-ups, which verified that changes the client made during treatment continued.
7. *Infer effectiveness*. This study used a modified multiple baseline design to evaluate the impact of behavioral intervention on three ritualistic behaviors. In each case, introduction of treatment was followed immediately by a reduction in the target behavior. These results were confirmed using the celeration line. The fact that treatment was begun at different points in time for the three different target behaviors and was followed by immediate change lends credibility to the hypothesis that treatment produced the change, not historical events, maturation, or some other factor. Thus, we can be fairly safe in concluding that the intervention produced the observed changes in target behaviors. Intervention did not appear to influence general anxiety or depression.

This study is a good example of the extent to which a fairly rigorous single-subject evaluation design can be implemented in direct practice. It used clear, concrete measures of the target behaviors. The modified multiple baseline design is able to rule out most competing explanations for the observed change in target behavior. Although realities of the practice situation did not permit an exact implementation of the multiple baseline design, it could be closely approximated, which adds considerably to the therapist's ability to infer the effectiveness of the intervention. Even if the multiple baseline design could not have been implemented, a simple AB design (baseline-intervention) on any one of the target behaviors would have provided valuable information about change.

Source: Marlene Cooper, "Treatment of a Client with Obsessive-Compulsive Disorder," *Social Work Research and Abstracts* 26 (1990), pp. 26–32.

Assess Threats to Validity

Concomitant variation alone is not sufficient to establish causality; it is only suggestive of a causal relationship. We also must rule out other possible (and plausible) explanations for why the client changed. These competing explanations fall into several

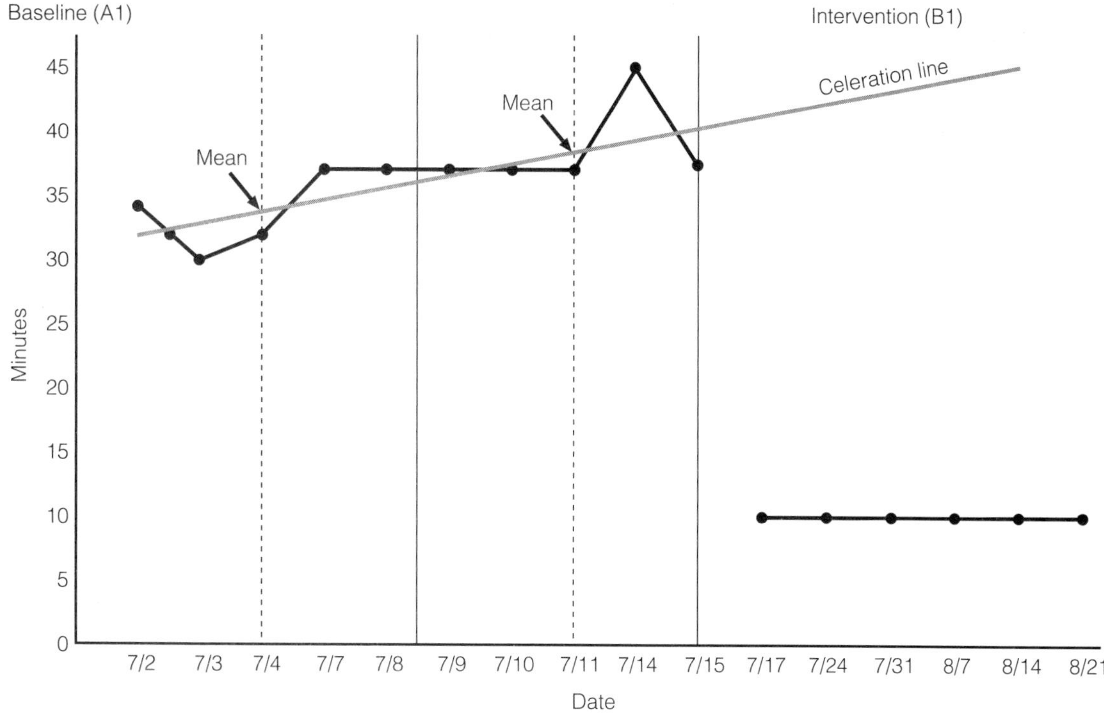

Figure 11.4
Number of twists, presses, and clicks of makeup case by client each morning at baseline (7/2 to 7/15) and after intervention (7/17 to 8/21).

Source: Marlene Cooper, "Treatment of a Client with Obsessive-Compulsive Disorder," *Social Work Research and Abstracts* 26 (1990), pp. 26–32. Social work research & abstracts by National Association of Social Workers. Copyright 1990 Reproduced with permission of National Association of Social Workers in the format Textbook via Copyright Clearance Center.

categories, which have been called threats to validity (Shadish, Cook, & Campbell, 2002). *Validity,* as the term is used here, refers to the best available approximation of truth regarding the cause of client change. Four important threats to validity are described below. Others are discussed by Shadish et al. (2002) and Kratochwill (1978).

History *History* refers to any event that may have occurred during the time the intervention was implemented that could also account for the change. Examples are events such as getting a promotion, getting a new classroom teacher, or having a birthday. Observed improvements in the client's functioning may result from such historical events rather than the intervention. Simple baseline intervention designs (AB designs) do not permit us to rule out the effects of history. Other more advanced designs are needed.

Maturation *Maturation* includes any processes within the client that operate as a function of the passage of time, such as growing up, becoming senile, or becoming tired. Maturation generally becomes more of a threat the longer it takes for the intervention to have an impact.

Statistical Regression Usually clients come to social workers for help when things have gotten worse—that is, they are in an extreme state. However, chances are good that things will look better at the next observation simply because of random fluctuations of the behavior. This threat to validity is called *statistical regression*. The best way to control statistical regression is to take an adequate baseline. If the baseline shows an upward or downward trend or an unusual amount of variability, you should continue to baseline to see whether the data stabilize or the pattern of normal variability becomes clear. The point is to not mistake normal variation in your client's behavior for a real change in behavior.

EP 2.1.6a, b

Multiple Intervention Interference When a client receives more than one intervention at a time, there is no empirical basis for knowing which intervention produced the change. This is a common problem, particularly in institutional settings where clients may participate in a variety of groups, receive individual therapy, and perhaps take medication. Again, simple AB designs are inadequate to control for this threat. Other designs, such as multiple baseline designs, are useful in ruling out multiple intervention interference.

Exercise 11.2: Applying the Single-System Evaluation Approach to a Problematic Behavior

Goal: This exercise is designed to assist you in understanding and applying the single-system evaluation approach.

Step 1: Identify a problematic behavior that you have that you can make a positive change in within a week. (Perhaps you are procrastinating about a paper or drinking to excess.) Specify this problematic behavior.

Step 2: Use the single-system approach for the next week. Complete the following list as soon as you complete each of the procedures.

a. Specify the goal.

b. Select suitable measures.

c. Record baseline data.

d. Select the intervention.

e. Implement the intervention and continue monitoring.

f. Assess change.

g. Infer effectiveness.

SINGLE-SYSTEM DESIGNS

The Basic AB Design

Thus far we have discussed only the simplest of single-system designs: the baseline intervention, or AB design. It is the simplest design because it provides the information necessary for determining that there has been change, it suggests the possibility that the intervention produced the change, but it is not able to control for many of the threats to validity mentioned earlier. The AB design generally is not adequate for inferring causality or intervention effectiveness. More advanced single-system designs are needed to control for such threats.

Withdrawal Designs

Withdrawal designs are characterized by repeated occasions in which the intervention is implemented and then withdrawn. The rationale underlying withdrawal designs is that the causal inference is stronger when there are more occasions on which client outcome can be shown to vary concomitantly with intervention. Common examples are the ABA and ABAB designs (see Figure 11.5). In the former, treatment is withdrawn after it has been implemented; in the latter, treatment is implemented again. Withdrawal designs are useful for controlling threats caused by history, maturation, and statistical regression, among others. Withdrawal designs are often difficult to implement in day-to-day practice, however, because they require withdrawal of intervention even when it appears to be working. This is one example in which the goals of research (demonstrating causality) may conflict with the goals of service (providing effective treatment).

It is important to be careful to distinguish between withdrawal phases and follow-ups. In withdrawal designs, the objective is for the client outcome to return to the pretreatment level to demonstrate repeatedly that it is under the control of the intervention. In follow-ups, however, the objective is to show that change is permanent and that it lasts even after treatment has been discontinued. You should be clear in your own mind about which objective you are addressing so you will know how to interpret the data.

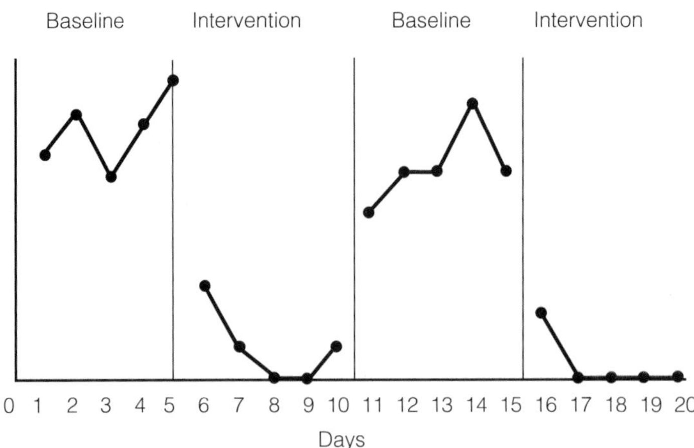

Figure 11.5
Withdrawal design.

Source: © Cengage Learning, 2013.

Multiple Baseline Designs

In multiple baseline designs several outcomes of interest are identified and baselined simultaneously. The intervention is then implemented on each outcome at staggered intervals (Figure 11.6). This type of design is stronger than simple AB designs because it provides for several occasions on which outcome can vary concomitantly with intervention. Further, it avoids the practical and ethical problems of withdrawing treatment as in ABA and ABAB designs.

Still other advanced single-system designs should be considered if the objective is to infer causality. The texts by Jayaratne and Levy (1979), Bloom et al. (2009), and Barlow and Hersen (1984) offer a more detailed discussion of single-system research designs.

EVALUATING PROGRAMS

Most of the discussion thus far has assumed that we are evaluating social work practice with individuals, groups, and families. There is nothing inherent in the single-system approach that limits it to clinical evaluation, however. Some of the first applications of single-system designs were to evaluate the impact of policy, such as a change in speed limits or a change in monetary policy. Single-system designs can easily be applied to the evaluation of policy and program interventions. The basic designs are the same; the primary differences are the conceptualization of the intervention and outcome and the selection of suitable measures.

In program evaluation, the policy or program becomes the intervention. Such interventions include providing incentives for able-bodied welfare recipients to obtain employment, instituting a token economy to reward good behavior in a group home, or starting a new procedure whereby staff ignore the obnoxious noises of children but give positive attention for appropriate talk.

Likewise, in program evaluation the desired outcome has to do with the behavior of the targets of the policy or program change, usually a group of people. Accordingly, the measures must be those that are suitable for all individuals. This usually rules out client-specific measures such as self-anchored scales. Frequently, the desired outcomes are observable behaviors, such as getting a job, cooperative play in the cottage, or appropriate table conversation. In program evaluation, you must be careful to define outcomes in sufficiently general terms so that the definitions will be relevant for all individuals in the target group. When the desired outcome is an internal state, you

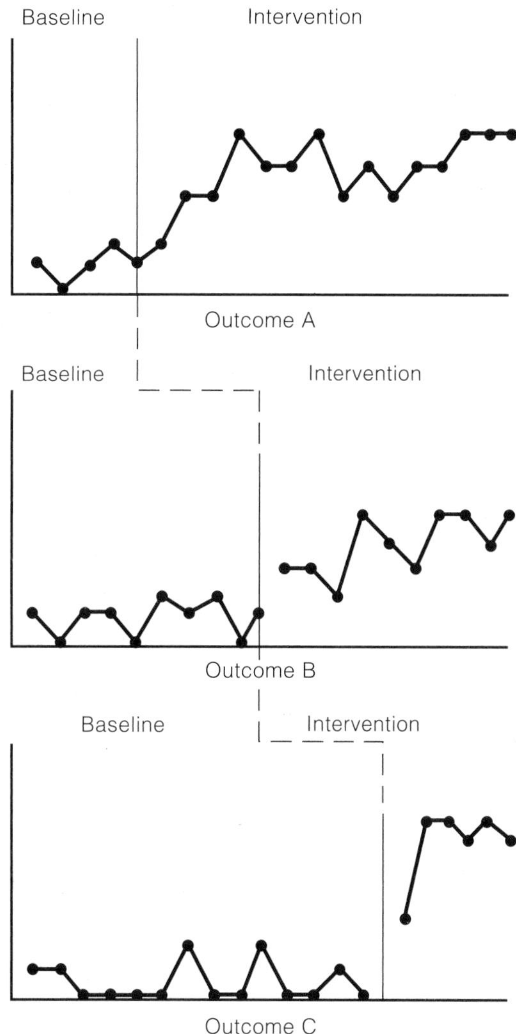

Figure 11.6
Multiple baseline design.

Source: © Cengage Learning, 2013.

may need to use some of the standardized measures or rapid assessment instruments mentioned earlier.

Program evaluation, then, is no different conceptually from clinical evaluation. The distinction is that the intervention is a policy or program rather than a therapeutic technique, and the outcome is reflected in the behaviors of a target group of individuals rather than a single individual or therapy group.

The single-system approach to evaluation has much to recommend it. Single-system designs are compatible with most of social work practice, and they provide a beginning basis for inferring that our interventions are effective. Single-system designs, including the more advanced designs, are not always sufficient, however. They cannot always rule out all threats to validity. Some social work interventions, particularly policy and program changes, cannot be implemented abruptly, and other interventions sometimes have a delayed effect on outcome. In both cases, it is difficult empirically to relate changes in outcome to the intervention. In such cases, traditional group designs may be justified.

The requirements of group designs—random assignment to groups, relatively large numbers of clients, and uniform treatment of all subjects within groups—make them costly and difficult to implement in normal practice settings. Frequently, the potential benefits of doing a group evaluation do not justify the costs involved. At times, however, group designs are warranted, particularly when single-system evaluation has provided cumulative evidence of effectiveness and a more rigorous test is desired. Group evaluation is a rather technical undertaking for which research expertise is advised. Texts by Kaufman and Thomas (1980); Posavac and Carey (1980); Rossi, Freeman, and Wright (1979); and Weiss (1972) and are recommended for further reading in this area.

EVALUATION IN A MANAGED CARE ENVIRONMENT

Systematic practice evaluation will help you know if your clients are improving, and it may provide evidence that your interventions are effective. This is reason enough to make evaluation part of your ordinary practice activities. However, as managed care becomes more prevalent in social work settings, there is added reason to evaluate your practice. Managed care agencies and others who fund social work services will increasingly ask for hard evidence that clients are benefiting from your services (Mullen & Magnabosco, 1997). "Hard evidence" almost always means a standardized measure of some sort and perhaps client-specific data also, such as the behavioral data or rating scales discussed earlier. Unstructured clinical impressions are not adequate for such purposes.

Increasingly, social workers will be required to use standardized measures to document client change, usually of the rapid assessment type described by Corcoran and Fischer (2007). The most widely used general-purpose instrument is the Short Form Health Survey (SF-36), which was designed for clinical use in health settings (Ware & Sherbourne, 1992). The SF-36 has well-established validity and reliability and includes subscales on general mental health and on limitations in role activities because of emotional problems. Another general-purpose measure is the Outcome Questionnaire (OQ-45.2), which is specifically designed to measure client progress and can be used at every meeting with the client if desired (American Professional Credentialing Services, 1996). The Questionnaire OQ-45.2 assesses three dimensions: intrapsychic functioning, interpersonal relationships, and social role performance. In addition, it includes screening items for suicidality, substance abuse, and physical violence. Depending on the setting, more specific measures such as the Beck Depression Inventory (Beck, Rush, Shaw, & Emery, 1979) or the Addiction Severity Index (McLellan, Luborsky, Woody, & O'Brien, 1992) may be used instead. In any case, it is advisable to identify one or more rapid assessment instruments relevant for your client population and administer them routinely at the beginning and end of treatment. Such a practice will help you accumulate evidence that your clients benefit from services. Make sure that the measure you use is relevant for the client goal you are working on, however, or it will likely show no change.

Rapid assessment instruments should not replace the repeated use of direct observations or rating scales as your primary measure of client change. Pre- and postmeasures give no information about how your client is progressing during intervention. Further, because standardized measures are designed for use across many clients, usually they are not as sensitive to client change as are client-specific measures. Thus, a good procedure is to use a client-specific measure (behavioral observation or rating scale) on a repeated basis (daily, if possible) and supplement it with an appropriate rapid assessment instrument at the beginning and end of treatment.

THE ETHICS OF EVALUATION

Most of the discussion in this chapter has assumed that we are conducting outcome evaluation as part of normal practice—that is, we identify goals, select measures of them, and monitor change to verify that the desired goals have been achieved. Outcome evaluation is integral to practice because it tells us if we are making progress and when we can terminate the helping process. Because it is a part of normal practice, outcome evaluation as a process is treated no differently than any other aspect of practice. Accordingly, the usual ethical requirements of confidentiality, informed consent, and client access to records discussed in earlier chapters apply.

When we undertake evaluative research to infer causality and advance our knowledge of effective practice, however, additional ethical guidelines are required to protect our clients as research subjects. The distinction between evaluation as a practice activity and evaluative research as a knowledge-building activity is often ambiguous. But as a general rule, if the primary purpose of your activity is to develop the knowledge base of the profession rather than deliver a service to your client, you are engaging in research. If you plan to present your results to a professional meeting or publish them in a journal, you are probably engaged in research. If in doubt, consider the activity to be research.

When clients are asked to participate in research activities, additional ethical standards apply (see the NASW *Code of Ethics,* section 5.02, "Evaluation and Research," at www.naswdc.org). We must be sure that clients will not be subjected to undue risk as a consequence of their participation in the research activity. Furthermore, clients must be fully informed of the nature of the activity, both the intervention itself and the measurement and design requirements of the research component. Finally, clients' participation must be completely voluntary, and there must be no adverse consequence if clients decide not to participate in the research. The principle of voluntary informed consent is a fundamental ethical requirement for all research activity and must be carefully followed and documented at all times.

INFORMATION TECHNOLOGY IN SOCIAL WORK PRACTICE

Although the computer is essential in industries such as banking, travel reservations, and medical care, it has yet to make a serious impact on social work practice. That is about to change, however, because of developments that make the technology more useful in the less structured situations characteristic of social work practice and because of the availability of extraordinary computing capability at steadily declining cost.

Today the most common use of information technology in social work practice is word processing. Increasingly, social workers use their computers to write assessments and progress notes and routine correspondence and reports. Some workers also use database programs to create electronic filing systems for their caseloads and to do reports and analyses of their caseload activities. Personal information managers help you keep track of your appointments, addresses and phone numbers, and business expenses. All of these applications are readily available in local computer stores at reasonable cost—many are included with the purchase of a new computer. With a little thought and effort, these applications can be customized to your particular setting and can be quite useful in your work. For additional information about computer applications in social work, see the resources listed in Exhibit 11.2.

In the rest of this section, we will look at applications that have been developed specifically for use in social work or, more broadly, human services practice.

Assessment and Testing

Assessment and testing applications constitute by far the largest number of computer applications in social work practice. More than 200 such programs are currently available, most of them consisting of computer-administered testing, scoring, and interpretation packages. The Minnesota Multiphasic Personality Inventory (MMPI) and various depression inventories were among the first instruments to be computerized. Most of the commonly used assessment devices are now available in computerized versions, including DSM-IV interviewing and diagnostic programs. The Clinical Measurement Package developed by Walter Hudson provides administration and scoring of all Hudson rapid assessment scales, now numbering more than 30 (Nurius & Hudson, 1993). In addition, this package will maintain a history of assessment scores for individual clients, enabling the graphic representation of client change over time. Demonstration

Exhibit 11.2 Resource Materials on Computer Applications for Social Work Practice

Gingerich, W. (2002a). "Computer Applications for Social Work Practice." In A. R. Roberts & G. J. Greene (Eds.), *Social Worker's Desk Reference* (pp. 23–28). New York: Oxford University Press.

Gingerich, W. (2002b). "Online Social Work: Ethical and Practical Considerations." In A. R. Roberts & G. J Greene (Eds.), *Social Worker's Desk Reference* (pp. 81–85). New York: Oxford University Press.

Grant, G. B., & Grobman, L. M. (1998). *The Social Worker's Internet Handbook*. Harrisburg, PA: White Hat Communications.

Grohol, J. M. (2003). *The Insider's Guide to Mental Health Resources Online 2002/2003 Edition*. New York: Guilford Press.

Hick, S. F., & McNutt, J. G. (2002). *Advocacy, Activism, and the Internet*. Chicago: Lyceum Books.

Holden, G., Rosenberg, G., & Weissman, A. (1996). "World Wide Web Accessible Resources Related to Research on Social Work Practice." *Research on Social Work Practice*, 6, 236–262.

Journal of Technology in Human Services. New York: Haworth Press.

Kjosness, J. Y., Barr, L. R., & Rettman, S. (2004). Research Navigator Guide: *The Helping Professions*. Boston: Allyn & Bacon.

Patterson, D. A. (2000). *Personal Computer Applications in the Social Services*. Boston: Allyn & Bacon.

Schoech, D. (1999). *Human Services Technology: Understanding, Designing, and Implementing Computer and Internet Applications in the Social Services* (2nd ed.). New York: Haworth Press.

Trabin, T. (1996). *The Computerization of Behavioral Healthcare*. San Francisco: Jossey-Bass.

and educational versions of this package are available free of cost. Information about many of these applications is readily available on the Internet.

Computerized Clinical Records

Computerized clinical record-keeping systems maintain the complete case record on the computer and usually incorporate case management and caseload management functions as well. Many of these systems also incorporate appointment scheduling, community resource directories, and billing and accounting functions. Typically, clinical record-keeping systems operate on a network or large computer, and the individual worker accesses the system through a computer located in his or her office. Because of the complexities and idiosyncrasies of record-keeping requirements, most of these systems have been custom-designed for a particular agency and are not available on the open market. In other cases, large software companies have developed packages that can be adapted for a particular agency's needs. In either case, these systems are very costly ($20,000 or more) and often require sophisticated equipment and trained systems staff to support them.

Other record-keeping programs emphasize treatment planning and case management. These systems assist the practitioner in conducting the assessment and selecting treatment goals and then help monitor client change over time (Corcoran & Gingerich, 1994; Gingerich, 1995b). In addition, case management programs can remind the worker of tasks that need to be done and even identify which clients are not making progress so that their plans can be reviewed. Increasingly, case management programs will be able to use the information contained in the case record to assist workers in managing their caseloads more efficiently and may even reduce the amount of time spent on paperwork.

Practice Management and Billing

Numerous psychotherapy practice management programs are now available commercially. Most of these systems are designed for small group practices and focus heavily on the clinical information needed to justify services (such as DSM diagnoses, target complaints, level of functioning, and service data) and maintain patient accounts (such as preparing insurance billings and tracking payments). Many of these programs are advertised in professional publications such as the *NASW News* and on the Internet. Because these applications are intended for solo use, they typically cost only several hundred dollars per workstation.

Managed Care Applications

Computer technology is rapidly being applied in the field of managed behavioral health care; many of the applications are designed for use by practitioners (Gingerich & Broskowski, 1996). These systems generally aim to maximize the efficiency of behavioral health interventions by advising on the level of treatment to be provided, the type of treatment to be used, and the most cost-effective management of particular types of cases. Some systems are designed to improve consistency in diagnosing problems and authorizing services. Others are designed to guide the practitioner on what kind of intervention to use and for how long. Managed care applications basically use information technology to implement the managed care firm's approved authorization criteria and practice guidelines. Many of these are based in part on research data, but they also inevitably incorporate the company's own practice philosophy. These applications may have the most value for practitioners interested in evaluating their own practice because they are most focused on client change and the interventions that seem to produce client change.

Expert Systems

Expert systems are computer programs that contain the expertise of a human expert on a specified problem area and advise the user on the specified problem area (Gingerich, 1990, 1995a). Expert systems grew out of research in artificial intelligence and have been implemented widely in industry, medicine, and computer software. Because of the newness of the technology and unresolved product liability issues, few if any clinical expert systems are in routine use in social work practice today. Experimental systems have been developed for assessing the risk of child abuse, advising on risk to women of domestic violence, advising on treatment interventions using a brief solution-focused therapy approach (see Module 4), or assessing suicide risk. Although expert-system applications have yet to be implemented in social work practice, the process of conceptualizing, designing, and testing an expert system can have valuable knowledge-building benefits and can be a useful educational experience. Inexpensive expert-system shells are available that perform the technical programming chores and allow the user to concentrate on developing the rules that go into the knowledge base and the inferencing strategy to be used.

Computer-Based Interventions

Computer programs have been used to administer cognitive therapy to patients experiencing anxiety and to provide sex therapy for couples. The systems carry out an assessment and assign homework. Based on the response of the client, the computer then provides additional advice and feedback. Another system has been developed for delivering exposure therapy to patients experiencing anxiety (see Module 2). This computer-administered program is available to patients via touch-tone telephone, making it accessible for people anywhere to access it at nearly any time. Computer-administered interventions can produce results similar to those delivered by human practitioners and are preferred by some clients.

Graphing Packages

Numerous packages have been developed that produce graphs or charts useful in assessment and intervention. Several packages are available that can draw family

Exhibit 11.3 World Wide Web Sites for Social Work

Information for Practice
ifp.nyu.edu
New Social Worker Online
www.socialworker.com
Social Work Search.com
www.socialworksearch.com
National Association of Social Workers
www.socialworkers.org
Association of Social Work Boards (licensing)
www.aswb.org
Mental Help Net
mentalhelp.net
International Society for Mental Health Online
www.ismho.org
Society for Social Work and Research
www.sswr.org
Social Work Policy Institute
www.socialworkpolicy.org
Council on Social Work Education
www.cswe.org
The Campbell Collaboration
www.campbellcollaboration.org
U.S. National Institute of Mental Health
www.nimh.nih.gov
U.S. Department of Health and Human Services
www.hhs.gov
U.S. Census Bureau
www.census.gov

genograms or eco-maps (see Chapter 8) based on information the user enters into the computer. Some of these programs can maintain a database of the ecosystem over time and permit the user to graph these changes. Some of the record-keeping and managed care systems previously mentioned also incorporate a variety of graphs. Increasingly, we will see programs that can present the target behavior in the form of a graph, which will provide immediate visual feedback on progress to the client and the worker.

Internet and Online Services

The rapid growth of the Internet and readily available access to it have opened up a vast array of potential applications in social work practice (Gingerich, 2002a). The Internet provides immediate access to a rich storehouse of information relevant to social work practice, and this is probably the most common use of the Internet today. The sites listed in Exhibit 11.3 contain links to many sites of interest and are organized to make it easy for you to find what you are looking for. Government sites give access to informative reports, regulations, and statistical data of value to social workers. State and local governments and increasingly many social service agencies have their own websites, which can be located through World Wide Web search engines such as Google.com. Some individual social workers have developed their own sites for professional use. Visit the author's site at gingerich.net and click on the Social Work Web Ring to visit many other social worker sites.

Unlike commercial and academic publishing houses that use rigorous review procedures to ensure the quality of the information they put out, the information on the Internet has passed no such test. Thus, it is important for you to think critically about the information you access over the Internet and judge for yourself whether it is reliable.

Another common use of the Internet is online support groups. These are discussion groups organized by users with a particular interest, such as coping with depression, incest survivors, Alzheimer's caregivers, parents of children who committed suicide, and hundreds of other topics. You can find information about these sites in books such as *Health Online* (Ferguson, 1996) and *The Insider's Guide to Mental Health Resources Online* (Grohol, 2003). Web portals such as Yahoo (www.yahoo.com) also provide easy access to many support group sites and other informative health-related sites.

The Internet is also used by many social workers (and social work students) for networking and professional development. You can join mailing lists organized around topics of particular interest, search for a graduate school or a job, or chat with other students or social workers about issues of mutual interest. The New Social Worker Online site (Exhibit 11.3) is a good place to start, as well as the *The Social Worker's Internet Handbook* (Exhibit 11.2).

Advocacy and fund-raising are exciting new uses of the Internet that take advantage of the Internet's capacity to network with millions of people (Hick & McNutt, 2002). Howard Dean, a presidential candidate in 2004, saw this potential and used the Internet to raise millions of dollars from ordinary Americans to support his political campaign. The potential for organizing clients and other stakeholders to advocate on behalf of social welfare issues is enormous.

Finally, the Internet is beginning to be used to deliver professional services (Gingerich, 2002b). Recently, a researcher offered a smoking cessation program over the Internet, and 360,000 people subscribed! Some social workers are beginning to offer professional services such as counseling over the Internet, via e-mail, chat rooms, or real-time voice and video. These services are called variously eTherapy, eHealth, TeleHealth, or simply online services. Types of services, mode of delivery, and payment mechanisms are still being developed, and it is impossible to tell now what form online services will eventually take. You should be aware, however, that difficult issues pertaining to legal liability, licensing, informed consent, and privacy and confidentiality have yet to be resolved. Social workers delivering services online place themselves at some risk until these issues can be clarified.

EP 2.1.3b

Exercise 11.3: Assessing Counseling over the Internet

Goal: This exercise is designed to assist you in understanding the merits and shortcomings of counseling over the Internet, which is an emerging form of clinical practice.

Step 1: Specify what you see as the merits and benefits of counseling over the Internet.

Step 2: Specify some of the unresolved issues of counseling over the Internet.

Step 3: Specify what you see as the shortcomings of counseling over the Internet.

SUMMARY

Outcome evaluation asks whether the desired client outcome was achieved, and evaluative research asks whether the observed change was the result of the intervention. Because it is an inherent part of the problem-solving approach to interventions, outcome evaluation should be done with all clients. Evaluative research requires more rigorous controls. It is more difficult to carry out and often requires research expertise.

The single-system approach to evaluation consists of seven steps: (1) Specify the outcome you and your client are interested in. (2) Select a suitable measure of the outcome, one that is adequate methodologically and is sensitive to the changes you expect your client to make. (3) Record baseline data on the outcome measure until the pattern of behavior before intervention is clear. (4) Select an effective intervention. (5) Implement your intervention and continue to monitor the outcome. (6) Analyze your data to decide whether there is significant change in the outcome. (7) If you have used an appropriate research design, you may be able to infer whether your intervention produced the change.

Although it uses research techniques to assess change and infer treatment effectiveness, the single-system approach to evaluation is compatible with most social work practice. In treatment you ordinarily make informal judgments about whether your client is getting better and whether your intervention is working. Evaluation simply makes the process more systematic and rigorous with a view to improving your information and making your conclusions more reliable. The goal of evaluation is to improve your information about outcomes and thereby improve your practice. Some research suggests that using practice evaluation techniques does in fact improve client outcomes (Faul, McMurtry and Hudson, 2001; Slonim-Nevo & Anson, 1998). Furthermore, several studies show that clients may actually prefer to work with practitioners who evaluate their practice (Campbell, 1988, 1990).

EP 2.1.6a, b

The chapter concludes with a summary of computer applications in social work practice. Not only are computers used in evaluation and research, they are beginning to have an impact on many other aspects of social work practice as well. The most common computer applications in social work fall into these areas: assessment and testing, record keeping, practice management, managed care, expert systems, clinical interventions, graphing packages, and Internet and online services.

EXERCISES

1. Selecting a Suitable Outcome Measure

Goal: To measure client outcomes.

Step 1: Form groups of three or four. A volunteer "client" in your group decides on an outcome that will become your focus for this exercise. The outcome can be a real one or a hypothetical one.

Step 2: Group members interview the "client" to find out more about the desired outcome. How would the "client" like things to be? What will he or she be doing differently when the outcome is achieved?

Step 3: Identify at least two possible measurement strategies to evaluate the outcome. Describe each measure in detail. What will the anchors be on the self-anchored scale, for example? What specific behavior will you observe or ask your "client" to observe?

Step 4: Ask the "client" to estimate what data he or she would have collected during the past week had he or she used each measure. What would the data be like when the problem has been solved?

Step 5: Group discussion of the pros and cons of each measure developed. Consider these questions: (a) How reliable (accurate and consistent) will the measurement data be? (b) How valid will the data be—that is, would the behavior counts or self-ratings be good indicators of the outcome the "client" is hoping to achieve? (c) Will the measure be sensitive to changes the "client" would like to see? Do you really expect to see changes in the measures you have selected? (d) Which measure does your "client" think is best? Why?

Step 6: Class presentation of group findings.

2. Threats to Inferring Causality

Goals: To experience some of the problems involved in inferring causality.

Step 1: Break into groups of five. You will conduct an evaluation of the following case. Your client, a mother of two children (ages 5 and 8), comes in complaining that her 8-yearold, Joey, clings to her too much and doesn't play with other children his age. You and she agree that the desired outcome is for Joey to play with neighbor children his own age. Mother agrees to record the number of 15-minute periods each evening after supper and before bedtime that Joey plays nicely with his peers. She dutifully collects baseline information as shown below.

After a week of baselining, you instruct the mother to invite a neighbor child over to play with Joey each evening to get the children started in an activity appropriate to their age level. Once the activity has started, she is to give specific praise to the children for their play and to continue to praise every 5 or 10 minutes as it seems appropriate. Also, she is instructed to ignore Joey when he clings to her dress and whines. After role-playing some situations in your office, you are convinced that she understands the intervention and is able to carry it out. Mother returns the next week for her appointment. You review the data and refine and rehearse again the intervention. The next week Mother reports the following data:

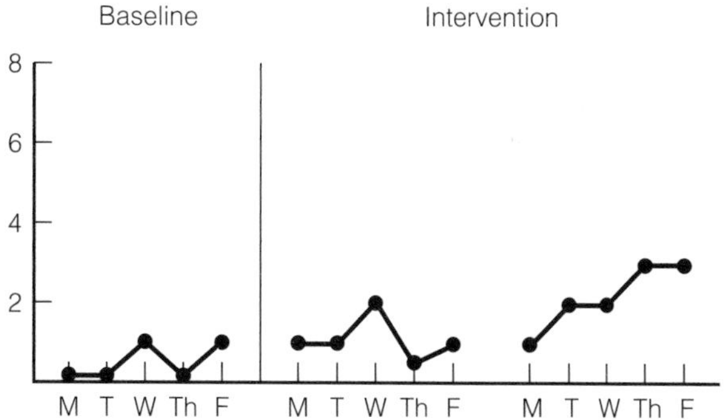

During the interview, she reports the following additional information. She has begun to think that Joey is a nice kid after all. Last week when she took him to the park to play, they had a really good time. Joey seemed to get along well with the other children on the playground too. Mother also mentioned that Joey seemed to enjoy his last two weekend visits with his dad. In general, Joey seems to be getting back to his good old self.

Step 2: Decide first whether you agree with Mother that Joey's behavior has changed. Is the standard of "clearly evident and reliable" met? Is the change experimentally or clinically significant?

Step 3: Enumerate other possible explanations of Joey's behavior change. What is the likelihood of these explanations? Does the simple AB design used allow you to rule out these explanations?

Step 4: Class discussion of group findings. Has the intervention been successful? How confident are you of your conclusions? Does the intervention seem promising enough to continue using it and observing the results?

COMPETENCY NOTES

The following identifies where Educational Policy (EP) competencies and practice behaviors are discussed in the chapter.

EP 2.1.6a *Use practice experience to inform scientific inquiry.*

EP 2.1.6b *Use research evidence to inform practice.* (pp. 343–370).

This chapter describes outcome evaluation and evaluative research, the single-system evaluation approach, evidence-based practice, program evaluation, and information technology in social work practice.

EP 2.1.6a *Use practice experience to inform scientific inquiry.*

EP 2.1.6b *Use research evidence to inform practice.* (pp. 344–345).

Exercise 11.1 is designed to demonstrate to students that they have already been involved, numerous times, in outcome evaluation.

EP 2.1.6a *Use practice experience to inform scientific inquiry.*

EP 2.1.6b *Use research evidence to inform practice.* (pp. 360–361).

Exercise 11.2 is designed to assist students in understanding and applying the single-system evaluation approach to one of their problematic behaviors.

EP 2.1.3b *Analyze models of assessment, prevention, intervention, and evaluation.* (p. 369).

Exercise 11.3 is designed to assist students in understanding the merits and shortcomings of counseling over the Internet, which is an emerging form of clinical practice.

EP 2.1.6a *Use practice experience to inform scientific inquiry.*

EP 2.1.6b *Use research evidence to inform practice.* (p. 370).

This exercise is designed to assist students in better understanding the process of selecting quality measurement strategies to measure client outcomes.

EP 2.1.6a *Use practice experience to inform scientific inquiry.*

EP 2.1.6b *Use research evidence to inform practice.* (p. 371).

This exercise is designed to have students experience some of the problems involved in inferring causality when conducting scientific studies.

CHAPTER 12

Social Work Practice with Diverse Groups

EP 2.1.4a, b, c, d; 2.1.5a, b, c; 2.1.10a

The social work profession prides itself on its recognition of the importance of ethnic, cultural, racial, and sexual differences.[1] Social workers helped to establish the National Association for the Advancement of Colored People (NAACP) and the National Urban League (Garvin & Cox, 2001, p. 74). The National Association of Social Workers' *Code of Ethics* (1996) specifically prohibits discrimination "on the basis of race, ethnicity, national origin, color, sex, sexual orientation, age, marital status, political belief, religion, or mental or physical disability." Judging from public pronouncements at least, one would expect social workers to perform admirably when working with people from diverse groups. Unfortunately, this benign view is not necessarily accurate. All of us were raised and socialized in a racist system. As a result, all of us are likely to have some racist stereotypes.

In addition, as many writers point out, much of our understanding of human development is based on studies of males (Jaffee & Hyde, 2000; Skoe, Cumberland, Eisenberg, Hansen, & Perry, 2002). It has been shown that females have very different developmental experiences than males, and that we cannot simply apply to one gender theories that were based on the other. So, not surprisingly, evidence indicates that social workers face a difficult task understanding and working with clients whose backgrounds differ from their own.

In this chapter, we consider barriers resulting from worker-client differences and point out reasons for the problematic nature of cross-cultural relationships. It is beyond the scope of this text to provide content on all populations at risk. Information covering a greater number of populations at risk can be found in *Culturally Competent Practice* (Lum, 2007).

This chapter will:

A. Present a perspective on stereotyping and multiculturalism
B. Describe barriers in worker-client cross-cultural relationships
C. Describe knowledge needed for cross-cultural social work practice
D. Describe culturally competent practice
E. Explain how social constructs adversely impact populations at risk
F. Describe macro strategies to promote social and economic justice

[1] Most of this chapter was specially written for this text by Grafton H. Hull, Jr., EdD. Dr. Hull is a retired director of the BSW Program at the University of Utah. The section titled "Macro Strategies to Promote Social and Economic Justice" was written primarily by Charles Zastrow.

STEREOTYPING AND MULTICULTURALISM: A PERSPECTIVE

Among the factors that social workers need to respect and appreciate are the following identified by the Council on Social Work Education's *Educational Policy and Accreditation Standards* (2008): "age, class, color, culture, disability, ethnicity, gender, gender identity and expression, immigration status, political ideology, race, religion, sex, and sexual orientation." Like most social work texts, this text presents descriptive information about the groups identified by the National Association of Social Workers (NASW) and the Council on Social Work Education (CSWE). It has traditionally been thought that such information will increase social workers' capacities to be culturally competent with these groups. But it is important to note that some social work authorities are now raising questions about whether presenting descriptive information actually leads to stereotypes and prejudices (Mor Barak, 2005). For example, if we describe women as being more emotional than men and men as being more rational than women, this perception and categorization may shape expectations. Such perceptions and categorizations are often inaccurate when applied to individuals as well as to the group as a whole.

Another example may help to clarify this issue. There is a perception that Asian Americans are a "model minority" because they achieve well in educational settings, experience little or no discrimination, and experience low levels of emotional illness (Grossman & Liang, 2008). This perception, however, raises a number of questions that may negatively affect people labeled "Asian American." A few of these questions are the following: Will it lead Asian American children to feel undue pressure to be supersuccessful? Will it lead Asian Americans who are not supersuccessful to view themselves as "failures"? Will social service agencies and policy makers tend not to develop human service programs for Asian Americans because they are perceived to be overachieving and supersuccessful? Will providers of services—dentists, car dealers, plumbers, electricians—tend to charge Asian Americans more because they perceive them as "wealthy"?

The stereotyping of Asian Americans as being overachieving and supersuccessful ignores the diverse experiences of Asian Americans. It glosses over huge differences within a group of people from more than two dozen countries, most of which have their own distinct languages and cultures. In this regard, Ziaddlin Sardar (2001, pp. 14–16) notes,

> White people . . . look at me and exclaim: "Surely, you're Asian." However, there is no such thing as an Asian. Asia is not a race or identity: it is a continent. Even in Asia, where more than half of the world's population lives, no one calls him or herself "Asian." . . . In the U.S., the Asian label is attached to Koreans, Filipinos, and Chinese. In Britain, we do not use the term *Asian* to describe our substantial communities of Turks, Iranians, or Indonesians, even though these countries are in Asia.

To repeat, there is a danger that presenting descriptive information about a group may lead to negative stereotyping and then overt discrimination. For example, descriptive information indicates African Americans tend to have higher rates (compared with whites) of poverty, homelessness, births outside of marriage, dropping out of school, criminal arrests, and criminal convictions (Schaefer, 2010). Does such information lead to the expectation by non–African Americans that African American individuals they meet are apt to "fit" such descriptive information? For example, the poverty rate for African Americans is about 20%, whereas for whites it is 10% (Schaefer, 2010, p. 203). Will this lead non–African Americans to expect that African American individuals they encounter are apt to be "poor"? What may be ignored by the non–African American is that most African Americans (80%) are not living in poverty.

This text uses the traditional approach of presenting descriptive information about the diverse categories identified in the CSWE's *Educational Policy and Accreditation Standards* (2008) for two reasons: (1) Most social work educators deduce that the *EPAS* was written with the expectation that descriptive information on these categories will be presented in the social work curriculum. (2) The social work authorities who are concerned about possibly negative effects of descriptive information have not arrived at a new definition of *diversity* that enables us to develop a knowledge base of information about the diverse groups identified in the *EPAS* who have been victimized in the past (and during the present time) by discrimination. I urge readers to be aware of the possibility that stereotypes may be generated by this descriptive information and to guard against falling victim to them.

Another caveat about diversity needs to be mentioned. Everyone has multicultural diversity. We differ from one another in age, economic status, education, family type, gender, personality type, ethnicity, religion, geographic origin, sexual orientation, communication types, native-born or immigrant status, attire, language, political views, physical abilities, lifestyle, and other ways. Therefore, when we meet someone who, for example, is Japanese American, it is essential for us to recognize that there are so many other facets of that individual besides his or her ethnicity. It is impossible to present information on all sources of diversity. If we consider ethnicity alone, there are literally thousands of different populations. In the United States alone, there are about 600 different Native American tribes, each with a distinctive culture. Therefore, in this chapter descriptive information is presented about a few illustrative groups—African American clients, Latino clients, Native American clients, female clients, and gay and lesbian clients.

PROBLEMS AND BARRIERS

The social work profession needs to recognize the reality of practice in a culturally diverse environment. Various studies demonstrate that social workers and other helping persons share many of the prejudices and misperceptions of the general society (Appleby, 2001; Green, Kiernan-Stein, & Baskind, 2005; Raiz & Saltzburg, 2007).

Multiple examples of sexism, for example, can be found in the social work knowledge base. DeJong and Berg (1998), in summarizing the work of several other social work authors, note, "For too long, the helping professions have operated with built-in preferences for the traits and behaviors of middle-class white males. Such preferences have minimized or ignored the characteristics more common among poor people, women, and people of color" (p. 204). For example, males working with depressed women may simply re-create old relationships between the dependent woman and the controlling male—relationships counter to the goals of intervention. Hall (2007) argues that all social workers have a special obligation to recognize the importance of gender in working with women and that, in particular, "male social workers are ethically bound to actively support gender equality" (p. 214).

The tendency to use our own cultural, social, or economic values as the norm poses additional dangers for well-meaning workers. The ease with which many workers confuse a healthy adaptation to a sick environment with pathology points up the difficulty. Both the habit of misreading strengths as deficits and the assumption that African Americans and other minorities are culturally deprived arise from the use of norms derived from the dominant white middle class. The problematic nature of cross-cultural counseling, however, does not preclude its effectiveness. Many white workers, for instance, can establish viable working relationships with minority clients. Despite rather disparate backgrounds and experiences, social workers and clients do develop productive relationships. This is not to say there are no difficulties in intercultural relationships. It is only natural that our life experiences affect how we view the world. They clearly can affect our ability to understand and assist others whose life experiences are markedly different from our own. It should not be surprising, then, that social workers don't always know how to respond when confronted with cultural or other differences. The problem becomes increasingly complex when we focus on some of the major barriers to effective cross-cultural social work practice. In the following sections we examine selected characteristics of a sample of diverse groups with whom social workers are likely to interact, and we identify some of the potential dangers facing the unwary helper. These issues are intended only to sensitize you to your upcoming tasks and are not designed to cover all possible situations. They should be viewed accordingly.

First Nations People Clients[2]

A social worker counseling a First Nations People client might readily assume that the client's quietness indicates an uncooperative attitude or that the worker and client are on the same wavelength (Lum, 2007). Unfortunately neither assumption may be correct. In fact, First Nations People may not correct or challenge a worker who is off track because to do so violates a basic tenet of their culture: noninterference. Noninterference in practice is similar but not identical to the social work value of self-determination. It requires First Nations People to meet unwanted attempts at intervention or intrusion with withdrawal—emotional, physical, or both. In other cases, this may take the form of changing the subject or pretending not to hear the offending words. Even the most well-intentioned worker may be perceived as a coercive authority figure whose efforts are resisted passively but firmly. Consequently, First Nations People are perhaps less likely to assert themselves than might be true of members of other protected classes. Assuming that clients will give feedback if you are off target is only one of several beliefs you must "unlearn" to practice effectively in a cross-cultural environment.

Another response pattern of social workers that frequently proves counterproductive is direct eye contact. Many First Nations People consider such face-to-face eye contact rude and intimidating. Lum (2007) noted that ethnic differences in eye contact exist and that some Native Americans in particular find eye contact disrespectful. Avoiding eye contact is a way of showing deference in this culture. A white worker who plans to practice in a Native American community needs to be aware of these factors to avoid worsening the already tenuous relationship that exists between cultures. Lacking thorough knowledge of Native American culture often results in failure to recognize its complexity, and workers do this at their peril.

In the dominant white culture, a firm handshake generally means that a person may be trusted, but many First Nations People view a firm handshake as aggressive and disrespectful (Harper & Lantz, 1996). In addition, white social workers should not be surprised if Native Americans do not trust them in the initial stage of intervention, as Native Americans have a long history of being victimized by the dominant white group in our society.

Middle-class white social workers may also be surprised to discover that many First Nations People consider it a sign of disrespect to question a person in detail about his or her personal life. A social worker taking a social history on a Native American client may unknowingly be acting in a very disrespectful manner if the client does not share the worker's views of the value of full self-disclosure. Honest and direct questioning by the worker is likely to be experienced by the Native American client as interrogation (Harper-Dorton & Lantz, 2007).

African American Clients

With African American clients, the picture is somewhat similar; workers frequently misread the meaning of client behavior, with harmful consequences. For example, the adaptive behavior of many African Americans, which includes "aloofness" or reserve, can be mistaken by whites as hostile or rejecting (Brammer, 2004). Lum (2007) suggests that a certain level of distrust by the African American client can intrude on the client–white worker relationship and that African Americans in

[2] The terms *First Nations People* and *Native American* are used interchangeably in this chapter because some members of this ethnic group prefer the former term and others prefer the latter.

particular experience frequent racism from government agencies. With these factors in mind, it is easy to understand why some writers and others feel that only a worker from the client's cultural background can effectively work with minority clients. At times a non–African American worker may attempt to overcompensate for these differences by unrealistic empathy. A worker may ascribe all the emotional and social difficulties experienced by African American clients to a racist society. This, in effect, denies clients their individuality and similarities with other human beings, a result that is, of course, unintended.

Some authors have argued that traditional Eurocentric views of human behavior provide additional barriers to understanding and helping African Americans (Lum, 2007). For example, our tendency to focus on individuals rather than seeing a person as a part of a larger social group ignores the cooperative and sharing traditions that represent untapped client strengths. Our lack of attention to spirituality and the role it plays in understanding African American clients is also cited as a problem. Finally, we may fail to recognize the importance that emotions play when we tend only to the rational side of the person's life situation. An Africentric view recognizes that emotions and thoughts are not independent and that thoughts "are no more superior to emotions than emotions are to thoughts" (Schiele, 1996, p. 287). Adopting this perspective is consistent with the social work sensitivity to feelings but can challenge more rational approaches to helping. The theoretical concepts of the Africentric perspective and worldview are receiving increased attention and recognition. These concepts are described in Exhibit 12.1.

Another barrier is the tendency to rely on research findings not applicable to African Americans for our understanding of certain family dynamics. For example, substantial evidence indicates that white women who are battered are much more likely to use community resources such as shelters than are African American women (Richie, 2003). Similarly, comparisons of homeless men and women show very different patterns depending on whether clients are white or nonwhite. Socioeconomic factors and lack of institutional resources are much more likely to account for the homeless state of African Americans, whereas white homeless individuals and families are more likely to suffer from substance abuse and various psychiatric illnesses, which contribute to their present situation (North & Smith, 1994; Tessler, Rosencheck, & Gamache, 2001).

Schaefer (2008, pp. 226–246) notes that African American children in foster care experienced several major barriers. For example, although blacks comprise only about 14% of the population of children in the United States, they represent more than a third of the children in foster care, and they remain in foster care for months longer than white children. In Utah, for example, black children were in foster care at a rate of six times their proportion in the general population. In several other states, black children were four times as likely to end up in foster care. On average, across the United States, African American children are more than twice as likely as white children to end up in foster care. Factors such as poverty and lack of access to services represent one source of problems, but other sources include bias or cultural misunderstanding among social workers providing child welfare services. Here is one simple example: A white social worker spotted dark spots on the skin of a black child and jumped to the conclusion that the child was being abused. What the worker was observing was "Mongolian spots"—skin blotches often found on black children. When a worker lacks familiarity with a culture, snap judgments can have serious consequences.

Latino Clients

As noted earlier, even workers who share common characteristics with minority clients sometimes experience comparable difficulties in client interactions Bilingual white practitioners, for example, who work in a Latino community don't necessarily possess the requisite skills to understand all aspects of the language. The special language of the barrio in particular is not easily understood unless one has some shared experience

Exhibit 12.1 The Africentric Perspective and Worldview

African American culture includes elements from traditional African cultures; from slavery, Reconstruction, and subsequent exposure to racism and discrimination; and from "mainstream" white culture. The *Africentric perspective* (Belgrave & Allison, 2006) acknowledges African culture and expressions of African beliefs, values, institutions, and behaviors. It recognizes that African Americans retain, to some degree, a number of elements of African life and values.

The Africentric perspective asserts that applying Eurocentric theories of human behavior to explain the behavior and ethos of African Americans is often inappropriate. Eurocentric theories of human behavior reflect concepts developed in European and Anglo-American cultures. Eurocentric theorists historically vilified people of African descent and other people of color. Such theorists explicitly or implicitly claimed that people of African descent were pathological or inferior in their social, personality, or moral development (Belgrave & Allison, 2006). The origins of this denigration can be found in the slave trade, as slave traders and owners endeavored to justify the enslavement of Africans. Eurocentric theories portray the culture of people of African descent as "uncivilized" and as having contributed practically nothing of value to world development and human history.

The Africentric perspective seeks to dispel the negative distortions about people of African ancestry by legitimizing and disseminating a worldview that goes back thousands of years and that exists in the hearts and minds of many people of African descent today. (The concept of worldview involves perceptions of ourselves in relation to other people, objects, institutions, and nature. It focuses on our view of the world and our role and place in it.) The worldview of African Americans is shaped by unique and important experiences, such as racism and discrimination, an African heritage, traditional attributes of the African American family and community life, and a strong religious orientation.

The Africentric perspective also promotes a worldview that facilitates human and societal transformation toward moral, spiritual, and humanistic ends and that seeks to persuade people of different cultural and ethnic groups that they share a mutual interest in this regard. The Africentric perspective rejects the idea that individuals can be understood separately from others in their social group. Instead, it emphasizes a collective identity, which encourages sharing, cooperation, and social responsibility.

The Africentric perspective also emphasizes the importance of spirituality, which includes moral development and attaining meaning and identity in life. The Africentric perspective asserts that the major sources of human problems in the United States are oppression and alienation. Oppression and alienation are generated not only by prejudice and discrimination but also by the European worldview that teaches people to see themselves primarily as material, physical beings seeking immediate pleasure for their physical, material, or sexual desires. It is further asserted that the European worldview discourages spiritual and moral development.

The Africentric perspective has been used to explain the origins of specific social problems. For example, violent crimes by youths are thought to result from their limited options and choices for economic advancement. Black youths seek a life of street crime as a logical way to cope with and protest against a society that practices pervasive employment discrimination (associated with minimum wages, layoffs, lack of opportunities for education or training, and a wide gap between the rich and the poor). These youths understand that they can make more money from a life of street crime than from attending college or starting a legitimate business with little start-up capital. Choosing a life of crime is also thought more likely to occur in a society that uses the European worldview, which deemphasizes spiritual and moral development, because individuals have little or no awareness of collective social responsibility.

The Africentric perspective values a more holistic, spiritual, and optimistic view of human beings. It supports the "strengths perspective" and "empowerment" concepts of social work practice.

with the culture. Both the meaning of words and their usage differ, sometimes significantly. As a consequence, workers who speak Spanish must be acutely sensitive to the possibility that words can have other meanings.

Our ability to perceive communication accurately is enhanced by knowing the client's life experiences. All groups have problems and characteristics that arise from long-standing value systems, ethnic backgrounds, socioeconomic factors, languages, and behavior patterns. Workers who are familiar with these variables will be more effective practitioners. In the case of Latinos, bilingualism is not a sufficient condition for successful practice, but it is often necessary or helpful.

EP 2.1.1b

Lest you become discouraged about the difficulties inherent in cross-cultural social work, even counselors of the same ethnic or cultural background are not guaranteed freedom from problems. Issues such as different life experiences, language fluency, and gender influence the worker-client relationship even when client and worker share ethnicity.

Exercise 12.1: Some of My Stereotypes

Goal: This exercise is designed to identify some of your stereotypes that you need to be aware of so you can develop an objective approach to social work practice with diverse groups.

Step 1: Assume that you are single. Place an *X* by the name of each group into which you would hesitate to marry.

___ Russian

___ Cuban

___ French

___ Mexican

___ African American

___ White American

___ Native American

___ Puerto Rican

___ Italian

___ German

___ Polish

___ Norwegian

___ Samoan

___ Arab

___ Israeli

___ Chinese

___ Japanese

___ Filipino

___ Eskimo

___ Brazilian

___ Hungarian

___ Vietnamese

___ Pakistani

___ Korean

Step 2: Being as specific as possible, state the reasons for the groups you checked (next to each group that you checked).

Step 3: Do you hold stereotypes about the groups you checked?

Gay, Lesbian, Bisexual, and Transgendered Clients

In May 2010, President Barack Obama issued a proclamation declaring June 2010 as Lesbian, Gay, Bisexual, and Transgender (GLBT) Pride Month. The proclamation also identified a number of national initiatives designed to demonstrate a commitment to a community often subject to inequity, social and economic injustice, and discrimination. With some exceptions, members of the GLBT community are denied the same rights and responsibilities accorded to other married couples, experience barriers to adoption, and face an unsupportive environment when dealing with health facilities, employment, and governmental agencies. The community is at risk for several health threats, many deriving from the stigma they experience. Combating these experiences and the policies, rules, and laws that allow them is part of the obligation of social workers to secure social and economic justice and well-being throughout our society.

The terms used to describe this community have varied over time. The current use of *gay, lesbian, bisexual, and transgendered* is perhaps the most common description, although it does not necessarily capture all members of the community. For example, intersex individuals with some combination of male and female physical features are not often mentioned. The term *sexual minority* has been used at times to describe all community members, although it also evokes a sense of powerlessness that some members find offensive. Others have added a Q to the GLBT acronym, referring to those individuals who are questioning their sexual orientation. We will use the acronym GLBT here to refer to all members of this community, recognizing that no term is likely to capture the richness and individualism of all group members.

One of the more frustrating challenges for social scientists studying the unique needs and characteristics of the GLBT community is determining the percentage of the adult population who would be so classified. Many studies have been designed to gather this information, but most have multiple flaws (Pruitt, 2002). Range estimates from 3% to 13% are commonly cited, but these numbers usually refer only to those who self-identify as gay or lesbian. A report by the Urban Institute based on the 2000 U.S. Census used the figure of 5% of the U.S. population over age 18 (Gates, 2001).

Because many gay men and lesbian women choose not to publicly identify themselves as homosexual, it is difficult to get meaningful data. Predictably, antigay organizations provide estimates that are extremely low (1% to 3%) and gay-rights organizations are prone to use larger numbers (3% to 10%). Despite the lack of valid percentages, other reports indicate that the lives of many individuals and families are touched by homosexuality. Moreover, many social work practitioners work with clients who are struggling with their sexual identity or with gay/lesbian clients who are grappling with health, mental health, or social challenges unrelated to their sexual orientation. This suggests the importance of social workers understanding more about their clients' sexual orientations.

Unfortunately, homosexuality traditionally has been viewed variously as deviant, criminal, an illness, an emotional disturbance, and, among some groups, a sin. The result has been an irrational fear of homosexuality—homophobia—that is as serious a problem as other forms of prejudice, such as sexism and racism.

Helping professionals are as likely to be affected by these prejudices as the general public. Lack of knowledge, acceptance of stereotypes, and fear of the unknown are not limited to the layperson. Many social workers may have been exposed to minority group members, but the stigma associated with GLBT sexuality has kept a large number of members from sharing information with others. As a result, social workers who come in contact with GLBT clients are often no better prepared to help these groups than is the general public. The tendency to stereotype GLBT clients flies in the face of what is known about the differences and similarities among human beings. Kertzner (2007) argues that the personalities and developmental experiences of gay men and lesbian women reflect a similar level of diversity as those found in heterosexual individuals.

Sexual orientation often intersects with race and gender to compound the issues and challenges facing gay, lesbian, and transgendered people. Thus, to be an African American female who is also a lesbian can result in multiple forms of discrimination. In addition, cultural views on homosexuality can have a great bearing on the individual's level of adaptation to his or her sexual orientation. A culture that is more accepting of GLBT people may provide some degree of amelioration from the otherwise oppressive larger society.

Social workers who work with GLBT clients can start with the information on diversity yet still recognize common difficulties experienced by GLBT individuals in our society. The barriers and discrimination encountered by these clients should be acknowledged for their impact on the client's life as well as for their effect on the relationship between worker and client.

As a beginning, it is helpful to recognize that debate over causation of homosexuality is irrelevant in efforts to help. A focus on etiology does not assist the client with present functioning and tends to obscure the multiple problems resulting from societal reaction to GLBT members. Attempts to focus on cause have not been beneficial in coping with stereotypes and in fact have led to GLBTs being mistreated to correct for some presumed deficit in early life experiences. Furthermore, few gays and lesbians can be identified either by appearance or mannerisms. This, coupled with the risks in coming out (publicly identifying oneself as gay and lesbian), has resulted in a lack of attention to the needs of GLBT clients. At the same time, recent research shows that gay youth are at much greater risk for suicide, resulting, in part, from the pain of being isolated and discriminated against (Clements-Nolle, Marx, & Katz, 2006). Youth without adequate support systems are more likely to consider suicide as a coping mechanism. Later in this chapter we suggest several means by which social workers can assist GLBT clients by recognizing and dealing with the specialized needs of this group.

EP 2.1.1b

Exercise 12.2: Questionnaire about GLBTs

Goal: This exercise is designed to assess your views about GLTBs.

Step 1: Indicate whether you think the following statements are true or false.

1. Gay men are effeminate; they have a "swishy" walk, talk with a lisp, and are limp wristed.
   a. true b. false
2. Most lesbians are masculine; they have short hair, dress mainly in men's clothes, and appear manly.
   a. true b. false
3. Gay men desire to be women.
   a. true b. false
4. Lesbians desire to be men.
   a. true b. false
5. In a gay or lesbian couple, one partner will assume the dominant (sometimes called masculine) role, and the other will assume the submissive (sometimes called feminine) role.
   a. true b. false
6. Most gay men are child molesters.
   a. true b. false
7. People are either homosexual or heterosexual.
   a. true b. false

8. Most gays and lesbians are mentally ill.
   a. true b. false
9. Gays and lesbians are to blame for the AIDS epidemic.
   a. true b. false
10. People choose to be gay or lesbian.
    a. true b. false
11. Everyone who is bisexual is also transgendered.
    a. true b. false
12. Everyone who is transgendered has had, or is currently having, transsexual surgery.
    a. true b. false

Step 2: The instructor may want to tabulate students' responses. The instructor may then choose to present factual information on each of these questions.

Feminist Social Work

Increasing sensitivity to the impact of gender on the development, definition, and amelioration of social and personal problems has helped identify another barrier to effective social work practice: sexism. There is greater recognition today that many of the difficulties experienced by both men and women in society are related to gender inequality, specifically in the areas of privileges, power, and access to resources. The enormous role played by gender limits the effectiveness of social work practice and suggests ways in which the worker's own sex can be a contributing problem. Van Den Bergh and Cooper (1987, p. 610) identified situations in which a male worker may be less appropriate than a female practitioner:

1. All-female groups, which may reinforce stereotypic dependencies or set up competition for male attention
2. Women who are hostile to men unless they work as a co-therapist in the therapeutic process
3. Women who relate to male therapists primarily in a seductive manner
4. Extremely dependent, inhibited women who equate femaleness with passivity and docility
5. Women who are in the midst of a divorce crisis and, as a result of intense transference feelings, may see the male therapist as a surrogate spouse

Although these limitations do not mean that gender must always be a limiting factor in social work practice, both male and female social workers must be aware of ways that gender shapes a client's problems and how help can and should be provided. The significant consideration is the extent to which gender-related oppression encompasses all aspects of society—economic, social, religious, and political—and the fact that gender itself plays no less a role in social work practice than race, sexual orientation, and location. The difficulty in overcoming the bondage of sexism provides a challenge as great as dealing with factors that perpetuate racism and homophobia. Some methods of providing effective intervention within the context of nonsexist practice will be described later. (See Exhibit 12.3 on page 400 for a discussion of the feminist perspective on therapy.)

Persons with Disabilities

Another group of individuals served by social workers is those with disabilities. This group includes people with physical disabilities, developmental disabilities, and intellectual and emotional challenges. The year 2010 was the 20th anniversary of the Americans with Disabilities Act, a major attempt by the federal government to assure to resources and reduction in barriers for people with disabilities. Although the provisions of the ADA have helped reduce infrastructure, transportation, and communication barriers, those with a disability are still 50% more likely to be unemployed than those without a disability, as well as 60% more likely to be employed only part-time (Bureau of Labor Statistics, 2010).

Those with a disability encompass a very diverse group of people as evidenced by reports from the U.S. Census Bureau (2005, p. 19). The chart below identifies the disability statistics for people 15 years of age or older in the United States as of 2005.

DISABILITY DOMAIN	*PERCENTAGE*
With a disability	21.3%
Seeing/Hearing/Speaking	6.4%
Walking/Using Stairs	11.9%
Mental	7%
Two or more domains	8.5%

The kinds of assistance needed by people with disabilities reflect the diversity of this group. They range from help taking prescriptions to assistance with standing. The chart below suggests a few of the activities-of-daily-life challenges faced by this group (U.S. Census Bureau, 2005, pp. 17–18).

ACTIVITIES-OF-DAILY-LIFE CHALLENGES FACED BY SOME PEOPLE WITH DISABILITIES

Difficulty getting around

Difficulty getting into bed

Difficulty taking a bath

Difficulty dressing

Difficulty eating or preparing meals

Difficulty toileting

Difficulty managing money

Difficulty doing housework

Difficulty taking prescriptions

Difficulty using the phone

Identifying the numbers of people with disabilities and the kinds of impairments they experience is not meant to suggest that all people with disabilities require help. Many with disabilities pursue their daily activities and employment without any assistance, raise families, and participate in society at the same level as other citizens. As with the general population, many make significant contributions to our culture, political realm, and everyday existence. A list of those who have achieved greatly while experiencing disabilities reads like a who's who of American society, such as singers Hank Williams, Sr. and Lucinda Williams (spina bifida); sports figures Tiger Woods, Bill Walton, and Adrian Peterson (stuttering); actors James Earl Jones and Bruce Willis (stuttering); writers Edgar Allan Poe, Truman Capote, and Dame Agatha Christie (epilepsy); politicians President Franklin Delano Roosevelt, Senators Max Cleland, Robert Dole, John McCain, and Daniel Inouye, and others (physical disability); and Tommy Hilfiger, Terry Bradshaw, Sir Richard Branson, Charles Schwab, Orlando Bloom, Patrick Dempsey, and Whoopi Goldberg (learning disability and/or ADHD) (Family Village, 2010). The list could go on for pages, but it is clear that people can and do overcome their disability or find ways to manage it, with or without help. Finding ways to assist those with disabilities to help them achieve their goals is just another task of a social worker and will be discussed later in this chapter.

Other Examples

Many elements can separate worker and client and undermine the empathic quality of the relationship. Cultural, racial, and sexual differences that create this gulf have been discussed, but Lum (2007) and Brammer (2004) described additional worker-client characteristics that can also affect outcomes. The age difference between a younger worker and an older client, for instance, can be a barrier because of differences in values, perceptions, or physiological factors. At the same time, workers attempting to establish relationships with children will find that as adults they are potentially contaminated by their association with parents, a state of affairs that may have to be overcome if the child is to trust the counselor. Even a worker's preference for a particular type of intervention or treatment may be inappropriate when the client's environment provides no support. Similarly, some problems are chronic because of social and economic injustices that are not alleviated by counseling, no matter how competent the social worker.

Clearly, a social worker's role is complex. Critical and fundamental issues affecting the worker's practice, however, are generally categorized into four areas: (1) ignorance of the culture or characteristics of clients, (2) stereotypic perceptions of the target group, (3) lack of self-knowledge, and (4) reliance on standard counseling techniques and approaches without regard to their implications for the target group. Each of these areas can be overcome, providing you are willing and able to make the necessary adaptations. The task is not easy because, as Gross (1996) and others have noted, much of the research available to interested social workers paints an inaccurate picture of minority groups, misjudging such salient areas as family structure and lifestyle characteristics.

Part of the problem experienced in gathering factual data, of course, is that much of the research is based on the perceptions of middle-class white investigators. Despite this obstacle, workers who have a significant intercultural practice must seek appropriate information on their client groups. However, knowledge is only the beginning. Cross-cultural social work demands a high degree of self-knowledge and self-awareness by workers. Unlike sociological, psychological, and anthropological data, which are obtained with reasonable ease, self-knowledge is perhaps the most difficult to obtain because it can be anxiety producing. Few of us want to acknowledge our own prejudices in part because to do so reflects badly on our self-perception. Understandably, we prefer to view ourselves as enlightened and nondiscriminatory. However, the route to effective cross-cultural social work practice requires examining our beliefs, attitudes, and values and perhaps changing them. Complete elimination of every vestige of prejudice is difficult, but the effort is valid. Even though we must expect to practice in a prejudiced world, our own interventions must be culturally appropriate and sensitive.

KNOWLEDGE YOU WILL NEED FOR CROSS-CULTURAL WORK

Knowledge of Self

There is no substitute for self-awareness. The ability to be responsive to your own senses, feelings, behavior, and thoughts is a prime requisite for effective practice in the helping professions. This includes a thorough recognition, knowledge, and acceptance of your value system. Workers need to understand how their own professional actions contribute to social and economic injustice in the world and especially for those who are at risk because of their culture.

In some cases, our feelings about racism and the plight of minorities or other groups suffering from discrimination can effectively block our functioning by generating guilt, depression, or a sense of being overwhelmed. This process can be averted by recognizing the likelihood that we have grown up prejudiced. Laird (1998) and Dean (2001) point out that a postmodern perspective acknowledges the cultural baggage that we all bring to our work with clients. That baggage includes our own beliefs, biases, stereotypes, family experiences, theories, and knowledge about human behavior. This baggage can predispose us to arrive at certain conclusions, color our interpretations of the behavior of others, and interfere with critical thinking. As a result, we have an obligation to listen very carefully to our clients, resist jumping to conclusions about them, and willingly accept feedback that challenges our assumptions and preconceived

CASE EXAMPLE Unwritten Community Value Prevails

Marty Jacobsen has been an active member of her small community in a rural midwestern state. She has served on several community committees, attended the customary volunteer firefighters fund-raising chicken dinners, and was chair of her church's auxiliary. She is also a faculty member at Ravenswood University, a small institution that over time has become one of the largest employers in the area. When Marty decided to run for a seat on the Ravenwood City Council, she expected to receive strong support from her friends and acquaintances in the community. The current City Council has seven members, three of whom are university employees. She has heard about an unwritten community value that university employees will never constitute a majority on the City Council. Regardless, she waged a vigorous campaign, posted signs in the yards of scores of her "friends," and explained carefully her well-thought-out positions on important community issues. On election day Marty was soundly beaten by her opponent, a retired Army sergeant with no connection to the university who had campaigned very little. Once again, the norms of the community prevailed and power on the City Council remained in the hands of the nonuniversity population.

notions. The ability to correct our own tendencies toward racist thinking obviously requires sensitivity and effort. We must be willing to make fundamental changes in our thinking patterns, attitudes, and behavior. Still, such growth in self-knowledge (of and by itself) is insufficient without a concomitant growth in awareness of the uniqueness of the client group.

Knowledge of Differences

It has long been asserted that similar needs exist in all cultures, but how those needs are molded and shaped is culturally relative. Thus, although a basic acceptance of the worth and dignity of each human being is important, workers who practice with diverse groups must enhance this acceptance with hard facts. We believe ourselves to be grounded in reality, but our reality is nevertheless only a function of our perception of the real world. An individual who comes to a counseling situation from a different cultural background, especially one who has experienced racist or sexist behavior, will have a different reality. Therefore, we must be aware of the ways in which cultural and other background factors affect perceptions and feelings and the expression of these qualities.

The issues, concerns, problems, and situations of women are inextricably related to other factors in society. These include race and culture, social class and economics, power and resources, and political and legal factors. Women tend to be most affected by poverty and are the target of oppression, especially in those countries where they are treated as second-class citizens by the male-dominated political and social structures. In war-torn countries they are brutalized by rape, and in others they experience genital mutilation sanctioned by their own cultures. In almost all cultures they are expected to, and do, provide the vast majority of domestic duties (such as child care and housekeeping), even among supposedly more egalitarian societies such as the United States. Institutionized prejudice against women presents workers with additional problems. Thus, workers must be aware of the unique vulnerabilities of women, the absence of certain coping resources, and the stereotyping tendencies of much of society.

Also beneficial is some knowledge of the history and language of the client group. Becoming familiar with common phrases and vocabulary will be helpful even if you are not bilingual. You should endeavor to build a solid knowledge base in minority lifestyles so your clients' strengths and ability to adapt are not ignored or branded as abnormal behavior. For example, minority clients who appear hostile or suspicious of a white worker may be expressing a quite reasonable reaction based on past experiences with well-meaning professionals or other representatives of "helping" agencies. The growing incidence of ethnoviolence (conflict and violence motivated by prejudice) experienced in the United States during the past 20 years is testimony to the continued difficulties of members of minority groups (Brammer, 2004).

With a solid understanding of how social, economic, and other forces influence the individual, it becomes easier to recognize that what is thought to be "normal" is, in fact, an illusion. (As an illustration, see Case Example "Unwritten Community Value Prevails.") Normality is a function of what a particular culture defines as appropriate and reflects values rather than verifiable truth. Behavior considered strange in one culture may be highly valued in another. It becomes very difficult to understand other people's situation without looking at it in the context of their culture's expectation. Living with racism, prejudice, discrimination, and violence has important consequences for clients' feelings, thoughts, and behaviors. Workers cannot ignore this reality.

Simple behaviors that we take for granted often carry radically different meanings for people from different cultures. Even something as "simple" as personal space varies dramatically across cultures. If your class is diverse, take a class survey of culturally acceptable ways to point fingers, for example. Thus, workers must consider family and cultural norms as well as community organizations and structures.

The knowledge of how a given group responds to authority, to stress, and to dependency is invaluable because a worker without a sound grasp of the culture can easily mistake a reaction as inappropriate. This grounding can come from living in a minority area and taking part in community activities such as council meetings, powwows, and neighborhood get-togethers. Certainly, these activities should be pursued by all social workers serving a given population. A background of direct experience with minorities is ideal, but most social workers who begin practice lack this base. As a result, it behooves you to take advantage of the excellent bibliographic material available on cultural diversity, some of which can be found in the reference list at the end of this text. Workers, for example, who intend to work with First Nations People clients should carefully study the unique cultural heritage of this group. There are many Native American cultures, and each tribe has its own history, traditions, customs, and environment. This makes it difficult to generalize from tribal group to tribal group. However, there are some important similarities. For example, the fact that some First Nations People fathers play a strong disciplinarian role in their families may suggest to the unknowing worker that child abuse is occurring, when in fact the Native American family is perhaps less dependent on corporal punishment than the average non–Native American family. The failure to recognize cultural factors such as this inevitably results in misunderstanding and frustrations for the erring worker. Awareness of the principal values of First Nations People and an understanding of the cultural context in which they exist will lessen this possibility.

The First Nations People tradition of sharing is another area that confuses white workers unaccustomed to this kind of hospitality. Even if resources are meager, the Native American is willing to allow other family and friends to partake of what there is. Although this behavior may appear to be nonfunctional to many whites, the value is intrinsic to the Native American heritage. To do otherwise would be to ignore part of a value system that has helped the culture survive more than 400 years of racism.

Even the First Nations People's use of time can be a subject of confusion to the non–Native American. Green (1999, pp. 32–33) noted that some Native Americans observe "social time," which is "person-centered" and focuses on family and personal needs. "White time," or clock time, which exists primarily for business, is less important specifically because it is not oriented to human beings. Arriving on time for an appointment with the social worker may be much less important than stopping to help a friend or talking with a family member. This does not mean that all First Nations People ignore "white time" but that the use of time should be taken into account when working with this group.

Although some might suggest otherwise, Native Americans are not unaware of time; however, they do not subject themselves to its tyranny as many whites have done. Punctuality is not a pressing concern, a fact that confounds many time-conscious helping professionals. The time-bound worker may also misperceive the related Native American value of patience as evidence of laziness or lack of motivation. Respect for and appreciation of First Nations People culture is essential if the worker is to establish an effective relationship.

Similarly, the Latino experience will be sufficiently new to most workers that a dedicated effort must be made to replace ignorance with knowledge. As in the case of Native Americans, the family unit of Latinos is more likely to be characterized as extended. This expanded family network is another indication of the adaptability of Latinos. Workers therefore need to be alert for the boundaries of the family system so they do not exclude or overlook pertinent members. The fact that the elderly have an important role to play and must be included in planning places a special burden on workers. The significance of religion in Latino life is more commonly known to most non-Latinos, as is the importance of the male role. Although some evidence suggests that cross-cultural differences in these areas may be exaggerated in the literature, workers need to be aware of the significance of these factors in Latino life.

The diversity of cultural backgrounds in Native American culture is duplicated in Latino culture. The tendency to see any culture as one-dimensional fails to recognize the diversity within cultures. For instance, the term *Latino* encompasses Mexican Americans, Puerto Ricans, Colombians, Brazilians, and others whose ancestry can be traced to Spanish or Portuguese beginnings. It is probably more helpful for social workers to learn how clients describe themselves (such as Puerto Rican or Cuban American) rather than using less specific terms such as *Latino* or *Hispanic*.

Like Latinos, Asian Americans are such an extraordinarily diverse group that it is difficult to characterize them by identifying commonalities. Comparisons among Hmong, Laotian, and Japanese clients are especially difficult. The recent immigrant experiences of the Hmong and other Southeast Asian groups, coupled with cultural differences between these groups and others who have been here for several generations, make it unlikely that one set of guidelines would ever be helpful. In addition, the tendency to lump these groups together has been criticized, because it does not specifically address the unique needs of individual Asian cultures (Fong, 2003). Special programs involving interpreters, language classes, and other efforts aimed at helping new immigrants learn about American culture are needed for recent immigrant groups. Such programs are one way to promote social and economic justice for populations at risk.

The Hmong and Cambodians in the United States often speak little English, hold very low-paying jobs, and struggle with overt discrimination more often than do third- or fourth-generation Asian Americans. In one sense, the experiences of first-generation Hmong and Cambodians resemble those of immigrants in the nineteenth and early twentieth centuries. To be of help, one community used innovative school programs to ensure that Hmong students and their parents felt a part of the educational system. These included using bilingual aides to talk to parents about school programs, explain homework assignments, confirm parent-teacher conference times, and invite parents to participate in school programs (Alexander, 1993). The result of such programs has been almost 100% participation by parents in conferences and by children in after-school programs. Such programs exemplify the innovative efforts needed to reach at-risk populations.

It also may prove helpful to become familiar with the health-care practices of immigrants and refugees from other countries. For example, "cupping" is used by Vietnamese and Cambodian immigrants to help cure illnesses. Placing a heated cup on a person's skin to help draw out illness is a traditional Asian method to treat a sickness. Though painless, to the uninformed, the marks produced by this treatment may appear to be the result of abuse, potentially leading to unnecessary social work intervention. Awareness of alternative health-care practices among other cultures will assist social workers to avoid misunderstandings.

Although the client group and community may not be ethnically or racially different from that of workers, those who serve in rural environments must also possess a certain knowledge base to be effective. They must be aware of the network of nontraditional services often available in these areas. Service clubs and church groups, for instance, assume greater importance than in larger, more metropolitan communities. Likewise, the existence of natural support systems can be a real asset, but workers must know about them before they can use them effectively. (Natural support systems include family and friendship groups, local informal caregivers, volunteer service groups, and mutual or self-help groups.) Knowledge of the local power structure is perhaps more crucial than for urban workers because the effectiveness of rural workers may be seriously impaired without the necessary sanction and cooperation. As in the case of other diverse groups, ignorance of values, beliefs, and attitudes of the rural client system is inexcusable and counterproductive. If this need to be alert to, and operate within, local norms is seen as onerous by workers, then they should consider moving elsewhere.

As discussed earlier, age differences between worker and client can also affect practice. Maguire (2002) suggested, for example, that workers must be aware of the effect that the physical condition of the elderly can have on the interview. Among other factors, lack of energy and hearing difficulties can impair the aged client's ability to participate in the relationship. Thus, competent workers must have a firm foundation in human behavior and development as well as sensitivity to the nuances of communication in helping relationships.

It is also important to increase one's knowledge about people with disabilities. This includes not only the kinds of disabilities encountered in one's agency among clients, but also the resources available to assist clients to become successful despite the disability. You will need to know which agencies provide specific kinds of support for people with disabilities—transportation, companion services, occupational training, advocacy, and many others. You will also have to acquire knowledge of how best to work with people when they need help with their disability. This includes the dos and don'ts of working with people with physically disabilities, those with hearing and vision deficits, and those with less obvious challenges.

It is common for social workers to identify and build on clients' strengths. Assessment of these strengths, however, requires recognizing their clients' vast and diverse experiences. Too often, a strength that is overlooked is the spiritual element. Spiritualism takes many forms, especially among the diverse groups in our society. Social workers might consider whether clients regularly attend church or belong to religious organizations. Such activities often serve as a source of support in tough times and can also be both an emotional and an economic resource. Religious values may dictate appropriate behavior toward other family members and nonfamily individuals, as well as how clients express pain and suffering. In addition, in Caribbean, Hispanic, and some Asian cultures (Lum, 2007; Brammer, 2004), spiritualism is used to explain a variety of physical and emotional problems. The importance of spirituality is relevant to understanding human behavior, affects social work practice, and has an impact on social policy and research.

APPLYING YOUR KNOWLEDGE: TECHNIQUES OF INTERVENTION

Once a sufficient knowledge base is acquired, you must incorporate this into practice to increase the effectiveness of your intervention activities. In this section, we review specific intervention approaches and techniques designed to enhance your capabilities. The material presented is not intended to be exhaustive, and obviously there is no substitute for direct experience. Workers whose practice encompasses any of these areas must do more extensive reading than is presented here (and, it is hoped, receive formal training).

Basic to any relationship, according to Ivey and Ivey (1999), is empathy, clearly communicated to clients, plus warmth and genuineness. Workers in a bicultural relationship must pay special heed to this advice because authenticity is even more crucial when differences are great between client and helper. Moreover, workers must use their own patterns of communication and avoid the temptation to adopt the client's vocabulary and speech. A worker who does not follow this stricture may find clients either withdrawing from the relationship or attacking the helper for lack of sincerity. In many cross-cultural relationships, the client has a greater need to know the worker as a person. A helper who is uncomfortable stepping outside the professional role will have difficulty working with many minority clients or practicing in a rural environment, as greater informality is expected in both settings.

There are clear limits to the time and place for informality in intercultural counseling. Generally, the kind of informality that marks the effective relationship does not occur immediately. For example, in the initial interview, Kirst-Ashman and Hull (2009a) recommend using all the formalities associated with culturally prescribed displays of respect. This should include use of the client's proper full name, title (Mr., Miss, Mrs., Ms., Dr.), greeting with a handshake, and the other courtesies usually extended. Workers must also be up-front with clients about the reasons for their presence. For example, if the contact was worker initiated, the worker should give identification, state the reasons for the meeting, and avoid placing the client in the position of having to guess the purpose.

It is important to remember that a power differential exists in every helping relationship. The worker, by virtue of his or her expertise and position, is accorded a certain degree of power by the client. The client, who by definition is seeking or needing help, has a lesser degree of power. This power differential can become especially problematic with clients who have a history of being oppressed by those in positions of power. Workers in empathic relationships must be alert to power differentials engendered by race and other differences and strive to reduce or eliminate them. Proper protocol aids in this effort.

Awareness of these differences and a degree of sensitivity to the subtle impact of racial prejudice should help workers avoid the related trap of color blindness that often confuses the novice. To avoid appearing prejudiced, the new worker may decide to adopt the strategy of color blindness and ignore the client's race or ethnic background. There are several major problems with color blindness. First, it denies the existence of individual differences influenced by one's experiences, culture, and other life factors. Second, it reduces a client to being an amorphous creature indistinguishable from other human beings. Third, it perpetuates racist thinking and actions based on the premise that everybody is exactly like everyone else, a notion not even accepted as true of identical twins. Those who believe everyone else should be "like me" are predisposed to look down upon those who differ.

It is understandable if on occasion the worker's feelings about racism get in the way of the relationship; guilt, depression, or a sense of being overwhelmed are not uncommon reactions. But helpers must reject sympathy when empathy is required. Conversely, even though some impact of racism will almost always exist, its impact on the presenting problem may be greater or less. It may be a contributing factor in the client's problem, the cause of the problem, or entirely unrelated to the issues at hand. Workers should not automatically attribute all difficulties to racism.

Like the culturally sensitive worker, an agency can be equally dedicated to providing services to different client groups. The agency's responsiveness can be demonstrated through relatively simple measures such as establishing hours that coincide with the needs of the groups to be served. This may include evening hours to avoid the need for some clients, already economically marginal, to lose time from jobs, and it could extend to weekend hours and walk-in arrangements. The fact that the poor are frequently afflicted by crises requires more flexible means of dealing with immediate client needs and greater accessibility to services for the here-and-now, present-oriented client. Logically, the immediacy of the situation coupled with the economic and political existence of many minority clients suggest that first-level needs must be attended to on a priority basis. This orientation is basic to the social work principle of starting where the client is. It is most unlikely that the client whose housing needs are urgent and tenuous will tolerate a worker who insists on focusing on the dynamics of the marital interactions. Clients from all cultures will reject an incompetent and insensitive social worker.

Within the relationship, workers will have to judge the need to be more or less active. As you will see later, a high level of intervention by the worker dealing with a Native American family may well prove less productive than with a client from another cultural or racial group. Lum (2007) recommended that the focus in the relationship be on specific problems and behaviors.

African American Client and White Worker

African Americans can easily be defined as a historically oppressed group. The patterns of discrimination they have encountered since colonial times and their history, intertwined with the institution of slavery, have combined to create a population at risk. For more than three centuries, racism and mistreatment have enveloped the experiences of individuals and families. This places African Americans in a disadvantaged position relative to community institutions, including social welfare agencies. Fortunately, most of the guides to practice discussed earlier are directly applicable to the relationship between the non–African American worker and the African American client. In addition, however, Lee (1999) stressed the need to avoid placing African American clients in a position of dependency. The power discrepancy often results when this is neglected. Both workers and agencies serving African American clients, according to Franklin (1999), must recognize the value of supporting African American manhood as well as efforts aimed at maintaining the male's role in the family. This may require that the agency arrange to have male social workers available in situations where a sex differential would be counterproductive to the goal of supporting African American males as males. Same-sex workers are by no means required in all cases, but agencies should be sensitive to the possibility that individual cases may necessitate using a same-gender worker.

In the area of group services to minority clients, Toseland and Rivas (2007) point out the importance of paying attention to group membership when deciding who will be in a group. For example, it would probably be unwise to have the African American members vastly outnumbered by other ethnic groups. Such situations can repeat the sense of minority status experienced in other aspects of the client's life. In addition, Corey (2004) suggests that it may be more helpful to have African American men and African American women in different groups because the presence of women may inhibit the men's willingness to talk about issues such as racism and other experiences. As always, if workers are alert and responsive to clients' feelings and reactions, needed adjustments in the intervention approach can be made and the use of standard formulas for success can be tempered by judgment.

Because the client's exposure to and experience with professional therapeutic relationships may be limited, workers may need to educate their clients about the processes of counseling. The use of unambiguous jargon is the best way to convey this information and should be the rule for most worker-client interaction. Also suggested is the promotion of concrete activities by worker and client, including greater use of role-playing, gaming, and simulations to supplant or supplement, as appropriate, more verbal techniques. Clients from lower socioeconomic backgrounds may better understand and appreciate direct action.

EP 2.1.1b

Exercise 12.3: Victimized in Syria

Goal: This exercise is designed to assist you in understanding the worries and fears of certain ethnic and racial groups when they seek help from a social service agency in this country.

Step 1: Imagine that you and a friend are traveling in Syria. In a medium-size city in central Syria, your knapsacks are stolen, and they contain your passports, other forms of identification, travelers checks, and money. What are your fears and trepidations?

Step 2: If you decide to go to a social service agency for help, would you be wary of how you will be treated? Would you be worried the agency may not believe your story and perhaps will turn you over to the police—who may throw you in jail?

Step 3: Because you do not speak the national language, would you be worried about how you will communicate your predicament?

Some general guidelines for practice with African Americans include the following:

1. Assume nothing about your client. For example:
   a. Don't assume he or she wants to talk to someone of the same race.
   b. Don't assume you completely understand the experiences of African American clients.
   c. Don't assume that the client's beliefs, actions, behaviors, or speech will match those of other African Americans you have known.
2. Don't comment on the client's clothes, hair, or other personal characteristics.
3. When assessing client strengths, consider such often-overlooked resources as spiritual or religious values. For example, the church has played a major role in the African American community over the centuries and is a significant source of support for many individuals and families.
4. When assessing potential family strengths and resources, consider the possibility of "kinship care" when out-of-home placement of children is required (Hull & Mather, 2006). Kinship care uses relatives as primary caretakers of children when they cannot remain in their own homes.
5. Recognize that past experiences with white authority figures can lead African Americans to distrust white workers. Consider explaining the reasons behind your request for information to help reduce what Grier and Cobbs (1968) called "healthy paranoia."
6. Be particularly conscious of your nonverbal messages to ensure they are congruent with your verbal communications. Incongruence in this area may be seen as a sign of insincerity.
7. Orient clients to the helping process to facilitate trust between worker and clients.

These practice suggestions increase the likelihood that an intervention will not be marred by inappropriate or stereotyped behaviors on your part.

Latino Client and Non-Latino Worker

With Latino clients, as with other groups, the verbal tradition of social work may need to be supplemented by other means of communication. Workers must bear direct responsibility for communicating when language difficulties compound the situation and the need for an interpreter is apparent. Lest the worker err by commission, however, certain rules apply to the use of such individuals. First, bilingual children should not be used as family interpreters. Respect for the individual and for the family relationships dictates that children maintain their culturally established place. Serving as conduits for sensitive family information is not an acceptable role for children to play and places an unfair and unpleasant burden on them. In addition, children lack an adult's knowledge base, a fact that further reduces their value as interpreters. This prohibition on the use of children applies equally to other ethnic groups, including Asian Americans. Described in the following paragraphs is a situation in which a probation officer ignored some of the basic caveats of relationship building with unfortunate consequences for the client:

> The purposes in mind for this first interview were accomplished, to meet Mr. and Mrs. X personally and to establish a comfortable relationship that would lead to a partnership once they were able to share their problems with the social worker. The next step is to share a common purpose, in this case, helping Freddy.
>
> Mr. X was included in the helping process from the beginning. Had he been left out, it would have meant that Mrs. X was assuming an improper role, that Mr. X was being put down by her, and that his role as head of the household plus his macho role were being jeopardized.
>
> The following day Mr. and Mrs. X came a little late to the meeting and were reluctant to talk about their conference with the probation officer. Mr. X remained silent, looking down. Mrs. X, red-eyed, finally said, "I am very ashamed. You should have heard what the probation officer said about us. He blamed us for all the troubles with Freddy and said that if we were not able to speak English we should go back to Mexico. Perhaps worst of all, our daughter heard all of this because she had to translate for us."
>
> I suggested that they arrange to meet with the probation officer the next time at the center; there the social worker could translate for them and make the necessary interpretations. Thus the harmful effect of the probation officer's prejudices against them would be minimized. Mr. and Mrs. X were assured that they had certain legal and moral rights that had to be respected—among them the right to be treated as human beings. Major differences between the systems of law in the United States and Mexico were explained, as were the functions of the probation department and the role of its officers.
>
> Mr. and Mrs. X then seemed somewhat relieved and looked less tense and fearful. Mrs. X thanked the social worker and, looking at her husband, said: "We are not ignorant and dumb. We just did not understand anything about what was happening." (Aguilar, 1972, p. 189)

A second guide to the use of interpreters is equally important. Workers must at all times relate and talk to their clients, not to the interpreter. Addressing the translator diverts attention from clients and places them in the position of a bystander to, rather than a central figure in, the relationship. The opportunity to enhance client dignity and individual autonomy should be vigorously pursued, as the same goal of helping clients to help themselves is applicable both between and within cultures.

Workers beginning a relationship with Latino clients should be prepared for a longer assessment period and should be more leisurely, warm, personal and informal, and more low-key than otherwise might be the case (Zuniga, 2003). Directness is considered rude and should be minimized in these situations. Galan (2001) suggested that a cognitive approach would be an appropriate methodology to employ in working with Mexican Americans, Zuniga (2003) noted that obstacles faced by Mexican American families include prejudice, ignorance, fear of formal social and legal systems, and a reluctance to deal with these system. This would suggest some areas to which workers could direct their attention during the early stages of the relationship. Mexican Americans often make decisions more quickly than is typical of Anglo clients. Once alternatives have been explored, the worker should be prepared for a decisive response from the client.

Successful intervention with Latino families, however, requires greater knowledge of their culture. For example, close family ties exist in Puerto Rican culture, and these ties are a source of pride. Anglo culture, in contrast, values independence from the family. Ghali (1992) also pointed out that practices frowned on in American society are more readily accepted among many Puerto Ricans. Examples include common-law marriages among those with low incomes; the bearing of a child by a teenager, which often accords the mother the status of adulthood; and the relatively supreme position of the father in the family.

One of the special dilemmas of Puerto Ricans is that they have two countries, two languages, and two cultures. The role confusion this can entail, the resultant family problems, and the value conflicts inherent in this duality must be recognized. Workers should keep these in mind during interviews. Other suggestions include the following:

- Determine how important the client's ethnic values are and whether the values are a source of conflict. (This could be ascertained by asking which, if any, of the old traditions, such as holidays, are still observed.)
- Focus on the short-term benefits and on strengthening the worker-client relationship.
- Recognize that some measure of client dependence is likely.
- Demonstrate competence, respect, and warmth toward the client.
- Share a personal experience.
- Respect the role of the father in the family.
- Ask "What do you see as the problem here?" rather than "How do you feel about this?"
- Be alert to nonverbal cues to feelings, such as facial expressions and tone.
- Be prepared to explain the therapeutic process to the client.
- Begin and end the session with a handshake (the man extends his hand to the woman first).
- Use formal greetings to convey respect.
- Accept food or drink offered in the client's home (not doing so may offend the host).
- Recognize that the client may verbally agree with the worker to show respect for authority but may not follow through.
- Remember that Puerto Rican culture does not look favorably on laughing at oneself, so humor must not be of the self-deprecatory type.
- Remember that strangers do not touch little girls, even to be friendly.
- Place signs in both Spanish and English in the agency.

Zuniga (2003) suggests other ways to provide assistance to Latino families. The use of natural support systems is one recommendation. Resource systems important for Latino clients may include extended family, folk healers, religious institutions, and merchants' and social clubs. Included in the category of extended family are the family of origin, nuclear family members, and others related by marriage or blood or custom. Godparents also become an important resource for Latino children in the event that anything befalls the natural parents.

Folk healers include a variety of individuals, including spiritists and *santeros* who focus on emotional and interpersonal problems, herbalists and *santiguadors* who deal primarily with physical ailments, and the *curanderos,* whose interventions include both emotional and physical realms. In Mexican American, Cuban, and Puerto Rican communities any one of the five, or a combination, may exist. The *santero* is more common in the Cuban community, and the *curandero* is found frequently in Mexican American communities. Some folk healers use treatments that blend natural healing methods with spiritual or religious beliefs. This is not surprising given the importance of religion, particularly Roman Catholicism, in Latino life.

Exhibit 12.2 Needs Served by Latino Natural Support Systems

	Natural Support Systems			
Needs Served	Extended Family	Folk Healers	Religious Institutions	Merchants' and Social Clubs
1. Accessibility to community	X	X	X	X
2. Communication in Spanish	X	X	X	X
3. Continuation of cultural traditions	X	X	X	X
4. Crisis intervention	X	X	X	X
5. Emotional support for interpersonal problems	X	X	X	X
6. Friendship, companionship, trust	X	X	X	X
7. Identification with Hispanic role models, leaders, or experts	X	X	X	X
8. Information and referral	X	X	X	X
9. Care and treatment of the disabled or aged	X	X	X	
10. Financial aid or credit	X		X	
11. Medical care and pharmaceutical products	X	X		X
12. Recreation	X		X	X
13. Translation or interpretation	X		X	
14. Advocacy	X		X	
15. Physical and emotional		X	X	
16. Religious or spiritual affiliation rehabilitation		X	X	
17. Babysitting, day care, respite care, foster care, or adoption	X			
18. Child rearing and parent education	X			
19. Educational alternative to public school			X	
20. Housing	X			

Source: Reprinted from Melvin Delgado and Denise Humm-Delgado, "Natural Support Systems: Source of Strength in Hispanic Communities," *Social Work* 27, no. 1 (January 1982), Table 1, p. 87. Copyright 1982, National Association of Social Workers, Inc. Social work research & abstracts by National Association of Social Workers. Copyright 1982 Reproduced with permission of National Association of Social Workers in the format Textbook via Copyright Clearance Center.

Religious institutions that serve as a resource include the Roman Catholic church as well as such denominations as the Jehovah's Witness, Seventh-Day Adventist, and Pentecostal. Among the services offered are pastoral counseling, housing and job-locating assistance, emergency money, and specialized programs in areas such as drug abuse (Aguilar, 2001).

Finally, merchants' and social clubs provide herbs and native foods, credit and information, referrals to other resources, recreation, prayer books, and the services of healers. Exhibit 12.2 identifies the types of needs served by these various resource systems in the Latino community.

Natural support systems are highly significant. Such groups help clients maintain their culture, language, and traditions with a strong emphasis on personal relationships and a diminution of stigmatization for seeking help. Formal agencies that provide services to Latinos should benefit from the availability of these additional community resources. The reluctance of some clients to come to the formal agency could be reduced if the agency staff made greater use of the natural support system and increased attempts to reach the target population. Outreach can be done at merchants' and social clubs, at churches, through radio and newspaper ads or public service announcements, and through notices on barrio grocery bulletin boards. Agencies should consider developing community resource directories in both English and Spanish and including nontraditional resources within the directory.

Workers who serve the Latino community must be much more alert to the unique resources available as well as to the many cultural issues that impinge on social work practice with what has become the fastest-growing minority group in the United States.

Native American Client and Non–Native American Worker

"Social agencies mandated to provide services to American Indian populations are staffed predominantly by non-Indian social workers whose professional education may not have provided the tools to deliver culturally appropriate services" (Williams & Ellison, 1996, p. 147). They may not know, for example, that involving yourself in the affairs of others is rude and contrary to the culture (Green, 1999). With these statements in mind, the well-meaning worker might respond, "Well, how can I help if I can't intervene?" The difficulty of this dilemma is at the heart of the problems faced by many non–Native American social workers. First Nations People will request intervention only infrequently, and white workers must develop patience and wait for the necessary acceptance. How long this will take varies from client to client. During this period, the non–Native American should be available and may offer assistance as long as there is no hint of coercion accompanying the offer. Once help is accepted, the worker's competence will be tested and, if found wanting, the word will spread. Conversely, the worker's ability to do what he or she says will spread equally fast. The results of the former will be a cessation of clients; in the latter case, the opposite is true. The situation described in the following extract indicates noninterference with a First Nations People family:

> The Redthunder family was brought to the school social worker's attention when teachers reported that both children had been tardy and absent frequently in the past weeks. Since the worker lived near Mr. Redthunder's neighborhood, she volunteered to transport the children back and forth to school. Through this regular but informal arrangement, the worker became acquainted with the entire family, especially with Mrs. Redthunder, who expressed her gratitude to the worker by sharing her homegrown vegetables.
>
> The worker sensed that there was much family discomfort and that a tumultuous relationship existed between Mr. and Mrs. Redthunder. Instead of probing into their personal and marital affairs, the worker let Mrs. Redthunder know that she was willing to listen should the woman need someone to talk to. After a few gifts of homegrown vegetables and Native American handicrafts, Mrs. Redthunder broke into tears one day and told the worker about her husband's problem of alcoholism and their deteriorating marital relationship.
>
> Realizing Mr. Redthunder's position of respect in the family and his resistance to outside interference, the social worker advised Mrs. Redthunder to take her family to visit the minister, a man whom Mr. Redthunder admired. The Littleaxe family, who were mutual friends of the worker and the Redthunder family, agreed to visit the Redthunders more often. Through such frequent but informal family visits, Mr. Redthunder finally obtained a job, with the recommendation of Mr. Littleaxe, as recordkeeper in a storeroom. Mr. Redthunder enjoyed his work so much that he drank less and spent more time with his family. (Lewis & Ho, 1975, p. 381)

White workers who serve Native Americans can expect that the interview will also be a new experience. Periods of silence at the start of the interview, for example, are not uncommon. Neither is the practice of some clients of switching from English to their native tongue and back as they address other members of the family. The use of Native American languages is not necessarily meant to keep the message from the worker but rather indicates that this is the easiest way to translate a particular idea.

Establishing intervention objectives should also be consistent with the environment of the Native American client, as must the specific techniques to be used. Culturally repugnant approaches will not succeed regardless of the worker's good intentions. Any type of manipulation is likely to fail also, although providing alternative choices for the Native American client to choose from is generally acceptable. Cognitive-behavioral approaches have been reported as effective with Native Americans (Brammer, 2004). Approaches that emphasize acceptance and are low-key, nondirective, and non-threatening are likely to be useful (Green, 1999).

Brave Heart (2001) discusses the use of groups for treating Native Americans dealing with historical trauma issues. The use of both indirect and extra-group means of influence is particularly recommended. For example, careful planning and implementation of program activities is preferred to more direct and unwelcome techniques. The use of group pressure on individuals is a tactic to avoid if the worker and setting are not to appear coercive. Also recommended are self-help groups and other family support networks that are group based and are consistent with the values and culture of Native American clients.

Williams and Ellison (1996) provide a number of useful suggestions for social workers who serve Native Americans. For example, during assessments, workers would be wise to consider the recent literature that recognizes that most Native Americans exist on a "cultural continuum" that includes traditional, marginal, middle-class, and pan-Indian lifestyles. As might be expected, more traditional Native American clients observe the customs of their tribal group. This affects their view of problems they encounter, especially those involving health difficulties.

Native Americans who are marginal typically live between two worlds, sometimes fitting into neither. It is important to assess the clients' reliance on traditional approaches to problem solving and their willingness to work within the values of the dominant society. Middle-class Native Americans include those who have adopted mainstream middle-class values and beliefs. At the same time, their connections to more traditional patterns need to be considered. Acceptance of most middle-class attitudes and ways of behaving does not always rule out links to traditional patterns. Finally, pan-Indians are those who seek a return to more traditional Native American culture. They will not routinely access non–Native American health and social services because these services are not sensitive to traditional Native American values.

Client with a Disability

The enormous diversity in the types of disabilities that a social worker may encounter limits somewhat the suggestions that we can make about the best ways of helping. We have already suggested the importance of knowing the specific resources that will be most helpful to the individual client. This requires a thorough knowledge of resources covering a variety of disabilities—physical, intellectual, and so on. For example, school systems and universities often provide substantial assistance to students with disabilities, including determining whether a disability is present. Agencies that serve the older adults often provide services to allow the individuals to remain in their own home by offering assistance with meals, housekeeping, yard work, and the like. Visiting nurses can help with medical needs, including proper use of medication and nutrition.

It is important to use typical social work interviewing skills such as eye contact and careful listening. Sometimes novices avoid speaking directly to the client with a disability and address the parent or other adult accompanying the client. This reduces the client to being a spectator and should be avoided. Likewise, some beginners invade the space of a client using a wheelchair by touching him or her or the chair without being invited to do so. Interpersonal space is just as important for clients who use wheelchairs as it is for those who do not.

Equally useful is recognizing and building on the strengths of the client. As we have seen, building a successful life while coping with a disability is possible. Too often we tend to define the individual client by the disability. We use terms such as "confined to a wheelchair," "she's handicapped," or "he's dyslexic" to refer to a client when we would not use such descriptions of other clients. Imagine referring to a client as she's a blond," "he's short," or "she's got spikey hair." We would not pigeonhole someone based on one part of their being, and this is equally true for those with a disability. Care with the words we use is clearly important when working with such clients.

Clients with a disability may need a social worker to advocate for them in some situations. The client may have been denied Social Security for a disability and not know what to do. She may have been refused a reasonable accommodation at her job that would let her continue to be employed. He may be faced with eviction because a landlord refuses to build a ramp that would allow him to access his front door. In each of these cases, and in others, social workers may need to become advocates, negotiators, and/or mediators between the needs of the client and the resources that the client requires to pursue his or her lie. These roles are in addition to whatever counseling, therapy, or other clinical needs the client may require.

Female Client and Male Worker

Evidence shows that women continue to be at risk from a number of forces. Women's salaries continue to lag behind men's, and the concept of the "glass ceiling," which limits upward mobility of women, is discussed often in the media. Women constitute almost three-quarters of the elderly poor (Kornblum & Julian, 2004). The statistics for elderly women of color are even worse. Factors accounting for such discrepancies include family obligations (women as primary caregivers) and employment histories (often affected by job discrimination). If it were not for the success of the Social Security system, impoverishment among women would be much greater. Until 1983, even private pension plans were allowed to pay women lower retirement benefits than they paid men.

Women are also more likely to shoulder the burden of caring for elderly family members. This can have devastating economic consequences when it comes at the expense of employment. When these factors are coupled with the concentration of women in low-paying jobs with few fringe benefits, women are clearly a population at risk. These factors reflect institutional sexism, which can impede cross-sex social work interventions and challenge the worker-client relationship.

Although it is generally conceded that a difference in gender between client and worker is not an insurmountable barrier to an effective relationship, some issues should be considered when such differences exist. Important considerations to keep in mind when a male practitioner is working with women is the lack of shared experiences. Men and women do experience the world differently; the latter are more likely to have encountered oppression, stereotyping, and other forms of discrimination. The male social worker must work with women using mutually agreed interventions designed to empower the client. It is also important to identify client sources of strengths and build or restore informal networks that can reinforce the view that women are "unique and worthwhile human beings whose common emotionally bonding experiences are unifying. The goal is the development of an intrinsic self-esteem which is not based on gender role performance" (Freeman, 1994, p. 131).

Some authors feel that female social workers engage in more modeling for women clients and are more likely to take the client's problems seriously. Some topics may be more comfortably discussed with a counselor of the same sex, and workers and agencies must not overlook this possibility. However, as in many other situations where dissimilarities between client and worker exist, the relationship can usually transcend the differences.

Because the sexist nature of much of society in part contributes to the problems experienced by women, various authors on women and feminism have identified some salient guidelines for use in working with women clients (Davis, 1994; Julia, 2000; Lie & Lowery, 2007). Most of these are equally effective whether employed by a male or female social worker:

- Respond to the client's negative self-statements with alternative views emphasizing strengths.
- Point out instances where the client is showing signs of perfectionism leading to stress and negative self-talk.
- Help clients identify ways in which society devalues women.
- Encourage clients to reinforce other women in their attempts to recognize their strengths.
- In groups of women, incorporate opportunities for mutual compliments, sharing of positive observations about the strengths of others.
- When appropriate, assist clients to reframe symptoms not as pathology but as logical responses to external oppressive events.
- Help clients recognize when their behaviors are often responses to society's gender expectations and to consider alternative behaviors.
- Encourage the expression of feelings as valid means of increasing power.
- Reduce the power differential between worker and client by employing self-disclosure.
- Ensure that assessments reflect strengths.
- Help the client focus on her needs and wants rather than those of others in her life.
- Assist clients to identify specific positive actions they can take to build their sense of efficacy and move toward achievement of their goals.
- Employ techniques such as journaling to help clients identify themes, stressors, and other events that occur on a daily basis, and use the journal in sessions.
- Help clients make conscious choices in their lives as a way of building self-confidence.
- Assist clients to realistically evaluate and challenge their fears and poor self-concepts.

Pro-feminist social work is practiced by both men and women. It requires a commitment to challenging the oppression that pervades much of our society and to empowering clients to act in their own behalf. It means being willing to alter everything from the client-worker relationship to the larger institutions of society. On a one-to-one basis, it includes reducing client-worker distance and power differentials and encouraging clients to redefine experiences to recognize oppression they have encountered. It also means recognizing sexist assumptions regarding appropriate gender behavior; encouraging assertive, independent client behavior; building on client strengths; encouraging woman-to-woman bonding rather than competition between women; and advocating equalitarian rights for women. This stance does not necessarily mean that workers must develop an entire new intervention model, but it does require recognition that some traditional approaches are inconsistent with a pro-feminist stance. Psychoanalytic social work is largely inappropriate because of its focus on the intrapsychic and its failure to consider environmental influences. Humanistic practice approaches, problem-solving interventions, and systems perspectives are largely functional if used by workers who also recognize that many problems develop precisely because of the systemic inequities structured into society.

In summary, pro-feminist workers will be more sensitive to ecological factors in the etiology of problems, oriented to prevention whenever possible, and supportive of client empowerment strategies. This approach is consistent with good social work practice, in keeping with the values of the profession, and will help ensure that workers do not perpetuate gender-based oppression of women. The principles of feminist intervention are presented in Exhibit 12.3.

Exercise 12.4: Roles of Men and Women in Your Family

EP, 2.1.1b

Goal: This exercise is designed to assist you in examining gender-role patterns in your family.

Step 1: Who are the primary caregivers in your family?

___ Men

___ Women

___ Shared equally between the sexes

Why do you think this has occurred?

Step 2: Who primarily has performed the domestic tasks in your family?

___ Men

___ Women

___ Shared equally between the sexes

Why do you think this has occurred?

Step 3: Who have been the primary financial providers in your family?

___ Men

___ Women

___ Shared equally between the sexes

Why do you think this has occurred?

Step 4: For yourself, do you want these gender roles to continue in your future in your family?

___ Yes

___ No

If your answer is "no," specify what you intend to do to change the gender roles you will fulfill in the future.

Exhibit 12.3 Principles of Feminist Intervention

Barker (2003, p. 161) defines *feminism* as "the social movement and doctrine advocating legal and socioeconomic equality for women. The movement originated in Great Britain in the eighteenth century." Barker (2003, p. 161) then defines *feminist social work* as "the integration of the *values,* skills, and knowledge of social work with a feminist orientation to help individuals and society overcome the emotional and social problems that result from *sex discrimination.*"

Barker (2003, p. 161) defines *feminist therapy as* follows:

> A psychosocial treatment orientation in which the professional (usually a woman) helps the client (usually a woman) in individual or group settings to overcome the psychological and social problems largely encountered as a result of *sex discrimination* and sex-role stereotyping. Feminist therapists help clients maximize potential, especially through *consciousness-raising,* eliminating sex stereotyping, and helping them become aware of the commonalities shared by all women.

Nine principles of feminist intervention have been identified (Kirst-Ashman & Hull, 2009a; Van Den Berg, 1992, pp. 95–110; Van Den Berg & Cooper, 1987):

1. *A client's problems should be viewed "within a sociopolitical framework"* (Van Den Berg & Cooper, 1987, p. 613). Feminist intervention is concerned with the inequitable power relationship between women and men and is opposed to all "power-over" relationships, regardless of gender, race, class, age, and so on. Such relationships lead to oppression and domination. Feminism is concerned with changing all social, economic, and political structures based on the relationships between the haves and the have-nots. The problems of the have-nots are often rooted in a sexist social and political structure. Another way of stating this principle is that the "personal is political." According to Van Den Bergh (1992, p. 103):

   > This principle maintains that what a woman experiences in her personal life is directly related to societal dynamics that affect other women. In other words, an individual woman's experiences of pejorative comments based on sex are directly related to societal sexism. For ethnic minority women, racism and classism also are factors that affect well-being.

   A primary distinguishing characteristic of feminist treatment is to help the client analyze how her problems are related to systematic difficulties experienced by women in a sexist, classist, and racist society.
2. *Traditional sex roles are pathological, and clients need encouragement to free themselves from traditional gender-role bonds.* Women are put in a double bind because of *femininity achievement incompatibility.* There is a traditional view in our society that a woman cannot be both feminine and an achiever. Achievement, erroneously, is thought to reduce a woman's femininity, and the truly feminine woman is thought to be someone who does not seek to be an achiever. Traditionally, women have been socialized to fill a "learned helplessness" role. Van Den Bergh (1992, p. 101) describes the effects of such sex-role stereotyping:

   > Sex-role stereotypes suggest that women should be submissive, docile, receptive, and dependent. The message is one of helplessness; that women cannot take care of themselves and are dependent upon others for their well-being. This sets up a dynamic in which a woman's locus of control is external to her self, preventing her from believing that she can acquire what she needs on her own in order to develop and self-actualize. In other words, oversubscription to sex-role stereotypes engenders a state of powerlessness in which a woman is likely to become involved in situations where she becomes victimized. . . . For example, because young girls are socialized to be helpless, when they become women they tend to have a limited repertoire of responses when under stress; e.g., they respond passively.

   In feminist treatment, clients are helped to see how their difficulties may be related to oversubscription to traditional sex-role stereotypes. They are shown that by internalizing traditional sex roles, women are inevitably set up to play passive, submissive roles and experience low self-esteem and self-hatred. The feminist approach asserts that clients need encouragement to make their own choices and pursue the tasks and achievements they desire, rather than be constrained by traditional sex roles.
3. *Intervention should focus on client empowerment.* Van Den Bergh (1992, p. 104) describes the empowerment process:

   > Helping women to acquire a sense of power, or the ability to affect outcome in their lives, is a crucial component of feminist practice. Empowerment means acquiring knowledge, skills, and resources that enhance an individual's ability to control her own life and to influence others. Traditionally women have used indirect, covert techniques to get what they want, such as helplessness, dependency, coyness, and demureness.

   Empowerment is fostered in a variety of ways: (1) by helping the client define her own needs and clarify her personal goals so she can derive a sense of purposefulness; (2) by providing the client with

Exhibit 12.3 *(continued)*

education and access to resources; (3) by helping the client see that the direction and ability to change lie within herself (that is, alterations in her life will result only from her own undertakings); and (4) by focusing on the identification and enhancement of the client's strengths rather than on her pathologies. Women need to be empowered so they can increase their ability to control their environments to get what they need.

4. *Clients' self-esteem should be enhanced.* Self-esteem and self-confidence are essential for empowerment. Self-esteem can be enhanced in a variety of ways. The worker should try to be an encouraging person. The worker should help clients identify and recognize their unique qualities and strengths. Many clients with low self-esteem tend to blame themselves for everything that is wrong. For example, a battered woman typically tends to blame herself for being battered. These clients need to look more realistically at those areas in which they are blaming themselves and feeling guilt. They need to distinguish where their responsibility for dysfunctional interactions ends and other individuals' responsibility begins.
5. *Clients should be encouraged to develop their identity (sense of self) on the basis of their own strengths, attributes, qualities, and achievements.* It is a serious mistake for a woman to develop her identity in terms of her spouse or dating partner. Women need to develop an independent identity that is not based on their relationships with others.
6. *Clients need to value and develop social support systems with other women.* In a society that devalues women, it is all too easy for some women to view other women as insignificant. With social support systems, women can ventilate their concerns and share their experiences and the solutions they've found to similar problems. They can serve as brokers in identifying resources and can provide emotional support and nurturance to one another.
7. *Clients need to find an effective balance between work and personal relationships.* Feminist intervention encourages both women and men to share in the nurturant aspects of their lives and in providing economic resources.
8. The *nature of the relationship between practitioner and client should approach equality as much as possible.* Feminist practitioners do not view themselves as experts in resolving clients' problems but, rather, as catalysts whose role is helping clients empower themselves. Feminist practitioners try to eliminate dominant-submissive relationships. Regarding an egalitarian relationship, Van Den Bergh (1992, p. 104) notes,

   > Obviously, there is an innate power differential between practitioner and client because the former has expertise and training as an "authority." However, the feminist admonition is to avoid abusing that status; "abuse" in this sense might be, for example, taking all credit for client change, or using terminology and nomenclature that are difficult for the client to understand.

9. *Many clients can benefit from learning to express themselves assertively.* The steps in assertiveness training are described in Module 2. As indicated earlier, many women are socialized to be passive and nonassertive, and as a result, they have difficulty expressing themselves assertively. Clients can be helped through individual and group counseling.

Clients who learn to express themselves assertively will experience increased self-confidence and self-esteem. They will be better able to communicate their thoughts, feelings, and opinions. Also, learning to express oneself assertively is an important component of empowerment.

Many women feel considerable anger over being victimized by sex discrimination and gender stereotyping. Some of these women turn these feelings inward, resulting in depression. Assertiveness training can help women recognize their right to be angry and also help them identify and practice constructive ways to express their anger assertively, rather than aggressively.

EP, 2.1.1b

Exercise 12.5: Feminist Intervention

Goal: This exercise is designed to further your understanding of feminist issues and feminist intervention.

Step 1: Describe the plight of a female who you know could benefit from feminist intervention. Do not give identifying information (such as last name) of this person in your description.

Step 2: Speculate about how a social worker could use principles of feminist therapy to counsel this person.

GLBT Clients

The bigotry of some homophobic elements of society, in conjunction with the ignorance and fear of many Americans, produces another population at risk—namely, the GLBT community. This perspective has been carefully documented by Brammer (2004) and others. Some evidence suggests that social workers as a group may be as homophobic as other groups of helping professionals (Harper & Lantz, 1996). This evidence, coupled with the need to educate all social workers about sexual orientation, led the Council on Social Work Education to highlight this area as a key aspect of diversity that all social work programs must address (CSWE, 2008).

Pierce (1993, p. 5) identified four person-in-environment issues that all gay men and lesbians face in the workplace: (1) the unusual situation of being part of a group yet remaining invisible in terms of sexual orientation, (2) facing a potential of physical violence and harassment, (3) dealing regularly with discrimination and prejudice, and (4) living in a society that characterizes homosexuality as "bad." These experiences must be considered when working with lesbian and gay clients and recognized as affecting the lives of your colleagues as well.

Ongoing debates about whether gays and lesbians should serve in the military are evidence of the ignorance and homophobia that exist. Arguments against allowing gay and lesbian persons in the military mirror similar arguments made against allowing African Americans to serve with whites several decades ago. Social workers have an obligation to help gay and lesbian clients with the same degree of professionalism accorded other clients and to work in the political process to overturn homophobia-based barriers that hinder gays and lesbians from enjoying the same rights and privileges as other Americans.

In individual worker-client relationships, the role of social work in providing assistance to gay and lesbian clients is clear. The worker's responsibility is to help clients meet basic human needs and provide linkages with resources that further these goals. The problems of gay and lesbian clients are often similar to those of heterosexuals. In other situations, the problems are unique to gays and lesbians. For younger gays and lesbians, the stress associated with identity confusion regarding their sexuality is a difficulty that often requires intervention. The goal of such help is self-acceptance by the client. Workers can also help with finding peer support if clients have decided to adopt or maintain their identity as a gay or lesbian person. Such a decision may also necessitate dealing with the client's parents, employers, and friends. Here again, social workers can be of help. Significant others can be worked with individually or in groups to assist them in dealing with their own feelings and reactions.

For older gays and lesbians, the tasks and problems are considerably different. Davidson (2000) identified problem areas facing elderly gays and lesbians: institutional, legal, emotional, and medical. The older gay may find that institutional rules prohibit visits to a hospitalized patient by anyone but a member of the immediate family, thus excluding a lover of many years. Similarly, medical decisions in case of emergency often require consent by next of kin, thus ignoring the gay or lesbian partner completely. Services to the grieving spouse are common, but almost no efforts are made to provide similar help to the partner of the deceased gay or lesbian person. The need for companionship and dealing with loneliness in old age are also problems confronting many gays and lesbians that can be ameliorated by professional assistance. Workers can help clients prepare relationship contracts and encourage them to make other arrangements, such as wills.

The difficulties of older gays and lesbians differ somewhat from those of younger gays and lesbians. For instance, the task of coming out may be easier when one is older, because the most common problem, dealing with one's parents, often no longer exists. At the same time, older gays and lesbians may prefer not to address the issue of sexual orientation directly, and workers would be advised to follow suit. This requires workers who are open to their client's needs but feel no compulsion to press the client into coming out or openly communicating his or her sexuality.

For some gay and lesbian clients, homophobia is indeed a problem requiring assistance. The stigma associated with sexual orientation sometimes creates self-loathing among gays and lesbians themselves. Such a reaction is at odds with the goal of self-acceptance and can be dealt with accordingly. Social workers should be aware of local support groups and should encourage the development of such organizations when absent. Likewise, agencies that provide specialized services to gays and lesbians or that are especially sensitive to their needs can be supported by referrals and by other means.

On another level, there are equally concrete activities in which social workers can engage. Support for legislation to decriminalize same-sex acts would help reduce the psychological risks of being gay or lesbian, and civil rights protection would help ensure that discrimination in employment and housing would be avoided. Many cities and states have adopted such laws, removing another burden to those whose sexual orientation is gay or lesbian.

Adequate sex education in schools, in churches, and within the family can also be encouraged. In-service training for agency staff on the topic of homosexuality and multiagency efforts to combat prejudice and discrimination toward gays and lesbians can also be undertaken. Refusing to accept homophobic behavior from colleagues and pointing out that such actions are a violation of the NASW *Code of Ethics* is an option.

EP 2.1.1b

Certainly, to be of help to gay and lesbian clients, we must become more comfortable with the topic of homosexuality and begin to deal with our own homophobic tendencies. Just as in other areas of practice, ignorance and confusion about sexual orientation must be dealt with directly and openly.

Exercise 12.6: Should Same-Sex Marriages Be Legalized?

Goal: This exercise is designed to assist you in arriving at your opinion on an issue that has become highly controversial.

Step 1: Some states and countries are now permitting same-sex marriage. Are you in favor of legalizing same-sex marriage?

___ Yes

___ No

Step 2: Explain your views.

Rural Settings

Social workers who elect to practice in rural settings are likely to discover that a multiplicity of differences exist in the way they conduct business. For example, social workers who comfortably assume the role of advocate in an urban setting will quickly find that this is more difficult in a rural setting. Rural advocates risk losing the trust of the community that they nurtured so carefully in such other roles as broker, mediator, and problem solver. The degree of risk must be assessed as one step in the problem-solving process (Kirst-Ashman & Hull, 2009a). The fact that workers become more a part of the area they serve means that there is greater informality and less professional detachment than would be true in an urban setting. The need to have relationships with, and the support of, community power sources makes it more difficult to pursue changes that threaten those interests.

Workers, especially in-migrant practitioners, are often perceived as outsiders, and it takes time for the community to develop trust and confidence in their competence. Thus, to advocate strongly for anything under these conditions is not recommended if other effective alternatives can be pursued. The greater autonomy of rural workers is an asset, but it also carries additional responsibilities. Workers need to develop the ability to form relationships quickly because the geographical distance to be covered means less time can be devoted to long-term projects. Making each contact with a client count is essential because those contacts are more infrequent than would otherwise be the case.

Knowledge of natural and informal rather than formal support systems is crucial, as is the ability to work with other professionals and nonprofessionals in achieving change. Rural workers must also be patient, however, because changes, when they come, can be exceedingly slow. "Attempting to impose one's ideas before understanding what the community's ideas and wishes are is generally a mistake. It is equally a mistake in metropolitan and nonmetropolitan areas. However, it can be a fatal mistake in a nonmetropolitan community" (Ginsburg, 1998, p. 12). Workers must be knowledgeable and compliant with local norms and etiquette. Workers may need to adjust their personal lifestyles to the community and to the job to be done. Clearly not every social worker will be willing or able to accomplish this. It follows from what we have indicated previously that existing cultural or ethnic differences can complicate understanding of, and practice in, rural communities.

Social workers new to rural areas and small towns sometimes ignore the many ways their private actions affect the way they are seen as professionals. For example, workers finding higher prices in smaller communities have often resorted to shopping in nearby communities that are larger. Purchases of groceries, automobiles, clothes, and other items are often made without regard to how this affects the local community. This pattern of shopping may result in a lower price paid for goods and services, but the net result may be that the worker is not seen as a member of the community. Shopping in the community where you practice helps link you with that community, supports the local economy, and gives you an opportunity to talk regularly with businesspeople and leaders in the area. This makes it easier to approach community leaders later on when you are pursuing a macro-change opportunity.

Similarly, participating in local community activities helps ensure that you are seen as a member of the community. Workers who serve a community but do not live there, shop there, or participate in community activities have greatly diminished ability to exert influence within that setting. In smaller communities, becoming part of the community is key to influencing local events. Workers are encouraged to attend the local chicken dinners sponsored by church or civic groups, participate in the volunteer fire department fund-raising effort, serve on the centennial committee, and accept membership in local service organizations. Other ways to become involved include volunteering to work on special projects (such as historical museum renovations, tree planting, and community beautification efforts). In the long run, the worker who is seen as part of the community will be better able to influence the course of events within that community.

Other Differences Affecting Practice

A variety of potential and actual differences between client and worker can impinge on the relationship and affect the outcome of interventive efforts. Age differences, as mentioned earlier, will dictate certain adaptations to your usual style. When serving older clients, for example, workers should exercise greater patience and understanding of the problems of the elderly and, if feasible, elect to conduct the interview out of the office, in a location more suitable to the client. Home interviews are suggested when possible.

Similar care should be used when workers are engaged in a practice with young children. As an adult, you may need to place some distance between yourself and the child's parents to gain the youngster's confidence. Although children are more open in many ways, they are also quick to tune out questions, thus reducing your reliance on standard verbal techniques. The child's medium is play, and workers would be advised to use such activities in the helping process. Adult rules of conversation are more strict, whereas an interview with a child may appear both random and disorganized. This places a special responsibility on workers to be sensitive to the unspoken aspects of the interview and to stay attuned to the bits and pieces of information that are generated in these situations. Although the process can be somewhat disjointed, the rewards are substantial.

CULTURALLY COMPETENT PRACTICE

Traditionally, professional social work practice has used the medical model for the delivery of services. The medical model is a deficit model, which focuses on identifying problems or deficits in a person. It largely ignores environmental factors that can affect the person-in-situation. Also, with its focus on deficits, strengths and resources are ignored. (When only shortcomings are emphasized, a client's self-esteem is likely to be severely affected negatively. Defining oneself in terms of shortcomings overlooks strengths and resources.)

Culturally competent practice seeks to incorporate understanding of diverse ethnic, cultural, and minority groups into the theories and principles that guide social work practice (Devore & Schlesinger, 1996). It is based on the view that practice must be attuned to the values and dispositions related to clients' ethnic group membership and social-class position. Culturally competent practice requires that social workers have an in-depth understanding of the effects of oppression on racial and ethnic groups.

Another important conceptual framework is that of the "dual perspective" (Norton, 1978). This concept is derived from the view that all people are part of two systems: (1) the dominant system (the society that one lives in), which is the source of power and economic resources; and (2) the nurturing system, composed of the physical and social environment of family and community. The dual perspective concept asserts that the adverse consequences of an oppressive society on the self-concept of a person of color can be partially offset by the nurturing system.

Culturally competent practice asserts that social workers have a special obligation to be aware of and to seek to redress the oppression experienced by ethnic groups. It assumes that each ethnic group and its members have an ethnic history with roots in the past that have a bearing on the members' perceptions of current problems. For example, the individual and collective history of many African Americans leads to the expectation that family resources will be available in times of trouble (Devore & Schlesinger, 1996). Culturally competent practice also recognizes the importance of the present. This is especially true when immigrants, refugees, and others from different cultures struggle to adjust to norms, gender roles, and other expectations associated with life in the United States. The tensions and stress engendered by such transitions are real, and social workers can be helpful in ameliorating them.

Culturally competent practice does not always necessitate new practice principles or approaches but urges adaptation of prevailing therapies, social work principles, and skills to take account of ethnic reality. Regardless of which practice approach is used, empowerment and the strengths perspective should be emphasized.

Empowerment has been defined as "the process of helping individuals, families, groups, and communities increase their personal, interpersonal, socioeconomic, and political strength and develop influence toward improving their circumstances" (Barker, 2003, p. 147). In working with an ethnic or a racial group, empowerment counters the negative image or stereotypes of a group (rendered through a long history of discrimination) with a positive value or image and an emphasis on the ability of ethnic group members to influence the conditions of their lives. Empowerment counters hopelessness and powerlessness by emphasizing the ability of each person to address problems competently, beginning with a positive view of self. Empowerment counters oppression and poverty by helping ethnic groups and their members increase their ability to make and implement basic life decisions.

The strengths perspective is closely related to empowerment. The *strengths perspective* seeks to identify, use, build, and reinforce individuals' abilities and strengths, emphasizing their interests, aspirations, resources, beliefs, and accomplishments. This is in contrast to the pathological perspective, which focuses on deficiencies.

EP 2.1.7a

For example, strengths of African Americans in the United States include the following. There are more than 100 predominantly African American colleges and universities; fraternal and women's organizations; and social, political, and professional organizations. Many of the schools, businesses, churches, and organizations that are predominantly African American have developed social service programs—such as family support services, mentoring programs, food and shelter services, transportation services, and educational and scholarship programs. Through individual and organized efforts, self-help approaches and mutual aid traditions continue among African Americans. African Americans tend to have strong ties to immediate, extended family. They also tend to have a strong religious orientation, a strong work and achievement orientation, and egalitarian role sharing (Billingsley, 1993).

Exercise 12.7: The Strengths Perspective Applied to a Homeless Family

Goal: This exercise is designed to have you apply the strengths perspective to a case scenario.

Step 1: Read the following scenario:

> Ms. Kerr was recently evicted from her two-bedroom apartment. She had been working at a small business that did not offer health insurance coverage to her. She is a single mother with three children, ages 7, 9, and 10. She developed pneumonia, which hung on because she could not pay to see a physician. The small business experienced financial problems, and her employment was terminated. She has been seeking another job but has not found one. She wants a job that has health benefits. Being unable to pay rent, she was evicted from her apartment. She cares a lot for her children, and they display respect for her. The children are all doing well in school. Ms. Kerr and her children lived on the street for 3 days and nights but then located a homeless shelter at the Salvation Army. They have been at the homeless shelter for the past 2½ weeks. The children are fairly healthy and are respectful of the services they are receiving from the shelter. Ms. Kerr has largely recovered from her pneumonia, partly because of the physician's visit she asked the Salvation Army to arrange for her.

Step 2: List the strengths that you identify in this family.

SOME GENERAL OBSERVATIONS

In this chapter, we have focused extensively on the unique differences of various groups, such as people of color, women, rural populations, and gay and lesbian individuals. Although the emphasis has been on characteristics that differentiate these groups and on social work practice as it relates to the groups, there are some important commonalities that affect our efforts to help. In this section, we will attempt to highlight some of these similarities.

Any intervention effort that is ethnically sensitive should take into account those individuals affected by the problem. Social workers, for example, who plan to work with minority families should be certain they understand "who the appropriate actors are" (Devore & Schlesinger, 1996, p. 187). This might include nuclear family members as well as other relatives and friends who are "like family." Most minorities of color evidence a sound respect for elders and seek their advice and opinions. In addition, most are also tolerant of other ethnic groups to a degree not found among the dominant majority. Even though religious orientations and spiritual beliefs may differ markedly among groups, each is likely to be characterized by some degree of religiosity or belief in a supreme being (Green, 1999).

People of color also share their commonality of color, their oppression, and their victimization by white society. Most have experienced conflict with this society ranging from colonization to slavery to economic injustice (Brammer, 2004). The result of this conflict can be distrust of traditional social service institutions, pride in and reliance on one's own kind, and a sense of impotence when dealing with the typical government agency.

To provide competent social services within the framework outlined earlier, workers must attend to a variety of issues. First, it is helpful to keep in mind that feelings, emotions, and thoughts are all shared. Differences most often lie in how we choose to express them. Our own culture influences us to the extent that some say we are culture-bound. As a result, feelings, thoughts, and ideas we felt were firmly under control or previously resolved may become aroused during one-on-one encounters with those of a different race. It is healthier to recognize this possibility than to be surprised by it at an inopportune time. Our attempts to provide sensitive and effective social work intervention can be enhanced by observing the following guidelines:

1. Avoid color blindness.
2. Avoid jargon and clichés, such as referring to clients as culturally deprived.
3. Concentrate on building the relationship first and showing sensitivity to the client's culture and difficulty.
4. Consider client behavior as functional/dysfunctional rather than normal/abnormal based on an a priori standard.
5. Recognize and accept that client distrust is likely to be the norm.
6. Accept the limits of your own knowledge.
7. Acquire some familiarity with clients' language whenever possible.
8. Recognize that culture is fluid, not static.
9. Acquire and maintain a sound working knowledge of programs, services, agencies, and workers providing specialized assistance to diverse groups.
10. Keep abreast of new rules and laws affecting diverse groups.
11. Support training and education for agency staff related to diverse groups.
12. Take active steps to combat discrimination within your own agency and programs.
13. Place greater emphasis in your practice on developing community-based alternatives to reduce the discriminatory reliance on institutional placements for people of color.
14. Recognize that all clients are individuals and may share all, some, or none of the customs, norms, values, or beliefs of their racial or ethnic group.

Dean (2001) argues correctly that the process of working cross culturally requires an ever increasing awareness of oneself, constant learning about the cultural groups with which one works, and a healthy skepticism that what we know is adequate or accurate. The 2008 accreditation standards promulgated by CSWE highlight this by requiring that students "view themselves as learners and engage those with whom they work as informants." This expectation underscores the importance of learning from our clients rather than making too many assumptions based on past learning. The process of becoming an effective practitioner with clients from different cultures and backgrounds is an ongoing one with the reservation that complete cultural competence is unlikely to be achieved.

SOCIAL CONSTRUCTS THAT ADVERSELY IMPACT POPULATIONS AT RISK

Ashley Montague (1964) considered the concept of race to be one of the most dangerous and tragic myths in our society. Race is erroneously believed by many to be a biological classification of people. Yet, surprisingly to some, there are no clearly delineating characteristics of any race. Throughout history, the genes of different societies and racial groups have occasionally been intermingled. No racial group has any unique or distinctive genes. In addition, biological differentiations of racial groups have gradually been diluted through various sociocultural factors. These factors include changes in preferences of desirable characteristics in mates, effects of different diets on those who reproduce, and such variables as wars and diseases in selecting those who will live to reproduce (Johnson, 1973).

Despite definitional problems, it is common to use racial categories in the social sciences. Race has important (though not necessarily consistent) social meanings for people. In order to have a basis for racial classifications, social scientists have used a social, rather than a biological, definition. A social definition is based on the way in which members of a society classify each other by physical characteristics. For example, a frequently used social definition of an African American is anyone who either displays overt African American physical characteristics or is known to have an African American ancestor (Schaefer, 2004).

A social definitional approach to classifying races sometimes results in different societies using different definitions of *race*. For example, in the United States anyone who is known to have an African American ancestor is considered to be African American; in Brazil, anyone known to have a white ancestor is considered to be white (Schaefer, 2004).

Race, according to Montague (1964), becomes a dangerous myth when people assume that physical traits are linked with mental traits and cultural achievements. Johnson (1973) summarized the need for an impartial, objective view of the capacity of different racial groups to achieve: "Race bigots contend that, the cultural achievements of different races being so obviously unlike, it follows that their genetic capacities for achievements must be just as different. Nobody can discover the cultural capacities of any population or race . . . until there is equality of opportunities to demonstrate the capacities" (p. 50). Nevertheless, every few years, it seems, some noted scientist stirs up the country by highlighting supposedly race-based differences. For example, Herrnstein and Murray (1994) asserted that whites, on the average, are more intelligent, because IQ tests show that whites average scores of 10 to 15 points higher than African Americans. Herrnstein and Murray's findings have been sharply criticized by other authorities as falsely assuming that IQ is largely genetically determined (Lefrancois, 1996). These critics contend that IQ is substantially influenced by environmental factors and that it is likely that the average achievement of African Americans, if given similar opportunities to realize their potentialities, would be the same as whites'. Also, it has been charged that IQ tests are racially slanted, for the tests ask the kinds of questions that whites are more familiar with and thereby more apt to answer correctly.

Most scientists, both physical and social, now believe that in biological inheritance all races are alike in everything that really makes any difference (such as problem-solving capacities, altruistic tendencies, and communication capacities). With the exception of several very small, inbred, isolated, primitive tribes, all racial groups appear to show a wide distribution of every kind of ability. All important race differences that have been noted in personality, behavior, and achievement (for example, high school graduation rates) appear to be primarily due to environmental factors.

The term *gender* is also socially constructed. Social scientists distinguish between "sex," which is a biologically based category, and "gender," which refers to the particular set of socially constructed meanings that are associated with each sex. For example, the traditional sex role for women is to be "sugar and spice and everything nice"; males, in contrast, are to be "sturdy oaks." Sex-role stereotypes vary over time and place so that what is understood as "naturally" masculine or femine behavior in one society may be the exact opposite of what is considered "natural" for women or men in another culture. Rothenberg (2007, p. 8) notes:

> Whereas in many cultures strenuous physical activity is considered to be more appropriate to men than to women, in one society where women are responsible for such labor the heaviest loads are described as being "so heavy only a woman can lift it." In some societies it is women who are responsible for agricultural labor, and in others it is men. Even within cultures that claim that women are unsuited for heavy manual labor, some women (usually women of color and poor, white working women) have always been expected and required to perform back-breaking physical work—on plantations, in factories, on farms, in commercial laundries, and in their homes. The actual lives of real women and real men throughout history stand in sharp contrast to the images of masculinity and femininity that have been constructed by society and then rationalized as reflecting innate differences between the sexes.

Social class is also a term that is socially constructed. Differences between rich and poor, which result from particular ways of structuring the economy, are often erroneously believed as innate differences among people.

There are many other terms related to social work that are socially constructed. A few will be mentioned. Elders in our society are believed to be unproductive even though many are productive for decades after turning 65. There are many erroneous stereotypes of GLBT individuals. For example, prior to the late 1960s, the American Psychiatric Association classified them as being mentally ill. People with a serious physical disability are often shunned by employers when they apply for a job, for they are viewed as "unproductive." Yet many have made outstanding contributions to our society.

Rothenberg (2007) has noted that such social constructs have led to the development of structures and processes in our society that result in the following: men being privileged and women being oppressed, whites being privileged in the economic arena and people of color being oppressed, people 65 years and older being oppressed in the economic arena, GLBT people being oppressed, people with a serious physical disability being oppressed in the economic arena, and so on.

How can such oppression and discrimination be alleviated? Two categories of changes are needed: (1) The structures and processes that privilege some groups and oppress others need to be changed in an egalitarian direction. (2) The negative social constructs surrounding oppressed groups need to be changed in a direction that respects and appreciates all persons (including members of diverse groups).

What are some strategies to alleviate oppression and discrimination? In the next section, we consider some macro strategies (this list of strategies is not exhaustive).

MACRO STRATEGIES TO PROMOTE SOCIAL AND ECONOMIC JUSTICE

Social Programs

Thousands of social programs have been enacted at national, state, and local levels to promote social and economic justice for a variety of populations at risk. A few examples are presented here.

The 1935 Social Security Act initiated a variety of programs for several populations at risk. Aid to the Blind provides financial assistance to low-income people of any age whose vision is 20/200 or less with correction. Aid to the Disabled provides financial assistance to low-income people, ages 18 to 65, who have a permanent disability. Old Age Assistance provides financial assistance to the low-income elderly (ages 65 and older). Aid to Dependent Children provides financial assistance to low-income mothers with children under age 18 and no father in the home.

In the 1960s President Lyndon Johnson declared a War on Poverty. Various anti-poverty programs were created, including Head Start, Medicare, and Medicaid. (Medicare helps the elderly pay the high cost of health care; Medicaid primarily provides medical care for recipients of public assistance.)

In 1975, the U.S. Congress passed the Education for All Handicapped Children Act. This legislation mandates that all school districts identify students with physical, developmental, learning, and social-emotional problems that hamper their education. Once the children are identified, school districts are then required to develop specialized programs to meet their needs.

In 1990, the U.S. Congress passed the Americans with Disabilities Act. This act prohibits discrimination against persons with a disability, in employment or by limiting access to public accommodations (such as restaurants, stores, museums, and theaters). The law requires that new public buildings be accessible to persons with a disability and requires that barriers in existing public buildings be removed if the changes can be accomplished without much difficulty or expense.

In 1996, the Personal Responsibility and Work Opportunity Reconciliation Act established the Temporary Assistance for Needy Families (TANF) program. TANF replaced the Aid to Families with Dependent Children (AFDC) program originally created in 1935. Each state receives a block grant from the federal government and is allowed substantial flexibility in setting up and operating the TANF program. Program purposes include providing assistance to needy families so that children can remain in their own homes; reducing dependency by helping recipients acquire job skills, encouraging work and marriage; eliminating out-of-wedlock pregnancies; and encouraging two-parent families. Unlike AFDC, TANF sets time limits and work requirements for recipients.

Social workers have an obligation to be involved in enacting and implementing social programs to meet the needs of individuals and groups subjected to discrimination and oppression. Ways that social workers can participate in the enactment of needed social programs include running for political office, calling and writing to political officials to express their views about needed programs, campaigning for persons running for office who support the enactment of needed social programs, lobbying for needed programs, and joining and becoming active in groups that support the enactment of needed social programs. A more detailed list and discussion of macro-level strategies appears in Kirst-Ashman and Hull (2009b).

Mass-Media Appeals

Newspapers, radio, and television at times present programs designed to explain the nature and harmful effects of prejudice and to promote social and economic justice for populations at risk. Mass media reaches large numbers of people simultaneously. By expanding public awareness of the existence of discrimination and its consequences, the media can strengthen control over highly prejudiced people. But it has limitations in changing prejudiced attitudes and behaviors; it primarily provides information and seldom has a lasting effect in changing deep-seated prejudices through propaganda. Broadcasting platitudes like "all people are brothers and sisters" and "prejudice is un-American" is not very effective. Highly prejudiced people are often unaware of their own prejudices. Even if they are aware, however, they generally dismiss mass-media appeals as irrelevant to them or as propaganda. Mass media has probably had a significant impact in reducing racial discrimination by showing nonwhites and whites working harmoniously in commercials, on news teams, and on TV shows.

The Internet and Other Technology

The Internet is proving an effective venue for promoting social and economic justice. Bloggers write about issues that mainstream media ignore and thus bring attention to instances of social and economic justice. Use of websites to promote political agendas and raise funds for political purposes is commonplace. Candidates for office announce their candidacy on the Internet and raise millions of dollars in support of their campaigns. Websites are used to attract people who will work for candidates or otherwise promote their cause. Websites also are created to help communities address problems ranging from criminal behavior to civic improvements.

In countries across the world, citizens use the Internet and cell phones to transmit information about government misbehavior and deprivation of civil rights and to call attention to current problems. In places where government-owned mass media are the only source of news and information, the Internet allows people to receive unbiased news and to communicate with the outside world. The Internet frequently functions as a bulwark against tyranny and oppression.

Likewise, e-mail and phone text messaging are useful in allowing almost instantaneous communication. In a recent campus attack at a midwestern state university, text messaging via cell phones helped warn students about a gunman on campus, thereby potentially saving a number of lives. E-mail and text messaging by cell phone can be used to quickly assemble supporters, coordinate planning, and engage in concerted effort to promote social and economic justice.

Cell phones also are used to record photographs and videos showing police mistreatment of people of color and others. These images draw attention to injustices and abuse, forcing communities and organizations to take action to address long-standing problems. The potential for this technology to advance social and economic justice is great.

Civil Rights Laws

In recent decades, equal rights laws have been enacted in areas such as employment, voting, housing, public accommodation, and education for a variety of populations at risk. Populations benefiting from federal civil rights laws include people of color, women, persons with disabilities, and the elderly.

Civil rights laws prohibit overt discrimination in specified areas. For example, in 1986 the U.S. Congress outlawed most mandatory age-related retirement policies, which had discriminated against the elderly. The passage of a civil rights law protects the population at risk only in the area or areas specified in the law. The legislation does not provide protection in areas that are not specified. As a result, subtle discrimination often persists because it is hidden and therefore difficult to document.

How effective are laws in curbing discrimination and reducing prejudice? Proponents of civil rights legislation make certain assumptions. The first is that new laws will lessen discriminatory behavior. The laws redefine what was once "normal" behavior (discrimination) as now being "deviant." It is expected that attitudes over time will change and become more consistent with the mandated nondiscriminatory behavior. The second assumption is that the laws will be enforced.

Civil rights laws enacted after the Civil War, however, prohibited discriminatory behavior against African Americans but were seldom enforced and gradually eroded. It is also unfortunately true that some officials find ways to evade the intent of the law by eliminating only extreme, overt symbols of discrimination without changing other practices. Thus, the enactment of a law is only the first step in the process of changing prejudiced attitudes and practices. However, as Martin Luther King, Jr., noted, "The law may not make a man love me, but it can restrain him from lynching me, and I think that's pretty important" (www.quotationspage.com, 2004).

It should be noted that even current civil rights laws are often not enforced. For example, a recent report by the Citizens' Commission on Civil Rights (Taylor, Piché,

Rosario, & Rich, 2007) looked at the enforcement of civil rights during the administration of George W. Bush. The report found that "the erosion of civil rights across our nation over the past six years is the result of willful neglect and calculated design. The Bush administration continues to use the courts and the judicial appointment process to narrow civil rights protections and repeal remedies for legal redress while allowing the traditional tools of the executive branch for civil rights enforcement to wither and die. The resulting inequality of opportunity, deteriorating civil liberties, and rising religious and racial discrimination are sad commentaries on the priorities of the current administration" (p. 1). In the absence of determination by government officials to enforce civil rights laws, their usefulness as a means of promoting social and economic justice is limited.

Activism

The strategy of activism attempts to promote social and economic justice through direct confrontation of policies involving discrimination and oppression. Activism has three types of politics: the politics of creative disorder, the politics of disorder, and the politics of escape (Johnson, 1973, pp. 374–379).

The *politics of creative disorder* operates on the edge of the dominant social system and includes school boycotts, rent strikes, job blockades, sit-ins (for example, at segregated restaurants), public marches, and product boycotts. This type of activism is based on the concept of nonviolent resistance. A classic illustration of nonviolent resistance began on December 1, 1955, when Rosa Parks, an African American in Montgomery, Alabama, refused to give up her seat on a bus to a white person. (Exhibit 12.4 describes Rosa Parks's act of courage.)

The *politics of disorder* reflects alienation from the dominant culture and disillusionment with the political system. In this type of activism, those being discriminated against resort to mob uprisings, riots, and other forms of violence.

In 1969, the National Commission on Causes and Prevention of Violence reported that 200 riots had occurred in the previous 5 years, when inner cities in the United States erupted (Johnson, 1973, p. 376). In the early 1980s, there were again some riots in Miami and in other U.S. inner cities. In 1992, race riots devastated parts of Los Angeles after the acquittal of four white police officers charged with using excessive force to arrest Rodney King, an African American; the brutal arrest had been videotaped. The focus of most of these riots has been aggression by people of color against white-owned property.

Riots and similar forms of activism have a long history in the United States, including draft riots in New York in 1863 and race riots in Chicago in 1919. The 1969 Stonewall riots involving gays against the police in New York is sometimes considered the beginning of the gay rights movement in this country. Riots are common across the globe as a tool to bring about change. The sparks that set off riots can be as diverse as citizens lacking basic goods and services (for example, gas riots in Jamaica, 1999) to responding to oppression and ethnic/religious differences, as happened in India in 2004. Typically, riots are used as a tool when other efforts to end long-standing grievances and oppression have not been successful.

The *politics of escape* engages in passionate rhetoric about the oppression of populations. Because the focus is not on arriving at solutions, the rhetoric is not productive, except perhaps for providing an emotional release.

The principal value of activism or social protest seems to be that it informs the public of the existence of certain problems. The civil rights protests in the 1960s made practically all Americans aware of the discrimination to which nonwhite groups were being subjected. Since then, at least some of the discrimination has ceased, and race relations have improved. Continued protest beyond a certain (although indeterminate) point, however, appears to have little additional value (Sullivan, Thompson, Wright, Gross, & Spady, 1980).

Exhibit 12.4 Rosa Parks's Act of Courage Sparked the Civil Rights Movement

On December 1, 1955, Rosa Parks was in a hurry. She had a lot of things to do. When the bus came to the boarding area where she was standing in Montgomery, Alabama, she got on without paying attention to the driver. She rode the bus often and was aware of Montgomery's segregated seating laws, which required blacks to sit at the back of the bus.

In those days in the South, black people were expected to board the front of the bus, pay their fare, then get off and walk outside the bus to reboard on the back. But Rosa Parks noted the back was already crowded, standing-room only, with black passengers even standing on the back steps of the bus. It was apparent to Rosa that it would be all but impossible to reboard at the back. Besides, bus drivers sometimes drove off and left black passengers behind, even after accepting their fares. Rosa Parks spontaneously decided to take her chances. She paid her fare in the front of the bus, then walked down the aisle, and took a seat toward the back of the bus that was still in the area reserved for whites. At the second stop after boarding, a white man got on and had to stand.

The bus driver saw the white man standing and ordered Rosa Parks to move to the back. She refused, thinking, "I want to be treated like a human being."

Two police officers were called and they arrested Rosa. She was taken to city hall, booked, fingerprinted, jailed, and fined. Her arrest and subsequent appeal all the way to the U.S. Supreme Court were the catalyst for a year-long boycott of the city buses by blacks, who composed 70% of the bus riders. The boycott inspired Martin Luther King, Jr., to become involved. The boycott ended when the Supreme Court declared Montgomery's segregated seating laws unconstitutional.

Rosa Parks's unplanned defiance of the segregated seating law sparked the civil rights movement. This movement not only has promoted social and economic justice for African Americans but also has served to inspire other groups to organize to advocate for their civil rights. These groups include other racial and ethnic groups, women, the elderly, persons with a disability, and GLBT individuals.

Affirmative Action Programs

Affirmative action programs provide for preferential hiring and admission requirements (for example, admission to medical schools) for minority applicants. Affirmative action programs cover minority groups, including women, many groups of color, and persons with a disability. (Women—though in the majority in the United States—are considered a minority group because for generations they have been subjected to discrimination and have been denied equal opportunities.) Affirmative action programs also require that employers must (1) make active efforts to locate and recruit qualified minority applicants, and (2) in certain circumstances, have hard quotas under which specific numbers of minority members must be accepted to fill vacant positions (for example, a university with a high proportion of white, male faculty may be required to fill half of its faculty vacancies with women and members of other minority groups). Affirmative action programs require that employers must demonstrate, according to a checklist of positive measures, that they are not guilty of discrimination.

A major dilemma with affirmative action programs is that preferential hiring and quota programs involve reverse discrimination, which sometimes arbitrarily excludes qualified majority group members. Several successful lawsuits have claimed reverse discrimination. The best-known case has been that of Alan Bakke, who was initially denied admission to the medical school at the University of California, Davis, in 1973. He alleged reverse discrimination because he had higher grades and higher scores on the Medical College Admissions Test than several minority applicants who were admitted under the university's minorities quota policy. In 1978, his claim was upheld by the U.S. Supreme Court in a precedent-setting decision (Sindler, 1978). The Court ruled that strict racial quotas were unconstitutional, but the Court did not rule that race could not be used as one among many criteria in making admissions decisions.

Supporters of affirmative action programs note that the majority group expressed little concern about discrimination when its members were the beneficiaries instead of the victims of discrimination. They also assert there is no other way to rapidly make up for past discrimination against minorities—many of whom may presently score slightly lower on qualification tests because they have not had the opportunities and the quality of training that the majority group members have had.

With affirmative action programs, some minority group members are given preferential treatment, which results in some whites being discriminated against. But minority group members still face more employment discrimination than whites do. Affirmative action programs raise delicate and complex questions about achieving equality through giving preferences in hiring and admissions to minorities. Yet no other means has been found to end subtle discrimination in hiring and admissions.

Admission to educational programs and well-paying jobs are crucial elements in working toward integration. The history of immigrant groups who have "made it" (such as the Irish, Japanese, and Italians) suggests equality will be achieved only when minority group members gain middle- and upper-class status. Once such status is achieved, the minority group members become an economic and political force to be reckoned with. Dominant groups are then pressured into modifying their norms, values, and stereotypes. For this reason, numerous authorities have noted that the elimination of economic discrimination is a prerequisite for achieving equality and harmonious race relations (Kornblum & Julian, 2009). Achieving educational equality between races is also crucial because lower educational attainments lead to less prestigious jobs, lower incomes, lower living standards, and the perpetuation of racial inequalities from one generation to the next.

Critics of affirmative action assert that it is a highly politicized and painful remedy that stigmatizes many of those it was meant to help. Affirmative action is now perceived by many in our society as a system of preferences for the unqualified. Critics further assert that although affirmative action may have been necessary 30 years ago to make sure that minority candidates received fair treatment to counter the social barriers to hiring and admission that stemmed from centuries of unequal treatment, such programs are no longer needed. They assert that it is wrong to discriminate against white males for the sole purpose of making up for an injustice that somebody's great-grandfather may have done to somebody else's great-grandfather. They assert that it is wrong for the daughter of a wealthy African American couple, for example, to be given preference in employment over the son of a homeless alcoholic who happens to be white.

In 1996, voters in the state of California passed Proposition 209, which explicitly rejects the idea that women and other minority group members should get special consideration when applying for jobs, government contracts, or university admission. This affirmative action ban became law in California in August 1997. In addition, numerous lawsuits have been filed objecting to reverse discrimination. If the courts rule in favor of those filing the lawsuits, the power of affirmative action programs will be sharply reduced. In November 1997, the U.S. Supreme Court rejected a challenge to the California law that ended racial and gender preferences in that state. This Supreme Court action clears the way for other states and cities to ban affirmative action. The states of Washington and Michigan have since voted to abolish the use of affirmative action in public university admissions.

Supporters of affirmative action believe that if we abandon affirmative action, we return to the old-boy network. They assert that affirmative action has helped a number of women and people of color to attain a good education and higher-paying positions and thereby to remove themselves from the ranks of the poor. They assert that in a society in which racist and sexist attitudes remain, affirmative action is necessary to give women and people of color a fair opportunity at attaining a quality education and well-paying jobs.

Is there a middle ground for the future of affirmative action? Zuckerman (1995) recommends:

> The vast majority of Americans would probably accept a return to the original notion of affirmative action—an aggressive outreach to minorities to make sure they have a fair shot. They would probably see a social benefit in accepting that racial justice might be relevant in a tiebreaker case, or might even confer a slight advantage. The goal must be a return to policies based on evenhandedness for individuals rather than for groups. Then employers can concentrate on whether a minority applicant is the right person for the job rather than being moved by whether the applicant looks litigious. All employees could take it for granted that they had a fair shot. (p. 112)

EP 2.1.7a

Exercise 12.8: Your Thoughts on Affirmative Action Programs

Goal: This exercise is designed to assist you in analyzing the merits and shortcomings of affirmative action programs.

Step 1: Specify the merits and benefits of affirmative action programs. (With affirmative action programs, some minority group members are given preferential treatment, which results in some whites being discriminated against.)

Step 2: Specify the shortcomings of affirmative action programs.

Step 3: Specify your recommendation about whether affirmative action programs should be (a) continued, (b) discontinued, or (c) changed in a direction you suggest. Explain your rationale.

Confrontation of Jokes and Discriminatory Actions

Jokes and sarcastic remarks about people of color, women, persons with a disability, and other populations at risk perpetuate stereotypes and prejudices. It is important that we all seek to tactfully but assertively indicate that we do not view such remarks as humorous or appropriate. We must also tactfully and assertively point out the inappropriateness of discriminatory actions by others against populations at risk. Such confrontations make explicit that jokes and discriminatory actions involving populations at risk are harmful; this has a consciousness-raising effect. Gradually, such confrontations will help reduce prejudices and discriminatory actions.

Grassroots Approaches to Improving Deteriorating Neighborhoods

Deteriorating neighborhoods in cities are a national disgrace. The United States is the richest and most powerful country in the world, yet we have been unable to improve living conditions in deteriorating neighborhoods.

Our country has tried a variety of approaches to improve living conditions in deteriorating neighborhoods. Programs and services provided include work training, job placement, financial assistance through public welfare, low-interest loans to start businesses, Head Start, drug and alcohol treatment, crime prevention, housing programs, rehabilitation programs, day-care services, health-care services, and public health services.

One of the most comprehensive undertakings to assist inner cities was the Model Cities Program, which was part of the War on Poverty in the 1960s. Several inner cities were targeted for this massive intervention. The program tore down dilapidated housing and constructed comfortable living quarters. Salvageable buildings were renovated. In addition, these Model City projects had a variety of programs that provided job training and placement, health-care services, social services, and educational opportunities. The results are more than depressing. The communities have again become slums, and living conditions are as bleak as, or bleaker than, they were at the start of the Model City interventions (Schaefer, 1993).

To date, practically all programs that have endeavored to improve deteriorating neighborhoods have had, at best, only short-term success. No other conclusion can be made. Deteriorating neighborhoods continue to have abysmal living conditions. The federal government appears to have given up trying to improve living conditions; federal programs for deteriorating neighborhoods have either been eliminated or sharply cut back.

Our society, for better or worse, is materialistic. The two main legitimate avenues for acquiring material goods are getting a good education and obtaining a high-paying job. It appears that many residents in deteriorating neighborhoods realize that prospects are bleak for them getting a good education (when only inferior schools exist in their areas) or obtaining a high-paying job (when they have few marketable job skills). As a result, many turn to illegitimate ways to get material goods (shoplifting, drug trafficking, robbery, and con games). Many also turn to immediate gratification (including sex and drug highs). A value system is developing that includes being resigned to being dependent on the government through welfare for a substandard lifestyle.

One promising approach to improving inner cities is grassroots organizations. These organizations can sometimes effect positive, long-lasting changes in a variety of settings, including inner cities. Grassroots organizations are community groups composed of community residents who work together to improve their surroundings. (It may be that lasting changes can be made only in neighborhoods whose residents are inspired to improve their community.) The following is a description of a successful grassroots effort in Cochran Gardens in St. Louis, Missouri (Boyte, 1989; Deparle, 2007).

Cochran Gardens was once a low-income housing project typical of many deteriorating housing projects in large urban areas. It was strewn with rubbish, graffiti, and broken windows, and its residents were plagued by frequent shootings, crime, and drug trafficking. Bertha Gilkey grew up in Cochran Gardens. Had it not been for her, this neighborhood might have continued to deteriorate. As a youngster, Gilkey believed the neighborhood could improve if residents worked together. As a teenager she attended tenant meetings in a neighborhood church. When she was 20 years old, she was elected to chair this tenants' association. The neighborhood has since undergone gradual, yet dramatic, positive changes.

Gilkey and her group started with small projects. They asked tenants what realistically achievable things they really wanted. There was a consensus that the housing project needed a self-service laundry. The project's previous laundries had been vandalized, and the only one working had no door and no locks (the entry door had been stolen). Bertha and her group requested and received a door from the city housing authority. The organization then held a successful fund-raiser for a lock. The organization next held a fund-raiser for paint, and that too was a success. The organization then painted the laundry. The residents were pleased to have an attractive, working facility, and its presence increased their interest in joining and supporting the tenants' association. The association then organized to paint the hallways, floor by floor, of the housing project. All the residents on every floor were responsible for getting involved in painting their floor's hallway. Gilkey recalled:

> Kids who lived on the floor that hadn't been painted would come and look at the painted hallways and then go back and hassle their parents. The elderly who couldn't paint prepared lunch so they could feel like they were a part of it too. (qtd. in Boyte, 1989, p. 5)

The tenants' association continued to initiate and successfully complete new projects to spruce up the neighborhood. Each success inspired more and more residents to take pride in their neighborhood and to work toward making improvements. While improving the physical appearance of this housing project, Gilkey and the tenants' organization also reintroduced a conduct code for the project. A committee formulated rules of behavior and elected monitors on each floor. The rules included no loud disruptions, no throwing garbage out of the windows, and no fights. Slowly, residents got the message, and living conditions improved, one small step at a time.

The building was renamed Dr. Martin Luther King, Jr., Building. (Symbols are important in community-development efforts.) The organization also held a party and a celebration for each successfully completed project.

Another focus of Gilkey's efforts was to reach out to children and adolescents. The positives were highlighted. The young people wrote papers in school on "What I like about living here." In art class, they built a cardboard model of the housing project that included the buildings, streets, and playground. Such efforts were designed to boost the self-esteem of the young people and to instill a sense of pride in their community.

In the 1980s, Cochran Gardens was a public housing project with flower-lined paths, trees, and grass—a beautiful and clean neighborhood filled with trusting people who had a sense of pride in their community. The high-rise buildings were completely renovated. There was a community center, and there were tennis courts, playgrounds, and townhouse apartments to reduce density in the complex. Cochran Gardens was managed by the tenants. The association (named Tenant Management Council) ventured into owning and operating certain businesses: a catering service, day-care centers, health clinics, and a vocational training program.

The Cochran success was based on principles of self-help, empowerment, responsibility, and dignity. Gilkey stated,

> This goes against the grain, doesn't it? Poor people are to *be* managed. What we've done is cut through all the bullshit and said it doesn't take all that. People with degrees and credentials got us in this mess. All it takes is some basic skills. . . . If we can do it in public housing, it can happen anywhere. (qtd. in Boyte, 1989, p. 5)

In the 1990s, Bertha Gilkey focused her attention, nationally, as she served as co-chair of the New York–based National Congress of Neighborhood Women, where she negotiated for government grants that supported the establishment of tenant management associations in New York and other cities.

Gilkey hired a professional manager, an accountant, and other staff to run Cochran Gardens in the early 1990s. In 1998 city authorities took over the management of Cochran Gardens, citing mismanagement by the tenant association. The buildings rapidly deteriorated under city management. Rental vacancies rapidly increased. By the end of 2008, all but one of the Cochran Gardens buildings had been demolished.

Although Cochran Gardens had a sad ending, the community prospered for over 30 years. It remains a symbol of the viability of grassroots efforts.

> The accomplishments of Cochran Gardens suggest that federal, state, and city governments to improve inner-city conditions by encouraging and supporting (including financially) grassroots efforts. Social workers can use their macro-practice skills as catalysts in the formation of grassroots organizations. Once such organizations are formed, social workers can provide invaluable assistance by helping them identify community needs and then plan and implement interventions to meet these needs.

SUMMARY

This chapter reviews some of the barriers inherent in worker–client differences and discusses some of the obstacles to workers' forming relationships with clients who differ in race, culture, age, gender, disability, or sexual orientation. The chapter provides information about how such obstacles and barriers can be overcome. Another section provides specific techniques and approaches that can be used (or should be avoided) in social work practice with Native Americans, African Americans, Latinos, women, GLBT individuals, children, rural clients, and clients with disabilities.

Generally, the difficulties workers experience can be attributed to four fundamental issues: (1) ignorance of the culture or characteristics of those with whom they are working; (2) retention of stereotypic perceptions of the target group; (3) insufficient knowledge of self; and (4) a tendency to rely on standard interventive techniques without regard to their appropriateness for the client group. The existence of these barriers may give you the impression that client and worker differences present obstacles that only superhuman effort by the helper can overcome. In actuality, the similarities between helper and client often outweigh the dissimilarities. Workers can de-emphasize some of the differences that do exist through those mechanisms that are important to all relationships.

A belief in (and practice consistent with) respect for the worth and dignity of the client is significant. A worker who is genuinely interested in the problems and situation of the client and who gives hope for improvement will assuage much of the division caused by racial, ethnic, cultural, or sexual orientation differences. Adhering to the values of the profession, though not a panacea, increases the likelihood that the worker in these situations will be accepted and accorded the status of a competent and sensitive professional. When coupled with a thorough knowledge of the client group, a depth of self-understanding, and a repertoire of culturally relevant techniques, the applied values of the profession provide an effective means to this end. Culturally competent practice seeks to incorporate understanding of diverse ethnic, cultural, and minority groups into the theories and principles that guide social work practice. Two concepts that are emphasized in culturally competent practice are empowerment and the strengths perspective.

EP, 2.1.1b

The chapter concludes with a presentation of macro strategies to promote social and economic justice for populations at risk. The strategies included social programs, mass media appeals, use of the Internet and technology, civil rights laws, activism, affirmative action programs, minority-owned businesses, confrontation of jokes and discriminatory actions, and grassroots approaches to improving inner cities.

EXERCISES

1. Diversity Self-Assessment

Goal: To confront your own attitudes toward various groups.

Step 1: Look over the "Diversity Self-Assessment Checklist."

Step 2: Take 10 minutes to complete the self-assessment guides. *Do not* note your name on these.

Step 3: Break into groups of six to eight and discuss your findings, focusing on what you have learned about yourself.

Step 4: Class discussion of the class profile and its implications for social work practice.

DIVERSITY SELF-ASSESSMENT CHECKLIST

The following table lists a number of individuals with whom you may come in contact in your role as a social worker. The questions should be answered with each of the individuals mentioned in mind. This exercise works best if you strive for honesty. Your responses will not be revealed to anyone in the class.

INSTRUCTIONS

a. Answer only one question at a time. Continue until you have answered the first question for each individual listed. Then proceed to question 2.
b. Place an X in the columns when your answer is "no." Also place an X if you hesitate before answering "yes."

Question 1: Can I greet this person warmly and sincerely?

Question 2: Am I comfortable interviewing this person? Can I really listen to his or her problems?

Question 3: Can I comfortably help this person deal with his or her problems?

Individuals	Question		
	1	2	3
1. Asian American			
2. Mexican Amercian			
3. Jew			
4. Gay male			
5. Native American			
6. Senile senior citizen			
7. Ku Klux Klan member			
8. Prostitute			
9. Blind person			
10. Alcoholic			
11. Drug pusher			
12. Farmer			
13. African American			
14. Lesbian			
15. Puerto Rican			
16. Person in a wheelchair			
17. Person with cerebral palsy			
18. Jehovah's Witness			
19. Pimp			
20. Person with a badly disfigured face			

DIVERSITY SELF-ASSESSMENT

This assessment will help you recognize areas of potential difficulty in working with various groups.

Be alert to any concentration of X's under the categories given, for they may indicate potential barriers to your efforts to work with certain groups. Transpose your answers from the "Diversity Self-Assessment Checklist" to this guide.

Question 1: Can I greet this person warmly and sincerely?

Question 2: Am I comfortable interviewing this person? Can I really listen to his or her problems?

Question 3: Can I comfortably help this person deal with his or her problems?

Categories	Question		
	1	2	3
ETHNIC OR RACIAL			
1. Asian American			
2. Mexican American			
3. Native American			
4. African American			
5. Puerto Rican			

(continued)

Categories (*continued*)	Question		
	1	2	3
LIFESTYLE			
6. Gay male			
7. Prostitute			
8. Alcoholic			
9. Drug pusher			
10. Farmer			
11. Lesbian			
12. Pimp			
RELIGIOUS OR SPIRITUAL			
13. Jew			
14. Jehovah's Witness			
MENTAL OR PHYSICAL DISABILITY			
15. Senile senior citizen			
16. Blind person			
17. Person in a wheelchair			
18. Person with cerebral palsy			
19. Person with a badly disfigured face			
POLITICAL			
20. Ku Klux Klan member			

EP 2.1.1b

2. Racial and Ethnic Prejudices*

Goal: To identify your racial and ethnic prejudices and to demonstrate that every one of us has racial and ethnic stereotypes.

Step 1: Assume you are single. Place an X by the following groups that you would hesitate to marry into. Do not write your name on this sheet. Briefly note your reasons for your answers.

___ Russian
___ Cuban
___ French
___ Mexican
___ African American
___ Native American
___ Puerto Rican
___ Italian
___ German
___ Polish
___ Norwegian
___ Samoan
___ Arab
___ Israeli
___ Chinese
___ Japanese
___ Filipino
___ Eskimo
___ Brazilian
___ Hungarian
___ Vietnamese
___ Pakistani
___ Korean
___ Anglo-American

* This exercise was written by Charles Zastrow.

Step 2: Class tally of student answers. Which group is viewed as least "marriageable"? Class discussion of reasons and the implications of profiling.

a. Do class results suggest that everyone has racial and ethnic stereotypes and prejudices?
b. How do stereotypes and prejudices develop in people?
c. How would you feel if you were a member of a racial or ethnic group being disparaged by others?
d. How can we eradicate stereotypes and prejudices?
e. Is such profiling ever justified? Why or why not?

COMPETENCY NOTES

The following identifies where Educational Policy (EP) competencies and practice behaviors are discussed in the chapter.

EP 2.1.4a *Recognize the extent to which a culture's structures and values may oppress, marginalize, alienate, or create or enhance privilege and power.*

EP 2.1.4b *Gain sufficient self-awareness to eliminate the influence of personal biases and values in working with diverse groups.*

EP 2.1.4c *Recognize and communicate their understanding of the importance of difference in shaping life experiences.*

EP 2.1.4d *View themselves as learners and engage those with whom they work as informants.*

EP 2.1.5a *Understand forms and mechanisms of oppression and discrimination.*

EP 2.1.5b *Advocate for human rights and social and economic justice.*

EP 2.1.5c *Engage in practices that advance social and economic justice.*

EP 2.1.10a *Substantively and affectively prepare for action with individuals, families, groups, organizations, and communities.* (pp. Chapter 12).

This chapter provides content on all of these practice behaviors, as it covers social work practice with diverse groups.

EP 2.1.1b *Practice personal reflection and self-correction to assure continual professional development.* (pp. 379–380).

Exercise 12.1 is designed to identify some of the stereotypes that students need to be aware of so that they can develop an objective approach to social work practice with diverse groups.

EP 2.1.1b *Practice personal reflection and self-correction to assure continual professional development.* (pp. 381–382).

Exercise 12.2 is designed to assist students in reflecting on their views about GLBTs.

EP 2.1.1b *Practice personal reflection and self-correction to assure continual professional development.* (pp. 391).

Exercise 12.3 is designed to assist students in understanding the worries and fears of certain ethnic and racial groups when they seek help from a social service agency in this country.

EP 2.1.1b *Practice personal reflection and self-correction to assure continual professional development.* (pp. 399).

Exercise 12.4 is designed to assist students in examining gender-role patterns in their families.

EP 2.1.1b *Practice personal reflection and self-correction to assure continual professional development.* (pp. 401–402).

Exercise 12.5 is designed to further students' understanding of feminist issues and feminist intervention.

EP 2.1.1b *Practice personal reflection and self-correction to assure continual professional development.* (p. 403).

Exercise 12.6 is designed to assist students in arriving at an opinion on whether same-sex marriages should be legalized.

EP 2.1.7a *Utilize conceptual frameworks to guide the process of assessment, intervention, and evaluation.* (p. 406).

Exercise 12.7 is designed to have students apply the strengths perspective to a homeless family.

EP 2.1.7a *Utilize conceptual frameworks to guide the process of assessment, intervention, and evaluation.* (p. 415).

Exercise 12.8 is designed to assist students in analyzing the merits and shortcomings of affirmative action programs.

EP 2.1.1b *Practice personal reflection and self-correction to assure continual professional development.* (pp. 418–420).

This exercise is designed to have students reflect upon their attitudes toward various groups.

EP 2.1.1b *Practice personal reflection and self-correction to assure continual professional development.* (pp. 420–421).

This exercise is designed to help students identify their racial and ethnic prejudices, and to demonstrate that every one of us holds racial and ethnic stereotypes.

CHAPTER 13

Spirituality and Religion in Social Work Practice

EP 2.1.7a

You are a social worker for the following clients. An older male client who displays manic-depressive symptoms informs you that he recently had an intense spiritual experience. As a result, he wants to quit his job, separate from his wife and grown children, and make pilgrimages to holy sites. How do you respond to his stated intentions?

A married mother of seven children who is a devout Roman Catholic is pregnant. Her husband and she both work full-time, but their combined earnings are well below the poverty level for their family size. She and her husband come to see you about their options for this pregnancy. They ask whether you believe abortion is a morally acceptable option. How do you respond?

A 75-year-old male with a terminal degenerative illness is in intense pain that painkillers are unable to relieve. He asks you for a referral for physician-assisted suicide. How do you respond?

A married couple contacts you for advice about a plan to physically kidnap their son from a religious cult. The son dropped out of college after joining this cult and now lives in a distant state in a cult commune. How do you respond to their request for advice?

Such questions pose various moral, ethical, and value dilemmas. Bullis (1996) notes,

> The spiritual issues clients raise are as diverse as the clients themselves. For some, grief over the loss of a loved one, a job or career, a marriage, or a child is spiritual. For some, decisions over pregnancy, marriage, separation and divorce, disease, terminal illness, or debilitating illness are spiritual. For others, the experience of depression, alienation, isolation or ennui evokes spiritual issues. For still others, crises of war, immigration, child custody disputes, child abuse, or domestic violence trigger spiritual concerns. Spiritual questions deserve thoughtful, deliberate, and authentic responses. (p. 9)

This chapter will:

A. Present a rationale for the use of spirituality and religion in social work practice
B. Describe four prominent religions
C. Describe spiritual and religious assessments of clients
D. Describe spiritual and religious interventions with clients
E. Describe social work and religion in limited partnership

SPIRITUALITY AND RELIGION

A major thrust of social work education is to prepare students for culturally sensitive practice. Because religion and spirituality play important roles in all cultures, it is essential that social workers comprehend the influence of religion and spirituality in human lives. The Council on Social Work Education's *Educational Policy and Accreditation*

Standards (2008) requires that accredited baccalaureate and master's programs provide practice content in this area so that students will develop approaches and skills for working with clients with differing spiritual backgrounds.

Spirituality and religion are separate though often related dimensions. *Spirituality* can be defined as "the general human experience of developing a sense of meaning, purpose, and morality" (Miley, 1992, p. 2). Key components of spirituality include the personal search for meaning in life, having a sense of identity, and having a value system. In contrast, *religion* refers to the formal institutional contexts of spiritual beliefs and practices.

Social work has historical roots in religious organizations. The philanthropic founders of social work were inspired by Judeo-Christian religious traditions. Jewish scriptures and religious law requiring the emulation of God's creativity and caring have spurred social welfare activities for many centuries. Similarly, the Christian biblical command to love one's neighbor as oneself is interpreted as establishing a moral responsibility for social service. This idea drove the development of charity organizations and philanthropy in the United States during the nineteenth century. Social workers need to be trained for effective practice with religiously oriented clients. Many social issues today—abortion, use of contraceptives, acceptance of gay, lesbian, bisexual, and transgendead (GLBT) individuals, reproductive technology, roles of women, prayer in public schools, physician-assisted suicide—have religious dimensions.

Social workers need to have an appreciation and respect for religious beliefs that differ from their own chosen beliefs. There is a danger that those who believe that their religion is the "one true religion" will tend to view people with divergent religious beliefs as ill guided, evil, or mistaken or in need of being "saved." More wars have been fought over religious differences than for any other reason. A major source of intolerance, discrimination, and oppression is this notion: "My religion is the one true religion. Anyone who believes as I do will go to heaven. Those who follow in some other religion are heathens condemned to eternal damnation."

Furman (1994, p. 10) notes, "The goal of incorporating religious and spiritual beliefs in social work curricula should include a broad array of knowledge of many different religious and spiritual beliefs, primarily to expand students' understanding and sensitivity." As a beginning effort to move in this direction, Exhibit 13.1 summarizes information on four prominent religions: Judaism, Christianity, Islam, and Buddhism. These religions were selected because of their prominence, but there are hundreds of other religions in the world. Practicing social workers should have a knowledge and appreciation of the religious beliefs and value systems of their clients.

RATIONALE FOR THE USE OF SPIRITUALITY AND RELIGION IN SOCIAL WORK PRACTICE

Traditionally, social work literature has tended to ignore the impact of religion or spirituality on social work practice. Loewenberg (1988) identified several reasons for this neglect: The psychoanalytic movement (which social work was involved with for many years) rejected religious approaches to furthering the personal and social well-being of people. Economic, political, and professional competition has at times existed between members of the clergy and secular social workers. In the United States, the separation of church and state led many social workers to avoid spiritual assessments and interventions with clients. Some social workers avoid spiritual aspects of human behavior because of their perception that spirituality and social work are totally distinct from one another. Spirituality has been viewed (erroneously) as having only heavenly concerns, and social work has been viewed (erroneously) as having only earthly concerns.

As noted in Chapter 1, the pioneers of the social work profession (such as Jane Addams, who founded Hull House) often used interventions that had religious or spiritual components (such as initiating and leading Bible classes) in providing services to their communities. In addition, many religious organizations are heavily involved in providing social services. Examples of such organizations include Jewish Social

Exhibit 13.1 Four Prominent Religions

Judaism Judaism is the religion of the Jews. Jews believe in one God, the creator of the world who delivered the Israelites out of their bondage in Egypt. The Hebrew Bible is the primary source of Judaism. (The Hebrew Bible was adopted by Christians as part of their sacred writings, and they now call it the "Old Testament.") God is believed to have revealed his law (Torah) to the Israelites; part of this law was the Ten Commandments, which were given to Moses by God. The Israelites believed God chose them to be a light to all humankind.

Next in importance to the Hebrew Bible is the Talmud. The Talmud is an influential compilation of rabbinic traditions and discussions about Jewish life and law. The Talmud consists of the Mishnah (the codification of the oral Torah) and a collection of extensive early rabbinical commentary. Various later commentaries and the standard code of Jewish law and ritual (Halakhah) produced in the later Middle Ages have been important in shaping Jewish practice and thought.

Abraham (who lived roughly 2,000 years before Christ) is viewed as an ancestor or father of the Hebrew people. According to Genesis, he came from the Sumerian town of Ur (now part of modern Iraq) and migrated with his family and flocks via Haran (the ancient city of Nari on the Euphrates) to the "Promised Land" of Canaan, where he settled at Shechem (modern Nablus). After a sojourn in Egypt, he lived to be 175 years old and was buried with Sarah, his first wife. By Sarah, he was the father of Isaac (whom he was prepared to sacrifice at the behest of the Lord) and grandfather of Jacob ("Israel"). By his second wife, Hagar (Sarah's Egyptian handmaiden), he was the father of Ismael, the ancestor of 12 clans. By his third wife, Keturah, he had six sons who became the ancestors of the Arab tribes. He was also the uncle of Lot. (Interestingly, Abraham is regarded as being an important ancestor or father in Judaism, Christianity, and Islam.)

All Jews see themselves as members of a community with origins around the time in which Abraham lived. This past lives on in its rituals. The family is the basic unit of Jewish ritual, although the synagogue plays an important role. Observation of the Sabbath, which begins at sunset on Friday and ends at sunset on Saturday, is the central religious ritual. The synagogue is the center for community worship and study. Its main feature is the "ark," a cupboard containing the handwritten scrolls of the Pentateuch (the five books of Moses in the Hebrew Bible, comprising Genesis, Exodus, Leviticus, Numbers, and Deuteronomy). Rabbis are primarily teachers and spiritual guides.

There is an annual cycle of religious festivals and days of fasting. Rosh Hashanah, the Jewish New Year, falls in September or October. During the New Year's Day service, a ram's horn is blown as a call to repentance and spiritual renewal. The holiest day in the Jewish year is Yom Kippur, the Day of Atonement, which comes at the end of 10 days of penitence following Rosh Hashanah; Yom Kippur is a day devoted to fasting, prayer, and repentance for past sins. Another important festival is Hanukkah, in December, commemorating the rededication of Jerusalem after the victory of Judas Maccabees over the Syrians. Pesach, the Passover festival, occurs in March or April, commemorating the exodus of the Israelites from Egypt; the festival gets its name from God's passing over the houses of the Israelites when he killed the firstborn children of Egyptian families.

Christianity Developed out of Judaism, Christianity is practiced in numerous countries and is centered on the life and work of Jesus of Nazareth in Israel. The earliest followers were Jews who, after the death and resurrection of Jesus, believed Jesus to be the Messiah, or Christ, promised by the prophets in the Old Testament. He was declared to be the Son of God. During his life he chose 12 men as disciples who formed the nucleus of the church. This communion of believers believed that Jesus would come again to inaugurate the "Kingdom of God." God is believed to be one in essence but threefold in person, comprising the Father, Son, and Holy Spirit, or Holy Ghost (known as the Trinity). Jesus Christ is also wholly human because of his birth to Mary. The Holy Spirit is the touch or "breath" of God, which inspires people to follow the Christian faith. The Bible is thought to have been written under the Holy Spirit's influence.

Jesus Christ was the son of Mary and Joseph yet also the Son of God, created by a miraculous conception by the Spirit of God. He was born in Bethlehem (near Jerusalem) but began his ministry in Nazareth. The main records of his ministry are the New Testament Gospels, which show him proclaiming the coming of the Kingdom of God and, in particular, the acceptance of the oppressed and the poor into the Kingdom. The duration of his public ministry is uncertain, but from John's Gospel we get the impression of a 3 year period of teaching. Jesus was executed by crucifixion under the order of Pontius Pilate, a Roman ruler. The date of death is uncertain, but it is considered to be when Jesus was in his early 30s.

At the heart of the Christian faith is the conviction that through Jesus' death and resurrection, God has allowed humans to find salvation. Belief in Jesus as the Son of God, along with praying for forgiveness of sin, brings forgiveness of all sin. Many Christians believe that those who ask for forgiveness of their sins will join God in heaven, while unbelievers who do not ask for forgiveness of their sins will be consigned to hell. The Gospel of Jesus was proclaimed at first by word of mouth, but by the end of the first century A.D. it was written and became accepted as the authoritative scripture of the New Testament. Through the witness of the 12 earliest leaders (Apostles) and their

(continued)

Exhibit 13.1 *(continued)*

successors, the Christian faith, despite sporadic persecution, spread through the Greek and Roman world, and in A.D. 315 it was declared by Emperor Constantine to be the official religion of the Roman Empire. Christianity survived the break-up of the Empire and the "Dark Ages," largely through the life and witness of groups of monks in monasteries. The religion helped form the basis of civilization in the Middle Ages in Europe. Since the Middle Ages, major divisions of Christianity have separated as a result of differences in doctrine and practice.

Islam Islam is the Arabic word for "submission" to the will of God (Allah). Islam is also the name of the religion originating in Arabia during the seventh century through the prophet Muhammad. Followers of Islam are known as Muslims, or Moslems.

Muhammad was born in Mecca. He was the son of Abdallah, a poor merchant of the powerful tribe of Quaraysh, hereditary guardians of the shrine in Mecca. Muhammad was orphaned at age 6 and raised by his grandfather and uncle. His uncle Abu Talib trained him to be a merchant. At the age of 24, Muhammad entered the service of a rich widow, Khadijah, whom he eventually married. They had six children. While continuing as a trader, Muhammad became increasingly drawn to religious contemplation. Soon afterward he began to receive revelations of the word of Allah, the one and only God. These revelations given to Muhammad by the angel Gabriel over a period of 20 years were eventually codified into the Quran (Koran). The Quran commanded that the numerous idols of the shrine should be destroyed and that the rich should give to the poor. This simple message attracted some support but provoked a great deal of hostility from those who felt that their interests were threatened. When his wife and uncle died, Muhammad was reduced to poverty, but he began making a few converts among pilgrims to Mecca. Muhammad eventually migrated to Hegira. The name of this town was changed to Medina, "city of the prophet." This migration marks the beginning of the Muslim era. After a series of battles with warring enemies of Islam, Muhammad was able to take control of Mecca, which recognized him as chief and prophet. By A.D. 630, he had control over all Arabia. Two years later he fell ill and died in the home of one of his nine wives. His tomb in the mosque at Medina is venerated throughout Islam.

The religion of Islam embraces every aspect of life. Muslims believe that individuals, societies, and governments should all be obedient to the will of God as set forth in the Quran. The Quran teaches that there is one God, who has no partners. He is the Creator of all things and has absolute power over them. All persons should commit themselves to lives of praise-giving and grateful obedience to God, for everyone will be judged on the Day of Resurrection. Those who have obeyed God's commandments will dwell forever in paradise; those who have sinned against God and have not repented will be condemned eternally to the fires of hell. Since the beginning of time, God has sent prophets (including Abraham, Moses, and Jesus) to provide the guidance necessary for the attainment of eternal reward.

Devout Muslims have five essential religious duties, known as "the pillars of Islam." (1) The Shahadah (profession of faith) is sincere recitation of the twofold creed: "There is no god but God" and "Muhammad is the Messenger of God." (2) The Salat (formal prayer) must be performed at fixed hours five times a day while facing toward the holy city of Mecca. (3) Alms giving through the payment of Zakat ("purification") is regarded primarily as an act of worship and is the duty of sharing one's wealth out of gratitude for God's favor, according to the uses stated in the Quran. (4) There is a duty to fast (Saum) during the month of Ramadan (the ninth month of the Muslim year, during which Muslims abstain from eating and drinking between sunrise and sunset). (5) The pilgrimage to Mecca is to be performed if at all possible at least once during one's lifetime.

Shariah, the sacred law of Islam, applies to all aspects of life, not just religious practices. This sacred law is found in the Quran and in the sunnah (the sayings and acts of Muhammad).

Buddhism Buddhism originated in India about 2,500 years ago and is derived from the teachings of Buddha (Siddharta Gautama). Buddha is regarded as one of a continuing series of enlightened beings.

Buddha was born the son of the rajah of the Sakya tribe in Kapilavastu, north of Benares. His personal name was Siddharta, but he was also known by his family name of Gautama. At about age 30 he left the luxuries of the court, his beautiful wife, and all earthly ambitions. He became an ascetic, practicing strict self-denial as a measure of personal and spiritual discipline. After several years of severe austerities, he saw in meditation and contemplation the way to enlightenment. For the next four decades he taught, gaining many followers and disciples. He died at Kusinagara in Oudh.

The teaching of Buddha is summarized in the Four Noble Truths, the last of which asserts the existence of a path leading to deliverance from the universal human experience of suffering. A central tenet of Buddhism is the law of Karma, by which good and evil deeds result in appropriate rewards or punishments in this life or in a succession of rebirths. It is believed that the sum of a person's actions is carried forward from one life to the next, leading to an improvement or deterioration in that person's fate. Through a proper understanding of the law of Karma and by obedience to the right path, humans can break the chain of Karma.

The Buddha's path to deliverance is through morality (Sila), meditation (samadhi), and wisdom (panna). The goal is nirvana, which is the "blowing out" of the

Exhibit 13.1 *(continued)*

fires of all desires and absorption of the self into the infinite. All Buddhas are greatly revered, with a place of special accordance being given to Gautama.

There are two main branches of Buddhism, dating from its earliest history. Theravada Buddhism adheres to the strict and narrow teachings of the early Buddhist writings; in this branch, salvation is possible for only the few who accept the severe discipline and effort to achieve it. Mahayana Buddhism is more liberal and makes concessions to popular piety; it teaches that salvation is possible for everyone. It introduced the doctrine of the bodhisattva (or personal saviour). A bodhisattva is one who has attained the enlightenment of a Buddha but chooses not to pass into nirvana. Rather, this person voluntarily remains in the world to help lesser beings attain enlightenment. This view emphasizes charity toward others. Mahayana Buddhism asserts that all living beings have the inner potential of Buddha nature. Buddha nature is a kind of spiritual embryo that holds out the promise to all people that they can eventually become Buddhas because they all have the potential for Buddhahood.

Source: From *Chambers Dictionary of Beliefs and Religions,* 2010. Reproduced by permission of Hodder Education.

Services, Catholic Charities, Lutheran Social Services, YMCA (Young Men's Christian Association), and YWCA (Young Women's Christian Association). Twelve-step self-help groups also have a spiritual component, emphasizing recognition of a "higher power." Examples of 12-step self-help groups include Alcoholics Anonymous, Emphysema Anonymous, Smokers Anonymous, Gamblers Anonymous, Narcotics Anonymous, Overeaters Anonymous, and Families Anonymous.

Social work, historically and philosophically, has links to spirituality. Philosophically, social work and spirituality are natural allies in working for personal and social well-being. Social workers and the clergy have numerous similar goals. Both promote personal and community welfare, both urge the ending of interpersonal violence, and both are advocates for family values.

EP 2.1.1b

The spiritual aspects of a person's life should be an important area of assessment by both social workers and the clergy. To ignore this aspect is a serious error. As indicated earlier, spiritual beliefs often are major determinants in clients' decisions in such areas as terminating a pregnancy, seeking a divorce, seeking physician-assisted suicide, entering the military (which may lead to deadly combat with an enemy), and using reproductive technology.

Exercise 13.1: Understanding Your Religious Beliefs

Goal: This exercise is designed to assist you in understanding and becoming comfortable with your religious beliefs.

Step 1: Summarize your religious beliefs.

Step 2: If you have questions about religion that you experience discomfort about (and many people have questions), specify these questions.

Step 3: If you wrote questions in the previous step, specify what you hope to do to obtain answers—such as talking to a member of the clergy or taking a course in the philosophy of religion.

Step 4: Do you believe there is "one true religion"?

___ Yes ___ No

If your answer is "yes," what is this religion, and what evidence do you have?

Step 5: If a social worker firmly believes that his or her religion is the one true religion, can that worker fully accept clients who adhere to other religious faiths?

___ Yes ___ No

Explain your view.

In a study from a national probablity sample of clinical social workers ($N = 283$) in the United States, Kuarfordt and Sheridan (2009) found that these social workers received limited content on religion and spirituality in their social work educational program. The authors highly recommend:

> attention to religious and spiritual diversity should be addressed in the curriculam to the same degree as other aspects of human diversity, such as race, gender, age, class, or sexual orientation. (p. 401)

In another study, Sheridan and Amatovon Hemert (1999) found that while social work students want more content on religion and spirituality in their social work education, they are receiving relatively little exposure to content on religion and spirituality in their educational program.

SPIRITUAL AND RELIGIOUS ASSESSMENTS OF CLIENTS

In the twentieth century many social workers (and psychologists and psychiatrists) ignored religious and spiritual aspects of clients' lives in their assessments. Today, helping professions increasingly recognize the importance of attending to religious and spiritual matters in assessments. The CSWE *Educational Policy and Accreditation Standards* (2008) identifies religion and spiritual development as important areas for social workers to attend to in their work with individuals, groups, families, organizations, and communities. The American Psychiatric Association's *Diagnostic and Statistical Manual–IV* (2000) recognizes spiritual and religious issues as an important area of assessment. For example, section V62.89, titled "Religious or Spiritual Problem," states,

> This category can be used when the focus of clinical attention is a religious or spiritual problem. Examples include distressing experiences that involve loss or questioning of faith, problems associated with conversion to a new faith, or questioning of spiritual values that may not necessarily be related to an organized church or religious institution.

What kinds of questions are useful in a spiritual or religious assessment with a client? Here are a few suggestions:

1. What are your main religious and spiritual beliefs?
2. What is your current religious or spiritual affiliation?
3. Would you describe yourself as strict or lenient (casual) in following the values and principles of your religious or spiritual affiliation?
4. What changes have occurred in your religious and spiritual orientation since your childhood years? What events or experiences were associated with these changes?
5. What was the religious or spiritual faith of your parents? Were they strict or casual in their beliefs?
6. How have your parents' beliefs influenced you in the past? Do their beliefs still influence you? If "yes," how?
7. What do you think are the most important spiritual beliefs held by your parents? Do you currently hold these same beliefs?
8. What are the main religious beliefs of the people closest to you (such as a spouse or partner)?
9. In what religious or spiritual orientation were they raised? Have they remained with this orientation? Why, or why not?
10. What, if any, religious or spiritual issues have caused problems with those you are closest to? Are there some current unresolved spiritual issues with your partner?
11. How comfortable are you with your current religious and spiritual beliefs?
12. Are you currently struggling with religious or spiritual issues? If "yes," what are those issues?

EP 2.1.7a

Exercise 13.2: A Religious and Spiritual Assessment

Goal: This exercise is designed to give you practice in conducting a religious and spiritual assessment.

Step 1: Ask a friend or acquaintance the 12 questions for conducting a religious and spiritual assessment. Summarize the answers here.

Step 2: If the person has current religious or spiritual issues, specify your recommendations for resolving these issues.

When you are conducting a spiritual assessment, your clients may ask you what your religious affiliation is. How should you respond? If your spiritual or religious affiliation differs from that of your clients, they may erroneously believe that the difference will interfere with rapport, with your comprehension of their spiritual dilemmas, and with solutions you may suggest. Therefore, a useful response is, "Our agency has a policy that instructs us not to share our religious affiliation." (To ensure honesty, you may well want to request that your agency adopt such a policy.) The underlying reason for a client asking this question may be that the client is trying to determine if the worker has the necessary knowledge, skills, and qualifications to help him or her. Therefore, it may be useful for the worker to add something like the following: "I think it is highly desirable for clients to assess whether a professional person they are beginning to work with has the necessary expertise to assist them in problem-solving the challenges they are facing. Let me briefly summarize my background and training related to your personal challenges." (The worker then summarizes his or her background and training.) The worker then adds: "If you have further questions, now or in the future, about my background and training, I'd be happy to answer such questions."

Nelson and Wilson (1984) identify an exception to the guideline that social workers generally should not share their religious beliefs with clients. In their view it is ethical for social workers to share their religious beliefs with a client if three conditions are met: (1) There is a high probability that such sharing will assist in problem-solving the client's issues. (2) The discussions related to sharing are held within the client's own belief systems. (3) Such sharing is defined within the intervention contract. (At the present time, few intervention contracts discuss such sharing.)

SPIRITUAL AND RELIGIOUS INTERVENTIONS WITH CLIENTS

Which spiritually related interventions should social workers use, and which should not be used? This is an important question! Spiritually related interventions vary widely, from referring clients to 12-step self-help groups, using or recommending religious literature in counseling, teaching spiritual meditation to clients, meditating spiritually with clients, praying privately for clients, praying with clients in counseling, using religious language or metaphors in counseling, touching clients for "healing" purposes, reading scripture with clients in counseling, helping clients clarify religious or spiritual values in counseling, referring clients to religious counselors or to members of the clergy, exploring religious elements in dreams, recommending religious penance or some other religious ritual in counseling, to performing exorcism. Which of these interventions are appropriate, and which are inappropriate? The social work profession and the judicial system have not established clear-cut guidelines, but a review of social work literature provides some ideas. However, many questions remain unanswered.

Sherwood (1981) and Keith-Lucas (1985) provide some guidelines for social workers with strong religious beliefs:

1. At times you may encounter major conflicts between the values of the social work profession and your religion. Possible areas of conflict include abortion, rights to be accorded to GLBT individuals, military combat service, use of contraceptives, use of reproductive technology, and physician-assisted suicide. Integrating faith and practice involves difficult judgments and compromise because every choice will advance certain values at the expense of other values.
2. It is possible to work with clients whose values are at variance with yours. It is acceptable for you to express your own values, when appropriate, as long as they are clearly labeled as yours and as long as you emphasize that clients have the right and responsibility to make their own choices (and to then be accountable for the consequences).
3. A social agency, particularly a secular one, is not an appropriate setting for a social worker espousing his or her religious beliefs.
4. When working in a social agency, you have an obligation to carry out the policy of the agency. For example, in a public health clinic, you must adhere to the agency's policies on issues such as discussing the use of condoms with gays and with unmarried clients as a means of AIDS prevention, providing birth control information to teenagers, discussing abortion as an option to a problem pregnancy, and discussing strategies for obtaining clean needles with IV drug addicts. Keith-Lucas

(1985, p. 32) notes, "One has no right to ignore policies or give them subtly some other meaning than that which the agency intends. Clients have a right to rely on an agency's consistency and Government or a Board of Trustees that its money be spent as it directs."

5. Should you be asked at the employing agency to do something that you cannot in good conscience do, you have three choices. One is to resign. The second is to refuse to carry out the policy (in which case you may be fired). The third is to advocate for a change in agency policy.

Many religiously affiliated agencies employ social workers who are not very religious. What should you do when a religiously affiliated agency asks you to do something that runs counter to the values of your profession? For example, what should pro-choice social workers do when employed by a Catholic agency that has a strict policy against discussing abortion as an option for clients? Workers in such a setting certainly have an obligation to follow agency policy and to not discuss abortion—but they also have an obligation to follow the pro-choice position of the social work profession. Workers in such a setting can resign, request that the agency change its policy (which a Catholic-affiliated agency in this situation will not do), adhere to the policy of the agency, or ask to be reassigned to another unit of the agency where they will not be serving pregnant clients. (It is perfectly ethical for a Catholic-affiliated agency to have a pro-life policy as long as clients know about it ahead of time. It is not ethical for an agency to call itself a "Pregnancy Counseling Center"—implying it offers all options—if it does not offer abortion as an option.)

The following guidelines may be useful in helping you decide which spiritual or religious interventions are appropriate (and inappropriate) to use:

1. Social workers should not use interventions that have the potential of resulting in harm to the client or to others whom a client interacts with. If you were to use such an intervention, you would be at risk of being sued for malpractice. For example, an intervention that is inappropriate for social workers to engage in with clients is a religious ritual involving the sacrifice of an animal.
2. Social workers should never engage in actions that can be construed as seeking to convert a client to the social worker's religious beliefs. Thus, encouraging a devout Buddhist to read the Bible is inappropriate.
3. Some interventions (such as leading a Bible class with clients that emphasizes adherence to Christian principles and values) may be appropriate in some sectarian (religiously affiliated) settings but will be inappropriate in most secular (not religiously affiliated) settings.
4. When you have questions about which spiritually related interventions are appropriate (or inappropriate), consult with your supervisor.
5. Social workers should use interventions with proven therapeutic value and generally avoid using techniques with no proven value.
6. Interventions that are clearly beyond the purview of social work should not be used. For example, administering sacraments (such as Communion) is the purview of designated members of the clergy and certainly beyond the purview of social workers.
7. Spiritually related interventions should generally be limited to those specifically identified in the intervention contract with the client. Such an intervention contract should be approved by the worker's supervisor or agency director.
8. It is crucial that social workers gain an understanding of their clients' religious and spiritual beliefs, traditions, and rituals—and of the laws related to these religious and spiritual practices. Three examples will be presented. Members of the Native American Church, a religious organization, use peyote (a hallucinogenic drug derived from a cactus plant) for ceremonial purposes; 23 states have now passed statutes allowing this church to use this illegal drug for sacramental purposes (Bullis, 1996, p. 89). In a major 1993 U.S. Supreme Court decision, *Church of the Lukumi Babalu Aye v. City of Hialeah* (Bullis, 1996, pp. 89–92), the Court ruled that the City

of Hialeah, Florida, could not prohibit members of the Santeria faith from sacrificing live animals (including chickens, pigeons, pigs, doves, ducks, goats, sheep, and turtles); this decision follows the precedent of other Supreme Court decisions that unusual or popularly distasteful spiritual practices are sometimes afforded First Amendment protection when the religious practice is a central ritual component of spiritual importance for a religious organization. In another area, Bullis (1996) notes several court decisions that have generally sided with cult members when their parents have sought to rescue or kidnap them from seemingly unusual and even bizarre spiritual groups. The courts have generally asserted that cult members' First Amendment rights and their ethical rights of self-determination outweigh the wishes of parents and other family members. Social workers who assist or even encourage parents in rescuing and deprogramming an adult son or daughter from an unpopular cult should be prepared to defend themselves against a suit for false imprisonment, intentional infliction of emotional distress, and other torts.

Bullis (1996) conducted a study to determine whether clinical social workers believe it is professionally ethical to use a variety of religious and spiritual interventions. Survey questions were sent to 294 clinical social workers in Virginia; 116 (44%) responded. Most clinical social workers in this survey believe that it is professionally ethical to use a variety of religious and spiritual interventions. The study also found that these clinical social workers use a wide variety of such interventions in their practice. Most social workers in the survey reported that they use the following religious and spiritual interventions in their practice:

- Explore client's religious background
- Explore client's spiritual background
- Use or recommend spiritual books
- Pray privately for client
- Use religious language or metaphors
- Use spiritual language or metaphors
- Recommend participation in religious program (Sunday school, religious education)
- Recommend participation in spiritual programs (meditation groups, 12-step programs, men's/women's groups)
- Help clients clarify religious values
- Help clients clarify spiritual values
- Refer clients to religious counselors
- Refer clients to spiritual counselors
- Help clients develop ritual as a clinical intervention (house blessings, visiting graves of relatives, and so on)
- Explore religious elements in dreams
- Explore spiritual elements in dreams
- Recommend religious/spiritual, forgiveness, penance, or amends
- Share their (the workers') own religious/spiritual beliefs or views

With the recent attention to spirituality by a variety of helping professionals (including social workers, psychologists, and psychiatrists), it is anticipated that ethical guidelines increasingly will be developed related to the use of spiritual and religious interventions.

In a review of court decisions involving which spiritual and religious interventions are appropriate (and inappropriate) to use in social work practice, Schoener (2000) concludes that spiritual and religious interventions are appropriate if *all* of the following conditions exist: (1) There is no evidence the interventions physically or emotionally harm clients. (2) The helping professionals inform clients of the spiritual and religious interventions that they use before contracting with clients for services. (3) The helping professionals are *in no way* using the spiritual and religious interventions to persuade clients to join a particular religious faith.

SOCIAL WORK AND RELIGION IN LIMITED PARTNERSHIP

Ram Cnann in *The Newer Deal* (1999) indicates that in the United States the "devolution revolution" (the federal government's surrender of its responsibility for the welfare of its citizens) has been gaining momentum since the 1980s (see Chapter 2). Devolution of social welfare is a broad national process that originated with the Reagan administration to shift responsibility for the administration of funding of social and health services to state and local governments and to nonprofit organizations. Devolution includes two complementary trends: privatization of service delivery and the end of some entitlements (such as the replacement of the program Aid to Families with Dependent Children with the program Temporary Assistance to Needy Families). Cnaan (1999) notes,

> Devolution is the antithesis of the welfare state in which the central government assumes full responsibility for the social and health needs of individuals with low income. In the United States, the process of devolution has resulted in the replacement of federal allocations for social services by smaller block grants to states. The states, in turn, asked counties and cities to do more with less and to engage nonprofit organizations in the provision of services. This process culminated in 1996 welfare reform legislation. This legislation not only substantially reduced the responsibility of the federal government for social welfare but also heightened both the visibility and the role of the religious-based services providers as a viable replacement. (pp. x and xi)

An important outcome of the devolution revolution is that the religious community (as it was in the 1800s) is again becoming a major provider of social services. The role of religious-based services provision in maintaining the local social services infrastructure is stronger than ever. Most religious groups now provide social and community services as a means to witness their faith, to fulfill religious teachings and beliefs, and to simply "do good" in providing for those in need in the community.

From 2008 to the time of this revision (2011), the United States, and many other countries, were in a very serious economic recession. Because of the shortage of funds, states and the federal government made serious cutbacks in federal funding for social welfare and social work programs. As a result, church-affiliated social service organizations were asked to expand their services to people in need, and as a result are becoming even more prominent in the provision of social services.

In regard to the principle of church and state separation in the United States, Cnann (1999) notes,

> Despite all the attempts to separate church and state in the United States, the two are quite interwoven.
>
> We would like to believe that church and state can be fully separated. However, this is not the case. In a country that calls upon the religious community to do more for the welfare of strangers and that willingly pays religious-based groups to do so, church-state separation is merely an ideal. Politicians recognize that the separation does not exist. Managers of religious-based social services also know it. After all, more than 50 percent of the budgets of Catholic Charities, Jewish Family and Children's Services, and Lutheran Social Ministries, to name just a few agencies, comes from the public coffers. It is now time for the profession of social work, its leaders, its scholars, and its practitioners to acknowledge the same: the church-social work separation is unwarranted.
>
> If the religious community is to be even more deeply involved in social services provision, then we must learn how to cooperate with organized religion to improve the lot of those whom we serve and whose interests we represent. We must apply a more pluralistic model, one that enables both sides to maintain their ideological and value stances while collaborating where possible and when beneficial for both. (pp. 300–301)

Congregations and church-affiliated organizations provide a wide range of social services, many of them partly financed by the purchase of care arrangements with federal, state, and local governmental units. Examples of social services provided by congregations and church-affiliated organizations include counseling; telephone reassurance; free use of church buildings for meetings by self-help groups, such as Alcoholics Anonymous, Narcotics Anonymous, Al-Anon, Alateen, and Overeaters Anonymous; emergency food assistance; congregate meals; soup kitchens; emergency shelter; mobile meals; cash assistance; housework for elderly and those with a disability; food preparations; legal help; brokering services; child care; after-school care; adult day care; tutoring; employment help; pregnancy counseling; foster care; housing for health clinics; food banks; housing rehabilitation; adoption services; and refugee resettlement.

Religious congregations and organizations are not solely "member-serving" organizations but also are "other-serving" organizations that are committed to improving the quality of life in their communities. Clearly, a limited partnership is emerging between social work and the religious community. Cnaan (1999) recommends the following:

1. That baccalaureate and master's programs in social work teach students about the increasing role of the religious community in the provision of local social services, which would include field placements that prepare graduates to work more effectively within religious-based social service organizations.
2. That social work professionals form coalitions with religious-based social services and other religious groups when planning and implementing community projects as a means of increasing both the legitimacy and the resource base of the projects, because religious organizations have the trust and support of many local residents.
3. That social work professionals offer consultative services to religious congregations to assist them in expanding or reorganizing the programs they provide to the community.
4. That baccalaureate and master's programs in social work educate students on the boundary issues between social work and religious organizations. At times the values and principles of the profession of social work and those of religious organizations will conflict. When conflicts occur (for example, between the pro-choice position of social work and the pro-life position of some religious organizations), social work professionals need strategies for resolving such conflicts.

EP 2.1.10e

Exercise 13.3: Benefits and Dangers of the Religious Community Being a Major Provider of Social Services

Goal: This exercise is designed to assist you in analyzing the merits of social services being provided by the religious community.

Step 1: Specify the merits and benefits of the religious community being a major provider of social services.

Step 2: Specify the dangers and questions raised by the religious community being a major provider of social services.

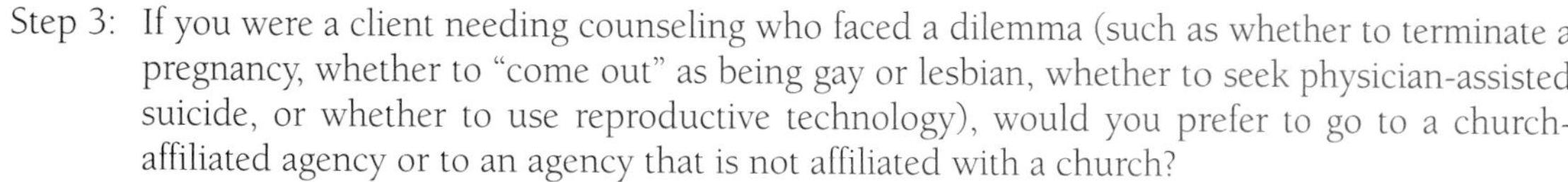

Step 3: If you were a client needing counseling who faced a dilemma (such as whether to terminate a pregnancy, whether to "come out" as being gay or lesbian, whether to seek physician-assisted suicide, or whether to use reproductive technology), would you prefer to go to a church-affiliated agency or to an agency that is not affiliated with a church?

___ Church-affiliated agency

___ Agency that is not affiliated with a church

Explain your rationale.

SUMMARY

A major thrust of social work education is to prepare students for culturally sensitive practice, including helping social workers comprehend the influence of religion and spirituality in human lives. The philanthropic founders of social work were inspired by Judeo-Christian traditions to pursue social work. Social workers need to have an appreciation and respect for religious beliefs that differ from their own chosen beliefs. Although social work literature has largely ignored religion's or spirituality's impact on social work practice, there has been a resurgence in recent years to attend to the spiritual aspects of clients' lives. Philosophically, social work and spirituality are natural allies in working for personal and social well-being. Spiritual beliefs are major determinants in a wide variety of clients' decisions.

This chapter summarizes the kinds of questions that are useful in a spiritual and religious assessment of clients. Some guidelines regarding appropriate and inappropriate interventions are provided. However, many questions remain unanswered in this area. It is crucial that social workers gain an understanding of their clients' religious and spiritual beliefs, traditions, and rituals—and of the laws and court decisions related to these religious and spiritual practices.

EP 2.1.1b

A limited partnership between social work and religion is emerging in the provision of social services in communities.

EXERCISES

1. Respecting Clients' Spiritual and Religious Beliefs and Practices

Goals: To gain background information about diverse religions, learn to respect religious beliefs that differ from your own, and become more comfortable with your own religious beliefs.

Step 1: Read Exhibit 13.1.

Step 2: Form groups of three and discuss the following questions:

a. Some religions assert that God is all-good, all-knowing, and all-powerful. If God has these three characteristics, why would God allow diseases like AIDS or send people to eternal damnation?
b. What evidence is there that God ever existed or currently exists?
c. Most prominent religions have a "bible"—that is, a book of sacred scriptures. Is one of these bibles more accurate in being the word of God than the others? If your answer is "yes," which book is it, and what evidence do you have?

d. Is there "one true religion"? If your answer is "yes," what is it, and what evidence do you have?
e. Can a social worker who believes strongly that his or her religion is the one true religion fully accept clients who adhere to other religious faiths?

Step 3: Class discussion of group thoughts.

Step 4: How does intolerance of others' religious beliefs contribute to other forms of prejudice, such as racism, sexism, and homophobia?

EP 2.1.1b

2. Timeline of Your Religious and Spiritual Journey

Goal: To describe the chronology of your religious and spiritual journey.

Step 1: Draw a timeline of your religious and spiritual experiences. Begin by drawing a straight line at the bottom of a sheet of paper and numbering the line with numbers corresponding to your current age; a 22-year-old student would have 22 numbers. Note significant religious and spiritual events that occurred at various ages—significant experiences with people, places, ideas, books, movies, churches, and so on. End with a summary of your current religious and spiritual beliefs and values.

Step 2: Form groups of three or four and share your timelines. (You may choose not to share.)

EP 2.1.2d

3. Using Religious and Spiritual Interventions

Goal: To explore the ethics of using religious and spiritual interventions in practice.

Step 1: You are a social worker at a *secular* (not religiously affiliated) agency. For each intervention in the following table, mark on a separate sheet of paper whether you believe the intervention is professionally ethical for you to use and whether you personally would be comfortable using this intervention at your agency.

Step 2: List the 26 numbers and the possible responses on the chalkboard. Ask each student to mark his or her responses on the chalkboard.

Step 3: Lead a discussion of the items and student responses.

Interventions	Professionally Ethical to Use		Personally Comfortable Using	
	Yes	No	Yes	No
1. Lead a Bible class				
2. Explore client's spiritual background				
3. Help clients clarify spiritual values				
4. Recommend participation in spiritual programs (meditation groups, 12-step programs, men's/women's groups)				
5. Explore client's religious background				
6. Explore spiritual elements in dreams				
7. Help clients develop ritual as a clinical intervention (house blessings, visiting graves of relatives, and so forth)				
8. Refer clients to religious counselors				

Interventions *(continued)*	Professionally Ethical to Use		Personally Comfortable Using	
	Yes	No	Yes	No
9. Use or recommend spiritual books				
10. Use spiritual language or metaphors				
11. Refer clients to spiritual counselors				
12. Pray privately for client				
13. Explore religious elements in dreams				
14. Help clients clarify religious values				
15. Recommend participation in religious programs (Sunday school, religious education)				
16. Teach spiritual meditation to clients				
17. Use religious language or metaphors				
18. Recommend religious/spiritual forgiveness, penance, or amends				
19. Share your own religious/spiritual beliefs or views				
20. Participate in client's rituals as a clinical intervention				
21. Use or recommend religious books				
22. Meditate spiritually with clients				
23. Pray with client in session				
24. Read scripture with client				
25. Touch client for "healing" purposes				
26. Perform exorcism				

EP 2.1.2d

4. Providing Services in Cases with Religious or Spiritual Issues

Goal: This exercise is designed to assist students in setting goals and objectives in working with cases involving religious or spiritual issues.

Step 1: State the goal of the exercise. Ask students to form subgroups of about five students each. Ask the subgroups to arrive at a consensus as to the goals and objectives they would set for each of the following situations. Have each subgroup select a representative to summarize the goals and objectives they arrived at for each case scenario.

a. You are a social worker at a secular agency. A married couple asks your help in rescuing (kidnapping) their 19-year-old daughter from a religious cult. The daughter dropped out of college and joined this cult. She is living in a distant state in a commune sponsored by this cult. Her parents ask for a referral to an organization that rescues adult children from such cults and also asks your help in deprogramming her once she is rescued (kidnapped). How do you respond?

b. You are a social worker at a secular agency in a community where a religious group that practices voodoo wants to relocate (voodooism includes the practice of witchcraft). An organization forms in your community with the objective of stopping this religious group from relocating to your community. The organization contacts your agency requesting any help you can provide. How do you respond?

c. You are a hospital social worker, and a nurse approaches you for help. A Haitian patient has requested that his spiritual adviser conduct a healing ceremony in his hospital room. The patient and his spiritual adviser practice voodooism. The nurse is concerned that the ceremony may be inappropriate in a hospital that is loosely affiliated with the Catholic church and that the ceremony may upset other patients. How do you respond to this nurse's concerns?

d. You are a protective services worker. A child abuse report comes in from a teacher at an elementary school that an 8-year-old boy is being emotionally abused. His parents practice the Santeria religion and require that their son attend ritual slaughters of lambs, pigs, and turtles. The schoolteacher asserts that forcing the child to attend such sacrifices is upsetting to him and therefore constitutes emotional abuse. You investigate and find that the child does become upset after attending such ceremonies but does not appear to be unduly traumatized. How would you proceed with this case? What would be your goals?

Step 2: After the subgroups conclude their discussions, ask the representatives for the subgroups to share their responses to the first case scenario with the class. After the representatives give their summaries, briefly discuss how you would proceed. The second, third, and fourth case scenarios are processed in the same manner. (Point out that some statutes and court decisions discussed in this chapter may provide guidance in setting goals and objectives for these case scenarios.)

COMPETENCY NOTES

The following identifies where Educational Policy (EP) competencies and practice behaviors are discussed in the chapter.

EP 2.1.7a *Utilize conceptual frameworks to guide the process of assessment, intervention, and evaluation.* (Chapter 13).

This chapter presents a rationale for the use of spirituality and religion in social work practice, describes four prominent religions, describes spiritual and religious assessments of clients, describes spiritual and religious interventions with clients, and describes social work and religion in limited partnership.

EP 2.1.1b *Practice personal reflection and self-correction to assure continual professional development.* (pp. 427–428).

Exercise 13.1 is designed to have students better understand and become more comfortable with their religious beliefs.

EP 2.1.7a *Utilize conceptual frameworks to guide the process of assessment, intervention, and evaluation.* (pp. 429).

Exercise 13.2 is designed to give students practice in conducting a religious and spiritual assessment.

EP 2.1.10e *Assess client strengths and limitations.* (pp. 434–435).

Exercise 13.3 is designed to have students assess the merits and shortcomings of social services being provided by the religious community.

EP 2.1.1b *Practice personal reflection and self-correction to assure continual professional development.* (pp. 435–436).

This exercise is designed to have students gain background information about diverse religions, learn to respect religious beliefs that differ from their own, and become more comfortable with their own religious beliefs.

EP 2.1.1b *Practice personal reflection and self-correction to assure continual professional development.* (pp. 435).

This exercise has students describe the chronology of their religious and spiritual journey.

EP 2.1.2d *Demonstrate professional demeanor in behavior, appearance, and communication.* (pp 436–437).

This exercise is designed to have students explore the ethics of using religious and spiritual interventions in practice.

EP 2.1.2d *Demonstrate professional demeanor in behavior, appearance, and communication.* (pp 437–438).

This exercise is designed to assist students in setting goals and objectives in working with cases involving religious or spiritual issues.

CHAPTER 14

Surviving and Enjoying Social Work

To be of help to others, helping professionals must first take care of themselves. Good emotional and physical health are internal resources that helping professionals need to be able to help others. In this chapter, we focus on how to survive and enjoy a career in social work. This chapter will:

A. Present common concerns of students related to majoring in social work

B. Provide safety guidelines for social workers

C. Describe burnout, stress, and stress management techniques

D. Present strategies for enjoying social work and your life

STUDENTS' COMMON CONCERNS

EP 2.1.1b

One of the surprises I found in teaching social work students is that although they have a number of common concerns, they believe their concerns are so unique and "secret" that they are reluctant to share and discuss them with others. In this section, I examine a number of these concerns and offer some suggestions for resolving them.

Will I Be Able to Make It in Field Placement?

Associated with this concern are numerous specific concerns: Will I be accepted and liked by the agency staff? Will I be accepted and liked by the clients who are assigned to me? Will I be able to help clients? Will the clothes I wear be acceptable? Will my shortcomings do me in? (*Every* student perceives a number of personal shortcomings—such as unusual tone of voice, inability to speak clearly, a low level of interviewing skills, questionable personal appearance, or inability to start and maintain a conversation. Students by far are their own harshest critics.) Am I emotionally stable enough to handle field placement? Will I be able to speak on the telephone? Will I be able to learn to do all the paperwork? Will I be attacked by clients? Will my car hold up, or will I be able to get where I'm supposed to be? Will I become too anxious and get stage fright when I'm assigned certain tasks?

In 30 years of supervising students in field placement, I have heard these and many similar concerns from practically every student. The students I worry about when arranging field placements are those who deny having such concerns; I have found that they generally are not perceptive about themselves. If people are not perceptive about personal concerns and emotions, it generally means they won't be perceptive about the thoughts and emotions of clients and therefore won't make skillful counselors.

Practically every student is anxious before field placement and during at least the first few weeks at placement. This anxiety is to be expected. You will find in field placement that your moderate level of anxiety will drain your energy. When you leave in the evening, you may be exhausted.

Although such anxiety and concerns are normal, there are ways to reduce some of these concerns.

1. In many social work programs, students have considerable input in choosing their field placement setting. If you have such input, use this opportunity to visit the agency you are considering for a placement. Meet with agency staff, ask them to describe the agency's programs and also discuss the expected tasks for student interns. Certain other concerns, such as expected dress code, can also be discussed. If after the visit you have serious reservations about taking a placement at that agency, discuss your reservations with the faculty who coordinate field placements. If your concerns are not allayed after this discussion, many programs allow you to visit another agency to explore doing a field placement there.
2. Ask other students who are currently in field placement or who have completed field placement to share and discuss their experiences and concerns. This will give you a better idea of what placement is like and may provide answers to some of your concerns. It is particularly useful to talk with students who have worked at the agency you are considering.
3. Discuss your concerns with faculty who coordinate field placements at your school. They will be able to answer some of your concerns and provide additional information about the agency.
4. Volunteer in your classes to role-play simulated counseling situations. Videotaping these sessions is particularly useful. Reviewing the tapes will enable you to assess and further develop your interviewing skills. Zastrow and Navarre (1979) found that videotaped role-playing of counseling situations also develops students' confidence in their counseling capacities.
5. Express any concerns you have to your agency supervisor. Make sure you understand agency procedures and policies and expectations for student interns. Open communication between you and your agency supervisor is an important key to making it in field placement.

These suggestions will reduce some, but certainly not all, of your concerns about whether you will make it in field placement. It is normal to be anxious at the beginning. As the weeks pass and you receive feedback that you are doing well, you will become more relaxed.

Will I Conduct a Satisfactory Interview with My First Client?

Concerns that relate to this question include the following: How will I know what to say? How will I keep the conversation going? If I say the wrong thing, won't it be a calamity for the client? How will I introduce myself? Will clients discover that I am only a student and therefore feel they are being used as guinea pigs to train me? What if I become tongue-tied and am unable to say anything? Am I really ready to assume the awesome responsibility of counseling others? I've got personal problems that are unresolved—how can I possibly help others?

Before seeing their first client, some students become so concerned that they can't sleep the night before; others develop tension headaches. A few students have told me they couldn't eat or developed diarrhea or were nauseated. It happens. If you have severe reactions, you are not alone. Just remember, it is highly unlikely that you will "bomb" during your first interview. Most anxious students report that once the interview began they relaxed and the interview went fairly well.

Here are suggestions for reducing your concerns:

1. Role-play simulated counseling situations, ideally playing the roles of both counselor and client. Videotaping and reviewing the tape is particularly helpful. Such role-playing will give you practice in counseling.
2. To prepare for the interview, identify your objectives, and think about the kinds of questions you will need to ask to accomplish them. Review the material in

Chapters 4 and 5 on how to begin and end interviews, how to build a relationship, and how to begin to explore the client's problems.

3. Clients are much less fragile than beginning counselors believe they are. If you fail to cover something, you can probably do so at some future interview. If you fail to phrase a question properly, you won't cause a calamity in the client's life. It is irrational to expect that if you make some mistakes in the first interview you will cause a disaster for the client. No one has that kind of power. Clients have been exposed to situations much more traumatic and chaotic than talking to you; they survived those experiences; they will survive talking to you.
4. Review the interview with your agency supervisor or your faculty supervisor to identify which aspects you did well and which ones you need to improve. Don't expect perfection—in your first interview or in *any* interview. You *will* make mistakes; everyone does. Remember, the main purpose of field placement is *training*—helping you test and further develop your social work skills and techniques. Therefore, agency staff expect you to make mistakes. The students who generally do best in placement are those who readily seek to apply the theoretical material they have learned about social work practice, because this facilitates the development of their social work skills. It is a serious mistake to "hang back" in field placement for fear of making mistakes. Focusing on making few errors in order to get a high grade usually leads student interns to "hang back," and this usually *lowers* their grade.
5. If you have specific questions before the first interview, ask your agency supervisor. Perhaps you are wondering whether you should inform the client that you are a student. Different agencies handle this question differently. Your agency supervisor wants to hear your questions and concerns. Only by hearing your questions can your agency supervisor determine "where you are" and how to be most helpful to you. Agency supervisors were once in training themselves. They are fully aware of the pressures and anxieties of being in field placement and are committed to helping you. Many have told me that the questions students ask frequently bring a fresh, new perspective to their practice, which leads them to make improvements in their counseling and interviewing approaches.

Will I Ever Be Able to Interview as Well as My Supervisor?

When student interns observe the interviewing and counseling skills of their agency or faculty supervisor, many become disheartened because they realize their skills are not as highly developed. They tend to "awfulize" and erroneously conclude they never will do well at interviewing and counseling. *Of course* your skills are not as good as your supervisor's; you haven't had 30 years in the field! Rome was not built in a day, and neither are interviewing skills. You *will* get better. Be patient, observe carefully, and *don't* think negatively!

How Do I Separate the Roles of Counselor and Friend?

Students generally have a small caseload in field placement, which allows them to spend considerable time with clients. It is not uncommon for clients to begin to become attracted to their worker because sharing personal concerns fosters an attachment. Students are also generally young and physically attractive, which also fosters attachments. Questions that students in field placement frequently have include, "Is this client beginning to see me as someone he wants to get socially involved with—how do I handle this?" "This client has invited me to her home—should I go?" "This client has suggested we have a cup of coffee (or dinner) together—should I go?" "This client has suggested we go to a park (or play golf, or go to a bar, or play cards)—should I go?"

There are no yes or no answers to these questions. Most agencies frown on and some prohibit fraternizing with clients. For example, if you as a probation officer socialize extensively with a probationee, problems may arise. The probationee might violate some conditions of probation and then try to use the friendship with you to avoid the consequences. Also, other probationees and parolees who become aware of the friendship may conclude they no longer have to rigidly adhere to the conditions of probation or of parole because you are "a nice guy" and "a soft touch." In addition, administrative officials will view the friendship as a conflict-of-interest situation and will disapprove highly of such a relationship.

Furthermore, if you become socially involved with a client, it is difficult to counsel that person effectively. The client, for example, may no longer be willing to accept suggestions from you—he may misinterpret the suggestions as being put-downs. Counseling someone you are socially involved with elicits clashes, not unlike when you tried to teach your sister how to drive a car.

Nevertheless, the attraction of client to counselor *can* be a component of a helping relationship and one that occasionally can be used positively. I've seen elderly, apathetic, depressed male clients in nursing homes become attracted to female student interns. These interns then used this attraction to motivate these elderly men to become involved in programs at the nursing home (such as hobbies and craft activities). Once involved in the programs, they started to enjoy them and as a result became more energetic, happier, and more active.

How, then, should counselors decide whether to accept social invitations from clients? The guideline is simple. *If* you believe doing something with your client will help you develop a working relationship and would be constructive for the client, then do it. Going to a park and talking helps some clients relax and develops the kind of atmosphere in which they will feel free to share and discuss their secret personal concerns. However, *if* you believe that accepting an invitation has the potential for being destructive to the helping process, then don't do it. If you believe going to a park will lead the client to conclude that you want to become romantically involved, then tactfully decline the invitation. (Establishing professional boundaries with clients is discussed at greater length in Chapter 2.)

It is useful for beginning workers to understand the essential difference between friendship with a client and a professional relationship. Friendship is for *both* of you to *give* and *receive;* a professional relationship involves the helping person *giving* and the client *receiving*.

Beginning counselors often wonder how, in practice, to separate the roles of counselor and friend. With experience, this problem usually disappears. Experienced counselors become more perceptive in determining the intents behind invitations from clients and more skillful in conveying the boundaries of the professional relationship. Experienced counselors also have more cases; this reduces the amount of time spent per client, which reduces socializing opportunities.

How Do I Avoid Becoming Too Emotionally Involved?

At one time or another, every counselor becomes overly emotionally involved in a case. I recently supervised a student in a child welfare unit at a public welfare department. One case assigned to this student involved a 14-year-old girl who had been in a series of foster homes since she was 3. The student, Linda H., became fairly attached to the girl. This client wanted to date, which her conservative foster parents could not accept. Considerable friction developed, and the foster parents suggested to the agency that it would be best for the girl to be placed in a different foster home. Because the girl felt rejected, Linda H. arranged a meeting between the foster parents and the girl to try to work out a compromise, but the meeting resolved nothing. After considerable effort, Linda H. found another foster home, and a trial visit was attempted. Linda H. indicated that she "felt like a nervous mother" about this visit. (Right away this statement led me to believe she was becoming overly involved.) The trial visit went fairly well, but after a day of reflecting, these foster parents decided they did not want to take a foster child at this time. Not only did the girl feel rejected, unloved, and depressed, but

Exhibit 14.1 Irrational Thinking Leads to Emotional Overinvolvement, Which Can Be Changed by Rational Self-Challenges

Irrational Thinking	Rational Self-Challenges
1. "This client has shared his problems, and therefore I must help this client resolve these problems." (Such thinking leads to taking ownership of the client's problems.)	1. "Clients own their problems and have the responsibility for resolving them. I do not have the power to resolve them. All I can do is help clients explore their problems, explore alternative solutions, and encourage clients to select a resolution approach."
2. "If things (events) don't work out for clients, I have failed. I am at fault for their problems. I am a failure."	2. "Everyone has ups and downs. We are all fallible, and we all have problems. If one resolution approach does not work out for a client, it only means that approach failed. It in no way means I am a failure. What the client and I need to do is to examine why that approach did not work out, explore other alternatives, select one, and try that."
3. "If things don't work out for clients, it is *awful, terrible, overwhelming, unbearable*."	3. "As Ellis and Harper (1977) pointed out, it is irrational to conclude that a problem is awful, overwhelming, or unbearable. Adverse events are often inconvenient and problematic, but assigning labels such as 'awful' only leads to unwanted emotions. Instead of viewing problems as being overwhelming, I need to take each problem one at a time and in a step-by-step fashion develop strategies to deal with each."
4. "If I don't solve the client's problems, the consequences for the client, the client's family, and others close to the client will be tragic, unbearable." (Overly involved counselors often view the consequences as being more tragic than the clients themselves view the consequences.)	4. "Clients own their problems and have the responsibility to resolve them. I am not God; I have no miracle power to resolve problems. All I can ever do is 'give it my best shot' in counseling. It is irrational and counterproductive to overexaggerate consequences. If the selected approach doesn't work, the client needs to select and try another."
5. "I've tried the only approach there is, and it failed. There is no hope. Things are certainly bleak for this client. I feel overwhelmed—I give up!"	5. "There is always hope. Even though I am unaware of other alternatives, there may well be others. I need to talk to an authority in this area to learn about other alternatives."

Linda H. became so depressed that she had to take 2 days off from her placement. She sympathized, rather than empathized, with the girl. Fortunately, she realized she was too emotionally involved at this point to search for another foster family. (She did ask the foster parents to keep the girl for a few more days until a new placement could be found, which they consented to do.)

As Linda H.'s example indicates, counselors who are too emotionally involved have a reduced capacity to help clients discuss their problems and to explore alternative solutions objectively with clients. Several types of irrational thinking lead to overinvolvement. Exhibit 14.1 lists these types of irrational thinking and presents rational self-challenges to counter them.

Beginning counselors are much more likely than experienced counselors to become overly involved. With experience, counselors increasingly learn that clients own their problems, that clients are the primary problem-solvers, and that to be of optimal assistance, counselors need to remain objective rather than exaggerating the consequences of resolution approaches that don't work out. (The main reason counselors are less successful in counseling close friends and relatives is because they are too involved to be objective.)

Yet even experienced counselors at times become involved. I speak from experience. A few years ago I was asked to provide professional help to a client for a number of personal problems—including burnout, grief over her husband's death, drinking problems, insomnia, depression, and lack of meaning in work or in living. She was highly respected in her profession. I realized I was giving myself the following irrational thinking that was leading to overinvolvement: "I must solve her problems. If she resigns her position this will be tragic, as several thousand people will be adversely affected. If this person resigns, it will be awful." By countering my thinking with rational self-challenges, I was able to help her explore her problems, one at a time, and we developed strategies to handle each.

What should you do when you feel emotionally involved in a case (for example, taking it home with you by thinking about it for several hours)? Here are three possible strategies:

1. Discuss the case with others, particularly your supervisor. Other people are often able to offer suggestions on alternatives and may be able to suggest ways to become more objective and less emotionally involved.
2. Do a rational self-analysis (described in Module 1) of your unwanted emotions about a case. This will help you identify your irrational thinking so that you can counter it with rational self-challenges.
3. Seriously consider transferring the case to another worker if your involvement is simply too intense. It is irrational to expect to be able to handle all cases optimally. You will handle some cases better than your fellow workers, and they will handle other cases better than you. Intense emotional involvement with a case for an extended period lessens your objectivity and indicates a transfer is necessary.

Do I Really Want a Career in Social Work?

Related concerns include the following: Do I have capacities to be a competent social worker? What area of social work (for example, mental health, corrections) should I pursue? Will a career in social work pay me enough money to live the way I want to live? (See Exhibit 14.2.) What do I really want to do with my life? What will my parents, friends, and relatives think of me if I become a social worker? Is there a profession or vocation that I would find more enjoyable and gratifying?

Most of these questions can be answered only by you. As far as the money question goes, faculty members in your social work department will be able to tell you about average starting salaries in your area for graduates of baccalaureate and master's programs in social work. Starting salaries vary considerably in different regions and in different positions. Pay increases are largely determined by you—your skills, your efforts to obtain advanced degrees, and your efforts to seek administrative and supervisory positions that generally pay more than direct services positions. Psychotherapists in private practice (who have an MSW degree and 2 or more years of counseling experience) can earn more than $100,000 per year. Skills at grant writing, consultation, public speaking, and developing new programs also are often financially rewarded.

But how do you determine whether social work is the right career for you and, if so, which area of social work to pursue? Only you can decide. Here are some suggestions that may help you:

1. Relax. Don't be in a hurry to make a final career decision. Some social work students think they have to make such decisions within a few weeks. Thinking about the pros and cons makes them so anxious they can't make any decision. In one sense you've got the rest of your life to make career decisions. Today people routinely start new careers in their 40s, 50s, 60s, and even 70s.

Exhibit 14.2 What Do Social Workers Make?

Social work, as most everyone knows, is not one of the highest-paying professions. What do social workers really make?

They make a teenager in a dysfunctional family find a focus in school and in his life. They locate two children to adopt for an infertile couple who yearn to be parents, and they rescue these two children from the alternative of being raised in a series of foster homes. They facilitate, through counselling, a marital couple problem-solving their marital issues, and thereby prevent a divorce.

They place a battered wife and her three children in a domestic violence shelter and then work with this family to find new directions in their lives. They empower a recently arrived Hmong refugee family living in poverty to learn English, to receive job training services, to be connected with necessary medical and dental care, and to find housing, and they place the parents in jobs that allow the family members to escape from poverty. They instruct and facilitate a young adult with anger management issues to learn to express her anger in an assertive manner and thereby empower her to get what she wants, rather than allowing her anger to get her involved in physical confrontations with others.

They empower a postpartum depressed mother with a young baby to challenge her negative and irrational thinking patterns and thereby alleviate the depression—and thereby also provide a better life for herself, her child, and her husband. They provide sexual assault services to a rape victim and thereby help her put her life back together. They assist a suicidal gay teenager to become aware and accepting of his sexual orientation and to begin to develop a lifestyle that provides direction and meaning to his life.

They provide a diversion program for first-time offenders for shoplifting (and similar offenses) that provides restitution to the victims and also deters these offenders from committing future crimes. They help organizations to recognize institutional patterns of racism and then make changes to reach out to better serve people of color.

They assist an older employee to make a solid financial plan for retiring and to also connect him with volunteer opportunities that will be gratifying for him and also benefit the community. They serve as a catalyst in a deteriorating community to form a grassroots organization to improve the neighborhood.

They provide family group conferencing to a family in which abuse is occurring, which empowers the family to end the abuse and keeps the family intact. They connect (broker) an alcoholic female in her 20s with AA and start her one-day-at-a-time recovery. They empower a secretary to become assertive to confront her employer about the sexual innuendoes that he makes, which thereby ends the sexual harassment.

They provide hospice services to a terminally ill male cancer patient, thereby relieving the pain associated with the disease and helping him make the most of his remaining days; they also provide services to the family members to help them through this difficult time—and then provide bereavement services to the family members after the patient dies. They find a quality group home for an autistic young adult and also place him in a job at a fast-food restaurant and job-coach him until he learns how to do the tasks that are assigned. They inform a 16-year-old pregnant teenager of her options and help her make plans for the adoption option she selects.

What do social workers make? They get paid to help other people—that's something most people would be inclined to do anyway. They make more than most people will ever make. They make a difference.

2. Try a trial-and-error approach. If you find one area of social work unsatisfying, try another. Skills learned in one area won't be wasted. You may find one area fulfilling for a while, but then find you need new challenges. If you really don't think you want a career in social work, fine; try something else—you may like it. Perhaps someday you'll change your mind and want to try social work again. No problem. You can take refresher or continuing education courses or attend workshops to polish your skills and learn new techniques and revised procedures. We have students in our undergraduate courses in their 40s, 50s, and 60s who are just now pursuing a career in social work. Do not think that this is your *final* career decision. Times change, agencies change, our interests and values change, and—yes, our careers change too.

Do not idly sit back and wait for some unknown force to decide your career path for you. You are in the driver's seat, and it's up to you to decide on the *first* destination of your journey and then to drive yourself there.

EP 2.1.1b

Exercise 14.1: My Concerns about Majoring in Social Work

Goal: This exercise is designed to have you identify your concerns about majoring in social work and to problem-solve these concerns.

Step 1: Specify your concerns about majoring in social work.

Step 2: Are your concerns consistent or inconsistent with the "common concerns" of other students?

___ Consistent___ Inconsistent___ Uncertain

Explain your view.

Step 3: If you have concerns that are not mentioned in this chapter, specify your plans for problem-solving those concerns.

SAFETY GUIDELINES FOR SOCIAL WORKERS

EP 2.1.7a

The social work perspective views violence as erupting in context rather than residing within the "violent individual." Rather than viewing some people as inherently violent, social workers understand that most violent behavior occurs because of interactions between the environmental context, the worker's interaction with the potentially violent client, and the client's internal dynamics. People differ in their tendency toward violent behavior and in the speed with which they convert emotions into violent behavior. The immediate context tempers whether a person with a shorter fuse (that is, more prone to violence) gets further agitated. Violent behavior is often a defensive reaction—the person expects harm or perceives a threat. Because the immediate environmental context is important, social workers are often able to use their skills to deter potentially violent behavior.

Environmental Signals of Danger

Context—the environment—may signal a violent situation. Certain situations have more potential for violence than others. Consider these scenarios. A protective services worker decides to remove a child from a home in which one, or both, of his parents are abusing him. A social worker at a battered women's shelter takes a resident to her home (where the batterer may be present) to pick up her belongings. A social worker at a police department goes with a police officer to a home where domestic violence is reportedly occurring. A social worker at a neighborhood center works with juvenile gang members to curb criminal activity. In assessing risk

Exhibit 14.3 Client Signals of Danger

Signal Type	Behavior
Angry verbalizations	Swearing, threatening statements, complaining, sarcasm
Emotional distress	Suspicious, hostile, irritable, unhappy, angry
Thinking difficulties	Confused, disoriented, hallucinations, paranoid ideas
Bodily changes	Trembling, heavy breathing, shakes, sweating
Speech	Sharp, loud, pressured speech
Signs of intoxication	Slurred speech, flushed face, unsteady gait, dilated pupils, lack of coordination
Body movements	Exaggerated movements, pacing, shifting positions, flailing arms, threatening gestures, clenched fists, pounding of fists on objects, wringing of hands, tense muscles
Facial cues	Muscle tension in face and neck, paleness, gritting teeth, dilated pupils, glaring, scowling
Agitation	Hyperactive, tenseness, ill at ease, overly anxious

in these and other potentially violent situations, social workers need to determine the following:

- Are there people present who are inciting the situation?
- Are colleagues present who can assist me?
- Are there obvious weapons present or objects that can be used as weapons?

Client Signals of Danger

Weinger (2001), in a review of the literature on social worker safety, has identified client signals that indicate an increased risk of violence. These are listed in Exhibit 14.3.

The best predictor of violent outbursts is a history of violent expressions. Clients who have a history of violent reactions stand a greater chance of becoming violent again. Therefore, if at all possible, workers should read clients' records before meeting with them. Diagnoses of antisocial personality disorder, borderline personality, and schizophrenia are also associated with proneness to violence.

Another indicator is a history of substance abuse. Alcohol intoxication lowers inhibitions and interferes with a client's judgment. Use of such drugs as cocaine, PCP, and amphetamines increases the risk of violence because these drugs increase the potential for agitation, suspicion, grandiosity, and delusional beliefs.

Yet another indicator is a history of child abuse or of witnessing repeated abuse at home when growing up. Sadly, children who have been abused are more prone to violence as adults. Other indicators of an increased risk of violence include fitting these categories: male, military combat experience, and having been incarcerated.

Regarding all these warning signals, Weinger (2001) astutely notes three caveats:

> First, although knowing the predictive factors may increase awareness, there are many false positives. Persons who do not resort to violence may also have these risk factors. . . . Second, in fueling the flames of racism we have often linked violence and crime to race. Although research has demonstrated that when different groups live in the same social, economic, and political environment their rate of violence is comparable, we have not always absorbed these findings into our mind-sets. Because of these distortions, for example, a social worker may too readily suspect an African American client and may overlook the warning signs exhibited in contact with a White client. . . .

> Finally, there is a potential to use predictors of violence in a way that will create more risk to the clinician. If clinicians forsake their level of alertness because a client doesn't meet the criteria for potential risk factors, they may overlook important signals. It is important to realize that a client who presents or does not present risk factors can exhibit assaultive behaviors. (p. 37)

Worker Signals of Danger

Pay attention to your gut feelings. This is crucial. You are already in social work because of your inherent ability to empathize and understand people. You pick up on signals probably a lot better than the proverbial "man on the street." *Use this ability here as well.* This doesn't always mean you will be correct in your assessment. You can be misled by personal biases, by cultural biases, and by misinformation. Also, always remember that gestures, body language, and verbal expressions have different meanings in different cultures.

The Assault Cycle

Kaplan and Wheeler (1983) note that most assaults follow a predictable pattern of five phases:

1. *Triggering phase:* Everyone has a baseline of normative behaviors. In the triggering phase, an event occurs that ignites the first deviation from the baseline demeanor. The event can be infinitely varied—such as receiving criticism or receiving a speeding ticket.
2. *Escalation phase:* Clients become increasingly emotionally aroused. Their speech, behavior, and emotions move away from their normative expressions. The best time to intervene is early in this cycle. Interventions can involve active listening, nonjudgmental listening, and problem solving, to prevent the agitation from escalating further.
3. *Crisis phase:* Clients are so aroused physiologically and psychologically that they are unable (or at least not inclined) to control angry and hostile feelings. They become verbally or physically aggressive. At this point, interventions such as active listening and problem solving are no longer effective. It is time to attend to your own safety, the safety of others, and the safety of the aggressive client.
4. *Recovery phase:* Clients begin to return to baseline behaviors but are still in a precarious state. If further events upset them, they can rapidly return to the crisis phase. To support the recovery, pace your interventions in response to clients' cues, and perhaps reassure them that they will be safe. Avoid disapproving comments, and do not explore the reasons for, and consequences of, the behavior.
5. *Postcrisis depression phase:* At this point, clients have calmed down and returned to baseline behaviors. They may even be more subdued than their normal baseline behaviors. They may be mentally and physically exhausted. They are likely to feel remorse and shame, which then make them more receptive to social work interventions. In this phase, Weinger (2001) notes,

   > It may be appropriate to reflect on the assaultive episode with the client . . . to help the client discuss the consequences of the behavior and deal with feelings of fear or guilt that someone got hurt . . . to understand the dynamics or events that preceded her or his losing control, and to consider appropriate choices and behavioral options for the future when she or he becomes anxious or angry. (p. 35)

This progression of reactions provides clues about when and how interventions can deescalate the situation. Thus, during the crisis and recovery phases, active listening and problem solving probably won't be helpful, yet these same techniques may be more than usually effective during the postcrisis phase.

Preventing Violence

The best way to deal with violence, of course, is to prevent it from happening in the first place. Usually the most constructive way to do this is to lessen perceived threats and feelings of helplessness. Fortunately, a variety of options help do just this.

Deescalate Verbal Communication Help clients express their feelings and thoughts—that is, let them vent. To do this, use your skills of active listening and reflecting feelings. This helps clients feel worthy. Use disarming (see Chapter 7)—that is, find some truth in what the client is saying, and then express this "agreement." Disarming also helps the client feel understood and validated and perhaps more open to examining another point of view. Use empathy (see Chapter 7)—that is, paraphrase what clients say. Restating their thoughts and feelings helps them reflect and move to problem solving.

Encourage clients to problem-solve. This can also help deescalate verbal communication. Weinger (2001, p. 38) notes that violence-prone clients have difficulty generating nonviolent solutions. They may need help thinking of nonviolent options.

It may be time for small talk. Sometimes redirecting clients' attention to less emotionally charged subjects deescalates verbal communication. For example, say, "It's really getting warm in here. Let's take a walk. We'll come back to this later."

Avoid aggressive, confrontational, or macho responses when a potentially violent client is emotionally upset. Such responses increase the likelihood of violence.

Deescalate Nonverbal Communication Weinger (2001, p. 39) recommends approaching the client from an angle (rather than head-on or from the back) in order to convey a nonconfrontational approach. Approach the client casually and gradually, so as not to appear aggressive. Maintain some distance, so that the client doesn't feel his or her personal space is being violated. Individuals with a history of violence often require a wider personal space than do less violent individuals (Weinger, 2001, p. 39). Avoid touching the client (other than shaking hands). Touching can be perceived as a challenge, or it may arouse emotionally charged memories of past physical abuse.

Some eye contact with potentially violent clients may be useful. It conveys interest, and it enables you to be watchful. However, sustained eye contact (and definitely glaring) should be avoided.

If your client's body language is agitated, mirror his or her body language, but do so at a somewhat slower and softer pace. This conveys that you are "in sync" with the client, that you are an ally. Once the client feels in sync with you, gradually reduce the intensity of your movements; often unconsciously the client will model this reduced level of activity. With this approach, you are literally leading the client to a more relaxed state.

Set Limits Many angry clients fear losing control. For such clients, Weinger (2001, p. 40) recommends that you say something like, "It's okay to be angry, but it's not okay to strike out. What can I do to help you feel more in control right now?" This statement clarifies that physical aggression is not acceptable. The tone and wording should support the client's worth and should not increase feelings of powerlessness. Don't come across as a parent. Don't be nonassertive. Both can trigger additional arousal. Set limits in a confident, assertive, but neutral tone.

Stay Calm and Generate Options As much as possible, remain calm. Communicate calmness, both verbally and nonverbally, even if you are agitated and frightened. An even, slow, soft-toned voice and a confident nonjudgmental, nonauthoritarian approach will reassure an agitated person but won't pressure him or her. Conveying your agitation can provoke aggression.

Remaining calm also helps you figure out constructive options (including escape strategies). Fear and anxiety interfere with generating and assessing appropriate options. Use relaxation techniques (described later in this chapter) and self-talk (Module 1) to calm yourself.

Safeguards in the Workplace

The nature of your work setting can increase or decrease the risk of violence. Disorganization, cold-appearing surroundings, staff conflict, isolated offices, overcrowding, and lack of an alarm system can contribute to the likelihood of client violence.

Safety accommodations in the workplace vary according to the field of social work practice and the type of clients. Different settings need different safeguards. Typical workplace safeguards include the following:

1. Metal detectors. Some settings (such as some schools and courthouses) now use metal detectors that screen for weapons. There should also be a dependable planned-response system when a weapon is detected.
2. Alarm systems and other security devices include cellular phones, intercoms, panic buttons, and handheld or mounted buzzers. Again, when using these systems, have a dependable, planned, and *rehearsed* response system in place.
3. Possible weapons. Be aware of items in the workplace that can be used as weapons. Limit the presence of potential weapons such as soda bottles, pens, ashtrays, vases, pictures, and radios. When interviewing potentially violent clients, remove your clothing accessories that can be used in harmful ways, such as neckties, dangling earrings, and necklaces.
4. Interview rooms should be in view and have two exits (for escape purposes). The agency may also choose to have a special interview room with a large window that other staff can view into or have a one-way mirror for viewing from the outside.
5. Furniture should be arranged so that staff (and clients) can make quick exits. Chairs that are light in weight can be picked up by workers and used as shields.
6. Pleasant surroundings. Waiting rooms and interview rooms should be designed for comfort and for stress reduction. Try to have soft lighting, comfortable chairs, current magazines, and calming color schemes (such as pastel colors).

Response Planning

Planning for "what if" scenarios needs to be an ongoing part of staff training and meetings. The following guidelines are useful:

1. Report and record all violent incidents. Agency administration should keep records.
2. Have a policy that informs clients and workers that violence will not be tolerated.
3. Schedule initial interviews with clients at times when other staff are present. Workers should never be alone in the office or building with clients who are identified as potentially violent.
4. Have strategies in place for summoning immediate help from other staff—such as cell phones or panic buttons.
5. Plan how the agency will respond to agitated clients—including when and how police should be called and how other staff are expected to respond.
6. Role-play and rehearse what staff will say and do when clients are verbally combative or physically combative.
7. Keep your colleagues informed of potentially violent clients.
8. Keep waiting time to a minimum. Clients waiting for service should be treated in a respectful, courteous manner and given an approximate estimate of the length of time they will have to wait.

Home Visits

Specific safety precautions need to be tailored to the individual situation. However, the following are some safety guidelines for home visits.

If possible, have clients come to the office, where safety is more easily achieved. If the meeting cannot be held in the office, try to hold it in some other public place, such as a library or restaurant.

If the visit must be held in the home, arrange for two workers (or a worker and a supervisor) to attend. If the potential for violence is especially high (as in helping a woman at a battered women's shelter retrieve belongings from home when the batterer is present), arrange for a police officer to accompany you.

Before home visits, obtain as much information as possible about your clients. Review the file for evidence of a history of violence and for risk factors (such as alcohol or other drug abuse). Determine whether others in the household present a risk. Also, find out whether there is an aggressive dog in the home or yard.

At the beginning of the visit, note exit routes. Wear shoes that facilitate a rapid exit. Don't wear expensive jewelry and clothes in deteriorating neighborhoods. Such items underscore that you are from a different socioeconomic class and thus unlikely to relate to the client's circumstances. They also tempt muggers and others in the neighborhood. Wear professional attire that presents you as a nonthreatening person. Make certain your agency knows your itinerary and location. Have a staff "partner"—you know your partner's location and approximate departure times, and your partner knows yours. Carry a cell phone and have it on. (Workers should call the agency if they anticipate being late.) Cellular phones should be programmed with agency and emergency numbers for quick dialing.

Present yourself as a confident, assertive person. Timid or aggressive behavior can elicit aggressive responses. If other people are present and appear threatening near your destination, you may choose to return at another time or day—and perhaps take another staff member along.

Park your vehicle in a place that allows for a quick escape. If a noisy argument is occurring at your destination, consider returning at another time.

As you enter a house, do a quick visual scan looking for signs of danger, such as weapons or drugs. Be watchful of *all* persons in the home. Ask who else besides your client is at home. If there are signs of danger, promptly and politely postpone the visit, saying something like, "I'm sorry, you're going to have to excuse me. I just remembered I'm supposed to be at another meeting. I'll call you this afternoon to arrange another time when we can meet." It's best, at least at first, to stay near the entrance door, in case a quick exit is needed. The bottom line when conducting a home visit is to *remain calm*. Being calm helps you generate and assess your options. And always trust your gut feelings. If it feels dangerous, it probably is.

BURNOUT, STRESS, AND STRESS MANAGEMENT

Ron Pakenham is 10 days behind in his paperwork. He has been a juvenile probation and parole officer for the past 3½ years. Both his agency director and the juvenile judge are pressuring him to do his paperwork. Mr. Pakenham also has problems at home. His mother has emphysema, and he and his wife are going through a divorce. While working on his paperwork, he receives a call from a houseparent at a group home for adolescent youths, inquiring when high school is starting in fall. (Mr. Pakenham supervises two teenage boys at this home.) Mr. Pakenham replies, "Hey, I don't know. You'll have to call the school system. I'm not your errand boy. Don't you know I have more important things to do than to hunt information for you?" Moments later, Mr. Pakenham regrets his response. Pondering his family problems and his mountain of paperwork, Mr. Pakenham realizes he is nearing burnout.

Definitions and Symptoms of Burnout

Burnout is a serious problem for helping professionals. Pines and Aronson (1981) defined *burnout* as

> a state of mind . . . accompanied by an array of symptoms that indicate a general malaise: emotional, physical, and psychological fatigue; feelings of helplessness, hopelessness, and a lack of enthusiasm about work and even about life in general. (p. 3)

Maslach and Pines (1977) studied burnout extensively among social workers, psychiatrists, psychologists, prison personnel, psychiatric nurses, legal aid attorneys, physicians, child-care workers, teachers, ministers, and counselors. They summarized a number of symptoms:

> Burnout involves the loss of concern for the people with whom one is working. In addition to physical exhaustion (and sometimes even illness), burnout is characterized by an emotional exhaustion in which the professional no longer has any positive feelings, sympathy, or respect for clients or patients. A very cynical and dehumanized perception of these people often develops, in which they are labeled in derogatory ways and treated accordingly. As a result of this dehumanizing process, these people are viewed as somehow deserving of their problems and are blamed for their own victimization, and thus there is a deterioration of the quality of care or service that they receive. The professional who burns out is unable to deal successfully with the overwhelming emotional stresses of the job, and this failure to cope can be manifested in a number of ways, ranging from impaired performance and absenteeism to various types of personal problems (such as alcohol and drug abuse, marital conflict, and mental illness). People who burn out often quit their jobs or even change professions, while some seek psychiatric treatment for what they believe to be their personal failings. (pp. 100–101)

Freudenberger (1977) described burnout as follows:

> Briefly described, burnout includes such symptoms as cynicism and negativism and a tendency to be inflexible and almost rigid in thinking, which often leads to a closed mind about change or innovation. The worker may begin to discuss the client in intellectual and jargon terms and thereby distance himself from any emotional involvement. Along with this, a form of paranoia may set in whereby the worker feels that his peers and administration are out to make life more difficult. (pp. 90–91)

Burnout as a Reaction to High Levels of Stress

We don't always differentiate being "burned out" from feeling alienated, indifferent, apathetic, cynical, discouraged, mentally or physically exhausted, and overwhelmed by stress. To better understand burnout, it is useful to conceptualize it as one reaction to high levels of stress. This suggests that stress management strategies can be used to prevent and treat burnout.

Stress is a contributing factor in most illnesses, including heart attacks, migraine headaches, diabetes, allergies, colds, cancer, arthritis, insomnia, emphysema, hypertension, and alcoholism (Sapolsky, 1998). It is also a contributing factor in numerous emotional and behavioral difficulties, including depression, anxiety, suicide attempts, spouse abuse, child abuse, physical assaults, irritability, and stuttering (Sapolsky, 1998). Becoming skillful in reducing stress is an effective way to prevent emotional and physical disorders, and it is also an effective adjunct to treatment for emotional and physical disorders (Sapolsky, 1998).

Stress can be defined as an emotional and physiological reaction to stressors. A stressor is a demand, situation, or circumstance that disrupts our equilibrium and initiates the stress response. Possible stressors include crowding, noise, death of a friend, excessive cold, loss of a job, toxic substances, arguments—the list is infinite.

Hans Selye (1956), one of the first authorities on stress, found that we have a three-stage reaction to stress—alarm, resistance, and exhaustion—and he called this three-stage response the "General Adaptation Syndrome."

In the *alarm* stage, the body recognizes the stressor, such as an argument, then reacts to it by preparing to fight or flee. Our physiological reactions are complex and numerous and are summarized only briefly here (for an extended discussion, see Sapolsky, 1998). The body sends messages from the brain (hypothalamus) to the pituitary gland to release its hormones. These hormones trigger the adrenal glands to release adrenaline. Adrenaline increases the rate of breathing and heartbeat, increases perspiration, raises blood sugar level, dilates the pupils, and slows digestion. This results in a huge burst of energy, better hearing and vision, and greater muscular strength—all reactions that increase our capacity to cope with the situation. During the alarm stage, the body's immune system functions at a sharply reduced

Exhibit 14.4 Conceptualizing Stressors, Stress, and Stress-Related Illnesses

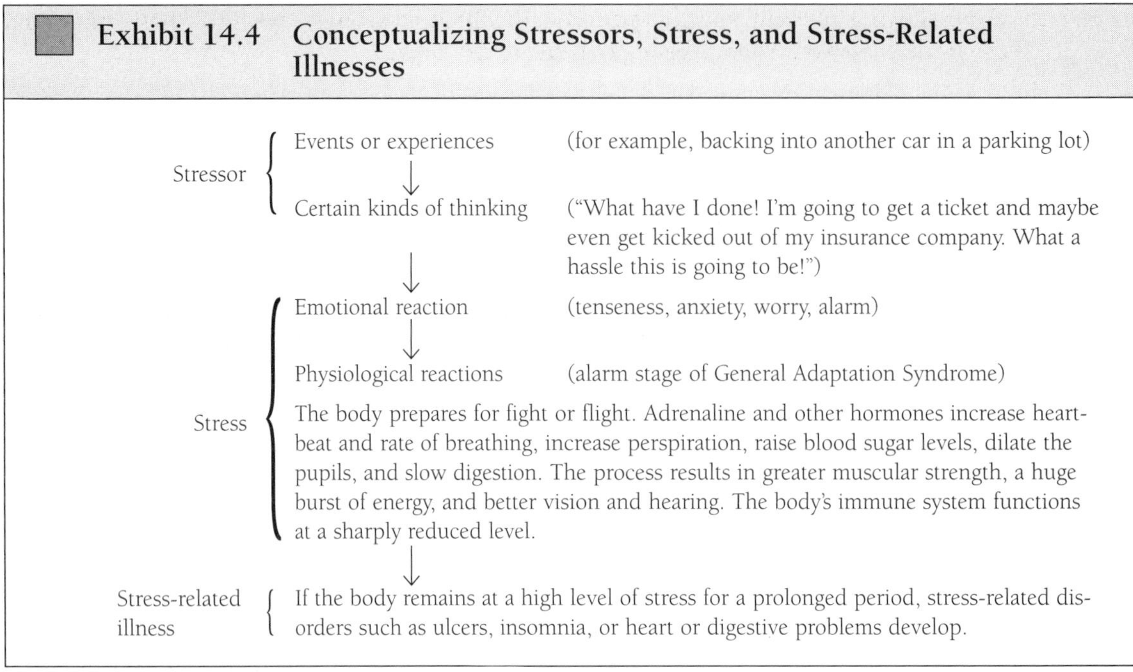

level. (The immune system fights germs, bacteria, and viruses and facilitates healing within the body.)

In the *resistance* stage, the body becomes relaxed. When the body is relaxed, the immune system functions at its optimal capacities. During this stage, the body (and the immune system) repair any damage caused during the alarm stage. Most stressors cause the body to go through only the alarm and resistance stages. During our lifetimes we experience these two stages innumerable times.

Are you aware that stress can be beneficial? It increases concentration and enhances our capacities to accomplish physical tasks. A life without stress would be boring and might even be impossible. Even dreaming produces some stress.

Stress that causes long-term damage results when the body remains in a stage of high stress for an extended period. When this happens, the body is unable to repair the damage and eventually reaches the *exhaustion* stage. This stage is characterized by the development of one or more stress-related illnesses, such as ulcers, hypertension, or arthritis.

EP 2.1.1b

Numerous authorities on stress note two components of stressors: the events or experiences encountered and our thoughts and perceptions about these events. This conceptualization of stressors, stress, and stress-related illnesses (Exhibit 14.4) suggests two general approaches for reducing stress: Change the distressing events, or change your thoughts and perceptions about the events.

Exhibit 14.6 provides material on traumas and stress disorders.

Exercise 14.2: Events and Self-Talk as Stressors

Goal: This exercise is designed for you to recognize your current stressors and to assist you in realizing that stressors consist of distressing events and self-talk associated with those events.

Step 1: Specify the events that are currently stressors in your life.

Step 2: For each stressful event, specify your self-talk associated with the event. (Self-talk may intensify or decrease your overall feeling of being under stress.)

Step 3: Which form of a stressor (the event or the associated self-talk) do you believe is the major contributor to the level of stress that you experience? Explain your views on this issue.

EP 2.1.1b

Exercise 14.3: My Physiological Reactions to High Levels of Stress

Goal: This exercise is designed to assist you in recognizing how you physiologically react to high levels of stress.

Step 1: Specify two events in the past week that were very stressful to you—where you physiologically were in the alarm phase.

Step 2: What physiological reactions do you remember having? Review the material on reactions to stress. Specify the physiological reactions that you remember having.

Step 3: Specify the stress-related illnesses that you have experienced. Also indicate (as well as you can) the starting and ending times for these illnesses.

Step 4: Rate the importance to you of learning and using stress management strategies:

______	______	______	______	______
Not important	Somewhat important	Fairly important	Very important	Absolutely essential

Exhibit 14.5 Burnout Is a Reaction to High Levels of Stress

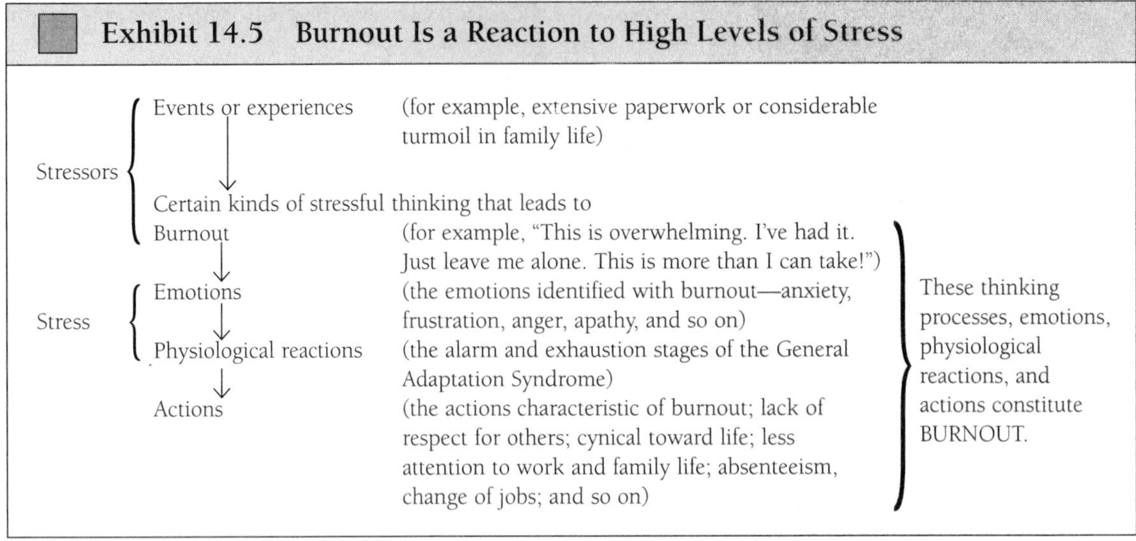

As noted earlier, burnout is one reaction to high levels of stress (Exhibit 14.5). Burnout is caused primarily by what we tell ourselves about events or experiences: "I've had it." "What's the use, whatever I try won't work." "I'm going to give up—I am no longer going to make an effort." Avoiding self-defeating thoughts reduces burnout.

Structural Causes of Stress That May Lead to Burnout

Because burnout is one possible reaction to, or consequence of, high stress levels, it therefore follows that events (structural factors) that contribute to high stress levels also contribute to burnout. Edelwich (1980) identified structural factors associated with work that contribute to high stress levels and lead to burnout:

- Too many work hours
- Career dead end
- Too much paperwork
- Insufficient training
- Not appreciated by clients
- Not appreciated by supervisor
- Not paid enough money
- No support for important decisions
- Powerlessness
- System not responsive to clients' needs
- Bad office politics
- Sexism
- Too much travel
- Isolation from peers
- No social life

Edelwich added that people who seek careers in the helping professions are particularly vulnerable to burnout because many enter this field with unrealistic expectations. They expect (1) that the services they provide will decisively improve the lives of practically all their clients, (2) that they will be highly appreciated by the employing agency and practically all clients, (3) that they will be able to substantially change bureaucracies to be more responsive to clients' needs, and (4) that there will be many opportunities for rapid advancement and high status. The frustrations experienced at work and the gradual recognition that many of these expectations are unrealistic are contributing factors to stress and to burnout.

Maslach (1976) found that large caseloads in the helping professions are a major cause of stress and burnout:

> Burnout often becomes inevitable when the professional is forced to provide care for too many people. As the ratio increases, the result is higher and higher emotional overload until, like a wire that has too much electricity flowing through it, the worker just burns out and emotionally disconnects. (p. 19)

A lack of approved *timeouts* at work is another source of stress and may be a factor in burnout. Timeouts are not merely short coffee breaks; they are opportunities for professionals having a stressful day to switch to less stressful tasks. Timeouts are possible in large agencies that have shared work responsibilities.

Additional causes of burnout include poor time management, inability to work effectively with other people, lack of purpose or undefined goals in life, and inability to handle effectively emergencies that arise (Pines & Aronson, 1981).

Clients can add to staff burnout (Maslach, 1978). Some clients cause high levels of stress, particularly those with depressing or emotionally draining problems (such as terminally ill clients, belligerent clients, suicidal clients, obnoxious clients, incest cases, and severe abuse cases). Chronic clients who show no improvement (such as an alcoholic family in which the problem drinker denies a drinking problem) can lead to frustration and high stress levels for workers. So can clients who remind workers of personal difficulties they presently face, such as providing marriage counseling services when workers are having marital difficulties at home. Extensive home responsibilities, such as taking care of a terminally ill parent, can also drain energy needed at home and at work.

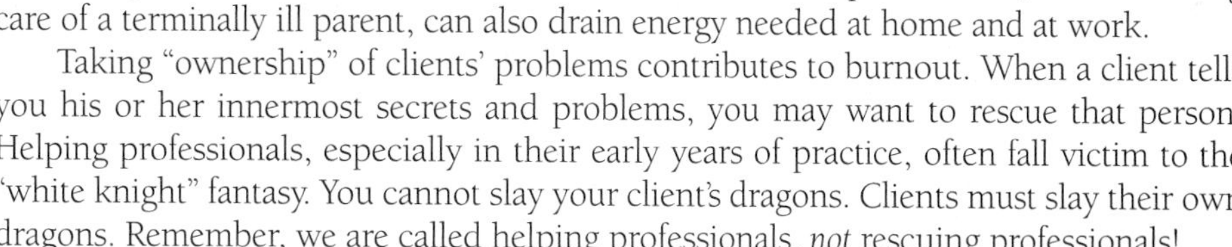

EP 2.1.1b

Taking "ownership" of clients' problems contributes to burnout. When a client tells you his or her innermost secrets and problems, you may want to rescue that person. Helping professionals, especially in their early years of practice, often fall victim to the "white knight" fantasy. You cannot slay your client's dragons. Clients must slay their own dragons. Remember, we are called helping professionals, *not* rescuing professionals!

Exercise 14.4: A Time When I Burned Out

Goal: This exercise is designed to help you recognize what you can do when you experience burnout.

Step 1: Describe a time in your life when you experienced burnout. When you were experiencing burnout, did you conclude (for a while), "I can't take this anymore"?

Step 2: If you have recovered from feeling burned out, describe what helped you to recover. If you are still feeling burned out, speculate about what you need to do to make progress in recovering.

Approaches to Manage Stress and Prevent Burnout

Okay, you ask, so what can I do to avoid burnout? Lots of things, it turns out. What follows is a small sampling of strategies. The key is to select strategies you will be most motivated to use. These strategies parallel healthy diet plans—they work for those who put forth effort to make them work. (The references provide expanded reading on these strategies.)

Exhibit 14.6 Traumas and Stress Disorders

Physical trauma is an injury to the body caused by violence or accident, such as a fracture, bruise, and so forth. Psychological trauma is an emotional wound or shock, often having long-lasting effects. Physical traumas often lead to psychological traumas.

Traumatic experiences often involve a threat to life or safety, but any situation that leaves one feeling overwhelmed and alone can be traumatic even if it does not involve physical harm. It's not the objective facts that determine whether an event is traumatic, but one's subjective emotional experience of the event.

A stressful event is most likely to be traumatic if:

- It happened unexpectedly.
- One is unprepared for it.
- It happened repeatedly.
- One felt powerless to prevent it.
- Someone was intentionally cruel.

Traumas can come in a huge variety of ways. The following is a short list: serving in combat in the military, being physically or sexually abused as a child, a sexual assault, an auto accident, the breakup of a significant relationship, a humiliating or deeply disappointing experience, and the discovery of a life-threatening illness or disabling condition.

People are more likely to be traumatized by a stressful experience if they are already under a heavy stress load or have recently suffered a series of losses. Not all potentially traumatic events lead to lasting psychological and emotional damage, some people rebound quickly from even the most shocking and tragic experiences, while others are devastated by experiences that appear on the surface to be "mildly upsetting."

Traumatic experiences in childhood can have a severe and long-lasting impact. Children who have been traumatized see the world as a dangerous and frightening place. When childhood trauma is unresolved, this sense of fear and helplessness carries over into adulthood, setting the stage for further trauma.

Emotional symptoms of trauma include:

- Denial, shock, or disbelief
- Anxiety and fear
- Withdrawing from others
- Feeling numb or disconnected
- Anger, irritability, mood swings
- Confusion, difficulty concentrating
- Guilt, self-blame, shame
- Feeling hopeless or sad

Physical symptoms of trauma include:

- Aches and pains
- Fatigue
- Muscle tension
- Being startled easily
- Racing heart beat
- Agitation and edginess
- Difficulty concentrating

These emotional and physical symptoms gradually fade *if* the impacted person makes progress in coming to terms with the trauma. But even if the person is progressing in resolving the trauma, the person may be troubled from time to time by painful memories and emotions. Triggers for reliving the painful event include the anniversary of the event, or sounds and images of the situation that remind the traumatized individual of the traumatic experience.

There are two stress disorders associated with severe traumas: acute stress disorder and posttraumatic stress disorder (PTSD). Acute stress disorder is an anxiety disorder in which fear and related symptoms are experienced soon after a traumatic event and last less than a month (American Psychiatric Association, 2000).

Posttraumatic stress disorder is an anxiety disorder in which fear and related symptoms continue to be experienced long after a traumatic event (American Psychiatric Association, 2000). Primary symptoms of PTSD include flashbacks or intrusive memories, living in a constant state of "red alert," and avoiding things that remind the impacted person of the traumatic event.

Working through trauma can be painful, scary, and potentially retraumatizing. The "healing" work is best done with a competent trauma expert, Trauma treatment involves:

- Processing the trauma memories and feelings
- Discharging the pent-up emotions/energy associated with the trauma
- Learning how to control strong emotions
- Rebuilding the capacity to trust other people

Treatment approaches for PTSD include the following:

- Cognitive-behavioral therapy, such as rational therapy (described in Module 1), in which the person learns to reframe the disturbing traumatic thoughts.
- Antianxiety drugs, which help control the anxieties and tensions associated with PTSD. Such medication provides some relief but needs to be combined with a "talk" therapy approach.
- Eye movement desensitization and reprocessing (EMDR), which incorporates elements of cognitive-behavioral therapy, in which the impacted persons move their eyes in a rhythmic manner from side to side while flooding their minds with images of the objects and situations they try to avoid. These back-and-forth eye movements are thought to work by "unfreezing" traumatic memories, which then can be processed and resolved.

Goal Setting and Time Management Not knowing what you want out of life is distressing and even depressing. Many people muddle through life without ever setting goals. The result? Frustration and boredom. (Boredom, by the way, is highly stressful.) The solution? Realistic goal setting. What do you get? Increased self-confidence, improved decision making, a greater sense of purpose, and an improved sense of security. Do you set goals, or do you muddle?

Time is life, and to waste time is to waste life. Managing your time well is empowering. Time management approaches help you set goals and use your time effectively to reach short-term and lifetime goals (Lakein, 1973). First, set lifetime and short-term goals. (Admittedly this can be a lengthy process, but failure to set goals almost guarantees feeling unfulfilled and dissatisfied.) Next, write down tasks that will help you accomplish your high-priority goals—both short-term and lifetime. Then prioritize tasks according to what is most important to do to accomplish each goal. Do the high-priority tasks first and—generally—ignore doing the low-priority (low-payoff) tasks. Low-priority tasks consume time and interfere with your high-priority tasks.

EP 2.1.3a

Exercise 14.5: My High-Value Goals and Tasks

Goal: This exercise is designed to assist you in specifying your short-range and long-range goals, and to identify tasks that will help you achieve these goals.

Step 1: List your goals for the next 6 months on one sheet of paper, and list your long-range goals on another.

Step 2: Prioritize your goals by assigning "A" to high-value goals, "B" to medium-value goals, and "C" to low-value goals. Next, rank the A, or high-value, goals in order: A-1, A-2, A-3, and so on.

Step 3: List the tasks needed to achieve the specified A goals.

Step 4: Prioritize each task's value in achieving each of your A goals using the A, B, C, and so forth approach.

Note: If this process is conscientiously followed, you will have a clear vision of your goals in life and what you need to do to achieve these goals.

Positive Thinking Is your cup half full or half empty? You and you alone choose how you view your "cup of life." Negative self-talk ("I've had it. I'm no longer going to try. I'm just going to go through the motions. I'm giving in.") becomes self-fulfilling.

Choose positive thinking. Taking a positive view and positive action not only leads to others' liking you, but you will also feel worthwhile, you will like yourself, you will be productive and creative, and good things will happen. (Positive thinking is discussed more fully later in this chapter.)

Travel through life at a "relaxed cruising speed." Look at the scenery with enjoyment, remain calm during crises and emergencies, approach work thoughtfully and strive to be creative, and enjoy your leisure.

Changing "Burnout Thoughts" Rational therapy (Module 1) demonstrates that what we tell ourselves about our experiences causes our emotions and shapes future actions. Burnout is thus primarily determined by our thinking processes.

Although we cannot change events that happen to us, we can think rationally and positively about events. Challenge your "burnout thoughts": "I am *not* going to give up. I've handled challenges in the past, and I can handle this one. One step at a time, that's what I have to do. When the going gets tough, I get going."

Keys to changing "burnout thoughts": (1) Recognize when you are thinking them. (2) Select positive thoughts that challenge burnout ones. And (3) every time you start thinking burnout thoughts, replace them with positive thoughts.

Relaxation Techniques Burnout doesn't happen in a day, but it does happen one day at a time. The days accumulate, and bingo, you're in burnout. So challenge burnout one day at a time. How? By taking the time to relax. The relaxation response is a powerful challenge to burnout. Use it. Three relaxation techniques are described in Exhibit 14.7.

Exhibit 14.7 Three Relaxation Techniques

There is considerable evidence that relaxation techniques reduce stress and anxiety through a simple set of general procedures that can be learned without elaborate rituals or large expense (Seaward, 2005). A strong advocate of this view is Herbert Benson, a Harvard cardiologist who carefully reviewed contemporary relaxation techniques. Benson (1975) identified the following four elements as key to eliciting the relaxation response in any relaxation approach:

1. *Being in a quiet environment* that facilitates tuning out external distractions and internal stimuli.
2. *Being in a comfortable position,* such as sitting or lying down. The position should be one in which the person relaxing can feel comfortable for at least 20 minutes.
3. *Having an object to dwell on,* which also facilitates tuning out thoughts about day-to-day concerns. Examples of suitable objects include one's breathing, a word or phrase chanted to oneself, an audiotape of ocean waves, a symbol to be gazed at steadily, or the sights and sounds of a relaxing place, visualized with one's eyes closed.
4. *Having a passive attitude,* in which the user of the relaxation technique "lets go" of day-to-day concerns. A passive attitude appears to be key to eliciting the relaxation response; people become relaxed when they focus their cognitions on relaxing thoughts and stop thinking about everyday problems. If day-to-day concerns drift into the person's awareness, he or she should allow them to pass on as effortlessly as possible.

The following three relaxation techniques will be presented here: deep breathing, imagery relaxation, and meditation.

Deep-Breathing Relaxation

Brown (1977) describes the deep-breathing technique:

RELAXATION TECHNIQUE: DEEP BREATHING (5 MINUTES)

1. Select a comfortable sitting position.
2. Close your eyes and direct your attention to your own breathing process.
3. Think about nothing but your breath, as it flows in and out of your body.
4. Say to yourself something like this: "I am relaxing, breathing smoothly and rhythmically. Fresh oxygen flows in and out of my body. I feel calm, renewed, and refreshed."
5. Continue to focus on your breathing as it flows in and out, in and out, thinking of nothing but the smooth, rhythmical process of your own breathing.
6. After 5 minutes, stand up, stretch, smile, and continue with your daily activities.*

Imagery Relaxation

Brown (1977) describes this approach:

1. Select a comfortable sitting or reclining position.
2. Close your eyes, and think about a place that you have been before that represents your ideal place for physical and mental relaxation. (It should be a quiet environment, perhaps the seashore, the mountains, or even your own backyard. If you can't think of an ideal relaxation place, then create one in your mind.)
3. Now imagine that you are actually in your ideal relaxation place. Imagine that you are seeing all the colors, hearing the sounds, smelling the aromas. Just lie back, and enjoy your soothing, rejuvenating environment.
4. Feel the peacefulness, the calmness, and imagine your whole body and mind being renewed and refreshed.
5. After 5 to 10 minutes, open your eyes and stretch. You have the realization that you may instantly return to your relaxation place whenever you desire, and experience a peacefulness and calmness in body and mind.** (pp. 259–260)

Meditation

An example of a simplified, nonreligious meditation approach is as follows:

1. Find a quiet environment, such as a quiet room, where you will not be interrupted.
2. Sit quietly in a comfortable position.
3. Close your eyes.
4. Breathe in and out through your nose at a relaxed, natural pace. As you breathe out, silently say the word *relax* slowly to yourself.
5. Continue this process for 10–20 minutes: Slowly breathe in, as you exhale slowly say "relax" to yourself.
6. Do not focus your thoughts on day-to-day concerns, and do not worry whether you will achieve a deep level of relaxation. Deep levels of relaxation are gradually achieved with continued practice. The state of being relaxed comes slowly as you let go of your worries and concerns. When distracting thoughts enter your mind, allow them to drift

---

*Names and other identifying information in this case example have been changed.

*From *Stress and the Art of Biofeedback,* by Barbara B. Brown. Copyright © 1977 by Barbara B. Brown. By permission of Bantam Books, New York. All rights reserved.

**Ibid.

Exhibit 14.7 *(continued)*

away as effortlessly as possible. Focusing your thoughts on your breathing and on silently saying "relax" as you exhale facilitates your "letting go" of worries and concerns.

7. When you finish, sit quietly for several minutes, first with your eyes closed and then with your eyes open. Practice this technique once or twice daily. With practice, you will gradually achieve more rapid and deeper levels of relaxation.

A word of caution when using any relaxation technique: Walk around for 15 or more minutes before driving because you are likely to be lethargic and your response reaction time may be lengthened considerably.

Research has demonstrated that using a relaxation technique is physiologically and psychologically more refreshing and energy restoring than deep sleep (Seaward, 2005). Many users, in fact, have reported that they needed less sleep after they began relaxing, which suggests that a regenerative process occurs during relaxation (Seaward, 2005). Relaxation techniques have been used successfully in the treatment of many stress-related disorders including hypertension and asthma (Seaward, 2005). They also have been effective in decreasing the use of drugs, alcohol, and cigarette smoking (Seaward, 2005); alleviating sleep disorders; and accelerating the bodily healing process.

Relaxation techniques have been found to have a number of other positive effects. They are useful in treating phobias and in treating people with emotional problems (Seaward, 2005). Regular practice of a technique improves learning ability, perceptual motor performance, ability to recover from stress, perceptual acuity, work productivity and job satisfaction, and creativity (Seaward, 2005). Using a technique improves psychological health; heightens self-awareness; increases self-actualization; reduces anxiety, depression, and aggression; reduces reaction time; increases recall ability; and improves academic performance (Seaward, 2005).

The potential medical value in eliciting the relaxation response is dramatically described by Benson (1975):

> The prevention of stress-related diseases carries with it enormous significance, certainly for the individual and his family in terms of their own physical and mental well-being, and for society as a whole through huge dollar savings in health expenditures. It is possible that the regular elicitation of the Relaxation Response will prevent the huge personal suffering and social costs now being inflicted on us by high blood pressure and its related ailments. (pp. 156–157)

EP 2.1.1b

Exercise 14.6: Learning to Relax with Relaxation Techniques

Goal: This exercise is designed to help you determine if practicing one or more relaxation techniques will be beneficial to you.

Step 1: Review the three practice techniques in Exhibit 14.7, Practice one or more several times—for about 15 minutes each time.

Step 2: Do the results that you receive lead you to commit to use one or more of these techniques in the future when you want to relax? (If the techniques do not help you to relax, that is okay.)

___ Yes___ No

Explain your view.

Step 3: Do you think it would be worthwhile to teach highly stressed clients that you will have in the future to use one or more of these techniques?

___ Yes___ No

Explain your view.

Exercise Regular exercise reduces stress (period). Choose an exercise program that you enjoy (be it softball or belly dancing). You will get fit (which of course you will feel good about), and you will have increased energy to meet crises and emergencies. Negative aspects of your job and home life won't seem so bad. Exercising uses up fuel, reduces heart rate and blood pressure, and sets off numerous physiological changes that reduce stress and induce the relaxation response (Seaward, 1994).

And don't forget to eat properly, get sufficient sleep, and get appropriate medical care.

Outside Activities Have a life. Family and friends, church and meditation, hobbies and travel, fun—find the mixture that makes you healthy. These are your antidotes to stress and burnout and the sources of your inner strengths.

Reward yourself for tasks done well. We don't hesitate to compliment others for jobs done well; don't forget to take pride in your own work well done and in a life well lived. Take a mental health day. In periods of extended stress, take a day off and do only the things you want to do. (Some agencies now allow a certain number of mental health days with pay.) You will return to work more effective and ready to face challenges.

Social Support Systems Develop trusting and mutually caring relationships at work. We all need a "lifeline." Maslach (1976) noted,

> Our findings show that burnout rates are lower for those professionals who actively express, analyze and share their personal feelings with their colleagues. Not only do they consciously get things off their chest, but they have an opportunity to receive constructive feedback from other people and to develop new perspectives of their relationship with patients/clients. This process is greatly enhanced if the institution sets up some social outlets such as support groups, special staff meetings or workshops. (p. 19)

Social support groups (at work or outside work) let us let our hair down, help us "kid around," share our lives, keep in touch, and give us a source of security that helps when crises arise. Support groups have several essential features (Greenberg, 1980): (1) The group meets regularly. (2) The same people attend. (3) A feeling of closeness has developed. (4) There is an opportunity for spontaneity and informality. Possible support groups come in many "shapes and sizes": coworkers, friends, sport or hobby groups, family, church groups, and community organizations such as Parents Without Partners.

Variety at Work No doubt about it—doing the same thing day in and day out becomes exhausting. The simple fact is, emotionally draining work (such as suicide counseling or hospice work) can be done only for limited periods, or burnout will rear its ugly head. Therefore, it is important to structure your practice so that you have a variety of job tasks during the week. Also, participating in workshops, conferences, continuing education courses, and in-service training programs adds variety and helps you grow professionally.

Humor It is impossible to say enough about laughter as a coping mechanism. Humor relaxes us, makes work more enjoyable, and takes the edge off. Humor at work and at home relieves stress and helps prevent burnout.

Distressing Events Bad things happen—to us, to friends and family we care about, and to clients we care about. Competent people lose their jobs, friends die, romantic relationships end, we question our faith—the list is endless.

When distressing events arise, what can you do? Actually, many things. It is important to confront events head-on to attempt to improve the situation. Power is always better than helplessness. For example, if you feel beginning burnout, identify what is frustrating and exhausting you at work and then develop new approaches for handling these responsibilities. One worker finds incest cases particularly exhausting, whereas another finds working with the terminally ill more draining—consider exchanging these cases. If you are frustrated because program objectives and job expectations are unclear, get clarification from your supervisor.

EP 2.1.1b

Many distressing events get less distressing when we confront them head-on and take positive action. Not all events or situations can be changed. For example, you may not be able to change certain distasteful aspects of your job. In such situations, the only constructive remaining alternative is to bite the bullet and accept them. It is counterproductive to spend time complaining about a situation you cannot change.

Exercise 14.7: Stress Management Techniques for Me

Goal: This exercise is designed to familiarize you with available stress management techniques.

Step 1: Review the material in this chapter on stress management techniques. List those techniques that you have used. Briefly describe whether the technique was beneficial to you in helping reduce the level of stress you were experiencing.

Step 2: Specify stress management techniques that you are planning to use in the future.

ENJOYING SOCIAL WORK AND YOUR LIFE

To gather material to write this section, I asked friends who have practiced social work for several years to summarize their satisfactions and frustrations about pursuing a career in social work. Here is one reply.

> It is difficult to find the right words to describe my satisfaction with having made a decision to be a social worker. I have worked in a protective services unit of a public welfare department for two years, as a probation and parole officer for three years, and now am a director of a group home for teenage males who have conflicts with their parents.
>
> One of the satisfying aspects of social work is that there are a wide variety of areas where a person can work. When I found myself becoming stale as a probation officer, it was inspiring to look forward to moving on to something else. If this job becomes routine and no longer something I would look forward to doing, I would again move on to some other social work position.
>
> I truly find it gratifying to work with people. If you don't like working with people, then certainly this is the wrong job to have. I know this sounds "naive," but when I feel I've been of some help in assisting someone to better handle a personal or social problem, it really makes me feel good. It should be noted I'm no longer as idealistic as I was when I was going to college and thought I would be able to help the vast majority of my clients. I've learned that most clients simply aren't sufficiently motivated to put forth the time and effort needed to improve their lives—it's like exercising; we all know exercising will

improve our health and keep us trim, but only a few people are willing to put forth the time and effort.

Social work is a challenging profession. Every client's problem is unique. For that matter every client's personality is unique. Interacting with new people, and developing somewhat different treatment strategies with each client is a challenge. Through helping clients I also grow as a person and learn more about myself. Also challenging, and often learning experiences, are speaking to groups in the community, and seeking to develop new services when a need arises. Also educational (and a way of seeing old friends) are in-service training sessions that are held at the agencies I've worked at.

I don't want to give an ever-glowing picture of social work. There are also frustrations. At every agency there seem to be occasional personality conflicts between staff. (Such conflicts are furthered by staff members being pitted against each other for merit increases, for desired task assignments, and for who will get to go to conferences.)

Another frustration is the amount of paperwork. At the three agencies I've worked at, 10 to 15 hours per week are spent on paperwork.

Some social workers complain this profession doesn't pay enough. I've found that in social work there are some jobs that pay a lot more than others. When I first started out, my annual salary was pretty low, but now that I'm a director of this group home I have no complaints.

Another thing that is frustrating is being aware that there are a few workers who are cynical, who always look at the negative side of things, and who really appear to be only interested in drawing their paycheck, rather than helping people. With their negative attitude, I frankly don't see how they can ever help anyone. If I was a client of theirs, I would become even more discouraged and apathetic. To me, these social workers are "deadwood" and are on "welfare" themselves as they are drawing a check without doing anything productive. These people either burned out years ago or were never "encouraging" persons who were motivated to help others.

All in all I really am delighted I chose a career in social work. I enjoy working with most clients (certainly not all of my clients as some I do find obnoxious) and with most of the other staff. I hope this information will be useful to you, and if you ever want someone to speak in your classes, give me a "jingle."

One factor identified by this social worker is the importance of being an "encouraging" person. Chapter 5 noted this as a crucial characteristic of effective counselors. Closely related to this is positive thinking, which is important not only in working with clients but also in enjoying life.

Become a Positive Thinker

In *A Treasury of Success Unlimited,* W. Clement Stone (1966) presented some of the basic principles of positive thinking:

> Your most precious, valued possessions and your greatest powers are invisible and intangible. No one can take them. You, and you alone, can give them. You will receive abundance for your giving. The more you give—the more you will have!
>
> Give a smile to everyone you meet (smile with your eyes)—and you'll smile and receive smiles. . . .
> Give a kind word (with a kindly thought behind the word)—you will be kind and receive kind words. . . .
> Give appreciation (warmth from the heart)—you will appreciate and be appreciated. . . .
> Give honor, credit and applause (the victor's wreath)—you will be honorable and receive credit and applause. . . .
> Give time for a worthy cause (with eagerness)—you will be worthy and richly rewarded. . . .
> Give hope (the magic ingredient for success)—you will have hope and be made hopeful. . . .
> Give happiness (a most treasured state of mind)—you will be happy and be made happy. . . .
> Give encouragement (the incentive to action)—you will have courage and be encouraged. . . .
> Give cheer (the verbal sunshine)—you'll be cheerful and cheered. . . .
> Give a pleasant response (the neutralizer of irritants)—you will be pleasant and receive pleasant responses. . . .
> Give good thoughts (nature's character builder)—you will be good and the world will have good thoughts for you. . . . (pp. 9–10)

> Few living Americans can write or speak on the power of positive thinking with more authority than W. Clement Stone. Beginning as a newsboy on the streets of Chicago, Stone applied the principles of positive thinking to amass and share with others a fortune in excess of $160 million (Mandino, 1966).

Harold Sherman (1966), in "The Surest Way in the World to Attract Success—or Failure," further elaborated on positive thinking:

> "You might know this would happen to me!" Is this a comment you have made, not once, but many times, when things have gone wrong? . . . Certainly—you *knew* it was going to happen—and it did. Your *faith* in "things going wrong" caused the "power of TNT" [thinking negative thoughts] within you to work *against* you instead of for you. There is a great law of mind by which your thinking and your conduct should always be guided: "Like attracts like."
>
> Think good thoughts; you will eventually attract good things. Think bad thoughts, you will ultimately attract bad things.
>
> Simple—easy to remember—but also easy to forget. . . .
>
> Get this point clearly in mind: *you* supply the material (by the nature of your thoughts) out of which your creative power builds your future. If the material is inferior, comprised of mental pictures of failure, despair, defeat and the like, you can readily see that only unhappy results can be materialized from them. . . .
>
> Whatever conditions you are facing at the moment are the result of your past thinking—good and bad. These conditions cannot change until you have first changed your thinking. . . .
>
> Things first happen in your mind before they can happen in this outer world. What are you picturing? Do you want it to happen? If not, you are the only one who can prevent it. Your future success or failure is in your hands—where it should be. (pp. 111–113)

Numerous books have been written about positive thinking philosophy (*Looking Out for No. 1,* by Robert Ringer, 1977; *Move Ahead with Possibility Thinking,* by Robert Schuller, 1973; *Positive Thinking Everyday,* by Norman Vincent Peale, 1993; and *Positive Thinking,* by Vera Pfeiffer, 1993—to name but a few). Positive thinking certainly has considerable merit. However, there is a potential danger. Every accomplishment requires certain abilities. For those who set goals above their capacities, positive thinking creates a false sense of hope. When people (particularly those suffering from emotional problems like anxiety or depression) fail to achieve unrealistic goals, they are headed for a downturn. Authorities now suggest replacing *positive thinking* with *optimal thinking* to avoid the pitfall noted above. In optimal thinking, we look for all *realistic* options for a situation. Then we assess the merits and shortcomings of those options, and finally we select the option that appears to be most constructive. (The optimal thinking approach uses the principles of the problem-solving process described in Chapter 1.)

Positive thinking usually gets people started on a project. Many people don't realize their own potential, and a bright outlook and positive action help them achieve their goals. It is your choice. You can think and act negatively about events that happen to you, or you can think and act positively about those same events. Positive thinking helps you enjoy your career and your life.

Develop an Identity[1]

What kind of person are you? What do you want out of life? What kind of person do you want to be? These questions are among the most important ones you will ever face. Without answers, you are not prepared to make major life decisions. Unfortunately,

[1] This section is adapted from Charles Zastrow, "Who Am I? The Quest for Identity," in *The Personal Problem Solver,* edited by Charles Zastrow and Dae H. Chang, © 1977, pp. 365–370. Adapted by permission of Prentice-Hall, Inc., Englewood Cliffs, New Jersey.

many people muddle through life and never contemplate these questions. Those who don't have a clue about these questions may find themselves depressed, indecisive, anxious, and unfulfilled. All too often, their lives are carbon copies of Stan Sinclair's.

At age 18, Stan graduated from high school. Unable to find a job, he enlisted in the army for a 3-year hitch. At 20, he started dating Julia Johnson while he was stationed in Illinois. He liked Julia. She became pregnant, and they decided to get married. Money was tight, and Julia wanted to live near her relatives. Two months after his discharge, Stan became a father. Needing a job in the area, he became a gas station attendant because it was the only employment he could find. Two and one-half years later, an opening occurred in an auto assembly plant. The pay was better, so Stan applied and was hired. The job was relatively easy but monotonous. Stan faithfully attached mufflers to new cars, over and over, for 40 hours a week. During the next 8 years, Stan and Julia had three more children. The pay and fringe benefits, combined with his family and financial responsibilities, locked Stan into this assembly-line job until he retired at age 65. The morning after he retired, he looked into the mirror and began asking, finally, the key questions. Was it all worth it? Why did he feel empty and unfulfilled? What did he want out of the future? Never having in the past figured out what he wanted out of life, his only answer was a frown.

Identity Development Identity is our sense of who we are—knowledge and a feeling of the ways in which we are separate, distinct persons. Identity development is a lifelong process, and our identity changes throughout our lifetime. During the early years, our sense of who we are is largely determined by the reactions of others. A long time ago, Cooley (1902) suggested that this labeling process results in the *looking glass self*—that is, people experience their self-concept through their perceptions of how others relate to them. For example, if a neighborhood identifies a male youth as a "troublemaker" (a delinquent), the neighbors will not trust him, may accuse him of delinquent acts, and will label his semidelinquent and aggressive behaviors as "delinquent." The youth begins to realize that this label gives him prestige and status, at least among his peers. In the absence of objective ways to gauge whether he is, in fact, a delinquent, the youth will rely on the subjective evaluations of others. Thus, gradually, as people relate to him as a delinquent, he begins to perceive himself in that way and begins to become a delinquent in earnest.

Fortunately, identity development is a lifetime process, and positive changes are possible even for those with negative self-concepts. There are two key principles to remember: (1) We cannot change the past. (2) What we want out of the future and our motivation to achieve what we want are more important than any past experiences in determining our future.

How to Determine Who You Are Forming an identity involves thinking about, and arriving at, answers to these questions: (1) What do I want out of life? (2) What kind of person am I? (3) What kind of person do I want to be? The most important decisions you make in your life may well depend on your answers to these questions.

This is not to say that these questions are easy to answer. They require considerable contemplation and trial and error. But if you are to lead a gratifying, fulfilling life, it is imperative to find a direction so you can live the kind of life you find meaningful. Here are some questions to consider:

1. What is satisfying/meaningful/enjoyable to me? (Only after you know this will you be able to consciously seek activities that make your life fulfilling and avoid those activities that are meaningless or stifling.)
2. What is my moral code? (One possible code is to seek to fulfill your needs and to do what you find enjoyable, doing so in a way that does not deprive others of the ability to fulfill their needs.)

3. What are my religious beliefs?
4. What kind of career do I want? (Ideally, you should choose work that you find stimulating and satisfying, that you are skilled at, and that earns you enough money to support the lifestyle you want.)
5. What are my sexual mores? (Find a code that you are comfortable with and that helps you meet your needs without exploiting others. There is no one right code. What works for one may not work for another because of differences in lifestyles, life goals, and personal values.)
6. Do I want to marry? (If yes, to what type of person and when? How consistent are your answers here with your other life goals?)
7. Do I want to have children? (If yes, how many, when, and how consistent are your answers here with your other life goals?)
8. What area of the country/world do I want to live in? (Climate, geography, type of dwelling, rural or urban setting, closeness to relatives or friends, and characteristics of the neighborhood.)
9. What do I enjoy doing with my leisure time?
10. What kind of image do I want to project to others? (Your image will be composed of your dressing style and grooming habits, your emotions, personality, degree of assertiveness, capacity to communicate, material possessions, moral code, physical features, and voice patterns. You need to assess your strengths and shortcomings honestly in this area and seek to make improvements.)
11. What type of people do I enjoy being with and why?
12. Do I desire to improve the quality of my life and that of others? (If yes, in what ways, and how do you hope to achieve these goals?)
13. What types of relationships do I want to have with relatives, friends, neighbors, and people I meet for the first time?
14. What are my thoughts about death and dying?
15. What do I hope to be doing 5 years from now? 10 years? 20 years?
16. How can I achieve the goals that I identified here?

To have a well-developed sense of identity, you will at some time need answers to most, but not all, of those questions. Very few of us arrive at rational, consistent answers to all the questions. But having at least contemplated them will provide a reference for you as you embark on life after college.

EP 2.1.3a

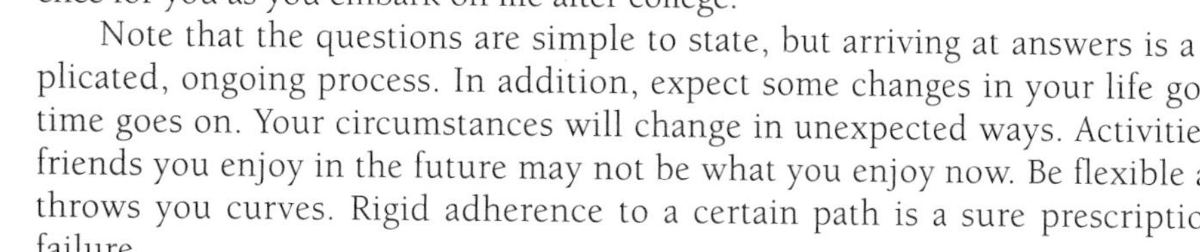

Note that the questions are simple to state, but arriving at answers is a complicated, ongoing process. In addition, expect some changes in your life goals as time goes on. Your circumstances will change in unexpected ways. Activities and friends you enjoy in the future may not be what you enjoy now. Be flexible as life throws you curves. Rigid adherence to a certain path is a sure prescription for failure.

Exercise 14.8: Arriving at a Better Sense of Who You Are

Goal: This exercise is designed to assist you in identifying who you are and what you want out of life.

Step 1: Answer the 16 questions listed above.

Step 2: Has this exercise been useful in focusing you on who you are and what you want out of life?

___ Yes___ No

Explain your view.

Use Rational Challenges to Develop a Success Identity

Some people muddle through without a clear sense of what they want or who they are; others wallow in self-pity, seeing themselves as failures. I once compared people who have a success identity with those who have a failure identity:

> Success identities are characterized by the following kinds of self-talk. "I have accomplished many of the things I have tried in the past." "I am a competent, worthwhile person." "I, similar to other people, have certain special talents." "Trying something new is challenging and stimulating." "I look forward to trying something more complicated that has the opportunity for substantial payoffs, and which will test and further develop my special talents." "Trying new things helps me grow as a person, and helps provide meaning to living." "I look forward to each new day with its opportunities for involvement in activities that will be gratifying and fulfilling."
>
> Do you give yourself these types of positive self-talk, or do you give yourself the following negative kinds of self-talk, . . . characteristic of those with a "failure identity"?: "I can't accomplish anything I try." "I'm inferior to other people." "Why can't I be as competent, capable, or attractive as others?" "I'm a failure." "I can't afford to risk trying anything new as it will reveal my weaknesses to others." "I wish people would stop picking on me, and making cutting comments about my shortcomings." "I've got a number of personal problems that are overwhelming me, and draining my energy." "There just is no hope for a brighter tomorrow." "My problems are certainly more confusing and unresolvable than those that other people have." "Life is certainly the 'pits' and really not worth living." "I wish I was someone else." "I wonder why such and such hurt me so badly—I just can't stop thinking about it." "What did I do wrong to deserve all this misery?"
>
> Such self-talk by people with failure orientations generates a variety of negative emotions, including excessive worry, fatigue, anxiety, boredom, depression, loneliness, and general feelings of misery. (Zastrow, 1979, pp. 92–93)

Manley (1977) also noted:

> A sense of failure becomes a further problem since it limits the amount of risk-taking behavior in which we are willing to engage. If we feel that we are failures, we will feel threatened by any new behavior patterns that we perceive as risky. Accordingly, we will be very reluctant to try any such behaviors. This means that we will continue to operate as we have in the past, thereby creating somewhat of a "rut." To the degree that we follow this practice, we are precluded from growing psychologically or expanding our behavioral responses. We are stultifying ourselves from greater use of our potential and becoming a more complete individual. We learn and grow by our experiences. If we limit ourselves to only the "tried and true" modes of behavior, we are putting disabling constraints on ourselves and seriously limiting our growth potential. (p. 38)

To be an "encouraging" person as you work with clients and to feel good about yourself, it is essential that you have a positive, success self-concept. A very simple formula helps people who view themselves as failures improve their lives; they shift their thinking from focusing on negative items to focusing on positive items.

One way to change a failure identity into a success identity is to identify the failure self-talk and then challenge this with rational self-talk (see Module 1 for how to write a rational self-analysis). A feeling of failure is an emotion similar to any other emotion. This feeling results mainly from negative self-talk, and this emotion can be changed by rational self-challenges. (See Case Example "Developing a Positive Self-Concept.")

CASE EXAMPLE Developing a Positive Self-Concept

*Since her early teenage years Sarah had viewed herself as a failure.** *Her sense of being a failure was temporarily alleviated during her junior and senior years in high school, when she steadily dated and became overly dependent on Tom. However, her failure concept returned shortly after Tom left to attend the Air Force Academy. In this case example, Sarah describes her deep sense of being a failure and how she used rational self-challenges to develop a more positive self-concept.*

An excerpt from Sarah's journal:

Breakfast at the airport appeared cheerful enough. His parents, full of optimistic talk of his future, kept the conversation light and promising. And I, my real feelings hidden by a facade of carefully planned cheerfulness, made attempts at bright small talk, which seemed to add to the somehow phony color and splendor of the day.

At that point, after all of the months of waiting and preparation, all was ready. Every last detail had been checked, and it was time. Tom was ready to embark on a new and challenging lifestyle—without me!

Later, as I recall that first painful good-bye, our words edged with emotion, full of promises for the future, and yet our every thought charged with the upcoming agony of being apart from one another, I do not once remember thinking of how I was going to adjust to his absence. Tom was the most significant person in my life to that date, and yet I had not realized the powerful effect our new "separateness" would take in relation to my life from there on.

The sequence(s) of events and emotions that followed seemed to me to be normal or what I thought as being normal reactions for a person to feel when a loved one is away for a prolonged period of time. That is when I began my "Poor Me" syndrome!

It was summer, and I was very lonely and didn't have enough to keep me busy. I worked at a local restaurant as much as I possibly could to pass the time, but it didn't seem to be enough—I still had those lonely nights to myself.

"Poor me," I'd say to myself. "I'm alone and no one cares enough to spend time with me, I must be worthless, boring, etc." This became repetitious with me to the point that whenever I felt a bit depressed I would reinforce those feelings with other intense feelings of worthlessness. I could really bring myself down, you see, because I truly felt that I could never be happy, feel my personal worth, expand myself unless Tom was with me. I guess that was a rather natural feeling for me to have because while he was home I allowed myself to be dependent upon him to fill my every need and whim. And gladly he filled them. Call it "ego" or whatever, but it somehow filled a need in him to have me need him so desperately. It seemed to be a very workable arrangement while he was home with me. My belief was that we were "in love" and it was a very positive point to "need" someone I loved. What I hadn't considered was how my dependency upon him was, in fact, setting me up for a lifetime of unhappiness. Time progressed, and I felt myself more and more alone. I walled myself off from my "helpful friends," people who did in fact care for me and who wanted to include me in their activities. I did join them on occasion, but generally if I did, I'd begin to feel sorry for myself and bring out my tale of woe. Of course they listened, but one can listen to the same negative thoughts only so many times. I remember having feelings of bitterness and hostility toward these friends, people who had things going their way. I was jealous.

It seemed as though everything was going wrong. I began to drink more and to experience the effects of drugs. At times this seemed to be a haven for me, an escape from what seemed to be insurmountable problems.

I took an apartment with an acquaintance who was pregnant. (It created many problems.) I overextended myself financially, knowing full well that I was. I was enrolled in classes but had neither the motivation nor goal to attend all of them.

All around I began to see myself as a failure. Whenever I'd receive a poor grade on a test, paper, or quiz, I'd tell myself that I was stupid. If it came time to pay the bills and I did not have the money, I'd tell myself that I was a failure at supporting myself. Then, to pay those same bills for which I spent the money on extravagances, I'd have to work doubly hard.

Well, eventually I became tired of feeling negative all the time. After all, if I could feel good about myself when I was with Tom, then somehow I should be able to feel good about myself at other times. I had to—either that, suicide, or stay miserable. Neither of the latter two sounded too appealing, so I decided to make the best of it and give myself a positive try. Many times, over tears on the telephone, I would explain to Tom my fears and anxieties and it would hurt him some, as he felt a bit responsible. He is a person whom I genuinely care for, and I began to have my doubts as to what I should and shouldn't tell him. After all, I really don't intend to make those I care for feel responsible for my feelings and actions. I'm responsible for myself.

*Names and other identifying information in this case example have been changed.

(continued)

CASE EXAMPLE *(continued)*

Fortunately, it was at this point in my life that I enrolled in a course on counseling, which exposed me to the concepts of rational therapy, and I proceeded to write the following rational self-analysis (RSA) on my personal concerns.

Perhaps the quickest way to improve our self-concept is to challenge our self-downing thoughts with positive/rational self-challenges. The following illustrates this approach.

A
EVENT

In August my boyfriend left for the Air Force Academy. At his leave-taking the two of us promised to wait until the end of his education and then to marry. I had little confidence in myself as a person to begin with. When he left, I became less confident and began to discount myself as a person having no worth or value. As time progressed, I began to do poorly in several aspects of life: poor grades, too much financial responsibility (too many extravagances), poor organization of my life's plans (work or school, which has priority?), hostile attitude toward friends, etc. I generally felt worthless and sad because Tom left.

D[1]
CAMERA CHECK

This is all factual.

B
SELF-TALK

1. "I am able to be happy only if Tom is with me." (bad)
2. "I'm dependent upon Tom in all ways if I allow his leaving to affect me this way." (bad)
3. "I'm a failure in my studies." (bad)
4. "I'm worthless." (bad)
5. "My friends won't like me if I react to them in a hostile manner." (bad)
6. "I can't support myself sufficiently. I buy extravagant items." (bad)

D[2]
RATIONAL SELF-CHALLENGES TO THE SELF-TALK IN SECTION B

1. *False*. If I hope to be a self-sufficient and satisfied person in my lifetime, I know that I must do it alone—for myself. Others may make it easier for me, but essentially, I have to make myself happy.
2. *True*. But I'm not allowing myself my own rights as a person. I realize that I could never mold my life around another's wants and likes. I've got to have my own identity.
3. *False*. I'm not a failure and never have been. At my lowest point, I still received C's for grades. I received those C's with a minimal amount of effort; so if I really tried, I could do better.
4. *False*. Every person has some worth. I do too. At times when I'm depressed I may like to tell myself I'm worthless, but I really know that I'm not. Every human being has some worth. I'm as valuable as any other person, just because I'm human.
5. *True*. My friends don't like to spend time with me when I react to them in a negative, hostile way. It doesn't do much for the friendship, which was built of positive, mutual concern to begin with. I really don't like to treat them in this way, and from now on I will make a conscious effort to be more pleasant.
6. *False*. In the past I've done quite well. It is when I take trips to visit Tom or buy a new wardrobe that I feel depleted financially. At other times I manage quite well, and even if I overextend myself, I still work to pay for my expenses.

CASE EXAMPLE (continued)

B
SELF-TALK

7. "Because Tom has left me, all things go wrong in my life." (bad)

8. "The only thing I can look forward to is becoming Tom's wife and then I will hopefully feel better." (bad)

9. "Tom is responsible for my feeling so rotten. It's all his fault!" (bad)

D²
RATIONAL SELF-CHALLENGES TO THE SELF-TALK IN SECTION B

7. *False*. Things do not go wrong because Tom left me but because of circumstances or something I do to allow things to go wrong. Tom is away; there is no possible way he can control what happens to me here.

8. *False*. I intend to become a counselor if I really put forth an effort. If I do decide to become Tom's wife, that will be a major event to look forward to—a life together—but that is not all I'm looking forward to. For 2½ years I've struggled with college—certainly not for nothing!

9. *False*. Tom is away and has no control over my life. He never did. In the past I felt the way I wanted to, did what I liked because that is the power that I have as a person. When Tom left, it was an unfortunate circumstance. I allowed myself to blame him for all the "wrongs" and unhappiness in my life when actually he had nothing to do with it. I'm the person living my life—choosing my own feelings, situations, etc., over which Tom has no control.

C
MY EMOTIONS

Depression, sadness, insecurity, inferiority, and loneliness. I had nine "bad" self-talk statements. That doesn't say much for my ability to adjust well to a given situation.

E
EMOTIONAL AND BEHAVIORAL GOALS

In the future I'd like to try to build my self-image so that I will be capable of accepting and utilizing change in my life in a positive way. A way in which I can do this is through my self-talk—what I tell myself about occurrences. The given (A) situation is a continuing occurrence—it happens at least once every summer. Having worked on the problem since September, I've begun to realize what I need to do in this situation to make myself happy. I need to see myself happy. I need to see myself as a strong, self-sufficient, happily functioning person—with a "separate" life and identity from Tom. These qualities (strength, independence, self-sufficiency) have been hidden in me for some time, and I've yet to cultivate them totally, but instead I'm working on them slowly. This, I expect, will make me a more satisfied person, and for others more pleasant and satisfying to be with.

(Sarah also wrote the following summary of the usefulness of this approach.)

I used rational therapy with the belief that I really did have the power to control my emotions and then, in turn, to control my life. I have always been a person of a negative nature—I had too much to say about all the "bads" and "wrongs" in my life that happened, and too little to say of the good.

I saw myself as a worthless, weak, submissive, and stupid person who really didn't matter in the course of this big world. There was one person who made me feel valuable, and when he left I allowed myself to feel useless again. This was followed by a succession of negative thoughts about myself, and fears.

A strong point of doing an RSA is what I found to be my ability to look at myself objectively on paper. What is written on paper looks factual and truthful. I found myself debating those facts and truths and actually finding out more of how I really

(continued)

CASE EXAMPLE (*continued*)

felt inside. I had an outsider's view of myself on the objective side. This allowed me to weigh the pros and cons of my behavior, emotions, etc., and to take positive, realistic means to change what I didn't like.

Also, doing a rational self-analysis on my emotional and behavioral problems helped me to become more rational and realistic in regard to living my everyday life. In a world that is so disproportionate in itself, I find it easy to stretch many aspects of my personal life out of proportion. A rational self-analysis doesn't allow me to do that. A person must face the facts, debate the thoughts underlying his or her dysfunctional behaviors and unwanted emotions, and determine what he or she chooses to feel from there on. A rational self-analysis allows only honesty and a willingness to change those feelings that one is not comfortable with. A person who does his or her rational self-analysis dishonestly will get nowhere.

Ultimately, rational therapy taught me the power of control. A human person is a complex, highly intelligent organism. Then why should he or she not have the power of controlling what could turn out to be his or her own destiny in life?

An excerpt from Sarah's journal 2 years later:

Inside myself, I guess that I'm really satisfied with the person I'm becoming. Sure, it can be a long, hard struggle at times, and often frustrating, but it is a part of my life. That is how things become imporant and significant in life—through the living of such experiences. Sometimes I'm amazed when I think that I was born a person in my own right, with potential emotional growth, strength, and abilities, to become what I choose to become.

Source: This case example is reprinted from Charles Zastrow, *Talk to Yourself: Using the Power of Self-Talk*, © 1979 pp. 99–105. Reprinted by permission of Prentice-Hall, Inc., Englewood Cliffs, New Jersey.

EP 2.1.1b

Exercise 14.9: Changing a Failure Identity into a Success Identity

Goal: This exercise is designed to demonstrate that by changing your failure self-talk to success self-talk, you will move in the direction of having a success identity.

Step 1: Review the material on writing a rational self-analysis in Module 1, and also review the case example in this chapter, "Developing a Positive Self-Concept."

Step 2: Write a rational self-analysis in which you identify your failure self-talk, and then challenge this with rational self-talk.

Step 3: Do you believe that if you practice using rational self-talk to challenge your failure self-talk, you will move in the direction of having a success identity?

___ Yes___ No___ Uncertain

Explain your views.

SUMMARY

To be of help to others, social workers must first take care of themselves. Good emotional and physical health are internal resources that social workers need to have to be of help to others. This chapter presents material on how to survive and enjoy social work and, in a broader sense, how to enjoy living.

Although social work students have a number of common concerns, often they are reluctant to share them with others. The following concerns are discussed, and suggestions for resolving them are given: Will I be able to make it in field placement? Will I be able to handle my first interview with my first client? I'm really depressed because my supervisor is able to handle an interview much better than I—will I ever be able to do that well? How should I separate the role of counselor from that of friend? How can I avoid becoming too emotionally involved with clients' problems? Do I really want to pursue a career in social work?

Safety guidelines for social workers are presented. In the social work perspective, violence erupts in context, rather than residing within the "violent individual." The immediate environmental context is important, so social workers are often able to use their skills to deter potentially violent behavior. Social workers need to be aware of the following signals of danger: environmental cues, client cues, and worker cues. Most assaults follow a predictable pattern of five phases: triggering, escalation, crisis, recovery, and postcrisis depression.

Numerous strategies for preventing violence are summarized. Techniques to de-escalate verbal communication and nonverbal communication are discussed. In some situations, it is important for social workers to state acceptable limits for clients to express their discontent. Agencies need environmental safeguards (such as workers having cellular phones) and response systems to deter potential violence. Guidelines were presented to increase worker safety during home visits.

Burnout is a major problem encountered by helping professionals. The symptoms and causes of burnout are discussed and suggestions given for reducing stress and preventing burnout. Because burnout is one reaction to high levels of stress, it follows that stress management techniques are also useful in preventing burnout.

EP 2.1.1b

The chapter ends by providing tips on how to enjoy social work and life. The value of positive thinking is described. Also, the importance of developing a sense of who you are and what you want out of life is discussed, and suggestions are given for developing such an identity. Having a failure identity is contrasted with having a success identity, and rational self-analysis is presented as one approach that is useful in challenging and changing a failure identity.

EXERCISES

1. Reducing Stress and Preventing Burnout

Goal: This exercise is designed to help students reduce stress and prevent burnout.

Step 1: Describe the purpose of this exercise. Using the material in this chapter, define stress and burnout. Indicate that burnout is one reaction to high stress levels. Also summarize a variety of strategies to reduce stress and prevent burnout. (These strategies are outlined in this chapter. It may be helpful to prepare and distribute a handout that identifies these strategies.)

Step 2: Ask students to write answers to the following questions on a sheet of paper:

a. A few problematic situations that are presently causing high levels of stress in my life are___.
b. My current ways of handling these high levels of stress are___.
c. Ways in which I could better handle these situations and become more relaxed are___.

Step 3: Ask students to form subgroups of three and have them share what they wrote. Indicate that the subgroups may be able to offer additional suggestions on how to handle the stress-producing situations and on how to relax. Also indicate that each student has a right to privacy and is not expected to self-disclose what he or she wants to keep private.

Step 4: After the subgroups have concluded their discussions, ask whether there are questions or comments about what was discussed.

EP 2.1.1b

2. Positive and Negative Thinking Become Self-Fulfilling Prophecies

Goal: This exercise is designed to help students become aware that positive and negative thinking often become self-fulfilling prophecies.

Step 1: Indicate the purpose of the exercise. Indicate that we always have a choice of thinking either positively or negatively about events that happen to us. Also indicate that both positive and negative thinking frequently become self-fulfilling prophecies. For example, if we go for a job interview and think we have a good chance to get the job, we will be more relaxed and probably better able to sell ourselves. If we think negatively, we will be more anxious and probably less able to present ourselves with confidence. Give additional examples if desired.

Step 2: Ask students to write on a sheet of paper a situation in which positive thinking led to a self-fulfilling prophecy for themselves or for someone close to them. Also ask students to write a situation in which negative thinking led to a self-fulfilling prophecy for themselves or for someone close to them.

Step 3: Ask for volunteers to share what they wrote. Also ask the class if they are aware of any situations in which positive thinking led to undesirable results or negative thinking resulted in desirable consequences.

EP 2.1.3a

3. Law of Attraction

Goal: This exercise presents a unique strategy to help students improve their lives.

Step 1: Ask students to brainstorm about the qualities that they admire in others. The instructor lists all these qualities on the board. (The instructor should seek to elicit a long list.)

Step 2: The instructor then indicates that the Law of Attraction asserts that a person's thoughts (both conscious and unconscious) dictate the reality of that person's life, whether or not he or she is aware of it. The Law further asserts that if you really want something and truly believe it's possible, you'll get it. Furthermore, if you place a lot of attention and thought onto something you don't want, you'll probably get that too. For example, if you continue to worry and dwell on your belief that your romantic life "is in the pits," that belief system (along with the way you present yourself in accordance with this belief system) will lead you to have unhappy romantic relationships.

The instructor adds that the Law of Attraction asserts that we are always sending out vibes/vibrations of what we are thinking/feeling. If we are thinking bad thoughts, we will have bad feelings, and will be sending out negative vibes. If we are thinking good/positive thoughts, we will have good feelings, and will be sending out good vibes.

We like to be with people who send out good vibes, and who have the qualities you listed in this exercise. We generally do not like to associate with people who are sending out bad vibes.

In order for a salesperson to be successful, he or she needs to be sending out good vibes, so that customers will want to converse with him or her. In order for a social worker to be effective with clients, he or she also needs to be sending out good vibes, so that clients will want to converse with him or her. This rule applies to most professionals—physicians, attorneys, psychologists, psychiatrists, guidance counselors, teachers, and so on.

The Law of Attraction asserts that if you present yourself as exhibiting the qualities you listed in this exercise, many doors will be opened up for you; and you will be successful, happy, contented, relaxed, and so on.

Are you willing to make a commitment to presenting yourself to others as having the characteristics you listed in this exercise?

COMPETENCY NOTES

The following identifies where Educational Policy (EP) competencies and practice behaviors are discussed in the chapter.

EP 2.1.1b *Practice personal reflection and self-correction to assure continual professional development.*(pp. 439–446).

This section summarizes common concerns of students majoring in social work, and provides some ways of addressing these concerns.

EP 2.1.1b *Practice personal reflection and self-correction to assure continual professional development.*(p. 446).

Exercise 14.1 is designed to have students reflect upon their concerns about majoring in social work and to then problem-solve these concerns.

EP 2.1.7a *Utilize conceptual frameworks to guide the process of assessment, intervention, and evaluation.* (pp. 446–451).

Material is presented on safety guidelines for social workers; burnout, stress, and stress management; traumas and stress disorders; and enjoying social work and life.

EP 2.1.1b *Practice personal reflection and self-correction to assure continual professional development.*(pp. 453–454).

Exercise 14.2 is designed to have students recognize their current stressors, and to assist them in realizing that stressors consist of distressing events and self-talk associated with those events.

EP 2.1.1b *Practice personal reflection and self-correction to assure continual professional development.*(p. 454).

Exercise 14.3 is designed to have students reflect upon how they physiologically react to high levels of stress.

EP 2.1.1b *Practice personal reflection and self-correction to assure continual professional development.*(p. 456).

Exercise 14.4 is designed to have students reflect upon what they can do when they experience burnout.

EP 2.1.3a *Distinguish, appraise, and integrate multiple sources of knowledge, including research-based knowledge and practice wisdom.* (p. 458).

Exercise 14.5 is designed to assist students in specifying their short-range and long-range goals, and to then identify tasks that will help them achieve these goals.

EP 2.1.1b *Practice personal reflection and self-correction to assure continual professional development* (pp. 460–461).

Exercise 14.6 is designed to have students reflect upon whether relaxation techniques will be beneficial to them.

EP 2.1.1b *Practice personal reflection and self-correction to assure continual professional development.* (p. 462).

Exercise 14.7 is designed to have students reflect about using available stress management techniques.

EP 2.1.3a *Distinguish, appraise, and integrate multiple sources of knowledge, including research-based knowledge and practice wisdom.* (pp. 466–467).

Exercise 14.8 is designed to assist students in identifying who they are, and what they want out of life.

EP 2.1.1b *Practice personal reflection and self-correction to assure continual professional development.* (p. 471).

Exercise 14.9 is designed to demonstrate to students that they can change a failure identity to a success identity by changing their failure self-talk to success self-talk.

EP 2.1.1b *Practice personal reflection and self-correction to assure continual professional development.* (pp. 472–473).

This exercise is designed to help students reflect upon high levels of stress they have experienced, and to then problem-solve how to reduce high stress levels.

EP 2.1.1b *Practice personal reflection and self-correction to assure continual professional development.* (p. 473).

This exercise is designed to reflect upon the fact that positive and negative thinking often become self-fulfilling prophecies.

EP 2.1.3a *Distinguish, appraise, and integrate multiple sources of knowledge, including research-based knowledge and practice wisdom* (pp. 473–474).

This exercise, involving the Law of Attraction, presents a unique strategy to help students improve their lives.

Counseling Theories Resource Manual

Prominent theories of counseling are summarized and critiqued in this manual. Use it as a reference guide in your future practice and as a primer in your current coursework.

An effective social worker needs knowledge of comprehensive counseling theories and specialized intervention techniques to determine precisely what problems exist and how to intervene effectively. In a comprehensive counseling theory, the theorist proposes a counseling approach that can be used to treat practically all personal problems. There are a number of contemporary comprehensive counseling theories, including rational therapy, behavior modification, and reality therapy. These theories typically present material on (1) personality theory, or how normal psychosocial development occurs; (2) behavior pathology, or how emotional and behavioral problems arise; and (3) intervention, or how to change emotional and behavioral problems.

An effective counselor generally knows several intervention approaches and, depending on the problems being presented by the client, is able to select a strategy with a high probability of success. In addition to comprehensive counseling theories, social workers also use specialized intervention techniques for specific problems—for example, assertiveness training for people who are shy or overly aggressive and parent effectiveness training for parent-child relationship difficulties. Conscientious workers strive to gain working knowledge of a wide variety of intervention techniques, but it is nearly impossible to acquire working knowledge of all the comprehensive and specialized intervention approaches that are available. The material in this manual summarizes approaches that social workers commonly use. Case examples illustrate how each approach is used.

MODULE 1

Rational Therapy

ALBERT ELLIS

EP 2.1.10a, j

The founder of rational therapy, Albert Ellis (1913–2007) practiced psychoanalytic approaches to therapy during the late 1940s and early 1950s. He became disenchanted with both the results and the approach when he observed that even patients who achieved incredible insight into their childhood and unconscious processes continued to experience emotional difficulties.

Ellis developed a new approach, *rational therapy* (also called *rational-emotive therapy*), in which he treated clients by challenging and changing their irrational beliefs. Ellis (1957) was able to demonstrate significant effectiveness using this new approach.

In 1959, Ellis established the Institute for Rational Living in New York City, which provides adult education courses in rational living and a moderate-cost psychotherapy clinic for clients. In 1968, Ellis founded the Institute for Advanced Study in Rational Psychotherapy, which provides helping professionals with extensive training in rational therapy and also provides seminars and workshops throughout the country. Ironically, toward the end of his life, Ellis's relationship with this institute became strained. Ellis (2008, p. 193) recalled:

> In September 2005, the Board of Trustees of the Albert Ellis Institute removed Ellis from the board and dismissed him from all duties at the institute. In January 2006, the State Supreme Court in Manhattan ruled that the board was wrong in ousting Ellis at a meeting from which Ellis was excluded. The judge's decision reinstated him to the board. The judge called the institute's position regarding Dr. Ellis "disingenuous" citing case law saying that such a "dismissal, accomplished without notice of any kind or the right of confrontation, is offensive and contrary to our fundamental process of democratic and legal procedure, fair play and the spirit of the law."

The Albert Ellis Foundation was established in 2006 to promote rational-emotive behavior therapy and the works of Albert Ellis. The foundation was created to ensure that Ellis's lifework would be protected and promoted and to advocate for the legal and human rights of Ellis himself.

Ellis was also recognized nationally as an authority on sexuality. In addition to running workshops and seminars and being a practicing psychotherapist, he wrote 54 books and more than 600 articles.

Rational therapy has had an enormous impact on both professionals and the public. The principles of rational therapy have been applied to assertiveness training, sexuality, adolescence, law and criminality, religion, executive leadership, children's literature, music, feminism, philosophy, personal problems, alcoholism, marriage and the family, and sex adjustment and therapy.

This module will:

A. Present the theory that self-talk determines our feelings and behaviors

B. Describe three constructive ways to change unwanted emotions

C. Describe assessing and changing dysfunctional behavior

D. Explore the idea that the restructuring of thinking is the key therapeutic agent in producing positive changes in clients

SELF-TALK DETERMINES OUR FEELINGS AND ACTIONS

Most people believe that our emotions and our actions are determined primarily by the events that happen to us. According to rational therapists, however (Ellis, 2000), the primary cause of all our emotions and actions is *self-talk*—what we tell ourselves about the events that happen to us:

This is not a new idea. The Stoic philosopher Epictetus wrote in the first century A.D., "Men are disturbed not by things, but by the view which they take of them" (Ellis, 2000). Exhibit M1.1 illustrates this process.

Self-talk determines how we feel and act. By changing our self-talk, we can change how we feel and act. We cannot always control events that happen to us, but we do have the power to think rationally about them and thereby change our unwanted emotions and ineffective actions.

Maultsby (1977) indicated that thinking is irrational if it does one or more of the following:

1. Does not fit the facts (is not based on objective reality)
2. Hampers you in protecting your life

Exhibit M1.1 How Self-Talk Determines Events

Event: A husband unexpectedly arrives home early and on walking into his living room sees his wife and an acquaintance embracing.

↓

Self-talk: "My wife and this guy are having an affair—this is awful!"
"This guy is threatening my personal life."
"This is morally wrong—this is the worst thing that could happen to me."
"This guy is violating my rights—I've got to forcefully protect my rights."

↓

Emotion: Anger, rage, and a vengeful feeling

↓

Action: Running at the acquaintance and physically getting into a fight.

If, however, the husband remembers that his wife and the acquaintance are preparing to put on a romantic play at a nearby college, the following may occur:

Event: A husband unexpectedly arrives home early and on walking into his living room sees his wife and an acquaintance embracing.

↓

Self-talk: "Well, apparently they're practicing for the play"
"I'll watch closely, but I don't think anything romantic is occurring."
"There is no reason for me to get upset and make a fool of myself."

↓

Emotion: More emotionally relaxed and calm, though somewhat wary.

↓

Action: Casually making small talk with his wife and the acquaintance while observing their interactions.

3. Hampers you in achieving your short- and long-term goals
4. Causes significant trouble with other people
5. Leads you to feel emotions that you do not want to feel

We cannot always control events, but we can think rational thoughts about each experience. Lembo (1974) notes,

> We can think rationally or irrationally about *the things that will happen to us* and insist that we will not be a failure if our boss fires us or that we will be a worthless no-account if we are dismissed from our job; that nothing catastrophic will happen if our parents die or that it will be horrible and unbearable if they do die. (p. 9)

EP 2.1.1, b

Because we determine our feelings and our behaviors by means of self-talk, we truly are in control of our lives. If we are unhappy, unfulfilled, unsatisfied, frustrated, depressed, grief-stricken, or whatever, it is primarily our own doing. Lembo (1974, p. 10) notes, "We have the ability to create a satisfying life for ourselves, and we will succeed in doing so if we rationally manage the thoughts we tell ourselves."

Exercise M1.1: Self-Talk Causes Our Emotions

Goal: This exercise is designed to illustrate that it is primarily self-talk (rather than the event) that causes our emotions.

Step 1: Specify a negative emotion that you recently experienced.

Step 2: Describe the event associated with this emotion.

Step 3: Specify your self-talk associated with this event.

Step 4: Review the discussion of self-talk being the primary source of our emotions. Is it not true that if you had given yourself a different set of self-talk about this event, you would have felt differently?

____Yes ____No ____Uncertain

Step 5: Do you now believe that self-talk is the primary source of our emotions? Explain your views.

ADDITIONAL ASPECTS OF SELF-TALK

Our emotional reactions to repeated occurrences of an event become nearly automatic because we rapidly give ourselves a set of self-talk responses to them. For example, a few years ago I counseled a woman who became intensely emotionally upset every time her husband (who had a drinking problem) came home intoxicated. As we examined this situation, it became clear that because of repeated occurrences, she routinely gave herself the following self-talk on seeing him inebriated:

Self-talk: "He's foolishly spending the money we desperately need in this family."
"He's making a fool of himself and me in that condition."
↓ "He's setting a terrible example for our children."
"One of these days he's going to have a serious accident, get hurt, and then what will we do?"

Emotion: Anger, frustration, some depression, general unhappiness.

We are often unaware of how self-talk affects us, and it behooves counselors to discover this self-talk. Several years ago I counseled a married woman who expressed a strong desire to continue having extramarital affairs but was afraid her husband would find out about them and end the marriage. Although she was fully aware of her emotional desire for having affairs, she was unaware of the self-talk that generated this feeling. I got her to look at the self-talk that was driving her desire to have extramarital sex, and she gradually discovered the underlying self-talk: "I enjoy the feeling of being able to seduce someone to whom I am attracted." "The people I seduce feel somewhat obligated to me." "The conquest of someone who is very attractive is three-quarters of the thrill."

Another aspect of self-talk is *layering*, in which what Ellis termed the "emotional Consequence" (*C*) becomes a new "Activating Event" (*A*) by "Tom" giving himself additional self-talk (*B*) about his initial reaction. Ellis (1973) described layering as follows:

> Once the individual [Tom] becomes emotionally upset—or, rather, upsets himself—another startling human thing frequently occurs. Most of the time, he *knows* that he is anxious, depressed, enraged, or otherwise agitated; and he also generally knows that his symptoms are undesirable and (in our culture) socially disapproved. For who approves or respects highly agitated or "crazy" people? He therefore makes his emotional Consequence (*C*) or symptom into another Activating Event (*A*).
>
> Thus, he originally starts with something like "(*A*) I did poorly on my job today; (*B*) Isn't that horrible! What a worm I am for failing!" and he winds up with (*C*) feelings of anxiety, worthlessness, and depression. He now starts all over: "(*A*) I feel anxious and depressed, and worthless. (*B*) Isn't *that* horrible! What a worm I am for feeling anxious, depressed, and worthless!" Now he winds up with (*C*) even greater feelings of anxiety, worthlessness, and depression. Or, in other words, once he becomes anxious, he frequently makes himself anxious about being anxious. Once he becomes depressed, he makes himself depressed about *being* depressed. Et cetera! He now has two consequences or symptoms for the price of one; and he often goes around and around in a vicious cycle of (1) condemning himself for doing poorly at some task; (2) feeling guilty or depressed because of his self-condemnation; (3) condemning himself for his feelings of guilt and depression; (4) condemning himself for condemning himself; (5) condemning himself for seeing that he condemns himself and for still not stopping condemning himself; (6) condemning himself for going for psychotherapeutic help and still not getting better; (7) condemning himself for being more disturbed than other individuals; (8) concluding that he is indubitably hopelessly disturbed and that nothing can be done about it; and so on, and so forth. (p. 178)

EP 2.1.1b

Although self-talk is often based on our attitudes, beliefs, and values, it is a distinct entity. It has a here-and-now quality; it represents those thoughts we tell ourselves in the present. Although we hold thousands of beliefs, attitudes, and values, our self-talk at a given time is based on only a fraction of them. Self-talk is also driven by our needs, wants, and motives.

Exercise M1.2: Understanding Layering

Goal: This exercise is designed to help you understand the concept of "layering."

Reflect on a time when your awfulizing about an event led you to feel "bad." Then, because you were feeling "bad," you proceeded to awfulize about other "bad" things happening in your life—which led you to feel even worse. Specify (a) the original bad event, (b) your original set of negative self-talk, (c) how you then felt, (d) your second set of negative self-talk because you were feeling "bad," and (e) how you then felt.

CHANGING UNWANTED EMOTIONS

Rational therapy is increasingly used to change unwanted emotions. Rational therapy asserts that all emotions are primarily determined by self-talk, even the emotion of love. Individuals often believe that love is a feeling beyond their control. The language of love reinforces this erroneous belief: "I just *couldn't help it,* he swept me off my feet," "I *fell* in love," and "*It was* love at first sight." But in reality, the emotion of love is based primarily on self-talk:

Event: A woman's ideal date is a man who is tall and athletic, has dark hair, is a good conversationalist, and likes pop music. She meets a man in one of her classes who is 6 feet tall, a football player, has dark hair, is personable, and likes pop music.

↓

Her self-talk: *I can hardly believe I've finally met someone I'm really attracted to. This person is really handsome, charming, the kind of person I'd really like to get to know better and to go out to dinner with.*

↓

Her emotion: Feelings of infatuation.

There are five ways to change an unwanted emotion. Three are constructive: getting involved in a meaningful activity, changing the negative and irrational thinking underlying the unwanted emotion, and changing the distressing event. Two are destructive: abuse of alcohol, drugs, and food; and suicide. We will discuss each of the five in turn.

Getting Involved in Meaningful Activity

Practically everyone encounters day-to-day frustrations and irritations—having a class or two that aren't going well, working at a job that's unpleasant, coping with a dull social life. Dwelling on such irritations will spawn such unwanted emotions as depression, anger, frustration, despair, or feelings of failure. Which of these emotions a person has will directly depend on the person's self-talk.

Meaningful enjoyable activity, however, produces satisfaction and a healthful distraction from unwanted emotion. Individuals can learn the value of meaningful activity by writing an "escape" list of activities they find motivating, energizing, and enjoyable—taking a walk, playing golf or tennis, going to a movie, shopping, knitting, visiting friends, and so on. By having an "escape" list of things they enjoy doing, individuals can nip unwanted emotions in the bud. They can use enjoyable activities to take their minds off their day-to-day concerns and irritations. The positive emotions they experience will stem directly from the things they tell themselves about the enjoyable things they are doing.

EP 2.1.1b

In urging individuals to compile and use an escape list, rational therapy is not suggesting that people should avoid doing something about unpleasant events. If something can be done to change a distressing event, all constructive efforts should be tried. However, we often do not have control over unpleasant events and cannot change them. But we always have the capacity to control and change what we tell ourselves about the unpleasant events.

Exercise M1.3: Using Meaningful Activities to Change Unwanted Emotions

Goal: This exercise demonstrates that when we are awfulizing about something and therefore feeling bad, we can alleviate the unwanted emotions by getting involved in meaningful activities.

Step 1: Describe a time when you were awfulizing about something and therefore feeling bad and then alleviated the unwanted emotions by getting involved in something you enjoyed doing.

Step 2: Reflect on this experience. Is it not true that getting involved in enjoyable activities stopped you from awfulizing (that is, you stopped thinking about the unpleasant event and instead switched to thinking about an activity you were enjoying)? Also, when you stopped awfulizing, did you find your unwanted emotions alleviated?

Changing Self-Talk[1]

A second approach to changing unwanted emotions is to identify and then alter the negative and irrational thinking that leads to them. Maultsby (1977) developed *rational self-analysis* (RSA), which is very useful for alleviating undesirable emotions. The goal in RSA is to change unwanted emotions (such as anger, guilt, depression, or shyness). An RSA is done by recording the event and self-talk on paper. An RSA has six parts (see Exhibit M1.2).

1. *Part A (facts and events):* Simply state the facts or events that occurred.
2. *Part B (self-talk):* Write all of your thoughts about A. Number each statement (1, 2, 3, 4, and so on). Write "good," "bad," or "neutral" after each self-talk statement to show how you believe each B-section statement reflects on you as a person. (The RSA case example on page 486 illustrates the mechanics of an RSA.)

[1]This description of rational self-analysis is adapted from Charles Zastrow, *Talk to Yourself: Using the Power of Self-Talk*, © 1979, pp. 32–36, Prentice-Hall, Inc., Englewood Cliffs, New Jersey. Reprinted by permission of the author.

Exhibit M1.2 Format for RSA

A Facts and Events B Self-Talk	D(a) Camera Check of A D(b) Rational Debate of B
1. __________	1. __________
2. __________	2. __________
and so on	and so on
C Emotional Consequences of B	E Emotional Goals and Behavioral Goals for Similar Future Events

3. *Part C (emotional consequences)*: Write simple statements describing your gut reactions and emotions stemming from your self-talk in part B.

4. *Part D(a)* is written *only* after you have written sections A, B, and C and *only* after you have reviewed all five guidelines for rational thinking. Part D(a) is a "camera check" of part A. Reread part A and ask yourself, "If I had had a video of what happened, would it verify what I wrote as 'fact'?" Videos record facts, not personal beliefs or opinions.

An example in part B of a personal opinion that is mistaken as a fact is "Karen made me look like a fool when she laughed while I was trying to make a point." In D(a) (the video check of A), you correct the opinion part of this statement by writing only the factual part: "I was attempting to make a serious point when Karen laughed." Then add the personal opinion part of the statement to B ("Karen made me look like a fool").

5. *Part D(b)* challenges and thus may change negative and irrational thinking. Take each B statement separately. Read B–1 first and ask yourself whether it is inconsistent with any of the five criteria for rational thinking. According to Maultsby (1977), thinking is irrational if it does one or more of the following:

1. Does not fit the facts (is not based on objective reality)
2. Hampers you in protecting your life
3. Hampers you in achieving your short- and long-term goals
4. Causes significant trouble with other people
5. Leads you to feel emotions that you do not want to feel

If the self-talk statement is consistent with the five criteria for rational thinking, merely write "that's rational." If, however, the self-talk statement meets one or more of the criteria for irrational thinking, then think of an alternative self-talk to that B statement. This new self-talk statement is crucially important in changing your undesirable emotion and needs to be rational and to be a self-talk statement you are willing to accept as a new opinion for yourself. After writing down this D(b–1) self-talk in the D(b) section, then consider B–2, B–3, and so on, in the same way.

6. Under *part E*, write down the new emotions you want to have in similar future A situations. In writing these new emotions that you desire, keep in mind that they will follow from your self-talk statements in your D(b) section. Section E may also contain a description of certain actions you intend to take to help you achieve your emotional goals when you encounter future A's.

Rational self-challenges will work only if clients actively practice using the rational self-challenges they develop. Self-challenges work best when used by clients every time they start the original negative, irrational self-talk.

CASE EXAMPLE Rational Self-Analysis: Coping with a Sexual Affair

Cindy sought counseling after her boyfriend Jim told her that a few months earlier he had become sexually involved with Linda. Jim and Cindy had dated for 2 years. But they began to argue frequently and so decided not to see each other during the summer. In the fall, they again felt strongly about each other and resumed their relationship. A few weeks later, Jim (after Cindy questioned him) informed her about Linda.

Cindy told the counselor that she wanted to better handle her unwanted feelings about this affair. After discussing them in some depth, the counselor informed her that she could counter her undesirable emotions with a rational self-analysis, and Cindy wrote the following RSA.

A (FACTS AND EVENTS)	D(a) VIDEO CHECK OF A
My boyfriend, Jim, informed me that he had sex with Linda, after a party where they had both been drinking.	This is all factual. I know this because Jim told me himself. Jim and I are very close, and I know he wouldn't lie to me.

B (SELF-TALK)	D(b) CINDY'S RATIONAL DEBATE OF B
B–1 It's not fair! How could Jim do such a thing to me? (bad)	D(b–1) Jim had sex with Linda. I'll just have to accept that. People are human and fallible, I can't expect to always be treated with fairness. Besides, Jim and I had broken up, so I'm sure they didn't have me in mind when they did it. At the time they were sexually involved, neither Jim nor I had any commitment to each other. Truth be told, I also considered having a fling this summer and would have had I met the right guy.
B–2 That creep just had sex with Linda because he wanted a piece of _____. (bad)	D(b–2) Jim probably had sex with Linda for other reasons. I know he's not the type who uses a woman merely for relief of his sexual tensions. It is also a mistake to label him a creep. No one is a creep. People are humans. If I mislabel him a creep, it may lead me to view him in terms of an inaccurate label.
B–3 Jim and Linda had no good reasons for doing what they did. They only did it because they were both drunk. What a couple of jerks! (bad)	D(b–3) Alcohol obviously had something to do with their having sex. I know that Jim is much less inhibited when he has had a few drinks. I don't know about Linda, though. The drinking can't be the only reason they had sex. Maybe they felt attracted to each other and wanted to have sex. I've got to remember that this summer Jim and I had no commitments to each other, and therefore I do not have the right to expect that he would be celibate to please me. Also, it is a mistake for me to refer to Jim or Linda as being a "jerk." People are people.
B–4 Linda must be some kind of cheap tramp. Only a tramp would have sex with a guy she didn't love. (bad)	D(b–4) I don't even know Linda, so I shouldn't judge her like this. Furthermore, I have no way of knowing how Linda felt about Jim. Maybe she felt she loved him at the time. A woman isn't necessarily loose if she has sex with a guy.

CASE EXAMPLE *(continued)*

A (FACTS AND EVENTS)		D(a) VIDEO CHECK OF A
B–5 Jim must think he's some kind of stud now. (bad)	D(b–5)	Jim has told me that he has had sex with only two women. My idea of a "stud" is a guy who thinks he can have sex with any woman who comes along. I know Jim better than that. He doesn't think he could, nor would he try to, conquer just any woman.
B–6 Jim and I will never again be able to have a good sexual relationship of our own now that he has someone else to compare me to. I just know that he'll be thinking of Linda from now on. (bad)	D(b–6)	Jim and I love each other. Jim told me that he does not love Linda. Just because Jim had sex with Linda does not mean our relationship will always be adversely affected. We can communicate easily during sex, and it has always been satisfying so far. It would be silly for Jim to compare our entire relationship to the one night he spent with Linda.
B–7 This is the worst thing that Jim could have done. (bad)	D(b–7)	This is not the worst thing that Jim could have done. What he did was not a crime, like murder or rape, which would have been worse. The situation would be worse if Jim had slept with Linda while he was still seeing me. I'm glad to know that he would never do that.
B–8 Now that I know Jim had sex with Linda, our whole relationship will be ruined. (bad)	D(b–8)	The fact that Jim had sex with Linda does not have to ruin our relationship. The event occurred in the past. It's over. Past sexual experiences should have no bearing on the future of our relationship. I want the relationship to continue, and I don't want to see it ruined.
B–9 I should never have broken up with Jim. Then he would never have slept with Linda. It's all my fault. (bad)	D(b–9)	It's not my fault at all. I broke up with Jim because I felt it was the best thing to do at the time. I know Jim would not have been unfaithful to me had we still been dating, but we weren't dating at the time this happened. I had no way of knowing he would some day go to bed with Linda, and knowing would not have changed my decision to break up with him. It's not my fault because I wasn't even involved.
B–10 From now on, whenever I hear Linda's name mentioned I'm going to have a fit! I won't be able to handle it! (bad)	D(b–10)	When I hear Linda's name mentioned, I don't have to respond by having a fit. I can handle my feelings by being calm and not letting the mention of her name bother me.

C MY EMOTIONS	E MY EMOTIONAL AND BEHAVIORAL GOALS
I feel guilty, hurt, angry, upset, and jealous. (very bad)	I want to get over my unwanted emotions that I have had about this affair. I want to put this affair in our past. At the time it happened, Jim and I had no commitments to each other. What is important to Jim and me is our present and future relationship and not what happened one evening when Jim and I had broken up.

EP 2.1.1b

Exercise M1.4: Changing Unwanted Emotions with a Rational Self-Analysis

Goal: This exercise demonstrates that writing and then using the rational debates will change unwanted emotions.

Step 1: Review the material on a rational self-analysis. Write a rational self-analysis on an unwanted emotion you recently experienced.

Step 2: Do you believe that if you apply the rational debates to your negative and irrational self-talk, you will be able to change unwanted emotions? Explain your views.

Changing the Distressing Event

A third way to change unwanted emotions is to change the distressing event. There is an infinite number of distressing events: losing a job, the breakup of a romantic relationship, receiving failing grades, being in an automobile accident, and so on. In some cases, constructive action can be taken to change the distressing event. For example, if a man is terminated from a job, he can seek another; when he finds one, he will feel better. If a student is getting failing grades, a conference with the instructor may give the student some ideas about how to improve the grades. If the suggestions appear practical and have merit, the student will feel better.

Not all distressing events can be changed. For example, a woman may have a job that she needs and be forced to interact with other employees who display behaviors she dislikes. If that individual cannot change the behaviors of the others, the only other constructive option is to "bite the bullet" and adapt to the circumstances. However, when it is practical to change distressing events, they should be changed. When constructive changes in events are made, a person probably will feel better because he or she will then (in all likelihood) be having more positive self-talk related to the constructive changes that have been made.

EP 2.1.1b

Exercise M1.5: Changing Unwanted Emotions by Changing Events

Goal: This exercise demonstrates that unwanted emotions can be changed by changing the event that is associated with the unwanted emotion.

Step 1: Describe a time in your life when you were awfulizing about something and therefore feeling bad and you then changed the event—which resulted in your stopping awfulizing. For example, you may have had an unpleasant job, which you then changed. Or you may have been in an abusive relationship, which you then ended.

Step 2: Is it not true that you stopped feeling bad after changing the unpleasant event because you stopped awfulizing and then had more positive self-talk related to the constructive changes that you made? Explain your views on this.

Exhibit M1.3 Explaining How to Change an Unwanted Emotion to a Client

The following is a step-by-step guide for a counselor to use in using rational therapy concepts with a client who has an unwanted emotion:

Step 1: Introductions are made between the counselor and the client. (The counselor may engage in some small talk to facilitate forming a therapeutic relationship.)

Step 2: The counselor asks the client to summarize why he (we will assume the client is a male) came in today? We will also assume the client indicates he has an unwanted emotion that he is struggling with. The unwanted emotion may be: depression, anger, anxiety, frustration, or some other painful emotion.

Step 3: The counselor asks the client what he believes is the cause of the unwanted emotion. Practically all clients will indicate the cause is due to external events. For illustrative purposes, let us take the example of the client saying, "I am really sad because my wife is ending our marriage."

Step 4: The counselor briefly summarizes that, in almost all cases, it is not so much the external event, but what he is telling himself about the event, that is the cause of his unwanted emotion. (Expect the client to be puzzled by this statement.) To clarify, ask the client to ponder the following. Are you thinking some of the following thoughts about the impending divorce: "I love her so much—I don't want her to leave." "My life is ruined without her." "I'll never find anyone as good as her." "My life is no longer worth living." "I am such a loser—I drove her away." "I'm just not a lovable person."

You may want to ask the client, in this situation: "Would you not feel very different if you were thinking the following about her leaving: "This is good—I will find someone better than her." "Thank God she is leaving; we've haven't gotten along for the past few years." "There are plenty of other fish in the sea."

Step 5: Spend time clarifying with the client that it is our self-talk (thoughts) that are the major source of unwanted emotions, perhaps with additional examples. Add, that we have the power to change our thoughts, which will then lead to our painful unwanted emotion going "poof"; that is, leaving us.

Step 6: Indicate there are only three constructive approaches to making an unwanted emotion go "poof". The first is to seek to change the external event. For example, ask the client if he thought offering to go to marriage counseling with his wife may lead the wife to decide to work on maintaining their marriage. It should be noted some events can be changed, while others can't. For example, an event that cannot be changed is being involved in a bad car accident. An event that may be changed is going to marriage counseling, instead of seeking a divorce.

Step 7: Indicate the second option for changing an unwanted emotion is to change one's self-talk about the external event. One way of doing this is for the client to write out a rational self-analysis, in which he specifies: The external event, his self-talk about that event, his unwanted emotions that he is feeling, his rational debates of his irrational self-talk; and his emotional and behavioral goals. (An example is provided in this chapter.) It is generally helpful to have a copy of an RSA that can be given to the client, for illustrative purposes.

Step 8: Indicate the third option is to make the unwanted emotion go "poof" by getting involved in some meaningful activities. Ask the client to indicate what activities he truly enjoys, that would then stop him (at least for while) from thinking about his wife leaving. Indicate, "We sometimes cannot control external events, but we always have the power to change our thoughts." For example, "If you are awfulizing about your wife leaving you, and suddenly you are informed you had just won a lottery, would you not think happy thoughts for awhile?"

Step 9: Ask the client to summarize the three constructive options for seeking to change an unwanted emotion. (If the client has a few challenges in summarizing these options, help him with this.)

Step 10: Ask the client which of these three options, or strategies, he wants to try. The client may choose a combination of these three strategies, which is "good".

Step 11: Wish the client the best with his strategies, and check back with him in a week or two as to how he is doing.

Two Destructive Ways of Dealing with Unwanted Emotions

I strongly discourage using either of the following two ways of dealing with unwanted emotions. I present them here only to complete the list of ways to deal with unwanted emotions.

One method is to relieve intense unwanted emotions temporarily through the use of alcohol, other drugs, or food. When the effects of the drug wear off, the person's problems and unwanted emotions remain, and there is a danger that through repeated use the person will become dependent on the drug. Some people overeat for the same reasons—loneliness, insecurity, boredom, and frustration. The process of eating and the feeling of having a full stomach provide temporary relief from intense unwanted emotions. Such people are likely to become overweight or bulimic—or both.

EP 2.1.1b

The other destructive way to relieve unwanted emotions is suicide. This is the ultimate destructive approach to dealing with unwanted emotions. If you know of someone who is contemplating suicide, you have a legal right and an ethical obligation to seek to connect that person with professional help—even when the suicidal person requests that you do not inform anyone else of his or her intentions.

Exercise M1.6: Changing Unwanted Emotions by Abusing the Use of Alcohol, Other Drugs, or Food

Goal: This exercise demonstrates that unwanted emotions can be changed temporarily through the abusive use of alcohol, other drugs, or food.

Step 1: Describe someone you know who emotionally was feeling bad and turned to abusive use of alcohol, other drugs, or food. If you do not know anyone who did this, describe a time in your life when you were feeling bad and resorted to the abusive use of alcohol, other drugs, or food.

Step 2: Is it not accurate that the abusive use of alcohol, other drugs, or food only provides temporary relief? Give a short explanation of your views on this question.

ASSESSING AND CHANGING DYSFUNCTIONAL BEHAVIOR

Self-talk is the primary determinant not only of our emotions but also of our actions:

In a nutshell, our actions are primarily determined by self-talk (our cognitions). Our thoughts determine our actions. To demonstrate this principle, reflect on the last time you did something bizarre or unusual. What self-talk statements were you giving yourself (that is, what were you thinking) before and during the time when you did what you did?

Rational therapy maintains that the reasons for any dysfunctional act (including crime) can be determined by examining what the offender was telling himself or herself before and during the time when the act was being committed. Two examples of cognitions that lead to dysfunctional behavior are the following:

Cognition: A 16-year-old sees an unlocked Audi with the keys in it and thinks, "Hey, this is the ultimate car to drive. Let me take it for a ride."

Behavior: Car theft.

Cognition: A 23-year-old male is on his third date with the same woman. He brings her to his apartment and thinks, "She is really sexy. Since I've wined and dined her three times, now it's time for her to show her appreciation.

"I'll bet she wants it as much as I do. I'll show her what a great lover I am. If she says, 'Don't,' I know she really means 'Don't stop.' I'll use a little force if I have to. When it's over, she'll really love me."

Behavior: Date rape.

It should be noted that the cognitions underlying each dysfunctional behavior may vary considerably among perpetrators. For example, possible cognitions for shoplifting a shirt might be the following. "This shirt would look really nice for the wedding I'm going to on Saturday. Since I'm buying a number of other items from this store, they still will make a profit from me even if I take this without paying for it." Another may be: "This will be a challenge to see if I can get away with taking this shirt. I'll put it on in the fitting room and put my own shirt and coat on over it, and no one will even see me walk out of the store with it. Since I've taken a number of things in the past, I'll act real casual as I walk out of the store." Or: "My son really needs a decent shirt. He doesn't have any nice ones to wear. I don't get enough money from public assistance to buy my children what they need. I know my son is embarrassed to wear the rags that he has. I'll just stick this shirt under my coat and walk out with it."

Assessing human behavior is largely a process of identifying the cognitions that underlie unwanted emotions or dysfunctional behavior. The stages of this process are as follows:

1. Identify as precisely as possible the unwanted emotions or dysfunctional behavior that a client has.
2. Identify the cognitions, or thinking patterns, that the client has during the time when the client is having unwanted emotions or is displaying dysfunctional behavior. There are two primary ways of identifying these cognitions. One way is to ask the client what he was thinking before and during the time when the client was having unwanted emotions or displaying dysfunctional behavior. If this approach does not work (perhaps because the client refuses to divulge what he was thinking), a second approach is to obtain information about the client's life circumstances at that time. Once these life circumstances are identified, the professional conducting the assessment needs to place herself mentally into the life circumstances of the perpetrator and then reflect on the kinds of cognitions that would lead this client to have his specific unwanted emotions or dysfunctional behavior. For example, if the client is a 16-year-old female who has run away from home and is unemployed, it is fairly easy to identify (to some extent) the kinds of cognitions that would lead such a person to turn to prostitution.

EP 2.1.1b

One deduction that can be made from the principle that thinking processes determine dysfunctional behaviors and unwanted emotions is that *to change dysfunctional behaviors or unwanted emotions it is necessary for the affected person to change his or her thinking patterns.* This concept is illustrated in Exhibit M1.4. Also see the Case Example "Using Rational Therapy to Change Irresponsible Behavior" on page 494.

Exercise M1.7: Our Actions Are Determined by Our Thoughts

Goal: This exercise demonstrates that most of our actions are determined by what we think.

Step 1: Describe something embarrassing that you did.

Step 2: Describe what you were thinking that led you to do the embarrassing thing that you described.

Step 3: Can you identify any actions that you engaged in that were not partially influenced by what you were thinking? If "yes," specify such actions.

Step 4: In criminal court proceedings, prosecuting attorneys are expected to identify the "motive" for why the defendant committed the alleged crime. Is not the search for the motive a search to identify the thinking patterns that led the defendant to commit the alleged crime? Explain your views.

Step 5: Is it not true that to stop engaging in dysfunctional or deviant behaviors, a person needs to change the thought patterns underlying the dysfunctional behaviors? Explain your views.

Step 6: As an example, what interventions might be used to change the abusive behavior of a husband who abuses his wife?

Exhibit M1.4 Our Thinking Determines Our Behaviors and Our Emotions

A few years ago I was describing to a class the concept that our thinking primarily causes our emotions and our actions. A male student voluntarily self-disclosed the following:

> What you're saying makes a lot of sense. It really applies to something that happened to me. I was living with a female student whom I really cared about. I thought, though, that she was going out on me. When I confronted her about it, she always said I was paranoid and denied it.
>
> Then one night I walked into a bar in this town and I saw her in a corner in a "clutch" position with this guy. I told myself things like "She really is cheating on me. Both of them are playing me for a fool." Such thinking led me to be angry.
>
> I also told myself "I'm going to set this straight. I'm going to get even with them. I'll break the bottoms off these two empty beer bottles and then jab each of them with the jagged edges." I proceeded to knock off the bottoms on the bar, and then started walking toward them. I got to within eight feet of them and they were still arm in arm and didn't see me. I began, though, to change my thinking. I thought that if I jabbed them, the end result would be that I would get 8 to 10 years in prison, and I concluded she isn't worth that. Based on this thinking I decided to drop the beer bottles, walk out, and end my relationship with her—which is what I did.

RATIONAL THERAPY IS AN EDUCATIONAL PROCESS

Learning how to think rationally and to counter irrational and negative self-talk is a process. Clients can learn to analyze and change irrational self-talk in a variety of ways: instruction by their counselor, viewing videotapes and films, reading books and pamphlets, and attending workshops or seminars on rational therapy. Ellis demonstrated that the basic principles of analyzing irrational self-talk and thinking rationally can be successfully taught both to adults and to elementary and secondary school students.

Rational therapists teach clients how to analyze irrational self-talk using probes, confrontation, explanations, interpretations, humor, and suggestions that help clients discover their irrational thinking. Once clients become aware of their irrational self-talk, rational therapists use a variety of techniques to help them change.

AN ECLECTIC APPROACH

Rational therapists use whatever approaches show promise in changing irrational self-talk. Ellis (1979, p. 186) noted, "The rational therapist uses role playing, assertion training, desensitization, humor, operant conditioning, suggestion, support, and a whole bag of other 'tricks.'"

Rational self-challenges (including RSAs) are often used to change unwanted emotions. For certain unwanted emotions, such as depression, rational therapists may attempt to get clients involved in meaningful or enjoyable activities (for example, playing golf, joining a social club). Reality therapists (see Module 3) use this approach to change unwanted emotions. Rational therapists theorize that getting clients involved in enjoyable activities works because it switches their negative focus to a positive one, which then changes their emotions.

For people who are shy or prone to temper outbursts, rational therapists may use assertiveness training techniques (see Module 2). For clients with drinking problems, rational therapists may supplement therapy by getting clients involved in Alcoholics Anonymous.

Homework assignments are frequently given. Shy clients try out assertive approaches that they role-played in counseling. They may write an RSA in which

CASE EXAMPLE Using Rational Therapy to Change Irresponsible Behavior

Dan Barber, age 4½, was taken to the emergency room of St. Mary's Hospital in a midwestern city. He was unconscious and severely bruised, and he had a broken arm. Dan was brought in by neighbors after Mr. Barber telephoned them. Dan had a concussion, sustained from what appeared to be several blows. Seven weeks earlier Dan had been rushed to the hospital for a broken leg. That time Mr. Barber stated Dan fell down a stairway. Protective Services was contacted by the hospital, and in the initial interview Mr. Barber acknowledged that he beat Dan on both of these occasions. Why? The following is Mr. Barber's account of the thinking processes (self-talk) that led him to abuse his son.

> Dan is my only son. His mother and I got a divorce 8 months ago. I'm an accountant and up until about a year ago I really thought I had it made. Mary is very attractive, and we got along well. We had a nice house, and I had a good income—many days I worked 11 or 12 hours, getting overtime pay. Mary primarily took care of our son.
>
> One day I arrived home and there was a note from my wife saying she was leaving me. I was shocked and couldn't believe it. A few weeks later I received papers indicating she had gotten a divorce in Mexico. Shortly afterward I heard she married a person from the same church I used to go to. I really don't understand how she could leave both Dan and me, without even talking about it. I guess I've been so involved with my work that I didn't realize how she felt.
>
> As time went by after she left I discussed my problems with some of our neighbors. A few indicated that several men over the years visited with my wife during the day when I was at work. Apparently she had been having affairs for a long time.
>
> My mother moved in after Mary left, to help take care of Dan.
>
> In the past few months, I have been wondering if Dan is really my own son.

At this point Mr. Barber was asked to indicate what he was thinking during the last time he abused Dan. The events and self-talk are put into the format presented earlier.

Event: That evening I came home from work feeling exhausted. I wanted just to relax and have a peaceful evening. My mother went grocery shopping, and I guess I was feeling sorry for myself. Dan was quite noisy, and I told him to stop making so much noise. But he continued.

↓

Self-talk: "I can't take any more of this."
"Here I have to take care of a kid who may not even be my own."
"This kid reminds me of the hurt that Mary has caused me. I have a right to even the score."
"I can't stand this! I've got to shut this brat up!"
"My father beat me when I did wrong—that's the best way to show kids who's the boss."

↓

Emotion: Anger, revenge, hostility, frustration.

Actions: Hitting Dan, knocking him down several times. (Mr. Barber added, "Once I started hitting Dan, I thought I was evening the score with Mary, and didn't want to stop.")

At first, Mr. Barber indicated he couldn't understand how he could lose control and abuse his son. He appeared remorseful and desirous of changing his actions. Through therapy, he gradually came to understand that he controlled his emotions and actions and that he could change his unwanted emotions and actions by changing his self-talk. He knew he had severely hurt his son and that he could lose him if the abuse was not curbed.

Mr. Barber's concerns about being Dan's biological father were relieved by the results of DNA testing, and he learned through rational therapy how to challenge and change the self-talk that led him to abuse his son. Mr. Barber was also instructed to leave Dan in the care of his mother whenever he felt an urge to abuse Dan. If the grandmother wasn't available, Mr. Barber agreed to call the Protective Services worker to ventilate his feelings over the phone rather than at Dan. Mr. Barber also received counseling about his feelings toward his wife and about the importance of focusing his thoughts and energies on the present and future rather than wallowing in self-pity and dwelling on the past.

they identify and challenge the negative and irrational self-talk that makes them feel shy. A male client who states he can't stand to be rejected by the opposite sex might ask three different females out on dates to test the hypothesis that he can indeed survive rejection. Clients also read books to help them learn and apply the basic concepts.

COMMON IRRATIONAL BELIEFS

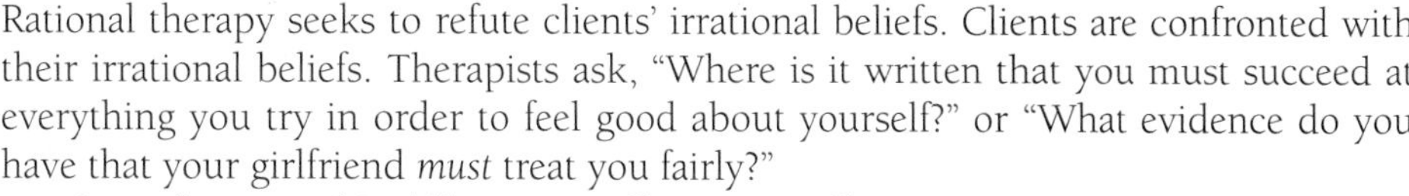

Rational therapy seeks to refute clients' irrational beliefs. Clients are confronted with their irrational beliefs. Therapists ask, "Where is it written that you must succeed at everything you try in order to feel good about yourself?" or "What evidence do you have that your girlfriend *must* treat you fairly?"

EP 2.1.1b

Several writers (Criddle, 1974; Ellis, 1958; Ellis & Harper, 1977; Hauck, 1972; Raimy, 1977; Zastrow, 1979, 1993) have identified common beliefs that generate negative or irrational self-talk. For a list, see Exhibit M1.5. Thinking of "needs," "shoulds," "musts," "awful," and "unbearable" distorts reality and frequently leads us to overact. A more rational philosophy is "I would like to be treated reasonably well by people and life."

Exercise M1.8: Changing My Irrational Beliefs

Goal: This exercise is designed to assist you in identifying and eliminating your irrational beliefs.

Step 1: Review the irrational beliefs in listed in Exhibit M1.4. Write down any irrational beliefs that you have (which may or may not be listed in the exhibit). For each irrational belief that you have, write down the rational belief that you should instead focus on developing for yourself.

Step 2: Do you think you can make progress in changing your irrational beliefs by seeking to refute your irrational beliefs by challenging them with your rational beliefs? Explain your views.

WHAT REALLY CAUSES CHANGE?

Client-centered therapy, psychoanalysis, rational therapy, feminist intervention, behavior therapy, transactional analysis, reality therapy, hypnosis, meditation, and crisis intervention are all used to treat a wide range of emotional and behavioral problems: people who are depressed, who are lonely, who have marital or other interpersonal relationship problems, who have disabling fears and phobias, who are overly aggressive, who have drinking problems, or who suffer from grief, shame, or guilt. These therapies differ substantially in explaining why therapeutic change occurs. How can all these distinct and diverse therapies produce positive change in clients? What produces changes in therapy? Is there a single explanation?

Practically every theory postulates a different view of why change occurs. In reviewing this dilemma, Raimy (1977) stated,

> Psychotherapists today are faced with an insistent, nagging problem: since widely diverse methods of treatment for similar problems have their successes as well as their failures, how can one defend a given set of treatment procedures as superior to others? Clearly, since quite different, even contradictory, methods of treatment produce similar results, explanations for the success of treatment must be sought outside the realm of method or technique. (p. 1)

Exhibit M1.5 Common Beliefs That Generate Negative Self-Talk

1. The belief that it is a dire necessity to be loved or approved of by everyone for everything you do. A more rational idea is to do the things you want to do as long as you do not hinder others. No matter how hard you try, you will never get everyone to like you as what will please one may displease another. Your opinion of yourself is much more important than others' views of you.
2. The belief that you should be thoroughly competent, skilled, and achieving in all possible respects if you are to consider yourself worthwhile. This idea represents a demand for perfection that is simply impossible to achieve. All humans are fallible. We all make mistakes. Achieving something does not make you a "better person." We all have intrinsic worth because we exist. If you fail at something, it does not make you a failure but only a person who has failed at something.
3. The belief that it is awful and catastrophic when things are not the way you would like them to be. In actuality, nothing is awful. Awful connotes that certain circumstances are more than "100 percent" negative. Events or circumstances are at times inconvenient, but they never are "awful." By telling ourselves that certain inconvenient events (such as a broken engagement) are awful, we are causing ourselves to overreact emotionally. In actuality we have limited control over events that happen to us. You can try to change reality, but you better stop *demanding* that it be as you say—there is a great deal of evidence that neither you nor I runs the world. Rational therapy seeks to "deawfulize" thinking.
4. The belief that there will be justice in the world and in interpersonal relationships. Humans are fallible, and injustices can be expected to occur. To expect justice in all interactions is unrealistic and will lead you to react with anger or frustration when an injustice occurs. "Complete justice" does not exist, and it never did. A more rational philosophy is to seek to change conditions so they become more fair. But if you come to realize that it is impossible to change an "unfair" situation, you had better become resigned to its existence and stop telling yourself how awful it is.
5. The belief that human unhappiness (and happiness) is externally caused and that you have little or no ability to control your unwanted emotions. The external environment can only cause you physical pain, never emotional pain. You cause all your emotions by your self-talk, and thereby you can control and relieve any uncomfortable emotion by changing your negative or irrational self-talk.
6. The belief that if something is or may be dangerous or fearsome you should be terribly concerned about it and should keep dwelling on the possibility of its occurring. Worriers frequently believe the act of worrying has a "magical" value of preventing the worst from occurring. Of course, worrying has no magical power. Chronic worrying seldom achieves the results that calm deliberation and careful study do. Excessive worry often incapacitates a person to the point that the feared event is not avoided but often brought about. If you are a chronic worrier, analyze your self-talk to discover what is rational fear and what is irrational fear. Worriers will find that most of their fears are irrational and can be countered with rational self-challenges.
7. The belief that you should depend on others and that you need someone stronger than yourself on whom to rely. Any time you enter into a dependent relationship, you become vulnerable to the whims of the person you are dependent on. It is usually far better to stand on your own feet and gain faith in yourself by doing what you can for yourself and for others. There is no guarantee that someone else's judgment is right—in fact, all humans are fallible. The only way you become efficient at acting on your own judgment is to practice doing it.
8. The belief that your past is an all-important determinant of your present behavior and that because something once strongly affected your life it will indefinitely have a similar effect. In actuality, what you want out of life, now and in the future (along with your motivation to achieve what you want), is a much stronger determinant of what your life will be.
9. The belief that what other people do is vitally important to your existence and that you should make great efforts to change them in the direction you would like them to be. Forcing others to behave in a certain way frequently makes them rebel. In actuality, you have a right to live the way you want to as long as you do not hinder others in living the way they want to. You own your life and others own theirs, and you should respect their right to live the way they want to.
10. The belief that other people's problems are also yours and that you should become quite emotionally involved in other people's problems. You can do very little in controlling the emotions and behaviors of others, although you can do a great deal about controlling your own. When other people have problems, they *own* them; you don't. Becoming emotionally involved by psychologically taking on joint ownership usually is more destructive than helpful. The best way to help others is to recognize their problems are theirs and be an emotionally calm person who is available to help arrive at a sensible attack on the problems.

Exhibit M1.5 *(continued)*

11. The belief that people with a stereotyped label (for example, ex-convict, mentally ill, mentally retarded, whore, juvenile delinquent, welfare mother) are somehow categorically different from "normal" people and should be viewed with suspicion and avoided. In actuality, such a label (at best) refers only to a small proportion of their past or present behavior. Every person is unique. Stereotypes that are based on labels are frequently myths without a factual base. We will get to know other people much more realistically if we interact with them as "unique persons" rather than in terms of expectations based on labels. The same approach is applicable to interacting with people having labels with more positive stereotypes; — for example, priests, professors, executive directors, police officers, counselors, school principals, judges.
12. The belief that human happiness can be achieved by inaction. There is no magical way in which happiness is suddenly going to happen to you. We get out of life what we put into it. If you are bored or unhappy, there are two ways of counteracting these problems: challenging the irrational self-talk or getting involved in meaningful activities. People are the happiest when they are fully absorbed in satisfying activities.
13. The belief that what you *want* are needs that *must* be fulfilled. In actuality, you have very few *needs*— you need food, water, and shelter to exist. The consequences of thinking in terms of needs are often self-defeating. Thinking in terms of needs implies life-and-death consequences. Faced with such consequences, you will tend to panic and think and behave irrationally, and thus self-defeatingly. Ellis (1973) coined the term *musterbation* for people who behave irrationally because they erroneously perceive their wants to be needs that *must* be fulfilled.
14. The belief that people and life *should* always be pleasing, and if they are not, they are awful and unbearable. This erroneous belief is operating when you give yourself the following self-talk about an unpleasant experience: "I *should* be treated in a totally satisfying way; it is *awful* when I'm not." But where is the evidence that people and life *should* treat anyone in a perfectly gratifying way? Everything in life is imperfect. Nothing completely lasts or fully satisfies. All people are fallible. Demanding "I should be treated in a certain way" requires that othets act and that events unfold according to your private wishes. You have neither the control over others nor are you (or for that matter, anyone) such a superspecial person that the world *should* revolve around you.

Thinking psychologically in terms of "needs," "shoulds," "musts," "awful," and "unbearable" is a distortion of reality and frequently leads us to overact. Instead of using "shoulds" and "musts" in our interactions with others, a more rational philosophy is "I would like to be treated reasonably well by people and life."

What Causes Disturbing Emotions and Ineffective Actions?

Before we attempt to provide an explanation of what produces positive changes in therapy, it is important to identify the primary determinants of emotional and behavior problems. The most important point about the rational therapy formula (Event → Self-talk → Emotion → Actions) is that self-talk determines how we act.

By changing our self-talk, we can change how we act. Generally we cannot control events that happen to us, but we have the power to think rationally and thereby change *all* of our unwanted emotions and dysfunctional behaviors. Self-talk is hypothesized as the primary determinant of all actions and all emotions, including love, fear, anger, grief, depression, anxiety, shame, happiness, hate, and frustration. Zastrow (1979, 1993) has also shown that self-talk is the primary determinant of our self-concept, our sense of success or failure, our personality, and stress-related illnesses.

EP 2.1.1b

Restructuring Thinking: Is This the Key Therapeutic Agent?

Rational therapy asserts that discomforting emotions and dysfunctional actions arise primarily from negative or irrational self-talk. If this conceptualization is accurate, an important corollary is that any therapy technique that succeeds in changing emotions or actions is effective primarily because it changes self-talk. In other words, self-talk appears to be the key therapeutic agent in all approaches that produce positive changes.

Exercise M1.9: Is Restructuring Thinking the Key Therapeutic Agent?

Goal: This exercise is designed to have you reflect on what causes therapeutic change.

Step 1: Describe an unwanted emotion that you recently had that you no longer have.

Step 2: Did restructuring your thinking lead to the unwanted emotion ceasing to exist? Describe what you believe led to your unwanted emotion ceasing to exist.

Step 3: Describe a dysfunctional behavior (such as procrastinating about something) that you recently engaged in but no longer engage in.

Step 4: Did restructuring your thinking lead you to stop engaging in this dysfunctional behavior? Describe what you believe led you to no longer engage in this dysfunctional behavior.

Step 5: Provide your thoughts on the assertion that changing self-talk in a more positive and rational direction is the key therapeutic agent in changing unwanted emotions and dysfunctional behaviors.

EVALUATION OF RATIONAL THERAPY

Rational therapy is one of the most widely used therapy approaches. DiGiuseppe, Miller, and Trexler (1977) summarized a large number of outcome studies conducted on rational therapy and found that more than 90% of these studies supported its claims. Ellis (2008) noted that more than 200 outcome studies have been published showing that rational therapy is effective in changing the thoughts, feelings, and behaviors of individuals with various kinds of disturbances. DiGiuseppe, Terjesen, Rose,

Doyle, and Vadalakis (1998) stated that studies conducted on rational therapy show that the approach usually works better than no therapy and that rational therapy is often more effective than other methods of psychotherapy.

Rational therapy has been used successfully to treat clients with a wide range of problems, including unwanted emotions (depression, anxiety, fears and phobias, guilt, shame), sexual problems and sexual dysfunctions, worrying, marital problems, interaction problems, alcoholism, shyness, and such irresponsible actions as committing crimes, procrastination, and jealous actions. Its major hypotheses are also useful in child rearing, education, and executive management.

By asserting that we primarily cause our unwanted emotions and irresponsible behaviors by what we think, the approach squarely puts responsibility on us for improving our lives. We are in charge of our lives and have the power to alleviate unwanted emotions and change ineffective actions. Zastrow (1979, 1993) theorized that our self-talk has immense effects on our lives that we only now are beginning to understand. Self-talk, for example, plays a major part in chronic stress, and chronic stress causes a wide range of stress-related illnesses, including ulcers, migraine headaches, insomnia, diarrhea, heart problems, digestive problems, cancer, hypertension, and obesity. It is also hypothesized that success at any competitive game is substantially determined by the kind of self-talk we give ourselves.

Rational therapy has made a substantial contribution to psychotherapy. Yet there are some important unanswered questions:

1. *Physiology of self-talk and emotions.* As yet we do not precisely know the physiological components of thinking or of emotions. The brain, of course, is important in enabling us to think. But what precisely takes place in the brain that leads us to conceptualize our thoughts? Are other parts of the body involved in thinking? Thinking is related to memory. But what precisely is memory, and how do we "store" and "recall" experiences that we have? And how are memory and thinking physiologically related?

   If self-talk primarily causes our emotions, what are the physiological processes involved? What different physiological processes occur for such varied emotions as love, depression, happiness, anger, sorrow, and so on? And how, physiologically, do certain types of self-talk and certain kinds of emotional states influence our health?
2. *Separating the effects of self-talk from the effects of physiological factors.* For people with injuries or abnormal conditions in the brain, it is at times extremely difficult to separate the effects of their medical conditions from those of self-talk. Injuries in different areas of the brain cause changes in a person's emotions and behaviors (Rosenhan & Seligman, 1995). Abnormal conditions of the brain result from a wide range of factors, including brain tumors, disorders such as cerebral palsy, chronic alcoholic intoxication, Alzheimer's disease, general paresis, AIDS, and cerebral arteriosclerosis. Such medical conditions are a factor in causing confusion, incoherence, clouding of consciousness, loss of recent or past memory, reduction in reasoning capacities, listlessness, apathy, reduction in intellectual capacities, and sometimes perceptual changes. Although these conditions can have permanent or long-lasting effects on thinking patterns and emotional reactions, other factors also change mental activity—such as high fever, toxins or poisons, and the intake of drugs and alcohol.

   Even with the presence of these factors, one's self-talk about these conditions also affects one's emotions and behaviors. Separating which effects result from other factors and which from self-talk often is difficult.
3. *Nature versus nurture. Nurture* can be defined as the sum of the influences modifying the expression of the genetic potentialities of a person. The theory of human behavior presented in this module focuses on nurture determinants, as it states human behavior is determined by events and self-talk. This theory fails to include genetic factors, which obviously influence human behavior.

4. *The importance of experiences or events themselves.* According to critics of rational therapy, the events that happen to a person are as important in determining behavior as the self-talk about such experiences (and perhaps even more important). These critics point out that events such as poverty, discrimination, child abuse, overprotective parents, inadequate education, and being victimized by crime are major determinants of human behavior.
5. *Boundaries of self-talk.* Rational therapy theorizes that self-talk has immense effects on our lives, and many of these effects are summarized in this module. But what are the limits of the effects of self-talk? In reference to this question, Zastrow (1979) presented the following example:

> A college student recently asked if her mother's long-time concern about giving birth to a child with a "dwarf" arm might have led to her youngest being born with a malformed arm.
>
> The student mentioned that her mother had been mildly concerned for a number of years that she would give birth to a child with a malformed arm. This young woman and her older brother were born without having such a malformation. However, shortly after the mother became pregnant the third time, a neighbor woman gave birth to a child with a malformed arm. This led the mother to have intense concerns that the child she was carrying would be born with a "dwarf" arm. When the child was born, it in fact was born with a "dwarf" arm.
>
> After I had given several lectures on the effects of self-talk in one of my classes, the student asked whether I thought this malformation was partly caused by self-talk or was just a matter of coincidence.
>
> In truth, I answered I didn't know—and I still don't know. We know certain drugs (such as thalidomide and excessive drinking) can cause malformations. So can having certain illnesses, such as German measles, during the time when the mother is pregnant. There is also speculation that the mother's emotional state while pregnant can influence the emotional and physiological development of the unborn child (Ainsworth et al., 1966; Dunn, 1977). Is it possible that this mother's thoughts and fears about having a malformed child might have been a factor in the child's being born with a malformed arm?...
>
> Daily I become aware of new ways in which my life, and that of others, is being influenced by self-talk. And, as I discuss the concept with others, the discussion usually ignites their relating to me specific incidents in which their self-talk has had a powerful effect on them.
>
> At this point I frankly do not know what the boundaries are for the effects of self-talk. It may well be that we are only at the "tip of the iceberg" in understanding all its effects. (pp. 327–328)

SUMMARY

Rational therapy asserts that the primary cause of all our emotions and actions is not our experiences but rather what we tell ourselves about events that happen to us. Generally we cannot control events, but we can think rationally and thereby change unwanted emotions and dysfunctional actions. Self-talk has a here-and-now quality because it represents our present thoughts. Self-talk is frequently based on our attitudes, beliefs, values, wants, needs, drives, and motives.

Rational therapy maintains that the reasons for deviant acts can be determined by examining what offenders tell themselves before and during the act.

The initial focus of rational therapy is to help clients become aware of the irrational and negative self-talk that is the primary source of their unwanted emotions and dysfunctional actions. Once the irrational self-talk is identified, a wide range of techniques is used to change the irrational self-talk. A frequently used technique is to have the client develop and practice using rational self-challenges to counter the irrational self-talk. Clients also write rational self-analyses.

Rational therapy has a wide variety of applications. It is used to reduce stress, change negative self-concepts, improve negative aspects of personalities, help clients become more assertive, and treat sexual dysfunctions.

EP 2.1.1b

The question "What really causes therapeutic change?" is raised. Proponents of rational therapy assert that therapy techniques that succeed in changing emotions or actions are effective primarily because they change negative or irrational self-talk.

Unanswered questions remain about rational therapy, including how self-talk physiologically leads to emotions and what the limits of the effects of self-talk are.

EXERCISES

1. Changing Unwanted Emotions

Goal: This exercise is designed to illustrate many of the principles of rational therapy and to demonstrate to students how to change unwanted emotions.

Step 1: Begin by asking students to think about the last time they were "sad" or "angry." Ask what made them sad or angry. List three or four responses on the chalkboard under each heading. The students in all probability will give you "events" as being the source of these emotions.

Step 2: Indicate to the students that what they told you was *not* the primary source of their emotions. Indicate instead that emotions are determined primarily by self-talk rather than events. For each "event" response given by a student, have the student tell you about personal self-talk that led to the emotion or guess what the self-talk is. For example, if a student says, "I became sad because I received a speeding ticket," you might suggest the self-talk that led to being sad was something like "This is awful. I sure am stupid for driving so fast. Now my insurance rates will go up. Woe is me. I don't have enough money to pay for tickets and increased insurance payments. I'm a bad person for getting a ticket."

Step 3: Further demonstrate the principles of rational therapy by asking the students, "What would be your self-talk if the person you were dating for the past 4 years informed you that he or she no longer wanted to date you?" Write this event on the chalkboard. Ask students what would be their self-talk, and what would be the resulting emotions from each self-talk statement. Write these self-talk statements and the resulting emotions on the board. Using the five criteria for determining rational thinking, ask the students to identify which of the self-talk statements are irrational and to give the reasons they are irrational. For each irrational self-talk statement, ask the class to come up with rational self-challenges to challenge and change the irrational self-talk statement.

Step 4: Explain to students how to write a rational self-analysis. (Show them examples from this module or distribute a handout of a completed RSA.)

Step 5: Indicate that there are only three constructive ways to change an unwanted emotion:

a. Challenge negative and irrational thinking with rational self-challenges.
b. Get involved in meaningful and enjoyable activities, which stops a person from thinking negatively and irrationally.
c. Change the distressing event(s). If you are successful in doing this, you are likely to feel better because you will then give yourself more positive self-talk.

Step 6: As a homework assignment, ask students to write a rational self-analysis on an unwanted emotion they have. Ask students their thoughts on the merits and shortcomings of rational therapy.

EP 2.1.1b

2. Positive Affirmations

Goal: This exercise is designed to provide students with another approach to change negative and irrational thinking.

Step 1: Indicate that some people find writing a rational self-analysis too time-consuming and cumbersome. An alternative is to use positive affirmations. A positive affirmation is a positive assertion that helps in achieving emotional and behavioral goals. The process of writing a positive affirmation also enables a person to identify negative and irrational thinking that he or she may be unaware of.

Step 2: Instruct the students in the following process of writing a positive affirmation. Have each student select a realistic emotional or behavioral personal goal that he or she is currently struggling with. The following are examples:

"I believe I am a person of worth."
"I will no longer be depressed about _____."
"I will no longer get angry and aggressive when _____ occurs."
"I will lose 5 pounds in 2 months."
"I will stop smoking today."
"I will limit my drinking of alcoholic beverages to two drinks when I go out."
"I will no longer feel guilty about _____."
"I believe I am an attractive person."
"I will assertively express myself when _____ occurs."

Step 3: Have each student start writing on a sheet of paper the selected positive affirmation. When negative thoughts enter students' minds, have them record those thoughts and then continue writing the positive affirmation, using the following format:

Positive Affirmation	Negative Thoughts
"I will lose 5 pounds in 2 months."	
"I will lose 5 pounds in 2 months."	
"I will lose 5 pounds in 2 months."	"I overeat when I'm bored, depressed, or lonely."
"I will lose 5 pounds in 2 months."	
"I will lose 5 pounds in 2 months."	"I will need to develop an exercise program, which I hate to do."
"I will lose 5 pounds in 2 months."	"One reason I'm fat is because I snack between meals."
"I will lose 5 pounds in 2 months."	"I will have to limit the number of beers that I have when I go out—beer is putting a lot of weight on me."
"I will lose 5 pounds in 2 months."	"I wonder if I really want to make all the changes that I will have to make to lose 5 pounds."
"I will lose 5 pounds in 2 months."	
"I will lose 5 pounds in 2 months."	
"I will lose 5 pounds in 2 months."	

Step 4: Ask students to write for 10 to 15 minutes. Ask for volunteers to share what they wrote. Have the class discuss the merits and shortcomings of writing positive affirmations. One advantage of repeated writing of the affirmation is that it trains the mind to accept the positive affirmation more readily.

EP 2.1.1b

3. Assessing and Changing Dysfunctional Behaviors

Goal: This exercise is designed to have students evaluate the merits and shortcomings of focusing on cognitions in assessing and changing dysfunctional behaviors.

Step 1: Explain the theory, described in this module, that thinking processes primarily determine behavior. The theory asserts that the reasons for unusual or dysfunctional behavior can always be identified by determining what the perpetrator was thinking before and during the time the act was being committed.

Step 2: Divide the class into several subgroups (ranging in size from three to six). Give each subgroup a different problematic or dysfunctional behavior. Examples include (a) alcoholism, (b) child abuse, (c) bulimia, (d) date rape, (e) suicide attempt, and (f) compulsive gambling.

Step 3: Instruct each subgroup to (a) identify the *thinking processes* that would lead a person to engage in the dysfunctional behavior and (b) identify the interventions that would be most effective in changing the thinking patterns of the perpetrator to "curb" the dysfunctional behavior. Instruct each subgroup to identify several intervention strategies or options, because (in one sense) social work practice involves "options planning." Give the subgroups 10 or more minutes to arrive at their answers.

Step 4: Ask each subgroup to select a representative to share with the class what the subgroup arrived at for both thinking processes and interventions. Ask a representative to share what his or her subgroup arrived at. Then ask the class to discuss whether the representative identified thinking processes (as the exercise instructed) or focused on describing events and personality characteristics that the subgroup thought were related to the dysfunctional behavior. Also ask the class whether the subgroup may have overlooked some important intervention strategies and options. Continue this process for each subgroup: A representative of the group presents the group's findings, and then the class discusses them.

Step 5: After the presentations and discussions end, ask the class for their thoughts on the merits, difficulties, and shortcomings of focusing on cognitions to assess and change dysfunctional behaviors.

COMPETENCY NOTES

The following identifies where Educational Policy (EP) competencies and practice behaviors are discussed in the chapter.

EP 2.1.10a *Substantively and affectively prepare for action with individuals, families, groups, organizations, and communities.*

This module presents the rational therapy approach to changing unwanted emotions and dysfunctional behaviors of individuals, family members, and group members.

EP 2.1.10j *Help clients resolve problems.* (pp. 479–504).

This module presents the rational therapy approach to changing unwanted emotions and dysfunctional behaviors of individuals, family members, and group members.

EP 2.1.1b *Practice personal reflection and self-correction to assure continual professional development.* (p. 481).

Exercise M1.1 is designed to have students reflect on the assertion that it is primarily their self-talk that causes their emotions.

EP 2.1.1b *Practice personal reflection and self-correction to assure continual professional development.* (pp. 482–483).

Exercise M1.2 is designed to have students reflect on the concept of "layering."

EP 2.1.1b *Practice personal reflection and self-correction to assure continual professional development.* (p. 484).

Exercise M1.3 demonstrates that when we are awfulizing about something and therefore feeling bad, we can alleviate the unwanted emotions by getting involved in meaningful activities.

EP 2.1.1b *Practice personal reflection and self-correction to assure continual professional development.* (p. 488).

Exercise M1.4 demonstrates that unwanted emotions can be changed with a rational self-analysis.

EP 2.1.1b *Practice personal reflection and self-correction to assure continual professional development.* (p. 488).

Exercise M1.5 demonstrates that unwanted emotions can be changed by changing the event that is associated with the unwanted emotion.

EP 2.1.1b *Practice personal reflection and self-correction to assure continual professional development.* (p. 490).

Exercise M1.6 demonstrates that unwanted emotions can be changed temporarily through the abusive use of alcohol, other drugs, or food.

EP 2.1.1b *Practice personal reflection and self-correction to assure continual professional development.* (p. 492).

Exercise M1.7 demonstrates that most of our actions are determined by what we think.

EP 2.1.1b *Practice personal reflection and self-correction to assure continual professional development.* (p. 495).

Exercise M1.8 is designed to assist students in identifying and eliminating their irrational beliefs.

EP 2.1.1b *Practice personal reflection and self-correction to assure continual professional development.* (pp. 497–498).

Exercise M1.9 is designed to have students reflect upon what causes therapeutic change.

EP 2.1.1b *Practice personal reflection and self-correction to assure continual professional development.* (p. 501).

This exercise is designed to illustrate many of the principles of rational therapy and to demonstrate to students how to change unwanted emotions.

EP 2.1.1b *Practice personal reflection and self-correction to assure continual professional development.* (pp. 501–502).

This exercise is designed to show students that positive affirmations can be used to change negative and irrational thinking.

EP 2.1.1b *Practice personal reflection and self-correction to assure continual professional development.* (pp. 502–503).

This exercise is designed to have students evaluate the merits and shortcomings of focusing on cognitions in assessing and changing dysfunctional behaviors.

MODULE 2

Behavior Therapy

EP 2.1.10a, j

No one person is credited with developing behavioral approaches to psychotherapy. Behavior therapists vary considerably in both theory and technique. The main assumption in this counseling approach is that maladaptive behaviors are acquired primarily through learning and can be modified through additional learning. This module will:

A. Describe three types of learning processes
B. Present several behavior therapy intervention strategies

FOUNDERS

Learning theory has been the philosophical foundation for behavior therapy even though there has never been agreement about which learning theory is the core of behavior therapy. Numerous authorities have advanced somewhat different theories of how people learn. Pavlov, a Russian who lived between 1849 and 1936, was one of the earliest. Other prominent learning theorists include E. L. Thorndike (1913), E. R. Guthrie (1935), C. L. Hull (1943), E. C. Tolman (1932), and B. F. Skinner (1938). Behavior therapists who have achieved international recognition for developing therapies based on learning principles include R. E. Alberti and M. L. Emmons (1970), A. Bandura (1969), B. F. Skinner (1948), J. B. Watson and R. Rayner (1920), and J. Wolpe (1958).

Despite the wide variation in behavior therapy approaches and techniques, there are some common emphases. One is that the maladaptive behavior (such as bedwetting) is the problem and needs to be changed. This approach is in sharp contrast to the psychoanalytic approach that views the problematic behavior as a *symptom* of some underlying, unconscious causes. Psychoanalysts assert that the underlying causes must be treated to prevent the substitution of new symptoms or the return of old symptoms, but behavior therapists assert that treating the problematic behavior will not result in symptom substitution.

Behavior therapists assert that counseling approaches must be tested and validated by rigorous experimental procedures. This focus requires that the goals of therapy be articulated in behavioral terms that can be measured. Baseline levels of problematic behaviors are established before counseling to measure whether the approach is producing the desired change in the rate or intensity of responding.

The use of behavior modification therapy in counseling has increased dramatically during the past 40 years. Behavior therapy intervention techniques are now among the most widely used techniques in counseling and psychotherapy (Wilson, 2008).

Behavior therapists have devoted little attention to developing a behavioral model of personality. Behaviorists generally believe that environmental conditions or experiences are of much greater influence in controlling behavior than are internal personality traits.

TYPES OF LEARNING PROCESSES

Before we examine the prominent behavior therapy techniques, it behooves us to discuss three types of learning processes: operant conditioning, respondent conditioning, and modeling. These three learning processes form the theoretical basis of behavior therapy techniques.

Operant Conditioning

According to learning theory, much of human behavior is determined by positive and negative reinforcers. A *positive reinforcer* is any stimulus that, when applied following a behavior, increases or strengthens that behavior. Common examples include food, water, sex, attention, affection, and approval. The list of positive reinforcers is inexhaustible and highly individualized. Praise, for example, is a positive reinforcer when and only when it maintains or increases the behavior with which it is associated (for example, efforts to improve one's writing skills). A *negative reinforcer* (or *aversive stimulus*) is any stimulus that a person will terminate or avoid if given the opportunity. Common examples include frowns, electric shock, and criticism. The same stimulus—for example, the smell of Limburger cheese—can be a negative reinforcer for one person and a positive reinforcer for another.

There are four basic learning principles involving positive reinforcers and aversive stimuli:

1. If a positive reinforcer (for example, food) is presented to a person following a response, the result is positive reinforcement. With positive reinforcement, the occurrence of a given behavior is strengthened or increased.
2. If a positive reinforcer is withdrawn following a person's response, the result is punishment.
3. If an aversive stimulus (for example, an electric shock) is presented to a person following a response, the result is punishment. (As can be seen, there are two types of punishment.)
4. If an aversive stimulus is withdrawn following a person's response, the result is negative reinforcement. In negative reinforcement, a response (behavior) is increased by removing an aversive stimulus (for example, fastening one's seat belt to turn off the obnoxiously loud and annoying buzzer).

EP 2.1.7a

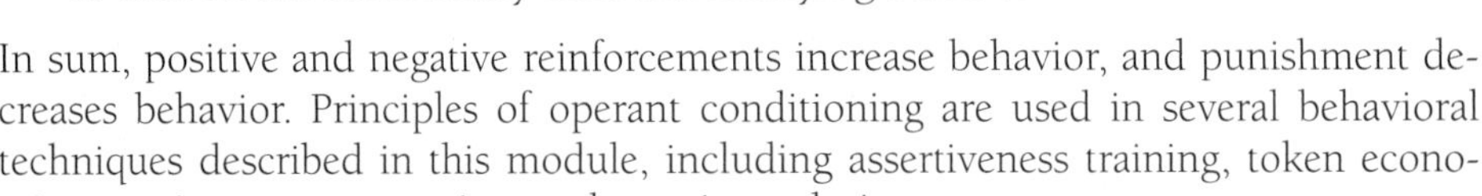
In sum, positive and negative reinforcements increase behavior, and punishment decreases behavior. Principles of operant conditioning are used in several behavioral techniques described in this module, including assertiveness training, token economies, contingency contracting, and aversive techniques.

Exercise M2.1: Operant Conditioning

Goal: This exercise is designed to assist you in understanding and applying operant conditioning.

Step 1: Describe an experience in which a behavior of yours was increased by a positive reinforcer.

Step 2: Describe an experience in which a behavior of yours was decreased by a negative reinforcer.

Respondent Conditioning

Respondent learning has also been called "classical" or "Pavlovian" conditioning. Many diverse everyday behaviors are considered respondent behaviors—perspiring, salivating, and, more important, many anxieties, fears, and phobias. A key concept in respondent learning is *pairing:* the idea that behaviors are learned by being consistently paired over time with other behaviors or events.

To explain respondent conditioning, let's first define the following key terms:

- *Neutral stimulus (NS):* a stimulus that elicits little or no response
- *Unconditioned stimulus (UCS):* a stimulus that elicits an innate, or unlearned, response
- *Unlearned response (UR):* a response that is innate—for example, salivating because of food in the mouth
- *Conditioned response (CR):* a new response that has been learned
- *Conditioned stimulus (CS):* an original neutral stimulus that, through pairing with an unconditioned stimulus, now begins to elicit a conditioned response

Respondent learning asserts that when a neutral stimulus (NS) is paired with an unconditioned stimulus (UCS), the neutral stimulus will elicit a response similar to the response elicited by the UCS. That new response is called a conditioned response (CR) because it has been learned. The originally neutral stimulus, once it begins to elicit the response, becomes the conditioned stimulus (CS). Thus, it is possible for an event that originally elicited no fear whatsoever (for example, being in the dark) to elicit fear when it is paired with a stimulus that does elicit fear (for example, horrifying stories about being in the dark). This learning process is indicated in the following paradigm:

1. *UCS* (horrifying stories about being in the dark) → elicits *UR* (fear)
2. *NS* (being in the dark) paired with *UCS* → elicits *CR* (fear)
3. *NS* becomes *CS* → elicits *CR* (fear)

The *CS-CR* bond can be broken by respondent extinction or by counterconditioning. *Respondent extinction* involves continuing presentation of the conditioned stimulus without any further pairing with the unconditioned stimulus. Respondent extinction gradually weakens and eventually eliminates the CS-CR bond. Implosive therapy, discussed later in this module, is based on this principle.

EP 2.1.7a

Counterconditioning is based on the principle that the CS-CR bond can be broken by using new responses that are stronger than, and incompatible with, old responses that are elicited by the same stimulus. For example, it is possible to teach a person to relax (new response) instead of becoming anxious (old response) when confronted with a particular stimulus (for example, the prospect of flying in a small plane). In vivo desensitization (also discussed later in this module) is based on counterconditioning.

Exercise M2.2: Respondent Conditioning

Goal: This exercise is designed to assist you in understanding and applying respondent conditioning.

Describe an experience in which a behavior of yours was shaped by respondent conditioning.

Modeling

Modeling is a technique in which the client changes his or her behavior as a result of observing another person's behavior—that is, learning by vicarious experience or imitation. Much of everyday learning is thought to take place through modeling—using both live models and symbolic models (such as films). Modeling has been used in behavior modification to develop new behaviors that are not in a person's repertoire—for example, showing a youngster how to swing a bat. Modeling has also been used to eliminate anxieties and fears—for example, using a model in assertiveness training. Anxieties and fears are reduced or eliminated through modeling by exposing fearful observers to modeled events in which the model performs the feared activity without experiencing any adverse effects and even enjoys the experience.

EP 2.1.7a

Exercise M2.3: Modeling

Goal: This exercise is designed to assist you in understanding and applying the principles of modeling.

Describe an experience in which you learned a new behavior by modeling.

THEORY OF COUNSELING

Behavior therapy rests on the assumption that all behavior occurs in response to stimulation, internal or external. The first task of the behavior therapist is to identify the probable stimulus-response (S-R) connections that are occurring for the client. This part of the counseling process is called a *behavioral,* or *functional, analysis*. The following illustrates an S-R connection: For a person who fears heights, the stimulus (S) of flying in a small plane elicits the response (R) of intense anxiety and avoidance of the stimulus.

Before and during the time the behavior therapist performs a behavioral analysis, he or she also attempts to establish a working relationship with the client. (The characteristics of a working relationship are described in Chapter 5.) In regard to this emphasis on establishing a working relationship, Chambless and Goldstein (1979) stated,

> Although behaviorists are often portrayed as cold and mechanical, a study of recordings of therapy sessions yields a different picture. When measured on variables used in the study of client-centered therapy, behavior therapists showed high warmth and positive regard for their clients (equal to other psychotherapists in the study) and higher empathy and self-congruence than the other therapists. (p. 243)

Chambless and Goldstein (1979) also described sources of information for making a behavioral analysis:

> The behavior therapist may base the [behavioral] analysis on interviews with the client and important people in the client's life or on information gained by having the client keep a journal. Questionnaire data are often useful. Interpersonal problems may be more clearly defined if the therapist and client role play interactions with which the client reports difficulty. When the therapist has a difficult time making the analysis, observing the client in the situation where the problem occurs may lead to a wealth of information. Obviously, there are times when this would be impossible or in poor taste, but direct observation is used much less frequently than it should be. (pp. 244–245)

During the analysis, the behavior therapist attempts to determine the stimuli associated with the maladaptive responses. Through this analysis, both client and counselor arrive at an understanding of the problem and generally how it developed. This insight does not treat the problem but is useful because it reduces client anxiety; clients no longer feel possessed or overwhelmed by unknown, mysterious forces. Errors about hypothesized S-R connections at this diagnostic stage usually lead to ineffective interventions because the interventions will be focused on treating S-R connections that are *not* involved in perpetuating the maladaptive behavior.

A behavioral analysis begins with the behavior therapist taking a detailed history of the presenting problem, its course, and particularly its association with current experiences. In making such an analysis, it is crucial to obtain specific, concrete details about the circumstances in which the presenting problem arises. If, for example, clients are shy in some situations, it is important to identify the specific interactions in which they are shy. Furthermore, it is important to determine why they are shy: Is it because they do not know how to express themselves, or is it because they have certain fears? The choice of an intervention depends on such information. If clients do not know how to express themselves, a *modeling* approach through role-playing might be used. However, if they have the response potential but are inhibited by certain fears, a desensitization procedure (described later in this module) to reduce these fears might be used.

The objective in the behavioral analysis is to identify the antecedent stimuli that are generating the maladaptive responses. Once the behavior therapist identifies these connections, he or she discusses them with the client, to help the client gain insight and to obtain from the client feedback on possible erroneous connections. Client and counselor then agree on the goals for the treatment. How counseling will proceed and the techniques to be used are described to the client. This information gives the client some idea of her or his role in the intervention. Orne and Wender (1968) found that this knowledge fosters positive outcomes and reduces the dropout rate.

ASSERTIVENESS TRAINING

Assertiveness training has become the most frequently used method in modifying unadaptive interpersonal behavior. It is particularly effective in changing both timid behavior and aggressive behavior. Wolpe (1958) originally developed this approach, and it has been further developed by a variety of authors, including Alberti and Emmons (1970) and Fensterheim and Baer (1975). Interest in assertiveness training has grown enormously in the past four decades, sparked by the recognition that sex-role stereotyping has led to a general lack of assertiveness in women. Assertiveness training groups are now widely offered. During the past few decades, increasing numbers of men are also getting involved, either individually or through groups, in assertiveness training. Outcome research on assertiveness training has found the approach to be effective in assisting participants to become more assertive (Cormier & Cormier, 1991).

Overview of Assertiveness Training[1]

Do you handle put-downs well? Are you reluctant to express your feelings and opinions openly and honestly in a group? Are you frequently timid in interacting with people in authority? Do you react well to criticism? Do you sometimes explode in anger when things go wrong, or are you able to remain calm? Do you find it difficult to

[1]This material on assertiveness training is adapted from Charles Zastrow, "How to Become More Assertive," in *The Personal Problem Solver*, edited by Charles Zastrow and Dae H. Chang, © 1977, pp. 236–243. Adapted by permission of Prentice-Hall, Inc., Englewood Cliffs, New Jersey. Reprinted by permission of the author.

maintain eye contact when talking? If you are uncomfortable with someone smoking near you, do you express your feelings? Are you timid in arranging a date or social event? If you have trouble in any of these situations, there is, fortunately, a useful technique—assertiveness training—that helps people become more effective in such interpersonal interactions.

Assertiveness problems range from extreme shyness, introversion, and withdrawal to inappropriately flying into a rage that results in alienating others. A nonassertive person is often acquiescent, fearful, and afraid of expressing his or her real, spontaneous feelings. Frequently, resentment and anxiety build up, which may result in general discomfort, feelings of low self-esteem, tension headaches, fatigue, and perhaps a destructive explosion of temper, anger, and aggression. Some people are overly shy and timid in nearly all interactions. Most of us, however, encounter occasional problems in isolated areas in which it would be to our benefit to be more assertive. For example, a bachelor may be quite effective and assertive in his job as store manager but still awkward and timid when attempting to arrange a date.

There are three basic styles of interacting with others: *nonassertive, aggressive,* and *assertive.* Alberti and Emmons (1975) summarized characteristics of these styles:

> In the *nonassertive* style, you are likely to hesitate, speak softly, look away, avoid the issue, agree regardless of your own feelings, not express opinions, value yourself "below" others, and hurt yourself to avoid any chance of hurting others.
>
> In the *aggressive* style, you typically answer before the other person is through talking, speak loudly and abusively, glare at the other person, speak "past" the issue (accusing, blaming, demeaning), vehemently expound your feelings and opinions, value yourself "above" others, and hurt others to avoid hurting yourself.
>
> In the *assertive* style, you will answer spontaneously, speak with a conversational tone and volume, and look at the other person, speak to the issue, openly express your personal feelings and opinions (anger, love, disagreement, sorrow), value yourself equal to others, and hurt neither yourself or others. (p. 24)

Simply stated, *assertive behavior* is being able to express yourself without hurting or stepping on others.

Assertiveness training is designed to lead people to realize, feel, and act on the assumption that they have the right to be themselves and to express their feelings freely. Assertive responses generally are not aggressive responses. The distinction between these two types of interactions is important. Let's look at two examples of nonassertive, aggressive, and assertive behavior.

You are a social worker driving in a car with an associate to a conference in another city. The associate lights up a pipe; you soon find the smoke irritating and the odor somewhat stifling. What are your choices?

1. *Nonassertive response:* You attempt to carry on a "cheery" conversation for the 3-hour trip without commenting about the smoke.
2. *Aggressive response:* You increasingly become irritated until exploding, "Either you put out that pipe or I'll put it out for you—the odor is sickening."
3. *Assertive response:* In a firm, conversational tone, you look directly at the associate and state, "The smoke from your pipe is irritating me. I'd appreciate it if you put it away."

At a party with friends, during small-talk conversation, your husband gives you a subtle put-down by stating, "Wives always talk too much." What do you do?

1. *Nonassertive response:* You don't say anything but feel hurt and become quiet.
2. *Aggressive response:* You glare at him and angrily ask, "John, why are you always criticizing me?"
3. *Assertive response:* You carry on as usual. On the drive home, you calmly look at him and say, "When we were at the party tonight, you said that wives always talk too much. I felt you were putting me down when you said that. What did you mean by that comment?"

Steps in Assertiveness Training[2]

You can train yourself to be more assertive. Here are 12 steps.

Step 1: Examine your interactions. Are there situations that you need to handle more assertively? Do you at times hold back your opinions and feelings for fear of what would happen if you expressed them? Do you occasionally lose control and lash out angrily at others? To study your interactions, keep a diary for a week or longer, recording the situations in which you acted timidly, aggressively, and assertively.

Step 2: Select those interactions in which it would be to your benefit to be more assertive. They may include situations in which you were overly polite, overly apologetic, timid, or allowed others to take advantage of you while you were harboring feelings of resentment, anger, embarrassment, fear of others, or self-criticism for not having the courage to express yourself. Overly aggressive interactions in which you exploded in anger or walked over others also need to be dealt with. For each set of nonassertive or aggressive interactions, you can become more assertive, as shown in the next steps.

Step 3: Concentrate on a specific incident in the past in which you were either nonassertive or aggressive when you wanted to be assertive. Close your eyes for a few minutes and vividly imagine the details, including what you and the other person said, and how you felt at the time and afterward.

Step 4: Write down and review your responses. Ask yourself the following questions to determine how you presented yourself:

a. *Eye contact.* Did you look directly at the other person in a relaxed, steady gaze? Looking down or away suggests a lack of self-confidence. Glaring is an aggressive response.
b. *Gestures.* Were your gestures appropriate, free flowing, and relaxed and used effectively to emphasize your messages? Awkward stiffness suggests nervousness; other gestures (such as a clenched fist) signal an aggressive reaction.
c. *Body posture.* Did you show the importance of your message by directly facing the other person, by leaning toward that person, by holding your head erect, and by sitting or standing appropriately close?
d. *Facial expression.* Did your facial expression show a stern, firm pose consistent with an assertive response?
e. *Voice tone and volume.* Was your response stated in a firm, conversational tone? Shouting may suggest anger. Speaking softly suggests shyness, and a cracking voice suggests nervousness. Tape recording and listening to one's voice is a way to practice increasing or decreasing the volume.
f. *Speech fluency.* Did your speech flow smoothly, clearly, and slowly? Rapid speech or hesitation in speaking suggests nervousness. Tape recording assertive responses that you try out in problem situations is a way to improve fluency.
g. *Timing.* Were your verbal reactions to a problem situation stated at a time close to the incident that would appropriately permit you and the other person time to review the incident? Generally, spontaneous expressions are the best, but certain situations should be handled at a later time. For example, a challenge to some of your boss's erroneous statements should be made in private rather than in front of a group in which he or she is making a presentation.
h. *Message content.* For a problem situation, which of your responses were nonassertive or aggressive and which were assertive? Study the content and consider why you responded in a nonassertive or aggressive style. (At this point, it is very helpful to identify the self-talk that led you to act nonassertively or aggressively, and to challenge this self-talk with rational, assertive self-challenges—see Module 1.)

---

[2]These self-training steps are a modification of assertiveness training programs developed by Robert E. Alberti and Michael L. Emmons, *Your Perfect Right,* 9th ed. (San Luis Obispo, CA: Impact Publishers, 2008), and by Herbert Fensterheim and Jean Baer, *Don't Say Yes When You Want to Say No* (New York: Dell Publishing Co., 1975).

Step 5: Observe one or more effective models. Watch the verbal and nonverbal approaches that are assertively used to handle the types of interactions with which you are having problems. Compare the consequences between their approach and yours. If possible, discuss their approach and their feelings about using it.

Step 6: Make a list of alternative approaches for being more assertive.

Step 7: Close your eyes and visualize yourself using each approach. For each one, think through what the full set of interactions would be, along with the consequences. Select one, or a combination of approaches, that you believe will be most effective for you to use. Through imagery, practice using this approach until you feel comfortable with it.

Step 8: Role-play the approach with a friend or counselor. If certain segments of your approach appear clumsy, awkward, timid, or aggressive, practice modifications until you become comfortable with the approach. Obtain feedback from the other person on the strengths and shortcomings of your approach. Compare your interactions to the verbal and nonverbal guidelines for assertive behavior in step 4. It may be useful for the other person to role-play one or more assertive strategies that you could then practice using.

Step 9: Repeat steps 7 and 8 until you develop an assertive approach that you believe will work best for you and that you are comfortable with.

Step 10: Use your approach in a real-life situation. The previous steps are designed to prepare you for the real event. Expect to be somewhat anxious when first trying to be assertive. If you are still too fearful of attempting to be assertive, repeat steps 5–8. For those few individuals who fail to develop the needed confidence to try being assertive, professional counseling is advised—expressing yourself and effective interactions with others are essential for personal happiness.

Step 11: Reflect on the effectiveness of your effort. Did you remain calm?[3] Considering the nonverbal guidelines for assertive behavior discussed in step 4, what components of your responses were assertive, aggressive, and nonassertive? What were the consequences of your effort? How did you feel after trying out this new set of interactions? If possible, discuss how you did in regard to these questions with a friend who observed the interactions.

Step 12: Expect some success, but not complete personal satisfaction, with your initial efforts. Personal growth and interacting more effectively with others is a continual learning process. Quite appropriately, "pat yourself on the back" for what you did well—you earned it. But also note the areas in which you need to improve.

Use these steps for improving your assertive efforts. These steps are not to be followed rigidly. You need to develop a process that works best for you.

Helping Others Become More Assertive

Either as a friend or as a social worker, you can be very helpful in assisting another person—your "client"—to become more assertive. The following guidelines are suggested:

1. Together identify situations or interactions in which your client needs to be more assertive. Get information about such interactions from your observations and knowledge of the person and from discussing in depth the interactions in which the person feels a need to be more assertive. You may also ask the person to keep a diary of interactions in which she or he feels resentment over being nonassertive and interactions in which she or he was overly aggressive.

---

[3]Getting angry at times is a normal human emotion, and it needs to be expressed. However, the anger should be expressed in a constructive, assertive fashion.

2. Develop together some strategies for the person to be more assertive. Small assignments with a high probability of successful outcomes should be given first. A great deal of discussion and preparation should take place between the two of you in preparing for the "real event." For a person who is generally shy, introverted, and nonassertive in all interpersonal relationships, it may be necessary to explore in great detail the connection between nonassertive behavior and feelings of resentment or low self-esteem. In addition, for very shy people, certain attitudes, such as "don't make waves" or the "meek will inherit the earth," may need to be dealt with before developing strategies for the person to be more assertive.
3. Role-playing is a very useful technique in preparing for being assertive. The helper first models an assertive strategy by taking the shy person's role. Shy clients concurrently role-play the role of the person with whom they want to be more assertive. Then the roles are reversed; clients role-play themselves, and the helper plays the other role. Besides the previously mentioned benefits of modeling and practice experience, role-playing has the added advantage of reducing the shy person's anxiety about attempting to be assertive. For feedback purposes, if possible, record the role-playing on audio or videotape.
4. Explain the 12 steps described earlier that your client can use on his or her own to handle future problem situations involving assertiveness. If possible, provide reading material on these steps.

Although individuals must be able to express themselves in their own unique styles, an additional guideline is often useful. A good rule is to start sentences with "I feel" rather than making threatening or aggressive statements. (I-messages are further described in Module 4.) Frequently, we don't take the time to express our real feelings to others. As a result, we end up creating serious misunderstandings, hurt feelings, and verbal fights that take 10 times as long to work through.

Consider the following example of two busy people, a working mother and her 15-year-old son:

Mother: John, please do the dishes for me tonight.
John: I can't, I'll do them tomorrow.
Mother: (*Getting angry*) You never do anything for me.
John: I said I'll do the dishes tomorrow.
Mother: And you always forget. I asked you to clean your room 2 weeks ago, and you still haven't done that. (*Now angry*) I just don't know what I'm going to do with you. Just for that you can't go camping this weekend.

And the argument has ignited. Contrast this to the following approach:

Mother: John, I feel very tired this evening. I had a bad day at work, and I still have to do all the washing and ironing tonight. Could you please help me out by doing the dishes?
John: I'm sorry you had a bad day. I'm supposed to be at basketball practice in 5 minutes. I'll be back at 8:30, would it be all right if I did them then?
Mother: Yes, if you don't forget.
John: I won't.

Assertiveness training is relatively simple to comprehend. Skill, common sense, and ingenuity, however, are needed to create an effective strategy for a real-life situation. The joy and pride resulting from being able to express oneself assertively are nearly unequaled.

EP 2.1.7a

Exercise M2.4: Becoming Assertive

Goal: This exercise is designed to assist you in understanding and applying the principles of assertiveness training.

Step 1: Describe a behavior in which you are routinely nonassertive and want to become more assertive.

Step 2: Review the material on assertiveness training. Visualize yourself being assertive in this situation. Describe what you will say, and describe what you want to communicate with your nonverbal behavior.

Step 3: Describe a behavior in which you are routinely aggressive and want to become more assertive.

Step 4: Visualize yourself being assertive in this situation. Describe what you will say, and describe what you want to communicate with your nonverbal behavior.

Step 5: Are you now committed to trying to be assertive when these problematic situations in which you have been nonassertive or aggressive arise again?

BEHAVIOR REHEARSAL

This technique enlarges the client's repertoire of coping behaviors. Behavior rehearsal has four stages.

First, the counselor prepares the client by explaining the importance of acquiring new behaviors (for example, to express anger assertively rather than aggressively), getting the client to accept behavioral rehearsal as a useful device, and reducing any initial anxiety over the prospect of role-playing. The second stage involves selecting target situations.

Together, counselor and client select one or more rehearsal situations that relate directly to the situations in which the client is having difficulty (for example, learning to respond assertively rather than aggressively when the client is criticized by his coworkers). The third stage is the actual behavior rehearsal. Counselors sometimes model an appropriate response pattern first. For example, the client may take on the role of a critical coworker while the counselor role-plays an assertive response to receiving criticism from a coworker. Frequently, then, the roles are reversed and the client role-plays responding assertively to being criticized by a coworker (with the counselor as coworker). The fourth stage is the client's actual use of the newly acquired skills in real-life situations.

After the final stage, client and counselor review the client's performance and feelings about the experiences. Sometimes clients are asked to keep diaries describing the real-life situations they encounter, their behavior, its consequences, and so on.

TOKEN ECONOMIES

Tokens are symbolic reinforcers, not unlike poker chips or lines on a tally sheet, that can be exchanged for reinforcement rewards such as candy or increased privileges. An exchange system—an "economy"—is set up that specifies exactly what the tokens can be exchanged for and how many tokens are needed to get particular items or privileges. Target behaviors (such as going to school or making a bed) are specified. These earn tokens; a certain response rate earns a particular number of tokens. For example, attending school every day for 2 weeks earns 10 tokens at an adolescent group home, and 10 tokens can be exchanged for attending a sports event.

Token economies have been successfully used in a wide variety of institutional settings, including mental hospitals, training schools for delinquents, classrooms for students with emotional problems, schools for individuals with cognitive disabilities, sheltered workshops, and group homes for adolescents. Considerable evidence supports the effectiveness of token economies (Kazdin, 1977b), which have been used to effect positive changes in a wide variety of behaviors, including personal hygiene, social interactions, job attendance and performance, academic performance, domestic tasks such as cleaning, and personal appearance. At times, token economies are arranged so that clients not only earn tokens for desired behaviors but also lose tokens for undesired behaviors (for example, instigating a fight).

Effective token economies are, however, more difficult to establish than it appears at first glance. Prochaska (1979) summarized important factors that need to be given attention in establishing a successful token economy:

> Some of the more important considerations include staff cooperation and coordination, since the staff must be more observant and more systematic in their responses to clients than in a noncontingent system. A variety of attempts at establishing token economies have failed because the staff did not cooperate adequately in monitoring the behavior of residents. Effective token economies must also have adequate control over reinforcements, since an economy becomes ineffective if residents have access to reinforcements by having money from home or being able to bum a cigarette from a less cooperative staff member. Problems must be clearly defined in terms of specific behaviors to be changed in order to avoid conflicts among staff or patients. Improving personal hygiene, for example, is too open to interpretation by individuals, and patients may insist that they are improving their hygiene even though staff members may disagree. There is much less room for misunderstandings if personal hygiene is defined as clean fingernails, no evidence of body odor, clean underwear, and other clear-cut rules. Specifying behaviors that are positive alternatives to problem behavior is very critical in teaching residents what positive actions they can take to help themselves rather than relying on just a negative set of eliminating responses. Perhaps most important for more lasting effectiveness of token economies is that they be gradually faded out as problem behaviors are reduced and more adaptive responses become well established. Obviously the outside world does not run according to an institution's internal economy, and it is important that clients be prepared to make the transition to the larger society. Using an abundance of social reinforcers along with token

EP 2.1.7a

reinforcers helps prepare clients for the fading out of tokens, so that positive behaviors can be maintained by praise or recognition rather than by tokens. Also encouraging patients to reinforce themselves, such as by learning to take pride in their appearance, is an important step in fading out tokens. Some institutions use transitional wards where clients go from token economies and learn to maintain adaptive behaviors through more naturalistic contingencies, such as praise from a fellow patient. In such transitional settings, backup reinforcers are available if needed, but they are used much more sparingly than in the token economies. Without the use of fading, token economies can become nothing more than hospital management procedures that make the care of patients more efficient without preparing patients to live effectively in the larger society.[4]

Exercise M2.5: Token Economy

Goal: This exercise is designed to assist you in understanding a token economy.

Describe a token economy that you participated in. Perhaps it was a token economy that a former teacher used with the class. Perhaps it was a system that your parents used to pay you for you doing work that they wanted completed.

CONTINGENCY CONTRACTING

Closely related to token economies is contingency contracting. Contingency contracts provide clients with a set of rules that govern the change process. Contracts may be *unilateral* —that is, clients may make contracts with themselves. For example, a person with a weight problem may limit himself to a certain calorie intake, using a system of rewards for staying within the calorie limit and negative consequences for going over the limit. Contracts may be *bilateral* and specify the obligations and the mutual reinforcements for each party. Kanfer (1975, p. 321) noted that a good contingency contract has the following seven elements:

1. A clear and detailed description of the required instrumental behavior.
2. Criterion for the time or frequency limitations that constitute the goal of the contract.
3. Specified positive reinforcements, contingent on fulfillment of the criterion.
4. Aversive consequence(s), contingent on nonfulfillment of the contract within the specified time or with the specified frequency.
5. Bonus clause with additional positive reinforcements obtainable if the person exceeds the minimal demands of the contract.
6. Specified means by which the contracted response is observed, measured, and recorded and a procedure for informing clients of their achievements during the contract's duration.
7. Delivery of reinforcement contingencies to follow the response as quickly as possible.

Helping professionals increasingly find contingency contracts useful. Such contracts specify desired goals, tasks to be performed to meet these goals, tasks for the client and for the therapist, and the deadline for completing tasks. Kanfer (1975) indicated that marriage counseling is one area in which contingency contracts are especially effective. Each spouse agrees to change behaviors that irritate the other. There is a specified system of reinforcements and consequences depending on the extent to which the contract provisions are met.

Formulating contracts with clients in both one-to-one settings and in group settings has a number of advantages. Contracts guide clients for specific actions they need to take to improve their situations. Contracts have a motivational effect because when people commit to the terms of a contract, they usually feel a moral obligation to follow through. In addition, reviewing whether commitments made in contracts are being met provides counselors and clients with a method for measuring progress.

---

[4]James O. Prochaska, *Systems of Psychotherapy: A Transtheoretical Analysis.* © 1979 Cengage Learning, pp. 324–325.

EP 2.1.7a

Exercise M2.6: Contingency Contracting

Goal: This exercise is designed to assist you in understanding and applying contingency contracting.

Step 1: Identify a behavior that you want to change (such as stopping smoking, stopping procrastinating on a project, or having only two alcoholic beverages when you go out).

Step 2: State your behavioral goal.

Step 3: Specify what tasks you need to accomplish to reach your goal.

Step 4: State your time frame for accomplishing the tasks.

Step 5: Specify the means of monitoring your progress toward accomplishing the tasks.

Step 6: Specify how you will reward yourself if you achieve your goal.

Step 7: Specify what you will do whenever you engage in behavior inconsistent with your goal (for example, donating $5.00 to a charity).

IN VIVO DESENSITIZATION[5]

In vivo (from the Latin "in life") *desensitization* is a real-life desensitization process in which a person gradually approaches an actual feared event or stimulus while being in a relaxed state. To carry out in vivo desensitization, the following three steps should be taken:

1. Make a ranked list of fear-producing situations, arranging items from least to most anxiety-producing. (This step is identical to the construction of anxiety hierarchies in systematic desensitization.)
2. Learn to produce or achieve relaxation, perhaps by meditation, muscle relaxation, deep—breathing relaxation, or imagery relaxation.[6]
3. Gradually approach an actual feared event while remaining relaxed.

A 22-year-old male college student used in vivo desensitization to overcome several situations (themes) connected with a fear of heights. He first became skilled at producing the relaxation response by imagery of his ideal relaxation place. (His ideal relaxation place was lying on the beach in Acapulco. With practice he became skilled at relaxing himself by fully focusing his thinking on relaxing in Acapulco.) He then gradually approached feared situations while remaining in a relaxed state with his imagery of Acapulco. For example, he countered his fear of tall buildings by looking out the window in the lower floors and gradually moving upward while thinking about being relaxed in Acapulco. He also used this approach to overcome his fears of taking amusement park rides and of flying in small planes.

Watson and Tharp (1972) indicated that in vivo desensitization is an effective method for eliminating fear and anxiety reactions associated with specific stimuli (events).

EXPOSURE THERAPY

Exposure therapy is based on the principle of *extinction*. In exposure therapy, clients expose themselves to stimuli or situations that they previously feared and avoided. The "exposure" can be in real life (*in vivo*) or in fantasy (*in imagino*). In the latter case, clients are asked to imagine themselves in the presence of the feared stimulus (for example, a snake) or in the anxiety-producing situation (for example, giving a presentation in class). The theory behind exposure therapy is that the occurrence of an anxiety response will gradually lessen when the fear-producing stimulus situation is continuously presented in the absence of the reinforcement that perpetuates the fear.

Exposure therapy has been found by researchers to be effective in treating panic disorders, specified phobias, agoraphobia (abnormal fear of crossing or being in open spaces), social phobia, posttraumatic stress disorder, and obsessive-compulsive disorder (Emmelkamp, 1994). Several researchers suggest that the following features must be present in exposure treatments for the client to achieve maximum benefits (Barlow & Cerny, 1988):

1. Exposure should be of long duration.
2. Exposure should be repeated until all fear and anxiety is eliminated.
3. Exposure should be graduated, starting with low-anxiety stimuli or situations and progressing to high-anxiety stimuli or situations.
4. Clients must attend to the feared stimulus and interact with it as much as possible.
5. Exposure must produce anxiety.

---

[5]Excerpted from Charles Zastrow, "In Vivo Desensitization," in *Talk to Yourself: Using the Power of Self-Talk*, © 1979, pp. 190–193. Reprinted by permission of author.

[6]These four relaxation techniques are described in Chapter 14.

According to exposure therapy, panic attacks or phobias are essentially "false alarms" issued by the body in response to a cue or signal that the client has learned to associate with danger or threat. Through the process of extinction, it is theorized, the anxiety or fear elicited in reaction to the false alarm will gradually subside as the client learns that there is no basis for the fear associated with the false alarm.

A recent innovation with exposure therapy is the use of virtual reality computer-simulated environments. For example, at the University of Washington in Seattle, people with serious fears of spiders are treated by using virtual reality in which they simulate entering a kitchen, chasing a tarantula around a countertop, and flushing it down a sink (Ritter, 2000). At U.S. Department of Veterans Affairs medical centers in Atlanta and Boston, some Vietnam veterans with posttraumatic stress disorder are visiting "Virtual Vietnam," a re-creation of the wartime environment that still haunts them (Ritter, 2000). Virtual reality is also being used to treat a wide variety of other phobias—including fear of flying, fear of public speaking, and fear of heights (Ritter, 2000). The idea is to teach people how to manage fears and then (through virtual reality) take them to whatever situations terrify them. There they learn that they can control their emotions and that these situations are not so scary after all. The advantage of virtual reality is that it can provide the feared environment in the counselor's office, which saves time and money. No more driving to the airport for fear-of-flying treatment!

AVERSIVE TECHNIQUES

An *aversive stimulus* is any stimulus that an organism (person) will avoid or terminate if given the opportunity. Examples include electric shock, unpleasant imagery, holding one's breath, stale cigarette smoke, vile-smelling substances, white noise, and shame.

In a review of aversive methods, Sandler (1986) found aversive therapy has been used to treat self-injurious behavior (such as head banging and self-biting), enuresis, sneezing, stuttering, alcoholism, cigarette smoking, overeating, gambling, sexual deviations (for example, fetishes and transvestism), and aggressive behavior. The following are some illustrations of aversive techniques.

Vogler, Lunde, Johnson, and Martin (1970) served cocktails to alcoholic clients in a simulated lounge arrangement. Each time clients took a drink, they were given an electric shock, and the shock was maintained until they spat out the drink. The investigators did a follow-up and concluded the treatment led to abstinence. Alcoholic clients have also been treated using aversive therapy by giving them an emetic drug (for example, Antabuse) that produces nausea or vomiting when they take a drink. Sometimes the emetic drug is mixed with the drink. This combination of alcohol and emetic is usually given for a week to 10 days. Eventually, just the sight of a drink is sufficient to induce nausea and discomfort in many clients (Phares & Trull, 1997, p. 390).

Regarding the use of aversive techniques, Chambless and Goldstein (1979) cautioned,

> When reporting on behavior therapy, the popular press emphasizes such techniques and often gives the impression that punishment is the behaviorist's major tool. On the contrary, punishment is used quite infrequently by behavior modifiers even though many clients initially ask for help via punishment in curbing unwanted behavior. To begin with, no behavior should be punished if no alternative behavior is available. For example, if a client complains of sexually deviant behavior, the first therapeutic intervention is usually directed toward reducing any inhibitions about normal sexual contact. This may be accomplished by a combination of desensitization procedures and training in appropriate expression. Generally the unwanted urges decrease when anxieties about "normal" sex, that is, sex with a consenting partner, diminish.
>
> Such an approach is dictated not only by the moral imperative to employ the least painful method when there is a choice but also by the experimentally demonstrated futility of eliminating behavior through punishment when no alternative modes of satisfaction are available. Opening up alternatives is important in most cases in which punishment might otherwise be used. (p. 252)

Phares and Trull (1997) add,

> Many critics, both within and without the behavior therapy movement, have been highly critical of aversion therapy. The concentration of punishment and the use of what are sometimes terrifying stimuli often seem totally incompatible with human dignity. Whether or not patients present themselves voluntarily for treatment is beside the point. Such techniques as inducing vomiting, using a curare-like drug so that the patient will experience the sensation of suffocating, or injecting stale smoke into the nostrils seem better relegated to the status of torture than dignified as treatment. (p. 391)

Positive reinforcement approaches are generally more effective than approaches based on punishment. Punishment is often counterproductive because it can lead to the client's becoming hostile about the treatment procedures. Also, punishment may have only temporary effects. When clients realize they are no longer under surveillance, they may engage in the dysfunctional behavior again. Aversive techniques probably should be used only when all other intervention approaches have failed. In general, aversive procedures should be applied only to people with seriously debilitating problems (such as alcoholism o sexual deviations) and who are in despair because nothing else has worked.

COGNITIVE BEHAVIORAL–MODIFICATION TECHNIQUES

A major trend in behavior therapy in the past four decades has been toward recognizing the role of cognition (thinking processes) in human behavior. Following the observations of cognitive therapists such as Albert Ellis (1962) and A. T. Beck (1976), cognitive-behavioral therapists have accepted the notion that changing one's thoughts often changes one's feelings and behavior.

The traditional paradigm of behavior therapy has been *S* (stimulus) → *R* (response). Cognitive-behavioral therapists insert an additional element into this paradigm:[7]

S	→	O	→	R
(stimulus)		(cognitions of organism)		(response)

The following techniques developed to change cognitions—thought stopping and covert assertion, diversion, and reframing—are examined in this section.

Thought Stopping and Covert Assertion

Thought stopping helps clients whose major problems involve obsessive thinking and ruminations about events that are very unlikely to occur (such as worrying that a plane they will be taking in 2 weeks will crash or that they are becoming mentally ill). The client is first asked to concentrate on and express aloud her obsessive, anxiety-inducing thoughts. As she begins to express those thoughts, the counselor suddenly and emphatically shouts "Stop." This procedure is repeated several times until the client reports that her thoughts are being successfully interrupted. Then responsibility for the intervention is shifted to the client, so that the client now tells herself "Stop" out loud when she begins to think about the troubling thoughts. Once the overt shouting is effective in stopping the troubling thoughts, the client begins to practice saying "Stop" silently to herself whenever the troubling thoughts begin.

Rimm and Masters (1974) supplemented the thought-stopping technique with covert assertion. In addition to interrupting obsessive thoughts by saying "Stop," the client is encouraged to produce a positive, assertive statement that is incompatible with the content of the obsession. For example, a client who worries about becoming mentally ill (when there is no basis for such thinking) may be encouraged to add the covert assertion "Screw it! I'm perfectly normal" whenever he interrupts the obsessive thinking with "Stop."

[7]This paradigm is similar to the paradigm of rational therapists: Events → Self-talk → Emotion → Actions. See Module 1 on rational therapy.

Mahoney (1973) successfully used thought stopping and covert assertion as part of a comprehensive program for overweight clients. Mahoney first instructed clients to become aware of such self-statements as "I just don't have the willpower" and "I sure can taste a strawberry sundae." Clients then were trained to use thought stopping and covert assertion to combat these thoughts.

EP 2.1.7a

Exercise M2.7: Applying Thought Stopping and Covert Assertion

Goal: This exercise is designed to demonstrate how to use thought stopping and covert assertion.

Step 1: This may sound strange, but start awfulizing about a current problem in your life. Awfulize for about 5 minutes about this problem. After 5 minutes, yell "Stop" to yourself (either out loud or silently).

Step 2: Think of a positive, assertive statement that is incompatible with the content of the obsession. From now on, whenever you start awfulizing about your problem, yell "Stop" and use your covert assertion.

Step 3: Specify what you were awfulizing about.

Step 4: Specify the covert assertion you came up with.

Step 5: Indicate whether the thought stopping and covert assertion approach worked for you.

Step 6: If the technique did not work very well, indicate why you believe it did not.

Diversion

Diversion is used with clients who have strong unwanted emotions such as loneliness, bitterness, depression, frustration, and anger. As indicated in Module 1, unwanted emotions stem primarily from negative and irrational thinking. When clients with unwanted emotions engage in physical activity, work, social interaction, or play, they will usually switch their negative cognitions to more positive cognitions related to the new activity. Once they focus their thinking on the diversion activity that they are finding meaningful and enjoyable, they experience more pleasing emotions.

Diversion is used in both rational therapy (see Module 1) and cognitive-behavioral therapy, which are closely related. In fact, rational therapy is often classified as a cognitive-behavioral approach.

EP 2.1.7a

Exercise M2.8: Applying the Diversion Technique

Goal: This exercise is designed to demonstrate that most people can change an unwanted emotion by means of diversion.

Step 1: Think about a situation in your past that you tended to awfulize extensively about, until you used diversion to stop the awfulizing and thereby diverted your thoughts away from the unwanted emotion. (For example, you may have awfulized about someone breaking up with you.)

Step 2: Specify what you were awfulizing about. Also describe your resulting unwanted emotion(s).

Step 3: Describe the diversion technique that you used.

Step 4: Describe the effects of your diversion technique.

Step 5: Are you willing to try diversion the next time you start awfulizing?

_____ Yes _____ No

Explain your view.

Reframing

Reframing is assisting a client to change cognitions that are causing unwanted emotions or dysfunctional behaviors. Six categories of cognitions are described here.

Positive Thinking When unpleasant events occur (such as receiving a lower grade on an exam than anticipated), we always have the choice of thinking positively or negatively. If we take a positive view and focus on problem solving, we are likely to identify and initiate actions to improve the circumstances. However, if we think negatively, we often develop unwanted emotions (such as depression and frustration) and fail to focus on how to solve the problem. With negative thinking, we may not do anything constructive and may even engage in destructive behavior.

When a client is thinking negatively, a counselor can use reframing to help the client realize he is thinking negatively. At times it is helpful to remind clients that both negative and positive thinking become self-fulfilling prophecies (see Module 1). Then, by asking clients to identify some positive aspects of the situation, counselors assist clients in thinking more positively. (If clients are unable to identify any positives, counselors suggest some.) Clients may then be encouraged to tell themselves "Stop" whenever they begin to think negatively and instead to focus on telling themselves positive aspects of the situation. Some people take a negative view of most events; for such people, reframing through using positive cognitions is difficult and time-consuming. However, if they succeed in learning to think positively, they often make substantial gains.

Deawfulizing When distressing events occur, most of us tend to awfulize—we exaggerate the negatives. When we awfulize, we focus only on the negatives and do not identify constructive actions to improve the situation. When clients are awfulizing, counselors can usually help them identify such thought processes by simply inquiring, "I wonder if you're awfulizing?" Counselors can then assist their clients to give themselves positive cognitions oriented toward problem solving.

When clients awfulize about distressing events that occurred, it is also helpful for the counselor to reframe the awfulizing by relating stories such as "Good luck? Bad luck? Who knows?" (De Mello, 1978):

> There is a Chinese story of an old farmer who had an old horse for tilling his fields. One day the horse escaped into the hills and when all the farmer's neighbors sympathized with the old man over his bad luck, the farmer replied, "Bad luck? Good luck? Who knows?" A week later the horse returned with a herd of wild horses from the hills and this time the neighbors congratulated the farmer on his good luck. His reply was, "Good luck? Bad luck? Who knows?" Then, when the farmer's son was attempting to tame one of the wild horses, he fell off its back and broke his leg. Everyone thought this very bad luck. Not the farmer, whose only reaction was, "Bad luck? Good luck? Who knows?" Some weeks later the army marched into the village and conscripted every able-bodied youth they found there. When they saw the farmer's son with his broken leg, they let him off. Now was that good luck? Bad luck? Who knows? (p. 140)

The point here is that distressing events often are crises but they also frequently lead those involved to make positive changes in their lives.

Decatastrophizing This technique (Beck & Weishaar, 1989) is used when clients are "catastrophizing" over anticipated feared events. Decatastrophizing involves continually asking clients "what if" an anticipated, undesired consequence occurs. The following is a dialogue with a 21-year-old college student who fears expressing his thoughts and feelings in class:

Counselor: What do you think will happen if you begin expressing your views in your classes?

Client: My voice may crack, and the others may laugh at me.

Counselor: It is unlikely that your voice will crack. But even if it does and the students happen to laugh a little, is that really worse than your anger and frustration over not sharing your thoughts?

Client: I don't know.

Counselor: Which is worse when you're asked a question in class? Shrugging your shoulders and appearing tongue-tied, or responding as well as you can even though your voice may crack?

Client: I hear what you're saying.

Counselor: What other negative consequences might occur if you begin expressing yourself in class?

Client: *(pause)* None that I can think of.

Counselor: What positives may come from your speaking up in class?

Client: I'd probably get more out of the class and feel better about myself. Enough of this. I get the message loud and clear. I will commit myself to speaking up at least once a week in each of my classes.

People who catastrophize usually exaggerate the feared consequences. Decatastrophizing demonstrates that even if such consequences occur (which they seldom do), they aren't as severe as feared.

Separating Positive Intents from Negative Behaviors The intent here is that the positive intents become linked to new positive behaviors. A physically abusive parent has the positive intent of raising her child well, but when she is under stress and the child is misbehaving, that parent may not be aware of other, much more constructive options. A counselor can assist such a parent by helping her reframe her thinking so that when the child misbehaves in the future she focuses her thinking processes on alternative responses, such as asking her husband to handle the child's misbehavior when she is under stress or by punishing the child with a time-out.

Redefining This is used for clients who believe a problem is beyond their personal control (Beck & Weishaar, 1989). A person who believes "Life is boring" may be encouraged to think, "The only reason I'm bored is because I don't have special interests and because I'm not initiating activities. It's not life that is boring; it's my thinking processes that make me feel bored. I need to get involved in activities I enjoy and initiate interactions with people I like." Redefining is accomplished by counselors first demonstrating that emotions, such as boredom, stem primarily from thoughts (see Module 1). Next, counselors demonstrate that if clients think more positively and realistically, they will feel better. Together, client and counselor then identify the negative thinking patterns that are causing clients to believe the problem is beyond their personal control. Finally, they identify cognitions that the client commits to using to counter cognitions that are causing unwanted emotions and ineffective behaviors.

Decentering This is used with anxious clients who erroneously believe they are the focus of everyone's attention (Beck & Weishaar, 1989). Clients are asked to observe the behaviors of others rather than focusing on their own anxiety; thereby they come to realize they are not the center of attention. Beck and Weishaar (1989) gave an example:

> One student who was reluctant to speak in class believed his classmates watched him constantly and noticed his anxiety. By observing them instead of focusing on his own discomfort, he saw some students taking notes, some looking at the professor, and some daydreaming. He concluded his classmates had other concerns. (p. 310)

Additional cognitive change methods that hold considerable promise for behavior therapists' becoming increasingly involved in changing unwanted emotions and maladaptive behaviors of clients by changing their troubling thoughts are being developed (Hepworth, Rooney, & Larson, 1997).

It is somewhat difficult to specify what is and is not a cognitive-behavioral technique. In addition to techniques described here, Cormier and Cormier (1991) identified the following as cognitive-behavioral techniques: role-playing, problem-solving efforts, meditation, muscle relaxation, and paradoxical suggestions (see Module 4). Module 1 notes that changing irrational and negative cognitions may be the key psychotherapeutic change agent. Because practically all effective psychotherapeutic techniques change cognitions, then, in a broad sense, practically all psychotherapeutic techniques can be considered cognitive-behavioral techniques.

EP 2.1.7a

Exercise M2.9: Applying Reframing

Goal: This exercise is designed to assist you in understanding and applying reframing.

Step 1: Specify an unwanted emotion you are currently (occasionally) experiencing or a dysfunctional behavior you sometimes engage in.

Step 2: Specify the cognitions that underlie your unwanted emotion or dysfunctional behavior.

Step 3: Specify a "reframe" for each of those cognitions.

Step 4: When you have this unwanted emotion in the future or when you are tempted to engage in your dysfunctional behavior, do you think it will be useful to focus your thinking by using your specified "reframes"? Explain your views.

EVALUATION OF BEHAVIOR THERAPY

Behavior therapy comprises a range of intervention techniques, some of them more effective than others. Also, behavior therapy rests on a variety of different learning theories, and behaviorists have never agreed on which learning theory should be the main focus of behavior therapy. Particularly controversial among behavior therapists is the learning approach advocated by cognitive-behavioral therapists that states that emotions and actions are largely determined by our thoughts. Cognitive techniques are incompatible with the traditional principles of behaviorism, which has ignored cognitive processes because they cannot be measured and tested. Traditional behaviorism has endeavored to explain all behavior in terms of stimuli-response connections.

During the past 60 years behavior therapy has experienced a dramatic growth in new treatment techniques and in their adoption by members of the helping professions. Two pivotal books that inspired this development were *Science and Human Behavior* (Skinner, 1953) and *Psychotherapy by Reciprocal Inhibition* (Wolpe, 1958). Behavior therapists have developed, and are continuing to develop, more intervention techniques than therapists in any other psychotherapeutic area are developing.

Behavior therapy is to be highly commended for its emphasis on testing the effectiveness of its intervention techniques. This is consistent with the demand by the public that human services be accountable. Approaches shown to be effective that are widely being used include assertiveness training, behavior rehearsal, contingency contracting, token economies, and systematic desensitization and exposure therapy. The future for behavior therapy is indeed bright. Helping professionals (psychologists, psychiatrists, social workers, guidance counselors, psychiatric nurses) are increasingly being trained in behavior techniques.

Some criticisms can be made of behavior therapy:

1. Research has focused on applying the techniques to problems that are readily tested in laboratory situations, with successful results, but these problems are not the kinds of problems that clients commonly face. As Prochaska (1979) noted,

   > So what if desensitization can reduce a college coed's fear of white rats? Does that have anything to do with the devastating problems that therapists are confronted with daily in their clinical practices? Whoever sees a snake phobic in a clinic? Most behaviorists would do themselves justice when planning a study if they asked the key clinical question for any outcome research—the so-what question. So what if having college students imagine vomiting in their lunches leads to a loss of a pound a week? So what if some of the loss lasts for four months? There is plenty of evidence that eighty-five percent of the people who lose weight through any means regain it within two years. How come only a tiny fraction of their studies use a two-year follow-up? Are the authors more concerned with completing a thesis quickly or rushing to publish than with establishing a really useful therapy? (p. 354)

2. Problems that clients face in the real world often involve arriving at some decision. Should a pregnant 17-year-old teenager have an abortion or carry the pregnancy to full term? How do you get a person with a drinking problem to admit he has a problem and make a decision to seek help? Should sons and daughters of an elderly parent seek to place him or her in a nursing home? How do you help a teenager who has run away from home make future plans about where to live? Behavior therapy does not help clients arrive at such decisions. The focus of behavior therapy is on changing maladaptive behavior, not on arriving at decisions.
3. Behavior therapy is an amalgam of techniques, which leads to the potential for theoretical chaos. Some techniques are based on operant conditioning, others on classical conditioning and modeling principles, still others on cognitive theories. Phares and Trull (1997) note,

   > Without an integrating theoretical framework, individual clinicians may find themselves flailing about in a morass of competing techniques, each claiming to be forms of behavior therapy. What is needed is a systematic theoretical position that will incorporate the techniques, classify them, and help the clinician decide when and under what conditions to employ one technique over another. Such a theoretical framework would be infinitely more efficient than multiple rules of thumb. (p. 404)

SUMMARY

Behavior therapy is based on learning theory. Behavior therapists assume that maladaptive behaviors are acquired primarily through learning and can be modified through additional learning. Numerous learning theories have been developed, and no consensus exists about which learning theory should be the basis of behavior therapy. Intervention techniques are tested with rigorous experimental procedures.

The main trend in behavior therapy is growing recognition of the role of cognition in human behavior. Some behavior therapists now identify themselves as cognitive-behavioral therapists and accept the notion that changing thoughts often changes feelings and behaviors. These theorists use techniques such as thought stopping and covert assertion, diversion, and reframing.

Behavior therapy assumes that all behavior occurs in response to stimulation, internal or external. Behavior therapists do a behavioral analysis, which involves identifying the probable stimulus-response connections of the maladaptive behavior. Behavior therapists attempt to establish working relationships with their clients. Once the behavioral analysis is completed, the findings are discussed with the client, and client and counselor agree on treatment goals.

EXERCISES

EP 2.1.1b

1. Learning to Be Assertive

Goal: This exercise is designed to help students learn how to be assertive in problematic interactions where in the past they were either nonassertive or aggressive.

Step 1: Describe the purpose of this exercise. Explain the differences between nonassertive, aggressive, and assertive behavior. Indicate that everyone is nonassertive or aggressive in some situations in which it would be more constructive to be assertive. Ask students to silently identify a situation in the past in which they wished they had been assertive rather than aggressive or nonassertive. Give some examples such as the following: The situation may involve being told to do something you did not want to do. Or perhaps someone was smoking a cigarette near you, which bothered you. Or perhaps someone made a put-down comment about you. Or perhaps you're unable to express what you feel about certain situations to your parents or to someone you're dating. Before proceeding further, ask whether the students have identified such a situation in which they wished they had been assertive. Do not proceed to the next step until everyone has identified a situation.

Step 2: State the following: "We will now do a visualization exercise that is designed to help you learn to be more assertive in the situation you identified. There will be no tricks in this exercise. Close your eyes and keep them closed during this exercise. Get as comfortable as possible in your chair, and slowly take a couple of deep breaths to become relaxed.

"Focus on a specific incident in your past when you wanted to be assertive but instead were either nonassertive or aggressive. Visualize all the details of what happened. *(Pauses a few seconds after asking each of the following questions.)* What was said to you? What did you fail to say that you wanted to say? What did you say that you didn't want to say? How did you feel about what was said? How do you now feel about this incident? Your nonverbal communication is as important in being assertive as is verbal communication. Think about your nonverbal communication. What did you communicate with your facial expressions? What did you communicate with your body posture? Did you look down or away from the other person? Did you glare at the other person? What did your gestures communicate? What were your voice tone and volume like? Did your voice crack? Did you yell or speak softly? Did you speak rapidly or with hesitation? During this incident, which of your verbal and nonverbal communications were nonassertive? Which were aggressive? Which were assertive?

"Now, let's turn to focus on how to handle this situation more assertively when it arises again. Continue to keep your eyes closed. What might you say that would assertively handle this situation? *(Pause.)* What changes do you need to make in your nonverbal communication to present yourself more assertively? *(Pause.)* Is there someone you know who would be good at handling this situation assertively? *(Pause.)* If there is someone, what would this person say or do? *(Pause.)* Does this assertive model give you some ideas on how you might assertively handle this situation? *(Pause.)*

"Continue to visualize various approaches that might work for you. Also, visualize yourself using each of these approaches. For each approach, imagine the full set of interactions that would occur if you were to use the approach. *(Pause.)*

"Now select an assertive approach that you believe would best work for you when the nonassertive or aggressive situation arises again in the future. Are you now sufficiently prepared and confident to use this approach in a real-life situation? If not, you may want to visualize further what you might say or do to increase your confidence. Or you may want to select another approach that you would be more comfortable in using. Or you may want to role-play your approach with a friend so that you become more comfortable using the approach. *(Pause.)*

"The real test will come when you try out your assertive approach in a real-life situation. The next time your problematic situation arises, use your assertive approach. After trying it out, analyze how it turned out. Pat yourself on the back for what you did well. Identify aspects of your nonverbal and verbal communication that you need to improve to express yourself more assertively. Visualize ways in which you might more assertively express yourself in the areas you need to work on.

"Above all, congratulate yourself on your efforts to become more assertive. You've earned feeling good about yourself. Learning to express yourself in situations that you're comfortable in is one of the greatest thrills you'll ever experience. Okay, gradually open your eyes, and take a little while to relax."

Step 3: Ask whether there are any questions or comments about the exercise. Then ask whether there are any situations students would like to see others in the class role-play. If students suggest some-situations, have other students role-play these. If no situations are suggested, ask for volunteers to role-play situations you suggest, such as these:

a. Ask someone to put out a cigarette that is bothering you.
b. Refuse to accept an alcoholic drink that a friend wants to buy for you when you prefer not to drink any more alcoholic beverages that day.
c. Say "no" when someone asks to borrow something you don't want to lend, such as a sweater.

EP 2.1.1b

2. Expressing Anger Assertively

Goal: The purpose of this exercise is to help students learn assertive and constructive ways to express their anger.

Step 1: Describe the goal of this exercise. Indicate that many people have not learned to express their anger assertively for a variety of reasons. Some of us have been brought up to believe it is wrong to get angry, so we deny our anger. Some of us, through modeling, have learned to express our anger aggressively, thereby lashing out and hurting others. Indicate that we have a right to all our emotions. It is normal to become angry at times. Others do not have a right to try to convince us that we should not be angry when we are angry.

When anger is not expressed assertively, it is often expressed destructively. We may aggressively hurt others. Or we may try to deny we are angry and instead turn the anger inward and become depressed. Or we may recognize the anger but fail to express it, which can result in anxiety. Or anger may lead to guilt if we punish ourselves for getting angry when we erroneously believe we should not get angry. Or we may seek to relieve our angry feelings through excessive drinking or eating.

Step 2: Explain that there are assertive and constructive ways to express anger. These ways include the following:

a. Express angry feelings assertively so no one is hurt. When expressing anger assertively, it is advisable to use nonblaming I-messages rather than you-messages. (See Module 4 for a description of I-messages.)
b. Express angry feelings at the time we become angry so we do not stew about it. If we delay expressing anger, the hostility may build, and we may explode and lash out at others.

c. Admit to ourselves when we are angry, so that we do not try to hide our anger from ourselves. Through acknowledging our anger, we are better able to focus on finding constructive ways to express our anger.
d. Blow off steam nondestructively through physical activities such as jogging, hitting a pillow or a punching bag, taking a walk, or lifting weights whenever it is counterproductive to express our anger or when we feel we seem about to explode.
e. Seek to counter negative and irrational self-talk by writing out a rational self-analysis (see Module 1).

Step 3: Ask each student to complete the following three statements on a sheet of paper:

a. Three or four things that make me angry are
b. I usually express my anger by
c. Things that I can do to better handle and express my anger are

Step 4: Have students form subgroups of three people each to share what they wrote and to receive additional suggestions on how to express their anger more effectively. (Indicate that students have a right to privacy and therefore do not have to self-disclose anything they want to keep private.)

Step 5: Form a circle and ask students whether they have any questions or comments about the exercise or about what was discussed in the subgroups.

EP 2.1.1b

3. Reframing

Goal: This exercise is designed to demonstrate to students how to reframe cognitions resulting from awfulizing.

Step 1: Describe the technique of reframing, and illustrate the process of awfulizing by giving a few examples of occasions in which you awfulized.

Step 2: Instruct each student to record his or her responses to the following questions and instructions on a sheet of paper. Indicate that students will not be required to reveal their responses.

a Briefly describe a distressing event over which you awfulized.
b. Specify your awfulizing cognitions about this distressing event.
c. For each awfulizing cognition, specify a more positive and realistic cognition that you could give yourself about this event. (Ideally, many of these countering cognitions will facilitate problem solving.)
d. Indicate the approximate length of time that you awfulized over this event.
e. Are you still awfulizing about this event?
f. Do you believe that countering the awfulizing cognitions with more positive and realistic cognitions would have shortened the time you spent awfulizing?

Step 3: Ask for volunteers to share their responses to those questions. End by asking students to indicate their thoughts on the merits and shortcomings of the use of reframing in therapy.

COMPETENCY NOTES

The following identifies where Educational Policy (EP) competencies and practice behaviors are discussed in the chapter.

EP 2.1.10a *Substantively and affectively prepare for action with individuals, families, groups, organizations, and communities.*

EP 2.1.10j *Help clients resolve problems.* (pp. 505–530).

This module presents the rational therapy approach to changing unwanted emotions and dysfunctional behaviors of individuals, family members, and group members.

EP 2.1.7a *Utilize conceptual frameworks to guide the process of assessment, intervention, and evaluation.* (p. 506).

Exercise M2.1 is designed to assist students in understanding and applying operant conditioning.

EP 2.1.7a *Utilize conceptual frameworks to guide the process of assessment, intervention, and evaluation.* (p. 507).

Exercise M2.2 is designed to assist students in understanding and applying respondent conditioning.

EP 2.1.7a *Utilize conceptual frameworks to guide the process of assessment, intervention, and evaluation.* (p. 508).

Exercise M2.3 is designed to assist students in understanding and applying the principles of modeling.

EP 2.1.7a *Utilize conceptual frameworks to guide the process of assessment, intervention, and evaluation.* (p. 514).

Exercise M2.4 is designed to assist students in understanding and applying the principles of assertiveness training.

EP 2.1.7a *Utilize conceptual frameworks to guide the process of assessment, intervention, and evaluation.* (p. 516).

Exercise M2.5 is designed to assist students in understanding a token economy.

EP 2.1.7a *Utilize conceptual frameworks to guide the process of assessment, intervention, and evaluation.* (p. 517).

Exercise M2.6 is designed to assist students in understanding and applying contingency contracting.

EP 2.1.7a *Utilize conceptual frameworks to guide the process of assessment, intervention, and evaluation.* (p. 521).

Exercise M2.7 is designed to demonstrate how to use thought stopping and covert assertion.

EP 2.1.7a *Utilize conceptual frameworks to guide the process of assessment, intervention, and evaluation.* (p. 522).

Exercise M2.8 is designed to demonstrate that most people can change an unwanted emotion by means of diversion.

EP 2.1.7a *Utilize conceptual frameworks to guide the process of assessment, intervention, and evaluation.* (p. 525).

Exercise M2.9 is designed to assist students in understanding and applying reframing.

EP 2.1.1b *Practice personal reflection and self-correction to assure continual professional development.* (pp. 527–528).

This exercise is designed to help students learn how to be assertive in problematic interactions where, in the past, they were either nonassertive or aggressive.

EP 2.1.1b *Practice personal reflection and self-correction to assure continual professional development.* (pp. 528–529).

This exercise is designed to help students learn assertive and constructive ways to express their anger.

EP 2.1.1b *Practice personal reflection and self-correction to assure continual professional development.* (p. 529).

This exercise is designed to demonstrate to students how to reframe cognitions resulting from awfulizing.

Reality Therapy

WILLIAM GLASSER

EP 2.1.10a. j

The founder of reality therapy is William Glasser (1925–). Glasser developed two versions of reality therapy. The first, developed in the 1960s, is based on identity theory (Glasser, 1965). The second, developed during the past two decades, is based on choice theory (Glasser, 1998). This second version is described in this module.

Glasser is an internationally recognized psychiatrist. He graduated from Case Western Reserve Medical School in Cleveland, Ohio, in 1953. In 1956, he became a consulting psychiatrist to the Ventura School for Girls, a California state institution for the treatment of delinquent girls. Glasser grew skeptical of the value of orthodox psychoanalysis. At the Ventura School, he set up a new treatment program based on the principles of his reality therapy. The program showed promise, and participants expressed enthusiasm. In 1966, Glasser began consulting in the California school system and applied the concepts of reality therapy to education. His emphasis on the need for schools to highlight involvement, relevance, and thinking continues to have a profound impact on the educational system.

Glasser does not believe in the concept of mental illness. His point of view on mental illness is presented later in this chapter. He has written more than 20 books. In 1967, he founded the Institute for Reality Therapy, which has trained over 60,000 people worldwide in reality therapy. In recent years, Glasser's major focus has been to teach the world his views on choice theory, the new psychology described in this module.

This module will:

A. Describe choice theory and present the axioms of choice theory
B. Describe the principles of reality therapy

OVERVIEW OF CHOICE THEORY

Choice theory is an *internal* control psychology: It explains why and how we make the choices that determine the course of our lives. According to Glasser (1998), we choose everything we do. A major assumption of choice theory is that we carry around in our heads pictures of what reality is like and of how we would like it to be. Glasser (1984, p. 32) asserts, "All our behavior is our constant attempt to reduce the difference between what we want (the pictures in our heads) and what we have (the way we see situations in the world.)" By *pictures*, Glasser means *perceptions* from our senses of sight, hearing, touch, smell, and taste. Some examples will clarify this idea. Each of us has a detailed idea of the type of person we would like to date or form a relationship with; when we find someone who closely matches these characteristics, we seek to form a relationship. Each of us carries around a mental picture album of our favorite foods; when we're hungry, we select an item and go about obtaining that food.

How do we develop these pictures/albums/ideas that we believe will satisfy our needs? According to Glasser, we begin to create our albums at an early age (perhaps even before birth), and we spend our whole life enlarging them. Essentially, whenever what we do gets us something that satisfies a need, we store the picture of it in our personal albums. Glasser (1984) gives the following example of this process by describing how a hungry child added chocolate-chip cookies to his picture album:

> Suppose you had a grandson and your daughter left you in charge while he was taking a nap. She said she would be right back, because be would be ravenous when he awoke and she knew you had no idea what to feed an eleven-month-old child. She was right. As soon as she left, he awoke screaming his head off, obviously starved. You tried a bottle, but he rejected it—he had something more substantial in mind. But what? Being unused to a howling baby, and desperate, you tried a chocolate-chip cookie and it worked wonders. At first, he did not seem to know what it was, but he was a quick learner. He quickly polished off three cookies. She returned and almost polished you off for being so stupid as to give a baby chocolate. "Now," she said, "he will be yelling all day for those cookies." She was right. If he is like most of us, he will probably have chocolate on his mind for the rest of his life. (p. 19)

When this child learned how satisfying chocolate-chip cookies are, he placed the picture of these cookies in his personal picture album.

The pictures in our albums do not have to be rational. Anorexics picture themselves as fat and starve themselves to come closer to their irrational picture of unhealthy thinness. Rapists have pictures of satisfying their power needs and perhaps sexual needs through sexual assault. To change a picture, we must replace it with one that will reasonably satisfy the need in question. People who are unable to replace a picture may endure a lifetime of misery. Some battered women, for example, endure brutal beatings and humiliations in marriage because they cannot picture themselves as worthy of a loving relationship.

Glasser notes that whenever the picture we see and the one we want to see differ, a *signal* generated by this difference leads us to behave in a way that will obtain the picture we want. We examine our behaviors and choose one or more that we believe will help us reduce this difference. These behaviors include straightforward problem-solving efforts as well as manipulative strategies such as anger, pouting, and guilt. People who act irresponsibly or ineffectually either have failed to choose responsible behaviors from their repertoires or have not yet learned responsible courses of action.

Glasser believes we are driven by five innate needs and that as soon as one need is satisfied another need or perhaps two or more needs acting together push for satisfaction. Our first need is *survival*. This includes such vital functions as breathing, digesting food, sweating, regulating blood pressure, and meeting the demands of hunger, thirst, and sex. Our second need is *love and belonging*. We generally meet this need through family, friends, pets, plans, and material possessions.

Our third need is *power*. Glasser says this need involves getting others to obey us and to then receive the esteem and recognition that accompanies power. Our drive for power sometimes conflicts with our need to belong. Two people in a relationship may struggle to control it rather than create an equalitarian relationship.

Our fourth need is *freedom*. People want the freedom to choose how they live their lives, to express themselves, to read and write what they choose, to associate with whom they select, and to worship or not worship as they believe.

Our fifth need is *fun*. Glasser believes learning is often fun; it gives us a great incentive to assimilate what we need to satisfy our needs. Classes that are grim and boring are major failings of our educational system. Laughing and humor help fulfill our needs for fun. Fun is such a vital part of living that most of us have trouble conceiving of life without it.

AXIOMS OF CHOICE THEORY

Glasser has a list of principles of choice theory. He calls these principles "axioms." A summary of these axioms follows:

EP 2.1.1 b

1. The only person whose behavior we can control is our own. No one can make us do anything we do not want to do—as long as we are willing to endure the consequences: punishment for not doing what others want us to do. If we choose to do what others want us to do under the threat of severe punishment, we tend to become passive-aggressive and not perform very well. When we try to force others to do what they do not want to do, they may choose not to do it—or resort to passive aggression and not perform well.

Exercise M3.1: Seeking to Change Someone and Being Controlled by Someone

Goal: This exercise is designed to illustrate that we are inclined to attempt to change others and that others sometimes attempt to control us. The consequences of attempting to control others are also examined.

Step 1: Describe a situation in which you attempted to change someone's behavior—perhaps the irritating actions of someone you were dating.

Step 2: Were you successful in changing the behavior of this person? What were the emotional reactions of this person to your attempts at change?

Step 3: If the person changed the behavior that you found irritating, do you think the change occurred because you forced this person to change or because he or she "chose" to change?

Step 4: Describe a situation in which someone (perhaps a parent or someone you were dating) sought to change some behavior of yours that he or she found irritating.

Step 5: Did you change your behavior? How did you feel about someone trying to change (or control) you?

Step 6: If you change the behavior, did you do so because someone forced you to change or because you "chose" to change?

Note: Isn't it interesting that we think we have a right to attempt to change irritating behavior of people we are dating, but we don't like others to attempt to change us!

2. All we can give to or get from other people is information. How each person deals with that information is his or her own choice. For example, a teacher can assign readings but is not responsible if some students choose to ignore the assignment. The teacher should not feel personally responsible for students who choose not to do the reading. The teacher, of course, can choose the consequences that students who fail to do the assignment will face—such as lower grades.
3. According to Glasser, all we can do from birth to death is "behave," and behavior consists of four inseparable components: acting, thinking, feeling, and physiology. Each of these components of what Glasser terms "total behavior" interacts with and affects the other three. (Axioms 4 and 5 elaborate on this interaction.)
4. All long-lasting psychological problems are relationship problems. Our usual way of dealing with an important relationship that is not working out the way we want it to is to choose misery—emotional misery and physical misery. Relationship problems are a partial cause of many other problems, such as fatigue, pain, weakness, and autoimmune diseases (such as fibromyalgia and rheumatoid arthritis). Glasser (1998) states,

   > Most doctors believe that adult rheumatoid arthritis is caused by the victims' immune systems attacking their own joints as if these joints were foreign bodies. Another way of putting it is that their own creative systems are trying to protect these people from a perceived harm. If we could figure out a way to stop this misguided creativity, millions of people who suffer from this disease and a host of other relentless diseases, called autoimmune diseases, could be helped. (pp. 137–138)

5. The human brain is very creative. A woman who was sexually abused as a child may develop a dissociative identity disorder to psychologically shield herself from the emotional pain of the abuse. Glasser believes that almost all medical problems for which physicians are unable to identify a cause are partially created by the ill person's brain to deal with the unhappiness that the person is experiencing. Unhappiness is the force that inspires the creativity inherent in the brain to be a partial cause of symptoms described in the *DSM-IV* (American Psychiatric Association, 2000): aches and pains (such as migraine headaches), physical illnesses (such as heart disease, cancer, adult asthma, and eczema).

   Regarding the brain creating the symptoms in the *DSM-IV,* Glasser (2003) describes how unhappiness may lead the brain to create hallucinations:

   > Suppose, instead of your creativity presenting an idea to you as a thought, it created a voice uttering a threat or any other message directly into the auditory cortex of your brain. You would hear an actual voice or voices; it could be a stranger or you might recognize whose voice it was. It would be impossible, just by hearing it, for you to tell it from an actual voice or voices. (p. 114)

Because we can hear voices, our brain can create voices that we hear when no one else is around. Because we can see, our brain can create visual hallucinations. Because we can feel pain, our brain can create pain—perhaps in greater severity and duration than what we experience from an injury or illness. Because we are able to fear, our brain can and does create disabling phobias. (See Exhibit M3.1.)

Exhibit M3.1 Our Thoughts Impact Our Physiological Functioning: Healing Thoughts versus Disease-Facilitating Thoughts

Diseases and medical conditions are caused by a variety of factors: what we eat; exposure to germs, viruses, and bacteria; genetics; too much or too little exposure to sun; lack of exercise; lack of sleep; and thoughts. The following are examples of how our thoughts impact our physiological functioning.

1. Under hypnosis, "I will feel no pain" —> painless surgery without anesthesia
2. Under hypnosis, "Something hot is burning my arm" —> blister
3. Deep-breathing relaxation, "I am relaxing" —> painless dental drilling without anesthesia
4. "I no longer want to live" —> death within a few years
5. "I don't want to die yet" —> a person ravaged by cancer continues to live
6. When I have a cold, the thought "I must get all these things done" —> cold lasts for weeks
   When I have a cold, the thought "I will take time off to rest and relax" —> cold lasts for only a few days
7. Hangover, "My head is killing me" —> intense headache
   Hangover, "I will relax and ignore the pain in my head" —> headache soon subsides (the same is true for most other headaches)
8. "I am worried about such and such," or "I have *so* much to do tomorrow" —> unable to fall asleep
9. "I will have serious complications if I have this surgery" —> complications likely
10. "The plane I'am going to fly on is going to crash" —> anxiety, panic attacks (panic attacks, if frequent, will lead to a variety of illnesses, including hypertension and heart problems)
11. A woman thinks she is pregnant but isn't —> morning sickness and enlarged stomach
12. Relaxing thoughts —> immune system functions well, fights off illnesses, and facilitates healing
13. Alarming thoughts (such as "I miss ___ *so much!*" —> high stress level —> various illnesses, such as heart problems, colitis, stomach problems, skin rashes, ulcers, aches and pains, headaches, cancer, colds, and flus. (Immune system is suppressed when a person experiences high levels of stress.)
14. "I will do well today in this sport, by focusing on___" —> success at tennis, golf, bowling, baseball, etc.
15. "I am too fat; but by controlling my eating, I can control part of my life" —> anorexia and various health problems
16. "By throwing up after eating, I can maintain my weight and figure and also enjoy the taste of food" —> bulimia and various health problems
17. "I need several drinks each day to get through the day and numb my pain" —> alcoholism
18. "I love food *so much that I don't care what happens to me*" —> compulsive overeating, obesity, diabetes, and various other health problems
19. "I need to get more work done, in a shorter time, for the next 10 years" —> Type A personality, hypertension, heart problems, and strokes
20. "I'll never forgive ___ for what s/he did," or "I'll get even with her/him if it's the last thing I do" —> hostility and heart problems and strokes
21. "Sex disgusting," or "My partner stinks," or "My partner is inept at lovemaking" —> lack of sexual arousal and other sexual dysfunctions

Note: Module 1 demonstrates that all our emotions and all our actions/behaviors are largely determined by our thoughts. Module 3 suggests our thoughts have a major impact on our physiological functioning. It appears our thoughts have a major impact on our lives!

EP 2.1.1 b

Exercise M3.2: The Creativity in Our Brains

Goal: This exercise is designed to assist you in understanding that our thoughts are sometimes a cause of somatic problems, emotional difficulties, and behavioral dysfunctions.

Step 1: Identify a somatic problem (such as migraine headaches) of unknown physical cause that you or someone close to you has. Speculate how thoughts may be a factor in causing the somatic problem.

Step 2: Identify an emotional or behavioral problem that you or someone close to you has. Speculate on how thoughts contributed to this emotional or behavioral problem.

6. Barring untreatable physical illnesses or severe poverty, unsatisfying relationships are the primary source of crimes, addictions, and emotional and behavioral disorders.
7. It is a serious mistake (and irrational to expect positive results) to seek to control others by nagging, preaching, punishing, or threatening to punish them. As indicated earlier, the only person we can effectively control is ourself. To progress in improving human relationships, we need to give up seeking to control others through nagging, preaching, putting down, or threatening punishment.

EP 2.1.1 b

Exercise M3.3: The Effects of Nagging and Preaching

Goal: This exercise is designed to increase your awareness of the effects of nagging, preaching, put-downs, or threats of punishment.

Step 1: Describe a situation in which someone tried to control you by nagging, preaching, putting you down, or threatening punishment.

Step 2: How did you feel about someone attempting to control you with those external control strategies?

Step 3: Did you change your behavior? If you did, was it because you were forced to change or because you "chose" to change?

Step 4: Describe a situation in which you attempted to change someone by nagging, preaching, put-downs, or threats of punishment.

Step 5: How did that person emotionally react to your external control attempts?

Step 6: Did that person change his or her behavior? If the person did change, was it because you forced him or her to change or because he or she "chose" to change?

8. The unsatisfying (problematic) relationship is always a current one. We cannot live happily without at least one satisfying relationship. In a quality relationship between two people, each person seeks to meet his or her own needs and wants and those of the other person too.
9. The *solving circle* is a good strategy for two people who know choice theory to use to redefine their freedom and improve their relationship. Glasser advocates its use in marital and dating relationships. Each person pictures his or her relationship inside a large circle—the solving circle. An imaginary circle is drawn on the floor. Each person sits on a chair within the circle. The two persons are told there are three entities in the solving circle: the two persons and the relationship itself. The two persons are asked to agree that maintaining the relationship takes precedence over what each person wants. In the circle, each person tells the other what he or she will agree to do to help the relationship. Within those limits, the two persons must reach a compromise on their conflicts.
10. Painful events that happened in the past have a great deal to do with what we are today, but dwelling on the painful past contributes little or nothing to what we need to do now—which is to improve an important, present relationship.

EP 2.1.1 b

Exercise M3.4: Improving an Unhappy Relationship

Goal: This exercise is designed to assist you in improving, through problem solving, a significant relationship in your life.

Step 1: Identify and briefly describe a significant relationship in your life that you would like to improve.

Step 2: Do you believe the unhappy components in this relationship may be having an adverse impact on your physical or mental well-being? Please explain. (If you cannot identify a problematic current relationship, describe a past unhappy relationship and indicate how it negatively affected your physical and mental well-being.)

Step 3: Speculate about what you might do to improve a current problematic relationship.

11. It is not necessary to know our past before we can deal with the present. It is good to revisit the parts of our past that were satisfying, but it is even better to let go of what was unhappy.

EP 2.1.1 b

Exercise M3.5: Letting Go of Grudges

Goal: This exercise is designed to assist you in letting go of strong feelings of being wronged by others.

Step 1: Describe a situation that you still awfulize about in which you feel that someone severely wronged you.

Step 2: Does it do you any good to continue to awfulize about this? Research shows hostility toward others is a major factor leading to heart disease and other stress-related illnesses (Leyden-Rubenstein, 1998). By holding a grudge, are you not adversely impacting your physical and mental well-being? Speculate about how holding a grudge may currently be affecting you.

Step 3: Speculate about what you can do to let go of this grudge.

12. We can satisfy our basic needs only by satisfying one or more pictures in our "quality world." Our quality world consists of three kinds of need-satisfying pictures: people (such as parents), things (such as a car and clothes), and beliefs (such as our religious and political beliefs). We experience the most freedom when we are able to satisfy one or more pictures in our quality world. We give up part of our freedom when we put pictures into our quality world that we cannot satisfy.
13. When we have difficulty in getting along with other people, we usually make the mistake of choosing to employ *external control psychology.* We attempt to coerce or control others by nagging, preaching, moralizing, criticizing, or using put-down messages.
14. Because relationships are central to human happiness, improving our emotional and physical well-being involves exploring how we relate to others and looking for ways to improve how we relate to others (particularly those people to whom we feel closest).

15. It is therapeutic to discuss our "total behavior" by means of verbs. For example, it is much more accurate to say "I am choosing to depress" or "I am depressing" than to think "I am suffering from depression" or "I am depressed." When we say "I am depressing," we are immediately aware that we are choosing to depress and have the option to do and feel something else (such as "I will go golfing and enjoy the day.") People who say "I am depressed" mistakenly tend to believe the depressing is beyond their control. In addition, they are likely to mistakenly believe the depressing has been caused by what someone else has done to them. To recognize that we have the power to choose to stop depressing (or to stop angering or frustrating, and so on) is a wonderful freedom that people who adhere to the view that they are largely controlled by others will never have.

EP 2.1.7a

Exercise M3.6: Expressing Negative Emotions by Means of Verbs

Goal: This exercise is designed to demonstrate that expressing our negative emotions by means of verbs assists us in recognizing that we are *choosing* to feel a certain way and could *choose* to feel positive emotions instead.

Step 1: List all the negative emotions you have felt in the past week.

Step 2: Rephrase all these negative emotions by means of verbs—for example, "I am angering" instead of "I am angry."

Step 3: Does this exercise help you to understand that we *choose* to feel negative emotions and could choose to feel positive ones instead? Explain your thoughts on this.

16. All four components of behavior (thinking, feeling, acting, and physiology) are subject to choice, but we have direct control over only the acting and thinking components. We do, however, control our physiology and our feelings through how we choose to act and think. It is not easy to change our actions and thoughts, but when we succeed in coming up with more satisfying actions and thoughts, we gain a great deal of personal freedom.

EP 2.1.1 b

Exercise M3.7: Changing Our Feelings and Improving Somatic Problems

Goal: This exercise is designed to demonstrate that negative emotions can be changed and some somatic problems can be improved by changing our thoughts and actions.

Step 1: Describe how you changed a negative emotion by changing your thoughts or actions.

Step 2: Describe how you improved a somatic problem (perhaps a headache) by changing your thoughts or actions.

17. Whenever you feel as if you lack the freedom you want in a relationship, it is because you, your partner, or both of you are unwilling to accept a key axiom of choice theory: *Only you can control your own life*. The more both you and your partner learn choice theory, the better you will get along with one another. Choice theory supports the golden rule.
18. People choose (although some are unaware of their choice) to play the mentally ill roles that are described in the *DSM-IV* (American Psychiatric Association, 2000). These people have the symptoms described in the *DSM-IV*, but they are not mentally ill (if mental illness is defined as a disease of the mind). These people do not have an untreatable or incurable mental illness. The symptoms are only an indication that these people are not as healthy as they could learn to be. See Exhibit M3.2 and Case Example "Reality Therapy."
19. According to Glasser, drugs prescribed by psychiatrists and doctors may make you feel better, temporarily, but in doing so they are no different from any prescription drug you may use on your own, such as alcohol, nicotine, or caffeine. Unless you solve the personal problems bothering you, the initial lift that prescribed drugs give you will wear off, and you may need a higher dose. Misguided psychiatric efforts have created an epidemic of drug-treated "mental illness."

Exhibit M3.2 Two Approaches to Mental Illness

Much of the language relating to emotional disturbances is a familiar part of our lexicon. We use *crazy, psychotic, neurotic, nervous breakdown, insane, sick, uptight, and mad* to express judgments (often unfavorable) about unusual behavior or unusual emotions. Whatever term we use, we often have only a vague idea of its technical meaning. Amazingly, though, we act as if the label is completely accurate and then relate to the person as if the label is absolutely correct. However, we all know it is impossible to define these terms precisely.

Helping professionals use two approaches to diagnose people who display emotional disturbances and abnormal behaviors: the medical model and the interactional model.

Medical Model

This model presents emotional and behavioral problems as illnesses comparable to physical illness. Mental illness labels use medical terminology (for example, *schizophrenia, paranoia, psychosis*, or *insanity*) to describe emotional problems. Adherents of this approach believe the disturbed person's mind is affected by an internal condition. This condition, they assert, results from genetic endowment, metabolic disorders, infectious diseases, internal conflicts, chemical imbalances, unconscious use of defense mechanisms, or traumatic early experiences.

The medical model has a lengthy classification of mental disorders defined by the American Psychiatric Association. (See Chapter 1 for a summary of the numerous specific mental disorders that are classified in *DSM-IV* [American Psychiatric Association, 2000].)

The medical model arose in reaction to the historical notion that the emotionally disturbed were possessed by demons and could therefore be blamed for their disturbances. The medical model treats the disturbed as in need of help and has stimulated enormous amounts of research into the nature of emotional problems. Therapeutic approaches owe their development to the medical model.

Interactional Model

Critics of the medical model assert that medical labels have no diagnostic or treatment value and may actually have an adverse effect. Thomas Szasz (1961) was one of the first authorities to assert that mental illness is a myth—that it does not exist. Szasz's theory is interactional; it focuses on the processes of everyday social interaction and the effects of labeling.

Exhibit M3.2 *(continued)*

Beginning with the assumption that the term *mental illness* implies a "disease of the mind," Szasz categorized all so-called mental illnesses into three types of emotional and behavioral disorders and discussed the inappropriateness of calling them "mental illnesses":

1. *Personal disabilities,* such as excessive anxiety, depression, fears, and feelings of inadequacy. Szasz said such so-called mental illnesses may be appropriately considered "mental" (in the sense that thinking and feeling are "mental" activities), but he asserts that they are not diseases.
2. *Antisocial acts,* such as bizarre homicides and social deviations. (Homosexuality used to be listed in this category but was removed from the American Psychiatric Association's list of mental illnesses in 1974.) Szasz said such antisocial acts are actually social deviations and not "mental" or "diseases."
3. *Deterioration of the brain with associated personality changes.* This category includes the "mental illnesses" in which personality changes result from brain deterioration caused by arteriosclerosis, chronic alcoholism, AIDS, general paresis, or serious brain injury. Common symptoms are loss of memory, listlessness, apathy, and deterioration of personal grooming habits. Szasz says these disorders can appropriately be considered "diseases" but are diseases of the brain rather than of the *mind.*

Szasz (1961) asserted that calling people with emotional problems "mentally ill" is as absurd as calling the emotionally disturbed "possessed":

> The belief in mental illness as something other than man's trouble in getting along with his fellow man is the proper heir to the belief in demonology and witchcraft. Mental illness exists or is "real" in exactly the same sense in which witches existed or were "real." (p. 84)

In reality, being labeled "mentally ill" occurs in three steps: the person displays some deviant behavior; the behavior is not tolerated by the family or community; and the professional labeler, usually a psychiatrist, believes in the medical model and assigns a mental illness label. Scheff (1966) and Mechanic (1962) offered evidence that family and community intolerance of deviant behavior and the professional labeler's belief in the medical model are more crucial than the behavior itself in determining whether someone will be labeled "mentally ill."

The point here is that people have emotional problems, not mystic "mental illnesses." Thus, reality therapists use the following terms to describe behavior: *depression, anxiety, obsession, compulsive, excessive fear, feelings of failure.* These are personal problems, not illnesses. Medical terms (for example, *schizophrenia* or *psychosis*) are not useful because no distinguishing symptom indicates whether a person has or does not have the "illness." In addition, Rosenhan and Seligman (1995) pointed out that considerable variation exists among cultures regarding what is mental illness. Indeed, psychiatrists themselves frequently disagree in their "medical" diagnoses.

In a dramatic study, psychologist David Rosenhan (1973) demonstrated that professional staff in mental hospitals could not distinguish between "sane" and "insane" people. Rosenhan and seven "normal" associates went to 12 mental hospitals in five different states and claimed to hear voices. After they were admitted, these pseudopatients said they had stopped hearing the voices. Although they then began to behave completely normally, the hospital personnel were unable to recognize the difference between their sanity and the "insanity" of the other patients. The pseudopatients were confined to the hospitals for an average of 19 days and then discharged with a diagnosis of "schizophrenia in remission."

Medical labels have several adverse labeling effects. People who are labeled *mentally ill* (and frequently their therapists) believe that they have a disease for which unfortunately there is no known "cure." The label gives them an excuse for not taking responsibility for their actions (for example, innocent by reason by insanity). Because there is no known "cure," the disturbed frequently idle away their time waiting for someone to discover a cure rather than assuming responsibility for their behavior, examining the reasons for their problems, and making efforts to improve. Other undesirable consequences of the label *mentally ill* are that those so labeled lose legal rights; can be stigmatized as dangerous, unpredictable, untrustworthy, or of "weak" character; and find it more difficult to secure employment or receive a promotion (Rosenhan & Seligman, 1995).

An even more harmful effect is that "mentally ill" people view themselves as different and therefore play the role of the "sick" person. Everyone needs to evaluate feelings, opinions, and abilities. In the absence of objective, nonsocial criteria, people rely on other people to gauge the validity of their beliefs and feelings. If others define us as mentally ill and react to us accordingly, we may begin to say, "I must be crazy, because other people treat me as if I were insane."

Authorities who adhere to the interactional model raise a key question, because expectations generally guide behavior: "If we relate to people with emotional problems as mentally ill, how can we expect them to act in emotionally healthy and responsible ways?" Also, a diagnosis of mental illness carries a greater stigma than does one of physical illness.

Szasz (1967) also argued that the mental model is used (perhaps unintentionally) to control people who do not conform to social expectations. The former Soviet Union had a long history of labeling dissenters

(continued)

Exhibit M3.2 *(continued)*

(including poets, writers, and intellectuals who would be respected in this country) as mentally ill and sending them to concentration camps or to insane asylums. In the past, psychiatrists in Russia often concluded that people who did not accept Marxist-Leninist philosophy were psychologically impaired. Are some psychiatrists using the mental illness label to control the behavior of nonconformists in our country? Szasz (1967) asserted that they are. As an example, he cited listing homosexuality as a mental disorder by the American Psychiatric Association. As another example, Szasz (1963) quoted Dana L. Farnsworth, a Harvard psychiatrist and an authority on college psychiatric services:

> Library vandalism, cheating and plagiarism, stealing in the college or community stores or in the dormitories, unacceptable or antisocial sexual practices (overt homosexuality, exhibitionism, promiscuity), and the unwise and unregulated use of harmful drugs are examples of behavior that suggest the presence of emotionally unstable persons. (p. 76)

Mental illness labels have a "boundary" effect, defining what behaviors a society considers "sick" and pressuring citizens to avoid such behaviors. Szasz's point is that nonconformists can be adversely affected by the use of the medical model.

Labeling as the Primary Cause of Chronic "Mental Illness"

We must, of course, ask "If mental illness does not exist, why do some people go through life as if they were mentally ill?" Scheff's theory (1966) provides an answer. Scheff hypothesizes that labeling is the most important determinant of chronic functional "mental illness."

Scheff began by first arriving at a definition of *mental illness:*

> One source of immediate embarrassment to any social theory of "mental illness" is that the terms used in referring to these phenomena in our society prejudge the issue. The medical metaphor "mental illness" suggests a determinant process which occurs within the individual: the unfolding and development of disease. In order to avoid this assumption, we will utilize sociological, rather than medical concepts to formulate the problem. (p. 31)

The symptoms of mental illness can thus be viewed as violations of social norms. For Scheff's purposes the term *mental illness* refers to persons assigned this label by professionals.

Literally thousands of studies have been conducted to identify the origins of long-term mental disorders. Practically all of these studies identified the causes as somewhere inside a person (for example, metabolic disorders, unconscious conflicts, heredity factors). These research efforts are based on medical and psychological models of human behavior. Yet, amazingly, despite this extensive research, the determinants of chronic mental disorders (such as schizophrenia) are largely unknown. Scheff suggested that the major determinants are not medical but are our social processes (that is, our interactions with others).

Scheff's theory is summarized here. Everyone, at times, violates social norms and commits acts that could be labeled symptoms of mental illness. For example, a person may on occasion angrily engage in fights with others, or experience intense depression or grief, or be highly anxious, or use drugs or alcohol to excess, or have a fetish, or be an exhibitionist, or commit a highly unusual and bizarre act.

Usually the person who has unwanted emotions or who commits deviant acts is not identified (labeled) as being mentally ill. In such cases, the unwanted emotions and deviant actions are usually not classified as symptoms of a mental illness but instead are ignored, unrecognized, or rationalized in some other manner.

Occasionally, however, such norm violations are perceived by others as being "abnormal." The offenders are then labeled *mentally ill* and consequently related to as if they are mentally ill. When people are publicly labeled, they are highly suggestible to cues from others. They realize they have done something unusual and turn to others to obtain an assessment of who they really are. In the absence of objective measures of their sanity, they rely on others for this assessment. If others relate to them as if they are mentally ill, they begin to define and perceive themselves as being mentally ill.

Traditional stereotypes of mental illness define the mentally ill role, both for those who are labeled mentally ill and for people they interact with. Frequently people they interact with reward them for enacting the social role of being mentally ill. The rewards may be sympathy and attention, such as not having to hold a job or not being held responsible for wrongdoing, or they fulfill the requirements of other roles.

In addition, the "mentally ill" are punished for attempting to return to conventional roles. They are viewed with suspicion and have considerable difficulty obtaining employment.

The effect of all this is a gradual change in one's self-concept. People thus labeled begin to view themselves as different, as insane, and a vicious circle is created. The more one enacts the role of being mentally ill, the more one is defined and treated as mentally ill, and so on. Unless interrupted, the cycle leads to a "career" of long-term mental illness. Scheff concluded that with this process, labeling is the single most important determinant of chronic mental illness.

If labeling is an important determinant of chronic functional mental illness, significant changes are suggested in certain diagnostic and treatment practices.

Exhibit M3.2 *(continued)*

Mental health personnel are frequently faced with uncertainty in deciding whether a person has a mental disorder. An informal norm has been developed to handle this uncertainty: When in doubt, it is better to judge a well person ill than to judge an ill person well. This norm is based on two assumptions taken from treating physical illness: (1) A diagnosis of illness results in only minimal damage to the status and reputation of a person. (2) Unless the illness is treated, the illness will become progressively worse. However, both of these assumptions are questionable. Unlike medical treatment, psychiatric treatment can drastically change a person's status in the community; for example, it can remove rights that are difficult to regain. Furthermore, if Scheff is right that labeling is the key determinant in leading to long-term mental illness, the exact opposite norm should be established to handle uncertainty—namely, when in doubt, do not label a person mentally ill. This would be in accord with the legal approach that follows the norm "When in doubt, acquit" or "A person is innocent until proven guilty."

If labeling is indeed a major determinant of mental illness, certain changes are also suggested in treating violators of social norms. One is to attempt to maintain people with problems in their local community without labeling them *mentally ill* or sending them to a mental hospital, where their playing the role of the mentally ill is likely to be reinforced. In the past few decades, the field of mental hygiene has been moving in this direction. Another outgrowth of Scheff's theory would be increasing public education efforts to inform the general public of the nature of emotional and behavioral problems and the adverse effects that result from inappropriate labeling.

The adverse effects of labeling ultimately raise the issue of the value of labeling anyone mentally ill.

Source: This material is adapted from the following articles: (1) Charles Zastrow, "When Labeled Mentally Ill," in *The Personal Problem Solver,* edited by Charles Zastrow and Dae H. Chang, © 1977, pp. 163–169. Adapted by permission of Prentice-Hall, Inc., Englewood Cliffs, New Jersey; (2) Charles Zastrow, "Understanding Deviant Behavior," in *Talk to Yourself: Using the Power of Self-Talk,* © 1979, pp. 117–124. Reprinted by permission of the author.

Considerable evidence indicates that the "brain drugs" used to treat mental illnesses act on the brain in ways that harm its normal functioning (Glasser, 2003). Many people who take brain drugs develop mental and physical illnesses that cannot be distinguished from Parkinson's disease. Manufacturers of brain drugs spend millions on public relations campaigns to sell the brain drugs they produce.

CASE EXAMPLE Reality Therapy

A number of years ago when I [the author] was employed as a social worker at a maximum security hospital for the criminally insane, my supervisor asked me to develop and lead a therapy group. When I wondered aloud who should be in the group and what its objectives should be, my supervisor indicated those decisions would be mine. He added that no one else was doing group therapy at the hospital and that the hospital administration thought it would be desirable to develop such a program.

Being newly employed at the hospital and wary because I had never been a group leader before, I asked myself, "Who is in the greatest need of group therapy?" and "If the group members do not improve, or even deteriorate, how will I be able to explain this—that is, cover my tracks?" I concluded that I should select those identified as being most ill (those labeled *chronic schizophrenics*). Because such patients are generally expected to show little improvement, I felt I would not be blamed if group members did not improve. However, if they did improve, I thought it would be viewed as a substantial accomplishment.

First I read the case records of the 11 residents who were diagnosed as chronic schizophrenics. I then met individually with each of these residents to invite them to join the group. (To my surprise, each of the residents appeared to be very different from the impressions I received from reading the case records.) I explained the purpose of the group and the probable topics to be covered. Eight of the 11 who were contacted decided to join; some frankly stated they would join primarily because it would look good on their records and increase their chances for an early release.

The approach I used in counseling these group members was based on reality therapy. I began the first group meeting by stating I knew what the "key" was to their being discharged from the hospital and asked if they knew what that might be. This statement got their attention. I indicated that the key was very simple—they

(continued)

CASE EXAMPLE *(continued)*

had to learn to "act sane" so that the medical staff would think they had recovered. At the first meeting the purpose and the focus of the group were presented and described. Our purpose was not to review the past but to make life in the present more enjoyable and meaningful and to plan for the future. Various topics would be covered: how group members could convince the hospital staff they no longer needed hospitalization; how they could prepare for returning to their home community (for example, learning an employable skill while at the institution); and what to do when they felt depression or some other unwanted emotion or had an urge to do something that would get them into trouble again after their release. Also to be covered were discussions on how to improve relationships with people who were important to them. Occasionally films covering some of these topics would be shown and discussed. The group would meet for about 1 hour each week for 12 weeks.

This focus on improving the current circumstances of the group members stimulated their interest, but soon they found it uncomfortable and anxiety-producing to examine what the future might hold for them. They also became uncomfortable after being told they had considerable control over their future. They reacted to this discomfort by stating that they were "mentally ill" and therefore had some internal condition that was causing their strange behavior. Further, since no cure for their schizophrenia had yet been found, they believed they could do little to improve.

I told them that their excuses were "garbage" (stronger terms were used) and spent a few sessions convincing them that the term *chronic schizophrenic* was a meaningless label. I spent considerable time in explaining the myth of mental illness—that people do not have a "disease of the mind," though they may have emotional problems. I went on to explain that what had gotten them locked up was their deviant behavior. The only way for them to get out was to stop such behavior and convince the staff that they would not exhibit it if released.

The next excuse they tried was that broken homes or inferior schools or broken romances or other misfortune had "messed up" their lives for good, and they could do little about their situation. "Garbage," I told them. True, their past experiences were important. But, I emphasized, what they *wanted* out of their future and the motivation they had to achieve their goals were more important in determining the future.

Finally, after working through a number of excuses, we focused on how they could better handle specific problems: how to handle being depressed, how to stop exhibiting behavior considered "strange," how to present themselves as being "sane" to increase their chances of an early release, and how to adjust to returning to their home communities. We also focused on what kind of work or career they desired upon their release and how they could prepare themselves for their selected careers by learning a skill or trade while at the institution. Another focus was to help them examine what they wanted out of the future and the specific steps they would have to take to achieve their goals. Also discussed was how they could improve relationships that were important to them.

The results of this approach were encouraging. Instead of idly spending much of the time brooding about their situation, group members became motivated to take action. At the end of the 12 weeks, the eight members spontaneously stated that the meetings were making a positive change in their lives and requested that another social worker from the hospital be assigned to continue the group after I left to return to school. This was arranged. Three years later on a return visit to the hospital, I was informed that five of the eight group members had been released to their home communities and two of the others had shown improvement. One group member's condition was described as "unchanged."

EP 2.1.1 b

Exercise M3.8: The Use of Psychotropic Drugs

Goal: This exercise is designed to assist you in assessing the merits and shortcomings of psychotropic drugs.

Step 1: Psychiatrists and other physicians use psychotropic drugs to help patients achieve psychological or emotional changes. These drugs include *antidepressant medications* (such as Prozac, Elavil, Norpramin, Pertofrane, Sinequan, Aventl, and Vivactil), *antianxiety drugs* (such as Valium, Librium, Tranxene, Ativan, Serax, and various barbiturates), *antipsychotic medications* (such as Thorazine, Haldol, Compazine, Selazine, Navane, Mellaril, Serentil, Trilafon, and Prolixin), and *antimanic medications* (lithium carbonate—that is, Eskalith, Lithane, or Lithonate) (Barker, 2003, p. 349). Are you aware of any family members or friends who have used psychotropic drugs? Have you used them? If "yes," specify if you can the name of the drug or drugs.

Step 2: Specify your thoughts on the benefits and side effects of these drugs for the person taking them.

Step 3: Do you agree with Glasser that psychotropic drugs are overprescribed and overused? Explain your thoughts.

20. A mentally healthy person enjoys being with most of the people he or she knows—especially important people such as family and friends. A mentally healthy person likes people and is more than willing to help an unhappy friend, colleague, or family member to feel better. A mentally healthy person laughs a lot and leads a mostly tension-free life. He or she enjoys life and has no trouble accepting others who are different. He or she does not focus on criticizing others or trying to change others. He or she is creative. A mentally healthy person, when unhappy (no one can be happy all the time), knows why she or he is unhappy and will attempt to do something about it.

EP 2.1.1 b

Exercise M3.9: A Mentally Healthy Person

Goal: This exercise is designed to help you identify what you need to work on to improve your mental well-being.

Step 1: Review Glasser's definition of a mentally healthy person. Describe components of your current life that are consistent with mental well-being.

Step 2: Identify components of your life that you need to work on to improve your mental well-being.

Step 3: For the components that you need to work on, speculate about courses of action to take to improve your mental well-being.

PRINCIPLES OF REALITY THERAPY

1. It is what you choose to do in a relationship, not what others choose to do, that is the focus of reality therapy.
2. People choose the behaviors that have led them into counseling because it is a way perceived by them as being their best effort to deal with an unsatisfying relationship or with no relationship at all. For example, an alcoholic chooses to drink because she or he sees such behavior as the best way to cope with the challenges in living that she or he is facing.
3. The task of the counselor is to help unhappy clients choose new relationship-improving behaviors. These new behaviors will also help clients satisfy one or more of their five basic needs: survival, love and belonging, power, freedom, and fun.
4. Satisfying the need for love and belonging is the key to satisfying the other four needs because the five basic needs can be satisfied only when we have good relationships with other people.
5. Because love and belonging (like all the other basic needs) can be satisfied only in the present, reality therapy focuses almost entirely on the here-and-now.
6. Although most of us have been traumatized in the past, we are victims of our past only if we currently choose to be. The solution to our problems is rarely found in explorations of the past; one exception may be a focus on past successes.
7. The symptoms or the pain that clients choose (because of their unhappiness) is not important to the counseling process. The focus in counseling needs to be on improving present relationships. (It is usually a fruitless endeavor to seek to determine why one discontented person may choose to depress, another to drink, a third to obsess, and a fourth to be crazy).
8. A continuing goal of reality therapy is to create a choice-theory relationship between the counselor and the client. By experiencing a satisfying relationship, the client can learn a lot about a model relationship and how to improve the troubled relationship that brought him or her into counseling.
9. As long as clients continue to use the choice-theory concepts they've learned in counseling, the therapy never ends.
10. During marriage or couple counseling, Glasser (2000) urges the use of *structured reality therapy*. This approach emphasizes that marriage is a partnership and the only way to help a troubled couple is to focus on what's best for their marriage, rather than on what may be best for one or the other spouse. Any marital counseling that allows one partner to blame the other will harm the marriage. Couples are urged to never say or do anything in a relationship that experience indicates will drive the two further apart. They are urged to say and do only what will bring them closer or keep them close. Couples are also instructed to use the solving circle (described earlier) extensively.

EP 2.1.7a

Exercise M3.10: The Solving Circle

Goal: This exercise is designed to have you speculate about the merits and shortcomings of the solving circle.

Step 1: Specify difficulties you are currently having in a relationship that is significant to you.

Step 2: Review the material on solving circles. Do you believe that using a solving circle with the person you are currently having difficulties with would be useful? (If possible, try to become involved in an actual solving circle with this person.) Speculate about the merits and shortcomings of the solving circle.

11. Reality therapy is a "doing" approach: Clients are guided in the direction of actually doing something about their problems.
12. Glasser notes that all of us are *responsible* for the behaviors we engage in because we can't be anything but *responsible* for everything we choose to do.
13. The reality therapist looks for every opportunity to teach choice therapy to clients and their families so that everyone involved can begin the process of replacing external control psychology with choice theory.
14. A symptom is a cry for help. People use symptoms to avoid situations that they fear will increase their frustration.
15. Good or bad, happy or sad, people choose everything they do all day long.

EP 2.1.1 b

Exercise M3.11: Symptoms as a Cry for Help

Goal: This exercise is designed to assist you in recognizing that emotional difficulties, dysfunctional behaviors, somatic problems, and relationship problems are cries for help.

Describe how someone you know is demonstrating that his or her emotional difficulties, relationship problems, dysfunctional behaviors, or somatic problems are cries for help.

EVALUATION OF REALITY THERAPY

Reality therapy is a commonsense approach to counseling. The first version (Glasser, 1965) has been found to be quite effective in producing positive changes (Eysenck, 1965; Glasser & Wubbolding, 1995; Stuart, 1970). It has been successfully applied in a variety of settings, including corrections, mental health, education, unemployment, public welfare, and treating delinquency. Relatively little research has been conducted on the newer version (Glasser, 2000). It does have potential to become a leading approach to counseling.

Critics of choice theory and reality therapy point out that the theory fails to explain why some people become depressed but others become highly anxious, or explode in anger, or are shy, or experience guilt and shame. Also, reality therapy does not explain why some people commit robbery but others commit murder or white-collar crimes, or neglect their children, and so on.

SUMMARY

Choice theory is an internal control psychology. According to choice theory, all behavior is an attempt to reduce the difference between what we want and what we have. Glasser believes that we are driven by five innate needs: survival, love and belonging, power, freedom, and fun.

The only behavior we can control is our own. All behavior is "total behavior" and is made up of four inseparable components: acting, thinking, feeling, and physiology.

All long-lasting psychological problems are relationship problems, human brains are very creative, and almost all medical problems for which physicians are unable to identify the cause are partially created by the ill person's brain to deal with unhappiness. Unsatisfying relationships are the primary source of crimes, addictions, and emotional and behavioral disorders.

It is a serious mistake to seek to control others by nagging, preaching, punishing, or threatening to punish them. The solving circle is a good strategy for two people who know choice theory to use in redefining their freedom and improving their relationship. It is not necessary to know our past before we can deal with the present. It is therapeutic to view our "total behavior" in terms of verbs.

All total behavior (thinking, feeling, acting, and physiology) is chosen, but we have direct control over only the acting and thinking components. People choose (although some are unaware of their choice) to play mentally ill roles. Mental illness is a myth. Considerable evidence indicates that all brain drugs used to treat nonexistent mental illnesses act on the brain in ways that harm its normal functioning.

Reality therapy focuses on improving unhappy relationships and on the here-and-now. Reality therapy focuses on having clients understand and apply the concepts of choice theory. During marriage or couple counseling, the solving circle is often used. Reality therapy is a "doing" approach. Clients are guided in the direction of doing something about their problems. A symptom is a cry for help.

EXERCISE

EP 2.1.7a

The Mental Illness Debate

Goal: To identify the arguments about whether mental illness exists.

Step 1. At a class session some students form two panels. One will argue that mental illness exists; the other, that mental illness is a myth. Panel members are given a few days to gather information and prepare their arguments. Panel members may interview counselors and therepists in the community and read reference materials.

Step 2. At the selected class date, a debate is held. At the end of the debate, students who did not participate on either panel summarize the strong points made by the debaters.

COMPETENCY NOTES

The following identifies where Educational Policy (EP) competencies and practice behaviors are discussed in the chapter.

EP 2.1.10a *Substantively and affectively prepare for action with individuals, families, groups, organizations, and communities.*

EP 2.1.10j *Help clients resolve problems.* (pp. 531–550).

This module presents content on choice theory's approach (and reality therapy's approach) to assessing and intervening with individuals, family members, and group members.

EP 2.1.1b *Practice personal reflection and self-correction to assure continual professional development.* (pp. 533–534).

Exercise M3.1 is designed to illustrate that we are inclined to attempt to change others and that others sometimes attempt to control us. The consequences of attempting to control others are also examined.

EP 2.1.1b *Practice personal reflection and self-correction to assure continual professional development.* (pp. 535–536).

Exercise 3.2 is designed to assist students in understanding that our thoughts are sometimes a cause of somatic problems, emotional difficulties, and behavioral dysfunctions.

EP 2.1.1b *Practice personal reflection and self-correction to assure continual professional development.* (pp. 536–537).

Exercise M3.3 is designed to increase students' awareness of the effects of nagging, preaching, put-downs, or threats of punishment.

EP 2.1.1b *Practice personal reflection and self-correction to assure continual professional development.* (pp. 537–538).

Exercise M3.4 is designed to assist students in improving, through problem solving, a significant relationship in their lives.

EP 2.1.1b *Practice personal reflection and self-correction to assure continual professional development.* (p. 538).

Exercise M3.5 is designed to assist students in letting go of strong feelings of being wronged by others.

EP 2.1.7a *Utilize conceptual frameworks to guide the process of assessment, intervention, and evaluation.* (p. 539).

Exercise M3.6 is designed to demonstrate that expressing our negative emotions by means of verbs assists us in recognizing that we are *choosing* to feel a certain way and could *choose* to feel positive emotions instead.

EP 2.1.1b *Practice personal reflection and self-correction to assure continual professional development.* (pp. 539–540).

Exercise M3.7 is designed to demonstrate that negative emotions can be changed and some somatic problems can be improved by changing our thoughts and actions.

EP 2.1.1b *Practice personal reflection and self-correction to assure continual professional development.* (pp. 544–545).

Exercise M3.8 is designed to assist students in assessing the merits and shortcomings of psychotropic drugs.

EP 2.1.1b *Practice personal reflection and self-correction to assure continual professional development.* (pp. 545–546).

Exercise M3.9 is designed to help students identify what they need to work on to improve their mental well-being.

EP 2.1.7a *Utilize conceptual frameworks to guide the process of assessment, intervention, and evaluation.* (p. 547).

Exercise M3.10 is designed to have students speculate about the merits and shortcomings of the solving circle.

EP 2.1.1b *Practice personal reflection and self-correction to assure continual professional development.* (p. 547).

Exercise M3.11 is designed to assist students in recognizing that emotional difficulties, relationship problems, dysfunctional behaviors, and somatic problems are cries for help.

EP 2.1.7a *Utilize conceptual frameworks to guide the process of assessment, intervention, and evaluation.* (p. 548).

This exercise is designed to identify the arguments, pro and con, about whether mental illness exists.

MODULE 4

Prominent Specific Intervention Techniques

EP 2.1.10a, j

Modules 1, 2, and 3 presented intervention techniques that are components of comprehensive theories of psychotherapy. Module 4 summarizes some intervention techniques that were developed independently of any comprehensive theory of psychotherapy. We'll call them *specific intervention approaches*. This module will:

A. Describe milieu therapy, psychodrama, and play therapy
B. Describe parental education, crisis intervention, and task-centered practice
C. Describe solution-focused therapy, mediation, and narrative therapy

MILIEU THERAPY

In milieu therapy, a learning or living environment is created in which the events that occur in day-to-day living are systematically regarded as opportunities for treating emotional and behavior problems. The idea is that our environment has an immense impact on behavior and can be structured to change deviant behavior and antisocial norms and values.

Milieu programs have been based on a wide variety of intervention approaches, including reality therapy, behavior therapy, and rational therapy. Some milieu programs emphasize individual therapy as part of the milieu; others emphasize changing behavioral and emotional problems in a group setting. A token economy (described in Module 2) is a milieu treatment program. Milieu programs typically use a team of professional staff members that may include social workers, psychiatrists, psychologists, special education teachers, occupational and physical therapists, and psychiatric nurses.

Although the components of milieu programs vary widely, there are some common focuses. Programs stress being democratic, permissive, and humanistic, and having reality-oriented living experiences. Milieu programs assume that lasting changes are more likely to take place through group interactional experiences. The community (including the professional staff, nonprofessional staff, and residents) meets and interacts regularly, often discussing common problems. An underlying philosophy is that personal problems primarily involve faulty interactions with others and that examining these difficulties through discussion can lead to understanding and resolution. Usually the traditional pyramid of authority is flattened in milieu programs; staff roles and ways of functioning are frequently reevaluated (Black, 1977).

Milieu programs have been used with juvenile delinquents, persons with mental illness, children and adults with cognitive disabilities, the elderly, alcoholics and drug abusers, emotionally disturbed children, and correctional clients. These programs have been used in mental hospitals, day hospitals for the emotionally disturbed, halfway houses, residential treatment centers, day-care programs for disturbed children, nursing homes, group homes, correctional institutions, therapeutic communities for alcohol and drug abusers, and sheltered workshops.

The therapeutic community is one of the intervention programs that is often selected in treating drug addiction in this country. The theory is that drug addiction is a form of behavior that is encouraged by a particular subculture and that therapeutic communities can provide group support to help people give up the drug subculture and also pressure them to replace previous norms and values with those acceptable to the general society.

PSYCHODRAMA

The primary developer of psychodrama was J. L. Moreno (1946). Its objective is to assist a client or client group to overcome personal problems through role-playing, drama, or action therapy. Through these media, clients are helped to express feelings of conflict, anger, aggression, guilt, and sadness. Moreno thought that the expression of pent-up emotions has a cathartic effect (eliminates emotional complexes by bringing them to consciousness and allowing the emotional energy to be expressed). Role-playing is a direct outgrowth of psychodrama (Blatner, 1995).

Moreno also thought psychodrama is therapeutic because people who want to change maladaptive behavior receive feedback about their behavior and are encouraged to try out and practice new behaviors. Psychodramas can be arranged to have other people model alternative behaviors and then to have clients practice new behaviors in a particular sequence to ensure success. Thus, clients can practice new behaviors in small bits until they incorporate them into their repertoire and gain mastery through practice.

Psychodrama is a group counseling approach. Whittaker (1974) provided a brief description of psychodrama:

> Psychodrama uses four major instruments: the stage, which is both the psychological and physical living space for the subject or client; the director, or worker; the staff of "auxiliary egos," or therapeutic aides; and the audience. Both the auxiliary egos and the audience are made up of other group members. The strategy is to enable the subject to project himself into his own world and draw responses from fellow group members. Below are several commonly used techniques:
>
> 1. Self-presentation. The client presents himself or a figure who is significant in his life.
> 2. Direct soliloquy. The client steps out of the drama and speaks to herself or to the group.
> 3. Double technique. An auxiliary ego acts with the client and does everything the client does and at the same time.
> 4. Mirror technique. An auxiliary ego acts in place of the client as clearly as he can. The client watches from the audience to see himself as others see him.
> 5. Role reversal. The client assumes the role of her antagonist and an auxiliary ego plays the client's part. (p. 230)

The director, or worker, functions as the producer and as the counselor. As the producer, the social worker selects and arranges the scenes and also directs the psychodrama action. The scenes are selected to reflect the client's problem—which is likely to be an emotionally charged situation for the client or one in which he or she behaves ineffectively or inappropriately. As the counselor, the worker provides the actors with support and clarification; at times the worker makes interpretations of the play action, often with the help of the other group members.

Psychodrama is used by practitioners who subscribe to various psychotherapeutic theories. Psychodrama is used in marital counseling, with children, with drug and alcohol abusers, with people having emotional problems, in prison settings, to train psychiatric residents, to train people with physical and mental impairments, in business and industry, and in education and decision making. Fine (1979) noted,

> We have all had experience with psychodrama. As children, one way we tested and mastered the world was to play roles. Lori put a coronet in her hair and became a queen and her girlfriend became her lady-in-waiting. Gary built satellites and took elaborate interstellar space explorations in his room. Children's play is an enactment of their fantasies in which they practice the social roles of their culture. The action and enacting world of the child is full of energy, excitement, and social learning. . . .
>
> Modern psychodrama is an extension of life in which catharsis and insight are available not only to the audience but to the players as well. (p. 487)

EP 2.1.1b

Barocas (1972) used psychodrama to train police officers to handle family crises more effectively. Domestic fights are a serious hazard for police officers; the "family disturbance call" is now the single most frequent source of officer injury and death. Barocas hired trained actors and actresses to perform skits developed from actual family fights reported by police officers. Actors developed the basic fight, and the police officer trainees practiced interventions. The skits were videotaped, and other police officer trainees observed the intervention approach, which was then discussed in a group. The trainees who role-played were also shown the videotape, and their performance was then critiqued further. Barocas concluded that this approach was effective in improving how police officers handled family disputes.

Exercise M4.1: Psychodrama in My Childhood

Goal: This exercise is designed to assist you in understanding that you, through role-playing in childhood, participated in psychodrama.

Step 1: As children, we role-played being our heroes and heroines. Perhaps we were batting a baseball and thought we would hit it as Barry Bonds did. Perhaps we were in a situation and acted like a famous actor or actress. Perhaps we were ice skating and pretended we were going for the gold at the Olympics. Specify a time in your childhood in which you role-played being someone famous. Also specify what you did in this role-play.

Step 2: Specify the beneficial effects of this role-play for you.

PLAY THERAPY

Play therapy is used with young children. Play is seen as a young child's most natural vehicle for self-expression and is therefore viewed by play therapists as a means for relating to, and communicating with, young children. Play therapy serves many purposes: making a diagnosis, forming a relationship, ventilating feelings, working through unwanted emotions, teaching desired new behaviors, modeling alternative behavior. Play therapists' approaches range from almost totally nondirective to highly directive. Play therapy is used by counselors with widely diverging orientations, including reality therapy, rational therapy, and behavior therapy.

CASE EXAMPLE Play Therapy

Dawn, age 7, was a second grader who was referred by her teacher to a school social worker. Academically and socially she was functioning far behind her peers, even though tests showed she was of normal intelligence. The social worker observed her in her play interactions with peers. She was withdrawn and tried to avoid competitive game situations. Forced to participate, she would quit whenever she fell behind. When the social worker discussed Dawn's behavior with her teacher, the teacher indicated that Dawn shied away from doing her assignments and seldom completed any. Dawn was observed for a few sessions in a playroom at school. At one point, Dawn held the mother doll and called the baby girl "stupid" and stated, "You'll never be able to do what your brother does." The social worker felt that Dawn's academic and social problems were resulting from Dawn's having such a low self-concept that she had virtually given up trying. Dawn's interactions with the dolls suggested her mother might be contributing to her low self-concept by disparaging her. Several meetings were then held with Dawn's parents, with Dawn present for two of these. The social worker observed that the mother was highly critical of Dawn without ever praising her. Dawn was placed in a special educational program for the next 18 months; here she received close attention and considerable praise for her academic and social efforts. The worker also counseled the parents on how they were contributing to her low self-concept and how they needed to praise Dawn for her efforts and to get her more involved in interests she had. On three separate occasions Dawn, her parents, Dawn's brother, and the social worker met in a playroom. The family members were encouraged to play together in various games, and the parents were instructed to praise Dawn whenever she made efforts to participate positively. Also, Dawn's mother was encouraged to refrain from disparaging Dawn. After this intensive program, Dawn was able to rejoin her class at the start of the fourth grade and had become much more outgoing and self-confident.

Source: In the classic *Play Therapy*, Axline (1947) provided a number of other case examples in which play therapy has been used for diagnostic purposes, for helping children to understand themselves and their problems better and to resolve their problems.

Whittaker (1974) described play therapy as follows:

> The therapist may use initial play sessions for diagnostic purposes to observe such things as relationship, attention span, areas of preoccupation, areas of inhibition, direction of aggression, wishes and fantasies, and self-perception. Depending upon orientation, the therapist typically encourages free play with a variety of available materials (paints, dolls, punching bags, puzzles, clay), interprets the child's affect to him ("You seem to be angry at the doll"), and finally offers insights into the child's behavior. The child may experience some regression to earlier levels of functioning while in the play situation and also may practice newly acquired skills and try on new behaviors. A central notion of play therapy is that the child is expressing symbolically through play the conflicts he is experiencing in the outside world. In the relative safety of the play situation, these conflicts can be worked through and—so the theory goes—transferred to the child's real-life situation. (pp. 225–226)

Play therapy generally takes place in a playroom, with only the child and the therapist present. At times other children are present, which helps the child learn to interact more effectively with others. Occasionally parents attend the play therapy sessions, which helps them better understand their child and learn more effective interaction approaches with their child. Play materials include dolls (usually a doll family), puppets, clay and finger paints, crayons, a sandbox, toy animals, soldiers and weapons, and cutting-out materials. In play therapy, children are generally allowed to express themselves as freely as they desire. Usually minimal limits are set: establishing the duration of the play sessions, forbidding the willful destruction of play materials, and forbidding the child from physically attacking others in the playroom. (See Case Example "Play Therapy.")

Some protective services programs use anatomically correct dolls to gather information from young children who are suspected victims of sexual abuse. A worker first forms a relationship with a child and then asks the child to show, with the dolls, what the alleged perpetrator did. In some jurisdictions, this process is videotaped and is available for court use if formal charges are brought against the alleged perpetrator.

EP 2.1.1b

Exercise M4.2: The Beneficial Effects of Playing for Me

Goal: This exercise is designed to assist you in understanding the beneficial effects of "play" for you in childhood and in adulthood.

Step 1: Specify your favorite play activities in your childhood.

Step 2: Summarize what you learned from play activities in your childhood.

Step 3: Specify your current "play" and "fun" activities.

Step 4: Specify the benefits of your current "play" and "fun" activities.

PARENTAL EDUCATION: PARENT EFFECTIVENESS TRAINING

The main goal of parental education programs is to help parents understand child behavior and develop child-rearing skills. Most programs rest on the assumption that rearing children is a difficult and complex task for which society ill prepares young people. Numerous theoreticians have developed somewhat different educational programs: Dreikurs (1964), Ginott (1965), Gordon (1970), Patterson (1971), and Spock (1957). These programs use a variety of educational formats: short courses, small discussion groups, and programmed self-instruction.

Probably the most popular program is Parent Effectiveness Training (PET), developed by Thomas Gordon (1970). PET courses are offered in hundreds of communities and have been endorsed by numerous public and private agencies serving parents and youth. The PET system has been found to work effectively with children of all ages. It fosters warmer and more harmonious relationships between parents and their children, and children learn to become more responsible. The basic concepts of this approach are presented here, partly because some of the techniques, such as active listening, I-messages, and no-lose problem solving, can be used by not only parents and parent surrogates (such as teachers, principals, counselors, and youth leaders) but also anyone who wants to interact more effectively with others.

Parents Are People, Not Gods

Gordon urges parents to be "real" in their relationships with children. "Realness" is much more important and more easily achievable than always being consistent in displaying feelings, putting up a "united front," and being unconditionally tolerant and accepting. In a close relationship, it is impossible to hide our true feelings, so it is normal and real for parents to be accepting of some behaviors of their children and nonaccepting of other behaviors. Parents should recognize their true feelings and not attempt to convey false acceptance when they dislike what their children are doing. It is normal and real for one parent to be more accepting than the other, and one parent may feel accepting and the other nonaccepting of the same behavior. Being honest and human in interacting with children will improve a relationship substantially more than will conveying false acceptance or trying to always be consistent.

Who Owns the Problem?

PET asserts that appropriate parental responses depend on the answer to the question "Who owns the problem?" We own a problem only when the situation affects our ability to get our needs met in a concrete and tangible way. If the *child* owns a problem, then *active listening* is an appropriate technique for a parent to use. If the *parent* owns the problem, then *I-messages* are appropriate for the parent to use. If the situation involves a conflict between the parent and the child in meeting the needs of both, then *no-lose problem solving* is an appropriate technique. If the situation involves a conflict in values between the parent and the child, Gordon provides guidelines for *resolving collisions of values*.

PET Techniques

Active Listening When a 16-year-old boy announces "I hate school, and I'm going to drop out," his parents can respond in a variety of ways: ordering him to stay in school, warning him that he'll be sorry if he drops out, moralizing by saying dropping out would not be proper or right, giving advice by saying he should discuss his intention with the high school counselor, and so forth. Such approaches are generally not effective or productive in helping children express their feelings, explore their problems, and arrive at a comfortable solution.

Active listening is a much more effective way of interacting: (1) The receiver of a message tries to understand what the sender's message means or what the sender is feeling. (2) The receiver then expresses this understanding in her or his own words and returns this understanding for the sender's verification. The receiver does *not* send any message of her or his own—such as a question, advice, feelings, or an opinion. The aim is to feed back only what the receiver feels the sender's message means. Active listening is a difficult skill to learn and takes practice to master.

In the following exchange, the parent consistently uses the active listening technique:

Youth: I hate school, and I'm going to drop out.
Parent: You're fed up with school and thinking about leaving.
Youth: Yes I am! My teachers are real bummers this year.
Parent: You're disappointed with your current teachers.
Youth: Especially my Spanish teacher. He asks us questions in Spanish and expects us to understand what he's saying. All I hear is words that I can't understand.
Parent: You're having trouble understanding your Spanish teacher when he speaks in Spanish.
Youth: I've been getting A's and B's on tests, but the other students appear to understand Spanish better when it is spoken.
Parent: Your grades show that you are doing well in Spanish, but you have trouble understanding Spanish when it is spoken.

Youth: Yeah, I wonder what I could do to learn to understand people better when they speak Spanish.
Parent: You're wondering how you can better learn to hear and speak in Spanish.
Youth: Maybe I could talk to my teacher. He'd know. He might have some ideas.

Gordon listed some advantages of using the active listening technique. It facilitates problem solving by the child, which fosters the development of responsibility. By talking a problem through, a person is more likely to identify the root of the problem and arrive at a solution than by merely thinking about a problem. A child who feels that his or her parents are listening is more likely to listen to their point of view. In addition, the relationship between parent and child is likely to improve because a child who feels he or she is being heard and understood by another person is likely to feel warmth toward the listener. Finally, the approach helps the child explore, recognize, and express personal feelings.

Gordon noted that parents need to have certain attitudes to use the technique effectively. Parents must view the child as a separate person with his or her own feelings. Parents must be able to accept the child's feelings, whatever they may be. Parents should genuinely want to be helpful and must want to hear what the child has to say. And parents must trust the child's capacities to handle personal problems and feelings.

Parents initially make three common mistakes as they use the technique: (1) They guide the child's behavior or thinking toward what the parents think the child should do. If parents have this intention, children are likely to feel they are being manipulated, and the approach may be counterproductive. (2) Parents parrot back the words rather than the intended meaning or feeling. For instance, if a daughter yells at her father "You stupid jerk," an appropriate response geared to the message would be "You're angry with me," rather than parroting the words "You think I'm a jerk." (3) Parents use active listening at the wrong time. If a child does not want to talk about her or his feelings or is simply too tired, the parent should respect the child's right to and need for privacy.

I-Messages Active listening is used when the child has the problem. However, many occasions arise when the child causes a problem for the parent. For example, a child talks loudly in church, or gets too close to a precious glass vase, or is about to walk on a new carpet with muddy shoes, or is driving recklessly. In such cases, entirely different communication skills are required. Confronted with such situations, many parents send either a *solution message* (they order, direct, command, warn, threaten, preach, moralize, or advise) or a *put-down message* (they blame, judge, criticize, ridicule, or name-call). Solution and put-down messages can have devastating effects on a child's self-concept and are generally counterproductive in helping a child become responsible.

Solution and put-down messages are primarily you-messages: "You do what I say," "Don't you do that," "Why don't you be good," "You're lazy," "You should know better." PET advocates that parents instead send *I-messages* on those occasions when a child is causing a problem for them. Suppose a child is walking on a clean carpet with dirty shoes. Instead of saying, "John, get off that carpet, you're a pig!," PET urges parents to use an I-message: "I shampooed the living room rug today and want to keep it clean as long as possible."

I-messages are nonblaming messages that communicate only how the sender of the message believes the receiver is adversely affecting the sender. I-messages do not provide a solution, and they are not put-down messages. It is possible to send an I-message without using the word *I*, for the essence of I-messages is a nonblaming statement of how the parent feels the child's behavior is affecting the parent. For example, a parent riding in a car driven by a 17-year-old son who is exceeding the speed limit may say, "Driving fast really terrifies me."

You-messages are generally put-down messages that convey to children either that they should do something or that they are bad. In contrast, I-messages communicate to children much more honestly the effect of the behavior on the parent. I-messages are also more effective because they help children learn to assume responsibility for their own behavior. An I-message tells children that the parent trusts them to respect the parent's needs, that the parent is leaving the responsibility with them, and that the parent is trusting them to handle the situation constructively.

You-messages frequently end up in a struggle between parent and child, whereas I-messages are much less likely to produce an argument. I-messages lead to honesty and openness in a relationship and generally foster intimacy. Children, as well as adults, often do not know how their behavior affects others. I-messages produce startling results. Parents frequently report that their children express surprise on learning how their parents really feel.

The following are examples of you-messages and I-messages:

YOU-MESSAGES	*I-MESSAGES*
1. Don't you ever kick me again; you're real pain.	Ouch! That kick really hurt me.
2. John, you stop pestering me now!	John, I am very tired today, and I just do not have the energy to play with you this evening.
3. You're a reckless driver, and someday you'll kill someone.	I'm afraid to ride with you when you drive so fast.

EP 2.1.1a

I-messages work only if the child does not want his or her actions to adversely affect his parent. A child who does not want to cause discomfort in his or her parent will seek to change the adversive behavior when an I-message is used. However, if a child enjoys causing discomfort in his or her parent, then I-messages may result in an *increase* in the adversive behavior, because the child is now more fully aware of how to cause parental discomfort.

Exercise M4.3: I-Messages and You-Messages

Goal: This exercise is designed to assist you in understanding I-messages and you-messages and to understand the consequences of each type of message.

Step 1: Reflect on your childhood. Did your parents primarily use I-messages or you-messages? Describe the kind of messages your parents sent to you.

Step 2: Summarize the affects of these messages on you.

Step 3: Reflect on your current life. Identify someone significant to you (perhaps a boss or someone you are dating or married to) who is currently interacting with you by using either I-messages or you-messages. Specify what this person tends to say to you with either I-messages or you-messages.

Step 4: Summarize the affect of these I-messages or you-messages on you.

No-Lose Problem Solving In every parent-child relationship, situations inevitably arise in which the child continues to behave in a way that interferes with the needs of the parent. Conflict is part of life and is not necessarily bad. Conflict occurs because people are different and have different needs and wants, which at times do not match. What is important is not how frequently conflicts arise but how they get resolved. Generally conflicts create a power struggle. In many families the power struggle is resolved by one of two win-lose approaches.

Most parents try to resolve the conflict by having the parent win and the child lose. Parents generally have the greater authority. When the parent wins, the child resents the parent, the child is less motivated to carry out the solution, and the child has no opportunity to develop self-discipline and self-responsibility. Such children may rebel or become dependent and withdrawn.

Alternatively, the win-lose conflict is resolved when parents give in to their children out of fear of frustrating their children or fear of conflict. These children come to believe their needs are more important than anyone else's, and they generally become self-centered, selfish, demanding, impulsive, and uncontrollable. They are viewed by others as being spoiled, they have difficulty interacting with peers, and they do not respect the property or feelings of others.

Of course, few parents use either approach exclusively. Oscillating between the two approaches is common. Evidence indicates that both approaches lead to the development of emotional problems in children (Gordon, 1970, p. 161). The two win-lose approaches are illustrated in the following situation:

Parent Wins—Child Loses

Mother: Since I'm now working, we need to divide the work tasks around the house. I'll continue to do most of the work, but from now on I'd like you to wash the dishes in the evening.

John: But I don't like washing dishes.

Mother: Well, I don't like cooking and washing and ironing clothes, but I have to do them. We all have to do things we don't like to do.

John: Washing dishes is for girls.

Mother: Look, I'm not going to argue with you about this. You're now old enough to help out. In this family we all have to contribute. If you don't do the dishes, you won't receive your allowance. In fact, from now on, every evening you do not wash dishes, 50 cents will be deducted from your weekly allowance.

Child Wins—Parent Loses

Mother: Since I'm now working, we need to divide the work tasks around the house. I'll continue to do most of the work, but from now on I'd like you to wash the dishes in the evening.

John: But I don't like washing dishes.

Mother: Why?

John: Washing dishes is for girls.

Mother: But many boys help their mothers with the dishes.

John: Tom and Gary don't help their mothers. What would they say about me washing dishes?

Mother: You may be right. Could you instead help me with washing clothes, or dusting, or cleaning your room?

John: Aw—Mom, those things are for girls, too.

Mother: (*Dejectedly*) Well, okay. I'll try to do these things while also working.

EP 2.1.1b

Exercise M4.4: My Win-Lose Struggles with My Parents

Goal: This exercise is designed to assist you in understanding the adverse consequences of win-lose struggles.

Step 1: Reflect on your childhood. Specify whether you were frequently, occasionally, or seldom involved in win-lose situations with your parents.

Step 2: Describe some of the win-lose situations that you had with your parents.

Step 3: Specify who tended to win and who tended to lose.

Step 4: Specify the affects of these win-lose situations on you and on your parents.

Step 5: Are you currently in a win-lose situation with someone important to you? If "yes," describe the situation and describe your current feelings about this situation.

Gordon seriously questioned whether power is necessary or justified in a parent-child relationship. As children grow older, they become less dependent, and parents gradually lose their power. Rewards and punishments that worked in younger years are less effective. Children resent those with power over them, and parents frequently feel guilty after using power. Gordon believed that parents continue to use power because they have little experience in using nonpower methods of influence.

Gordon describes a new approach, the *no-lose approach*, to resolve conflicts. In this approach, parent and child resolve their conflicts by finding their own unique solutions acceptable to both. Gordon (1970, p. 237) listed six steps of no-lose problem solving:

1. Identify and define the needs of each person.
2. Generate possible alternative solutions.

3. Evaluate the alternative solutions.
4. Decide on the best acceptable solution.
5. Work out ways of implementing the solution.
6. Follow up to evaluate how it worked.

The following example illustrates this approach:

Mother: Since I'm now working, I will have less time to do the work that needs to be done around the house. I would appreciate it if you would help me out with some of the things that need to be done.

John: I suppose I could help—what needs to be done?

Mother: The meals need to be cooked, dishes washed, the house cleaned, grocery shopping done, and the garbage taken out.

John: Let's see. I'd be willing to vacuum the floor and dust. Will my allowance be increased? I'd like to get a new bike.

Mother: Yes, since we'll have some more money now that I'm working, we could increase your allowance, with the increase dependent on how much additional work you do.

John: In addition to helping to clean the house, I'd be willing to wash the clothes if you show me what to do. I also could carry out the garbage.

EP 2.1.1b

The no-lose approach is simple to state: Each person in the conflict treats the other with respect, neither person tries to win by using power, and a creative solution acceptable to both parties is sought. There are two basic premises to no-lose problem solving: (1) All people have the right to have their needs met. (2) What is in conflict is not needs but solutions to those needs. This approach offers several advantages. It motivates children to carry out the solution because they participated in the decision. It develops children's thinking skills and responsibility. It requires less enforcement, eliminates the need for power, and improves relationships with parents.

Exercise M4.5: No-Lose Problem Solving

Goal: This exercise is designed to assist you in understanding and applying the no-lose approach to problem solving.

Step 1: Describe a situation in the past in which you had an interpersonal conflict with someone and you used no-lose problem solving, or describe a current situation in which you have an interpersonal conflict with someone and you now seek to apply no-lose problem solving.

Step 2: Specify the following for this situation:

a. Identify and define the needs of each person.

b. Generate possible alternative solutions.

c. Evaluate the alternative solutions.

d. Decide on the best acceptable solution.

e. Work out ways of implementing the solution.

f. Follow up to evaluate how the solution worked.

Step 3: Summarize the merits and shortcomings of no-lose problem-solving.

Resolving Collisions of Values Collisions of values are common between parents and children, particularly as the children become adolescents and young adults. Likely areas of conflict include sexual behavior, clothing and hairstyles, religion, choice of friends, education, plans for the future, use of drugs, and eating habits. On these topics, emotions run strong, and parents generally seek to influence their offspring to follow the values the parents consider important. Teenagers, however, often think their parents' values are old-fashioned and stupid and declare that they want to make their own decisions about these matters.

Gordon described three constructive ways in which parents and teenagers can seek to resolve such conflicts. (For the sake of simplicity, I use the term *mother* here, although a father or a teenager also can use these techniques.)

1. The mother models the values she holds important. If she values honesty, she should be honest. If she values responsible use of drugs, she should not get drunk or drink and drive, for example. If she values openness, she should be open. She asks herself if she is living according to the values she professes. If her values and behaviors are incongruent in certain areas, she needs to change either her values or her behavior in the direction of congruency. Congruence between behavior and values is important if she wants to be an effective model.
2. The mother acts as a consultant to her teen. A good consultant finds out whether the teen would like to consult with her. If the answer is "yes," she makes sure she

has all the available pertinent facts. She then shares these facts—once—so the teen understands them. She leaves the teen the responsibility of deciding whether to follow the advice. A good consultant is well informed and does not nag; otherwise, she may not be used as a consultant again.

3. The mother reduces tensions by modifying her own values. After she examines her teen's values, she may realize they have merit, and she can then move toward those values or at least toward understanding why the teen holds them.

In summary, PET is intended to improve relationships between parents and children and to develop responsibility in children. Many parents who participate in PET courses or read Gordon's *Parent Effectiveness Training* find them to be effective. In recent years, PET concepts have been found useful not only for improving relationships between parents and children but also for improving interactions and communication between people in all manner of transactions.

PET techniques work if influencees respect influencers and want a positive relationship with them. If the influencee neither respects nor wants a positive relationship with the influencer, these techniques don't work.

CRISIS INTERVENTION

Ell (1995) notes that crisis intervention is appropriate in an infinite number of situations, including serious illness or trauma, death of a loved one, disasters, violent crimes, moving away from home, and unplanned pregnancy. Crisis intervention (CI) is grounded in the belief that in a crisis situation current levels of functioning are disrupted and previously manageable internal psychological difficulties are stirred up. CI views the emotional disturbances presented by people facing crisis as the result of (1) the stressful situation they face and (2) underlying emotional dispositions that come to the surface only in crisis situations. CI postulates that underlying emotional difficulties are ingredients of all personalities. People are viewed as being fairly normal in their general adjustment, with the crisis being a major cause of a person's emotional difficulties. See Exhibit M4.1.

CI services often have two tasks. One is to resolve the current crisis. The other is to resolve problems the person has been denying or ignoring. For example, if a woman is fired from a job because of drinking problems, services might focus not only on helping her find another job but also on breaking down her denial of her drinking problem. Golan (1979, p. 500) noted that at the point of crisis "a minimal effort . . . can produce a maximal effect; a small amount of help, appropriately focused, can prove more effective than extensive help at a period of less emotional accessibility." (See Case Example "Crisis Intervention.")

Crisis intervention services are generally brief and provided when the client is in desperate need emotionally. The specific treatment techniques are borrowed from other approaches. Here are a few examples: Role-playing helps a pregnant single woman gather her nerve to inform her parents and her sexual partner. Confrontation helps a person arrested three times for drunken driving acknowledge that he has a drinking problem. A person whose engagement has been broken learns to counter unwanted emotions with a rational self-analysis. A young woman who has been raped is given immediate medical attention and counseling on both legal implications and on her thoughts and feelings about the assault. A counselor uses the active listening technique in counseling someone who is suicidal.

Whittaker (1974) provided a summary of crisis counseling services:

> Requisite worker skills include the ability to function effectively and efficiently in an emotionally tense atmosphere and to give support and direction while at the same time helping the client to develop autonomous coping skills.

Exhibit M4.1 The Effects of a Crisis

A. Prior to a crisis a person is functioning in a groove, that is, a relatively routine, stable kind of living with only minor changes.

B. A crisis arises (for example, being fired from a job) that places a person in an unfreezing position. This unfreezing position is emotionally charged, and the person's lifestyle is highly vulnerable to change. In such a crisis, a person may either take the constructive (C) path or the destructive (D) path.

C. This constructive path has the person (perhaps with the assistance of others) gaining an awareness of why the crisis arose. The person develops adaptive ways of handling the crisis, and thereby grows through acquiring problem-solving skills that will better enable him or her to solve future crisis situations.

D. If the destructive path is followed, the person does not satisfactorily resolve the crisis. Unsolved aspects of the crisis remain, and the person is apt to develop maladaptive coping patterns. The person remains in an emotionally charged situation, and is less able to face future crises that arise. Problems may well begin to snowball (for example, when a single, pregnant woman denies the pregnancy and makes no effort to begin making decisions that she will have to face).

CASE EXAMPLE Crisis Intervention

John Franzene (age 28) went to work intoxicated one day and was promptly fired. John became incensed and yelled obscenities at his supervisor. He then went to a local tavern and drank until he passed out. A friend took him home. When his wife found out that John had been fired from his job as a janitor, she packed her bags that evening and took the two children to live with her mother. She indicated that this was the "last straw."

John is an alcoholic and drinks an average of eight bottles of beer and a pint of whiskey every day. He has been drinking excessively for the past decade. Three years ago, his wife separated from him because he was abusive to her and the children, both physically and verbally, when intoxicated. At that time John promised to stop drinking if his wife would only return; she did, and 3 weeks later he again began drinking. Five years ago he lost his position as an elementary school teacher because of his drinking and his frequent absenteeism. Two years ago, he lost his driver's license for driving while intoxicated. In the past 5 years, he has lost three other jobs.

The next day John went to his mother-in-law's home to try to talk his wife into returning. She refused to speak to him. John, feeling sorry for himself, went to a local tavern and again got drunk. He blamed his supervisor for his current difficulties. While intoxicated he decided to "straighten this matter out." He went to the office where he had been fired and got into a fight with his supervisor. He was arrested. While in jail, he got the "DTs" (delirium tremens), which really scared him. He was transferred to a hospital. The doctor at the hospital explored his interest in receiving help for his drinking problem. John indicated he was willing to talk about it to someone, and he was referred to Tom Halaska, the hospital social worker.

For the first time in his life, John acknowledged that he had a drinking problem and needed help. Mr. Halaska met with John on several occasions during the next 4 days. The ways that alcohol was affecting his life (including his job and his family life) were traced, and John gained an awareness that he got into trouble only when he was drinking. Mr. Halaska explored the reasons John drank, and it became clear that he drank excessively either when he was with male friends in a tavern or when he sought to relieve unwanted emotions of feeling tense, moody, or depressed. John appeared at this time to be sincerely committed to giving up drinking. Mr. Halaska suggested that one thing he would have to do to give up drinking was to stop meeting his friends at a tavern. John indicated that saving his marriage meant more to him than hanging out with his friends. Mr. Halaska arranged a meeting between John and his wife. His wife agreed to return if John would first go 1 month without drinking, promise never to drink again, and actively participate in AA meetings. John agreed. Mr. Halaska referred him to an AA group and also referred him to the outpatient treatment unit of the mental health center. Among other services, this outpatient treatment service provided marriage counseling services to John and his wife and helped him explore job opportunities.

John occasionally stops by the hospital to visit Mr. Halaska briefly. It has now been 14 months since he had a drink. He is a sales clerk at a clothing store and is seeking a teaching position. He reports that he and his wife are getting along better than they ever have.

CASE EXAMPLE *(continued)*

Counseling Skills at Work in Generalist Practice

This case example illustrates that the social worker used the following roles that, as described in Chapter 1, are components of generalist social work practice: helping Mr. Franzene to acknowledge he had a drinking problem, mediating some of the issues between Mr. Franzene and his wife, encouraging him to attend AA meetings and to receive outpatient treatment at a mental health center, and brokering marriage counseling for Mr. and Mrs. Franzene.

Note: Additional case examples using crisis intervention are presented in Greenstone and Leviton (2011).

> Crisis intervention generally progresses in the following manner: (1) An attempt is made to alleviate the disabling tension through ventilation and the creation of a climate of trust and hope. (2) Next the worker attempts to understand the dynamics of the event that precipitated the crisis. (3) The worker gives his impressions and understanding of the crisis and checks out these perceptions with the client. (4) Client and worker attempt to determine specific remedial measures that can be taken to restore equilibrium. (5) New methods of coping may be introduced. (6) Finally, termination occurs—often after a predetermined number of interviews—when the agreed-upon goals have been realized. (p. 212)

EP 2.1.1b

Crisis intervention services are provided in traditional and nontraditional settings, including runaway centers, rape crisis centers, "hot lines," hospital emergency rooms, mental health clinics, suicide prevention services, neighborhood centers, crisis hostels, halfway houses, detention facilities, and self-help groups such as Parents Anonymous. Crisis intervention services are provided by both professionals and paraprofessionals and volunteers.

Exercise M4.6: Crisis Intervention in My Past

Goal: This exercise is designed to assist you in understanding crisis intervention services.

Step 1: Describe a crisis you had in the past.

Step 2: Specify how you resolved this crisis (crisis intervention services include both assistance from others and your own problem-solving resources).

TASK-CENTERED PRACTICE

The primary developers of task-centered practice are William J. Reid and Laura Epstein, social work faculty members of the School of Social Service Administration at the University of Chicago. Task-centered practice is described in Reid and Epstein (1977).

In the initial interview with clients, counselors seek to elicit, explore, and clarify clients' problems. During this interview, counselors may point out problems not recognized by clients or the consequences of allowing significant problems to go unattended.

In the first or second interview, counselor and client explicitly agree on the problems to be dealt with. The problems are defined in terms of specific circumstances to be changed. Counselor and client also agree on the duration and amount of service to be given. There are usually 6 to 12 interviews over a 2- to 4-month period. The kinds of services agreed on and the number of interviews to be held form the basis of the service contract, which can be modified by additional agreements as service proceeds.

Counselors and clients then identify tasks that clients can undertake to alleviate specific problems. These tasks may be general in nature in that they give the client a direction for action but do not precisely specify the expected behavior. For example, client Jim K will seek to establish a better relationship with his parents. Or tasks may be very specific. For example, Jim K will inform his parents how much he appreciates their financial support in sending him to college.

During the discussion of the tasks, counselors help clients structure the tasks to increase their chances of being accomplished. If clients are unable to arrive at alternatives for resolving the problems, counselors may suggest various possibilities. The counselor's primary roles in this change process are to help clients identify target problems, to help them identify tasks for resolving these problems, and to then carry out agreed-on tasks together with the client. The general tasks of clients, in this model, become the clients' own goals for change. In this change process, counselors use relationship skills (discussed in Chapter 5) and a variety of resolution approaches, such as contingency contracting and assertiveness training (both of which are described in Module 2).

During the intervention process, a substantial amount of the counselor's efforts goes into structuring communication during interviews to keep clients' attention and efforts focused on the tasks. Numerous efforts are made to enhance clients' awareness of their problems and to help them understand obstacles to task performance. Clients are given substantial encouragement about constructive actions they are contemplating or are undertaking. Clients also may be given suggestions or directions on how to proceed with the task.

Usually in the intervention process, there is an emphasis on counselors helping clients break down general tasks into more specific, operational tasks that they are then expected to carry out before the next treatment session. Incentives for task accomplishment are usually identified. Actions called for by the tasks are rehearsed or practiced (for example, through role-playing). This task-centered approach has been used with individual clients, families, and groups (Reid & Epstein, 1977).

Intervention is planned to be short-term. It is theorized that when a contract is made with clients for a set number of interviews (usually 6 to 12), clients will work hard to resolve their problems during this brief time period.

Another emphasis is to focus intervention sharply on target problems and resolution tasks—that is, to specify problems and tasks in operational and measurable terms. Thus, both counselor and client are more aware of precisely what needs to be done and what progress is being made during the intervention process in resolving the problems.

A final emphasis is the use of explicit agreements or contracts. These specify problems, goals, and tasks to be worked on during the intervention process. The contract is formed in the first or second interview and guides the intervention process. This contract may be oral or written; it may be modified later if both parties agree to changing it.

Numerous case examples of task-centered practice are given in Reid and Epstein (1977). The task-centered approach has many similarities to the counseling process described in Chapter 5.

SOLUTION-FOCUSED THERAPY

Solution-focused therapy is also called "solution-oriented therapy" and "strategic therapy." Solution-focused therapists ask clients *what* is happening now and *how* it should be changed. They do not ask *why*. This approach focuses not on pathology (the approach of fixing what is wrong) but on identifying clients' requests. This focus has a profound effect on what interventions are used. For clients, learning to be the persons they want to be is quite different (and often less time-consuming) than learning why they are the way they are. Solution-focused therapy has been developed by a variety of researchers, including Berg and Miller (1992), DeJong and Miller (1995), and de Shazer (1988).

Solution-focused therapy emphasizes two intervention techniques. One is developing well-formed goals with clients that are within their frame of reference. The other is developing solutions with the client based on "exceptions."

What are well-formed goals? Berg and Miller (1992) identify seven characteristics of well-formed goals in solution-focused therapy:

1. The goals are important to clients. Clients should want to achieve these goals, and the goals should be expressed in the clients' language. The only time the worker should object to the desired goals of a client is when a stated goal will result in danger to the client (such as the goal of terminating the client's life) or to others (such as the goal of physical retaliation for a perceived wrong).
2. The goals are modest. Small goals are easier to achieve than large goals.
3. The goals are concrete, specific, and behavioral, so that both client and worker can observe when progress is being made. For example, "going out to lunch with a friend three times a week" is a concrete, specific, and behavioral goal.
4. The goals describe the presence of something (for example, "taking walks") rather than the absence of something (for example, "no longer feeling discouraged").
5. The goals express beginnings ("arranging a pleasant vacation with my spouse for this summer") rather than endings ("having a happy marriage"). Stating goals as a beginning process helps clients conceptualize the first steps they need to take to achieve their desired ends.
6. The goals are realistic. Clients can achieve them within the context of their lives.
7. The goals are perceived by clients as involving "hard work." Goals call for changes in what clients do, and change is difficult. Clients are generally motivated to work hard to achieve highly desired goals.

Setting well-formed goals assumes that goals are negotiated between the worker and client. Expressing goals in such a way that they are consistent with these guidelines often requires considerable effort.

DeJong and Miller (1995) assert that a "miracle" question is often a superb way to assist clients in formulating goals:

> Suppose while you are sleeping tonight a miracle happens. The miracle is that the problem that has you here talking to me is somehow solved. Only you don't know that because you are asleep. What will you notice different tomorrow morning that will tell you that a miracle has happened? (p. 731)

Additional questions asked in this vein include

> What is the very first thing you notice after the miracle happens?
> What will your husband (child, friend) notice about you that gives him the idea that things are better for you?
> When he notices that, what might he do differently?
> When he does that, what will you do?
> And when you do that, what will be different around your house? (p. 731)

These questions shift clients' attention from their difficulties and pathologies to imagining a future in which their problems are resolved. The questions provide an opportunity for workers to help clients formulate goals consistent with the guidelines.

What are "exceptions"? In solution-focused therapy, exceptions are those occasions in clients' lives when their problems could have occurred but did not. For example, a married couple characterize their recent years as "continual fighting"; the worker asks the couple to describe times when they weren't fighting. Workers focus on the *who, what, when,* and *where* of exception times (rather than on the problem times), and an in-depth exploration of client problems is avoided. The result is growing awareness in both worker and client of the client's strengths relative to his or her goals rather than the client's deficiencies relative to his or her problems. Once these strengths are brought to clients' awareness, they can mobilize them to move in the direction of achieving their miracle.

In another example of the exceptions strategy, a worker asks a depressed client to do this homework assignment: "Pay attention to the times when you are not depressed or when the depression is less of a problem. What is different about those times?" During the next session, the worker asks the client what she did differently during those times when she noticed the depression was not a problem or was less of a problem. Such a question implies that the client already has the skills to function in a more satisfying manner.

Solution-focused therapy and problem-solving therapies are very different. The stages of problem solving are well known: specifying the problem; generating resolution strategies; evaluating the merits and shortcomings of the strategies; selecting and implementing a strategy; and evaluating at some later date how well the selected strategy is working. In contrast, the stages of solution-focused therapy are as follows: briefly describing the concern or problem in the client's words; developing well-formed goals; exploring for exceptions (successes or times in the client's life when problems do not happen or are less severe); evaluating client progress as the client defines it; and ending the session with feedback comprising affirmations of the client's goals and strengths. Homework assignments are often given in solution-focused therapy.

In a study of 275 clients, Berg and DeJong (1996) found a 77% success rate using solution-focused therapy. Forty-five percent of the clients indicated that their treatment goal was met, and another 32% indicated some progress in attaining their treatment goal.

Solution-focused therapy is highly consistent with the strengths perspective in social work, which is described in Chapter 3. Solution-focused therapy, task-centered therapy, and some forms of cognitive behavior therapy (see Module 2) are examples of brief therapies. Brief therapies are becoming increasingly popular with clients and with funding sources as society and individuals clamor for approaches that result in significant change in a short time and at a reasonable cost.

A shortcoming of solution-focused therapy is that the approach cannot be used with clients who deny a problem exists—for example, alcoholics who are in denial about their drinking problem. The approach cannot be used with people who are in denial because they do not want to change their problematic behavior. Solution-focused therapy can be used only with clients who want to change their problematic behavior(s).

MEDIATION

Moore (1986) defined *mediation* as follows:

> Mediation involves the intervention of an acceptable impartial and neutral third party who has no authoritative decision-making power to assist contending parties in voluntarily reaching their own mutually acceptable settlement of issues in dispute.... Mediation leaves the decision-making power in the hands of the people in conflict. Mediation is a voluntary process in that the participants must be willing to accept the assistance of the intervenor if the dispute is to be resolved. Mediation is usually initiated when the partners no longer believe that they can handle the conflict on their own and when the only means of resolution appears to involve impartial third-party assistance. (p. 6)

During the past three decades, mediation has been used increasingly to resolve conflicts between disputing groups. As far back as 1913, the federal government established the use of federal mediators to help resolve issues between employers and employees (Moore, 1986, p. 21). Mediated settlements were expected to prevent costly strikes or lockouts and to protect the welfare and safety of Americans. Federal use of mediation in labor disputes set a precedent, encouraging many states to pass laws and to train a cadre of mediators to handle intrastate labor conflicts.

Mediation is currently used in a variety of ways. The Civil Rights Act of 1964 created the Community Relations Service of the U.S. Department of Justice to use mediation to resolve disputes relating to discriminatory practices based on race, color, or national origin (Moore, 1986, pp. 21–22). Diverse private agencies, civil rights commissions, and state agencies now use mediation to handle charges of sex, race, and ethnic discrimination. The federal government funds Neighborhood Justice Centers that provide free or low-cost mediation services to the public to resolve disputes informally, inexpensively, and efficiently (Mayer, 1995, pp. 618–620). Disputes settled through mediation are resolved much more efficiently and creatively than those resolved in court. Mediation is also used in schools to resolve issues between students, between students and faculty, between faculty members, and between faculty and administration. The criminal justice system uses mediation to resolve disputes in correctional facilities—for example, for prison riots, hostage negotiations, and institutionalized grievance procedures. Mediation is used extensively in family disputes involving child custody and divorce proceedings, disputes between parents and children, conflicts involving adoption and the termination of parental rights, and domestic violence situations. Moore (1986, p. 23) stated, "In family disputes, mediated and consensual settlements are often more appropriate and satisfying than litigated or imposed court outcomes." Mediation also is used to settle disputes between business partners, private individuals, government agencies and individuals, landlords and tenants, businesses and customers, and disputants in personal injury cases.

Many professionals now occasionally act as mediators to help people or groups in conflict resolve their concerns. Such professionals include attorneys, social workers, psychologists, and guidance counselors. A few social workers, attorneys, and other professionals work full-time as mediators—often in public or private mediation agencies.

Various models describe the mediation process (Moore, 1986). The one developed by Blades (1985) is summarized here. Blades viewed the mediation process as involving five stages:

1. *Introduction/commitment:* This stage usually is accomplished in a 1- to 2-hour session. The mediator sets ground rules, describes mediation, answers questions, discusses fees, and seeks to gain a commitment to the process from the two parties. The mediator also seeks to develop an understanding of the more pressing issues, gains a sense of the personal dynamics of the two parties, and tries to ascertain whether they are ready and willing to mediate. If one or both parties are unwilling to mediate, then the mediation probably should not proceed. If one or both parties are hesitant to proceed, the mediator usually describes the alternatives to mediation—such as a lengthy and expensive court battle.
2. *Definition:* The two parties, with the mediator's assistance, define the areas in which they already agree and disagree. At this stage certain disputes, such as divorce mediation, require a considerable amount of information.
3. *Negotiation:* Once the two parties agree on the issues in conflict and relevant factual information on these issues is obtained, the two parties are ready to begin negotiating. At this stage, the mediator seeks to have the parties focus on one issue at a time. A problem-solving approach is used in which the needs of each party are first identified and alternatives are generated. The mediator recedes into the background when discussions are proceeding well and steps in when emotions intensify or when the two parties are overlooking creative solutions that will meet their needs.
4. *Agreement:* Once alternatives are generated and related facts are evaluated, the two parties are ready to begin making agreements on the issues. The role of the mediator is to maintain a cooperative atmosphere and to keep the two parties focused on a manageable number of issues. The mediator summarizes areas of agreement and provides legal or other information necessary to a discussion. The mediator helps the two parties examine the merits and shortcomings of the options. During this stage, the mediator praises the parties for the progress they are making and gets them to praise themselves for progress made. The mediator seeks to create a positive atmosphere.

5. *Contracting:* In this final stage of mediation, the two parties review the agreements and clarify any ambiguities. The agreements are almost always written in the form of a contract, which is available for future reference. Either party, the mediator, or everyone together may write the contract. The contract expresses what each party agrees to do, may set deadlines for the diverse tasks to be completed, and may specify consequences if either party fails to meet the terms of the contract. Mediators seek to have specific agreements stated in concrete form to prevent future controversies. The ultimate goal of mediation is a contract in which no one is a loser and by which both parties willingly abide.

One of the major techniques mediators use is a caucus (Moore, 1986). At times a mediator, or either party, may stop the mediation and request a caucus. During a caucus, the two parties are physically separated from each other, and there is no direct communication between them. The mediator meets with one of the parties or with each party individually. Caucuses are called for many reasons: to vent intense emotions privately, to clarify misperceptions, to reduce unproductive or repetitive negative behavior, to clarify a party's interests, to provide a pause for each party to consider an alternative, to convince an uncompromising party that the mediation process is better than going to court, to uncover confidential information, to educate an inexperienced disputant about the processes of mediation, or to design alternatives that will later be brought to a joint session.

Caucuses allow parties to express in private the concessions they are willing to make. Usually such concessions are contingent on the other party's making certain concessions. During caucuses, mediators go back and forth, relaying information from one party to the other to develop a consensus.

NARRATIVE THERAPY

Narrative therapy, originally developed by therapists in Australia and New Zealand, is a recent approach. Michael White (1995) and other narrative therapists assert that our sense of reality is organized and maintained by the stories through which we circulate knowledge about the outside world and about ourselves. People who present negative, dead-end stories about themselves feel inadequate, defeated, overwhelmed, and without future choices. Narrative therapists insist that "the person is never the problem; the person has a problem." In other words, a problem is something one has, not something one is. A person with a problem does not have to change his or her nature but does have to fight the influence of the problem in his or her life.

All of us need to select from the huge amount of information the world throws at us all the time. We need to organize what we see, hear, feel, and remember into a meaningful "story." This always introduces biases: We notice and remember things we find interesting, important, and in line with our beliefs, expectations, and prejudices. We ignore, forget, or play down things that are contrary to the way we see the world. Things we notice and remember tend to confirm and strengthen our story about ourselves and our world. This works fine for most people—because they live reasonably happily within their world. Problems arise when a person is stuck in a story that makes him, her, or others unhappy. Examples are stories involving beliefs like these:

- "I am a violent person; I have a short fuse (and can't help it)."
- "I am no good, useless, have no worth; no one could possibly love me."
- "The world is a terribly dangerous place, and I am helpless in the face of its threats."

Such beliefs lead the person to erroneously believe "there is something wrong with me." Narrative therapy is a search for events that prove these beliefs to be false.

There are always exceptions: events that occurred but didn't fit the story and so were ignored, played down, or forgotten. They can be used to "write a new story," one that separates the problem from the way the person sees himself or herself. Once the problem is found and named, it can be fought. In the process, the person does not have to change. He or she discovers a past, an identity, that was always there but hidden by the biases of the previous story. The new story liberates the person from the shackles of the problem. Therapeutic help comes in the form of learning to reduce the power of problem-saturated stories and reclaiming one's life by substituting previously subjugated stories in which the person was successful.

Techniques used by narrative therapists include the following:

- *Externalizing the problem:* The problem becomes the opponent and is not viewed as a characteristic of the client. If a client is "depressed" or has a "gambling addiction," the problem becomes the *oppressor* that the client and the therapist will work against. Externalizing places the problem outside the client. This technique facilitates the client's seeing that he or she can overcome this *oppressor,* which paves the way for finding different solutions rather than blaming the client for the problem. The therapist can then proceed to deconstruct a preferred story.
- *Exceptions:* Narrative therapists seek to find exceptions—that is, occasions in clients' lives when their problems could have occurred but did not. Such exceptions can facilitate the beginning of a new (more preferred) story.
- *Positive narratives:* Narrative therapists help clients search for positive stories (things that they are doing well or things that are going well) in their lives. Such positive stories can give clients a sense of empowerment.
- *Support for positive narratives:* Narrative therapists use letters and certificates and seek to involve significant others to help clients reauthor their stories in a positive direction. Sharf (2008) notes:

  > Letters written by the therapist summarize the session and externalize the problem. Such letters are positive and highlight the client's strengths. They focus on the unique outcomes of exceptions to the problem. Direct quotes from the session may be used. Also, questions or comments that the therapist thought about after the session can be included. Letters are mailed between sessions and at the end of therapy. Clients often report rereading the letters to help them to continue to make progress on the problem. Certificates, usually used with children, help to mark change and foster pride in having made changes. (p.425)

  Sharf (2008) also notes:

  > Support for client stories can also come from parents, siblings, friends, or others. In family therapy, a therapist may ask questions such as "Mother, how do you see Jennie overcoming Anger?" or "Dad, how do teachers see Jennie fighting Anger at school?" These questions support the client's stories and provide ways to have several people supporting client change. From a narrative point of view, the client has a receptive audience to applaud or appreciate her progress.
  >
  > Although narrative therapists may use a variety of other approaches related to understanding the client's story, all focus on how the client can look differently at her story to bring about a new sense of hope or accomplishment. Family and others work with the client to bring about a new narrative that fights the externalized "problem."

It is interesting to note that narrative therapy is a cognitive therapy approach as it seeks to change self-defeating stories (cognitions) into preferred (more positive) stories.

SUMMARY

This module presents intervention approaches that were developed independently of any comprehensive theory of psychotherapy. The techniques described here are milieu therapy, psychodrama, play therapy, parent effectiveness training, crisis intervention, task-centered practice, solution-focused therapy, mediation, and narrative therapy.

Parent effectiveness training has four techniques that anyone can use to improve interactions with others: active listening, I-messages, no-lose problem solving, and resolving collisions of values. Task-centered therapy focuses on helping clients identify and carry out specific tasks that will help them resolve their problems. Solution-focused therapy emphasizes the strengths of clients in achieving their own goals.

Mediation is used by a variety of professions to resolve conflicts between two or more people. Social workers have used the following intervention approaches for a number of years: crisis intervention, milieu therapy, play therapy, and psychodrama.

Narrative therapists insist that a problem is something a person has, not something a person is. The goal of narrative therapy is to help the client reclaim his or her life by "writing a new story" in which the person is successful and happy.

EXERCISES

EP 2.1.7a

1. Using I-Messages

Goal: This exercise is designed to demonstrate how to phrase I-messages.

Step 1: Explain the goal of this exercise. Indicate that I-messages are a nonblaming description of the effects a person is having on the sender of the message. I-messages do not involve giving a solution message or a put-down message.

Step 2: Ask the class how to formulate I-messages in a variety of situations. The following are examples:

a. Someone is smoking a cigarette near you, and the smoke is bothering you.
b. You're riding in a car that a friend is driving dangerously fast.
c. Someone is playing a stereo loudly in a building, which is interfering with your studying.
d. A friend has just made another comment about your being overweight.
e. A person you're dating continues to write to someone he or she dated in the past.

Step 3: Some of the responses given by students may well be you-messages. If that occurs, ask the class to indicate why the message is a you-message and not an I-message. If the class is having trouble formulating I-messages, ask students to discuss whether we are socialized in our society to use primarily you-messages.

EP 2.1.7a

2. Active Listening

Goal: This exercise is designed to have students practice and further develop their active listening skills.

Step 1: Explain the purpose of the exercise and describe what active listening is and what it is designed to accomplish. Indicate that active listening involves using two types of statements: reflecting feelings and restating content.

Step 2: Have students pair off. (Participate if there is someone without a partner.) Have one member of each pair select a topic to discuss for about 10 minutes. The topic may involve (a) a philosophical or moral issue such as abortion, (b) a problem with a friend or a relative, or (c) a problem at school.

Step 3: Ask the member who selected the topic to discuss it for about 10 minutes. The listener should try to respond solely with active listening statements.

Step 4: After the discussion, ask the presenter to discuss with the listener the quality of the active listening statements. Did the listener make the mistake of making suggestions, asking questions, or beginning to talk about personal experiences? Did active listening motivate the presenter to continue talking? Did the presenter perceive the active listening statements as primarily "natural" or "artificial"?

Have the listener discuss with the presenter his or her thoughts and feelings about using active listening statements. Did the listener want to make other types of statements? If so, what?

Step 5: Reverse the roles and repeat the process.

Step 6: Ask students to form a circle and discuss the merits and shortcomings of active listening. Did any unique or unusual events occur?

EP 2.1.7a

3. Narrative Therapy

Goal: This exercise is designed to assist students in comprehending narrative therapy.

Step 1: Students read the section on narrative therapy in the text.

Step 2: Each student writes down a problem that a friend or relative is having (students are told to withhold identifying information about this person). The problem might be excessive drinking, smoking too much, being depressed, excessive gambling, an eating disorder, and so on.

Step 3: Each student writes down his or her speculation about the self-defeating story that is leading to the problem.

Step 4: Volunteers are asked to share what they wrote. The class discusses what narrative therapy techniques may be useful in deconstructing the self-defeating story and reconstructing a preferred story.

COMPETENCY NOTES

The following identifies where Educational Policy (EP) competencies and practice behaviors are discussed in the chapter.

EP 2.1.10a *Substantively and affectively prepare for action with individuals, families, groups, organizations, and communities.*

EP 2.1.10j *Help clients resolve problems* (pp. 551–574).

This module describes a number of specific intervention approaches with individuals, family members, and group members.

EP 2.1.1b *Practice personal reflection and self-correction to assure continual professional development.* (p. 553).

Exercise M4.1 is designed to assist students in understanding that, through role-playing in childhood, they participated in psychodrama.

EP 2.1.1b *Practice personal reflection and self-correction to assure continual professional development* (p. 555).

Exercise M4.2 is designed to assist students in understanding the beneficial effects of "play" in childhood and in adulthood.

EP 2.1.7a *Utilize conceptual frameworks to guide the process of assessment, intervention, and evaluation.* (pp. 558–559).

Exercise M4.3 is designed to assist students in understanding I-messages and you-messages, and to understand the consequences of each type of message.

EP 2.1.1b *Practice personal reflection and self-correction to assure continual professional development.* (p. 560).

Exercise M4.4 is designed to assist students in understanding the adverse consequences of win-lose struggles.

EP 2.1.1b *Practice personal reflection and self-correction to assure continual professional development.* (pp. 561–562).

Exercise M4.5 is designed to assist students in understanding and applying the no-lose approach to problem solving.

EP 2.1.1b *Practice personal reflection and self-correction to assure continual professional development.* (p. 565).

Exercise M4.6 is designed to assist students in understanding crisis intervention services.

EP 2.1.7a *Utilize conceptual frameworks to guide the process of assessment, intervention, and evaluation.* (p. 572).

This exercise is designed to demonstrate how to phrase I-messages.

EP 2.1.7a *Utilize conceptual frameworks to guide the process of assessment, intervention, and evaluation*. (p. 572).

This exercise is designed to have students practice and further develop their active listening skills.

EP 2.1.7a *Utilize conceptual frameworks to guide the process of assessment, intervention, and evaluation*. (p. 573).

This exercise is designed to assist students in comprehending narrative therapy.

APPENDIX

Suggested Counselor's Responses to Client's Statements

The following are suggested responses to the client's statements in Exercise 3, Chapter 5 (pp. 162–163):

1. "I sense that you feel strongly about this and that you've given this a lot of thought. I'd like to explore this further with you, as I care very much about you as a person. It makes me uncomfortable if you think that the only reason I meet with you is because I'm getting paid. Working with you and with the other clients I have is personally very gratifying. Perhaps I have miscommunicated with you, verbally or nonverbally. I'd like to hear more about why you've reached the conclusion that I don't care about you as a person."
2. "You're really feeling as if you're caught in a dilemma. Obviously in this situation, as in many situations, you can't please everyone. But are you aware that the most important person to please is yourself? You're the one who has to live with your decisions. I'm wondering what your feelings are toward Kent and what your feelings are about getting married at this time in your life. I'm also wondering why your parents dislike Kent. Let's examine these one at a time. What are your feelings toward Kent?"
3. "Yes, I did, I took them two summers ago when I was vacationing in the Colorado Rockies. But we're here to talk about you and how your life is going. Let's begin by discussing how you're doing in school. Could you please tell me your midterm grades for each of your classes?"
4. "I sense this is extremely difficult for you to reveal. You are probably feeling very vulnerable at this point. I'm pleased that you shared this with me, and I want you to know that I have an open mind about sexual orientation. It took real courage for you to talk about this, and I now believe we are in a much better position to help you make some decisions about your future. Can you tell me more about this person you're involved with?"
5. "It's true that I am neither black nor have I lived in an inner city. But I'm interested in you and in working with you. Just because I'm white doesn't mean we can't work together. Everyone, including me, has personal problems. You, too, have some personal problems. By taking each one, one at a time, and examining them and then coming up with some realistic ways of resolving them, I firmly believe we can make progress. Just as a teacher doesn't have to be blind to teach students with a visual disability, a counselor doesn't need to have the same color of skin to work with people who have personal problems. Have I said or done anything to lead you to believe that I am prejudiced against people of color?"
6. "I'm sorry you're still involved with drugs, especially since you were using drugs when you committed the offenses that resulted in your being sent here. I don't like to see you get into trouble, but I have no choice. I have to report this. I made it

crystal clear to you at our first meeting that the consequences of drug involvement would probably be an extension of the time you spend here. As you know, we do have a drug treatment program. I suggest you seriously consider participating in this program. Participation in this program, now, may not only lead to an earlier release but may also help you become drug free. Are you interested in participating in this program?"

References

Addams, J. 1959. *Twenty Years of Hull House.* New York: Macmillan (original publication, 1910).

Aguilar, I. 1972. "Initial Contacts with Mexican-American Families." *Social Work 17* (May), pp. 186–189.

Aguilar, M. A. 2001. "Catholicism." In *Spirituality within Religious Traditions in Social Work Practice* eds. M. Van Hook, B. Hugen, & M. Aguilar, pp. 120–145. Pacific Grove, CA: Brooks/Cole.

Ahn, H. N., & N. Gilbert. 1992. "Cultural Diversity and Sexual Abuse Prevention." *Social Science Review 66,* no. 3, pp. 410–427.

Ainsworth, M. D., et al. 1966. *Deprivation of Maternal Care.* New York: Schocken Books.

Alberti, R. E., & M. L. Emmons. 1970. *Your Perfect Right: A Guide to Assertive Behavior.* San Luis Obispo, CA: Impact Publishers.

———. **1975.** *Stand Up, Speak Out, Talk Back!* New York: Pocket Books.

Alexander, C. A. 1982. "Professional Social Work and Political Responsibility." In *Practical Politics: Social Work and Political Responsibility,* eds. M. Mahaffey & J. W. Hanks. Silver Spring, MD: National Association of Social Workers.

Alexander, K. 1993. "Changes in Delivery of Services for Students with Limited English." *The Advocate 1,* no. 2, p. 1.

Alinsky, S. D. 1969. *Reveille for Radicals.* New York: Basic Books.

———. **1972.** *Rules for Radicals.* New York: Random House.

Alter, C., & W. Evens. 1990. *Evaluating Your Practice: A Guide to Self-Assessment.* New York: Springer.

American Association of Community Gardens. 2008. *Benefits of Community Gardening.* Retrieved March 2, 2008, from http://www.co.ramsey.mn.us/NR/rdonlyres/DA2B45C9-B882-4012-A161 7A826D4E40E4/857/Benefits_of_Community_Gardening.pdf.

American Professional Credentialing Services. 1996. *Administration and Scoring Manual for the OQ® 45.2.* Wharton, NJ: Author (September).

American Psychiatric Association. 2000. *Diagnostic and Statistical Manual of Mental Disorders, Fourth Edition Text Revision.* Washington, DC: Author.

Appleby, G. A. 2001. "Dynamics of Oppression and Discrimination." In *Diversity, Oppression, and Social Functioning: Person-in-Environment Assessment and Intervention,* eds. G. A. Appleby, E. Colon, & J. Hamilton, pp. 36–52. Boston: Allyn & Bacon.

Asch, S. E. 1955. "Opinions and Social Pressure." *Scientific American 193,* no. 5, pp. 31–35.

Bach, G., & P. Wyden. 1981. *The Intimate Enemy.* New York: Avon.

Baer, D. M., R. Harrison, L. Fradenburg, D. Peterson, & S. Milla. 2005. "Some Pragmatics in the Valid and Reliable Recording of Directly Observed Behavior." *Research on Social Work Practice 15,* pp. 440–451.

Bandura, A. 1969. *Principles of Behavior Modification.* New York: Holt, Rinehart & Winston.

Banfield, F. K., J. Terris, & N. Vorsanger. 2001. *Solving Sprawl Models of Smart Growth in Communities across America.* Washington, DC: Natural Resources Defense Council.

Barker, R. L. 2003. *The Social Work Dictionary,* 5th ed. Washington, DC: National Association of Social Workers.

Barlow, D. H., & J. A. Cerny. 1988. *Psychological Treatment of Panic.* New York: Guilford.

Barlow, D. H., S. C. Hayes, & R. O. Nelson. 1984. *The Scientist Practitioner.* Elmsford, NY: Pergamon Press.

Barlow, D. H., & M. Hersen. 1984. *Single Case Experimental Designs,* 2nd ed. Elmsford, NY: Pergamon Press.

Barocas, H. A. 1972. "Psychodrama Techniques in Training Police in Family Crisis Intervention." *Group Psychotherapy and Psychodrama 25,* pp. 30–31.

Beck, A. T. 1976. *Cognitive Theory and the Emotional Disorders.* New York: International Universities Press.

Beck, A. T., A. J. Rush, B. F. Shaw, & G. Emery. 1979. *Cognitive Therapy of Depression.* New York: Guilford.

Beck, A. T., & M. E. Weishaar. 1989. "Cognitive Therapy." In *Current Psychotherapies,* 4th ed., eds. R. J. Corsini & D. Wedding, pp. 284–320. Itasca, IL: Peacock.

Becker, D. G. 1968. "Social Welfare Leaders as Spokesmen for the Poor." *Social Casework 49,* no. 2 (Feb.), p. 85.

Belgrave, F. Z., & K. W. Allison. 2006. *African American Psychology: From Africa to America.* Thousand Oaks, CA: Sage.

Bellack, A. S., & M. Hersen, eds. 1998. *Behavioral Assessment: A Practical Handbook,* 4th ed. Boston: Allyn & Bacon.

Bemner, R. M. 1962. "The Rediscovery of Pauperism." In *Current Issues in Social Work Seen in Historical Perspective.* New York: Council on Social Work Education.

Benjamin, A. 1974. *The Helping Interview,* 2nd ed. Boston: Houghton Mifflin.

Benson, H. 1975. *The Relaxation Response.* New York: Morrow.

Berg, I. K., & P. DeJong. 1996. "Solution-Building Conversations: Co-Constructing a Sense of Competence with Clients." *Families in Society* (June), pp. 376–391.

Berg, I. K., & S. D. Miller. 1992. *Working with the Problem Drinker: A Solution-Focused Approach.* New York: Norton.

Bergman, A. 1989. "Informal Support Systems for Pregnant Teenagers." *Social Casework 70*, no. 9, pp. 526–533.

Bernanos, G. 1970. As quoted in J. C. DeBoer, *Let's Plan: A Guide to the Planning Process for Voluntary Organizations.* New York: United Church Press.

Bernstein, B. E. 1975. "The Social Worker as a Courtroom Witness." *Social Casework 56*, no. 9 (Nov.), pp. 521–525.

Berwick, D. 1980. "Nonorganic Failure to Thrive." *Pediatrics in Review 1*, pp. 265–270.

Billingsley, A. 1993. *Climbing Jacob's Ladder: The Enduring Legacy of African-American Families.* New York: Simon & Schuster.

Black, B. J. 1977. "Milieu Therapy." In *Encyclopedia of Social Work*, 17th ed., pp. 919–927. New York: National Association of Social Workers.

Blades, J. 1985. *Mediate Your Divorce.* Englewood Cliffs, NY: Prentice-Hall.

Blatner, A. 1995. "Psychodrama." In *Current Psychotherapies*, 5th ed., eds. R. J. Corsini & D. Wedding. Itasca, IL: Peacock.

Bloom, M. 1975. *The Paradox of Helping: Introduction to the Philosophy of Scientific Practice.* New York: Wiley.

———. **1983.** "Empirically Based Clinical Research." In *Handbook of Clinical Social Work*, eds. A. Rosenblatt & D. Waldfogel, pp. 560–582. San Francisco: Jossey-Bass.

Bloom, M., J. Fischer, & J. G. Orme. 2006. *Evaluating Practice: Guidelines for the Accountable Professional*, 5th ed. Boston: Allyn & Bacon.

———. **2009.** *Evaluting Practice: Guidelines for the Accountable Professional*, 6th ed. Boston: Pearson/Allyn & Bacon.

Blythe, B. J., & T. Tripodi. 1989. *Measurement in Direct Practice.* Newbury Park, CA: Sage.

Booth, A., K. Carver, & D. A. Granger. 2005. "Biosocial Perspectives on the Family." In *Exploring Family Theories*, eds. B. B. Ingoldsby, S. R. Smith, & J. E. Miller, pp. 227–246. Los Angeles: Roxbury.

Boyte, H. C. 1989. "People Power Transforms a St. Louis Housing Project." *Occasional Papers* (Jan.) Chicago: Community Renewable Society, pp. 1–5.

BPD. 2006 "Definition of Generalist Practice." Discussed and advanced by the BPD Social Work Continuum Committee and approved by the BPD Board of Directors.

Brammer, R. 2004. *Diversity in Counseling.* Belmont, CA: Brooks/Cole.

Branston, G., & R. Stafford. 2006. *The Media Student's Book*, 4th ed. London: Taylor & Francis.

Brave Heart, M. Y. H. 2001. "Culturally and Historically Congruent Clinical Social Work Interventions with Native Clients." In *Culturally Competent Practice*, eds. R. Fong & S. Furuto, pp. 285–298. Boston: Allyn & Bacon.

Brawley, E.A. 1983. *Mass Media and Human Services: Getting the Message Across.* Beverly Hills, CA: Sage.

______. **1995.** *Human Services and the Media: Developing Partnerships for Change.* Newark, NJ: Harwood Academic Publisher.

Brieland, D., L. B. Costin, & C. R. Atherton. 1985. *Contemporary Social Work: An Introduction to Social Work and Social Welfare*, 3rd ed. New York: McGraw-Hill.

Briggs, H. E., W. Feyerherm, & W. Gingerich. 2004. "Evaluating Science-Based Practice with Single-Subject Designs." In *Using Evidence in Social Work Practice: Behavioral Perspectives*, eds. H. E. Briggs & T. L. Rzepnicki. Chicago: Lyceum Books.

Brown, B. B. 1977. *Stress and the Art of Biofeedback.* New York: Bantam Books.

Bullis, R. K. 1996. *Spirituality in Social Work Practice.* Washington, DC: Taylor & Francis.

Bureau of Labor Statistics. 2010. *Persons with a Disability: Labor Force Characteristics Summary.* Washington, DC: Author.

Campbell, J. A. 1988. "Client Acceptance of Single-System Evaluation Procedures." *Social Work Research & Abstracts 24*, pp. 21–22.

———. **1990.** "Ability of Practitioners to Estimate Client Acceptance of Single-Subject Evaluation Procedures." *Social Work 35*, pp. 9–14.

Canadian Association of Social Workers. 2005. *Code of Ethics and Guideliners for Ethical Practice.* Retrieved from www.caswacts.ca.

Cartwright, T. J. 1973. "Problems, Solutions and Strategies: A Contribution to the Theory and Practice of Planning." *AIP Examination Readings.* Washington, DC: American Institute of Planners.

Center for Social Research and Development. 1974. *Analysis and Synthesis of Needs Assessment Research in the Field of Human Services.* Denver: University of Denver.

Chambless, D. L., & A. J. Goldstein. 1979. "Behavioral Psychotherapy." In *Current Psychotherapies*, 2nd ed., ed. R. Corsini. Itasca, IL: Peacock.

***Chicago Tribune*. 1998.** "Model Minority Doesn't Tell?" (Jan. 3), p. 18.

Christie, R., & F. Geis. 1970. *Studies in Machiavellianism.* New York: Academic Press.

Ciminero, A. R., K. S. Calhoun, & H. E. Adams, eds. 1986. *Handbook of Behavioral Assessment*, 2nd ed. New York: Wiley.

Clements-Nolle, K., R. Marx, & M. Katz. 2006. "Attempted Suicide among Transgender Persons: The Influence of Gender-Based Discrimination and Victimization." *Journal of Homosexuality 51*, no. 3, pp. 53–69.

Clifton, R. L., & A. M. Dahms. 1980. *Grassroots Administration: A Handbook for Staff and Directors of Small Community-Based Social-Service Agencies.* Belmont, CA: Wadsworth.

Cnaan, R. A. 1999. *The Newer Deal: Social Work and Religion in Partnership.* New York: Columbia University Press.

Cohen, N. E. 1958. *Social Work in the American Tradition.* Hinsdale, IL: Dryden Press.

Coleman, J. W., & D. R. Cressey. 1995. *Social Problems*, 8th ed. Englewood Cliffs, NJ: Prentice-Hall.

Compton, B., & B. Galaway. 1975. *Social Work Processes.* Homewood: IL: Dorsey Press.

———. **1999.** *Social Work Processes*, 6th ed. Pacific Grove, CA: Brooks/Cole.

Congress, E. P. 2000. "What Social Workers Should know About Ethics: Understanding and Resolving Practice Dilemmas." *Advances in Social Work* 1, no. 1 (Spring), pp. 1–25.

Cooley, C. H. 1902. *Human Nature and the Social Order.* New York: Scribner.
Cooper, M. 1990. "Treatment of a Client with Obsessive Compulsive Disorder." *Social Work Research & Abstracts 26,* pp. 26–32.
Corcoran, K., & J. Fischer. 2007. *Measures for Clinical Practice,* 4th ed. New York: Free Press.
Corcoran, K., & W. J. Gingerich. 1994. "Practice Evaluation in the Context of Managed Care: Case-Recording Methods for Quality Assurance Reviews." *Research on Social Work Practice 4,* pp. 326–337.
Corey, G. 2004. *Theory and Practice of Group Counseling.* Belmont, CA: Brooks/Cole.
Cormier, W. H., & L. S. Cormier. 1991. *Interviewing Strategies for Helpers.* Pacific Grove, CA: Brooks/Cole.
Council on Social Work Education. 1982. *Curriculum Policy for the Master's Degree & Baccalaureate Degree Programs in Social Work Education.* New York: Author, adopted May 24.
———. **1992a.** *Curriculum Policy Statement for Baccalaureate Degree Programs in Social Work Education.* Alexandria, VA: Author.
———. **1992b.** *Curriculum Policy Statement for Master's Degree Programs in Social Work Education.* Alexandria, VA: Author.
———. **2008.** *Educational Policy and Accreditation Standards.* Alexandria, VA: Author.
Cournoyer, B. R. 2004. *The Evidence-Based Social Work Skills Book.* Boston: Allyn & Bacon.
Criddle, W. D. 1974. "Guidelines for Challenging Irrational Beliefs." *Rational Living* (Spring), pp. 8–13.
Crosbie, J. 1993. "Interrupted Time-Series Analysis with Brief Single-Subject Data." *Journal of Consulting and Clinical Psychology 61,* pp. 966–974.
Davenport, J., & J. Davenport. 1982. "Utilizing the Social Network in Rural Communities." *Social Casework* 63 (Feb.), pp. 106–112.
Davidson, D. 2000. "Issues Facing Elderly Gay Men and Lesbians." Retrieved from www.keln.org/bibs/Davidson.html.
Davie, J. S., & A. P. Hare. 1956. "Button-Down Collar Culture: A Study of Undergraduate Life at a Men's College." *Human Organization 14,* pp. 13–20.
Davis, K., & W. Newstrom. 1989. *Human Behavior at Work,* 8th ed. New York: McGraw-Hill.
Davis, L. V. 1994. *Building on Women's Strengths.* New York: Haworth.
De Mello, A. 1978. *Sadhana: A Way to God.* Garden City, NY: Image Books.
de Shazer, S. 1988. "The Death of Resistance." *Family Process 23,* pp. 79–93.
Dean, R. (2001). "The Myth of Cross-Cultural Competence." *Families in Society* 82, no. 6 pp. 623–630.
DeBoer, J. C. 1970. *Let's Plan: A Guide to the Planning Process for Voluntary Organizations.* New York: United Church Press.
DeJong, P., & I. K. Berg. 1998. *Interviewing for Solutions.* Pacific Grove, CA: Brooks/Cole.
DeJong, P., & S. D. Miller. 1995. "How to Interview for Client Strengths." *Social Work 40,* no. 6 (Nov.), pp. 729–736.
Delbecq, A. L., & A. Van de Ven. 1971. "A Group Process Model for Problem Identification and Program Planning." *Journal of Applied Behavioral Science* (July–Aug.).
Deming, W. E. 1986. *Out of the Crisis.* Cambridge, MA: Massachusetts Institute of Technology, Center for Advanced Engineering Study.
Deparle, J. 2007. "Cultivating Their Own Gardens." *New York Times,* September 30.
Devore, W., & E. G. Schlesinger. 1996. *Ethnic-Sensitive Social Work Practice,* 4th ed. Boston: Allyn & Bacon.
Dickson, D. T. 1998. *Confidentiality and Privacy in Social Work.* New York: Free Press.
DiGiussepe, R., N. Miller, & L. Trexler. 1977. "A Review of Rational Emotive Psychotherapy Outcome Studies." *Counseling Psychologist 7,* no. 1.
DiGiuseppe, R. A., M. Terjesen, R. Rose, K. Doyle, & N. Vadalakis. 1998. "*Selective Abstractions Errors in Reviewing REBT Outcome Studies: A Review of Reviews.*" Poster presented at the 106th Annual Convention of the American Psychological Association, San Francisco (Aug.).
Dolgoff, R., & D. Feldstein. 1980. *Understanding Social Welfare.* New York: Harper & Row.
Dolgoff, R., F. M. Loewenberg, & D. Harrington. 2009. *Ethical Decisions for Social Work Practice.* Belmont, CA: Brooks/Cole.
Dorfman, D. 1998. *Mapping Community Assets Workbook.* Portland, OR: Northwest Regional Educational Laboratory.
Downs, S. W., E. Moore, E. J. McFadden, & L. B. Costin, 2000. *Child Welfare and Family Services,* 6th ed. Boston: Allyn & Bacon.
Dreikurs, R. 1964. *Children: The Challenge.* New York: Hawthorn Books.
Drucker, P. F. 1954. *The Practice of Management.* New York: Harper.
Dumont, M. 1968. *The Absurd Healer.* New York: Viking Press.
Dunn, J. 1977. *Distress and Comfort.* Cambridge, MA: Harvard University Press.
Earl, J. 2006. "Pursuing Social Change Online: The Use of Four Protest Tactics on the Internet." *Social Science Computer Review 24,* no. 3, pp. 362–377.
Edelwich, J. 1980. *Burn-Out.* New York: Human Sciences Press.
Egan, G. 1985. *Change Agent Skills in Helping and Human Service Settings.* Pacific Grove, CA: Brooks/Cole.
Ell, K. 1995. "Crisis Intervention: Research Needs." In *Encyclopedia of Social Work,* 19th ed. Washington, DC: National Association of Social Workers.
Ellis, A. 1957. "Outcome of Employing Three Techniques of Psychotherapy." *Journal of Clinical Psychology 13,* pp. 344–350.
———. **1958.** "Rational Psychotherapy." *Journal of General Psychology 58* (Jan.), pp. 35–49.
———. **1962.** *Reason and Emotion in Psychotherapy.* New York: Lyle Stuart.
———. **1973.** "Rational-Emotive Therapy." In *Current Psychotherapies,* ed. R. Corsini, pp. 167–206. Itasca, IL: Peacock.
———. **1979.** "Rational-Emotive Therapy." In *Current Psychotherapies,* 2nd ed., ed. Raymond Corsini, pp. 185–229. Itasca, IL: Peacock.
———. **2000.** "Rational Emotive Behavior Therapy." In *Current Psychotherapies,* 6th ed., eds. R. J. Corsini & D. Wedding, pp. 168–204. Itasca, IL: Peacock.
———. **2008.** "Rational Emotive Behavior Therapy." In *Current Psychotherapies,* 8th ed., eds. R. J. Corsini & D. Wedding, pp. 187–222. Belmont, CA: Brooks/Cole.
Ellis, A., & R. Harper. 1977. *A New Guide to Rational Living.* North Hollywood, CA: Wilshire Books.

Emmelkamp, P. M. G. 1994. "Behavior Therapy with Adults." In *Handbook of Psychotherapy and Behavior Change*, 4th ed., eds. A. E. Bergin & S. L. Garfield, pp. 379–427. New York: Wiley.

Eriksen, K. 1979. *Communication Skills for the Human Services.* Reston, VA: Reston Publishing.

Etzioni, A. 1964. *Modern Organizations*. Englewood Cliffs, NJ: Prentice-Hall.

Eysenck, H. J. 1961. "The Effects of Psychotherapy." In *Handbook of Abnormal Psychology*, pp. 697–725. New York: Basic Books.

———. **1965.** "The Effects of Psychotherapy." *International Journal of Psychiatry 1*, pp. 97–144.

Falck, H. E. 1966. "Integrating the Rural Welfare Department into the Community." In *Can Welfare Keep Pace?*, ed. M. Morton. New York: Columbia University Press.

Family Village Disability Culture. 2010. "Famous People and Disabilities." Retrieved September 13, 2010, from www.familyvillage wisc.edu/general/famous.html.

Faul, A. C., S. L. McMurtry, & W. W. Hudson. 2001. "Can Empirical Clinical Practice Techniques Improve Social Work Outcomes?" *Research on Social Work Practice, 11,* 277–299.

Fellin, p. 1987. *The Social Worker and the Community.* Itasca, IL: Peacock.

Fensterheim, H., & J. Baer. 1975. *Don't Say Yes When You Want to Say No.* New York: Dell.

Ferguson, T. 1996. *Health Online.* Reading, MA: Addison-Wesley.

Fine, L. J. 1979. "Psychodrama." In *Current Psychotherapies*, 2nd ed., ed. R. J. Corsini. Itasca, IL: Peacock.

Fischer, J., & K. Corcoran. 2006. *Measures for Clinical Practice*, 4th ed. New York: Oxford University Press.

Flanagan, J. 1977. *The Grass Roots Fundraising Book: How to Raise Money in Your Community.* Chicago: Swallow Press.

———. **1995.** *The Grass Roots Fundraising Book: How to Raise Money in Your Community.* Raleigh, NC: Contemporary Press.

Fong, R. 2003. "Cultural Competence with Asian Americans." In *Culturally Competent Practice,* pp. 261–281. Pacific Grove, CA: Brooks/Cole.

Ford, J., D. Young, B. Perez, R. Obermeyer, & D. Rohmer. 1992. "Needs Assessment for Persons with Severe Mental Illness: What Services Are Needed for Successful Community Living?" *Community Mental Health Journal 28*, no. 6, pp. 491–503.

Frank, J. D. 1973. *Persuasion and Healing*, 2nd ed. Baltimore: Johns Hopkins University Press.

Franklin, A. J. 1999. "Therapeutic Support Groups for African American Men." In *Working with African American Males,* ed. L. E. Davis, pp. 5–14. Thousand Oaks, CA: Sage.

Freedman, N., & R. Sherman. 1987. *Handbook of Measurements for Marriage and Family Therapy.* New York: Brunner/Mazel.

Freeman, E. M. 1994. "Women Who Work outside the Home: Multicultural and Multigenerational Influences on the Family Adjustment Process." In *Building on Women's Strengths,* ed. L. V. Davis. New York: Haworth.

French, J. R. P., & B. Raven. 1968. "The Bases of Social Power." In *Group Dynamics: Research and Theory,* 3rd ed., eds. D. Cartwright & A. Zander. New York: Harper & Row.

Freudenberger, H. J. 1977. "Burn-Out: Occupational Hazard of the Child Care Worker." *Child Care Quarterly 6*, pp. 90–99.

Frey, G. A. 1990. "A Framework for Promoting Organizational Change." *Families in Society 71,* no. 3, pp. 142–147.

Furman, L. E. 1994. "Religion and Spirituality in Social Work Education: Preparing the Culturally-Sensitive Practitioner for the Future." Paper presented at Midwest Biennial Conference on Social Work, April 28–29, St. Paul, MN.

Galan, F. 2001. "Interventions with Mexican American Families." In *Culturally Competent Practice,* eds. R. Fong & S. Furuto, pp. 255–268. Boston: Allyn & Bacon

Galper, J. H. 1975. *The Politics of Social Services.* Englewood Cliffs, NJ: Prentice-Hall.

———. **1980.** *Social Work Practice: A Radical Perspective.* Englewood Cliffs, NJ: Prentice-Hall.

Gambrill, E. 1999. "Evidence-Based Practice: An Alternative to Authority-Based Practice." *Families in Society: Journal of Contemporary Human Services 80,* no. 4, pp. 341–350.

———. **2006.** "Evidence-Based Practice and Policy: Choices Ahead." *Research on Social Work Practice 16,* pp. 338–357.

Ganz, M., 2009. *Why David Sometimes Wins: Leadership, Organization, and Strategy in the California Farm Worker Movement* New York: Oxford University Press.

Garland, J. A., H. Jones, & R. Kolodny. 1965. "A Model for Stages of Development in Social Work Groups." In *Explorations in Group Work,* ed. S. Bernstein. Boston: Milford House.

Garvin, C. D., & F. M. Cox. 2001. "A History of Community Organizing since the Civil War with Special Reference to Oppressed Communities." In *Strategies of Community Intervention,* 6th ed., eds. J. Rothman, J. L. Erlich, & J. E. Tropman, pp. 64–99. Itasca, IL: Peacock.

Gates. G.J. (2001). *Gay and Lesbian Families in the United States: Same-Sex Unmarried Partner Households.* Washington, DC: Urban Institute.

Ghali, S. B. 1992. "Understanding Puerto Rican Traditions." *Social Work 27,* no. 1 (Jan.), pp. 98–102.

Gibson, G., & K. Ottenbacher. 1988. "Characteristics Influencing the Visual Analysis of Single-Subject Data: An Empirical Investigation." *Journal of Applied Behavioral Science 24,* pp. 298–314.

Gingerich, W. J. 1979. "Procedure for Evaluating Clinical Practice." *Health and Social Work 4,* pp. 105–130.

———. **1983.** "Significance Testing in Single-Case Research." In *Handbook of Clinical Social Work,* eds. A. Rosenblatt & D. Waldfogel, pp. 694–720. San Francisco: Jossey-Bass.

———. **1990.** "Expert Systems and Their Potential Uses in Social Work." *Families in Society 71,* pp. 220–228.

———. **1995a.** "Expert Systems." In *Encyclopedia of Social Work,* 19th ed., ed. R. L. Edwards, pp. 917–925. Washington, DC: NASW Press.

———. **1995b.** "MY ASSISTANT: Computer-Assisted Record-Keeping for the Case Manager." Poster session at the Nineteenth Annual Symposium on Computer Applications in Medical Care, New Orleans, LA.

———. **2002a.** "Computer Applications for Social Work Practice." In *Social Worker's Desk Reference,* eds. A. R. Roberts & G. J. Greene, pp. 23–28. New York: Oxford University Press.

———. **2002b.** "Online Social Work: Ethical and Practical Considerations." In *Social Worker's Desk Reference,* eds. A. R. Roberts & G. J. Greene, pp. 81–85. New York: Oxford University Press.

Gingerich, W. J., & A. Broskowski. 1996. "Clinical Decision Support Systems." In *The Computerization of Behavioral Healthcare,* ed. T. Trabin, pp. 11–38. San Francisco: Jossey-Bass.

Ginott, H. G. 1965. *Between Parent and Child.* New York: Macmillan.

Ginsburg, L. 1998. *Social Work in Rural Communities,* 3rd ed. Alexandria, VA: Council on Social Work Education.

Glasser, W. 1965. *Reality Therapy.* New York: Harper & Row.

———. **1972.** *The Identity Society.* New York: Harper & Row.

———. **1984.** *Control Theory.* New York: Harper & Row.

———. **1998.** *Choice Theory: A New Psychology of Personal Freedom.* New York: HarperPerennial.

———. **2000.** *Reality Therapy in Action.* New York: HarperCollins.

———. **2003.** *Warning: Psychiatry Can Be Hazardous to Your Health.* New York: HarperCollins.

Glasser, W., & R. Wubbolding. 1995. "Reality Therapy." In *Current Psychotherapies,* 5th ed., eds. R. J. Corsini & D. Wedding, pp. 293–321. Itasca, IL: Peacock.

Golan, N. 1979. "Crisis Theory." In *Social Work Treatment,* 2nd ed., ed. F. J. Turner, pp. 499–531. London: Free Press.

Goldenberg, I., & H. Goldenberg. 1991. *Family Therapy, An Overview,* 3rd ed. Pacific Grove, CA: Brooks/Cole.

———. **2004.** *Family Therapy: An Overview,* 6th ed. Pacific Grove, CA: Brooks/Cole.

Googins, B., V. A. Capoccia, & N. Kaufman. 1983. "The Interactional Dimension of Planning: A Framework for Practice." *Social Work 18* (July–Aug.), pp. 273–278.

Google Maps User Guide. 2008. Retrieved March 8, 2008, from http://local.google.com/support/bin/answer.py?hl-en&answer-68480.

Gordon, T. 1970. *Parent Effectiveness Training.* New York: Wyden.

Green, J. W. 1999. *Cultural Awareness in the Human Services.* Boston: Allyn & Bacon.

Green, R. G., M. Kiernan-Stern, & F. R. Baskind. 2005. "White Social Workers' Attitudes about People of Color." *Journal of Ethnic & Cultural Diversity in Social Work 14,* nos. 1–2, pp. 47–68.

Greenberg, H. M. 1980. *Coping with Job Stress.* Englewood Cliffs, NJ: Spectrum.

Greenstone, J.L. & S. C. Levinton, 2011. *Elements of Crisis Intervention: Crisies and How to Respond to Them,* 3rd ed., Belmont, CA: Brooks/Cole.

Grier, W. H., & P. M. Cobbs. 1968. *Black Rage.* New York: Basic Books.

Grohol, J. M. 2000. *The Insider's Guide to Mental Health Resources Online, 2000/2001 Edition.* New York: Guilford Press.

———. **2003.** *The Insider's Guide to Mental Health Resources Online, 2002/2003 Edition.* New York: Guilford Press.

Gross, E. R. 1996. "Deconstructing Politically Correct Practice Literature: The American Indian Case." In *Multicultural Issues in Social Work,* eds. P. L. Ewalt et al., pp. 241–254. Washington, DC: NASW Press.

Grossman, J. M., & B. Liang. 2008. "Discrimination Distress among Chinese American Adolescents." *Journal of Youth Adolescence* 37, pp. 1–11.

Grotevant, H. D., & C. I. Carlson. 1987. "Family Interaction Coding Systems: A Descriptive Review." *Family Process* 26, p. 49.

Guthrie, E. R. 1935. *The Psychology of Learning.* New York: Harper & Row.

Hall, C. J. 2007. "Perceptions of Need and the Ethicality of the Male Social Work Practice." *Families in Society* 88, no. 2, pp. 214–222.

Hare, A. 1962. *Handbook of Small Group Research.* New York: Free Press.

Harper, K. V., & J. Lantz. 1996. *Cross-Cultural Practice: Social Work with Diverse Populations.* Chicago: Lyceum Books.

Harper–Dorton, K., & J. Lantz. 2007. *Cross-Cultural Practice: Social Work with Diverse Populations.* Chicago: Lyceum.

Hartman, A. 1978. "Diagrammatic Assessment of Family Relationships." *Social Casework 59* (Oct.), pp. 465–476.

Hauck, P. A. 1972. *The Rational Management of Children.* New York: Libra Publishers.

Hepworth, D. H., & J. Larsen. 1986. *Direct Social Work Practice: Theory and Skills,* 2nd ed. Pacific Grove, CA: Brooks/Cole.

———. **1993.** *Direct Social Work Practice,* 4th ed. Pacific Grove, CA: Brooks/Cole.

Hepworth, D. H., R. H. Rooney, & J. A. Larson. 1997. *Direct Social Work Practice,* 5th ed. Pacific Grove, CA: Brooks/Cole.

Herrnstein, R. J., & C. Murray. 1994. *The Bell Curve: The Reshaping of American Life by Differences in Intelligence.* New York: Free Press.

Hersen, M., & A. S. Bellack, eds. 1988. *Dictionary of Behavioral Assessment Techniques.* Elmsford, NY: Pergamon Press.

Hersey, P., & K. Blanchard. 1977. *Management of Organizational Behavior: Utilizing Human Resources,* 3rd ed. Englewood Cliffs, NJ: Prentice-Hall.

Hick, S. F., & J. G. McNutt. 2002. *Advocacy, Activism, and the Internet.* Chicago: Lyceum Books.

Hollis, F. 1972. *Casework: A Psychosocial Theory.* New York: Random House.

Hower, D. 1994. "David Hower's Definition of Total Quality." *Reporter* (Aug. 29), p. 10. Whitewater: University of Wisconsin–Whitewater.

Hudson, W. W. 1982. *The Clinical Measurement Package: A Field Manual.* Pacific Grove, CA: Brooks/Cole.

———. **1992.** *Walmyr Assessment Scales.* Tempe, AZ: Walmyr.

Hull, C. L. 1943. *Principles of Behavior.* New York: Appleton-Century-Crofts.

Hull, G. H. 1978. "The Parents' Anonymous Sponsor: A Professional Helping Role." Paper presented at the Child Welfare League of America Regional Conference, Omaha, NE.

———. **1990.** *Social Work Internship Manual.* Eau Claire: University of Wisconsin–Eau Claire, Department of Social Work.

Hyde, J. S., & J. DeLamater. 2006. *Understanding Human Sexuality,* 9th ed. New York: McGraw-Hill.

_______. **2011.** *Understanding Human Sexuality,* 10th ed. New York: McGraw-Hill.

International Federation of Social Workers and International Association of Social Workers. 2004.

Ethics in Social Work, Statement of Principles. Retrieved from www.ifsw.org.

Ivey, A. E., & M. B. Ivey. 1999. *Intentional Interviewing and Counseling*. Pacific Grove, CA: Brooks/Cole.

Jackson, D. D. 1965. "The Study of the Family."*Family Process 4,* pp. 1–20.

Jaffee, S., & J. S. Hyde. 2000. "Gender Differences in Moral Orientation: A Meta-Analysis." *Psychological Bulletin 126,* pp. 703–726.

Janis, I. 1971. "Group Think." *Psychology Today 15,* no. 6. (November), pp. 43–46, 74–76.

Jayaratne, S., & R. L. Levy. 1979. *Empirical Clinical Practice.* New York: Columbia University Press.

Johnson, D. W., & F. P. Johnson. 1975. *Joining Together.* Englewood Cliffs, NJ: Prentice-Hall.

———. **1987.** *Joining Together,* 3rd ed. Englewood Cliffs, NJ: Prentice-Hall.

———. **2000.** *Joining Together,* 7th ed. Boston: Allyn & Bacon.

———. **2009.** *Joining Together* 9th ed. Columbus, OH: Metrill.

Johnson, E. H. 1973. *Social Problems of Urban Man.* Pacific Grove, CA: Brooks/Cole.

Johnson, L. C. 1986. *Social Work Practice: A Generalist Approach,* 2nd ed. Boston: Allyn & Bacon.

Jones, R. R., R. S. Vaught, & M. R. A. Weinrott. 1977. "Time-Series Analysis in Operant Research." *Journal of Applied Behavior Analysis 10,* pp. 151–166.

Julia, M. 2000. *Constructing Gender.* Pacific Grove, CA: Brooks/Cole.

Juran, J. M. 1989. *Juran on Leadership for Quality: An Executive Handbook.* New York: Free Press.

Kadushin, A. 1972. *The Social Work Interview.* New York: Columbia University Press.

Kanfer, F. 1975. "Self-Management Methods." In *Helping People Change,* eds. F. H. Kanfer & A. P. Goldstein, pp. 309–355. Elmsford, NY: Pergamon Press.

Kaplan, S. G., & E. G. Wheeler. 1983. "Survival Skills for Working with Potentially Violent Clients." *Social Casework* 64, no. 6 (June), pp. 339–346.

Katz, A. H., & E. I. Bender. 1976. *The Strength in Us: Self-Help Groups in the Modern World.* New York: Franklin-Watts.

Kaufman, R., & S. Thomas. 1980. *Evaluation without Fear.* New York: New Viewpoints.

Kazdin, A. E. 1977a. "Assessing the Clinical or Applied Importance of Behavior Change through Social Validation." *Behavior Modification 1,* pp. 427–452.

———. **1977b.** *The Token Economy.* New York: Plenum.

Keegan, P. B. 1994. *Fundraising for Nonprofits: How to Build a Community Partnership.* New York: Harper Resource.

Keith-Lucas, A. 1972. *The Giving and Taking of Help.* Chapel Hill: University of North Carolina Press.

———. **1985.** *So You Want to Be a Social Worker: A Primer for the Christian Student.* St. Davids, PA: North American Association of Christians in Social Work.

Kelly, H. H., & A. J. Stahelski. 1970. "Social Interaction Basis of Cooperators' and Competitors' Beliefs about Others." *Journal of Personality and Social Psychology 16,* pp. 66–91.

Kelman, H. C. 1965. "Manipulation of Human Behavior: An Ethical Dilemma for the Social Scientist." *Journal of Social Issues 21,* no. 2, pp. 31–46.

Kertzner, R. M. 2007. "Developmental Issues in Lesbian and Gay Adulthood." In *The Health of Sexual Minorities: Public Health Perspectives on Lesbian, Gay, Bisexual, and Transgender Populations*, eds. I. H. Meyer & M. E. Northridge. New York: Springer.

Kilpatrick, A. C., & T. P. Holland. 2003. *Working with Families, an Integrative Model by Level of Need,* 3rd ed. Boston: Allyn & Bacon.

King, S. W., & R. S. Meyers. 1981. "Developing Self-Help Groups: Integrating Group Work and Community Organization Strategies." *Social Development Issues 5,* pp. 33–46.

Kiresuk, T. J., & S. H. Lund. 1978. "Goal Attainment Scaling." In *Evaluation of Human Service Programs,* eds. C. C. Attkisson, W. A. Hargreaves, M. J. Horowitz, & J. E. Sorensen, pp. 341–370. New York: Academic Press.

———. **2008.** Understanding Generalist Practice, 5th ed Pacific Grove, CA: Brooks/Cole.

———. **2009a.** *Understanding Generalist Practice,* 5th ed. Belmont, CA: Brooks/Cole.

———. **2009b.** *Generalist Practice with Organizations and Communities,* 4th ed. Belmont, CA: Cengage.

Knopf, R. 1979. *Surviving the BS (Bureaucratic System).* Wilmington, NC: Mandala Press.

Koop, J. 1988. "Self-Monitoring: A Literature Review of Research and Practice." *Social Work Research & Abstracts 24,* pp. 8–20.

Kornblum, W., & J. Julian. 2004. *Social Problems,* 11th ed. Upper Saddle River, NJ: Pearson Education.

———. **2009.** *Social Problems*, 13th ed. Boston: Allyn & Bacon.

Kratochwill, T. R., ed. 1978. *Single Subject Research: Strategies for Evaluating Change.* New York: Academic Press.

Krech, D., R. S. Crutchfield, & E. L. Ballachey. 1962. *Individual in Society.* New York: McGraw-Hill.

Kretzmann, J. P., & J. L. McKnight. 1993. *Building Communities from the Inside Out.* Chicago: Acta Publications.

Kuarfordt, C. L. & M. J. Sheridan. 2009. "Understanding the Pathways of Factors Influencing the Use of Spiritually Based interventions." *Journal of Social Work Education,* 45, no. 3, (Fall), pp. 385–405.

Kübler-Ross, E. 1969. *On Death and Dying.* New York: Macmillan.

Laird, J. 1998. "Theorizing Culture: Narrative ideas and Practice Principles." In *Re-visioning Family Therapy,* ed. M. McGoldrick, pp. 20–30. New York: Guilford:

Lakein, A. 1973. *How to Get Control of Your Time and Your Life.* New York: Signet.

Landers, S. 1993. "AIDS Deepens Duty-to-Warn Dilemma." *NASW News* (Jan.), p. 3.

Lee, C. C. 1999. "Counseling African American Men." In *Working with African American Males,* ed. L. E. Davis, pp. 39–44. Thousand Oaks, CA: Sage.

Lefrancois, G. R. 1996. *The Lifespan*, 5th ed. Belmont, CA: Wadsworth.

Lembo, J. 1974. *Help Yourself.* Niles, IL: Argus Communications.

Lewis, R. G., & M. Keung Ho. 1975. "Social Work with Native Americans." *Social Work 20* (Sept.), pp. 378–382.

Leyden-Rubenstein, L. 1998. *The Stress Management Handbook.* New Canaan: CT: Keats Publishing.

Liberman, R. 1971. "Behavioral Approaches to Family and Couple Therapy." *American Journal of Orthopsychiatry 40,* pp. 106–118.

Lie, G., & C. T. Lowery. 2007. "Cultural Competence with Women of Color." In *Culturally Competent Practice,* ed. D. Lum, pp. 351–388. Belmont, CA: Brooks/Cole.

Lieberman, M. A., E. D. Yalom, & M. B. Miles. 1973. "Encounter: The Leader Makes the Difference." *Psychology Today 6,* pp. 69–76.

Loewenberg, F. 1988. *Religion and Social Work Practice in Contemporary American Society.* New York: Columbia University Press.

Loewenberg, F., & R. Dolgoff. 2004. *Ethical Decisions for Social Work Practice,* 7th ed. Pacific Grove, CA: Brooks/Cole.

Loewenberg, F., & R. Dolgoff. 1971. *Teaching of Practice Skills in Undergraduate Programs in Social Welfare and Other Helping Services.* New York: Council on Social Work Education.

Losoncy, L. 1977. *Turning People On.* Englewood Cliffs, NJ: Prentice-Hall.

Lum, D. 2007. *Culturally Competent Practice,* 2nd ed. Belmont, CA: Brooks/Cole.

Maguire, L. 2002. *Clinical Social Work.* Belmont, CA: Brooks/Cole.

Mahoney, M. J. 1973. "Clinical Issues in Self-Control Training." Paper presented at the meeting of the American Psychological Association, Montreal.

Maier, N. R. F. 1970. *Problem Solving and Creativity in Individuals and Groups.* Pacific Grove, CA: Brooks/Cole.

Maluccio, A. 1979. "Perspectives of Social Workers and Clients on Treatment Outcome." *Social Casework 60,* pp. 394–401.

Mandino, O., ed. 1966. *A Treasury of Success Unlimited.* New York: Hawthorn Books.

Manley, M. J. 1977. "How to Cope with a Sense of Failure." In *The Personal Problem Solver,* eds. C. Zastrow & D. Chang. Englewood Cliffs, NJ: Prentice-Hall.

March, J. G. 1956. "Influence Measurement in Experimental and Semi-Experimental Groups." *Sociometry 19,* no. 4 (Dec.), pp. 260–271.

Marti-Costa, S., & I. Serrano-Garcia. 1987. "Needs Assessment and Community Development: An Ideological Perspective" In *Strategies of Community Organization: Macro Practice,* eds. F. M. Cox et al. Itasca, IL: Peacock.

Martinez-Brawley, E., & J. Blundall. 1989. "Farm Families' Preference toward the Personal Social Services." *Social Work 34,* no. 6, pp. 513–522.

Maslach, C. 1976. "Burned-Out." *Human Behavior 5* (Sept.), pp. 16–22.

———. **1978.** "The Client Role in Staff Burn-Out." *Journal of Social Issues 34,* pp. 11–24.

Maslach, C., & A. Pines. 1977. "The Burn-Out Syndrome in the Day Care Setting." *Child Care Quarterly 6,* pp. 100–113.

Masters, W. H., & V. E. Johnson. 1970. *Human Sexual Inadequacy.* Boston: Little, Brown.

Mauksch, H. O. 1975. "The Organizational Context of Dying." In *Death: The Final Stage of Growth,* ed. E. Kübler-Ross, pp. 7–26. Englewood Cliffs, NJ: Prentice-Hall.

Maultsby, M. C., Jr. 1977. "The ABC's of Better Emotional Self-Control." In *The Personal Problem Solver,* eds. C. Zastrow & D. Chang, pp. 3–18. Englewood Cliffs, NJ: Prentice-Hall.

Mayer, B. S. 1995. "Conflict Resolution." In *Encyclopedia of Social Work,* 19th ed., pp. 613–621. Washington, DC: National Association of Social Workers.

McGregor, D. 1960. *The Human Side of Enterprise.* New York: McGraw-Hill.

McLellan, A. T., L. Luborsky, G. E. Woody, & G. P. O'Brien. 1992. "An Improved Diagnostic Evaluation Instrument for Substance Abuse Patients: The Addiction Severity Index." *Journal of Nervous and Mental Diseases 168,* pp. 26–33.

Mead, M. 1935. *Sex and Temperament in Three Primitive Societies.* New York: Morrow.

Mechanic, D. 1962. "Some Factors in Identifying and Defining Mental Illness." *Mental Hygiene 46,* pp. 66–74.

Miley, K. 1992. "Religion and Spirituality as Central Social Work Concerns." Paper presented at the Midwest Biennial Conference on Social Work, April 9–10, LaCrosse, WI.

Milgram, S. 1963. "Behavioral Study of Obedience." *Journal of Abnormal and Social Psychology,* pp. 371–378.

Miller, W. R. & S. Rollnick. 1981. *Motivational Interviewing: Preparing People to Change Addictive Behavior.* New York: Guilford Press.

Minuchin, S., & H. C. Fishman. 1981. *Family Therapy Techniques.* Cambridge, MA: Harvard University Press.

Montague, A. 1964. *Man's Most Dangerous Myth: The Fallacy of Race,* 4th ed. Cleveland: World.

Mooney, L. A., Knox, D. & Schacht, C. 2011. *Understanding Social Problems,* 7th ed. Belmont, CA: Wadsworth.

Moore, C. W. 1986. *The Mediation Process.* San Francisco: Jossey-Bass.

Mor Barak, M. E. 2005. *Managing Diversity: Toward a Globally Inclusive Workplace.* Thousand Oaks, CA: Sage.

Moreno, J. L. 1946. *Psychodrama,* vol. 1. Boston: Beacon House.

Mullen, E. J., & H. L. Magnabosco, eds. 1997. *Outcomes Measurement in the Human Services.* Washington, DC: NASW Press.

National Association of Social Workers. 1982. *Standards for the Classification of Social Work Practice.* Washington, DC: Author.

———. **1996.** *Code of Ethics.* Revised and adopted by the 1996 Delegate Assembly of NASW.

National Highway Traffic Safety Administration. 2001. *Community How-to Guide: Needs Assessment and Strategic Planning.* Washington, DC: Author.

Nelson, A., & W. Wilson. 1984. "The Ethics of Sharing Religious Faith in Psychotherapy." *Journal of Psychology and Theology* 12, no. 1, pp. 15–23.

Netting, F. E., P. M. Kettner, & S. L. McMurtry. 1998. *Social Work Macro Practice,* 2nd ed. New York: Longman.

———. **2003.** *Social Work Macro Practice,* 3rd ed. Boston: Allyn & Bacon.

———. **2007.** *Social Work Macro Practice,* 4th ed. Boston: Allyn & Bacon.

Nichols, M. P., with R. C. Schwartz. 2005. *The Essentials of Family Therapy,* 2nd ed. Boston: Pearson.

North, C. S., & E. M. Smith. 1994. "Comparison of White and Nonwhite Homeless Men and Women." *Social Work 39,* no. 6, pp. 639–647.

Norton, D. G. 1978. "Incorporating Content on Minority Groups into Social Work Practice Courses." In *The Dual Perspective.* New York: Council on Social Work Education.

Nurius, P. S., & W. W. Hudson. 1993. *Human Services Practice, Evaluation, and Computers.* Pacific Grove, CA: Brooks/Cole.

O'Connor, G. 1972. "Toward a New Policy in Adult Corrections." *Social Service Review 46* (Dec.), pp. 482–493.

Ogles, B. J., M. J. Lambert, & S. A. Fields. 2002. *Essentials of Outcome Assessment.* New York: Wiley.

Omachonu, V. K., & J. E. Ross. 1994. *Principles of Total Quality.* Delray Beach, FL: St. Lucie Press.

Orne, M. T., & P. H. Wender. 1968. "Anticipatory Socialization for Psychotherapy: Method and Rationale." *American Journal of Psychiatry 124,* pp. 1202–1212.

Osborn, A. F. 1963. *Applied Imagination: Principles and Procedures of Creative Problem Solving,* 3rd ed. New York: Scribner.

Parsonson, B. S., & D. M. Baer. 1978. "The Analysis and Presentation of Graphic Data." In *Single Subject Research: Strategies for Evaluation Change,* ed. T. R. Kratochwill, pp. 101–165. New York: Academic Press.

Patterson, D. A. 2000. *Personal Computer Applications in the Social Services.* Boston: Allyn & Bacon.

Patterson, G. R. 1971. *Families.* Champaign, IL: Research Press.

Peale, N. V. 1993. *Positive Thinking Everyday.* New York: Fireside.

Pfeiffer, J. W., & J. E. Jones. 1976. "Role Functions in a Group." In *1976 Annual Handbook for Group Facilitators,* eds. J. W. Pfeiffer & J. E. Jones, pp. 136–138. La Jolla, CA: University Associates.

Pfeiffer, V. 1993. *Positive Thinking.* Rockport, MA: Element Books.

Phares, E. J., & T. J. Trull. 1997. *Clinical Psychology,* 5th ed. Pacific Grove, CA: Brooks/Cole.

Pierce, D. 1993. "Developing a Framework for Social Work Practice with Lesbian Women and Gay Men." Paper presented at CSWE Annual Program Meeting, New York, Feb.

Pincus, A., & A. Minahan. 1973. *Social Work Practice: Model and Method.* Itasca, IL: Peacock.

Pines, A., & E. Aronson. 1981. *Burnout: From Tedium to Personal Growth.* New York: Free Press.

Posavac, E. J., & R. G. Carey. 1980. *Program Evaluation: Methods and Case Studies.* Englewood Cliffs, NJ: Prentice-Hall.

Powell, T. J. 1987. *Self-Help Organizations and Professional Practice.* Silver Spring, MD: National Association of Social Workers.

Prochaska, J. O. 1979. *Systems of Psychotherapy.* Pacific Grove, CA: Brooks/Cole.

Prochaska, J. O. & C. C. DiClemente. 1982. "Trans-Theoretical Therapy—Toward a More integrative Model of Change." *Psychotherapy: Theory, Research and Practice* 19 no. 3, pp. 276–288.

Pruger, R. 1978. "Bureaucratic Functioning as a Social Work Skill." In *Educating the Baccalaureate Social Worker: Report of the Undergraduate Social Work Curriculum Development Project,* eds. B. L. Baer & R. Federico. Cambridge, MA: Ballinger.

Pruitt, M.W. 2002. "Size Matters:" A Comparison of Anti-and Pro-Gay Organizations' Estimates of the Size of the Gay Population." *Journal of Homosexuality 42,* no. 3, pp. 21–30.

Putnam, R. D. 2000. *Bowling Alone: The Collapse and Revival of American Community.* New York: Simon Schuster.

Raimy, V. 1977. *Misunderstandings of the Self.* San Francisco: Jossey-Bass.

Raiz, L., & S. Saltzburg. 2007. "Developing Awareness of the Subtleties of Heterosexism and Homophobia among Undergraduate, Heterosexual Social Work Majors." *Journal of Baccalaureate Social Work 12,* no. 2, pp. 53–69.

Reichert, E. 2007. *Challenges in Human Rights: A Social Work Perspective.* New York: Columbia University Press.

Reid, W., & L. Epstein. 1972. *Task-Centered Casework.* New York: Columbia University Press.

———. **1977.** *Task-Centered Practice.* New York: Columbia University Press.

Reid, W., & A. Shyne. 1969. *Brief and Extended Casework.* New York: Columbia University Press.

Richie, B. E. 2003. "Gender Entrapment and African American Women: An Analysis of Race, Ethnicity, Gender and Intimate Violence." In *Violent Crime: Assessing Race and Ethnic Differences,* ed. D. F. Hawkins, pp. 198–201. Cambridge, UK: Cambridge University Press.

Riessman, F. 1965. "The 'Helper Therapy' Principle." *Journal of Social Work 10,* no. 2 (April), pp. 27–34.

———. **1987.** "Foreword." In *Self-Help Organizations and Professional Practice,* ed. T. J. Powell. Silver Spring, MD: National Association of Social Workers.

Rimm, D., & J. Masters. 1974. *Behavior Therapy.* New York: Academic Press.

Ringer, R. J. 1977. *Looking Out for No. 1.* New York: Fawcett Books.

Ritter, M. 2000. "Virtual Reality Coming into Vogue as Therapy." *Wisconsin State Journal* (July 2), pp. 1A, 10A.

Rivera, F. G., & J. L. Erlich. 1992. *Community Organizing in a Diverse Society.* Boston: Allyn & Bacon.

Roethlisberger, F. J., & W. J. Dickson. 1939. *Management and the Worker.* Cambridge, MA: Harvard University Press.

Rogers, C. R. 1970. *Carl Rogers on Encounter Groups.* New York: Harper & Row.

Rome, S. H. & S. Hoehstetter. 2010. "Social Work and Civic Engagement: The Political Participation of Professional Social Workers." *Journal of Sociology and Social Work, 37,* no. 3, pp. 107–129.

Rosenhan, D. 1973. "On Being Sane in Insane Places." *Science 179,* pp. 250–257.

Rosenhan, D. L., & M. E. Seligman. 1995. *Abnormal Psychology,* 3rd ed. New York: Norton.

Rossi, P. H., H. E. Freeman, & S. R. Wright. 1979. *Evaluation: A Systematic Approach.* Newbury Park, CA: Sage.

Rothenberg, P. S. 2007. *Race, Class, and Gender in the United States,* 7th ed. New York: Worth.

Rothman, J., & J. E. Tropman. 1995. *Strategies of Community Intervention,* 5th ed., Itasca, IL: Peacock.

Rubin, A. 2007. "Proceedings of the Conference on Improving the Teaching of Evidence-Based Practice in Social Work" [Special issue]. *Research on Social Work Practice 17,* no. 5.

Rubin, A., & K. S. Knox. 1996. "Data Analysis Problems in Single-Case Evaluation: Issues for Research on Social Work Practice." In *Research on Social Work Practice 6,* pp. 40–65.

Rubin, H. J., & I. S. Rubin. 1992. *Community Organizing and Development.* New York: Macmillan.

Ruoss, M. 1970. As quoted in J. C. DeBoer. *Let's Plan: A Guide to the Planning Process for Voluntary Organizations.* Princeton, NJ: Pilgrim Press.

Saleeby, D. 1997. *The Strengths Perspective in Social Work Practice,* 2nd ed. Upper Saddle River, NJ: Pearson Education, Inc.

———. **2002.** *The Strengths Perspective in Social Work Practice,* 3rd ed. Boston: Allyn & Bacon.

Sandler, J. 1986. "Aversion Methods." In *Helping People Change,* 3rd ed., eds. F. H. Kanfer & A. P. Goldstein, pp. 191–235. Elmsford, NY: Pergamon Press.

Sandoval, J. 1985. "Crisis Counseling: Conceptualizations and General Principles." *School Psychology Review 14,* pp. 257–265.
Sapolsky, R. 1998. *Why Zebras Don't Get Ulcers.* New York: W. H. Freeman.
Sardar, Z. 2001. "More Hackney Than Bollywood," *New Statesman* 14 (July 30), pp. 14–16.
Satir, V. 1967. *Conjoint Family Therapy,* rev. ed. Palo Alto, CA: Science & Behavior Books.
———. **1972.** *Peoplemaking.* Palo Alto, CA: Science & Behavior Books.
Schachter, S. 1959. *The Psychology of Affiliation.* Stanford, CA: Stanford University Press.
Schaefer, R. T. 1993. *Racial & Ethnic Groups,* 5th ed. New York: HarperCollins.
———. **2004.** *Racial & Ethnic Groups,* 9th ed. Upper Saddle River, NJ: Pearson Education.
———. **2008.** *Racial & Ethnic Groups,* 10th ed. Upper Saddle River NJ: Pearson Education.
———. **2010.** *Racial & Ethnic Groups,* 12th ed. Upper Saddle River, NJ: Prentice Hall.
Scheff, I. 1966. *Being Mentally Ill.* Hawthorne, NY: Aldine.
Schiele, J. H. 1996. "Afrocentricity: An Emerging Paradigm in Social Work Practice." *Social Work 41* (May), pp. 284–294.
Schoener, G. R. 2000. "Duty to Warn or Protect." Paper presented at Professional At Risk: Ethical Dilemmas Workshop at the University of Wisconsin–Madison, Nov. 13.
Schuller, R., II. 1973. *Move Ahead with Possibility Thinking.* Moonachie, NJ: Pyramid Publications.
Schwartz, G. 1989. "Confidentiality Revisited." *Social Work* (May), pp. 223–226.
Seaward, B. L. 1994. *Managing Stress.* Boston: Jones & Bartlett.
———. **2005.** *Managing Stress,* 5th ed. Boston: Jones & Bartlett.
Selye, H. 1956. *The Stress of Life.* New York: McGraw-Hill.
Shadish, W. R., T. D. Cook, & D. T. Campbell. 2002. *Experimental and Quasi-Experimental Designs for Generalized Causal Inference.* Boston: Houghton Mifflin.
Sharf, R. S. 2008. *Theories of Psychotherapy and Counseling,* 4th ed. Belmont, CA: Brooks/Cole.
Sheafor, B. W., C. R. Horejsi, & C. A. Horejsi. 1988. *Techniques and Guidelines for Social Work Practice.* Boston: Allyn & Bacon.
Sheridan, M. J. & K. Amato-von Hemert. 1999. "The Role of Religion and Spirituality in Social Work Education and Practice: A Study of Student Views and Experiences." *Journal of Social Work Education 35,* no. 1, (Winter), pp. 125–141.
Sherif, M. 1936. *The Psychology of Social Norms.* New York: Harper & Row.
Sherman, H. 1966. "The Surest Way in the World to Attract Success—or Failure." In *A Treasury of Success Unlimited,* ed. O. Mandino, pp. 111–113. New York: Hawthorn Books.
Sherwood, D. A. 1981. "Add to Your Faith Virtue: The Integration of Christian Values and Social Work-Practice." *Social Work and Christianity 8* (Spring–Fall), pp. 41–54.
Shostrom, E. L. 1969. "Group Therapy: Let the Buyer Beware." *Psychology Today 2,* no. 12 (May), pp. 36–40.
Sindler, A. P. 1978. *Bakke, DeFunis and Minority Admissions: The Quest for Equal Opportunity.* New York: Longmans, Green.
Skinner, B. F. 1938. *The Behavior of Organisms.* New York: Appleton-Century-Crofts.
———. **1948.** *Walden Two.* New York: Macmillan.
———. **1953.** *Science and Human Behavior.* New York: Free Press.
Skoe, E. E. A., A. Cumberland, N. Eisenberg, K. Hansen, & J. Perry. 2002. "The Influence of Sex and Gender-Role Identity on Moral Cognition and Prosocial Personality Traits." *Sex Roles 46,* pp. 295–309.
Slater, P. E. 1958. "Contrasting Correlates of Group Size." *Sociometry 21,* no. 2 (June), pp. 129–139.
Slonim-Nevo, V., & Y. Anson. 1998. "Evaluating Practice: Does It Improve Treatment Outcome?" *Social Work Research 22,* pp. 66–74.
Spies, R. A., J. F. Carlson & K. F. Geisinger. 2010. *The Eighteenth Mental Measurements Yearbook.* Lincoln: University of Nebraska Press.
Spock, B. 1957. *The Common-Sense Book of Baby and Child Care.* New York: Duell, Sloan & Pierce.
Spranger, E. 1928. *Types of Men.* New York: Hafner.
Starkweather, C. L., & S. M. Turner. 1975. "Parents Anonymous: Reflections on the Development of a Self-Help Group." In *Child Abuse Interventions and Treatment,* eds. N. C. Ebeling & D. A. Hill. Littleton, MA: PSG.
Stephenson, M. M. 1983. "The Talking Circle: A Resource for Personal and Community Development." Paper presented at the Eighth Annual Institute on Social Work in Rural Areas, July, Cheney, WA.
Stone, W. C. 1966. "Be Generous." In *A Treasury of Success Unlimited,* ed. O. Mandino, pp. 9–10. New York: Hawthorn Books.
Stuart, R. B. 1970. *Trick or Treatment.* Champaign, IL: Research Press.
———. **1976.** "An Operant-Interpersonal Program for Couples." In *Treating Relationships,* ed. D. H. L. Olson. Lake Mills, IA: Graphic.
Suppes, M. A., & C. Wells. 2003. *The Social Work Experience, An Introduction to Social Work and Social Welfare,* 4th ed. New York: McGraw-Hill.
Szasz, T. 1961. "The Myth of Mental Illness." In *Clinical Psychology in Transition,* comp. J. R. Braun. Cleveland: Howard Allen.
———. **1963.** *Law, Liberty and Psychiatry.* New York: Macmillan.
———. **1967.** "The Psychiatrist as Double Agent." *Trans-Action 4,* pp. 3–25.
Taylor, F. W. 1947. *Scientific Management.* New York: Harper & Row.
Taylor, W. L., D. M. Piché, C. Rosario, & J. D. Rich. 2007. *The Erosion of Rights: Declining Civil Rights Enforcement under the Bush Administration.* Washington, DC: Citizens' Commission on Civil Rights.
Tessler, R., R. Rosenheck, & G. Gamache. 2001. "Gender Differences in Self-Reported Reasons for Homelessness." *Journal of Social Distress and the Homeless 10,* no. 3, pp. 243–254.
Thomas, E. J. 1978. "Research and Service in Single-Case Experimentation: Conflicts and Choices." *Social Work Research and Abstracts 14,* pp. 20–31.
———. **1984.** *Designing Interventions for the Helping Professions.* New York: Sage.
Thorndike, E. L. 1913. *The Psychology of Learning.* New York: Teachers College Press.
Thyer, B., & J. Wodarski. 2004. *Handbook of Empirical Social Work Practice.* New York: Wiley.
Thyer, B. A., & L. L. Myers. 2007. *A Social Worker's Guide to Evaluating Practice Outcomes.* Alexandria, VA: Council on Social Work Education Press.

Toch, H. 1970. "The Care and Feeding of Typologies and Labels." *Federal Probation 34* (Sept.), pp. 46–57.

Tolman, E. C. 1932. *Purposive Behavior in Animals and Men.* New York: Appleton-Century-Crofts.

Toseland, R. W., & R. F. Rivas. 2007. *An Introduction to Group Work Practice,* 6th ed. Boston: Allyn & Bacon.

Touliatos, J., B. F. Perlmutter, & M. A. Straus, eds. 1990. *Handbook of Family Measurement Techniques.* Newbury Park, CA: Sage.

Tripodi, T. 1994. *A Primer on Single-Subject Design for Clinical Social Workers.* Washington, DC: NASW Press.

Tubbs, S. I., & J. W. Baird. 1976. *The Open Person.* Columbus, OH: Merrill.

United Nations. 1948. *Universal Declaration of Human Rights.* Adopted December 10, 1948. General Assembly Resolution, 2200 AXXI. New York: United Nations.

***University of Pittsburgh Law Review.* 1975.** "*Tarasoff v. Regents of University of California:* The Psychotherapist's Peril" *37,* pp. 159–164.

U.S. Census Bureau. 2005. *Americans with Disabilities: 2005.* Washington, DC: Author

Van de Ven, A., & A. L. Delbecq. 1971. "Nominal versus Interacting Group Processes for Committee Decision-Making Effectiveness." *Academy of Management Journal 14,* no. 2 (June), pp. 203–212.

Van Den Bergh, N. 1992. "Feminist Treatment for People with Depression." In *Structuring Change,* ed. K. Corcoran, pp. 95–110. Chicago: Lyceum Books.

Van Den Bergh, N., & L. B. Cooper. 1987. "Feminist Social Work." In *The Encyclopedia of Social Work,* pp. 610–618. Washington, DC: National Association of Social Workers.

Vogler, R. E., S. E. Lunde, G. R. Johnson, & P. L. Martin. 1970. "Electrical Aversion Conditioning with Chronic Alcoholics." *Journal of Consulting and Clinical Psychology 34,* pp. 302–307.

Watson, D. L., & R. G. Tharp. 1972. *Self-Directed Behavior: Self-Modification for Personal Adjustment.* Pacific Grove, CA: Brooks/Cole.

Watson, J. B., & R. Rayner. 1920. "Conditioned Emotional Reaction." *Journal of Experimental Psychology 3,* no. 1, pp. 1–14.

Weick, A., C. Rapp, W. P. Sullivan, & W. Kisthardt. 1989. "A Strengths Perspective for Social Work Practice." *Social Work 34,* pp. 350–354.

Weil, M., & D. N. Gamble. 1995. "Community Practice Models." In *Encyclopedia of Social Work,* 19th ed., vol. 1, pp. 577–594. Washington, DC: NASW Press.

Weinger, S. 2001. *Security Risk: Preventing Violence against Social Workers,* Washington, DC: NASW Press.

Weiss, C. H. 1972. *Evaluation Research.* Englewood Cliffs, NJ: Prentice-Hall.

White, M. 1995. Reauthoring Lives: Interviews and Essays. Adelaide, South Australia: Dulwich Centre Publications.

Whittaker, J. K. 1974. *Social Treatment.* Hawthorne, NY: Aldine.

Wiger, D. E., & K. B. Solberg. 2001. *Tracking Mental Health Outcomes: A Therapist's Guide to Measuring Client Progress, Analyzing Data, and Improving Your Practice.* New York: Wiley.

Wigmore, J. H. 1961. *Evidence in Trials at Common Law,* vol. 8 (rev.), ed. J. T. McNaughton. Boston: Little, Brown.

Wilensky, H., & C. Lebeaux. 1965. *Industrial Society & Social Welfare.* New York: Free Press.

Williams, E. E., & F. Ellison. 1996. "Culturally Informed Social Work Practice with American Indian Clients: Guidelines for Non-Indian Social Workers." *Social Work 41,* no. 2, pp. 147–151.

Wilson, S. J. 1978. *Confidentiality in Social Work: Issues and Principles.* New York: Free Press.

Wilson, T. G. 2008. "Behavior Therapy." In *Current Psychotherapies,* 8th ed., eds. R. J. Corsini & D. Wedding, pp. 223–262. Belmont, CA: Brooks/Cole.

Winship, J., & A. Hall. 2004. "Social Exclusion: Understanding Barriers Facing Homeless and Immigrant Latino Students." A presentation at the Oxford Round Table: Addressing the Education Needs of At Risk Children, Oxford, England, March 22, 2004.

Wolpe, J. 1958. *Psychotherapy by Reciprocal Inhibition.* Stanford, CA: Stanford University Press.

www.quotationspage.com. (2004). Martin Luther King. Retrieved from www.quotationspage.com/quotes/ Martin Luther King Jr.

Yahoo News. 2004. "Report: CIA Gave False Info on Iraq," July 9.

Young, J. 1989. *Fundraising for Nonprofit Groups.* Bellingham, WA: Self Counsel Press.

Zastrow, C. 1973. "The Nominal Group: A New Approach to Designing Programs for Curbing Delinquency." *Canadian Journal of Criminology and Corrections* (Jan.), pp. 109–117.

———. **1979.** *Talk to Yourself: Using the Power of Self-Talk.* Englewood Cliffs, NJ: Prentice-Hall.

———. **1993.** *You Are What You Think: A Guide to Self-Realization.* Chicago: Nelson-Hall.

Zastrow, C., & R. Navarre. 1977. "The Nominal Group: A New Tool for Making Social Work Education Relevant." *Journal of Education for Social Work 13* (Winter), pp. 112–118.

Index